lo

Florence
& Tuscany

Northwestern Tuscany
(p221)

Florence
(p60)

Eastern Tuscany
(p264)

Central Coast & Elba
(p195)

Siena & Central Tuscany
(p126)

Elba

Southern Tuscany
(p177)

Nicola Williams, Virginia Maxwell

Contents

WINE IN CHIANTI P145

SAN GIMIGNANO P155

ON THE ROAD

Contents

TRATTORIA IN FLORENCE P60

Welcome to Florence & Tuscany

With its lyrical landscapes, world-class art and a superb cucina contadina (farmer's kitchen), the Tuscan experience is perfectly in symbiosis with the land.

Perfect Landscapes

Tuscany has a timeless familiarity, with its iconic Florentine cathedral dome, gently rolling hills dipped in morning mist and sculptural cypress alleys. But then, this *regione* in central Italy is postcard material. Golden wheat fields, silver olive groves and pea-green vineyards marching in terraced rows on hillsides form a graceful prelude to soul-soaring medieval hilltop villages, mountain ranges and fecund forests in the north, and a garland of islands along the coastal south. Get out, explore, hike and ding your bicycle bell, as this rousing landscape demands.

Sensational Slow Food

No land is more caught up with the fruits of its fertile earth than Tuscany, a gourmet destination whose residents spend an inordinate amount of time thinking about, discussing and consuming food and wine. Local, seasonal and sustainable is the Holy Trinity and Tuscans share enormous pride in the quality of their produce. Tuscan travel is grassroots: to wineries to taste blockbuster wines like Brunello di Montalcino and Vino Nobile di Montepulciano; to a family-run *pastificio tradizionale* where artisan pasta is cut by hand; and road trips in quest of the best *bistecca alla fiorentina* (chargrilled T-bone steak). *Buon appetito!*

Living History

Ever since the Etruscans dropped by to party and stayed, Tuscany has seduced. The Romans stocked their grain silos here, Christians walked stages of a medieval pilgrimage route, and Napoleon plundered art (and suffered terribly in exile in a beautiful neoclassical villa on the paradisiacal island of Elba). Florence's historic churches and monuments were a key stop for British aristocrats on the Grand Tour in the 19th century – and remain so. And at sundown when the River Arno turns pink, whether you like things old-fashioned and simple or boutique chic, know that this handsome city will oblige.

An Artistic Powerhouse

Then there's the art. And, oh, what art! The Etruscans indulged their fondness for a classy send-off with exquisite funerary objects, and the Romans left their usual legacy of monumental sculptures. But it was during the medieval and Renaissance periods that Tuscany really struck gold, with painters, sculptors and architects creating world-class masterpieces. Squirrelled away and safeguarded today in churches, museums and galleries all over the region, art in Tuscany is truly unmatched. Edgy street art in Florence and countryside sculpture parks bring the art scene right up to the 21st century.

Why I Love Florence & Tuscany

By Nicola Williams, Writer

Tuscany won me over at a farm in the Garfagnana. We were tucking into dinner when the farmer's wife rushed in mid-*secondi* and urged us to join her in the stable to watch a calf being born. Later, when she joyfully declared 'We'll call her Kaya after your daughter!' I was speechless. So my seven-year-old now has a cow in Tuscany and I the honour of being privy to yet another intimacy of this wildly diverse, soulful, earth-driven region. This (and its truffles, Florence, *aperitivi* tradition, Renaissance art and Chianti wine) is why I love Tuscany.

For more about our writers, see p352

Above: Florence (p60)

Florence & Tuscany

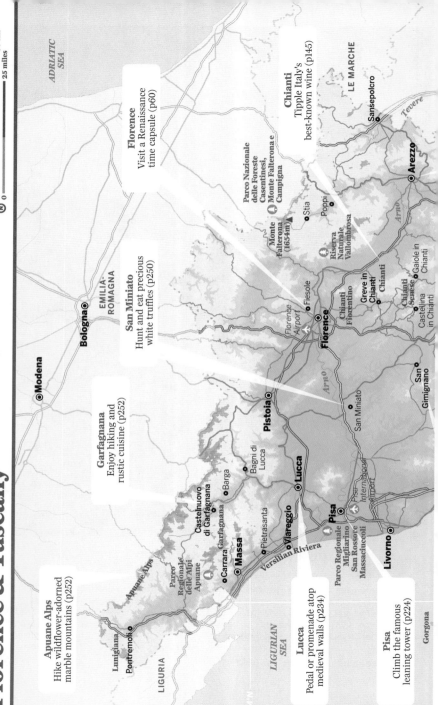

N 0 ____ 50 km
0 ____ 25 miles

ADRIATIC SEA

Florence
Visit a Renaissance time capsule (p60)

San Miniato
Hunt and eat precious white truffles (p250)

Garfagnana
Enjoy hiking and rustic cuisine (p252)

Apuane Alps
Hike wildflower-adorned marble mountains (p252)

Chianti
Tipple Italy's best-known wine (p145)

Lucca
Pedal or promenade atop medieval walls (p234)

Pisa
Climb the famous leaning tower (p224)

Modena
Bologna
EMILIA-ROMAGNA
LE MARCHE
Sansepolcro
Tevere
Arezzo

Parco Nazionale delle Foreste Casentinesi, Monte Falterona e Campigna
Monte Falterona (1654m)
Stia
Poppi
Fiesole
Riserva Naturale Vallombrosa
Greve in Chianti
Chianti Fiorentino
Chianti Senese
Gaiole in Chianti
Castellina in Chianti

Florence Airport
Florence
Arno

LIGURIA
Lunigiana
Pontremoli
Apuane Alps
Parco Regionale delle Alpi Apuane
Castelnuovo di Garfagnana
Barga
Garfagnana
Bagni di Lucca
Pistoia
Lucca
Pietrasanta
Viareggio
Versilian Riviera
Massa
Carrara

San Miniato
San Gimignano

Pisa International Airport
Pisa
Parco Regionale Migliarino San Rossore Massaciuccoli
Livorno

LIGURIAN SEA
Gorgona

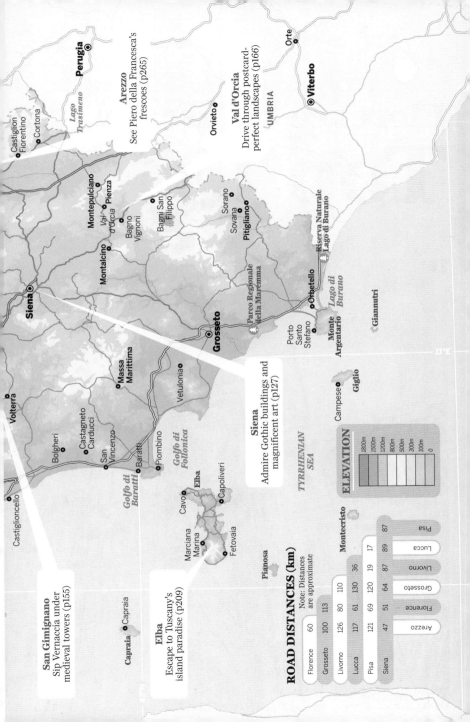

San Gimignano
Sip Vernaccia under medieval towers (p155)

Volterra

Castiglioncello

Bolgheri

Castagneto Carducci

San Vincenzo

Piombino

Golfo di Baratti

Baratti

Massa Marittima

Vetulonia

Golfo di Follonica

Capraia ● Capraia

Elba
Escape to Tuscany's island paradise (p209)

Elba

Cavo ●

Marciana Marina

Capoliveri ●

Fetovaia ●

Pianosa

Campese ● **Giglio**

TYRRHENIAN SEA

Montecristo

Siena
Admire Gothic buildings and magnificent art (p127)

Grosseto

Siena ◉

Montalcino

Montepulciano

Val d'Orcia **Pienza**

Bagno Vignoni

Bagni San Filippo

Sorano

Sovana

Pitigliano

Parco Regionale della Maremma

Orbetello ◉

Porto Santo Stefano

Monte Argentario

Lago di Burano

Riserva Naturale Lago di Burano

Giannutri ●

Castiglion Fiorentino

Cortona ●

Lago Trasimeno

Perugia ◉

Arezzo
See Piero della Francesca's frescoes (p265)

Orvieto ●

Val d'Orcia
Drive through postcard-perfect landscapes (p166)

UMBRIA

Orte ●

Viterbo ◉

11°E

ELEVATION

| 1800m |
| 1500m |
| 1200m |
| 800m |
| 500m |
| 300m |
| 100m |
| 0 |

ROAD DISTANCES (km)
Note: Distances are approximate

	Arezzo	Florence	Grosseto	Livorno	Lucca	Pisa
Florence	60					
Grosseto	100	113				
Livorno	126	80	110			
Lucca	117	61	130	36		
Pisa	121	69	120	19	17	
Siena	47	51	64	87	89	87

Florence & Tuscany's
Top 18

The Duomo, Florence

1 The Duomo (p74) isn't just the most spectacular structure in Florence – it's up there with Rome's Colosseum and Pisa's Leaning Tower as one of Italy's most recognisable icons. Its polychrome marble facade is vast, striking and magnificent. But what makes the building so extraordinary is Filippo Brunelleschi's distinctive red-brick dome, one of the greatest architectural achievements of all time. Scale the steep, narrow staircase up to the base of the dome and peer down on the toy-like cathedral interior far below – then climb some more for a stunning city panorama.

Piazza del Campo, Siena

2 Horses race around it twice a year, local teens hang out on it, tourists inevitably gasp on seeing it for the first time – Siena's strangely sloping, perfectly paved central piazza (p134) is the city's geographical and historical heart, staked out since the 12th century. Presided over by the graceful Palazzo Comunale and fringed with bustling cafe terraces, Piazza del Campo is the finest spot in Siena to promenade, take photographs and lap up the soul-soaring magic of this unique, gloriously Gothic and architecturally harmonious city.

AB_/CP/ALAMY ©

CEZARY WOJTKOWSKI/SHUTTERSTOCK ©

Chianti

3 This ancient wine region (p145) is the Tuscany of postcards, where cypress alleys give way to pea-green vineyards and silver olive groves, honey-coloured stone farmhouses and secluded Renaissance villas built for Florentine and Sienese nobility. Luxurious accommodation and the very best of modern Tuscan cuisine provide the ingredients for an idyllic short escape – peppered with romantic walks and road trips along narrow green lanes to wine cellars for tastings of Italy's best-known wine, the ruby-red, violet-scented Chianti Classico.

Uffizi Gallery, Florence

4 Few art galleries evoke such an over-whelming sense of awe and wonder-ment as the world-class Uffizi (p68), at home in a 16th-century Medici *palazzo* in Florence. Vast, labyrinthine, architectur-ally magnificent and rich in history, the building alone stuns. Add to this an art collection chock-full of Renaissance mas-terpieces, with works by Giotto, Botticelli, Michelangelo, da Vinci, Raphael, Titian and Caravaggio all jostling for the limelight, and you'll know you've arrived in art-lover heaven. Allow ample time to savour slowly, in several bite-sized visits if need be.

Flavours of Tuscany

5 'To cook like your mother is good, but to cook like your grandmother is better' says the Tuscan proverb. And indeed, in foodie Tuscany age-old recipes are passed between generations and form the backbone of the local cuisine – a highlight of any Tuscan trip. Devour feisty T-bone steak in a family-run trattoria such as Mario (p107) by Florence's central food market, savour modern Tuscan fare amid a sea of ancient Antinori vines at Rinuccio 1180, shop at local markets bursting with seasonal produce and wish fellow diners '*Buon appetito!*' Bistecca alla fiorentina (p42)

Relaxing in an Agriturismo

6 Whether you want to wallow in the idyllic beauty of the landscape from an infinity pool on a luxurious Tuscan estate or get your hands dirty in the fields, an *agriturismo* (rural accommodation on a working farm, winery or agricultural domain) is a five-star way of experiencing country life in Tuscany. Home-cooked dinners of seasonal farm produce and mountains of green space are a given. Barbialla Nuova (p251) has just the right mix of adventure (unpaved country roads) and panache (stylish decor and staggering views).

Hunting for Truffles

7 The most precious product in the Italian pantry, the pig-ugly white truffle is snuffed out by dogs in damp autumnal woods around the hilltop town of San Miniato. Much secrecy, mystique and cutthroat rivalry between local *tartufaio* (truffle hunters) surrounds the business – making a bite into a trufflelaced omelette all the more exciting and glam. From October to December, join a truffle hunt (p251), or follow your nose to San Miniato in November when the Mostra Mercato Nazionale del Tartufo Bianco (National White Truffle Market) takes over the town.

Medieval Festivals

8 Throw yourself into local life with an exuberant and eye-catching festival – a compelling snapshot of Tuscan culture, washed down with much food, wine and merrymaking. Come the warm days of spring and summer, almost every town hosts its own fest: locals don medieval costumes and battle with giant crossbows or lances, often re-enacting ancient political rivalries between different *contrada* (neighbourhoods). The prize? Wonderful trophies evocative of medieval pageantry such as the golden arrow and silk banners of Massa Marittima's Balestro del Girifalco (p182). Palio (p140)

Medieval Towers, San Gimignano

9 They form one of the world's most enchanting skylines, sheltering everything from family homes to contemporary art galleries, and bringing history alive for every visitor – San Gimignano's medieval towers (p155) are an iconic Tuscan sight. Few can be scaled these days – Torre Grossa in the Palazzo Comunale is a notable exception – but you can explore in their shadow and reflect on the civic pride and neighbourhood rivalry that prompted their construction and gave this diminutive hilltop town its unique appearance.

Val d'Orcia

10 Cruise in second gear along quiet, gently rolling roads along this unassuming valley laced with vines, the medieval abbeys of Sant'Antimo and San Galgano, splendidly Renaissance Pienza and the blockbuster wine towns of Montepulciano and Montalcino. Explore abbeys where pilgrims once overnighted en route along the Via Francigena from Canterbury to Rome, indulge in a long, lazy Brunello-fuelled lunch, and congratulate yourself on uncovering one of Tuscany's finest road trips – there's good reason why the Val d'Orcia (p166) is a Unesco World Heritage Site.

FLEGERE/SHUTTERSTOCK ©

SONGQUAN DENG/ALAMY ©

Sacred Art in Arezzo

11 It's a step off the trodden tourist trail, but that only adds to the impossible charm of laid-back Arezzo (p265), a small town in eastern Tuscany that shows Siena a thing or two when it comes to cinematically sloping central squares. Medieval churches safeguarding precious crucifixes, frescoes and sacred works of art stud Arezzo's shabby-chic streets and, should you be in the market for an artwork of your own, one of Italy's best-known antiques fairs is held here on the first weekend of each month. Fiera Antiquaria di Arezzo (p270)

Pedalling Around Lucca

12 Hire a bike, stock up on gourmet picnic supplies and freewheel along the cobbled streets of lovely Lucca (p234), zooming through a progression of tree-shaded piazzas and stone-paved alleys concealing medieval churches, a Romanesque cathedral and cinematic 17th-century *palazzi* (palaces). End with a gourmet lunch of local produce atop the monumental city walls, slicked with a circular, silky-smooth cycling path (a sweet loaf of *buccellato* from pastry shop Taddeucci is a Lucchese must), or hit the open road to swoon over opulent villas in the countryside.

ADAM EASTLAND/ALAMY ©

ALESSIO CATELLI/SHUTTERSTOCK ©

Aperitivo

13 *Aperitivo* (pre-dinner drinks accompanied by cocktail snacks) is one of Tuscany's finest food and wine rituals, best partaken of after a *passeggiata* (early-evening stroll) with seemingly half the town along Florence's boutique-beaded Via de' Tornabuoni, Lucca's Via Fillungo or another car-free urban strip. People-watching is an essential part of both elements. In Florence, grab a pew on the pavement terrace of wine bar Le Volpi e l'Uva (p119), with Florentine hipsters sipping garden cocktails in Santarosa Bistrot or between red-brick walls at Mad Souls & Spirits and enjoy.

Exploring the Apuane Alps

14 This rugged mountain range, protected within the Parco Regionale delle Alpi Apuane (p252), beckons hikers, bikers and drivers with a peaceful, soul-soothing trail of isolated farmhouses, medieval hermitages and hilltop villages. Its most spectacular sights are the slopes providing a backdrop to the town of , scarred with marble quarries worked since Roman times. Come here to visit a quarry and sample *lardo di colonnata* (thinner-than-wafer-thin slices of local pig fat), one of Tuscany's greatest gastronomic treats, in the tiny village of Colonnata.

Piazza dei Miracoli, Pisa

15 History resonates when you stand in the middle of this piazza (p226). Showcasing structures built to glorify God and flaunt civic riches (not necessarily in that order), this cluster of Romanesque church buildings possesses an architectural harmony that is remarkably refined and very rare. Hear the acoustics in the baptistry, marvel at Giovanni Pisano's marble pulpit in the *duomo* and confirm that, yes, the famous tower does lean. Living up to its name, this square really is a field full of miracles.

Island Life, Elba

16 Elba (p209) is the Tuscan paradise no one imagines. A Mediterranean island woven with sweetly scented orange trees, olive groves and century-old palms, Elba is a sensorial landscape clearly designed for beach lounging, coastal hikes and motoring from hilltop village to bijou fishing cove. Napoleon was banished here in 1814, meaning the island has a few historic sights to visit. And then there's the wine and olive oil, two glorious nectars crafted with pride and passion on family estates unchanged for centuries. Bedroom in Museo Nazionale della Residenze Napoleoniche (p212)

15

The Garfagnana

17 Head to the hills north of Lucca to feast on chestnuts, mushrooms, honey and other earthy fruits of the forest in this off-the-beaten-track corner of Tuscany. Hike through wildflower-festooned fields and meander slowly along bumpy back roads from one laid-back medieval mountain village to another. Stay in an *agriturismo* and spend your days hiking, mountain biking and devouring homemade dinners around a shared farmhouse table. From the Garfagnana (p252), the beaches and artistic enclaves of the Versilian coast aren't too far away should the need for modern civilisation kick in.

The Franciscan Pilgrim Trail

18 Offering a heady mix of scenery, art, history and religion, the Santuario della Verna (pictured bottom right; p277) in eastern Tuscany and the hilltop town of Assisi in neighbouring Umbria are two of the most important Christian pilgrimage sites in the world. Visit the windswept monastery in the Casentino where St Francis is said to have received the stigmata, and then move on to his birthplace, where Giotto's famous fresco series in the upper church stuns every beholder with its beauty and narrative power.

Need to Know

For more information, see Survival Guide (p325)

Currency
euro (€)

Language
Italian

Visas
Not needed for residents of Schengen countries or for many visitors staying for less than 90 days.

Money
ATMs widely available. Credit cards accepted at most hotels and many restaurants.

Mobile (Cell) Phones
Local SIM cards can be used in European and Australian phones. Other phones must be set to roaming.

Time
Central European Time (GMT/UTC plus one hour)

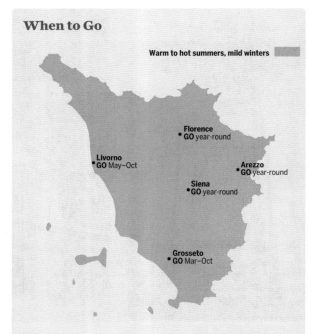

When to Go

Warm to hot summers, mild winters

Florence
• GO year-round

Livorno
• GO May–Oct

Arezzo
• GO year-round

Siena
• GO year-round

Grosseto
• GO Mar–Oct

High Season
(May, Jun, Sep & Oct)

➡ Accommodation prices rise by up to 50%.

➡ Perfect weather for travelling, but it can be crowded.

➡ Major festivals fall June to September.

Shoulder
(Apr, Jul & Aug)

➡ April weather is pleasant and prices are reasonable.

➡ High summer can be hot away from the coast and too crowded on the coast.

➡ Most attractions stay open to sundown during summer.

Low Season
(Nov–Mar)

➡ Accommodation bargains abound, but many hotels close for the season.

➡ Some tourist-information offices close.

➡ Many restaurants close for annual holidays.

Useful Websites

Visit Tuscany (www.visit tuscany.com) Official site of the Tuscany region.

The Florentine (www.thefloren tine.net) English-language newspaper covering Florence and much of Tuscany.

The Local (www.thelocal.it) Reliable one-stop shop for the day's regional and national Italian news in English.

Il Sole 24 Ore (www.italy24. ilsole24ore.com) Digital, English-language edition of Italian newspaper *Il Sole 24 Ore*.

Girl in Florence (http://girlinflorence.com) Up-to-the-minute city recommendations by a street-smart Texan Tuscan blogger very much at home in Florence.

Lonely Planet (www.lonely planet.com/italy/tuscany) Destination information, hotel bookings, traveller forum and more.

Important Numbers

Italy country code	📞39
International access code	📞00
Ambulance	📞118
Police	📞113
Emergency from mobile phone	📞112

Exchange Rates

Australia	A$1	€0.67
Canada	C$1	€0.72
Japan	¥100	€0.76
New Zealand	NZ$1	€0.58
UK	UK£1	€1.15
US	US$1	€0.75

For current exchange rates see www.xe.com.

Daily Costs

Budget: Less than €80

➡ Dorm bed: €16–36

➡ Sandwich: €5–8

➡ Trattoria dinner: €20

➡ Coffee standing at bar: €1

Midrange: €80–200

➡ Midrange-hotel double room: €110–200

➡ Restaurant meal: €35

➡ *Aperitivo*: €10

➡ Admission to museums: €5–20

Top end: More than €200

➡ Top-end-hotel double room: €200 and over

➡ Dinner of modern Tuscan cuisine: €50

➡ Coffee sitting on a cafe terrace: €4–5

➡ Tour guide for two hours: €140

Opening Hours

Opening hours vary throughout the year. We've provided summer (high-season) and winter (low-season) opening hours, but be aware that hours might differ in the shoulder seasons.

Banks 8.30am to 1.30pm and 3.30pm to 4.30pm Monday to Friday

Restaurants 12.30pm to 2.30pm and 7.30pm to 10pm

Cafes 7.30am to 8pm

Bars and pubs 10am to 1am

Shops 9am to 1pm and 3.30pm to 7.30pm (or 4pm to 8pm) Monday to Saturday

Arriving in Tuscany

Pisa International Airport LAM Rossa (red) bus line into central Pisa (€1.20). PisaMover automated trains run to Pisa's Stazione Pisa Centrale (€2.70); regular trains run to Florence's Stazione di Santa Maria Novella (€8.40). Taxis cost €10 to central Pisa.

Florence Airport Buses run to central Florence (€6). Taxis cost a fixed €20 to central Florence (€23 on Sunday and holidays, €22 between 10pm and 6am), plus €1 per bag and €1 supplement for a fourth passenger.

Dangers & Annoyances

➡ The region is a safe place generally.

➡ The usual street-smart rules apply in Florence, Siena and other key urban hubs: avoid wandering around town alone late at night; stick to main roads rather than narrow back alleys.

➡ Watch out for pickpockets in heavily touristed zones such as around Florence's Piazza del Duomo and Ponte Vecchio, Piazza dei Miracoli in Pisa and Piazza del Duomo in Siena.

➡ Keep alert on crowded buses to/from Florence and Pisa airports.

➡ Rural Tuscany is, well, rural: horseflies, mosquitoes and various other pesky insects come out in their droves in the height of summer. Bring repellent and/or cover up.

For much more on **getting around**, see p333

First Time Florence & Tuscany

For more information, see Survival Guide (p325)

Checklist

➡ Check passport validity and visa requirements

➡ Arrange travel insurance

➡ Confirm airline baggage restrictions

➡ Reserve accommodation and high-profile restaurants

➡ Buy tickets online for Florence's Uffizi and iconic cathedral dome, and Pisa's Leaning Tower

➡ Buy museum passes (eg Firenze Card)

➡ Book guided tours (eg to Siena's cathedral dome)

➡ Organise international roaming on your phone if needed

What to Pack

➡ Sturdy walking shoes for cobbled and unpaved streets

➡ Italian phrasebook

➡ Travel plug (adaptor)

➡ Driving map and GPS for the car (or phone app)

➡ Sunscreen, sunhat and sunglasses (summer)

➡ Umbrella and/or raincoat (except in high summer)

➡ Corkscrew – Italian winemakers dislike screw-tops

Top Tips for Your Trip

➡ Always carry some cash. Unattended petrol (gas) stations don't always accept foreign credit cards, and some restaurants and hotels operate on a cash-only basis.

➡ Don't rely solely on a GPS (which can occasionally lead you too far off the beaten track) – cross-check your route on a printed road map.

➡ You will often find that there is free wi-fi access in or around *palazzi comunale* (town halls) and tourist offices.

➡ To cut costs in Florence, plan your stay for the first Sunday of the month, when admission to state museums (including the Uffizi and the Galleria dell'Accademia) is free.

➡ Foodies should invest in *Osterie d'Italia,* published by Slow Food Editore as an App (iPhone and Android) and a printed book in English or Italian.

➡ Leave the selfie stick at home: they are forbidden in many museums in Tuscany.

What to Wear

A sense of style is vital to Tuscans, who take great pride in their dress and appearance. Maintaining *la bella figura* (ie making a good impression) is extremely important. Steer clear of shorts, miniskirts and flip-flops unless you're at the beach; and always dress up – not down – at restaurants, clubs and bars. Smart-casual outfits will cover you in most situations; trainers are definitely frowned upon after dark.

Cover yourself when entering a church (no shorts, short skirts or sleeveless or off-the-shoulder tops). Topless and nude bathing are unacceptable at most beaches.

Sleeping

Book accommodation in advance, particularly in spring, summer and autumn when the best addresses fill up fast. Check online for cheaper rates.

Agriturismi Accommodation on farms, wineries and rural estates: perfect for those with a car, and usually highly practical for those travelling with children.

Palazzo hotels Historic 'palace' hotels, designer in vibe, are the boutique option for those in towns and cities with a mid-range to top-end budget.

B&Bs Small family-run guesthouses with a handful of rooms, offering bed and breakfast; bathrooms are occasionally shared.

For more information, see p36.

Bargaining

Tuscans don't bargain, so neither should you.

Tipping

Taxis Round the fare up to the nearest euro.

Restaurants Many locals don't tip waiters, but most visitors leave 10% to 15% if there's no service charge.

Cafes Leave a coin (as little as €0.10 is acceptable) if you drank your coffee at the counter or 10% if you sat at a table.

Hotels Bellhops usually expect €1 to €2 per bag; it's not necessary to tip the concierge, cleaners or front-desk staff.

Language

Many locals in towns and cities speak at least one language other than Italian – usually English or French. But venture into the deep Tuscan countryside and you'll need that Italian phrasebook. Region-wide, many traditional places to eat have no written menu at all or a menu penned in Italian in spidery handwriting.

 What's the local speciality?
Qual'è la specialità di questa regione?
kwa·le la spe·cha·lee·ta dee kwes·ta re·jo·ne

A bit like the rivalry between medieval Italian city-states, these days the country's regions compete in speciality foods and wines.

 Which combined tickets do you have?
Quali biglietti cumulativi avete?
kwa·lee bee·lye·tee koo·moo·la·tee·vee a·ve·te

Make the most of your euro by getting combined tickets to various sights; they are available in all major Italian cities.

 Where can I buy discount designer items?
C'è un outlet in zona? che oon owt·let in zo·na

Discount fashion outlets are big business in major cities – get bargain-priced seconds, samples and cast-offs for *la bella figura*.

 I'm here with my husband/boyfriend.
Sono qui con il mio marito/ragazzo.
so·no kwee kon eel mee·o ma·ree·to/ra·ga·tso

Solo women travellers may receive unwanted attention in some parts of Italy; if ignoring fails have a polite rejection ready.

 Let's meet at 6pm for pre-dinner drinks.
Ci vediamo alle sei per un aperitivo.
chee ve·dya·mo a·le say per oon a·pe·ree·tee·vo

At dusk, watch the main piazza get crowded with people sipping colourful cocktails and snacking the evening away: join your new friends for this authentic Italian ritual!

Etiquette

Greetings Shake hands and say *buongiorno* (good morning) or *buonasera* (good afternoon/evening). If you know someone well, kissing both cheeks (starting with their left) is standard.

Polite language Say *mi scusi* to attract attention or to say 'I'm sorry', *grazie (mille)* to say 'thank you (very much)', *per favore* to say 'please', *prego* to say 'you're welcome' or 'please, after you', and *permesso* if you need to push past someone in a crowd.

Cafes Don't linger at the bar; drink your espresso and go.

Body language Be wary of making a circle with two hands (which in Italy means 'I'll kick your arse'), an A-OK signal ('You might be gay') or the devil horns with your hand ('Your wife is cheating on you').

In churches Never intrude on a mass or service.

Selfie sticks Officially banned in Florentine museums. Elsewhere don't stick them in front of other people's faces or those trying to view world-class art in relative peace.

What's New

Be Tuscan for a Day

Get under the region's skin with this enticing portfolio of unique, grassroots experiences in central Tuscany, designed to make you feel truly Tuscan for a day: think slow trekking, experimental archaeology, vineyard tours, medieval dining, cultural orienteering etc. (p143)

The Last Supper

Art lovers can feast on two recently restored masterpieces depicting the Last Supper: Domenico Ghirlandaio's 1476 fresco inside a medieval abbey in Badia a Passignano (p147) and Giorgio Vasari's 1546 oil painting, back inside Florence's Basilica di Santa Croce (p92) after 50 years of restoration.

Vignamaggio

Live the Tuscan dream on this magnificent Chianti estate with Renaissance villa, wine cellar and formal gardens near Greve in Chianti. During your stay you can spot shots from Kenneth Branagh's film adaptation of *Much Ado About Nothing*. (p146)

Centro Per l'Arte Contemporanea Pecci, Prato

If you tire of Renaissance art, head to Prato's dazzling new contemporary-art museum, at home in a striking piece of curvaceous, shiny-gold architecture by Dutch architect Maurice Nio. (p247)

Enoliteca Consortile, Montepulciano

Wine aficionados can swill, smell and sip their way into viticulturist heaven at this showcase of Vino Nobile di Montepulciano, with a heady 70-plus labels to taste and buy, inside the town's Medicean fortress. (p174)

Ground-breaking urban dining

Modern Tuscan cuisine is reaching fabulous new heights thanks to the dazzling talents of inventive young chef Simone Cipriani at Florence's loft-style Essenziale (p112) and Lorenzo Barsotti at cocktail bar–lounge hybrid Filippo Mud Bar (p261)

'Gate of Heaven' tour, Siena

Visiting Siena's remarkable Romanesque-Gothic *duomo* is now even more breathtaking thanks to spectacular Porta del Cielo tours up into, and around, the cathedral's roof and dome. (p131)

Craft cocktails

A powerful trio is driving the Florentine cocktail revolution: Mad Souls & Spirits (p117), crafting expertly mixed cocktails with crazy names; Balkan-Tuscan restaurant Gurdulù (p113), with its innovative food-cocktail pairings; and speakeasy Rasputin (p117).

For more recommendations and reviews, see lonelyplanet.com/tuscany

If You Like...

Food

There are so many ways to enjoy Tuscan food: from dining at one of the region's many fabulous restaurants to trawling local food markets or learning how to do it yourself.

Bistecca alla fiorentina Florence's iconic T-bone steak hails from the Val di Chiana; tuck in at Ristorante Da Muzzicone. (p281)

Antipasto toscano Open your meal with a mixed platter of cured meats, cheeses and pâté-topped toasts; in Florence try a traditional trattoria like Trattoria Le Massacce or Osteria Il Buongustai. (p104)

White truffles Decadent, unique and utterly memorable: hunt them at Barbialla Nuova. (p251)

Colonnata Discover *lardo* (pig fat) ageing in marble vats of olive oil in this mountain village near Carrara. (p257)

Mercato Centrale Excite taste buds with a foodie stroll around Florence's covered food market; lunch upstairs afterwards. (p106)

Farm to table Dine with one of Tuscany's top farm-to-table chefs in a fashionable Florence restaurant such as Culinaria Bistrot. (p112)

Street food Sink your teeth into a tripe *panini* from a traditional Florentine *trippaio* such as L'Antico Trippaio. (p108)

Wine

Aperitivi A pre-dinner glass of wine with feisty nibbles is a cornerstone of Florentine culture – indulge at Il Santino. (p118)

Antinori nel Chianti Classico The king of Chianti wine cellars: tasting and dining James Bond style. (p149)

Strada del Vino e dell'Olio Costa degli Etruschi Motor through Etruscan Coast wine country, visiting vineyards, *cantine* (cellars) and local artisan food producers. (p204)

Bolgheri Target the home of the ground-breaking Sassicaia 'Super Tuscan' on the Etruscan Coast. Fave wine bars include Enoteca Tognoni and Enoteca de Centro. (p204)

Montalcino Time your visit with the release of the new vintage of Brunello in February. (p166)

Montepulciano Taste and buy Vino Nobile de Montepulciano in this illustrious winemaking town. (p307)

Castello di Brolio Visit Italy's oldest winery, with museum, garden, tasting cellars and restaurant. (p154)

Renaissance Art

Galleria degli Uffizi It doesn't get any better than this Medici art collection in Florence. (p68)

Museo di San Marco No frescoes better portray the humanist spirit of the Renaissance than Fra' Angelico's. (p88)

Cattedrale di Santo Stefano Gorge on Filippo Lippi frescoes in crowd-free Prato. (p247)

Museo Diocesano Small but sensational collection of Renaissance art in Cortona. (p282)

Museo Civico Siena's most famous museum is a feast of secular art. (p132)

Piero della Francesca Trail eastern Tuscany's greatest Renaissance painter, beginning with his famous *Legend of the True Cross* in Arezzo. (p265)

Caprese Michelangelo Art aficionados adore this village in the remote Tuscan outback of Casentino where *David*'s creator was born. (p280)

Contemporary Art

Museo Novecento Modern and contemporary Italian art is brilliantly at home in a 13th-century Florentine *palazzo*. (p83)

Tuttomondo Who would guess that the last wall mural painted by American pop artist Keith Haring adorns a Pisan church facade? (p232)

Palazzo Fabroni Get acquainted with Pistoian contemporary artists at this riveting art museum. (p246)

Fattoria di Celle Count four hours to tour this extraordinary alfresco collection of installation art. (p245)

Castello di Ama Ancient winemaking traditions meet cutting-edge contemporary art on this Chianti wine estate. (p153)

Galleria Continua Ogle world-class contemporary art in medieval San Gimignano. (p157)

Giardino dei Tarocchi Franco-American artist Niki de Saint Phalle brings the tarot-card pack to life. (p193)

Garden of Daniel Spoerri Explore 16 hectares of countryside peppered with contemporary-art installations by 55 international artists. (p183)

Natural Landscapes

Parco Nazionale dell'Arcipelago Toscano Europe's largest marine-protected area has the magical island of Elba at its core. (p210)

Val d'Orcia Picturesque agricultural valley in central Tuscany, and a World Heritage–listed Natural Artistic and Cultural Park to boot. (p166)

Apuane Alps Not snow but marble whitens these dramatic mountain peaks around famous mining town Carrara. (p252)

Garfagnana A trio of remote valleys in northwestern Tuscany forested with chestnut groves and *porcini* mushrooms. (p252)

Top: Leaning Tower (p226), Pisa

Bottom: Montalcino (p166)

Parco Nazionale delle Foreste Casentinesi, Monte Falterona e Campigna Discover dense forests, sparkling rivers and medieval monasteries in Tuscany's northeast. (p277)

Parco Regionale della Maremma This spectacular regional park protects pine forests, marshy plains, unspoilt coastline and the Uccellina mountains. (p192)

Riserva Naturale Provinciale Diaccia Botrona Follow tens of thousands of migrating birds to coastal marshlands around Castiglione della Pescaia. (p191)

Scenic Drives

Passo del Vestito Twist down this hair-raising mountain pass from Castelnuovo di Garfagnana to Massa on the Versilian coast. (p253)

Colle d'Orano & Fetovaia A twinset of gorgeous golden-sand beaches are linked by a dramatic drive on Elba's western coast. (p219)

Monte Argentario Bring along nerves of steel to motor the narrow Via Panoramica encircling this rugged promontory. (p193)

Val d'Orcia Take your foot off the pedal in this serene World Heritage–listed valley of rolling hills and Romanesque abbeys. (p166)

Chianti Bump along age-old back roads woven through vineyards, olive groves and photogenic avenues of cypress trees. (p145)

Strada del Vino e dell'Olio From hilltop towns to the Etruscan Coast via cypress alleys and *enoteche* – this drive is gourmet. (p242)

Gardens

Giardino Torrigiani Explore Europe's largest privately owned green space within a historic town centre. (p98)

Giardino Bardini This quintessential Florentine garden boasts an orangery, marble maidens and Tuscany's finest garden restaurant. (p99)

Villa Grabau Skip, giddy as a child, around potted lemon trees and fountains in ornate villa gardens near Lucca. (p243)

Palazzo Pfanner Invite romance to a chamber-music concert in the baroque-styled garden of this Lucchese 17th-century palace. (p237)

Orto de' Pecci Track down peace, tranquillity, an organic farm, a medieval garden and an experimental vineyard in this Sienese oasis. (p136)

Museo di Casa Vasari Few know about the bijou Renaissance rooftop garden atop Giorgio Vasari's childhood home in Arezzo. (p269)

La Foce Enjoy a guided tour of these formal, English-designed gardens in the Val d'Orcia. (p171)

Vignamaggio These magnificent formal gardens featured in Kenneth Branagh's film adaptation of *Much Ado About Nothing*; bookings essential. (p146)

Pilgrimage Sites

Via Francigena Walk the Tuscan chunk of one of Europe's most important medieval pilgrimages – Siena's *duomo* is a highlight. (p52)

Assisi In neighbouring Umbria, the birthplace of St Francis of Assisi makes for a soulful day trip. (p284)

Santuario della Verna Visit the windswept monastery where St Francis received the stigmata – see his bloody gown. (p277)

Cattedrale di San Martino Pay your respects to the *Volto Santo,* Lucca's revered religious icon, carried through the streets by torchlight each September. (p235)

Siena Trail St Catherine in her home town; see where she was born, her embalmed head and her desiccated thumb. (p127)

Medieval Towers

Campanile Scale 414 steps to the top of Florence cathedral's bell tower for an uplifting city panorama. (p76)

Torre d'Arnolfo Admire one of Europe's most beautiful cities atop Palazzo Vecchio's 94m-tall crenellated tower. (p79)

Leaning Tower The bell tower of Pisa's cathedral leaned from the moment it was unveiled in 1372. (p226)

Torre Guinigi Bask in the shade of oak trees planted at the top of this 14th-century red-brick tower, one of 130 that once dotted medieval Lucca. (p238)

Torre del Mangia Views of Siena's iconic Piazza del Campo from atop this graceful tower are predictably swoon-worthy; count the 500 steps up. (p134)

Torre Grossa Gorge on spectacular views of San Gimignano's centuries-old streets and the picture-postcard countryside beyond. (p156)

Torre del Candeliere Quintessentially Tuscan views of a hilltop town and rolling landscape seduce from Massa Marittima's cute Candlestick Tower. (p181)

Month by Month

February

It's only towards the end of this month that locals are coaxed out of their winter hibernation. Windswept hill towns can appear all but deserted.

✱ Festa di Anna Maria Medici

Anna Maria Luisa de' Medici, the last Medici, bequeathed Florence its vast cultural heritage, hence this feast on 18 February marking her death in 1743: there's a costumed parade from Palazzo Vecchio to her tomb in the Cappelle Medicee, and free admission to state museums. (p103)

✱ Carnevale di Viareggio

The seaside resort of Viareggio goes wild during carnevale, an annual festival that kicks off in February. The famous month-long street party revolves around fireworks, floats featuring giant satirical effigies of topical personalities, parades and round-the-clock revelry. (p262)

March

Locals start to get into the springtime swing of things in the weeks leading up to Easter. Many visitors time their trips for this period to take advantage of low-season prices and uncrowded conditions.

✱ Torciata di San Giuseppe

An evocative torchlit procession down Pitigliano's mysterious, Etruscan-era *vie cave* (sunken roads) ends in a huge bonfire in the town. Held on the eve of the spring equinox (19 March), it's a symbol of purification and of winter's end.

✱ Settimana Santa

Easter Week is celebrated in neighbouring Umbria with processions and performances in Assisi. Other Easter celebrations in the region include Florence's dramatic Scoppio del Carro, aka Explosion of the Cart, in front of the *duomo* on Easter Sunday. (p103)

April

Wildflowers carpet the countryside, market stalls burst with new-season produce and classical music is staged in wonderfully atmospheric surrounds. Easter sees the tourist season kicking off in earnest.

☆ Maggio Musicale Fiorentino

Italy's oldest arts festival, a 1933 creation, brings world-class performances of theatre, classical music, jazz and dance to Florence's sparkling new opera house and other venues in the city. Concerts continue through April into June. (p103)

May

Medieval pageants take over the streets of towns and cities across the region from late spring to early autumn, highlighting ancient neighbourhood rivalries and the modern-day love of street parties.

✱ Balestro del Girifalco

Cinematic flag-waving opens this archery festival, held in Massa Marittima on the fourth Sunday in May

and again on 14 August. Archers from the town's three *terzieri* (districts) don medieval garb and, armed with 15th-century crossbows, compete for a symbolic golden arrow and painted silk banner. (p182)

June

It's summertime and, yes, the living is easy. The start of the month is the perfect time to tour the paradisiacal isle of Elba, and any time is right to gorge on seafood and strawberries.

🎉 Luminaria di San Ranieri

After dark on 16 June, Pisans honour their city's patron saint, San Ranieri, with thousands upon thousands of candles on window sills and doorways, and blazing torches along the banks of the Arno, climaxing at 11pm with a spectacular fireworks display.

🎉 Festa di San Giovanni

The feast of Florence's patron saint, San Giovanni (St John), on 24 June is a fantastic opportunity to catch a match of *calcio storico* (historic football) – headbutting, punching, elbowing, choking and all – on Piazza di Santa Croce. The grand finale is fireworks over Piazzale Michelangelo. (p103)

🎉 Giostra del Saracino

A grandiose affair deep-rooted in good old-fashioned neighbourhood rivalry, this tournament sees the four *quartieri* (quarters) of Arezzo each put forward

Top: J AX performing at Lucca Summer Festival (p239)

Bottom: Ferie delle Messi (p158)

ANA MURACA/SHUTTERSTOCK ©

Costumed teammates at Gioco del Ponte (p225)

a team of knights to battle on the beautiful Piazza Grande; jousts are held the third Saturday in June and the first Sunday in September. (p270)

☆ San Gimignano Estate

Battles between fearless knights in shining armour, archery contests, falconry displays, fiery tugs of war and theatre performances evoke all the fun and madness of San Gimignano's medieval heritage during the Ferie delle Messi, usually held the third weekend in June. (p158)

🎭 Gioco del Ponte

The atmosphere is electric during Pisa's Gioco del Ponte, when two teams in elaborate 16th-century costume battle to capture the city bridge, Ponte di Mezzo.

It's held on the last Sunday in June. (p225)

July

Cyclists and walkers take to the mountains, but everyone else heads to the beach, meaning that accommodation prices in inland cities and towns drop. Summer music and arts festivals abound.

🎭 Palio

The most spectacular event on the Tuscan calendar, the Palio is held on 2 July and 16 August in Siena. Featuring colourful street pageants, a wild horse race and generous doses of civic pride, it exemplifies the living history that makes Tuscany so brilliantly compelling. (p140)

☆ Cortona Festivals

The hill town of Cortona is alive with music during the sacred-music festival Cortona Cristiana (www.cortonacristiana.it). Late July ushers in the Cortona Mix Festival (www.mixfestival.it), an enticing cocktail of music, theatre, literature and film. Watch for the winter edition in February.

☆ Lucca Summer Festival

This month-long music festival lures big-name international pop, rock and blues acts to lovely Lucca, where they serenade crowds under the stars in some of the city's most atmospheric piazzas. (p239)

☆ Pistoia Blues

BB King, Miles Davis, David Bowie, Sting and Santana have all taken to the stage at Pistoia's annual blues festival, an electric alfresco fest around since 1980 that packs out central square Piazza del Duomo. (p248)

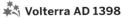 Giostra dell'Orso

Medieval jousting and other equestrian pranks fill Piazza del Duomo during Pistoia's Giostra dell'Orso (Joust of the Bear), a celebration of its patron saint San Giacomo on 25 July. (p248)

Medieval Evenings

Oh, how apt it is for Suvereto, one of Tuscany's most beautiful medieval villages on the Etruscan Coast, to host July's Serate Medievali (Medieval Evenings). The festival transforms the serene red-brick cloister of Convento di San Francesco into a bustling medieval marketplace. (p208)

☆ Puccini Festival

Opera buffs from around the world make a pilgrimage to the small town of Torre del Lago for this annual event in July and August (www.puccinifestival.it). Performances are staged in an open-air lakeside theatre next to the great man's house.

August

Locals take their annual holidays and the daily tempo of life in the cities slows to a snail's pace. The weather can be oppressively hot and beaches are inevitably crowded.

Volterra AD 1398

On the third and fourth Sundays of August, locals in Volterra roll back the calendar some 600 years, take to the streets in period costume and party like it's 1398. (p165)

Bravio delle Botti

Thick-armed men from Montepulciano's eight *contrade* (districts) flex their muscles and bust a gut to push 80kg wine barrels uphill in this compelling race, held in the wine-producing town on the last Sunday in August. (p175)

Antiques Fairs

Head to eastern Tuscany in late August or early September for antiques market Cortonantiquaria, inside Cortona's beautiful 18th-century Palazzo Vagnotti. Pair it with Tuscany's most famous antiques fair, Fiera Antiquaria di Arezzo, held in Arezzo the first Sunday and preceding Saturday of every month. (p282) (p270)

September

Gourmets, this is the Tuscan month for you. Autumn ushers in La Vendemmia (the grape harvest) and a bounty of scented *porcini* mushrooms and creamy chestnuts in the forests.

Festa delle Cantine

Wine aficionados, prepare your palate for plenty of dry and lively white Bianco di Pitigliano at the popular wine-cellar fest Settembre diVino – Festa delle Cantine, held the first weekend of September in the spectacular hilltop town of Pitigliano in southern Tuscany.

Palio della Ballestra

Sansepolcro's party-loving locals don medieval costumes and strut around town on the second Sunday of September while hosting a crossbow tournament between local archers and rivals from the nearby Umbrian town of Gubbio. (p274)

Expo de Chianti Classico

There is no finer or more fun opportunity to taste Chianti Classico than at Greve in Chianti's annual Expo del Chianti Classico, held on the second weekend in September. Festivities begin the preceding Thursday. Buy a glass and swirl, sniff, sip and spit your way round. (p145)

☆ Festival Barocco di San Gimignano

Lovers of baroque music will be in their element during this classical-music fest that graces the town of San Gimignano with a wonderful series of concerts (www.accademiadeileggieri.org) on September weekends. (p158)

November

November is when restaurateurs and truffle tragics come from every corner of the globe to sample and purchase Tuscany's bounty of strong-smelling and utterly delicious white truffles.

Mostra Mercato Nazionale del Tartufo Bianco

The old stone streets of San Miniato are filled with one of the world's most distinctive aromas at the National White Truffle Market, held on the last three weekends in November.

Itineraries

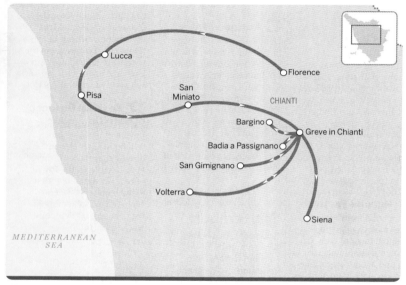

Only the Best

This road trip takes in a classic Tuscan mix of world-class art, medieval architecture, gorgeous countryside and outstanding food and wine.

Devote three days to exploring Renaissance **Florence**. Visit the Uffizi and meander the Arno riverbanks. Spend day two discovering opulent Medici chapels, extraordinary frescoes and Michelangelo's *David* in San Marco and San Lorenzo. On the third day, lose yourself in the Oltrarno's ancient web of squares and alleys laced with artists' workshops.

On day four, shift down a gear to go slow in 16th-century walled **Lucca**. Rent a bicycle to leisurely explore enchanting cobbled streets and graceful, butter-coloured piazzas. On day five, head to **Pisa** early to climb the Leaning Tower, then hit the east-bound road to Chianti with a break in foodie town **San Miniato** for lunch. Use a Tuscan farmhouse around **Greve in Chianti** as a base for three days to gorge on the magically preserved medieval town of **San Gimignano**, artistic enclave **Volterra** and Antinori wine cellars in **Bargino** and **Badia a Passignano**. End in Gothic **Siena** for a two-day gorge on breathlessly beautiful piazzas, churches, museums and eateries.

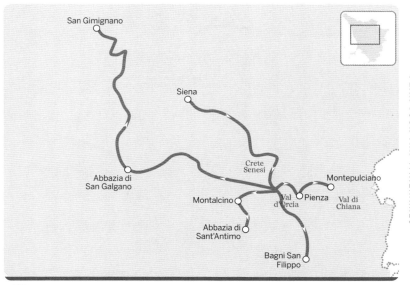

1 WEEK

The Heart of Tuscany

For those in the region for a limited amount of time, this itinerary through central Tuscany more than lives up to the Tuscan dream of gently rolling hills, medieval towns, Renaissance splendour and some very fine wine indeed.

Start in **Siena**, historical rival to Florence. A walking tour is the perfect prelude to the splendid Gothic symphony of this iconic Tuscan city. Gravitate towards the *duomo* and Museo Civico to explore each in greater depth. Break with a *caffè* on a pavement terrace on famously sloping Piazza del Campo, or nip down the street for traditional Sienese biscuits at nearby Il Magnifico. Continue your city exploration: Siena's delightfully intact *centro storico* (historic centre) is a Unesco World Heritage Site for good reason.

On day two (or three if Siena begs you to linger), motor southeast through the rounded hills and cypress alleys of Crete Senesi to Unesco-loved **Pienza**, a stroke of Renaissance architectural genius that, with a couple of lovely sleeping and eating options in and around town, is a brilliant base for exploring this tasty neck of the Tuscan woods. Or meander 15km east to blockbuster wine town **Montepulciano** in the gourmet Val di Chiana and use that as a base. Spend the next three days pandering to your culture-hungry soul and appetite for world-class wine and food: in the Val d'Orcia, tour vineyards around **Montalcino**, savour the serene beauty of **Abbazia di Sant'Antimo,** wander through the ruined Cistercian abbey of **San Galgano**, and soak in hot cascades at **Bagni San Filippo**. In Montepulciano, sink your teeth into a feisty slab of local Chianina beef, slicked in fragrant olive oil and accompanied by a glass of Brunello di Montalcino or Vino Nobile di Montepulciano (two of Italy's greatest wines).

End your sojourn in this idyllic area by looping back along scenic secondary roads to romantic **San Gimignano**, home to medieval tower houses, a lavishly frescoed *duomo* (cathedral) and cutting-edge contemporary art. Dine on delicate pasta dishes scented with locally grown saffron, drink the town's golden-hued Vernaccia wine and, whatever you do, don't miss out on the superb saffron and Vernaccia sorbet by former gelato world champion Sergio Dondoli.

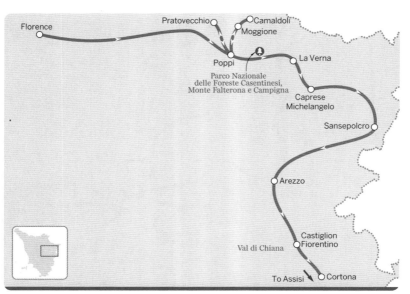

Into the East

12 DAYS

The perfect trip for Tuscan connoisseurs, this itinerary varies the pace with an edgy mix of well-known destinations and intriguing off-the-beaten-track alternatives.

Spend three days admiring the Renaissance splendour of **Florence** before motoring east into the little-known Casentino region, home to the idyllically isolated Parco Nazionale delle Foreste Casentinesi, Monte Falterona e Campigna. Base yourself around the fortified hill town of **Poppi** for three days and visit isolated, windswept medieval monasteries in **Camaldoli** and **La Verna**, hike trails in the national park, lunch on staunchly local, seasonal *cucina tipica casentinese* (typical Casentino cuisine) in family-run village restaurant Il Cedro in tiny **Moggione**, and dine exceedingly well after dark in **Pratovecchio**.

Next head southeast. Stop in the village of **Caprese Michelangelo** to see where *David*'s creator grew up. Then continue to **Sansepolcro**, proud possessor of masterpieces by the Renaissance painter Piero della Francesca.

Tear yourself away after two nights and continue to your final destination, the Val di Chiana, where you can spend a few days eating, drinking and sightseeing your way around the valley. Allow a full day for provincial capital **Arezzo**, with its marvellously sloping central square and laid-back cafe life. Get acquainted with the architect who designed Florence's world-famous Galleria degli Uffizi at the Museo di Casa Vasari, and spend a quiet moment in the town's beautiful churches – Cappella Bacci, Pieve di Santa Maria and the *duomo* are highlights. Join locals for lunch before enjoying a late-afternoon *passeggiata* (stroll) on shop-lined Corso Italia.

Foodies are obliged to make the medieval hilltop town of **Castiglion Fiorentino** a port of call. Tuscany's famed Chianina cow hails from this valley and the *bistecca alla fiorentina* (T-bone steak) served at Ristorante Da Muzzicone is the best there is.

Devote at least a half-day to **Cortona**. Walk up steep cobbled streets to its Fortezza Medicea, and admire the collections at the Museo dell'Accademia Etrusca and the Museo Diocesano. From Cortona it is an easy day trip to **Assisi**, one of Italy's most famous pilgrimage centres, in the neighbouring region of Umbria. Fans of Giotto's extraordinary frescoes will have a field day.

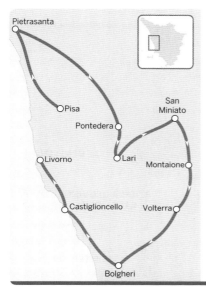

 ## Pisa & its Provinces

This part of Tuscany is not as well trodden as others. Tick off Pisa's blockbuster icon before indulging in a crowd-free road south to the coast.

Start in **Pisa**, allowing time for the Museo Nazionale di San Matteo as well as tourist-packed Piazza dei Miracoli. Scale the famous engineering project gone horribly wrong, aka the Leaning Tower. Come dusk, hit bijou art town **Pietrasanta** for an excellent dinner. On day two, pay homage to Italy's Vespa scooter at **Pontedera's** Museo Piaggio or see spaghetti being made in **Lari**. Lunch in the village, then motor to gourmet town **San Miniato**. Overnight at Barbialla Nuova near **Montaione** and, if the season's right, hunt white truffles.

From here, head to spectacularly sited **Volterra** in the Val di Cecina to visit alabaster ateliers and Etruscan art. On your fourth day, move to the coast, where wine-lovers can meander south to taste Super Tuscan Sassicaias in **Bolgheri**. Drive north along the Etruscan Coast: dip your toes in the sea in the delightfully old-fashioned resort of **Castiglioncello** and end the day on a gourmet high with a seafood feast at Vetto alle Vaglie or La Barrocciaia in port city **Livorno**.

 ## The Maremma

Outdoors-lovers will have a field day in southern Tuscany, where dramatic landscapes etched out of porous volcanic rock, local cowboy culture and a heap of wild activities provide a welcome adrenaline boost.

Start in the little-visited but delightful medieval town of **Massa Marittima** and spend a couple of days visiting its museums and sampling Maremmese food and wine in its rustic eateries. On day three, check out an archaeological dig, Etruscan tombs and an impressive museum at the ancient hilltop settlement of **Vetulonia**; overnight in a local *agriturismo*. From here, head down the coast to the wild and wonderful **Parco Regionale della Maremma** to walk, canoe, cycle or horse ride alongside the famous cowboys known as the *butteri*. End your journey inland amid the stunning surrounds of the Città del Tufo (City of the Tufo), where you should visit the towns of **Pitigliano**, **Sovana** and **Sorano**. Here you can sample the local Morellino di Scansano wine at Società Agricola Terenzi; explore the amazing Etruscan necropolises at the Parco Archeologico 'Città del Tufo'; and spend a day taking an 8km walk along the enigmatic sunken roads known as *vie cave*.

Off the Beaten Track

AL BENEFIZIO

Fragrant fig trees, olive groves, vines and acacia woods frame the nail-bitingly narrow road to this isolated farm where beekeeper Francesca welcomes guests like old friends. Learn to cook with her or help with the olive and honey harvests. (p257)

STRADA DEL VINO E DELL'OLIO

From Lucca, hit the empty road along a network of rural, postcard-Tuscan driving itineraries through the romantic vineyard-stiched hills of Colline Lucchesi and olive groves around the chic hilltop village of Montecarlo. Tastings obligatory. (p242)

PONTEDERA

It was in this small, little-known Tuscan town that Italy's iconic Vespa scooter was born in 1946. Discover the history, legends and romance surrounding the Hepburn-famous 'wasp' at the Museo Piaggio in Pontedera. (p246)

LARI

A pilgrimage to this medieval village between Pisa and Livorno is a must for curious foodies: it is home to the world's smallest pasta factory, aka an artisan workshop run by the Martelli family since 1926. (p233)

TERME DI SASSETA

Take a break from tasting super-hot Super Tuscans along Tuscany's Central Coast with a flop in natural hot springs in a remote chestnut wood near Sassetta, central Tuscany. (p208)

0
0
50 km
25 miles

IL CEDRO

Gourmet travel in Tuscany means tracking down far-flung dining legends, unchanged for decades and cooking up seasonal fruits of the land. Enter Il Cedro in the Parco Nazionale delle Foreste Casentinesi, Monte Falterona e Campigna. (p276)

CAPRESE MICHELANGELO

Dedicated Michelangelo fans won't do better than an off-track motor to the tiny medieval village in eastern Tuscany's Valle del Casentino where *David's* creator spent his childhood roaming the countryside and painting. (p280)

ABBAZIA DI MONTE OLIVETO MAGGIORE

Seek out solitude and soul-soaring fresco art at this medieval abbey, a forest retreat for Benedictine monks southeast of Siena. Its church, frescoed refectory, library and historic wine cellar are equally uplifting. (p176)

MONTE AMIATA

A contemporary sculpture park, an old mercury mine and thick forest are the quirky treats awaiting those who motor off the beaten track around Monte Amiata, an extinct volcano to boot. (p183)

GIARDINO DEI TAROCCHI SCULTURA

Never say Tuscany lacks variety. Franco-American artist Niki de Saint Phalle lived in a sculpture while creating the 22 oversized Gaudí-influenced sculptures that tumble down the hillside at this fantastical sculpture garden in southern Tuscany. (p193)

Map locations: Adriatic Sea, Parco Nazionale delle Foreste Casentinesi, Monte Falterona e Campigna, Monte Falterona (1654m), Florence Airport, Fiesole, Stia, IL CEDRO, Florence, Poppi, Chianti Fiorentino, CAPRESE MICHELANGELO, Greve in Chianti, Chianti, San Gimignano, Chianti Sense, Gaiole in Chianti, Arezzo, Castellina in Chianti, Arno, Siena, Cortona, ABBAZIA DI MONTE OLIVETO MAGGIORE, Montepulciano, Val d'Orcia, Pienza, Montalcino, Bagno Vignoni, Bagni San Filippo, MONTE AMIATA, Vetulonia, Grosseto, Sorano, Parco Regionale della Maremma, Sovana, Pitigliano, Porto Santo Stefano, Orbetello, GIARDINO DEI TAROCCHI SCULTURA, UMBRIA, Monte Argentario, Lago di Burano, Riserva Naturale Lago di Burano, Giannutri

Accommodation

Accommodation Types

Agriturismo A working farm or winery with rooms; family-run and often with evening dining. By definition, an *agriturismo* is required to grow at least one commercial crop, but beyond this common thread they run the gamut from a rustic country house with a handful of olive trees to a luxurious country estate with an attached vineyard to a fully functioning farm where guests can help with the harvest.

Albergo A hotel, be it budget or business, luxurious or a characterful midrange choice.

B&B A small guesthouse offering bed and breakfast; double rooms have a private bathroom.

Castello Literally a castle but in reality anything from a converted outbuilding on a farm to a fully fledged castle with crenellated towers. Whatever its architectural shape, bags of charm and atmosphere are guaranteed.

Locanda A country inn offering B&B in rustic surrounds; most provide dinner.

Ostello A hostel offering dorm beds and rooms to budget travellers.

Palazzo hotel Many urban hotels are housed in century-old palazzi – literally 'palaces' but in reality historic mansions; some have original frescoes and furnishings, others are thoroughly contemporary in design.

Pensione A small, family-run guesthouse offering B&B; the owners live on site.

Rifugio A mountain hut kitted out with bunk rooms sleeping two to a dozen or more people; rates include half board; open mid-June to mid-September.

Villa Self-catering villas and *fattorie* (farmhouses) can be rented in their entirety; most have swimming pools and dreamy green surrounds.

Booking Accommodation

Book well ahead, particularly in Florence and Siena and along the coast in summer. During busy periods, some hotels may impose a multinight stay (this usually applies at beach hotels over July and August, and always applies in Siena during the Palio). Country hotels, *locande,* villas and *agriturismi* often close in winter.

➡ Check hotel websites for good-value internet deals – the cheapest rates require advance payment and are non-reimbursable and non-exchangeable.

➡ Credit cards are accepted at many – but not all – places to stay.

Booking Services

Associazione Italiana Alberghi per la Gioventù (www.aighostels.com) Association of Italian Youth Hostels, affiliated with Hostelling International (HI).

Camping.it (www.camping.it) Directory of campsites in Tuscany.

Club Alpino Italiano (www.cai.it) Database of CAI-operated *rifugi*.

Lungarno Collection (www.lungarnocollection.com) Boutique collection of luxurious hotels owned by the Ferragamo fashion empire, ranging from penthouse suites in Florence to tropical paradise resorts on the Tuscan coast.

Monastery Stays (www.monasterystays.com) A well-organised online booking centre for monastery and convent stays.

Wtb Hotels (www.whythebesthotels.com) Florence-based hotel group.

Lonely Planet (lonelyplanet.com/italy/tuscany/hotels) Recommendations and bookings.

TASSA DI SOGGIORNO

Cities and towns in Tuscany charge a *tassa di soggiorno* (hotel occupancy tax) on top of advertised hotel, B&B or *agriturismo* rates. It is charged to your bill and must be paid in cash. The exact amount, which varies from city to city, depends on how many stars your hotel has and the time of year: expect to pay from €1.50 per person per night up to €5 in a four- or five-star hotel. Children under 10 or 12 are not taxed; 11 to 16s are usually charged 50% of the adult tax.

Top Choices

Best Agriturismi

Barbialla Novella (www.barbialla.it; €90-350) Stylish, self-catering farmhouses on a biodynamic farm and white truffle estate between Florence and Pisa.

Sant'Egle (www.santegle.it; €112-125) Luxurious B&B with bio pool, hot tub and yoga pavilion on an organic farm in southern Tuscany.

Podere San Lorenzo (www.agriturismo-volterra.it; €100) Olive-farm accommodation near Volterra with gourmet dining in a 12th-century chapel.

Podere Brizio (www.poderebrizio.it; €170-220) Splendid hotel on a wine estate near Montalcino.

Best Palazzi

Ad Astra (http://adastraflorence.com; €340) Fashionable Florence guesthouse in a 16th-century palazzo overlooking Europe's largest private garden.

Palazzo Puccini (www.lsmpistoia.it/residenza-storica; ; €105-130) Boutique guesthouse with uber-chic vintage interiors in Pistoia.

Pensione Palazzo Ravizza (www.palazzoravizza.it; €160-295) Renaissance-palace hotel in Siena, resolutely boutique in spirit.

Antica Torre di Via de' Tornabuoni (www.tornabuoni1.com; €350) Top-end Florence hotel in a 14th-century palazzo with sensational rooftop views.

Best for Families

La Bandita (www.la-bandita.com; €250-395) Urban chic meets rural charm at this sophisticated countryside hotel near Pienza, Montepulciano and Montalcino.

Rosselba Le Palme (www.rosselbalepalme.it; €69-198) Seaside campsite with 'glamping' tents, chalets and villa apartments on the island of Elba.

Villa Fontelunga (www.fontelunga.com; €240-365) Stylish self-catering villas in the grounds of a sublime 19th-century villa hotel in eastern Tuscany.

Borgo Corsignano (www.borgocorsignano.it; €120) Lavish medieval village with self-catering properties, two pools, playgrounds and sweeping mountain views.

Best on a Budget

Hotel Scoti (www.hotelscoti.com; €130) Superb *pensione* wedged between fashion boutiques on Florence's smartest shopping strip.

Hotel Alma Domus (www.hotelalmadomus.it; €90-140) Convent with uninterrupted views of Siena's *duomo*.

La Locanda di Pietracupa (www.locandapietracupa.com; €70-92) A rare budget option in posh Chianti.

La Casa di Adelina (www.lacasadiadelina.eu; €97) Art-strewn B&B with rustic-chic rooms in central Tuscany's Val d'Orcia.

Getting Around

For more information, see Transport (p332)

Travelling by Car

Urban meanderings aside, this is undoubtedly the best option for discovering the picture-postcard Tuscany – the romantic cypress alleys, the softly rolling mist-kissed hills, the patchwork of vineyards and fruit orchards and the medieval hilltop villages. Not only is it the quickest (and often only) way to get from A to B via C in this essentially rural region, but it's also the key to accessing some of the most authentic accommodation options, sights and traditional off-the-beaten-track experiences.

Car Hire

Major car-rental companies have desks at Florence and Pisa airports, making car hire upon arrival easy and straightforward. To rent a car you must be a last 25 years old and have a credit card. Make sure you understand precisely what is included in the price: Italian drivers can be unpredictable, streets are narrow and city parking is impossibly tight, meaning it might be worth paying extra to reduce the collision damage waiver excess to zero or at least a couple of hundred euros.

Driving Conditions

Tuscany has an excellent network of roads, ranging from toll-paying *autostradas* (motorways) to bucolic country lanes where two cars can just about squeeze past each another. The FI-PI-LI is a free motorway link between Florence, Pisa and Livorno.

Driving in towns and cities is best avoided. **Limited traffic zones** (ZTL; Zona a Traffico Limitato) make entry into historic city centres impossible, and parking is expensive and hard to find. Away from urban areas, the pace and mood changes: motorists can take their foot off the pedal and cruise at an enjoyable speed through drop-dead-gorgeous scenery.

Maps

Use a GPS device or smartphone app to map routes and navigate, but equip yourself with a decent road map too: in remote areas like the Val d'Orcia, Apuane Alps or Garfagnana, GPS coordinates can be wrong or direct you onto unpaved back roads. Phone reception can be poor or nonexistent.

No Car?

Bus

A reasonably extensive regional bus network links major towns. To get from Florence to Siena, for example, the *corse rapide* (express) bus service is your best bet. Many other routes can involve long trips, and services are reduced or nonexistent at weekends. Regional companies are loosely affiliated under the **Tiemme** (www.lfi.it) network.

On public buses in towns and cities, tickets must be time stamped or you risk a €50 on-the-spot fine.

Train

High-speed trains run by Trenitalia (p335) link Florence, Arezzo and Cortona, as well as Grosseto, Livorno and Pisa. Slow *regionale* (regional) trains link Florence, Lucca and Pisa. Otherwise, the train network throughout Tuscany is limited.

Time stamp your ticket before boarding or risk an immediate €50 fine.

Bicycle

Cycling is a national pastime and rewards in the countryside with grand views. Bikes can be taken on trains that have a bike logo, but they need a ticket – €3.50 for *regionale* services and €12 for international services. Bike hire outlets are common throughout the region and tourist offices in popular cycling areas like Chianti and along the Etruscan Coast have plenty of information on itineraries.

PLAN YOUR TRIP GETTING AROUND

DRIVING FAST FACTS

Right or Left? Right

Manual or automatic: Manual

Top speed limit: 130km/h

Legal driving age: 18

Signature car: Fiat 500 (preferably convertible)

Alternative vehicle: Vespa scooter

ROAD DISTANCES (MILES)

	Florence	Pisa	Lucca	San Miniato
Pisa	69			
Lucca	61	23		
San Miniato	37	47	70	
Siena	51	87	30	77

Don't Miss Drives

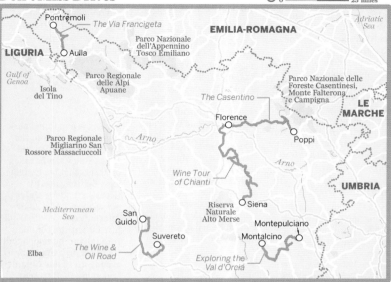

Wine Tour of Chianti (p150) Take your foot off the pedal and indulge in four days of slow meandering through Tuscan wine country.

Exploring the Val d'Orcia (p168) One of Tuscany's most beautiful road trips, this extraordinary Unesco World Heritage site of a valley in central Tuscany demands exploration.

Strada del Vino e dell'Olio Costa degli Etruschi (p206) Allow a full day for this coastal cruise

along the Etruscan Coast's Wine and Oil Road; book winery tastings in advance.

Go Slow in the Valle del Casentino (p278) An easy day trip from Florence, this short one-day itinerary delves into the wild and remote Casentino Valley in eastern Tuscany.

Via Francigena (p258) Trace the path of medieval pilgrims – by foot, bicycle or car – in the rural Lunigiana in northwestern Tuscany.

Fresh truffles and mushrooms

Plan Your Trip
Eat & Drink
Like a Local

For Tuscans, eating and drinking is a fine art to rival their masterpiece surroundings. Thanks to an ancient cuisine sourced in the
family farmstead from seasonal fruits of the land and sea, Tuscans eat exceedingly well – and around a shared table. Titillate
your taste buds with these food-trip essentials.

The Year in Food

Feasting is year round, with foodie festivals galore.

Spring (March–May)

Markets burst with baby violet artichokes, asparagus, fresh garlic and – towards the season's end – cherries, figs and zucchini flowers begging to be stuffed.

Summer (June–August)

There's strawberries and peppers, and the start of San Gimignano's saffron harvest (July to November). Beat the heat by the sea with seafood, and elsewhere with a gelato – chestnut, fig and honey, or saffron and pine-nut flavour.

Autumn (September–November)

Olives and grapes are harvested, forest fruits like chestnuts and *porcini* mushrooms (August to October) are gathered, and game is hunted. Oenophiles head to Greve in Chianti in September for Chianti's biggest wine fair. Mid-October opens the white truffle season near Pisa.

Winter (December–February)

The truffle season, which continues until mid-December, peaks with San Miniato's truffle market. Montalcino wine producers crack open the new vintage at February's Benvenuto Brunello.

Food Experiences

Dining in Tuscany covers the whole gamut, from street food to chic farm tables and posh-frock gastronomic temples. Plan ahead to cover all delicious bases.

Meals of a Lifetime

Enoteca Pinchiorri, Florence (p109) Tuscany's only Michelin-three-star address, stratospheric and smug in a 16th-century Florentine *palazzo*.

Peperino, San Miniato (p251) Dinner for two at the world's smallest, and possibly most romantic, restaurant.

Barbialla Nuova, Montaione (p251) Hunt white truffles in damp, musky woods, then head to a village trattoria to eat it shaved over steak.

Il Leccio, Sant'Angelo in Colle (p170) Simple but spectacular cuisine sourced from the garden, washed down with extraordinary Brunellos.

Osteria di Passignano, Chianti (p148) Elegant, wine-fuelled dining on an Antinori estate. It doesn't get more Tuscan glam.

Osteria del Castello, Gaiole in Chianti (p154) Classic Tuscan dishes with a modern twist courtesy of chef Silvia Zinato; find perfect pairings with the estate's well-regarded wines.

La Terrazza del Chiostro, Pienza (p172) Expert wine pairings honour chef Alessandro Rossi's dazzling modern Italian cuisine. The icing on the cake is the panorama from the terrace.

Cheap Treats

Pecorino Ewe's-milk cheese perfect in fresh, crunchy *pane* (bread).

Porchetta rolls Warm sliced pork (roasted whole with fennel, garlic and pepper) in a crispy roll.

Torta di ceci Savoury chickpea pancake.

Castagnaccio Hybrid cake-crepe, sweet and made from chestnut flour.

Gelato The best Tuscan ice cream uses seasonal, natural ingredients: figs, chestnuts, pine nuts, honey, saffron, wild strawberries...

Dare to Try

Bistecca alla fiorentina Blue and bloody is the only way to eat Florence's iconic T-bone steak; Trattoria Mario (p107) is the address.

Lampredotto Cow's fourth stomach, chopped, simmered and cooked up at every Florentine *trippaio*.

Trippa alla fiorentina Tripe in tomato sauce; once eaten, never forgotten at Da Nerbone (p107) in Florence's Mercato Centrale.

Lardo di colonnata Carrara's luscious pig lard, aged in marble vats, keeps cardiologists in the black.

Biroldo Local version of haggis, included in tastings at Osteria Vecchia Mulino (p252) in Castelnuovo di Garfagnana.

Mallegato San Miniato's Slow Food–accredited blood sausage, usually on the menu at the restaurant of butcher Sergio Falaschi (p251).

Local Specialities

Spicy green olives, extra-virgin olive oils, full-bodied red wines, smoky *porcini* mushrooms and bags of beans are culinary trademarks across the Tuscan board, but delve deeper to discover geographic differences every gourmet will revel in.

Florence

Tuscany's leading lady is a born-and-bred gourmet. Be it slow food or fine dining, *panino* in a piazza or tripe at a street cart, Florence meets every gastronomic taste with style and panache.

The day's end ushers in **aperitivi** (predinner drinks), a sacrosanct ritual big and buzzing in Tuscany's largest city: so copious are the complimentary buffets of snacks and nibbles laid out to accompany drinks that savvy young Florentines increasingly forgo dinner for **apericena** (*aperitivi* and dinner rolled into one).

Northwestern Tuscany

Wedged between wind-whipped sea and mountain, this unexpected culinary nest egg is known for its fresh *pecorino* cheese, *zuppe di cavolo* (cabbage soup) and other humble farm fare. Slow Food town San Miniato, near Pisa, is the source of Tuscany's exceptional white truffles.

In **Castelnuovo di Garfagnana**, fresh *porcini*, chestnuts and sacks of farmgrown *farro* (spelt) fill autumnal markets. Sweet *castagnaccio* (chestnut cake) is to

Cacciucco

locals in Garfagnana what *buccellato* (a sugared bread loaf studded with sultanas and aniseed) is to those in Lucca.

Not far from the coast, pig fat is aged in Carrara-marble vats and eaten 12 or 24 months later as wafer-thin, aromatic slices of *lardo di colonnata*.

Central Coast & Elba

Two words: sensational seafood. The grimy port of **Livorno** is the place to feast on superb affordable dining and **cacciucco**, a zesty fish stew swimming with octopus, rock fish and a shoal of other species.

Inland, vineyards around the walled village of **Bolgheri** produce Super Tuscan Sassicaia and other legendary full-bodied reds – a perfect match for *cinghiale* (wild boar). On **Elba**, sweet red Aleatico Passito DOCG is the nectar amid the raft of sun-drenched wines grown on the island; spunky olive oils too.

Siena & Central Tuscany

Siena is the GPS coordinate where Tuscan cuisine originates, say locals, for whom *caffè* (coffee) and a slice of *panforte* (a rich

---

BEST COOKING CLASSES

Desinare (☎055 22 11 18; www.desinare.it; Via dei Serragli 234r) Florence

Cucina Lorenzo de' Medici (Map p88; ☎334 3040551; www.cucinaldm.com; Mercato Centrale, Piazza del Mercato Centrale) Florence

La Dogana (p175) Montepulciano

Podere San Lorenzo (☎0588 3 90 80; www.agriturismo-volterra.it; Via Allori 80) Near Volterra

Strada del Vino Nobile di Montepulciano (p175) Montepulciano

Scuola di Cucina di Lella (p138) Siena

PLAN YOUR TRIP EAT & DRINK LIKE A LOCAL

Rosso di Montalcino wine

cake of almonds, honey and candied fruit) is a mandatory part of their weekend diet.

Chianti is for serious foodies: cheery, dry, full red wines; butcher legend Dario Cecchini (p148) in Panzano in Chianti; tip-top Chianti Classico DOP olive oils; *finocchiona briciolona* (pork salami made with fennel seeds and Chianti) from Antica Macelleria Falorni (p146) in Greve in Chianti; and some of Tuscany's most exciting modern Tuscan cuisine.

Montalcino is famed for red Brunello wine, the consistently good Rosso di Montalcino and prized extra-virgin olive oils. **Montepulciano,** home of Vino Nobile red and its equally quaffable second-string Rosso di Montepulciano, also produces fine beef and Terre di Siena DOP extra-virgin olive oil.

Cheese aficionados make a beeline for **Pienza**, where some of Italy's finest *pecorino* is crafted, and the **Val di Chiana**, where sheep cheese is wrapped in fern fronds to become *ravaggiolo*. The same gorgeous rolling green valley is also where the world-famous Chianina beef comes from, making it the perfect place to sample *bistecca alla fiorentina,* perhaps after a tasty *primo* (first course) of *pici* (a type of local hand-rolled pasta).

Something of a culinary curiosity, fiery red **San Gimignano** saffron was the first in Europe to get its own DOP (protected origin) stamp of quality. Saffron gelato at San Gimignano's Gelateria Dondoli (p158) is particularly memorable.

Southern Tuscany

When it comes to quality-guaranteed beef, chicken and game, Maremma is a byword. **Pitigliano** is a mecca for the sweet-toothed thanks to handmade biscuits crafted locally, including the traditional Jewish honey-and-walnut pastry *lo sfratto.*

BEST WINES
⇒ Brunello di Montalcino
⇒ Vino Nobile di Montepulciano
⇒ Chianti
⇒ Vernaccia di San Gimignano
⇒ Super Tuscan Sassicaia

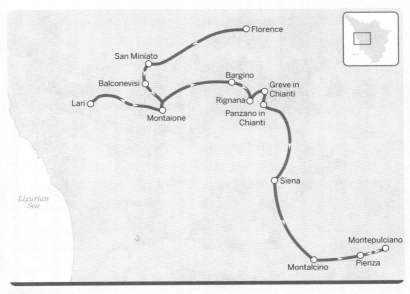

Ligurian Sea

Itinerary: A Foodie Tour of Tuscany

To taste, drink and dine exceedingly well, travel your taste buds through the gourmet heart of Tuscany.

No city plays the gourmet better than Florence (p60): shop for olive oils at La Bottega Della Frutta and Mercato Centrale, then lunch at Trattoria Mario. Round off your meal with an espresso at Ditta Artigianale. Later, indulge in a chocolate *degustazione* (tasting) with local foodie Alessandro Frassica at 'Ino and a gelato at Gelateria La Carraia. At dusk join Florentine gastronomes for *aperitivo* at All'Antico Vinaio (superb salami and cheese platters). Florence's *enoteche* (wine bars) such as Le Volpi e l'Uva and Enoteca Pitti Gola e Cantina are other superb pre-dinner drink stops. Complete the evening with the dazzling contemporary Tuscan cuisine of Simone Cipriani at warehouse-turned-lounge Essenziale or a theatrical supper rooted in the traditional Tuscan cuisine of legendary Florentine chef Fabio Picchi at Il Teatro del Sale.

On day two, motor 30km into hilltop San Miniato (p250), a Slow Food town with several stunning lunch options; nip into Sergio Falaschi's famous butcher shop for local cured meats. Head into the hills for a dinner of creative modern Tuscan fare at Osteria Il Papero in Balconevisi (p250). Overnight on white-truffle estate Barbialla Nuova in Montaione (p251).

Next morning, drive one hour west to Lari (p233) to watch artisan pasta makers at work at Martelli, or dive into Chianti for a cellar visit and lunch at the flagship Antinori nel Chianti Classico in Bargino (p149). Dine and overnight at Rignana (p148).

It's a short drive next day to Greve in Chianti (p146) to visit Enoteca Falorni, Chianti's biggest wine cellar. Buy *finocchiona briciolona* (fennel seed–studded pork salami) for a picnic lunch at Antica Macelleria Falorni and end the day at Badia a Passignano.

On day five, drive south to Panzano in Chianti (p148). Lunch with celebrity butcher Dario, then head to Siena (p127), where you could consider a cooking class at Scuola di Cucina di Lella, shop for *panforte* to take home at Il Magnifico and dine at La Taverna di San Giuseppe. On your final day, drive to Montalcino (p166) for a cellar tour at Poggio Antico, lunch at Il Leccio and – if you're mad about wine – a trip to the Enoliteca Consortile in wine town Montepulciano (p174). End the day on yet another culinary high at La Bandita in Pienza (p37).

GINA YESCOV/SHUTTERSTOCK ©

STEFANO EMBER/SHUTTERSTOCK ©

Top: *Ribollita* ('reboiled' bean, vegetable and bread soup)

Bottom: Shop in Volterra (p163)

Then there's Pitigliano's very own DOC Bianco di Pitigliano, a fresh and fruity, Trebbiano-based white wine.

How to Eat & Drink

It pays to know what and how much to eat, and when – adopting the local pace is key to savouring every last exquisite gastronomic moment of the Tuscan day.

When to Eat

Colazione (breakfast) is a quick dash into a bar or cafe for a short, sharp espresso and *cornetto* (croissant) or *brioche* (pastry) standing at the bar.

Pranzo (lunch) is traditionally the main meal of the day, though Tuscans now tend to share the main family meal in the evening. Standard restaurant times are noon or 12.30pm to 2.30pm; locals rarely lunch before 1pm.

Merenda (afternoon snack) is the traditional afternoon snack, much revered by school children, workers and actually pretty much anyone who loves their food. Indulged in around 4pm, it is often bread based.

Aperitivo (aperitif) is the all-essential post-work, early-evening drink that takes place any time between 5pm and 10pm when the price of your cocktail (€8 to €10 in Florence) includes a copious buffet of nibbles, finger foods, or even salads, pasta and so on.

Cena (dinner) is traditionally lighter than lunch. The legendary Tuscan belt-busting, five-course whammy only happens on Sunday and feast days. Standard restaurant times are 7.30pm to around 10pm (often later in Florence and across the board in summer); locals never eat before 8pm.

Where to Eat

In a **ristorante** (restaurant) expect to find crisp linen, classic furnishings, formal service and refined dishes**. A trattoria** is a restaurant, often family owned, with cheaper prices, more relaxed service and classic regional specialities. Intimate and relaxed, the **osteria** has its origins in a traditional inn serving wine with a little food on the side; these days it's hard

PLAN YOUR TRIP EAT & DRINK LIKE A LOCAL

WHITE TRUFFLES

They're not a plant, they don't spawn like mushrooms and cultivating them is impossible. Pig-ugly yet precious, these wild knobs of fungus excite and titillate. They're said to have aphrodisiacal qualities, and one whiff of their aroma is enough to convince: the smell of truffles, especially the more pungent white truffle, is seductive.

Truffles grow in symbiosis with oak trees and are *bianco* (white – actually a mouldy old yellowish colour) or *nero* (black – a gorgeous velvety tone). They are sniffed out by dogs from mid-October to late December, in San Giovanni d'Asso near Siena, and San Miniato, between Florence and Pisa. Truffles are typically served raw and thinly shaved over simple, mild-tasting dishes to give the palate full opportunity to revel in the subtle flavour. Some top truffle tastings:

Barbialla Nuova, Montaione (p251) Tuscany's golden ticket for hunting white truffles.

Boutique del Tartufo, Volterra (p166) Truffle shop selling fresh and conserved truffles, made-to-order truffle-infused cheese *panini* (sandwiches), truffle paste etc.

Pepenero, San Miniato (p251) Celebrity chef Gilberto Rossi gives truffles a creative spin.

Ristorante Da Ventura, Sansepolcro (p275) Nothing beats a simple omelette sprinkled with fresh truffle shavings.

I Sette Consoli, Orvieto (☑0763 34 39 11; www.isetteconsoli.it; Piazza Sant'Angelo 1a; meals around €45, 6-course tasting menu €42; ☺12.30-3pm & 7.30-10pm, closed Wed & dinner Sun) Special dishes of the day celebrate the truffle season.

L'Osteria di Casa Chianti, Fiano (p149) Speciality truffle dishes; cooking classes too.

La Taverna di San Giuseppe, Siena (p141) The address for truffle dining in Siena.

DIEGOMARIOTTINI/SHUTTERSTOCK ©

Pecorino in Pienza (p170)

to differentiate between an *osteria* and a trattoria. For a cheap feed, cold beer and a buzzing, convivial vibe, head for a **pizzeria**.

Enoteca (wine bars) are increasingly casual, atmospheric places to dine and taste Tuscan wines by the glass.

Dining on a farm at an **agriturismo** (farm stay) gives you the best of Tuscany – a copious, never-ending feast of homemade cooking using local produce, set against a quintessential Tuscan backdrop of old stone farmhouse, cypress alley and pea-green rolling hills.

At the **gelateria** (ice-cream shop), rain, hail or shine, a queue outside the door marks the best. The astonishing choice of flavours will have you longing for a gelato long after you've left Tuscany.

Menu Decoder

Menù di degustazione Tasting menu.

Coperto Cover charge, €1 to €3 per person, for bread.

Piatto del giorno Dish of the day.

Antipasto A hot or cold appetiser; for a mix of appetisers go for *antipasto misto* (mixed antipasto).

Primo First course, usually pasta, rice or *zuppa* (soup).

Secondo Second course, *carne* (meat) or *pesce* (fish).

Contorno Vegetable side dish.

Dolce Dessert, often *torta* (cake) or *cantucci* (dry almond-studded biscuits) dunked into a glass of sweet Vin Santo wine.

Acqua minerale (mineral water) Jugs of tap water aren't in, but a bottle of *frizzante* (sparkling) or *naturale* (still) with a meal is a Tuscan standard.

Vino della casa (house wine) Wine in restaurants is reasonably priced and good; the cheapest is *vino della casa,* ordered in carafes of 25cL, 50cL, 75cL or 1L.

Plan Your Trip
Activities

High mountains, gentle hills, pristine shores: Tuscany's natural environments deliver irresistible activities. Hiking, cycling, sailing, kayaking, diving, riding – you can do them all here amid superb scenery. In fact, along with the culture, food and wine, it's these memorable outdoor adventures that make Tuscany a must-come-back-to place.

When to Go

Lapping up all that sea and mountain air, heady with the scents of wild sage and pine, is an integral part of the Tuscan outdoor experience. Spring and autumn, with their warm, dry days, wildflowers and forest fruits, are the most picturesque times to be outdoors. July (less hot and crowded than August) is the best month for water sports and hiking in the Apuane Alps. Autumn, when the wine and olive harvests start, has a particularly mellow appeal and, with summer's warmth lingering well into October, there's plenty of daylight for dewy-morning hikes through mushroom-rich forests and crunchy leaves.

Times to Avoid

Easter The first key period of the Italian holiday year, this two-week slot in late March or April sees too many people jostle for too little trail space.

August Italians take their summer holidays, crowding paths, cycle routes and roads. On lower terrain, August's intense heat can be oppressive.

Winter This often means wet, slippery roads and poor visibility for cyclists.

Where to Go

Chianti (p145) Tuscany's key wine-growing area enables easy walking and cycling between achingly pretty vine and olive groves.

Top Outdoor Experiences

Best Short Walks
Along *vie cave* (Etruscan sunken roads) below Pitigliano (p185).

Guided nature walks in the hills around San Gimignano (p158).

From Montalcino to Abbazia di Sant'Antimo (p167), Val d'Orcia.

Best Easy Bike Rides
With elegance atop the city walls of Lucca (p234).

Around vineyards and olive groves in Chianti (p146).

Island touring on Elba (p212).

Best on the Water
Slicing silent waterways with a canoe in Parco Regionale della Maremma (p192).

Sea kayaking and diving offshore from Elba (p209).

Best Spa Towns
Old English literati fave Bagni di Lucca (p255).

Ancient Roman soak Terme di Saturnia (p188).

Puccini's favourite: Montecatini Terme (p235).

Apuane Alps & Garfagnana (p252) Ruggedly scenic and remote, with the region's most dramatic mountains, marble quarries and forested valleys: go hiking, caving, mountain biking and horse riding.

Etruscan Coast (p203) Hit the beach in July and August for sand, sea and water-sport action. Cycling is dirt track to silky smooth.

Elba (p195) A summer island idyll with stunning sea kayaking, sailing, diving and snorkelling; there's beautiful hiking between coves through scented *macchia* (herbal scrub) and parasol pines.

Val d'Orcia (p166) Family walking and cycling near Siena.

Parco Regionale della Maremma (p192) Hiking, biking, horse riding and backwater canoeing on Tuscany's southern coast.

Planning & Information

The tourist-board website (www.visittuscany.com) features background information, interactive maps and inspiring walking, cycling and horse-riding routes. It also covers caving, spas and water sports.

Throughout Tuscany, tourist offices and national-park offices have mountains of activity-related information, including lists of guides as well as accommodation options near trails. It's best to buy maps and guidebooks before leaving home.

Activity specialists:

Toscana Adventure Team (☑348 791 12 15; www.tateam.it) Organises everything from mountain biking and horse riding to coasteering, heli biking, abseiling, hiking and caving.

Hedonistic Hiking (☑Australia +61 3 5755 2307, Italy 333 319 42 03; www.hedonistichiking.com)

Treks around Volterra, Pisa, Elba, Lucca, Chianti and Siena with luxurious villa accommodation and gourmet meals.

Discovery Chianti (p146) Organises cycling and walking tours in Chianti.

Walking & Hiking

Hiking in Tuscany takes you straight to its soul. People have been criss-crossing this region on foot for millennia, and tracing those heritage-rich trails reveals the best of Tuscany today, opening up wine estates, town-crowned hills, mountains, marshes and sandy shores.

The Apuane Alps

On the spine of the Apennines, the challenging Apuane Alps and the stunning Garfagnana valleys (p252) are for serious hikers. Hundreds of trails encompass everything from half-day hikes to long-distance treks. The main town, Castelnuovo di Garfagnana, is the best base camp and the place to pick up information on *rifugi* (mountain huts with dorm-style accommodation). The Parco Regionale delle Alpi Apuane (www.parcapuane.it) has plentiful hiking information.

Grande Escursione Appenninica

This epic 400km trek takes in the Due Santi pass above La Spezia, Sansepolcro in eastern Tuscany and the Tuscan-Emilian Apennines. The route of ridge and valley hiking is split into 23 day-long stages, peaks at 2000m and can normally be tackled between April and October. Cicerone Press (www.cicerone.

BEST WALKS IF YOU LIKE...

Etruscan ruins Golfo di Baratti (p209), Pitigliano (p185)

Birdwatching Riserva Naturale Provinciale Diaccia Botrona (p191), Laguna di Orbetello (p193)

Geology Monterotondo Marittimo (p182)

Wine Chianti (p145), Montalcino (p166), Montepulciano (p173)

Pilgrim paths Marciana (p215), Abbazia di Sant'Antimo, (p167) Monteriggioni (p162), Siena (p127)

Coastal panoramas Monte Capanne (p215), Marciana (p215)

Art and sculpture Garden of Daniel Spoerri (p183), Fattoria di Celle (p245)

Cowboys Parco Regionale della Maremma (p192)

ALTERNATIVE ACTIVITIES

Can't face yet another impossibly graceful, vine-stitched hill or cypress alley to navigate? Consider one of these alternative activities to cast a whole new spin on your Tuscan perspective. For food-related things to do, see Eat & Drink Like a Local (p41).

Ballooning

Drifting noiselessly over Tuscany's pea-green vineyards and silvery olive groves is slow, serene and cinematic.

The ballooning season is late spring to early autumn. Take-off is around 6am; flights last 1¼ hours and cost €240 to €280 per person, often including a 'sparkling wine' breakfast.

Tuscany Ballooning (✆055 824 91 20, 335 6454036; www.tuscanyballooning.com; Via del Masso 14, San Casciano, Val di Pesa) Near Florence.

Ballooning in Tuscany (✆338 1462994; www.ballooningintuscany.com; adult/child under 12 from €280/220) South of Siena.

Chianti Ballooning (✆338 1462994; www.chiantiballooning.com; adult/child over 7 €280/220; ⏱mid-May–mid-Oct) Chianti based.

Beekeeping

Learn how acacia or chestnut nectar is extracted and made into a sweet single-flower honey (or take part in the olive harvest) at Al Benefizio (p257), a rustic *agriturismo* near Barga in northwestern Tuscany.

Caving

Typically, caving is inaccessible without the gear and expertise. But deep in the Apuane Alps, seasonal three-hour tours of the Grotta del Vento (p253) – 1200 steps past subterranean rivers and crystal-rimmed lakes – make for an extraordinary experience.

Photography

Photography tours are just one of the many fun and creative activities cooked up by Be Tuscan for a Day (p143), an innovative project designed to promote experiential travel in central Tuscany. Cultural orienteering and medieval dining and other experiences are on the packed agenda.

Urban Running

Runners, take note: in Siena, Siena Urban Running (p139) organises seasonal, 90-minute early-morning guided runs through the historic centre (€25 per person). From November to mid-May, runs take place in the evening. Check its Facebook page for the month's events. In Florence, ArtViva (p103) organises urban runs.

Summer Solstice

Joining locals in a solstice festival is just one of the many unique and inspiring activities organised by Sapori e Saperi (p256) in northwest Tuscany. Other fun stuff: watching a shepherd make *pecorino* (sheep's milk cheese) and ricotta with milk from the flock; foraging for wild herbs; textile tours with local artisans; and taking part in July's *farro* (spelt) harvest.

Vespa Tours

Don your Audrey Hepburn hat and hit the road on the back of a Vespa (p246).

Yoga

Tuscany is home to the real thing: head to the Dzogchen Community & Cultural Association (p183) in southern Tuscany for Yantra yoga, meditation and traditional dancing with Tibetan monks.

co.uk) publishes the guidebook *The GEA – The Grande Escursione Appenninica*.

Via Francigena

Devise a holiday with a difference by walking or driving parts of the **Via Francigena**, one of Europe's most important medieval pilgrimage routes, connecting English cathedral city Canterbury with Rome. In Central Tuscany, the route goes past or through towns including San Gimignano, Monteriggioni, San Quirico d'Orcia and Radicófani.

Touring Club Italiano publishes *Via Francigena Toscana* (€8), an English-language guide and hiking map (1:175,000) – you'll find it for sale in tourist offices and bookshops throughout the region. Also check www.viafrancigenatoscana.org (in Italian) or www.viefrancigene.org/en. The latter is packed with information and has an interactive map.

Chianti

For some this wine- and vine-laden region is the big hiking favourite. It'll see you rambling between vineyards, wine cellars and century-old farms, then sitting down at a shared table to dine on homemade pasta and homegrown oil and wine.

One of the most popular walks is between Florence and Siena. Routes head south out of Florence, across Chianti (often via Greve and Rada in Chianti) to Siena. Handily, there are plenty of restaurants, *enoteche* and *agriturismi* along the way. Factor on distances of around 80km to 120km between the two cities (five to seven days), depending on your chosen route.

Il Mugello

Starting a few kilometres northeast of Florence, the Mugello region (www.mugellotoscana.it) is ideal for half- and full-day hikes among gentle hills, river valleys and low mountains.

Elba

A prime hiking spot for dramatic scenery, Elba has only one really stiff hike: up Monte Capanne (p215).

Cycling

Whether you're out for a day's gentle pedal around Florence, a sybaritic Chianti weekend winery tour or a serious two-week-long workout, Tuscany has bags of cycling scope.

Regions & Routes

Via Francigena (p159) Cyclists are also welcome on this medieval pilgrimage trail.

Chianti The picturesque **Strada Chiantigiana** (SS222) waltzes through Chianti en route from Florence to Siena, opening up smooth cycling and short, challenging climbs. If you're fairly fit and have a multigear mountain bike, consider peeling off the SS222 onto Chianti's tranquil back roads (sometimes just gravel tracks), which snake between hamlets and vineyards. Either way, farmstay accommodation abounds.

Etruscan Coast Relatively gentle coastal cycling south from Livorno. Ask at the town's tourist office (p203) for the 20-route *Costa degli Etruschi: Cycling Itineraries* booklet.

NATIONAL & REGIONAL PARKS

PARK	FEATURES
Parco Nazionale dell'Arcipelago Toscano	Europe's largest marine park, covering 180 sq km of land & 600 sq km of sea; typical Mediterranean island flora & fauna
Parco Nazionale delle Foreste Casentinesi, Monte Falterona e Campigna	Source of the river Arno & Italy's most extensive, best-preserved forest: ancient pines, beech, five maple types & the rare yew; deer, wild boar, mouflon, wolves & 97 nesting bird species
Parco Alpi Apuane	Mountainous regional park cascading to the sea from the Garfagnana; golden eagles, peregrine falcons, buzzards & the rare chough (the park's symbol)
Parco Regionale Migliarino, San Rossore, Massaciuccoli	Coastal reserve stretching from Viareggio to Livorno; extraordinary birdlife (over 200 species) in its marshes, dunes & wetland
Parco Regionale della Maremma	Regional park comprising the Uccellina mountains, pine forest, agricultural farmland, marshland & 20km of unspoiled coastline; oak & cork oak, herbal maquis (scrubland); Maremma cows, horses & wild boar

Strada del Vino e dell'Olio (www.lastradadelvino.com) A wine- and olive-oil-themed 150km tourist itinerary winding south from Livorno to Piombino and then across to Elba. The 36km stretch from Bolgheri to Suvereto via the hill towns of Castagneto Carducci and Sassetta is particularly scenic; expect switchbacks galore.

Le Crete & Val d'Orcia Offer extensive, hilly itineraries where bursts of hill climbing are interspersed with cruises amid golden wheat fields and cypress alleys.

Monte Amiata A 1700m volcanic dome in southern Tuscany whose roads are a test for aspiring hill climbers.

Practicalities

Bike types All-terrain bikes, suitable for both paved and country routes, are the most versatile for Tuscan roads.

Equipment You'll need sun, wind and rain protection, plus a helmet. Carry enough liquids if you're heading into the high hills.

Bike transportation If bringing your own bike from home, check with your airline whether there's a fee and how much disassembling it requires. Bikes can be transported by train in Italy, either with you or to arrive within a couple of days (p333).

Bike hire Hire outlets are common in Tuscany. Book through EcoRent (www.ecorent.net) or on arrival in towns including Florence, Pisa, Lucca and Siena. Hotels and *agriturismi* often have bike rental.

Access While most historic town and city centres are closed to cars, cyclists are often free to enter at will – double-check the Zona a Traffico Limitato (ZTL; Limited Traffic Zones) signs locally.

Horse Riding

Sauntering serenely on horseback through chestnut and cork-oak woods, between vines and past fields of bright yellow sunflowers and wild red poppies is hypnotically calming, aromatic and oh so Tuscan.

Regions

Maremma Riding is particularly high profile in this rural slice of southern Tuscany – it's home to the famous *butteri* (Maremmese cowboys); experienced riders can sign up for a day herding cows with them at the Terre Regionali Toscani (p192). Or opt for two- to four-hour guided horseback tours (suitable for all experience levels); the Parco Regionale della Maremma (p192) can advise.

Etruscan Coast A horseback itinerary takes riders from Livorno 170km southeast to Sassetta along sun-scorched coastal paths (best in spring and

ACTIVITIES	BEST TIME TO VISIT	WEBSITE
sea kayaking, sailing, diving, snorkelling, water sports, walking, cycling, wine tasting	spring & summer	www.islepark.it
walking, hiking, birdwatching	spring & autumn	www.parcoforestecasentinesi.it
hiking, mountain biking, caving	summer & autumn	www.parcapuane.it
easy walking, cycling, horse riding, birdwatching, canoeing	spring, summer & autumn	www.parcosanrossore.org
walking, hiking, cycling, horse riding, canoeing	spring & autumn (mid-Jun–mid-Sep visits largely by guided tour only)	www.parco-maremma.it

GUIDED BIKE TOURS

Florence is a top spot to hook up with a cycling guide and venture into Chianti. On the following guided tours everything is supplied, including bike and helmet. Expect to pedal around 20km a day.

Florence By Bike (p146) Tour of northern Chianti (one day) with lunch and wine tasting; rents out bikes and suggests self-guided itineraries too.

I Bike Italy (p146) Two-day tour including accommodation and meals.

I Bike Tuscany (p146) One-day tours for all levels; tours include transport from Florence to Chianti.

Discovery Chianti (p146) Guided bike tours in Chianti and elsewhere in Tuscany.

Tuscany Ride A Bike (p239) Full-day guided bike tours departing from Lucca in northwestern Tuscany; themed wine, food and beach tours.

FiesoleBike (p124) Guided, 21km sunset pedal from Fiesole to Florence.

autumn) and shaded cart tracks. It recommends targeted accommodation en route; the tourist office (p203) in Livorno has more info.

Elba The Parco Nazionale dell'Arcipelago Toscano (p210) features old military and forest tracks that double as equestrian pathways; the Portoferraio tourist office (p213) has maps, brochures and trail details.

Water Sports

You could say Tuscany's best-kept secret is its coast, where a horizon of shimmering blue water is speckled with islands. Add sea kayaks, sailboats and sandy coves reached only from the sea, and you have the source of great outdoor action.

Diving & Snorkelling

Elba is among Italy's top year-round diving spots. Wreck-diving sites include Pomonte, where the *Elvisco* cargo boat sits on the seabed 12m down, and the German WWII plane *Junker 52,* wrecked at a more challenging 38m near Portoferraio.

Aquatic flora and fauna is protected and dramatic. Several Elba diving schools rent out gear and organise guides and courses. Less intrepid water lovers can snorkel.

You can also dive along the mainland **Etruscan Coast** and in Porto Ercole on **Monte Argentario**.

Kayaking & Canoeing

Hot summer afternoons are best spent lapping up the slow rhythm of Tuscan travel in a sea kayak or canoe – especially along

Elba's cove-clad coast. Adventure specialists Il Viottolo (p218) in Marina di Campo offer sea-kayaking treks.

The Parco Regionale della Maremma (p192) has a fabulous guided canoe trail.

Sailing & Surfing

The coves of the Tuscan archipelagos and around **Monte Argentario** are superb for sailing, windsurfing and kite surfing. Rent equipment and receive instruction at all the major resorts. **Viareggio** holds several annual sailing regattas.

White-Water Rafting

A handful of outfits in the spa town of **Bagni di Lucca** in northwestern Tuscany organise white-water rafting expeditions on the Lima River.

Spas

Tuscany is one of Italy's thermal-activity hot spots, with the province of Siena particularly rich in mineral-packed waters. Options range from swish indoor spas to natural woodland pools, and tracking them down – and trying them out – is a delight.

Terme di Saturnia (p188) A stunning, cascading cluster of free open-air pools near Pitigliano.

Bagni San Filippo (p172) Free alfresco backwoods bathing at its best in the Val d'Orcia.

Calidario Terme Etrusche (p205) Spa treatments and atmospheric outdoor swims on the Etruscan Coast.

Terme di Sassetta (p208) Elegant spa on a biodynamic farm, with quintessential 'Tuscan hills' panorama.

Plan Your Trip

Travel with Children

There is far more to Tuscany than churches and museums. The region is a quietly child-friendly destination and, with savvy planning, families can revel in a wonderful choice of creative, educational, culinary and old-fashioned fun things to see, do and experience.

Florence & Tuscany for Kids

Tuscany for children is wonderfully varied. Buckets, spades and swimming are a natural element of coastal travel (hit the Etruscan Coast or the island of Elba for the best sandy beaches), but there are mountains of things to see and do inland too. Urban centres such as Florence and Siena are finer (and more fun) than any school textbook when it comes to learning about Renaissance art, architecture and history – an increasing number of museums cater to younger-generation minds with superb multimedia displays, touchscreen gadgets, audio guides and creative tours.

The pace slows in the countryside. Rural farmsteads and *agriturismi* (accommodation on working farms or vineyards), wineries and agricultural estates inspire and excite young minds with traditional pastimes such as olive picking, feeding the black pigs, bread making in ancient stone ovens and saffron cultivation. There's bags of space to run around in, nature trails to explore, alfresco art sculptures and installations to gawp at and sufficient outdoor activities to keep a kid entertained for weeks.

Best Regions for Kids

Florence

Fascinating museums – some interactive, others with creative workshops and tours for children – make Florence a favourite for families with children who are school age and older. For the under fives, gentle riverside ambles, vintage carousels, fantastic *gelaterie* (ice-cream shops) and a vast choice of dining options add appeal.

Southern Tuscany

Marammese cowboys, archaeological ruins, sandy beaches and snowy mountains: this region might be rural, but it's a cracker when it comes to farmstay accommodation, outdoor action and quirky sights to pique kids' natural curiosity.

Central Coast & Elba

There's beaches and boats, Livorno's aquarium and 'Venetian' waterways to explore, and the paradise island of Elba to sail to.

Northwestern Tuscany

Head to the Apuane Alps and Garfagnana to stay on Tuscan farms, see marble being mined, and explore subterranean lakes and caverns. Then there's Pisa's Leaning Tower to climb and Lucca's fairy-tale city walls to cycle.

PLANNING

➡ Consider the best time of year you go for you, perhaps timing your visit with one of Tuscany's many vibrant festivals with particular appeal for kids, such as Siena's Palio, Viareggio's carnevale (p262) or Florence's Scoppio del Carro (p103).

➡ *Agriturismi* (accommodation on working farms or wine estates) and country resorts are invariably the best option for families; they often have self-catering facilities and plenty of kid-friendly activities like swimming, tennis, horse riding and mountain biking.

➡ Many museums and monuments are free for children, generally until they're aged six. In Florence state museums are free to EU passport holders aged under 18.

➡ On public transport, a seat on a bus costs the same for everyone (toddlers and babies on laps are free). Children under 12 pay half the fare on trains.

➡ Children under 150cm or 36kg must be buckled into an appropriate child seat for their weight and are not allowed in the front.

Children's Highlights

Museums

Museo Galileo, Florence (p67) Astronomical and mathematical treasures, with ample hands-on opportunities to explore how they work.

Palazzo Vecchio, Florence (p78) Guided tours for children and families through secret staircases and hidden rooms; led by historical personages.

Museo Piaggio, Pontedera (p246) Learn about Italy's iconic Vespa scooter at this fun museum near Pisa.

Museo Stibbert, Florence (p86) Life-size horses, and knights in suits of armour from Europe and the Middle East.

Museale Santa Maria della Scala, Siena (p134) Fantastic art space especially for kids in a fascinating museum in a 13th-century pilgrims' hospice.

Medieval to Modern Art

Parco Sculture del Chianti, Central Tuscany (p154) A 1km walking trail and lots of peculiar artworks to gawk at.

Giardino dei Tarocchi, Southern Tuscany (p193) Giant sculptures tumbling down a hillside.

Palazzo Comunale & Torre Grossa, San Gimignano (p156) Learn about medieval frescoes while wearing augmented-reality glasses.

Museo Novecento & Palazzo Strozzi, Florence (p83) Hands-on art workshops for children and families.

Museo Marino Marini, Pistoia (p247) Monthly family tours and hands-on activities in English.

Garden of Daniel Spoerri, Castel del Piano (p183) Fun contemporary-art installations in a 16-hectare garden in southern Tuscany.

Cool Stuff Outdoors

Cave di Marmo Tours, Carrara (p257) Take a Bond-style 4WD tour of the open-cast quarry or follow miners inside 'marble mountain'.

City walls, Lucca (p234) Hire a bike and ride along the top of the walls.

Grotta del Vento, Garfagnana (p253) Explore subterranean abysses, lakes and caverns.

Cabinovia Monte Capanne, Elba (p215) Ride a 'bird cage' up Elba's highest peak.

Pistoia Sotteranea, Pistoia (p247) Discover subterranean rivers underneath a 13th-century hospital.

Bagni San Filippo, Val d'Orcia (p172) Free backwoods bathing in thermal springs.

Terme di Saturnia, Southern Tuscany (p188) Not the plush luxe spa; rather the hidden cluster of natural pools by the actual springs.

Wildlife Encounters

Riserva Naturale Provinciale Diaccia Botrona, Southern Tuscany (p191) Spot flamingos and herons on a boat tour through the marshes.

Parco Regionale della Maremma, Southern Tuscany (p192) Hike, cycle or canoe through this huge coastal park.

Acquario di Livorno, Livorno (p199) A thoroughly modern aquarium by the seaside.

Regions at a Glance

Florence

Food
Art
Shopping

A Vibrant Culinary Scene

The city's exceptional dining scene ranges from *enoteche* (wine bars) bursting with cured meats and cheeses to no-nonsense trattorias, bustling food markets and the only restaurant in Tuscany to possess three Michelin stars.

Galleries & Museums

The Uffizi is one of the world's most famous art galleries, but it's not the only repository of artistic masterpieces in the city (the expression 'an embarrassment of riches' seems appropriate). Churches, chapels and a bevy of lesser-known museums showcase masterpieces galore.

Designers & Artisans

With everything from designer boutiques on chic Via de' Tornabuoni to tiny workshops hidden down a cobweb of alleys and backstreets in Oltrarno, the city where Gucci was born really is the last word in quality shopping.

p60

Siena & Central Tuscany

Food
Wine
Hill Towns

Sienese Treats

Sample Siena's famous cakes and biscuits, accompanied by a coffee or dunked in a glass of sweet Vin Santo wine.

Famous Wines

Tuscan wine hot shots Brunello, Vino Nobile, Chianti Classico and Vernaccia all hail from this rich part of Tuscany, with estates throughout the region opening their atmospheric cellar doors and vine-laced estates to the viticulturally curious for tastings and visits.

Architecture & Views

Explore scenic hill towns such as Montalcino, Montepulciano, Volterra and San Gimignano, where the intact medieval architecture is as impressive as the sweeping panoramic views that reward those who hike to the top.

p126

Southern Tuscany

Food
History
Nature

Local & Seasonal

This is a no-fuss zone when it comes to cuisine. Chefs buy local, stick to the season and subscribe to the concept of Slow Food. And the results are superb.

Archaeological Sites

The Etruscans certainly left their mark on the landscape: the countryside of the extraordinary Città del Tufo (City of the Tufo) is littered with their tombs. The Romans didn't shirk their duties here either, as a visit to the archaeological sites of Roselle or Vetulonia will confirm.

Untouched Landscapes

Europe's bird species stop here on their migration to North Africa for good reason – huge tracts of pristine landscape boast an impressive range of flora and fauna.

p177

PLAN YOUR TRIP REGIONS AT A GLANCE

Central Coast & Elba

Food
Beaches
History

Seafood

Livorno does seafood like nowhere else in Tuscany. Feisty locals in this waterside port city are staunchly proud of *cacciucco,* a remarkable seafood stew swimming with at least five types of fish.

Island Paradise

Visit Elba, the palm-tree-clad paradise where Napoleon was banished. This bijou island offers a sensational mix of sunbathing, sea kayaking, snorkelling and swimming.

Etruscan Ruins

Exploring the remains of ancient Etruscan tombs and temples hidden beneath sky-high parasol pines on the Golfo di Baratti's sandy shoreline is an extraordinary experience. Pair it with gentle walking and a picnic lunch for the perfect day.

p195

Northwestern Tuscany

Food
Mountains
Outdoors

White Truffles

No single food product is lusted over as much as the perfectly perfumed fresh white truffle – hunted in dew-kissed autumn forests around San Miniato and eaten with gusto during truffle season (mid-October to December).

The Apuane Alps

Take a drive through rugged peaks and richly forested valleys laced with walking trails to witness the majestic marble mountains of the Apuane Alps in their full glory.

The Garfagnana

The trio of valleys that form the Garfagnana region perfectly suits holiday-makers keen on hiking, biking and eating. Trails criss-cross chestnut woods and forests rich in berries and *porcini* mushrooms.

p221

Eastern Tuscany

Food
Holy Sites
Art

Steak

Come to the Val di Chiana to eat Italy's best *bistecca alla fiorentina,* the succulent, lightly seared piece of locally raised Chianina beef that is Tuscany's signature dish.

Shrines to St Francis

St Francis is closely associated with this part of Tuscany. Born in nearby Assisi, he is said to have received the stigmata at the Santuario della Verna in the wonderfully wild Casentino forest.

Masterpieces

The adage 'quality before quantity' applies here. Follow a trail highlighting the works of Piero della Francesca, but also look out for works by Cimabue, Fra' Angelico, Signorelli, Rosso Fiorentino, the Lorenzettis and the della Robbias.

p264

On the Road

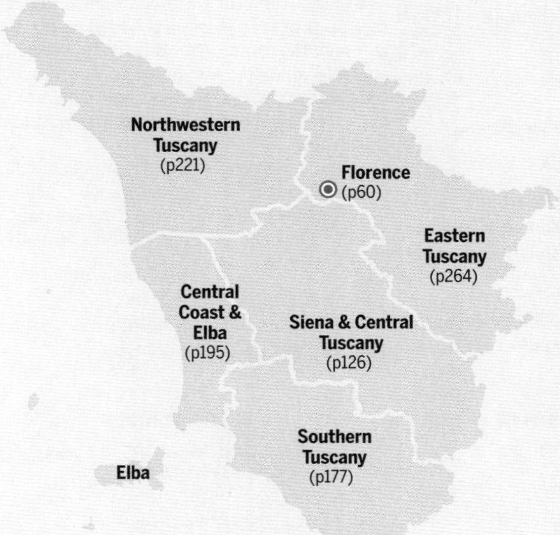

Northwestern
Tuscany
(p221)

Florence
⊙ (p60)

Eastern
Tuscany
(p264)

Central
Coast &
Elba
(p195)

Siena & Central
Tuscany
(p126)

Southern
Tuscany
(p177)

Elba

Florence

POP 377,635 / ☎ 055

Best Places to Eat

➜ Essenziale (p112)

➜ Trattoria Mario (p107)

➜ La Leggenda dei Frati (p99)

➜ Il Teatro del Sale (p108)

➜ Il Santo Bevitore (p113)

Best Summer Terraces

➜ Santarosa Bistrot (p118)

➜ Flò (p119)

➜ La Terrazza (p115)

➜ La Terrazza Lounge Bar (p115)

➜ Amblé (p115)

Why Go?

Return time and again and you still won't see it all. Stand on a bridge over the Arno river several times in a day and the light, mood and view changes every time. Surprisingly small as it is, this riverside city looms large on the world's 'must-sees' list. Cradle of the Renaissance and of tourist masses that flock here to feast on world-class art, Florence (Firenze) is magnetic, romantic and busy. Its urban fabric has hardly changed since the Renaissance, its narrow streets evoke a thousand tales, and its food and wine are so wonderful the tag 'Fiorentina' has become an international label of quality assurance.

Fashion designers parade on Via de' Tornabuoni. Gucci was born here, as was Roberto Cavalli, who, like many a smart Florentine these days, hangs out in wine-rich hills around Florence. After a while in this absorbing city, you might want to do the same.

Road Distances (km)

	Florence	Pisa	Lucca	San Miniato
Pisa	69			
Lucca	61	23		
San Miniato	37	47	70	
Siena	51	87	30	77

History

Florence's history stretches back to the time of the Etruscans, who based themselves in Fiesole. Julius Caesar founded the Roman colony of Florentia around 59 BC, making it a strategic garrison on the narrowest crossing of the Arno in order to control the Via Flaminia linking Rome to northern Italy and Gaul.

After the collapse of the Roman Empire, Florence fell to invading Goths, followed by Lombards and Franks. The year AD 1000 marked a crucial turning point in the city's fortunes, when Margrave Ugo of Tuscany moved his capital from Lucca to Florence. In 1110 Florence became a free *comune* (city-state) and by 1138 it was ruled by 12 consuls, assisted by the Consiglio di Cento (Council of One Hundred), whose members were drawn mainly from the prosperous merchant class. Agitation among differing factions in the city led to the appointment in 1207 of a foreign head of state called the *podestà,* aloof in principle from the plotting and wheeler-dealing of local cliques and alliances.

Medieval Florence was a wealthy, dynamic *comune,* one of Europe's leading financial, banking and cultural centres, and a major player in the international wool, silk and leather trades. The sizeable population of moneyed merchants and artisans began forming guilds and patronising the growing number of artists who found lucrative commissions in this burgeoning city.

Struggles between the pro-papal Guelphs (Guelfi) and the pro-Holy Roman Empire Ghibellines (Ghibellini) started in the mid-13th century, with power yo-yoing between the two for almost a century. Into this fractious atmosphere were born revolutionary artist Giotto and outspoken poet Dante Alighieri, whose family belonged to the Guelph camp.

The history of Medici Florence began in 1434, when Cosimo the Elder (Cosimo de' Medici), a patron of the arts, assumed power. His eye for talent and tact in dealing with artists saw Alberti, Brunelleschi, Luca della Robbia, Fra' Angelico, Donatello and Fra' Filippo Lippi flourish under his patronage.

Under the rule of Cosimo's popular and cultured grandson, Lorenzo il Magnifico (1469–92), Florence became the epicentre of the Renaissance ('Rebirth'), with artists such as Michelangelo, Botticelli and Domenico Ghirlandaio at work. Lorenzo's court, filled with Humanists (a school of thought begun in Florence in the late 14th century affirming the dignity and potential of mankind and embracing Latin and Greek literary texts), fostered a flowering of art, music and poetry, turning Florence into Italy's cultural capital.

Florence's golden age effectively died with Lorenzo in 1492. Just before his death, the Medici bank had failed and two years later the Medici were driven out of Florence. In a reaction against the splendour and excess of the Medici court, the city fell under the control of Girolamo Savonarola, a Dominican monk who led a stern, puritanical republic. In 1497 the likes of Botticelli gladly consigned their 'immoral' works and finery to the flames of the infamous 'Bonfire of the Vanities'. The following year Savonarola fell from public favour and was burned as a heretic.

The pro-French leanings of the subsequent republican government brought it into conflict with the pope and his Spanish allies. In 1512 a Spanish force defeated Florence and the Medici were reinstated. Their tyrannical rule endeared them to few and when Rome, ruled by the Medici pope Clement VII, fell to the emperor Charles V in 1527, the Florentines took advantage of this low point in the Medici fortunes to kick the family out again. Two years later though, imperial and papal forces besieged Florence, forcing the city to accept Lorenzo's great-grandson, Alessandro de' Medici, a ruthless transvestite whom Charles made Duke of Florence. Medici rule continued for another 200 years, during which time they gained control of all of Tuscany, though after the reign of Cosimo I (1537–74), Florence drifted into steep decline.

The last male Medici, Gian Gastone, died in 1737, after which his sister, Anna Maria, signed the grand duchy of Tuscany over to the House of Habsburg-Lorraine (at the time effectively under Austrian control). This situation remained unchanged, apart from a brief interruption under Napoleon from 1799 to 1814, until the duchy was incorporated into the Kingdom of Italy in 1860. Florence briefly became the national capital a year later, but Rome assumed the mantle permanently in 1871.

Florence was badly damaged during WWII by the retreating Germans, who blew up all of its bridges except the Ponte Vecchio. Devastating floods ravaged the city in 1966, causing inestimable damage to its buildings and artworks. Since 1997, amid a fair amount of controversy, the world-class Uffizi Gallery has been engaged in its biggest-ever expansion – a €65 million investment project, dubbed the 'New Uffizi project'. Its end date remains a mystery.

❶ Duomo & Piazza della Signoria (p66)

Hub of the Renaissance and now the cosmopolitan heart of modern Florence, the enchanting maze of narrow streets between the Duomo and Piazza della Signoria packs one almighty historic and cultural punch. A neighbourhood harking back to Dante, the Romans and beyond, this is where the city's blockbuster sights – and most tourists – can be found. Cafe life is naturally vibrant in this chic neck of the woods, as is shopping, which climaxes with the designer strip, uber-fashionist Via de' Tornabuoni.

❷ Santa Maria Novella (p83)

Anchored by its magnificent basilica, this ancient and intriguing part of Florence defies easy description – from the rough-cut streets around the central train station it's only a short walk to the busy social scene around increasingly gentrified Piazza di Santa Maria Novella and the hip boutiques on the atmosphere-laden, old-world 'back streets' west of Via de' Tornabuoni. Shopping here, intermingled with a multitude of attractive dining and drinking options, is among the best in Florence.

❸ San Lorenzo & San Marco (p86)

This part of the city fuses a gutsy market precinct – a covered produce market and noisy street stalls surrounding the Basilica di San Lorenzo – with capacious Piazza San Marco, home to Florence University and a much-loved museum. Between the two is the world's most famous sculpture, *David*. The result is a sensory experience jam-packed with urban grit, uplifting art and some fabulously authentic, local-loved addresses to eat, drink and shop.

❹ Santa Croce (p89)

Despite being only a hop, skip and jump from the city's major museums, this ancient part of Florence is far removed from the tourist maelstrom. The streets behind main sight Basilica di Santa Croce are home to plenty of locals, all of whom seem to be taking their neighbourhood's reinvention as hipster central – epicentre of the city's bar and club scene – with remarkable aplomb.

❺ Oltrarno (p96)

Literally the 'other side of the Arno', this achingly hip 'hood is traditionally home to Florence's artisans and its old-world, bohemian streets are sprinkled with *botteghe* (workshops), independent boutiques and hybrid forms of both. It embraces the area south of the river and west of Ponte Vecchio; its backbone is Borgo San Jacopo, clad with shops and a twinset of 12th-century towers, Torre dei Marsili and Torre de' Belfredelli. Cuisine – prepared using artisanal ingredients, of course – is a real strength here, with bags of fashionable restaurants and drinks to entice.

❻ Boboli & San Miniato al Monte (p98)

When museum overload strikes – a common occurrence in this culturally resplendent city – consider stretching your legs amid some urban greenery in this soul-soothing eastern neighbourhood on the Oltrarno (aka 'the other side of the river'). Fronted by the grandiose palace of Palazzo Pitti, jam-packed with museums, Boboli's magnificent tier of palaces, villas and gardens climbs up hill to San Miniato, a hilltop 'hood famously crowned by a copy of Michelangelo's *David* and one of the city's oldest and most beautiful churches. Views, predictably, are sweeping and soul-soaring.

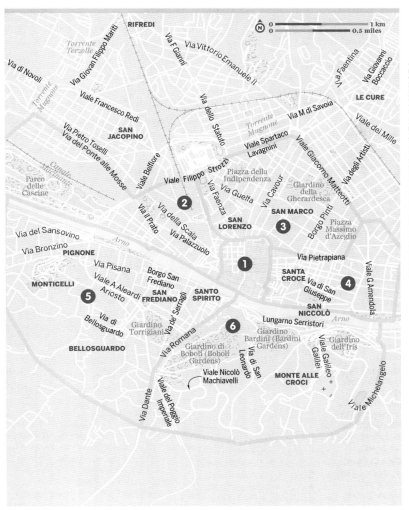

Florence Highlights

1 Galleria degli Uffizi (p68) Visiting the world's finest collection of Renaissance paintings in this world-class art gallery.

2 Duomo (p74) Climbing inside Brunelleschi's spectacular dome, superstar of the city skyline and crowning glory of Florence's Duomo.

3 Museo di San Marco (p88) Contemplating the artistic genius of Fra' Angelico with Reanissance frescoes inside this unsung monastery museum.

4 Piazzale Michelangelo (p99) Hiking uphill to meet David's lookalike and enjoy the most magnificent sunset show and city panorama.

5 Museo delle Cappelle Medicee (p87) Admiring hauntingly beautiful tomb sculptures by Michelangelo in the burial place of the Medici dynasty.

6 Cafe Culture (p116) Dipping into Florentine cafe culture at timeless classic Caffè Giacosa, trendsetter Ditta Artigianale or a backstreet address in artisanal Oltrarno.

7 Fiesole (p124) Escaping the city heat for a mooch between olive groves and Roman ruins in this hilltop retreat; cycling home to Florence at sunset with local guide Giovanni.

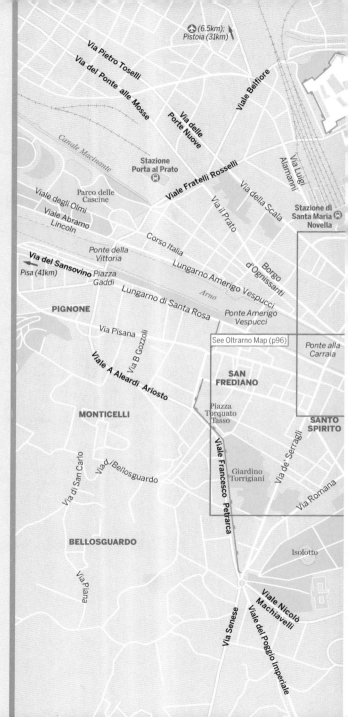

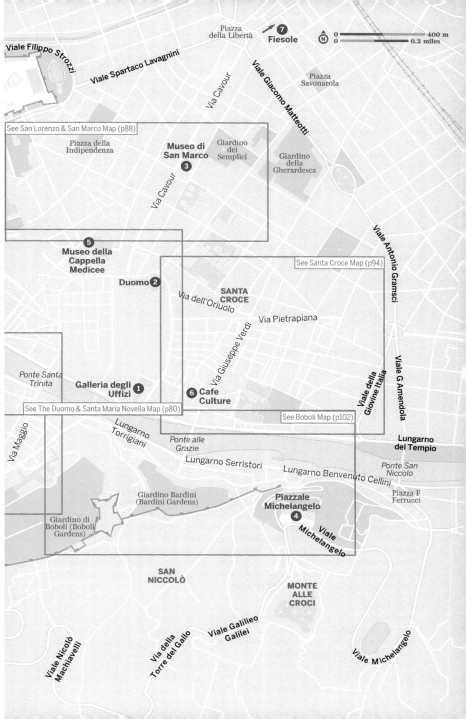

Piazza della Libertà

7 Fiesole

Piazza Savonarola

Viale Filippo Strozzi

Viale Spartaco Lavagnini

Via Cavour

Viale Giacomo Matteotti

N 0 ——— 400 m
0 ——— 0.2 miles

See San Lorenzo & San Marco Map (p88)

Piazza della Indipendenza

Museo di San Marco **3**

Giardino dei Semplici

Giardino della Gherardesca

Viale Antonio Gramsci

Via Cavour

Museo della Cappella Medicee **5**

Duomo **2**

SANTA CROCE

See Santa Croce Map (p94)

Via dell'Oriuolo

Via Pietrapiana

Via Giuseppe Verdi

Viale della Giovine Italia

Viale G Amendola

Ponte Santa Trinita

Galleria degli Uffizi **1**

6 **Cafe Culture**

See The Duomo & Santa Maria Novella Map (p80)

See Boboli Map (p102)

Via Maggio

Lungarno Torrigiani

Ponte alle Grazie

Lungarno Serristori

Lungarno Benvenuto Cellini

Lungarno del Tempio

Ponte San Niccolo

Piazza F Ferrucci

Giardino Bardini (Bardini Gardens)

Piazzale Michelangelo **4**

Giardino di Boboli (Boboli Gardens)

Viale Michelangelo

SAN NICCOLÒ

MONTE ALLE CROCI

Viale Nicolò Machiavelli

Via della Torre del Gallo

Viale Galileo Galilei

Viale Michelangelo

◉ Sights

Florence's wealth of museums and galleries house many of the world's most exquisite examples of Renaissance art, and its architecture is unrivalled. Yet don't feel pressured to see everything: combine your personal pick of sights with ample meandering through the city's warren of narrow streets broken by cafe and *enoteca* (wine bar) stops.

Churches enforce a strict dress code for visitors: no shorts, sleeveless shirts or plunging necklines. Photography with no flash is allowed in museums, but leave the selfie stick at home – they are offiicially forbidden.

◉ Duomo &
Piazza della Signoria

Florence's big-hit sights lie in the geographic, historic and cultural heart of the city – the tight grid of streets between Piazza del Duomo and cafe-strung Piazza della Signoria.

Piazza della Signoria   PIAZZA
(Map p80; Piazza della Signoria) The hub of local life since the 13th century, Florentines flock here to meet friends and chat over early-evening *aperitivi* at historic cafes. Presiding over everything is Palazzo Vecchio (p78), Florence's city hall, and the 14th-century Loggia dei Lanzi (Map p80) FREE, an open-air gallery showcasing Renaissance sculptures, including Giambologna's *Rape of the Sabine Women* (c 1583), Benvenuto Cellini's bronze *Perseus* (1554) and Agnolo Gaddi's *Seven Virtues* (1384–89).

In centuries past, townsfolk congregated on the piazza whenever the city entered one of its innumerable political crises. The people would be called for a *parlamento* (people's plebiscite) to rubber stamp decisions that frequently meant ruin for some ruling families and victory for others. Scenes of great pomp and circumstance alternated with those of terrible suffering: it was here that vehemently pious preacher-leader Savonarola set fire to the city's art – books, paintings, musical instruments, mirrors, fine clothes and so on – during his famous 'Bonfire of the Vanities' in 1497, and where he was hung in chains and burnt as a heretic, along with two other supporters a year later.

FLORENCE IN THREE DAYS

Day One
Journey into the Renaissance with a morning of mind-blowing 15th- and 16th-century art at the Uffizi (p68). Meander south to the river and cross Ponte Vecchio (p96) to the 'other side side of the Arno'. Explore Basilica di Santo Spirito (p96) and magnificent Cappella Brancacci (p97), grabbing a quick coffee or tea at the Oltrarno branch of Ditta Artigianale (p119). As the sun starts to sink, hike uphill to Piazzale Michelangelo (p99) for swoon-worthy views of the city. After dinner at Essenziale (p112), try to find Rasputin (p117), the city's secret speakeasy open until the wee hours.

Day Two
Prepare yourself for a sensational morning of sacred art and architecture on Piazza del Duomo: visit the cathedral (p74) then climb up its campanile (p76) and duck into its baptistery (p76). End on a giddy high with a hike up into the frescoed dome of Brunelleschi's cupola (p75), and complete the story with a tour of the insightful Grande Museo del Duomo (p76). Window shop on Via de' Tornabuoni (p82), with a break for a cheeky truffle panino at Procacci (p118). Travel west to the marvellous Basilica di Santa Maria Novella (p84). Stop for dinner at Il Santo Bevitore (p113) but leave space for dessert in the shape of a gelato from Gelateria La Carraia (p109), best enjoyed over a scenic riverside walk by night.

Day Three
Begin the day with a glorious 360-degree admiration of the world's most famous naked man, Michelangelo's original *David,* at the Galleria dell'Accademia (p90). Next up in this fascinating 'hood is the soulfully uplifting Museo di San Marco (p88), after which a cappuccino or specialist coffee beckons at Ditta Al Cinema (p116). Saunter south to Palazzo Vecchio (p78) in time to visit the fortress palace and catch sunset views from the top of its striking Torre d'Arnolfo – a Florentine landmark. If you're dining at Il Teatro del Sale (p108), sit back and enjoy the theatre show.

ℹ MUSEUM PASSES

Firenze Card

Firenze Card (www.firenzecard.it; €72) is valid for 72 hours and covers admission to some 72 museums, villas and gardens in Florence, as well as unlimited use of public transport and free wi-fi across the city. Its biggest advantage is reducing queueing time in high season – museums have a seperate queue for card-holders. The downside of the Firenze Card is it only allows one admission per museum, plus you need to visit an awful lot of museums to justify the cost. Buy the card online (and collect upon arrival in Florence) or in Florence at tourist offices or ticketing desks of the Uffizi (Gate 2), Palazzo Pitti, Palazzo Vecchio, Museo del Bargello, Cappella Brancacci, Museo di Santa Maria Novella and Giardini Bardini. If you're an EU citizen, your card also covers under 18 year olds travelling with you.

Friends of the Uffizi

If you prefer to split your Uffizi forays into a couple of visits and/or you're not from the EU and are travelling with kids, the annual Friends of the Uffizi Card (adult/reduced/family of four €60/40/100) is a good deal. Valid for a calendar year (expiring 31 December), it covers admission to 22 Florence museums (including Galleria dell'Accademia, Museo del Bargello and Palazzo Pitti) and allows return visits (have your passport on you as proof of ID to show at each museum with your card). Buy online or from the **Amici degli Uffizi Welcome Desk** (Map p80; ☏ 055 28 56 10; www.amicidegliuffizi.it; Galleria degli Uffizi, Piazzale degli Uffizi 6; ⊙10am-5pm Tue-Sat) next to Gate 2 at the Uffizi.

The same spot where both fires burned is marked by a bronze plaque embedded in the ground in front of Ammannati's **Fontana de Nettuno** (Neptune Fountain) with pin-headed bronze satyrs and divinities frolicking at its edges. More impressive are the equestrian statue of Cosimo I by Giambologna in the centre of the piazza, the much-photographed copy of Michelangelo's *David* guarding the western entrance to the Palazzo Vecchio since 1910 (the original stood here until 1873), and two copies of important Donatello works – *Marzocco,* the heraldic Florentine lion (for the original, visit the Museo del Bargello; p93), and *Giuditta e Oloferne* (*Judith and Holofernes;* c 1455; original inside Palazzo Vecchio).

Gucci Museo   MUSEUM
(Map p80; www.gucci.com; Piazza della Signoria 10; adult/reduced €7/5; ⊙10am-8pm, to 11pm Fri) Strut through the chic cafe and icon store to reach this museum. It tells the tale of the Gucci fashion house, from the first luggage pieces in Gucci's signature beige fabric emblazoned with the interlocking 'GG' logo to the 1950s red-and-green stripe and beyond. Don't miss the 1979 Cadillac Seville with gold Gs on the hubcaps and Gucci fabric upholstery. Displays continue to the present day.

Piazza della Repubblica   PIAZZA
(Map p80) The site of a Roman forum and heart of medieval Florence, this busy civic space was created in the 1880s as part of a controversial plan of 'civic improvements' involving the demolition of the old market, Jewish ghetto and slums, and the relocation of nearly 6000 residents. Vasari's lovely Loggia del Pesce (Fish Market) was saved and re-erected on Via Pietrapiana.

Chiesa e Museo di Orsanmichele   CHURCH, MUSEUM
(Map p80; ☏ 055 21 58 52; Via dell'Arte della Lana; ⊙museum 10am-5pm Mon, church 10am-5pm daily, closed Mon Aug) FREE This unusual and inspirational church, with a Gothic tabernacle by Andrea Orcagna, was created when the arcades of an old grain market (1290) were walled in and two storeys added during the 14th century. Its exterior is decorated with niches and tabernacles bearing statues. Representing the patron saints of Florence's many guilds, the statues were commissioned in the 15th and 16th centuries after the *signoria* ordered the city's guilds to finance the church's decoration.

Museo Galileo   MUSEUM
(Map p80; ☏ 055 26 53 11; www.museogalileo.it; Piazza dei Giudici 1; adult/reduced €9/5.50; ⊙9.30am-6pm Wed-Mon, to 1pm Tue) On the river next to the Uffizi in 12th-century Palazzo Castellani – look for the sundial telling the time on the pavement outside – is this state-of-the-art science museum, named after the great Pisa-born scientist who was invited by the Medici court to Florence in 1610 (don't miss two of his fingers and a tooth displayed here).

TOP SIGHT
GALLERIA DEGLI UFFIZI

Home to the world's greatest collection of Italian Renaissance art, Florence's premier gallery occupies the vast U-shaped Palazzo degli Uffizi. The world-famous collection, displayed in chronological order, spans the gamut of art history from ancient Greek sculpture to 18th-century Venetian paintings. But its core is the Renaissance collection – a morning can be spent enjoying its unmatched collection of Botticellis alone.

The Nuovo Uffizi

The gallery is undergoing a €65 million refurbishment (the Nuovi Uffizi project) that will see the doubling of exhibition space and possibly a new exit loggia designed by Japanese architect Arato Isozaki. Work is pretty much complete on the permanent collection, which has grown over the years from 45 to 101 revamped rooms split across two floors; but there is much to be done still on areas earmarked for temporary exhibitions. Until the project is completed (date unknown) expect some halls to be closed and the contents of others changed.

Tuscan 13th-Century Art

Arriving in the Primo Corridoio (First Corridor), the first room to the left of the staircase (Room 2) is designed like a medieval chapel to reflect its fabulous contents: three large altarpieces from Florentine churches by Tuscan masters Duccio di Buoninsegna, Cimabue and Giotto. They show the transition from Gothic to nascent Renaissance style.

DON'T MISS

➡ Michelangelo (2nd Floor, Rooms 33 to 35)

➡ Sala del Botticelli (2nd Floor, Rooms 10 to 14)

➡ Leonardo da Vinci (1st Floor, Room 79)

PRACTICALITIES

➡ Uffizi Gallery

➡ Map p80

➡ ☎ 055 29 48 83

➡ www.uffizi.beniculturali.it

➡ Piazzale degli Uffizi 6

➡ adult/reduced €8/4, incl temporary exhibition €12.50/6.25

➡ ⏱ 8.15am-6.50pm Tue-Sun

Sienese 14th-Century Art

The highlight in Room 3 is Simone Martini's shimmering *Annunciazione* (1333), painted with Lippo Memmi and setting the Madonna in a sea of gold. Also of note is *Madonna con il bambino in trono e angeli* (*Madonna with Child and Saints*; 1340) by Pietro Lorenzetti, which demonstrates a realism similar to Giotto's; unfortunately both Pietro and his artistic brother Ambrogio died from the plague in Siena in 1348.

Renaissance Pioneers

Perspective was a hallmark of the early-15th-century Florentine school (Room 8) that pioneered the Renaissance. One panel from Paolo Uccello's striking *Battle of San Romano* (1436–40), which celebrates Florence's victory over Siena in 1432, shows the artist's efforts to create perspective with amusing effect as he directs the lances, horses and soldiers to a central disappearing point. In the same room, don't miss the exquisite *Madonna con Bambino e due angeli* (*Madonna and Child with Two Angels*; 1460–65) by Fra' Filippo Lippi, a Carmelite monk who had an unfortunate soft spot for earthly pleasures and scandalously married a nun from Prato. This work clearly influenced his pupil, Sandro Botticelli.

Duke & Duchess of Urbino

Revel in the realism of Piero della Francesca's 1465 warts-and-all portraits of the Duke and Duchess of Urbino (Room 9). The crooked-nosed duke lost his right eye in a jousting accident, hence the focus on his left side only, while the duchess is deathly stone-white to convey the fact that the portrait was painted posthumously.

The First Botticelli

Learn about the seven cardinal and theological values of 15th-century Florence with the huge same-name painting by brothers Antonio and Piero del Pollaiolo in Room 9, commissioned for the merchant's tribunal in Piazza della Signoria. The only canvas in the theological and cardinal virtues series not to be painted by the Pollaiolos is *Fortitude* (1470), the first documented work by Botticelli.

Botticelli

The spectacular Sala del Botticelli, numbered 10 to 14 but really two light and graceful rooms, is always packed. Of the 18 Botticelli works displayed in the Uffizi in all, his iconic *La nascita di Venere* (*The Birth of Venus*; c 1485), *Primavera* (*Spring*; c 1482) and *Madonna del Magnificat* (*Madonna of the*

PALAZZO DEGLI UFFIZI

Cosimo I de' Medici commissioned Vasari to build the huge U-shaped Palazzo degli Uffizi in 1560 as a government office building (*uffizi* means 'offices'). Following Vasari's death in 1564, architects Alfonso Parigi and Bernando Buontalenti took over, with Buontalenti modifying the upper floor to house the artworks keenly collected by Cosimo I's son, Francesco I. In 1580 the building was complete. When the last Medici died in 1743, the family's enormous private art collection was bequeathed to Florence on the strict proviso that it never leaves the city.

Check the latest new rooms (and those temporarily closed during expansion works) in the 'News' section of www.uffizi.org.

THE CLOSED DOOR

Spot the closed door next to room 25 leading to the Medici's Corridoio Vasariano (p93) (Vasarian Corridor), a 1km-long covered passageway designed by Vasari in 1565 to allow the Medicis to wander between the Uffizi, Palazzo Vecchio (p78) and Palazzo Pitti (p98) in privacy and comfort.

Magnificat; 1483) are the best-known works by the Renaissance master known for his ethereal figures. Take time to study the lesser known *Annunciazione* (Annunciation), a 6m-wide fresco painted by Botticelli in 1481 for the San Martino hospital in Florence. True aficionados rate his twin set of miniatures depicting a sword-bearing Judith returning from the camp of Holofernes and the discovery of the decapitated Holofernes in his tent (1495–1500) as being among his finest works.

Northern Influences

Don't miss the *Adorazione dei Magi* (Adoration of the Magi; 1475) featuring Botticelli's self-portrait (look for the blond-haired guy, extreme right, dressed in yellow), tucked away in Room 15 alongside Botticelli's *Coronation of the Virgin* (1488–90) and works by Flemish painter Hugo van der Goes (1430–82). Study the altarpiece, painted by the latter for the church inside Florence's Santa Maria Novella hospital, to observe the clear influence artists in northern Europe had on Florentine artists.

The Tribune

The Medici clan stashed away their most precious art in this octagonal-shaped treasure trove (Room 18), created by Francesco I between 1581 and 1586. Designed to amaze, it features a small collection of classical statues and paintings on its upholstered silk walls and 6000 crimson-varnished mother-of-pearl shells encrusting the domed ceiling.

15th-Century Works

Rooms 19 to 23 delve into the work of painters in Siena, Venice, Emilia-Romagna and Lombardy in the 15th century. Note the ornate vaulted ceilings, frescoed in the 16th and 17th centuries with military objects, allegories, battles and festivals held on piazzas in Florence.

Teenage Michelangelo

Rooms 33 and 34, with sage-green painted walls, display sculptures from classical antiquity – of great influence on the young Michelangelo – and from the Medici-owned sculpture garden in San Marco where Michelangelo studied classical sculpture as an apprentice from the age of 13.

Tondo Doni

Michelangelo's dazzling *Tondo Doni,* a depiction of the Holy Family, hangs in Room 35. The composition is unusual and the colours as vibrant as when they were first applied in 1504–06. It was painted for wealthy Florentine merchant Agnolo Doni (who hung it above his bed) and bought by the Medici for Palazzo Pitti in 1594.

Madonna of the Goldfinch

Downstairs in the 1st-floor galleries, Rooms 46 to 55 display 16th- to 18th-century works by foreign artists, including Rembrandt (Room 49), Rubens and Van Dyck (who share Room 55), Andrea del Sarto (Rooms 57 and 58) and Raphael (Room 66), whose *Madonna del cardellino* (*Madonna of the Goldfinch;* 1505–06) steals the show. Raphael painted it during his four-year sojourn in Florence.

Medici Portraits

Room 65 showcases Agnolo Bronzino (1503–72), who worked as official portrait artist at the court of Cosimo I from 1539 until 1555 (when he was replaced by Vasari). His 1545 portraits of the Grand Duchess Eleonora of Toleto and her son Giovanni together, and the 18-month-old Giovanni alone holding a goldfinch – symbolising his calling into the church – are considered masterpieces of 16th-century European

Detail of *Annunciation* by Leonardo da Vinci

CEILING ART

Take time to study the make-believe grotesque monsters and unexpected burlesques (spot the arrow-shooting satyr outside Room 15) waltzing across the eastern corridor's fabulous frescoed ceiling. Admire more compelling ceiling art in Rooms 19 to 23 whose ornate vaulted ceilings were frescoed in the 16th and 17th centuries with military objects and allegories as well as illustrations of historical battles and traditional festivals that took place on Florence's many beautiful and distinctive piazzas.

Allow time to linger in the 2nd-floor Secondo Corridoio (Second Corridor) linking the Primo (First) and Terzo (Third) corridors – views of the Arno and Florentine hills beyond are intoxicating.

ROOFTOP CAFE

Visits are best kept to three or four hours maximum. When it all gets too much, head to the rooftop cafe (aka the terraced hanging garden, where the Medici clan listened to music performances on the square below) for fresh air and fabulous views.

portraiture. Giovanni was elected a cardinal in 1560 but died of malaria two years later.

Leonardo di Vinci

Four early Florentine works by Leonardo da Vinci are currently displayed in Room 79. (In due course, Leonardo could well be shifted back upstairs to the 2nd floor.) His *Annunciazione* (*Annunciation;* 1472) was deliberately painted to be admired not face on (from where Mary's arm appears too long, her face too light and the angle of buildings not quite right), but rather from the lower right-hand side of the painting. The eclectic style of his *Adorazione dei Pastori* (*Adoration of the Shepherds;* 1495–97) is typical of Florentine figurative painting in the 15th century. In spring 2017, one of Da Vinci's most dazzling early works, the partly unfinished *Adorazione dei Magi* (*Adoration of the Magi;* 1481–82), returned to the Uffizi after six lengthy years of intricate restoration.

Caravaggio

Room 90, with its canary-yellow walls, features works by Caravaggio, deemed vulgar at the time for his direct interpretation of reality. The *Head of Medusa* (1598–99), commissioned for a ceremonial shield, is supposedly a self-portrait of the young artist who died at the age of 39. The biblical drama of an angel steadying the hand of Abraham as he holds a knife to his son Isaac's throat in Caravaggio's *Sacrifice of Isaac* (1601–02) is glorious in its intensity.

The Uffizi

JOURNEY INTO THE RENAISSANCE

Navigating the Uffizi's chronologically-ordered art collection is straightforward enough: knowing which of the 1500-odd masterpieces to view before gallery fatigue strikes is not. Swap coat and bag (travel light) for floor plan and audioguide on the ground floor, then meet 16th-century Tuscany head-on with a walk up the *palazzo's* magnificent bust-lined staircase (skip the lift – the Uffizi is as much about masterly architecture as art).

Allow four hours for this journey into the High Renaissance. At the top of the staircase, on the 2nd floor, show your ticket, turn left and pause to admire the full length of the first corridor sweeping south towards the Arno river. Then duck left into room 2 to witness first steps in Tuscan art – shimmering altarpieces by ❶ **Giotto** et al. Journey through medieval art to room 9 and ❷ **Piero della Francesca's** impossibly famous portrait, then break in the corridor with playful ❸ **ceiling art**. After Renaissance heavyweight ❹ **Botticelli**, meander past the Tribuna (potential detour) and enjoy the daylight streaming in through the vast windows and panorama of the ❺ **riverside second corridor**. Lap up soul-stirring views of the Arno, crossed by Ponte Vecchio and its echo of four bridges drifting towards the Apuane Alps on the horizon. Then saunter into the third corridor, pausing between rooms 25 and 34 to ponder the entrance to the enigmatic Vasari Corridor. End with High Renaissance maestro Michelangelo in the ❻ **San Marco sculpture garden** and with ❼ **Doni Tondo**.

Giotto's Madonna
Room 2
Draw breath at the shy blush and curvaceous breast of Giotto's humanised Virgin (*Le Maestà di Ognissanti*; 1310) – so feminine compared with those of Duccio and Cimabue painted just 25 years before.

Portraits of the Duke & Duchess of Urbino
Room 9
Revel in realism's voyage with these uncompromising, warts-and-all portraits (1472–75) by Piero della Francesca. No larger than A3 size, they originally slotted into a portable, hinged frame that folded like a book.

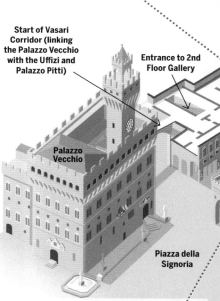

Start of Vasari Corridor (linking the Palazzo Vecchio with the Uffizi and Palazzo Pitti)

Entrance to 2nd Floor Gallery

Palazzo Vecchio

Piazza della Signoria

Grotesque Ceiling Frescoes
First Corridor
Take time to study the make-believe monsters and most unexpected of burlesques (spot the arrow-shooting satyr outside room 15) waltzing across this eastern corridor's fabulous frescoed ceiling (1581).

ALIZADA STUDIOS/SHUTTERSTOCK ©

The Genius of Botticelli
Room 10–14

The miniature form of *The Discovery of the Body of Holofernes* (c 1470) makes Botticelli's early Renaissance masterpiece all the more impressive. Don't miss the artist watching you in *Adoration of the Magi* (1475), oddly hidden in Room 15.

View of the Arno

Indulge in intoxicating city views from this short glassed-in corridor – an architectural masterpiece. Near the top of the hill, spot one of 73 outer towers built to defend Florence and its 15 city gates below.

Second Corridor

Tribuna

First Corridor

Arno River

❶ ❷ ❸ ❹ ❺ ❻ ❼

Entrance to Vasari Corridor

San Marco sculpture garden
Room 34

A 13-year-old Michelangelo studied classical sculpture as an apprentice at Lorenzo de Medici's sculpture school in San Marco. Admire relief-sculpted sarcophagi that had such a massive influence on this artist.

Third Corridor

Tribuna

No room in the Uffizi is so tiny or so exquisite. It was created in 1851 as a 'treasure chest' for Grand Duke Francesco and in the days of the Grand Tour, the Medici Venus here was a tour highlight.

VALUE LUNCHBOX

Try the Uffizi rooftop cafe or – better value – gourmet *panini* at 'Ino (www.ino-firenze.com; Via dei Georgofili 3-7r).

MATTER OF FACT

The Uffizi collection spans the 13th to 18th centuries, but its 15th- and 16th-century Renaissance works are second to none.

Doni Tondo
Room 35

The creator of *David*, Michelangelo, was essentially a sculptor and no painting expresses this better than *Doni Tondo* (1506–08). Mary's muscular arms against a backdrop of curvaceous nudes are practically 3D in their shapeliness.

TOP SIGHT
DUOMO

Properly titled **Cattedrale di Santa Maria del Fiore**
(Cathedral of St Mary of the Flower), but known as the
Duomo (cathedral), this is Florence's iconic landmark.
Designed by Sienese architect Arnolfo di Cambio,
construction began in 1296 and took almost 150
years. The result – Brunelleschi's distinctive red-tiled
cupola, graceful *campanile* (bell tower) and pink, white
and green marble facade – is breathtaking.

Facade

The neo-Gothic facade was designed in the 19th century by
architect Emilio de Fabris to replace the uncompleted original. The oldest and most clearly Gothic part of the structure
is its south flank, pierced by Porta dei Canonici (Canons'
Door), a mid-14th-century High Gothic creation (you enter
here to climb to the dome).

Interior

After the visual wham-bam of the facade, the sparse decoration of the Duomo's vast interior – 155m long and 90m
wide – is a surprise. Most of its artistic treasures have been
removed and those that remain are unexpectedly secular,
reflecting the fact that the Duomo was built with public
funds as a *chiesa di stato* (state church).

Down the left aisle two immense frescoes of equestrian
statues portray two *condottieri* (mercenaries) – on the left
Niccolò da Tolentino by Andrea del Castagno (1456), and on
the right Sir John Hawkwood (who fought in the service of
Florence in the 14th century) by Uccello (1436). In the same
aisle *La Commedia Illumina Firenze* (1465) by Domenico

DON'T MISS

➡ Climbing inside
Brunelleschi's cupola

➡ City view atop the
campanile

➡ Michelangelo's *La
Pièta* and Duomo
views from the rooftop
Terrazza Brunelleschi
at the Grande Museo del
Duomo

PRACTICALITIES

➡ Cattedrale di Santa
Maria del Fiore

➡ Map p80

➡ ☎ 055 230 28 85

➡ www.ilgrandemuseodel
duomo.it

➡ Piazza del Duomo

➡ ◷ 10am-5pm Mon-Wed
& Fri, to 4.30pm Thu, to
4.45pm Sat, 1.30-4.45pm
Sun

di Michelino depicts poet Dante Alighieri surrounded by the three afterlife worlds he describes in the *Divine Comedy:* purgatory is behind him, his right-hand points towards hell, and the city of Florence is paradise.

Mass Sacristy

Between the left (north) arm of the transept and the apse is the Sagrestia delle Messe (Mass Sacristy), its panelling a marvel of inlaid wood carved by Benedetto and Giuliano da Maiano. The fine bronze doors were executed by Luca della Robbia – his only known work in the material. Above the doorway is his glazed terracotta *Resurrezione* (Resurrection).

Crypt of Santa Reparata

A stairway near the main entrance of the cathedral leads down to the cathedral gift shop and Cripta Santa Reparata (Map p80; ◷10am-5pm Mon-Wed & Fri, to 4pm Thu, to 4.45pm Sat), the crypt where excavations between 1965 and 1974 unearthed parts of the 5th-century Chiesa di Santa Reparata that originally stood on the site. Should you be visiting on Sunday (when the crypt is closed), know your combined Duomo ticket is valid 48 hours.

Cupola

When Michelangelo went to work on St Peter's in Rome, he reportedly said: 'I go to build a greater dome, but not a fairer one', referring to the huge but graceful terracotta-brick dome (Brunelleschi's Dome; Map p80; ◷8.30am-7pm Mon-Fri, to 5pm Sat, 1-4pm Sun) atop Florence's Duomo. It was constructed between 1420 and 1436 to a design by Filippo Brunelleschi and is a highlight of any visit to Florence.

A Renaissance masterpiece, the cupola crowning the Duomo is a feat of engineering – it's 91m high and 45.5m wide – and one that cannot be fully appreciated without climbing its 463 interior stone steps. Taking his inspiration from Rome's Pantheon, Brunelleschi arrived at an innovative engineering solution of a distinctive octagonal shape of inner and outer concentric domes resting on the drum of the cathedral rather than the roof itself, allowing artisans to build from the ground up without needing a wooden support frame. Over four million bricks were used in the construction, laid in consecutive rings in horizontal courses using a vertical herringbone pattern.

The Climb

The climb up the spiral staircase is steep. Pause when you reach the balustrade at the base of the dome to admire the cathedral's octagonal *coro* (choir) below and seven round stained-glass windows piercing the

TICKETS

One ticket (adult/reduced incl cupola, baptistry, campanile, crypt & museum €15/3) covers all the sights and is valid for 48 hours (one visit per sight); purchase at online or at the ticket office, opposite the baptistery entrance at Piazza di San Giovanni 7.

Dress code is strict: no shorts, miniskirts or sleeveless tops.

A MATHEMATICAL WHIZZ

Architect, mathematician, engineer and sculptor, Filippo Brunelleschi (1377–1446) spent an incredible 42 years working on the dome of Florence's *duomo*. Starting work in 1419, his mathematical brain and talent for devising innovative engineering solutions enabled him to do what many Florentines had thought impossible: deliver the largest dome to be built in Italy since antiquity.

octagonal drum. The final leg – a straight, hazardous flight up the curve of the inner dome – rewards with a 360-degree panorama of one of Europe's most beautiful cities.

The Last Judgement

Giorgio Vasari and Federico Zuccari's late 16th-century *Giudizio Universale* (1572–79) fresco decorating the 4500-sq-metre surface of the cupola's inner dome is one of the world's largest paintings. Look for a spent Mother Nature with wrinkled breasts and the four seasons asleep at her feet. Less savoury are the poor souls in hell being sodomised with a pitch fork.

Bell Tower

Set next to the Duomo is its slender campanile (Bell Tower; Map p80; ⊘8.15am-8pm), a striking work of Florentine Gothic architecture designed by Giotto, the artistic genius often described as the founding artist of the Renaissance. The steep 414-step climb up the square, 85m tower offers the reward of a view that is nearly as impressive as that from the dome.

The first tier of bas-reliefs around the base of its elaborate Gothic facade are copies of those carved by Pisano depicting the Creation of Man and the *attività umane* (arts and industries). Those on the second tier depict the planets, the cardinal virtues, the arts and the seven sacraments. The sculpted Prophets and Sibyls in the upper-storey niches are copies of works by Donatello and others.

Baptistry

Across from the Duomo's main entrance is the 11th-century Battistero di San Giovanni (Baptistry; Map p80; ⊘8.15am-10.15am & 11.15am-7.30pm Mon-Fri, 8.15am-6.30pm Sat, 8.15am-1.30pm Sun), an octagonal, striped structure of white-and-green marble. Dante is among the famous people dunked in its baptismal font.

The Romanesque structure is most celebrated, however, for its three sets of doors illustrating the story of humanity and the Redemption. The gilded bronze doors by Lorenzo Ghiberti's at the eastern entrance, the *Porta del Paradiso* (Gate of Paradise), are copies – the originals are in the Grande Museo del Duomo. Andrea Pisano executed the southern doors (1330), illustrating the life of St John the Baptist, and Lorenzo Ghiberti won a public competition in 1401 to design the northern doors, likewise replaced by copies today.

The baptistry's interior gleams with Byzantine-style mosaics. Covering the dome in five horizontal tiers, they include scenes from the lives of St John the Baptist, Christ and Joseph on one side, and a representation of the Last Judgement on the other. A choir of angels surveys proceedings from the innermost tier.

Buy tickets online or at the ticket office at Piazza di San Giovanni 7, opposite the baptistry entrance.

Grande Museo del Duomo

This awe-inspiring museum (Cathedral Museum; ⊘9am-7.30pm) tells the magnificent story of how the Duomo and its cupola was built through art and short films. Its many sacred and liturgical treasures are immense.

The museum's spectacular main hall, Sala del Paradiso, is dominated by a life-size reconstruction of the original facade of the Duomo, decorated with some 40 14th- and early-15th-century statues carved for the facade by 14th-century masters. Building work began in 1296 but it was never finished and in 1587 the facade was eventually dismantled. This is also where you will find Ghiberti's original 15th-century masterpiece, *Porta del Paradiso (Doors of Paradise;* 1425–52) – gloriously golden, 16m-tall gilded bronze doors designed for the eastern entrance to the Baptistry – as well as those he sculpted for the northern entrance (1403–24).

Duomo interior

THE DUOMO CLOCK

Upon entering the Duomo, look up high to see its giant painted clock. One of the first monumental clocks in Europe, it notably turns in an anticlock-wise direction, counts in 24 hours starting at the bottom and begins the first hour of the day at sunset. The clock was painted by Florentine Paolo Ucello between 1440 and 1443.

Visit early in the morning to escape the crowds and avoid queuing in the hot sun.

CUPOLA RESERVATIONS

Reservations are obligatory for the Duomo's cupola; book a time slot when buying your ticket online or at a self-service Ticketpoint machine inside the Piazza di San Giovanni ticket office (Piazza San Giovanni 7; ⊙8.15am-6.45pm).

Michelangelo's achingly beautiful *La Pietà*, sculpted when he was almost 80 and intended for his own tomb, is displayed in the Tribuna di Michelangelo. Dissatisfied with both the quality of the marble and of his own work, Michelangelo broke up the unfinished sculpture, destroying the arm and left leg of the figure of Christ.

In Room 8, the Sala della Maddalena, it is impossible to miss Donatello's famous wooden representation of a gaunt, desperately desolate Mary Magdalene, a mid-15th-century work completed late in the sculptor's career.

Continuing up to the 1st floor, Rooms 14 and 15 explain in detail just how Brunelleschi constructed the ground-breaking cathedral dome. Look at 15th-century tools, pulleys, tackles and hoisting wagons used to build the cupola, watch a film and admire Brunelleschi's funeral mask (1446). On the 2nd floor, look at a fascinating collection of models of different proposed facades for the cathedral.

TOP SIGHT
PALAZZO VECCHIO

Dominating Florence's most glorious square, this fortress palace was the hub of political life in medieval Florence. Built for the *signoria* (city government) between 1298 and 1314, the 'Old Palace' hosted nine *priori* (consuls) – guild members picked out of a hat every two months. Cosimo I lived here in palatial ducal apartments from 1540 until 1549, and views from its iconic crenelated tower are mesmerising.

Salone dei Cinquecento

Cosimo I commissioned Vasari to renovate the interior of Palazzo Vecchio in 1540, living here for nine years before moving across the river to Palazzo Pitti. What impresses is the 53m-long, 22m-wide Salone dei Cinquecento with swirling battle scenes, painted floor to ceiling by Vasari and his apprentices. Cosimo commissioned Vasari to raise the original ceiling 7m in height and had himself portrayed as a god in the centre of the panelled ceiling. It took Vasari and his school, in consultation with Michelangelo, just two years (1563–65) to construct the ceiling and paint the 34 gold-leafed panels. The effect is dazzling.

Chapel of SS Cosmas & Damian

Off the huge Salone dei Cinquecento is this chapel, home to Vasari's 1557–58 triptych of the two saints. Cosimo the Elder is depicted as Cosmas (right) and Cosimo I as Damian (left).

DON'T MISS

➡ Vasari battle scenes in the Salone dei Cinquecento

➡ Cosimo's Studiolo on a 'Secret Passages' guided tour

PRACTICALITIES

➡ Map p80

➡ ☎ 055 276 85 58, 055 27 68 22

➡ www.musefirenze.it

➡ Piazza della Signoria

➡ adult/reduced museum €10/8, tower €10/8, museum & tower €14/12, archaeological tour €4, combination ticket €18/16

➡ ⊘ museum 9am-11pm Fri-Wed, to 2pm Thu Apr-Sep, 9am-7pm Fri-Wed, to 2pm Thu Oct-Mar, tower 9am-9pm Fri-Wed, to 2pm Thu Apr-Sep, 10am-5pm Fri-Wed, to 2pm Thu Oct-Mar

Studiolo

Cosimo I commissioned Vasari and a team of Florentine Mannerist artists to decorate this sumptuous study for his introverted, alchemy-mad son Francesco I; spot him disguised as a scientist experimenting with gunpowder in one of the 34 wall paintings. The lower paintings conceal 20 cabinets in which the young prince hid his treasures. Visit on a 'Secret Passages' tour.

Private Apartments

Upstairs, the private apartments of Eleonora and her ladies-in-waiting blare Medici glory. The ceiling in the Camera Verde (Green Room) by Ridolfo del Ghirlandaio was inspired by designs from Nero's Domus Aurea in Rome. The Sala dei Gigli, named after its frieze of fleur-de-lis, representing the Florentine Republic, is home to Donatello's original *Judith and Holofernes*.

Torre d'Arnolfo

Take a 418-step hike up this striking tower (adult/reduced €10/8) – the city panorama is breathtaking. Once up, you have 30 minutes to lap it up. No children under six years.

Backstage at the Palace

Imaginative guided tours take you into parts of Palazzo Vecchio otherwise inaccessible. You need a museum ticket in addition to the guided-tour ticket.

The 'Secret Passages' tour (adult/reduced €4/2, 1¼ hours) leads small groups along the secret staircase built between the palace's super-thick walls in 1342 as an escape route for French Duke of Athens Walter de Brienne, who seized the palace and nominated himself Lord of Florence, only to be sent packing back to France by the Florentines a year later. It follows this staircase to the Tesoretto (Treasury) of Cosimo I and Francesco I's sumptuous Studiolo (Study).

The 'Secrets of the Inferno' tour (adult/child €4/2, 1¼ hours), follows in the footsteps of Dan Brown's *Inferno* novel. The 'Invitation to the Court' tour (adult/child €4/2, 1¼ hours) ushers in actors dressed in Renaissance costume. Kid-specific tours include 'At Court with Donna Isabelle' (adult/child €4/2, 1¼ hours) led by a gregarious Spanish Isabel de Reinoso; and 'Life at Court' (adult/child €4/2, 1¼ hours), which ends with a 16th-century dressing-up session. There are also story-telling sessions and fresco and panel-painting workshops.

THE MAP ROOM

For a fascinating snapshot of how the world was viewed during the Renaissance, absorb Cosimo I's collection of maps displayed in the Sala delle Carte Geografiche (Map Room). His 16th-century maps chart everywhere in the known world at the time, from the polar regions to the Caribbean.

Vasari's battle scenes in the Salone del Cinquecentto glorify Florentine victories by Cosimo I over arch-rivals Pisa and Siena: unlike the Sienese, the Pisans are depicted bare of armour; play 'Spot the Leaning Tower'.

TOP TIPS

➡ Visit on a dry sunny day to ensure admission to the tower (closed when raining).

➡ Rent a tablet with multimedia guide (€5/4 for one/two people) at the ticket desk or download the Palazzo Vecchio app (€2) on your smartphone.

➡ Reserve guided tours by telephone (055 276 82 24, 055 276 85 58), email info@muse. comune.fi.it or at the Palazzo Vecchio ticket desk. You need a valid museum ticket in addition to the guided-tour ticket.

The Duomo & Santa Maria Novella

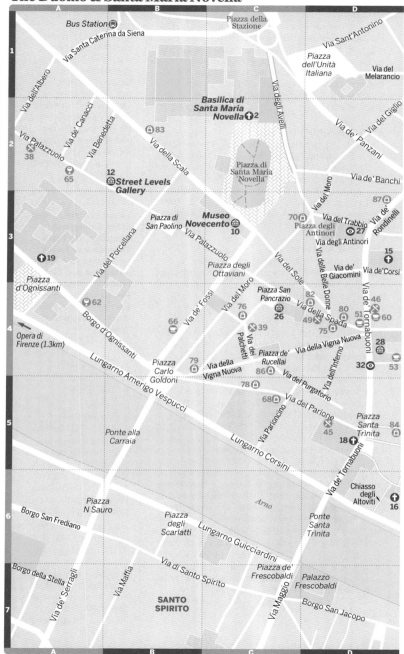

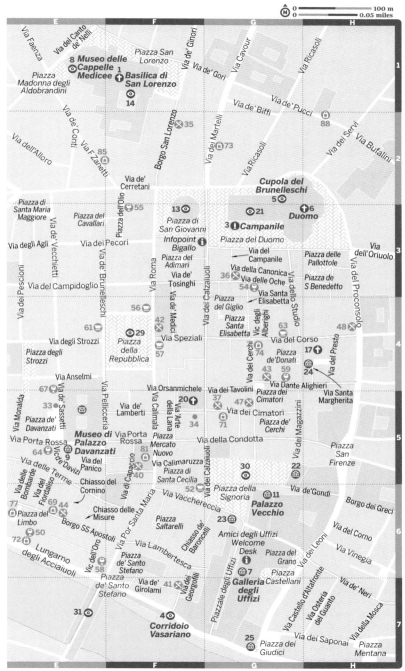

FLORENCE SIGHTS

The Duomo & Santa Maria Novella

Via de' Tornabuoni　　　　　LANDMARK
(Map p80) Renaissance palaces and Italian
fashion houses border Via de' Tornabuoni,
the city's most expensive shopping strip.
Named after a Florentine noble family
(which died out in the 17th century), it is referred to as the 'Salotto di Firenze' (Florence's
Drawing Room). At its northern end is Palazzo Antinori (Map p80; Piazza degli Antinori 3)
(1461–69), owned by the aristocratic Antinori
family (known for wine production) since
1506. Opposite, huge stone steps lead up
to 17th-century Chiesa dei Santi Michele
e Gaetano (Map p80; Piazza degli Antinori;
⊙ 7.15am-noon & 1-7.30pm Mon-Sat, 8am-1.15pm &
3.30-8pm Sun).

Palazzo Strozzi   GALLERY

(Map p80; ☑ 055 246 96 00; www.palazzostrozzi. org; Piazza degli Strozzi; adult/reduced €12/9.50, family ticket €22; ⊙10am-8pm Tue, Wed & Fri-Sun, to 11pm Thu) This 15th-century Renaissance mansion was built for wealthy merchant Filippo Strozzi, one of the Medicis' major political and commercial rivals. Today it hosts exciting art exhibitions. There's always a buzz about the place, with young Florentines congregating in the courtyard Caffé Strozzi (Map p80; ☑ 055 28 82 36; www.strozzicaffe.com; ⊙8am-8.30pm Mon, to 1am Tue-Sun; 🛜). Art workshops, tours and other activities aimed squarely at families make the gallery a firm favourite with pretty much everyone.

★Museo di Palazzo Davanzati   MUSEUM

(Map p80; ☑ 055 238 86 10; www.polomuseale. firenze.it; Via Porta Rossa 13; adult/reduced €6/3; ⊙8.15am-2pm, closed 1st, 3rd & 5th Mon, 2nd & 4th Sun of month) This is the address to see precisely how Florentine nobles lived in the 16th century. Home to the wealthy Davanzati merchant family from 1578, this 14th-century *palazzo* with a wonderful central loggia is a gem. Peep at the carved faces of the original owners on the pillars in the inner courtyard and don't miss the 1st-floor Sala Madornale (Reception Room) with its painted wooden ceiling, exotic Sala dei Pappagalli (Parrot Room) and Camera dei Pavoni (Peacock Bedroom).

◉ Santa Maria Novella

The main sights in this district are clustered on Piazza di Santa Maria Novella, fronted by the shimmering green-and-white facade of Santa Maria Novella's venerable basilica. Heading south towards the river, don't miss some of the city's finest frescoes in Chiesa di Santa Trinità; Chiesa d'Ognissanti, a must for Botticelli fans; and the small but fascinating Museo Marino Marini.

★Museo Novecento   MUSEUM

(Museum of the 20th Century; Map p80; ☑ 055 28 61 32; www.museonovecento.it; Piazza di Santa Maria Novella 10; adult/reduced €8.50/4; ⊙9am-7pm Mon-Wed, Sat & Sun, to 2pm Thu, to 11pm Fri summer, 9am-6pm Fri-Wed, to 2pm Thu winter) Don't allow the Renaissance to distract from Florence's fantastic modern art museum, in a 13th-century *palazzo* previously used as a pilgrim shelter, hospital and school. A well-articulated itinerary guides visitors through modern Italian painting and sculpture from

the early 20th century to the late 1980s. Installation art makes effective use of the outside space on the 1st-floor loggia. Fashion and theatre get a nod on the 2nd floor, and the itinerary ends with a 20-minute cinematic montage of the best films set in Florence.

A highlight of Room 10 is Arturo Martini's exquisite sculpture *La Pisana* (1933), next to one of Marino Marini's signature bronze horses – both representative of the archaeological rediscovery of the ancient world expressed by artists in Italy in the 1920s and 1930s.

Chiesa d'Ognissanti   CHURCH

(Map p80; ☑055 239 87 00; Borgo d'Ognissanti 42; ⊙9am-12.30pm & 4-6pm Mon-Sat, 9-10am & 4-5.30pm Sun) FREE Stroll along Borgo d'Ognissanti, from Piazza Carlo Goldoni towards ancient city gate Porta al Prato, past antiques shops and designer boutiques to reach this 13th-century church, built as part of a Benedictine monastery. Its highlight is Domenico Ghirlandaio's fresco of the *Madonna della Misericordia* protecting members of the Vespucci family, the church's main patrons. Amerigo Vespucci, the Florentine navigator who gave his name to the American continent, is supposed to be the young boy whose head peeks between the Madonna and the old man.

Museo Marino Marini   GALLERY

(Map p80; ☑ 055 21 94 32; http://museomarino marini.it/; Piazza San Pancrazio 1; adult/reduced €6/4; ⊙10am-7pm Sat-Mon, to 1pm Wed-Fri) Deconsecrated in the 19th century, Chiesa di San Pancrazio is home to this small art museum displaying sculptures, portraits and drawings by Pistoia-born sculptor Marino Marini (1901–80). But the highlight is the Cappella Rucellai with a tiny scale copy of Christ's Holy Sepulchre in Jerusalem – a Renaissance gem by Leon Battista Alberti. The chapel was built between 1458 and 1467 for the tomb of wealthy Florentine banker and wool merchant Giovanni Ruccellai.

Chiesa di Santa Trinita   CHURCH

(Map p80; Piazza Santa Trinita; ⊙8am-noon & 4-5.45pm Mon-Sat, 8-10.45am & 4-5.45pm Sun) Built in Gothic style and later given a Mannerist facade, this 14th-century church shelters some of the city's finest frescoes: Lorenzo Monaco's *Annunciation* (1422) in Cappella Bartholini Salimbeni and eye-catching frescoes by Ghirlandaio depicting the life of St Francis of Assisi in Cappella Sassetti, right of the altar. The frescoes

TOP SIGHT
BASILICA DI SANTA MARIA NOVELLA

This monastery complex, fronted by the striking green-and-white marble facade of its basilica, hides romantic church cloisters and a stunning frescoed chapel behind its monumental walls. The basilica itself is a treasure chest of artistic masterpieces, climaxing with frescoes by Domenico Ghirlandaio and a luminous painted _Crucifix_ by Giotto (c 1290).

Holy Trinity
As you enter, look straight ahead to see Masaccio's superb fresco _Holy Trinity_ (1424–25), one of the first artworks to use the then newly discovered techniques of perspective and proportion.

Cappella Maggiore
Look behind the main altar to find the basilica's highlight, a tiny chapel adorned in vibrant frescoes painted by Ghirlandaio between 1485 and 1490. Relating the lives of the Virgin Mary, the frescoes are notable for their depiction of Florentine life during the Renaissance. Spot portraits of Ghirlandaio's contemporaries and members of the Tornabuoni family (who commissioned the frescoes).

DON'T MISS
➡ Cappella Maggiore
➡ Chiostro Verde
➡ Cappellone degli Spagnoli

PRACTICALITIES
➡ Map p80
➡ ☎ 055 21 92 57
➡ www.smn.it
➡ Piazza di Santa Maria Novella 18
➡ adult/reduced €5/3.50
➡ ⏱ 9am-7pm Mon-Thu, 11am-7pm Fri, 9am-6.30pm Sat, noon-6.30pm Sun summer, shorter hours winter

Cappella Strozzi di Mantova

To the far left of the altar, up a short flight of stairs, is this wonderful chapel covered in soul-stirring 14th-century frescoes by Niccolò di Tommaso and Nardo di Cione. The fine altarpiece (1354–57) here was painted by the latter's brother Andrea, better known as Andrea Orcagna.

Chiostro Verde

From the church, walk through a side door into the serenely beautiful Green Cloister (1332–62), part of the vast monastery occupied by Dominican friars who arrived in Florence in 1219 and settled in Santa Maria Novella two years later. The cloister is named after the green earth base used for the frescoes on three of its four walls. On the west side of the Chiostro Verde, another passage leads to the 14th-century Cappella degli Ubriachi and a large refectory (1353–54) featuring ecclesiastical relics and a 1583 *Last Supper* by Alessandro Allori.

Cappellone degli Spagnoli

A door off the cloister's northern side leads into this chapel, named in 1566 when it was given to the Spanish colony in Florence (Spagnoli means Spanish). Its extraordinary frescoes (c 1365–67) by Andrea di Bonaiuto depict the Resurrection, Ascension and Pentecost (vault); on the altar wall are scenes of the Via Dolorosa, Crucifixion and Descent into Limbo.

were painted between 1483 and 1485 and feature portraits of illustrious Florentines of the time; pop a €0.50 coin in the slot to illuminate the frescoes for two minutes.

Museo Stibbert MUSEUM
(www.museostibbert.it; Via Federigo Stibbert 26; adult/reduced €8/6; ☺10am-2pm Mon-Wed, to 6pm Fri-Sun) Anglo-Italian, Florence-born Frederick Stibbert (1838–1906) was one of the grand 19th-century wheeler-dealers on the European antiquities market and amassed an intriguing personal collection of furnishings, tapestries and 16th- to 19th-century paintings, showcased in this villa museum. Fun for kids is the Sala della Cavalcata (Parade Room) with life-sized figures of horses and their riders in suits of armour from Europe and the Middle East. Take bus 4 from Stazione di Santa Maria Novella to the 'Gioia' stop on Via Fabroni, from where it is a short walk.

◎ San Lorenzo & San Marco

San Lorenzo is Medici territory – come here to see their palace, church, library and mausoleum, all decorated with extraordinary works of art. San Marco meanwhile offers far more than the city's most famous resident, one Signore David; the frescoes in the Museo di San Marco are nothing short of superb.

★Basilica di San Lorenzo BASILICA
(Map p80; www.operamedicealaurenziana.org; Piazza San Lorenzo; €6, with Biblioteca Laurenziana €8.50; ☺10am-5pm Mon-Sat, plus 1.30-5pm Sun Mar-Oct) Considered one of Florence's most harmonious examples of Renaissance architecture, this unfinished basilica was the Medici parish church and mausoleum. It was designed by Brunelleschi in 1425 for Cosimo the Elder and built over a 4th-century church. In the solemn interior, look for Brunelleschi's austerely beautiful Sagrestia Vecchia (Old Sacristy) with its sculptural decoration by Donatello. Michelangelo was commissioned to design the facade in 1518, but his design in white Carrara marble was never executed, hence the building's rough, unfinished appearance.

Inside, columns of *pietra serena* (soft grey stone) crowned with Corinthian capitals separate the nave from the two aisles. The gilded funerary monument of Donatello – who was still sculpting the two bronze pulpits (1460–67) adorned with panels of the Crucifixion when he died – lies in the Capella Martelli (Martelli Chapel) featuring Filippo Lippi's exquisitely restored *Annunciation* (c 1440).

Donatello's actual grave lies in the basilica crypt, today part of the Museo del Tesoro di San Lorenzo (San Lorenzo Treasury Museum); the crypt entrance is in the courtyard beyond the ticket office. The museum

---

❶ MUSEUM TICKETS

In July, August and other busy periods such as Easter, unbelievably long queues are a fact of life at Florence's key museums – if you haven't prebooked your ticket, you could well end up standing in line queuing for four hours or so.

For a fee of €3 per ticket (€4 for the Uffizi and Galleria dell'Accademia), tickets to nine *musei statali* (state museums) can be reserved, including the Uffizi, Galleria dell'Accademia (where *David* lives), Palazzo Pitti, Museo del Bargello and the Medicean chapels (Cappelle Medicee). In reality, the only museums where prebooking is vital are the Uffizi and Accademia – to organise your ticket, go online or call Firenze Musei (Florence Museums; www.firenzemusei.it), with ticketing desks (open 8.30am to 7pm Tuesday to Sunday) at the Uffizi (Door 3, Piazzale degli Uffizi) and Palazzo Pitti (Piazza dei Pitti).

At the Uffizi, signs point prebooked ticket holders to the building opposite the gallery where tickets can be collected; once you've got the ticket you go to Door 1 of the museum (for prebooked tickets only) and queue again to enter the gallery. It's annoying, but you'll still save hours of queuing time overall. Many hotels in Florence also prebook museum tickets for guests.

Admission to all state museums, including the Uffizi and Galleria dell'Accademia, is free on the first Sunday of each month and also on 18 February, the day Anna Maria Louisa de' Medici (1667–1743) died. The last of the Medici family, it was she who bequeathed the city its vast cultural heritage.

EU passport holders aged under 18 and over 65 get into Florence's state museums for free, and EU citizens aged 18 to 25 pay half price. Have your ID with you at all times. Note that museum ticket offices usually shut 30 minutes before closing time.

BACKSTREET FLORENCE: DANTE

Italy's most divine poet was born in 1265 in a wee house down a narrow lane in the back-streets of Florence. Tragic romance made him tick and there's no better place to unravel the medieval life and times of Dante than the Museo Casa di Dante (Map p80; ☑ 055 21 94 16; Via Santa Margherita 1; adult/reduced €4/2; ⊙ 10am-5pm Mon-Fri, 10am-6pm Sat & Sun).

When Dante was just 12 he was promised in marriage to Gemma Donati. But it was another Florentine gal, Beatrice Portinari (1266–90), that was his muse, his inspiration and the love of his life (despite only ever meeting her twice in his life): in *Divina Commedia (Divine Comedy)* Dante broke with tradition by using the familiar Italian, not the formal Latin, to describe travelling through the circles of hell in search of his beloved Beatrice.

Beatrice, who wed a banker and died a couple of years later aged just 24, is buried in 11th-century Chiesa di Santa Margherita (Map p80; Via Santa Margherita 4; ⊙ hours vary), in an alley near Dante's house; note the wicker basket in front of her grave filled with scraps of paper on which prayers and dedications evoking unrequited love have been penned. This chapel was also where the poet married Gemma in 1295. Dimly lit, it remains much as it was in medieval Florence. No wonder novelist Dan Brown chose it to set a scene in his most recent Dante-themed thriller, *Inferno* (2013), that takes place in Florence.

displays chalices, altarpieces, dazzling altar cloths, processional crucifixes, episcopal brooches and other precious sacred treasures once displayed in the church. Across from the plain marble tombstone of Donatello is the tomb of Cosimo the Elder, buried inside the quadrangular pilaster in the crypt supporting the basilica presbytery – his funerary monument sits directly above, in front of the high altar in the basilica.

Biblioteca Medicea Laurenziana   LIBRARY
(Medici Library; Map p80; ☑ 055 293 79 11; www.bml.firenze.sbn.it; Piazza San Lorenzo 9; €3, incl basilica €8.50; ⊙ 9.30am-1.30pm Mon-Sat) Beyond the Basilica di San Lorenzo ticket office lie peaceful cloisters framing a garden with orange trees. Stairs lead up the loggia to the Biblioteca Medicea Laurenziana, commissioned by Giulio de' Medici (Pope Clement VII) in 1524 to house the extensive Medici library (started by Cosimo the Elder and greatly added to by Lorenzo il Magnifico). The extraordinary staircase in the vestibule, intended as a 'dark prelude' to the magnificent Sala di Lettura (Reading Room), was designed by Michelangelo.

★ Museo delle
Cappelle Medicee   MAUSOLEUM
(Medici Chapels; Map p80; www.firenzemusei.it; Piazza Madonna degli Aldobrandini 6; adult/reduced €8/4; ⊙ 8.15am-1.50pm, closed 1st, 3rd & 5th Mon, 2nd & 4th Sun of month) Nowhere is Medici conceit expressed so explicitly as in the Medici Chapels. Adorned with granite, marble, semi-precious stones and some of Michelangelo's most beautiful sculptures, it is the

burial place of 49 dynasty members. Francesco I lies in the dark, imposing Cappella dei Principi (Princes' Chapel) alongside Ferdinando I and II and Cosimo I, II and III. Lorenzo il Magnifico is buried in the graceful Sagrestia Nuova (New Sacristy), which was Michelangelo's first architectural work.

It is also in the sacristy that you can swoon over three of Michelangelo's most haunting sculptures: *Dawn and Dusk* on the sarcophagus of Lorenzo, Duke of Urbino; *Night and Day* on the sarcophagus of Lorenzo's son Giuliano (note the unfinished face of 'Day' and the youth of the sleeping woman drenched in light aka 'Night'); and *Madonna and Child,* which adorns Lorenzo's tomb.

Palazzo Medici-Riccardi   PALACE
(Map p88; ☑ 055 276 03 40; www.palazzo-medici.it; Via Cavour 3; adult/reduced €7/4; ⊙ 8.30am-7pm Thu-Tue) Cosimo the Elder entrusted Michelozzo with the design of the family's townhouse in 1444. The result was this palace, a blueprint that influenced the construction of Florentine family residences such as Palazzo Pitti and Palazzo Strozzi. The upstairs chapel, Cappella dei Magi, is covered in wonderfully detailed frescoes (c 1459–63) by Benozzo Gozzoli, a pupil of Fra' Angelico, and is one of the supreme achievements of Renaissance painting.

Gozzoli's ostensible theme of *Procession of the Magi to Bethlehem* is but a slender pretext for portraying members of the Medici clan in their best light; spy Lorenzo il Magnifico and Cosimo the Elder in the crowd. The chapel was reconfigured to accommodate a baroque staircase, hence the oddly split fresco. The mid-15th-century altarpiece of the *Adoration*

San Lorenzo & San Marco

San Lorenzo & San Marco

of the Child is a copy of the original (originally here) by Fra' Filippo Lippi. Only 10 visitors are allowed in at a time; in high season reserve in advance at the ticket desk.

The Medici lived at Palazzo Medici until 1540, making way for the Riccardi family a century later. They remodelled the palace and built the 1st-floor Sala Luca Giordano, a sumptuous masterpiece of baroque art. Giordano adorned the ceiling with his complex *Allegory of Divine Wisdom* (1685), a rather overblown example of late baroque dripping with gold leaf and bursting with colour.

★ Museo di San Marco   MUSEUM
(Map p88; ☑ 055 238 86 08; Piazza San Marco 3; adult/reduced €4/2; ⊙ 8.15am-1.50pm Mon-Fri, 8.15am-4.50pm Sat & Sun, closed 1st, 3rd & 5th Sun & 2nd & 4th Mon of month) At the heart of Florence's university area sits Chiesa di San Marco and

an adjoining 15th-century Dominican monastery where both gifted painter Fra' Angelico (c 1395–1455) and the sharp-tongued Savonarola piously served God. Today the monastery, aka one of Florence's most spiritually uplifting museums, showcases the work of Fra' Angelico. After centuries of being known as 'Il Beato Angelico' (literally 'The Blessed Angelic One') or simply 'Il Beato' (The Blessed), the Renaissance's most blessed religious painter was made a saint by Pope John Paul II in 1984.

Enter via Michelozzo's Chiostro di Sant' Antonio (Saint Antoninus Cloister; 1440). Turn immediately right to enter the Sala dell'Ospizio dei Pellegrini (Pilgrims' Hospital Hall) where Fra' Angelico's attention to perspective and the realistic portrayal of nature comes to life in a number of major paintings, including the *Deposition from the Cross* (1432).

Giovanni Antonio Sogliani's fresco *The Miraculous Supper of St Domenic* (1536) dominates the former monks' Refettorio (Refectory) in the cloister. Fra' Angelico's huge *Crucifixion and Saints* fresco (1441–42), featuring all the patron saints of the convent and city, plus the Medici family who commissioned the fresco, decorates the former Capitolo (Chapterhouse). But it is the 44 monastic cells on the 1st floor that are the most haunting: at the top of the stairs, Fra' Angelico's most famous work, *Annunciation* (c 1440), commands all eyes.

A stroll around each of the cells reveals snippets of many more religious reliefs by the Tuscan-born friar, who decorated the cells between 1440 and 1441 with deeply devotional frescoes to guide the meditation of his fellow friars. Most were executed by Fra' Angelico himself, with others by aides under his supervision, including Benozzo Gozzoli. Among several masterpieces is the magnificent *Adoration of the Magi* in the cell used by Cosimo the Elder as a meditation retreat (Nos 38 to 39); only 10 people can visit at a time. The frescoes in the cell of San Antonino Arcivescovo (neighbouring Fra' Aneglico's *Annunication*) are gruesome: they show Jesus pushing open the door of his sepulchre, squashing a nasty-looking devil in the process.

Contrasting with the pure beauty of these frescoes are the plain rooms (Cell VI) that Savonarola called home from 1489. Rising to the position of prior at the Dominican convent, it was from here that the fanatical monk railed against luxury, greed and corruption of the clergy. Kept as a kind of shrine to the turbulent priest, the three small rooms house a portrait, a few personal items, fragments of the black cape and white tunic Savonarola wore, his rosary beads and the linen banner he carried in processions, and a grand marble monument erected by admirers in 1873.

⭐ **Museo degli Innocenti**   MUSEUM
(Map p88; ☎ 055 203 73 08; www.museodeglinnocenti.it; Piazza della Santissima Annunziata 13; adult/reduced/family €7/5/10; ☉10am-7pm) Shortly after its founding in 1421, Brunelleschi designed the loggia for Florence's Ospedale degli Innocenti, a foundling hospital and Europe's first orphanage, built by the wealthy silk weavers' guild to care for unwanted children. Inside, a highly emotive, state-of-the-art museum explores its history, climaxing with a sensational collection of frescoes and artworks that once decorated the hospital and a stunning rooftop cafe terrace (fab city views).

Brunelleschi's use of rounded arches and Roman capitals mark it as arguably the first building of the Renaissance.

Giardino dei Semplici   GARDENS
(Orto Botanico; Map p88; ☎ 055 275 64 44; www.unifi.it/msn; Via Pier Antonio Micheli 3; adult/reduced €4/2; ☉10am-7pm Apr–mid-Oct, 10am-4pm Sat & Sun mid-Oct–Mar) Founded in 1545 to furnish medicine to the Medici, Florence's botanical gardens – managed today by the university – are a wonderfully peaceful retreat in a stretch of the city with little green space. Its greenhouse is fragrant with citrus blossoms, and medicinal plants, Tuscan spices, 220 tree types and wildflowers from the Apennines pepper its 2.3 hectares. Don't miss the magnificent yew tree, planted in 1720, and an ornamental cork oak from 1805. Several themed footpaths wend their way through the gardens.

◉ **Santa Croce**

Presided over by the massive Franciscan basilica of the same name on the neighbourhood's main square, this area has a slightly rough veneer to it. The basilica aside, the other major sight is the Museo del Bargello with its sensational collection of Tuscan sculpture from the Renaissance period. Michelangelo's family lived in Santa Croce at what is now the Museo Casa Buonarotti house-museum.

Piazza di Santa Croce   PIAZZA
(Map p94) This square was cleared in the Middle Ages to allow the faithful to gather

---

I SPY ... STREET ART

Take a break from Renaissance art with urban street-art at Street Levels Gallery (Map p80; ☎ 347 3387760, 339 2203607; www.facebook.com/pg/StreetLevelsGalleriaFirenze; Via Palazzuolo 74r; ☉10am-1pm & 3-7pm). Exhibitions showcase the work of local street artists, including street-sign hacker Clet (p98), the stencil art of Hogre, and ExitEnter, whose work is easily recognisable by the red balloons holding up the matchstick figures he draws. A highlight is the enigmatic Blub, whose caricatures of historical figures wearing goggles and diving masks adorn many a city wall – his art is known as L'Arte Sa Nuotare (Art Knows how to Swim).

Check the gallery's Facebook page for workshops and events.

TOP SIGHT
GALLERIA DELL'ACCADEMIA

A lengthy queue marks the door to this gallery, purpose-built to house one of the Renaissance's greatest masterpieces, Michelangelo's *David*. Fortunately the world's most famous statue is worth the wait. Also here are Michelangelo's unfinished *Prigioni* sculpture and paintings by Andrea Orcagna, Taddeo Gaddi, Domenico Ghirlandaio, Filippino Lippi and Sandro Botticelli.

Michelangelo's David

Carved from a single block of marble already worked on by two sculptors, Michelangelo's most famous work was challenging to complete. Yet the subtle detail of the enormous work of art – the veins in his sinewy arms, the leg muscles, the change in expression as you move around the statue – is indeed impressive. Thankfully for Michelangelo, when the statue of the nude boy-warrior – depicted for the first time as a man rather than young boy – appeared on Piazza della Signoria in 1504, Florentines immediately adopted *David* as an emblem of power, liberty and civic pride.

DON'T MISS

➡ Michelangelo's *David*

➡ The Slaves

➡ Botticelli's *Madonna del Mare*

PRACTICALITIES

➡ Map p88

➡ www.firenzemusei.it

➡ Via Ricasoli 60

➡ adult/reduced €8/4, incl temporary exhibition €12.50/6.25

➡ ⊙ 8.15am-6.50pm Tue-Sun

The Slaves

Another soul-soaring work by Michelangelo, *Prigioni* (1521–30) evokes four 'prisoners' or 'slaves' so powerfully that the figures really do seem to be writhing and struggling to free themselves from the ice-cold marble. The work was intended for the tomb of Pope Julius II in Rome, which was never completed.

Coronation of the Virgin

This remarkable piece of embroidery – an altar frontal 4m long and over 1m wide – portrays the *Coronazione della Vergine* (*Coronation of the Virgin;* 1336; pictured above) in exquisite detail using polychrome silks and gold and silver thread. Completed by master embroiderer Jacopo Cambi, it originally covered the high altar of the Basilica di Santa Maria Novella.

Botticelli's Madonna

Madonna del Mare (*Madonna of the Sea;* 1477), a portrait of the Virgin and child by Sandro Botticelli, exudes a mesmerising serenity. Compare it with works in the gallery by Botticelli's master and mentor, Filippo Lippi (c 1457–1504), to whom some critics attribute it.

when the church itself was full. In Savonarola's day, heretics were executed here. Such an open space inevitably found other uses, and from the 14th century it was often the colourful scene of jousts, festivals and *calcio storico* (www.calciostorico.it) matches. The city's 2nd-century amphitheatre took up the area facing the square's western end: Piazza dei Peruzzi, Via de' Bentaccordi and Via Torta mark the oval outline of its course.

★ **Basilica di Santa Croce** CHURCH, MUSEUM
(Map p94; ☎ 055 246 61 05; www.santacroceopera.it; Piazza di Santa Croce; adult/reduced €8/4; ⏱ 9.30am-5.30pm Mon-Sat, 2-5.30pm Sun) The austere interior of this Franciscan basilica is a shock after the magnificent neo-Gothic facade enlivened by varying shades of coloured marble. Most visitors come to see the tombs of Michelangelo, Galileo and Ghiberti inside this church, but frescoes by Giotto in the chapels right of the altar are the real highlights. The basilica was designed by Arnolfo di Cambio between 1294 and 1385 and owes its name to a splinter of the Holy Cross donated by King Louis of France in 1258.

Some of its frescoed chapels are much better preserved than others – Giotto's murals featuring John the Baptist in the **Cappella Peruzzi** (1310–20) are in particularly poor condition. Those painted between 1320 and 1328 in the **Cappella Bardi** depicting scenes from the life of St Francis have fared better. Giotto's assistant and most loyal pupil, Taddeo Gaddi, frescoed the neighbouring **Cappella Majeure** (currently being restored) and nearby **Cappella Baroncelli** (1328–38); the latter takes as its subject the life of the Virgin.

Taddeo's son Agnolo painted the **Cappella Castellani** (1385), with frescoes depicting

FLORENCE'S FINEST LAST SUPPER

Once part of a sprawling Benedictine monastery, **Cenacolo di Sant'Apollonia** (Map p88; ☎ 055 238 86 07; www.polomusealetoscana.beniculturali.it; Via XXVII Apre 1; ⏱ 8.15am-1.50pm daily, closed 1st, 3rd & 5th Sat & Sun of month) FREE harbours arguably the city's most remarkable *Last Supper* scene. Painted by Andrea del Castagno in the 1440s, it is one of the first works of its kind to effectively apply Renaissance perspective. It possesses a haunting power with its vivid colours as well as the dark, menacing figure of Judas.

the life of St Nicholas, and was also responsible for the frescoes above the altar.

From the transept chapels a doorway designed by Michelozzo leads into a corridor, off which is the **Sagrestia** (Sacristy), an enchanting 14th-century room with Taddeo Gaddi's fresco of the Crucifixion. On the left as you enter, look for the late-15th-century glazed terracotta bust of Christ by Andrea della Robbia, all too often overshadowed by the large painted wooden cross (c 1288) by Cimabue suspended from the wooden ceiling. One of many priceless artworks to be damaged in the 1966 floods that inundated Santa Croce in more than 4m of water, the crucifix took 10 years to restore and has since become a symbol of the catastrophe that struck the city and its subsequent comeback.

Through the next room, the church bookshop, you can access the **Scuola del Cuoio** (Map p94; ☎ 055 24 45 33; www.scuoladelcuoio.com; Via di San Giuseppe 5r; ⏱ 10am-6pm), a leather school where you can see bags being fashioned and buy the finished products.

At the end of the corridor is a **Medici chapel** with a fine two-tone altarpiece in glazed terracotta by Andrea della Robbia. This was the original burial place of Galileo, from his death in 1642 until 1737 when arrangements were finally made for his reburial in the nave of the basilica. A small room to the left of the altar contains a bust of the scientist and a plaque marking the spot where his first tomb was.

Post-chapel, backtrack to the church and follow the 'Uscita' (exit) sign, opposite the main entrance, to access the basilica's two serene cloisters designed by Brunelleschi just before his death in 1446. His unfinished **Cappella de' Pazzi**, on the left at the end of the first cloister, is notable for its harmonious lines and restrained terracotta medallions of the Apostles by Luca della Robbia, and is a masterpiece of Renaissance architecture. It was built for, but never used by, the wealthy banking family destroyed in the 1478 Pazzi Conspiracy – when papal sympathisers sought to overthrow Lorenzo il Magnifico and the Medici dynasty.

Continue to the second cloister where a glass door leads into a gallery showcasing various artworks, climaxing with the cavernous **Cenacolo** (Refectory) where 150 Franciscan monks shared meals together in the 15th century, where warehouse goods were stored in the 20th century and where floodwaters hit a high of 5m in 1966. While Taddeo Gaddi's dazzling *The Last Supper* (1334–56) fresco fills the entire far wall, it is Georgio

THE VASARIAN CORRIDOR

Bathed in mystery, this must be the world's most infamous and enigmatic corridor. Look above the jewellery shops on the eastern side of Ponte Vecchio to see Florence's **Corridoio Vasariano** (Vasarian Corridor; Map p80; ⊙ by guided tour; 🖫 B), an elevated covered passageway joining the Palazzo Vecchio on Piazza della Signoria with the Uffizi and Palazzo Pitti on the other side of the river. Around 1km long, it was designed by Vasari for Cosimo I in 1565 to allow the Medicis to wander between the two palaces in privacy and comfort. From the 17th century, the Medicis strung it with self-portraits – today the collection of 700-odd artworks includes self-portraits of Andrea del Sarto (the oldest), Rubens, Rembrandt, Canova and others.

The original promenade incorporated tiny windows (facing the river) and circular apertures with iron gratings (facing the street) to protect those who used the corridor from outside attacks. But when Hitler visited Florence in 1941, his chum and fellow dictator Benito Mussolini had big new windows punched into the corridor walls on Ponte Vecchio so that his guest could enjoy an expansive view down the Arno from the famous Florentine bridge.

On the Oltrarno, the corridor passes by **Chiesa di Santa Felicità** (Map p102; Piazza di Santa Felicità; ⊙ 9.30am-noon & 3.30-5.30pm Mon-Sat), thereby providing the Medici with a private balcony in the church where they could attend Mass without mingling with the minions. Stand in front of the Romanesque church on Piazza di Santa Felicità and admire the trio of arches of the Vasarian Corridor that runs right above the portico outside the otherwise unnotable church facade. Inside, walk towards the altar and look backwards to see the Medici balcony up high (and imagine the corridor snaking behind it). Oh, and before leaving the church, don't miss Ghirlandaio's *Meeting of St Anne and St Joachim* hung at the end of its right transept.

Closed for renovation in 2017, the corridor will be open to just a privileged few by guided tour once work is complete (date unknown): contact Florence Town (p102) and Caf Tour & Travel (p103) for updated tour information, or check the Uffizi website (p68).

Vasari's magnificent *The Last Supper* (1546) that steals the show.

★ **Museo del Bargello**   MUSEUM
(Map p94; www.bargellomusei.beniculturali.it; Via del Proconsolo 4; adult/reduced €8/4; ⊙ 8.15am-1.50pm, closed 2nd & 4th Sun & 1st, 3rd & 5th Mon of month) It was behind the stark walls of Palazzo del Bargello, Florence's earliest public building redecorated in neo-Gothic style in 1845, that the *podestà* meted out justice from the 13th century until 1502. Today the building safeguards Italy's most comprehensive collection of Tuscan Renaissance sculpture with some of Michelangelo's best early works and several by Donatello. Michelangelo was just 21 when a cardinal commissioned him to create the drunken grape-adorned *Bacchus* (1496–97). Unfortunately the cardinal didn't like the result and sold it to a banker.

Other Michelangelo works to look out for in the ground-floor **Sala di Michelangelo e della Scultura del Cinque Cento** (first door on the right after entering the interior courtyard) include the marble bust of *Brutus* (c 1539), the *David/Apollo* from 1530–32 and the large, uncompleted roundel of the

Madonna and Child with the Infant St John (aka the *Tondo Pitti;* 1505). After Michelangelo left Florence for the final time in 1534, sculpture was dominated by Baccio Bandinelli (his 1551 *Adam and Eve,* created for the Duomo, is also displayed here) and Benvenuto Cellini (look for his playful 1548–50 marble *Ganymede* in the same room).

Back in in the interior courtyard, an open staircase leads up to the elegant, sculpture-laced **loggia** (1370) and, to the right, the **Salone di Donatello**. Here, in the majestic Sala del Consiglio where the city council met, works by Donatello and other early-15th-century sculptors can be admired. Originally on the facade of Chiesa di Orsanmichele and now within a tabernacle at the hall's far end, Donatello's wonderful *St George* (1416–17) brought a new sense of perspective and movement to Italian sculpture. Also look for the bronze bas-reliefs created for the Baptistry doors competition by Brunelleschi and Ghiberti.

Yet it is Donatello's two versions of *David,* a favourite subject for sculptors, that really fascinate: Donatello fashioned his slender, youthful dressed image in marble in 1408 and

Santa Croce

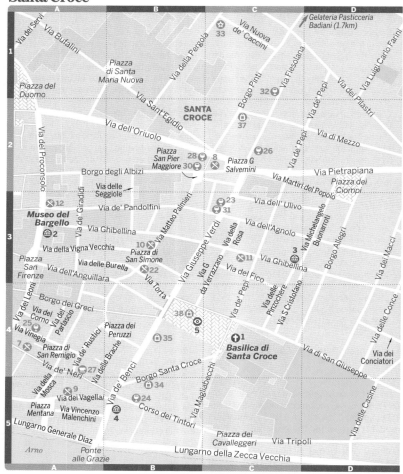

his fabled bronze between 1439 and 1443. The latter is extraordinary – the more so when you consider it was the first freestanding naked statue to be sculpted since classical times.

Criminals received their last rites before execution in the palace's 1st-floor Cappella del Podestà, also known as the Mary Magdalene Chapel, where Hell and Paradise are frescoed on the walls, as are stories from the lives of Mary of Egypt, Mary Magdalene and John the Baptist. These remnants of frescoes by Giotto were not discovered until 1840, when the chapel was turned into a storeroom and prison.

The 2nd floor moves into the 16th century with a superb collection of terracotta pieces by the prolific della Robbia family, including some of their best-known works, such as Andrea's *Ritratto idealizia di fanciullo* (*Bust of a Boy;* c 1475) and Giovanni's *Pietà* (1514). Instantly recognisable, Giovanni's works are more elaborate and flamboyant than either father Luca's or cousin Andrea's, using a larger palette of colours.

Museo Casa Buonarroti MUSEUM
(Map p94; ☎ 055 24 17 52; www.casabuonarroti.
it; Via Ghibellina 70; adult/reduced €6.40/4.50;
⊗10am-5pm Wed-Mon, to 4pm Nov-Feb) FREE

Though Michelangelo never lived in Casa Buonarotti, his heirs devoted some of the artist's hard-earned wealth to the construction of this 17th-century *palazzo* to honour his memory. The little museum contains frescoes of the artist's life and two of his most important early works – the serene, bas-relief *Madonna of the Stairs* and the unfinished *Battle of the Centaurs*.

Museo Horne   MUSEUM
(Map p94; ☑ 055 24 46 61; www.museohorne.it; Via de' Benci 6; adult/reduced €7/5; ⊙ 9am-1pm Mon-Sat) One of the many eccentric Brits who made Florence home in the early 20th century, Herbert Percy Horne bought and renovated this Renaissance *palazzo*, then installed his eclectic collection of 14th- and 15th-century Italian art, ceramics, furniture and other oddments. There are a few works by masters such as Giotto and Filippo Lippi. More interesting is the furniture, some of which is exquisite.

Oltrarno

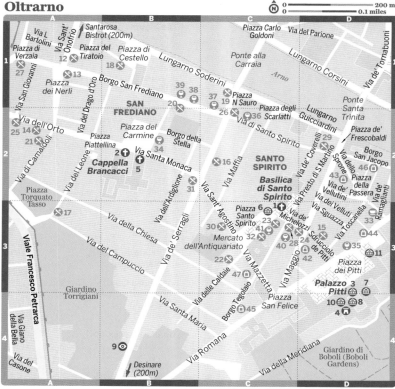

⊙ Oltrarno

The Oltrarno's main sights lie snug on Piazza Santo Spirito and nearby Piazza del Carmine. When you reach museum overload and need to stretch your legs and see some sky, meander east towards neighbouring Boboli where the tiers of parks and gardens behind Palazzo Pitti entice.

Ponte Vecchio   BRIDGE
(Map p80) Dating from 1345, Ponte Vecchio was the only Florentine bridge to survive destruction at the hands of retreating German forces in 1944. Above the jewellers' shops on the eastern side, the **Corridoio Vasariano** (Vasari Corridor) is a 16th-century passageway between the Uffizi and Palazzo Pitti that runs around, rather than through, the medieval **Torre dei Mannelli** at the bridge's southern end. The first documentation of a stone bridge here, at the narrowest crossing point along the entire length of the Arno, dates from 972.

Floods in 1177 and 1333 destroyed the bridge, and in 1966 it came close to being destroyed again. Many of the jewellers with shops on the bridge were convinced the floodwaters would sweep away their livelihoods; fortunately the bridge held.

★**Basilica di Santo Spirito**   CHURCH
(Map p96; Piazza Santo Spirito; ⊙9.30am-12.30pm & 4-5.30pm Thu-Tue) The facade of this Brunelleschi church, smart on Florence's most shabby-chic piazza, makes a striking backdrop to open-air concerts in summer. Inside, the basilica's length is lined with 38 semicircular chapels (covered with a plain wall in the 1960s), and a colonnade of grey *pietra forte* Corinthian columns injects monumental grandeur. Artworks to look for include Domenico di Zanobi's *Madonna of the Relief* (1485) in the Cappella Velutti, in which the Madonna wards off a little red devil with a club.

Oltrarno

★ **Cappella Brancacci**   CHAPEL
(Map p96; ☏055 238 21 95; http://museicivici fiorentini.comune.fi.it; Piazza del Carmine 14; adult/reduced €6/4.50; ☉10am-5pm Wed-Sat & Mon, 1-5pm Sun) Fire in the 18th century practically destroyed 13th-century **Basilica di Santa Maria del Carmine** (Map p96), but it spared the magnificent frescoes in this chapel – a treasure of paintings by Masolino da Panicale, Masaccio and Filippino Lippi commissioned by rich merchant Felice Brancacci upon his return from Egypt in 1423. The chapel entrance is to the right of the main church entrance. Only 30 people can visit at a time, limited to 30 minutes in high season; tickets include admission to the Fondazione Salvatore Romano.

Masaccio's fresco cycle illustrating the life of St Peter is considered among his greatest works, representing a definitive break with Gothic art and a plunge into new worlds of expression in the early stages of the Renaissance. *The Expulsion of Adam and Eve from Paradise* and *The Tribute Money,* both on the left side of the chapel, are his best-known works. Masaccio painted these frescoes in his early 20s, taking over from Masolino, and interrupted the task to go to

Rome, where he died, aged only 27. The cycle was completed some 60 years later by Filippino Lippi. Masaccio himself features in his *St Peter Enthroned;* he's the one standing beside the Apostle, staring out at the viewer. The figures around him have been identified as Brunelleschi, Masolino and Alberti. Filippino Lippi also painted himself into the scene of *St Peter's Crucifixion,* along with his teacher, Botticelli.

Fondazione Salvatore Romano   MUSEUM
(Cenacolo di Santo Spirito; Map p96; ☏055 28 70 43; http://museicivicifiorentini.comune.fi.it; Piazza Santo Spirito 29; adult/reduced €7/5; ☉10am-4pm Sat-Mon) For a change of pace from the Renaissance, head to this Gothic-style former refectory safeguarding an imposing wall fresco by Andrea Orcagna depicting the *Last Supper and the Crucifixion* (c 1370) – one of the largest 14th-century paintings to survive. The museum itself displays a collection of rare 11th-century Romanesque sculpture, paintings and antique furniture donated to the city by art collector and antiquarian Salvatore Romano (1875–1955). Tickets can only be bought at nearby Cappella Brancacci; the same ticket covers admission to both sights.

FLORENCE SIGHTS

CLET

Should you notice something gone awry with street signs in Oltrarno – on a No Entry sign, a tiny black figure stealthily sneaking away with the white bar, for example – you can be sure it is the work of French-born Clet Abraham, one of Florence's most popular street artists. In his Oltrarno **studio** (Map p102; www.facebook.com/CLET-108974755823172; Via dell'Olmo 8r; ⊙hours vary) you can buy stickers and postcards featuring his hacked traffic signs and, if you're lucky, catch a glimpse of the rebellious artist at work.

In 2011 Clet created quite a stir in his adopted city by installing, in the black of night, a life-sized figurine entitled *Uomo Comune* (Common Man) on Ponte alle Grazie (to which the city authorities turned a blind eye for a week before removing it). Should you fall completely and utterly head over heels in love with Clet's work, you can either order a reproduction street sign from his workshop (from €500) or purchase an original (numbered and signed, from €2500) limited edition from **Mio Concept** (Map p80; ☑ 055 264 55 43; www.mio-concept.com; Via della Spada 34r; ⊙10am-1.30pm & 2.30-7.30pm Tue-Sat, 3-7pm Mon) – Clet produces only 13 of each design.

Giardino Torrigiani   GARDENS
(Map p96; ☑ 055 22 45 27; www.giardinotorrigiani.
it; Via de' Serragli 144; 1½hr guided tours by donation; ⊙advance reservation via email) Astonishing. Behind the unassuming facades of Via
de' Serragli lies a vast, secret garden – Europe's largest privately owned green space
within a historic centre, owned by the Torrigiani Malaspina and Torrigiani di Santa
Cristina families. Well kept and loved, it's
possible to visit this leafy retreat in the engaging company of the charismatic Marquis
Vanni Torrigiani Malaspina and his wife,
Susanna. Tours (in English or Italian) are intimate and proffer a rare glimpse into a very
different and privileged Florentine world

◉ Boboli & San Miniato al Monte

The neighbourhood's sights are split between
Piazza dei Pitti – dominated by the vast Palazzo Pitti with its cache of museums – and Piazzale Michelangelo up the hill in San Miniato.

★ Palazzo Pitti   MUSEUM
(Map p96; www.polomuseale.firenze.it; Piazza dei
Pitti; ☑ 055 29 48 83; ⊙8.15am-6.50pm Tue-Sun)
Commissioned by banker Luca Pitta and
designed by Brunelleschi in 1457, this vast
Renaissance palace was later bought by the
Medici family. Over the centuries, it served
as the residence of the city's rulers until the
Savoys donated it to the state in 1919. Nowa-
days it houses an impressive silver museum, a
couple of art museums and a series of rooms
re-creating life in the palace during House of
Savoy times. Stop by at sunset when its entire
vast facade is coloured a vibrant pink.

➡ *Ground Floor*

Exquisite amber carvings, ivory miniatures,
glittering tiaras and headpieces, silver pill-
boxes and various other gems and jewels
are displayed in the **Tesoro dei Granduchi**
(Grand Dukes' Treasury; Map p96; adult/reduced
incl Museo delle Porcellane, Museo della Moda e del
Costume & Giardino di Boboli €7/3.50, during temporary exhibition €10/5), a series of elaborately
frescoed audience chambers, some of which
host temporary exhibitions. Notable (but
not always open) is the **Sala di Giovanni
da San Giovanni**, which sports lavish head-
to-toe frescoes (1635–42) celebrating the life
of Lorenzo il Magnifico – spot Michelangelo
giving Lorenzo a statue. 'Talk little, be brief
and witty' is the curt motto above the painted staircase in the next room, the public
audience chamber, where the grand duke
received visitors in the presence of his court.

➡ *1st Floor*

Raphaels and Rubens vie for centre stage
in the enviable collection of 16th- to 18th-
century art amassed by the Medici and
Lorraine dukes in the **Galleria Palatina**
(Map p96; adult/reduced incl Appartamenti Reali &
Galleria d'Arte Moderna €8.50/4.25, during temporary exhibition €13.50/6.50), reached by several flights of stairs from the palace's central
courtyard. This gallery has retained the
original display arrangement of paintings
(squeezed in, often on top of each other), so
can be visually overwhelming – go slowly
and focus on the works one by one.

Highlights include Fra' Filippo Lippi's
*Madonna and Child with Stories from the
Life of St Anne* (aka the *Tondo Bartolini;*
1452–53) and Botticelli's *Madonna with
Child and a Young Saint John the Baptist* (c

1490–95) in the Sala di Prometeo; Raphael's *Madonna of the Window* (1513–14) in the Sala di Ulisse; and Caravaggio's *Sleeping Cupid* (1608) in the Sala dell'Educazione di Giove. Don't miss the Sala di Saturno, full of magnificent works by Raphael, including the *Madonna of the Chair* (1511) and portraits of Anolo Doni and Maddalena Strozzi (c 1506). Nearby, in the Sala di Giove, the same artist's *Lady with a Veil* (aka *La Velata;* c 1516) holds court alongside Giorgione's *Three Ages of Man* (c 1500).

Past the Sala di Venere are the Appartamenti Reali (Royal Apartments; Map p96; adult/reduced incl Galleria Palatina & Galleria d'Arte Moderna €8.50/4.25, during temporary exhibition €13/6.50), a series of rooms presented as they were circa 1880–91 during House of Savoy times.

➡ *2nd Floor*

The Galleria d'Arte Moderna (Map p96; adult/reduced incl Appartamenti Reali & Galleria Palatina €8.50/4.25, during temporary exhibition €13.50/6.50) curates 18th- and 19th-century works. Paintings of the Florentine Macchiaioli school (the local equivalent of Impressionism) dominates the collection.

Crowning the palace are the Museo della Moda e del Costume (Fashion & Costume Museum; Map p96; admission incl Tesoro dei Granduchi, Museo delle Porcellane & Giardino di Boboli adult/reduced €7/3.50, during temporary exhibition €10/5), a parade of fashions from the times of Cosimo I to the haute couture 1990s.

⭐ Giardino di Boboli   GARDENS

(Map p102; ☎ 055 29 48 83; www.polomuseale.firenze.it; Palazzo Pitti, Piazza dei Pitti; adult/reduced incl Tesoro dei Granduchi, Museo delle Porcellane & Museo della Moda e del Costume €7/3.50, during temporary exhibition €10/5; ⏱ 8.15am-7.30pm summer, reduced hours winter, closed 1st & last Mon of month) Behind Palazzo Pitti, the Boboli Gardens were laid out in the mid-16th century to a design by architect Niccolò Pericoli. At the upper, southern limit, beyond the box-hedged rose garden and Museo delle Porcellane (Porcelain Museum; Map p102), beautiful views over the Florentine countryside unfold. Within the lower reaches of the gardens, don't miss the fantastical shell- and gem-encrusted Grotta del Buontalenti (Map p102), a decorative grotto built by Bernardo Buontalenti between 1583 and 1593 for Francesco I de' Medici.

Villa e Giardino Bardini   VILLA, GARDENS

(Map p102; ☎ 055 263 85 99; www.bardinipeyron.it; Costa San Giorgio 2, Via de' Bardi 1r; adult/reduced €8/6; ⏱ 10am-7pm Tue-Sun) This 17th-century villa and garden was named after 19th-century antiquarian art collector Stefano Bardini (1836–1922), who bought it in 1913 and restored its ornamental medieval garden. It has all the features of a quintessential Tuscan garden, including artificial grottos, orangery, marble statues and fountains. The villa houses two small museums: Museo Pietro Annigoni, with works by Italian painter Pietro Annigoni (1910–88), and Museo Roberto Capucci, showcasing Capucci-designed haute couture. End with city views from the romantic roof terrace.

Its Michelin-starred garden restaurant, La Leggenda Dei Frati (Map p102; ☎ 055 068 05 45; www.laleggendadeifrati.it; Costa di San Giorgio 6a; menus €60 & €75, meals €70; ⏱ 12.30-2pm & 7.30-10pm Tue-Sun; ☎), with stone loggia overlooking the Florentine skyline, is one of the most romantic spots in the city to dine.

Forte di Belvedere   FORTRESS

(Map p102; www.museicivicifiorentini.comune.fi.it; Via di San Leonardo 1; ⏱ hours vary) FREE Forte di Belvedere is a rambling fort designed by Bernardo Buontalenti for Grand Duke Ferdinando I at the end of the 16th century. From the massive bulwark soldiers kept watch on four fronts – as much for internal security as to protect the Palazzo Pitti against foreign attack. Today the fort hosts seasonal art exhibitions, which are well worth a peek if only to revel in the sweeping city panorama that can be had from the fort. Outside of exhibition times, the fort is closed.

Torre San Niccolò   CITY GATE

(Map p102; ☎ 055 276 82 24; http://musefirenze.it; Piazza Giuseppe Poggi; 30min guided visit €4; ⏱ 5-8pm daily 24 Jun-Sep) Built in 1324, the best preserved of the city's medieval gates stands sentinel on the banks of the Arno. In summer, you can scale the steep stairs inside the tower with a guide to enjoy blockbuster river and city views. Visits are limited to 15 people at a time (no children under eight years) making reservations essential; book online, by email or by phone. Tours are cancelled when it rains.

Piazzale Michelangelo   VIEWPOINT

(Map p102; Piazzale Michelangelo; ☒ 13) Turn your back on the bevy of ticky-tacky souvenir stalls flogging *David* statues and boxer shorts and take in the spectacular city panorama from this vast square, pierced by one of Florence's two *David* copies. Sunset here is particularly dramatic. It's a 10-minute uphill walk along the serpentine road, paths and steps that scale the hillside from the Arno and Piazza

100

PETER HORREE/ALAMY ©

1. Michelangelo's *David*, Galleria dell'Accademia (p90)

However many photographs you might have seen of the famous statue, nothing quite prepares you for the dazzling luminosity and gracefulness of the real thing.

2. Botticelli's *Calumny of Apelles*, Galleria degli Uffizi (p68)

The Galleria degli Uffizi is the jewel in Florence's crown. Its collection Renaissance art inlcudes masterpieces by Giotto, Botticelli, Michelangelo, Da Vinci, Raphael, Titan and Caravaggio.

3. Model for the Duomo's facade, Grande Museo del Duomo (p76)

Learn the magnificent story of how the cathedral and its cupola was built.

4. Gozzoli's *Procession of the Magi to Bethlehem*, Palazzo Medici-Riccardi (p87)

Cappella dei Magi is covered in wonderfully detailed fescoes by Benozzo Gozzoli. Spot members of the Medici family in the frescoes.

MICHELE BUZZI/SHUTTERSTOCK ©

Boboli

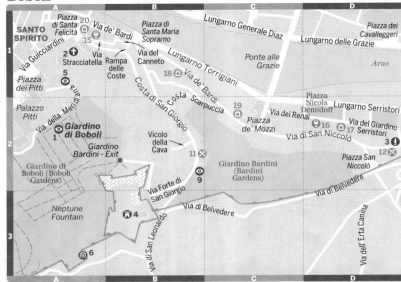

Giuseppe Poggi; from Piazza San Niccolò walk uphill and bear left up the long flight of steps signposted Viale Michelangelo. Or take bus 13 from Stazione di Santa Maria Novella.

👉 Tours

Muse Firenze TOURS
(☑ 055 276 82 24; http://musefirenze.it) Imaginative guided tours, including family-themed tours, in a handful of city museums, including Palazzo Vecchio (p78), Museo Novecento (p83), Basilica di Santa Maria Novella (p84), Cappella Brancacci (p97), Forte di Belvedere (p99) and Fiesole town. Reserve tours in advance by email or phone, or at its ticket desk inside Palazzo Vecchio (p78).

Curious Appetite TOURS
(www.curiousappetitetravel.com) Private and group food and wine tastings led by Italian-American Coral Sisk and a small team of guides. Tastings last 3½ hours (minimum four people) and are themed: at the market, craft cocktails and *aperitivi*, Italian food and wine pairings, and artisan gelato.

★500 Touring Club DRIVING
(☑ 346 8262324; www.500touringclub.com; Via Gherardo Silvani 149a) Hook up with Florence's 500 Touring Club for a guided tour in a vintage motor – with you behind the wheel!

Every car has a name in this outfit's fleet of gorgeous vintage Fiat 500s from the 1960s. Motoring tours are guided (hop in your car and follow the leader) and themed – families love the picnic trip, couples wine tasting.

City Sightseeing Firenze BUS
(Map p88; ☑ 055 29 04 51; www.firenze.city-sightseeing.it; Piazza della Stazione 1; 1/2/3 days adult €23/28/33, child €12/14/17) Explore Florence by red open-top bus, hopping on and off at 15 bus stops around the city. Tickets, sold by the driver or available in advance online, are valid for one, two or three days.

Tuscany Bike Tours CYCLING
(Map p94; ☑ 055 386 02 53, 339 1163495; www.tuscany-biketours.com; Via Ghibellina 34r; ☉ office 9-10am & 5-7pm Mar-Nov) Offers a fantastic range of cycling tours in and around Florence, including three-hour city tours by bike with a gelato break (adult/reduced €39/35) and a rather cool, Audrey Hepburn–styled one-day Vespa tour from Florence into the Chianti hills (adult/reduced/passenger €125/115/90, including lunch, castle visit and wine/olive-oil tasting). Bike hire too.

Florence Town WALKING
(Map p80; ☑ 055 28 11 03; www.florencetown.com; Via de' Lamberti 1) Organised tours, activities and workshops in and around Florence.

Cooking classes, market tours, pizza- and gelato-making courses and Tuscan wine trail tours too.

ArtViva   WALKING
(Map p80; ☑ 055 264 50 33; www.italy.artviva.com; Via de' Sassetti 1; per person from €29) One- to three-hour city walks led by historians or art history graduates: tours include Masterpieces of the Uffizi, the Original David tour and an adult-only 'Sex, Drugs & the Renaissance' art tour. Wine-tasting, cookery classes and running tours too.

De Gustibus   TOURS
(☑ 340 5796207; www.de-gustibus.it) This umbrella association for local farms in the surrounding Florentine countryside organises extremely tasty tours to small family-run organic farms. Tours are invariably themed – wine, truffles, olive oil – and can be by car, on foot or by bicycle. Check its website or Facebook page for details of upcoming tours.

Caf Tour & Travel   CULTURAL
(Map p88; ☑ 055 28 32 00; www.caftours.com; Via degli Alfani 151r; ⊙ 7.30am-8pm Mon-Sat, to 5pm Sun) Interesting guided tours in Florence, including a behind-the-scenes tour of the Duomo's restoration workshop (€45, 2¼ hours), the northern rooftop terrace of the Duomo (€50, 1½ hours) and the infamous Corridoio Vasariano.

⭐ Festivals & Events

Festa di Anna Maria Medici   CULTURAL
(⊙ 18 Feb) Florence's Feast of Anna Maria Medici marks the death in 1743 of the last Medici, Anna Maria, with a costumed parade from Palazzo Vecchio to her tomb in the Cappelle Medicee.

Scoppio del Carro   FIREWORKS
(⊙ Mar/Apr) A cart of fireworks is exploded in front of the cathedral in Piazza del Duomo at 11am on Easter Sunday.

Maggio Musicale Fiorentino   PERFORMING ARTS
(www.operadifirenze.it; ⊙ Apr-Jun) Italy's oldest arts festival features world-class performances of theatre, classical music, jazz, opera and dance. Events are staged at the Opera di Firenze (p120) and venues across town.

Festa di San Giovanni   RELIGIOUS
(⊙ 24 Jun) Florence celebrates its patron saint, John, with a *calcio storico* (historic football) match on Piazza di Santa Croce and fireworks over Piazzale Michelangelo.

✖ Eating

Quality ingredients and simple execution are the hallmarks of Florentine cuisine, climaxing with the *bistecca alla fiorentina,* a huge slab of prime T-bone steak rubbed with tangy Tuscan olive oil, seared on the char grill, garnished with salt and pepper and served beautifully *al sangue* (bloody). Be it dining in a traditional trattoria or contemporary, designer-chic space, quality is guaranteed.

✖ Duomo & Piazza della Signoria

Be it slow food in a trattoria, modern Tuscan in a hipster bistro or gourmet *panino* to picnic with riverside, this central neighbourhood cooks up some fantastic and wholly affordable meals.

★ Osteria Il Buongustai   OSTERIA $

(Map p80; ☑ 055 29 13 04; Via dei Cerchi 15r; meals €15-20; ☺ 8am-4pm Mon-Fri, to 11pm Sat) Run with breathtaking speed and grace by Laura and Lucia, this place is unmissable. Lunchtimes heave with locals who work nearby and savvy students who flock here to fill up on tasty Tuscan home cooking at a snip of other restaurant prices. The place is brilliantly no frills – expect to share a table and pay in cash; no credit cards.

Trattoria Le Massacce   TRATTORIA $

(Map p80; ☑ 055 29 43 61; www.trattoriale mossacce.it; Via del Proconsolo 55r; meals €20; ☺ noon-2.30pm & 7-9.30pm Mon-Fri) Strung with legs of ham and garlic garlands, this old-world trattoria lives up to its vintage promise of a warm *benvenuto* (welcome) and fabulous home cooking every Tuscan Nonna would approve of. A family address, it has been the pride and joy of the Fantoni-Mannucci family for the last 50-odd years and their *bistecca alla fiorentina* (T-bone steak) is among the best in town.

Mangiafoco   TUSCAN $$

(Map p80; ☑ 055 265 81 70; www.mangiafoco. com; Borgo SS Apostoli 26r; meals €40; ☺ 10am-10pm Mon-Sat) Aromatic truffles get full-page billing at this small and cosy *osteria* with buttercup-yellow walls, cushioned seating and an exceptional wine list. Whether you are a hardcore truffle fiend or a virgin, there is something for you here: steak topped with freshly shaved truffles in season, truffle *taglietelle* (ribbon pasta) or a simple plate of mixed cheeses with sweet truffle honey.

Obicà   ITALIAN $$

(Map p80; ☑ 055 277 35 26; www.obica.com; Via de' Tornabuoni 16; meals €30-50; ☺ noon-4pm & 6.30-11.30pm Mon-Fri, noon-11pm Sat & Sun) Given its exclusive location in Palazzo Tornabuoni, this designer address is naturally uber-trendy – even the table mats are upcycled from organic products. Taste 10 different types of mozzarella cheese in the cathedral-like interior or snuggle beneath heaters over pizza and salads on sofas in the enchanting star-topped courtyard. At *aperitivo* hour nibble on *taglierini* (tasting boards loaded with cheeses, salami, deep-fried veg).

★ Irene   BISTRO $$$

(Map p80; ☑ 055 273 58 91; www.roccoforte hotels.com; Piazza della Repubblica 7; meals €60; ☺ 12.30-10.30pm) Named after the accomplished Italian grandmother of Sir Rocco Forte of the same-name luxury hotel group, Irene (actually part of neighbouring Hotel Savoy) is a dazzling contemporary bistro with a pavement terrace (heated in winter) overlooking iconic Piazza della Repubblica. Interior design is retro-chic 1950s and celebrity chef Fulvio Pierangelini cooks up a playful, utterly fabulous bistro cuisine in his Tuscan kitchen.

✖ Santa Maria Novella

Dining in this down-to-the-earth 'hood tends to be traditional and reasonably priced: think vintage delis serving made-to-measure *panini* to take away and age-old family trattorias cooking up traditional Florentine fare.

Il Contadino   TRATTORIA $

(Map p80; ☑ 055 238 26 73; www.trattoriailcon tadino.com; Via Palazzuolo 69-71r; meals €11-15; ☺ noon-10.30pm) Come the weekend, this no-frills trattoria gets packed with families lunching with gusto on its astonishingly good-value Tuscan cuisine. Lunch, moreover, is served until 3.30pm when the dinner menu kicks in, meaning convenient all-day dining. The day's menu includes 10 or so dishes, including meaty classics like roast rabbit, tripe and oven-roasted pork shank. Two-course lunch/dinner menus start at €9/13.50.

Trattoria Marione   TRATTORIA $$

(Map p80; ☑ 055 21 47 56; Via della Spada 27; meals €30; ☺ noon-3pm & 7-11pm) For the quintessential 'Italian dining' experience, Marione is gold. It's busy, it's noisy, it's 99.9% local and the cuisine is right out of Nonna's Tuscan

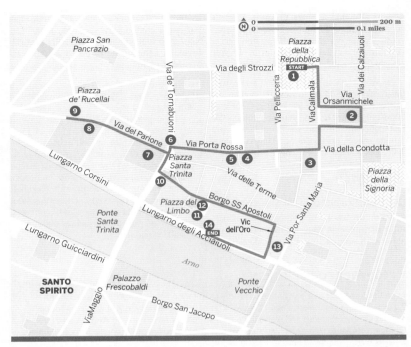

Walking Tour
Quintessential Florence

START PIAZZA DELLA REPUBBLICA
END AMBLÉ
LENGTH 2KM; TWO HOURS

Start with coffee on ① **Piazza della Repubblica** (p67), then walk one block south along Via Calimala and turn left onto Via Orsanmichele to ② **Chiesa e Museo di Orsanmichele** (p67), a unique church with ornate statuary adorning its facade and a fascinating museum inside. Backtrack to Via Calimala and continue walking south until you see the loggia of ③ **Mercato Nuovo** (p120), the 16th-century 'New Market'. Florentines know it as 'Il Porcellino' (The Piglet) after the bronze statue of a wild boar on its southern side. Rub its snout to ensure your return to Florence.

Walk past the market and along Via Porta Rossa to ④ **Palazzo Davanzati** (p83) with its magnificent studded doors and fascinating museum. A few doors down, next to the Slowly bar, peep through a sturdy iron gate and look up to admire the ancient brick vaults of this ⑤ **dark alley** – this is hidden Florence of 1001 fabulous doors and lost alleys at its best!

Continue to ⑥ **Via de' Tornabuoni** (p82) with its designer boutiques. Swoon over frescoed chapels in ⑦ **Chiesa di Santa Trìnita** (p83), then wander down Via del Parione to visit paper marbler ⑧ **Alberto Cozzi** (www.facebook.com/AlbertoCozzi1908; ⊙9am-1pm & 2.30-7pm Mon-Fri, 3-7pm Sat) and puppet maker ⑨ **Letizia Fiorini** (p121).

Backtrack to Via de' Tornabuoni and turn right, past 13th-century ⑩ **Palazzo Spini-Feroni**, home of Salvatore Ferragamo's flagship store, to Borgo Santissimi Apostoli. A short way ahead on Piazza del Limbo is the Romanesque ⑪ **Chiesa dei Santissimi Apostoli**, in a sunken square once used as a cemetery for unbaptised babies.

After browsing for Tuscan olive oil in ⑫ **La Bottega dell'Olio** (www.labottegadelloliofirenze.it; ⊙2.30-6.30pm Mon, 10am-1pm & 2-6.30pm Tue-Sat), continue east and turn right into Vicolo dell' Oro, home to the Hotel Continentale, whose sleek rooftop terrace ⑬ **La Terrazza Lounge Bar** (p115) is the perfect spot for a sundowner with a Ponte Vecchio view. If hipster Florence is more your cup of tea, indulge in an al fresco *aperitivo* at ⑭ **Amblé** (p115).

kitchen. No one appears to speak English so go for Italian – the tasty excellent-value traditional fare is worth it. If you don't get a complimentary *limoncello* with the bill, you clearly failed the language test.

Il Latini TRATTORIA $$
(Map p80; ☑055 21 09 16; www.illatini.com; Via dei Palchetti 6r; meals €30; ⊙12.30-2.30pm & 7.30-10.30pm Tue-Sun) A veteran guidebook favourite built around traditional *crostini,* Tuscan meats, fine pasta and roasted meats served at shared tables. There are two dinner seatings (7.30pm and 9pm). Reservations mandatory.

San Lorenzo & San Marco

San Lorenzo cooks up a mixed bag of traditional trattorias where slow food is king, along with sandwich shops and bakeries run by the same family for several generations. For more contemporary dining, make San Marco your focus – starting with ground-breaking concept store, bistro and bar La Ménagère (p107).

★**Mercato Centrale** FOOD HALL $
(Map p88; ☑055 239 97 98; www.mercatocen trale.it; Piazza del Mercato Centrale 4; dishes €7-15; ⊙10am-midnight; 🗊) Wander the maze of stalls rammed with fresh produce at Florence's oldest and largest food market, on the ground floor of a fantastic iron-and-glass structure designed by architect Giuseppe Mengoni in 1874. Head to the 1st floor's buzzing, thoroughly contemporary food hall with dedicated bookshop, cookery school and artisan stalls cooking steaks, burgers, tripe *panini,* vegetarian dishes, pizza, gelato, pastries and pasta.

FLORENCE FOR CHILDREN
....

Children are welcomed anywhere, anytime in Florence. Families frequently go out with young children in the evenings. However, it's not the easiest city to visit with very young children: green spaces and playgrounds are scarce, crowded cobbled streets make push-chairs (strollers) a challenge, and visiting museums requires meticulous advance planning.

Tours & Workshops

Museums Some imaginative and compelling family tours and hands-on art ateliers are organised by Firenze Musei (p86) at Palazzo Vecchio (p78), Museo Novecento (p83) and Basilica di Santa Maria Novella (p84). Palazzo Strozzi (p83) organises monthly family weekend activities, and out of town in Fiesole, the Museo Primo Conti (p124) hosts occasional art workshops for children.

Private tours For a private tour with children, contact professional licensed guide Molly McIlwrath (http://letterartemente.com) who leads family tours and organises creative art workshops for kids, which parents can also participate in. Her hands-on workshops range from calligraphy and frescoes to the art of mosaics, bookmaking, sketching and creating Arcimboldo-inspired self-portraits in vegetables and fruits. Many of Molly's city tours wind up in a local artisan workshop in the Oltrarno.

Group tours Small-group family tours are run by Context Travel (www.contexttravel. com), including a two-hour Symbols & Legends of Florence tour, a 2½-hour Florence art tour (for children aged from six years) focusing on the Uffizi, a two-hour Dissection Expedition (from eight years), which zooms in on science in the city, and a two-hour Renaissance Life-themed city walk (from six years).

Parks & Playgrounds

Playgrounds The best for those for under six years are near the Duomo on Piazza Massimo d'Azeglio and across the river on Lungarno Santa Rosa and Piazza Torquato Tasso.

Piazza della Repubblica (p67) The vintage carousel on this car-free, cafe-framed square in the historic centre never stops turning and is enchanting for all ages.

Gairdino di Boboli (p99) Fantastic statues, hidden paths, secret alleys, shell-decorated grottoes and bags of open green space to run around in.

Parco della Cascine (Viale degli Olmi) Open-air swimming pool and toddler-friendly playgrounds; a grassy footpath snakes along the banks of the Arno to the park.

★ Trattoria Mario TUSCAN $

(Map p88; ☑ 055 21 85 50; www.trattoria-mario.com; Via Rosina 2; meals €25; ☺ noon-3.30pm Mon-Sat, closed 3 weeks Aug; ⊛) Arrive by noon to ensure a stool around a shared table at this noisy, busy, brilliant trattoria – a legend that retains its soul (and allure with locals) despite being in every guidebook. Charming Fabio, whose grandfather opened the place in 1953, is front of house while big brother Romeo and nephew Francesco cook with speed in the kitchen. No advance reservations, no credit cards.

Trattoria Sergio Gozzi TRATTORIA $

(Map p88; ☑ 055 28 19 41; Piazza di San Lorenzo 8r; meals €25; ☺ 10am-4pm Mon-Sat) Keep things simple with a traditional Tuscan lunch at this two-room trattoria, tucked between cheap leather shops near Mercato Centrale. Dining is at marble-topped tables in a spartan vintage interior clearly unchanged since 1915 when it opened. Expect all the classics: plenty of pasta, roast meats, tripe and *bollito misto* (boiled beef, chicken and tongue) included.

Pugi BAKERY $

(Map p88; ☑ 055 28 09 81; www.focacceria-pugi.it; Piazza San Marco 9b; per kg €15 to €24; ☺ 7.45am-8pm Mon-Sat, closed 2 weeks mid-Aug) The inevitable line outside the door says it all. This bakery is a Florentine favourite for pizza slices and chunks of *schiacciata* (Tuscan flatbread) baked up plain, spiked with salt and rosemary, or topped or stuffed with whatever delicious edible goodies are in season.

Da Nerbone FAST FOOD $

(Map p88; Mercato Centrale, Piazza del Mercato Centrale; meals €10; ☺ 7am-2pm Mon-Sat) Forge your way past cheese, meat and sausage stalls on the ground floor of Florence's Mercato Centrale to join the lunchtime queue at Nerbone, in the biz since 1872. Go local and order *trippa alla fiorentina* (tripe and tomato stew) or follow the crowd with a feisty *panini con bollito* (a hefty boiled-beef bun, dunked in the meat's juices before serving). Eat standing up or fight for a table.

★ La Ménagère INTERNATIONAL $$

(Map p88; ☑ 055 075 06 00; www.lamenagere.it; Via de' Ginori 8r; meals €15-70; ☺ 7am-2am; ☎) Be it breakfast, lunch, dinner, good coffee or cocktails after dark, this bright industrial-styled space lures Florence's hip brigade. A concept store, the Housewife is a fashionable one-stop shop for chic china and tableware, designer kitchen gear and fresh flowers. For daytime dining and drinking, pick from retro

LOCAL KNOWLEDGE

STREET FOOD

'Bringing the countryside to the city' is the driver behind cherry-red artisan food truck **La Toraia** (☑ 338 5367198; www.latoraia.com; Lungarno del Tempio; burger €6, with cheese €7; ☺ noon-midnight 15 Apr-15 Oct), whose name translates as 'breeding shed'. Parked riverside, a 15-minute stroll east of Piazza di Santa Croce, the truck cooks up sweet 140g burgers, crafted from tender Chianina meat sourced at the family farm in Val di Chiana and topped with melted *pecorino* (sheep's milk cheese).

Real McCoy homemade fries (€4; made from organic Tuscan potatoes grown on the farm, of course), craft beers (€4) from the same valley, and a bunch of table, chairs and comfy loungers by the river cap off the bucolic alfresco experience.

sofas in the boutique area, or banquette seating and bar stools in the jam-packed bistro.

Antica Trattoria da Tito TRATTORIA $$

(☑ 055 47 24 75; www.trattoriadatito.it; Via San Gallo 112r; meals €30; ☺ noon-3pm & 7-11pm Mon-Sat) The 'No well done meat here' sign, strung in the window, says it all: the best of Tuscan culinary tradition is the only thing this iconic trattoria serves. In business since 1913, Da Tito does everything right – tasty Tuscan dishes like onion soup and wild boar pasta, served with friendly gusto and hearty goodwill to a local crowd. Don't be shy to enter.

✖ Santa Croce

Dining options in this delicious neck of the Florentine woods covers all moods, tastes and budgets; watch for new openings – a constant in Santa Croce.

★ All'Antico Vinaio OSTERIA $

(Map p94; ☑ 055 238 27 23; www.allantico vinaio.com; Via de' Neri 65r; tasting platters €10-30; ☺ 10am-4pm & 6-11pm Tue-Sat, noon-3.30pm Sun) The crowd spills out the door of this noisy Florentine thoroughbred. Push your way to the tables at the back to taste cheese and salami in situ (reservations recommended). Or join the queue at the deli counter for a well-stuffed focaccia wrapped in waxed paper to take away – the quality is outstanding. Pour yourself a glass of wine while you wait.

TRIPE: ORIGINAL FAST FOOD

When Florentines fancy a fast munch-on-the-move, they flit by a *trippaio* – a cart on wheels or mobile stand – for a tripe *panini* (sandwich). Think cow's stomach chopped up, boiled, sliced, seasoned and bunged between bread.

Those great bastions of good old-fashioned Florentine tradition still going strong include Il Trippaio del Porcellino (Map p80; ☑ 335 8070240; Piazza del Mercato Nuovo 1; tripe €4.50; ⊗ 9am-6.30pm Mon-Sat) on the southwest corner of Mercato Nuovo; L'Antico Trippaio (Map p80; ☑ 339 7425692; Piazza dei Cimatori; tripe €4.50; ⊗ 9.30am-8pm); Trippaio Sergio Pollini (Map p94; Piazza Sant'Ambrogio; tripe €3.50; ⊗ 9.30am-3pm Mon, to 8pm Tue-Sat) in Santa Croce; and hole-in-the-wall Da Vinattieri (Map p80; Via Santa Margherita 4; panini €4.50; ⊗ 10am-7.30pm Mon-Fri, to 8pm Sat & Sun). Pay €4.50 for a *panini* with tripe doused in *salsa verde* (pea-green sauce of smashed parsley, garlic, capers and anchovies) or garnished with salt, pepper and ground chilli. Alternatively, opt for a meaty-sized bowl (€5.50 to €7) of *lampredotto* (cow's fourth stomach that is chopped and simmered for hours).

The pew-style seating at staunchly local Osteria del Cocotrippone (☑ 055 234 75 27; www.facebook.com/OsteriaCocoTrippone; Via Vincenzo Gioberti 140; meals €25; ⊗ noon-3pm & 7-11pm) in the off-centre Beccaria neighbourhood is not a coincidence: Florentines come here to venerate the offal side of their city's traditional cuisine. The *trippa alla fiorentina* (tripe in tomato sauce) and *L'Intelligente* (fried brain and zucchini) are local legends.

Brac
VEGETARIAN $

(Map p94; ☑ 055 094 48 77; www.libreriabrac.net; Via dei Vagellai 18r; meals €20; ⊗ noon-midnight, closed 2 weeks mid-Aug; 📶🖋) This hipster cafe-bookshop – a hybrid dining-*aperitivi* address – cooks up inventive, home-style and strictly vegetarian and/or vegan cuisine. Its decor is recycled vintage with the occasional kid's drawing thrown in for that intimate homey touch; and the vibe is artsy.

Il Giova
TRATTORIA $

(Map p94; ☑ 055 248 06 39; www.ilgiova.com; Borgo La Croce 73r; meals €15; ⊗ noon-3pm & 7-11pm Mon-Sat) Pocket-sized and packed, this cheery trattoria with marigold walls and colourful ceramic-tiled tables is everything a traditional Florentine eating place should be. Dig into century-old dishes like *zuppa della nonna* (grandma's soup), *risotto del giorno* (risotto of the day) or *mafalde al ragù* (long-ribboned pasta with meat sauce) and pride yourself on finding the locals' lunchtime canteen.

★ Il Teatro del Sale
TUSCAN $$

(Map p94; ☑ 055 200 14 92; www.teatrodelsale.com; Via dei Macci 111r; lunch/dinner/weekend brunch €15/35/20; ⊗ 11am-3pm & 7.30-11pm Tue-Sat, 11am-3pm Sun, closed Aug) Florentine chef Fabio Picchi is one of Florence's living treasures who steals the Sant' Ambrogio show with this eccentric, good-value, members-only club (everyone welcome, membership €7) inside an old theatre. He cooks up weekend brunch, lunch and dinner, culminating

at 9.30pm in a live performance of drama, music or comedy arranged by his wife, artistic director and comic actress Maria Cassi.

Dinners are hectic: grab a chair, serve yourself water, wine and antipasti, and wait for the chef to yell out what's about to be served before queuing at the glass hatch for your *primo* (first course) and *secondo* (second course). Note: this is the only Picchi restaurant to serve pasta! Dessert and coffee are laid out buffet-style just prior to the performance.

Trattoria Cibrèo
TUSCAN $$

(Map p94; www.cibreo.com; Via dei Macci 122r; meals €40; ⊗ 12.50-2.30pm & 6.50-11pm Tue-Sat, closed Aug) Dine here chez Fabio Picchi and you'll instantly understand why a queue gathers outside before it opens. Once inside, revel in top-notch Tuscan cuisine: perhaps *pappa al pomodoro* (a thick soupy mash of tomato, bread and basil) followed by *polpettine di pollo e ricotta* (chicken and ricotta meatballs). No reservations, no credit cards, no pasta and arrive early to snag a table.

Vivo
FISH $$

(Map p94; ☑ 333 1824183; www.ristorantevivo.it; Largo Pietro Annigoni 9a/b; seafood platters €15-50, meals €45; ⊗ 12.30-2.30pm & 7.30-11pm Tue-Sun; 📶) Raw fish, shellfish, oysters and other fishy dishes – all caught in waters around Italy by the Manno family's 30-strong fleet of fishing boats – are cooked up by female chef Anna Maria at this fish restaurant, inside a hangar-styled contemporary space with a fishing-boat-shaped bar. Everything is ultra fresh and the daily changing menu includes many a rare or forgotten fish.

Gilda Bistrot TRATTORIA **$$**
(Map p94; ☑ 055 234 38 85; www.gildabistrot.it; Piazza Ghiberti 40r; meals €40; ☺ noon-3pm & 7-11pm Mon-Sat) Lap up Santa Croce's bustling market vibe on the pavement terrace of this classic trattoria, much-loved for its trad-tional Tuscan cuisine made with zero kilometre fruit and veg fresh from the market across the street. Colourful chequered tablecloths and potted plants inject a welcome dose of al fresco gaiety and the handwritten menu changes daily.

Antico Noè OSTERIA **$$**
(Map p94; http://anticonoe.com/; Volta di San Piero 6r; meals €40; ☺ noon-2am Mon & Wed-Sat) Don't be put off by the dank alley in which you'll find this old butcher's shop with marble-clad walls, wrought-iron meat hooks and a name inspired by an old Italian vermouth. The drunks loitering outside are generally harmless and the down-to-earth Tuscan fodder served is a real joy. For a quick bite, grab a *panini* (€4.50 to €5) at its *fiaschetteria* (small tavern). No credit cards.

Fishing Lab FISH **$$**
(Map p94; ☑ 055 24 06 18; www.fishinglab.it; Via del Proconsolo 16r; meals €40; ☺ 11am-midnight) All-day dining and a pick-and-mix, all-fish menu gives this stylish restaurant instant appeal. Savour finger-licking giant red shrimps, wild concave oysters and a shoal of raw fish – or go for something cooked (or smoked the old-fashioned Tuscan way in a walnut leaf). For *aperitivo* lovers, the 'street food' menu with fried anchovies, tuna buns and light nibbles hits the spot nicely.

Even if you're not dining, feel free to take a peek upstairs at the fragments of 14th- and 15th-century frescoes decorating the enchanting, vaulted dining area.

Enoteca Pinchiorri TUSCAN **$$$**
(Map p94; ☑ 055 24 27 77; www.enotecapinchiorri.com; Via Ghibellina 87r; 4-/7-/8-course tasting menu €150/225/275; ☺ lunch & dinner Tue-Sat, closed Aug) Niçois chef Annie Féolde applies French techniques to her versions of refined Tuscan cuisine and does it so well that this is the only restaurant in Tuscany to brandish three shiny Michelin stars. The setting is a 16th-century palace hotel and the wine list is mind-boggling in its extent and excellence. A once-in-a-lifetime experience. Reserve in advance.

✗ Oltrarno

New places to eat are forever popping up in this increasingly gentrified neighbourhood on the 'other side' of the Arno, home to some outstanding restaurants. Vegetarian, organic and raw cuisine is also at its Florentine best here. Several gourmet choices frame Piazza del Passera, an impossibly enchanting square with no passing traffic.

★ Raw HEALTH FOOD **$**
(Map p96; ☑ 055 21 93 79; Via Sant' Agostino 9; meals €7.50; ☺ 11am-4pm & 7-10pm Thu & Fri, 11am-4pm Sat, Sun, Tue & Wed; ☎) Be it a turmeric, ginger or aloe vera shot or a gently warmed, raw vegan burger served on a stylish slate-and-wood platter you desire, Raw hits the spot. Everything served here is freshly made and raw – to sensational effect. Herbs are grown in the biodynamic greenhouse of charismatic and hugely knowledgeable chef Caroline, a Swedish architect before moving to Florence.

TOP FIVE: GELATERIE

Grom (Map p80; ☑ 055 21 61 58; www.grom.it; Via del Campanile 2; cones €2.60-4.60, tubs €2.60-5.50; ☺ 10am-10.30pm Sun-Thu, to 11.30pm Fri & Sat) Top-notch gelato, including outstanding chocolate, near the Duomo.

Vivoli (Map p94; ☑ 055 29 23 34; www.vivoli.it; Via dell'Isola delle Stinche 7; tubs €2-10; ☺ 7.30am-midnight Tue-Sat, 9am-midnight Sun, to 9pm winter) Vintage favourite for coffee and cakes as well as gelato.

My Sugar (Map p88; ☑ 393 0696042; Via de' Ginori 49r; cones €2-2.50, tubs €2-5; ☺ 1-9pm) Sensational artisan gelateria near Piazza San Marco.

Gelateria La Carraia (Map p96; ☑ 055 28 06 95; Piazza Nazario Sauro 25r; cones & tubs €1.50-6; ☺ 10.30am-midnight summer, 11am-10pm winter) Florentine favourite on the other side of the river.

Carabé (Map p88; ☑ 055 28 94 76; www.parcocarabe.it; Via Ricasoli 60r; cones €2.50-4; ☺ 10am-midnight, closed mid-Dec–mid-Jan) Traditional Sicilian gelato and granita in San Marco.

LAZY DAYS

Florence is not just about gorging on art masterpieces, scaling the duomo and packing in too many museums. To get under the skin of Florentine culture and understand what makes this Renaissance city tick, take time out to laze with locals.

SERIOUS COFFEE

Weekending Florentines spend hours hanging out with friends, people-watching or discussing latte art over a picture-perfect al fresco cappuccino. Historic cafes like **Caffè Giacosa** (p118) and **Caffè Rivoire** (p118) are timeless. Or mingle with younger Florentines over a single-origin espresso or mug of V60 brew prepared by skillful baristas at new-generation cafe and speciality coffee roaster **Ditta Artigianale** (p116). **Santarosa Bistrot** (p118), wedged between river and ancient city wall, is the garden choice for a serious coffee.

A VERY LONG LUNCH

Food is of extreme importance to most Florentines, hence the lazy lunch. Join bon vivants on the chic Piazza della Repubblica terrace of bistro **Irene** (p104) or indulge at Michelin-starred **La Leggenda dei Frati** (p99), romantically at home in the Bardini Gardens. Alternatively grab your picnic rug, buy a gourmet burger at food truck **La Toraia** (p107), and flop on the grassy banks of the Arno for a lazy lunch riverside.

A GARDEN STROLL

Florentines have been flocking to the **Boboli** (p99) and **Bardini** (p99) gardens since the 16th century. But for a quieter change of scene, retreat to **Giardino dei Semplici** (p89), the city's peaceful botanical gardens in San Marco where fragrant citrus blooms mingle with ancient medicinal plants and Tuscan wild flowers.

1. Caffè Rivoire (p118)
2. Giardino Bardini (p99)

ARCO IMAGES GMBH/ALAMY ©

Carduccio ORGANIC $

(Map p96; ☑ 055 238 20 70; www.carduccio.com; Sdrucciolo de Pitti 10r; meals €15; ⊙ 8am-8pm Mon-Sat, 10am-5pm Sun; ☎) With just a handful of tables inside and a couple more al fresco, this *salotto bio* (organic living room) oozes intimacy. Miniature cabbage 'flowers' decorate each table, fruit and veg crates stack up by the bar, and the menu is 100% organic. Knock back a ginger and turmeric shot (€3) or linger over delicious salads, soups, vegan burgers or pumpkin and leek patties.

S.Forno BAKERY $

(Map p96; ☑ 055 239 85 80; Via Santa Monaco 3r; ⊙ 7.30am-7.30pm Mon-Fri, from 8am Sat & Sun) Shop at this hipster bakery, around for at least a century, for fresh breads and pastries baked to sweet perfection in its ancient *forno* (oven). Gourmet dried products stack up on vintage shelves and local baker Angelo cooks up soups, quiches and bespoke *panini* (€4 to €6) too, to eat in in or out.

Gesto TUSCAN $

(Map p96; ☑ 055 24 12 88; www.gestofailtuo.it; Borgo San Frediano 27r; meals €25; ⊙ 6pm-2am) Enter hipster Florence: candlelit Gesto is all about eco-sustainability, so much so that all the furniture in the well-scrubbed vintage space is salvaged or upcycled and diners write down their own order on a mini blackboard that subsequently doubles as a plate. Fish, meat and veg dishes (€3.50 to €5) are tapas style – order a few to share for the entire table.

Culinaria Bistrot TUSCAN $

(Map p96; ☑ 055 22 94 94; www.facebook.com/culinaria.degustibus.bistro/; Piazza Torquato Tasso 13; meals €25; ⊙ noon-3pm & 6.45-11.30pm) No dining address in Florence captures the culinary magic of 'farm to table' dining quite like this San Frediano bistro, an instant charmer with its exposed red-brick vaulted ceiling. Chefs only work with organic produce from local farms and small producers to cook up memorable Tuscan and Mediterranean dishes.

La Casalinga TRATTORIA $

(Map p96; ☑ 055 21 86 24; www.trattorialacasalinga.it; Via de' Michelozzi 9r; meals €25; ⊙ noon-2.30pm & 7-10pm Mon-Sat) Family run and locally loved, this busy unpretentious place is one of Florence's cheapest trattorias. Don't be surprised if Paolo – the patriarchal figure who conducts the mad-busy show from behind the bar – relegates you behind locals in the queue: it's a fact of life, and eventually you'll be rewarded with hearty Tuscan dishes, cooked to exacting perfection.

Gnam BURGERS $

(Map p96; ☑ 055 22 39 52; www.gnamfirenze.it; Via di Camaldoli 2r; burgers €10-12; ⊙ 7-11pm Tue-Sat, noon-2.30pm & 7-11pm Sun; ☎) Bread arrives at the table in a paper bag and fries come in a miniature copper cauldron at this artisanal burger joint in San Frediano. Ingredients are seasonal, locally sourced and organic – and there are vegetarian and gluten-free burgers as well as traditional beef. Delicious soups also (€8), to eat in or take away from Gnam's joint across the street.

★ Essenziale TUSCAN $$

(Map p96; ☑ 055 247 69 56; http://essenziale.me/; Piazza di Cestello 3r; 3-/5-/7-course tasting menu €35/55/75, brunch €28; ⊙ 7-10pm Tue-Sat, 11am-4pm Sun; ☎) There's no finer showcase for modern Tuscan cuisine than this loft-style

---

TIP-TOP PANINI

Semel (Map p94; Piazza Ghiberti 44r; panini €3.50-5; ⊙ 11.30am-3pm Mon-Sat) Irresistibly creative and gourmet sandwiches to take away in Sant'Ambrogio.

'Ino (Map p80; ☑ 055 21 45 14; www.inofirenze.com; Via dei Georgofili 3r-7r; bruschette/panini €6/8; ⊙ noon-4.30pm) ✐ Made-to-measure, gourmet *panini* by the Galleria degli Uffizi.

Mariano (Map p80; ☑ 055 21 40 67; Via del Parione 19r; panini €3.50; ⊙ 8am-3pm & 5-7.30pm Mon-Fri, 8am-3pm Sat) Local neighbourhood cafe serving super-fresh *panini* to boot.

Gustapanino (Map p96; www.facebook.com/pages/Gustapanino; Piazza Santa Spirito; focacce from €3.50; ⊙ 11am-8pm Mon-Sat, noon-5pm Sun) Hole-in-the-wall *enopaninoteca* (wine and sandwich stop) in Santa Croce.

Dal Barone (Map p80; ☑ 366 1479432; https://dalbarone.jimdo.com; Borgo San Lorenzo 30; sandwiches €5-10; ⊙ 11am-8pm) Hot 'n gooey *panini* to take away by San Lorenzo market.

I Due Fratellini (Map p80; ☑ 055 239 60 96; www.iduefratellini.com; Via dei Cimatori 38r; panini €4; ⊙ 10am-7pm) Memorable vintage kid on the block, around since 1875.

restaurant in a 19th-century warehouse. Preparing dishes at the kitchen bar, in rolled-up shirt sleeves and navy butcher's apron, is dazzling young chef Simone Cipriani. Order one of his tasting menus to sample the full range of his inventive, thoroughly modern cuisine inspired by classic Tuscan dishes.

If you're lucky, it will be the chef himself who brings the dish to your table and treats you to a detailed explanation: don't miss the tale behind his remarkable Fior d'Evo dessert, notably with kale (another of his desserts includes artichokes). Sunday ushers in brunch, a fabulously revolutionary affair with a choice of three courses, unlimited coffee and water, and most likely the most remarkable French toast, waffles and eggs (with purple cabbage) you've ever tasted. Reservations essential.

★ **Il Santo Bevitore** TUSCAN $$
(Map p96; ✆055 21 12 64; www.ilsantobevitore.com; Via di Santo Spirito 64-66r; meals €40; ⊗12.30-2.30pm & 7.30-11.30pm, closed Sun lunch & Aug) Reserve or arrive right on 7.30pm to snag the last table at this ever-popular address, an ode to stylish dining where gastronomes eat by candlelight in a vaulted, whitewashed, bottle-lined interior. The menu is a creative reinvention of seasonal classics: risotto with monkfish, red turnip and fennel; *ribollita* with kale; or chicken liver terrine with brioche and a Vin Santo reduction.

★ **Burro e Acciughe** TUSCAN $$
(Butter & Anchovies; Map p96; ✆055 045 72 86; www.burroeacciughe.com; Via dell'Orto 35; meals €35; ⊗noon-2pm & 7pm-midnight Fri-Sun, 7pm-midnight Tue-Thu) Carefully sourced, quality ingredients drive this fishy newcomer that woos punters with a short but stylish choice of raw (tartare and carpaccio) and cooked fish dishes. The gnocchi topped with octopus *ragù* (stew) is out of this world, as is the *baccalà* (salted cod) with creamed leeks, turnip and deep-fried polenta wedges. Excellent wine list too.

Gurdulù RISTORANTE $$
(Map p96; ✆055 28 22 23; www.gurdulu.com; Via delle Caldaie 12r; meals €40, tasting menu €55; ⊗7.30-11pm Tue-Sat, 12.30-2.30pm & 7.30-11pm Sun; ✆) Gourmet Gurdulù seduces fashionable Florentines with razor-sharp interior design, magnificent craft cocktails and seasonal market cuisine with a hint of Balkan spice by Albanian female chef Entiana Osmenzeza. A hybrid drink-dine, this address is as much about noshing gourmet *aperitivi* snacks over expertly mixed cocktails – thanks to talented

SILVER SPOON DINING

In Fabbrica (✆347 5145468; http://restaurant.pampaloni.com/; Via del Gelsomino 99; meal €45; ⊗8.30-10.30pm Wed-Sat), 1.5km south of Porto Romana along Via Senese on the Oltrarno, fuses Florence's outstanding tradition of craftsmanship with its equally fine cuisine. Meaning 'In the Factory', In Fabbrica is just that. By day, workers from third-generation Florentine silver house **Pampaloni** (Map p80; ✆055 28 90 94; www.pampaloni.com; Via Porta Rossa 97; ⊗10am-1.30pm & 3-7.30pm Mon-Sat) lunch here. Come dusk, the speakeasy canteen opens its doors to culturally curious diners.

Tables are laid with silver cutlery and majestic candelabras, waiters wear white gloves and cuisine is Tuscan. Reservations essential.

FLORENCE EATING

female mixologist Sabrina Galloni – as it is about dining exceedingly well.

Tamerò ITALIAN $$
(Map p96; ✆055 28 25 96; www.tamero.it; Piazza Santa Spirito 11r; meals €25; ⊗noon-3pm & 6.30pm-2am Tue-Sun; ✆) A happening pasta bar on Florence's hippest square: admire chefs at work in the open kitchen while you wait for a table. A buoyant, party-loving crowd flocks here to fill up on imaginative fresh pasta, giant salads and copious cheese and salami platters. Decor is trendy industrial, *aperitivo* 'happy hour' (€9) is 6.30pm to 9pm, and weekend DJs spin sets from 10pm.

Cuculia RISTORANTE $$
(Map p96; www.cuculia.it; Via dei Serragli 11; meals €40; ⊗10am-midnight Tue-Fri, to 1am Sat) This hybrid restaurant-bookshop is a wonderfully serene spot to while away a few hours in the company of classical music, shelves loaded with books, and a light, creative cuisine packed with seasonal flavours: beef tartare is spiced with fennel, mint and lime; beetroot gnocchi is purple and served with apple cubes, walnuts and a cheesy gorgonzola sauce.

All'Antico Ristoro di' Cambi TUSCAN $$
(Map p96; ✆055 21 71 34; www.anticoristorodicambi.it; Via Sant'Onofrio 1r; meals €35; ⊗noon-2.30pm & 6-10.30pm Mon-Sat) Founded as a wine shop in 1950, this Oltrarno institution sticks closely to the traditional, with its long list of fine Tuscan wines, dried meats

FLORENCE EATING

BEST PIZZA

Santarpia (Map p94; ☑ 055 24 58 29; www.santarpia.biz; Largo Pietro Annigoni 9; pizza €8.50-11; ⊗ 7.30pm-midnight Wed-Mon; ☎) Thin-crust Neapolitan pizza across the street from Mercato di Sant'Ambrogio.

Berberé (Map p96; ☑ 055 238 29 46; www.berberepizza.it; Piazza dei Nerli 1; pizza €6.50-13.50; ⊗ 12.30-2.30pm & 7pm-midnight Fri-Sun, 7pm-midnight Mon-Thu) Perfect pizza, craft beer and contemporary interior design in San Frediano.

Gustapizza (Map p96; ☑ 055 28 50 68; Via Maggio 46r; pizza €4.50-8; ⊗ 11.30am-3pm & 7-11pm Tue-Sun) Student favourite, Neapolitan-style, on the Oltrarno.

SimBIOsi (Map p88; ☑ 055 064 01 15; www.simbiosi.bio; Via de' Ginori 56r; pizza €6-10, salads €8-9; ⊗ noon-11pm; ☎) Hipster pizzeria cooking organic pizza, with craft beer and wine by small producers.

Caffè Italiano Pizzeria (Map p94; ☑ 055 28 93 68; www.caffeitaliano.it; Via dell'Isola delle Stinche 11-13r; pizza €8; ⊗ 7-11pm Tue-Sun) Just three pizza types in a bare-bones setting – or to take away.

Il Pizzaiuolo (Map p94; ☑ 055 24 11 71; Via dei Macci 113r; pizzas €5-10.50; ⊗ 12.30-2.30pm & 7.30pm-midnight Mon-Sat, closed Aug) Cosy pizzeria, lovely for an evening out, in Sant'Ambrogio.

hanging from beautiful red-brick-vaulted ceilings and a glass case proudly displaying its highly regarded *bistecca alla fiorentina* – it's one of the best places in town to try the city's iconic T-bone steak.

Olio   TUSCAN **$$**
(Map p96; ☑ 055 265 81 98; www.oliorestaurant. it; Via di Santo Spirito 4; tasting menus €40-49; ⊗ noon-3pm Tue-Thu, noon-3pm & 7-11pm Fri-Sun) A key address on any gastronomy agenda: your taste buds will tingle at the sight of the legs of ham, conserved truffles, wheels of cheese, artisanal bread and other delectable delicatessen products filling the shelves in this gourmet shop and restaurant. Elegant, white-clothed tables sit between bottle-lined shelves and tasting menus are themed.

Il Guscio   TUSCAN **$$**
(Map p96; ☑ 055 22 44 21; www.il-guscio.it; Via dell'Orto 49; meals €35; ⊗ 12.30-2pm & 7.30-11pm Mon-Fri, 7.30-11pm Sat) Exceptional dishes come out of the kitchen of this humble family-run gem in San Frediano, pleasantly off the beaten tourist track. Meat and fish get joint billing, with triumphs such as white bean soup with prawns and fish joining superbly executed mains on the short but sophisticated menu. Count €45 per kg for a *bistecca* (steak).

iO Osteria Personale   TUSCAN **$$$**
(Map p96; ☑ 055 933 13 41; www.io-osteriaper sonale.it; Borgo San Frediano 167r; 4-/5-/6-course tasting menus €40/48/55; ⊗ 7.30-10pm Mon-Sat) Persuade everyone at your table to order the

tasting menu to avoid the torture of picking just one dish – everything on the menu at this fabulously contemporary and creative *osteria* is to die for. Pontedera-born chef Nicolò Baretti uses only seasonal products, natural ingredients and traditional flavours – to sensational effect.

✖ Boboli & San Miniato al Monte

There might not be a wide range of eating options in this green part of Florence, but dining is at least gourmet and memorable.

★ **San Niccolò 39**   SEAFOOD **$$**
(Map p102; ☑ 055 200 13 97; www.sanniccolo39. com; Via di San Niccolò 39; meals €40; ⊗ 7-10.30pm Tue, 12.30-2.30pm & 7-10.30pm Wed-Sat; ☎) With a street terrace at the front and hidden summer garden out the back, this contemporary address in quaint San Niccolò is a gem. Fish – both raw and cooked – is the house speciality, with chef Vanni cooking up a storm with his creative salted-cod burgers, swordfish steak with radicchio, and famous *linguine* (fat spaghetti) with squid ink and Cetara anchovy oil.

★ **La Bottega del Buon Caffè**   TUSCAN **$$$**
(Map p102; ☑ 055 553 56 77; www.borgointhecity. com; Lungarno Benvenuto Cellini 69r; meals from €55; ⊗ 12.30-3pm Tue-Sat, 7.30-10.30pm Mon-Sat) Farm to table is the philosophy of this Michelin-starred restaurant where head chef Antonello Sardi mesmerises diners from the

stunning open kitchen. Veg and herbs arrive from the restaurant's own farm, Borgo Santo Pietro, in the Sienese hills. Breads and focaccia (the nut version is heavenly) are homemade and the olive oil used (special production from Vinci) is clearly only the best.

Drinking & Nightlife

Florence's drinking scene covers all bases. Be it historical cafes, contemporary cafes with barista-curated specialist coffee, traditional *enoteche* (wine bars, which invariably make great eating addresses too), trendy bars with lavish *aperitivo* buffets, secret speakeasys and edgy cocktail or craft-beer bars, drinking is fun and varied. Nightlife, less extravagant, revolves around a handful of dance clubs.

Duomo & Piazza della Signoria

★ La Terrazza Lounge Bar   BAR
(Map p80; ☎055 2726 5987; www.lungarnocollec tion.com; Vicolo dell' Oro 6r; ⊙2.30-11.30pm Apr-Sep) This rooftop bar with wooden-decking terrace accessible from the 5th floor of the 1950s-styled, design Hotel Continentale is as chic as one would expect of a fashion-house hotel. Its *aperitivo* buffet is a modest affair, but who cares with that fabulous, drop-dead-gorgeous panorama of one of Europe's most beautiful cities. Dress the part or feel out of place. Count on €19 for a cocktail.

Amblé   BAR
(Map p80; ☎055 26 85 28; Piazzetta dei del Bene 7a; ⊙10am-midnight Tue-Sat, noon-midnight Sun) You need to know about this cafe-bar, near Ponte Vecchio, to find it. Vintage furniture – all for sale – creates a hip, shabby-chic vibe and the tiny terrace feels delightfully far from the madding crowd on summer evenings. From the river head down Vicolo dell' Oro to the Hotel Continentale, and turn left along the alleyway that runs parallel to the river.

Coquinarius   WINE BAR
(Map p80; www.coquinarius.com; Via delle Oche 11r; ⊙12.30-3pm & 6.30-10.30pm Wed-Mon) With its old stone vaults, scrubbed wooden tables and refreshingly modern air, this *enoteca* run by the dynamic Nicolas is spacious and stylish. The wine list features bags of Tuscan greats and unknowns, and outstanding *crostini* and *carpacci* (cold sliced meats) ensure you don't leave hungry. The ravioli stuffed with silky *burrata* cheese and smothered in pistachio pesto is particularly outstanding.

Fiaschetteria Nuvoli   WINE BAR
(Map p80; ☎055 239 66 16; Piazza dell'Olio 15r; ⊙8am-9pm Mon-Sat) Pull up a stool on the street and chat with a regular over a glass of *vino della casa* (house wine) at this old-fashioned *fiaschetteria* (wine seller), a street away from the Duomo. Food too.

La Terrazza   CAFE
(Map p80; La Rinascente, Piazza della Repubblica 1; ⊙9am-9pm Mon-Sat, 10.30am-8pm Sun) Three canvas parasols and a dozen tables make this hidden terrace on the roof of Florence's central department store a privileged spot. Gloat with the birds over coffee or cocktaila at achingly lovely views of the Duomo, Piazza della Repubblica and Florentine hills beyond. The terrace is heated in winter.

RED   CAFE
(Map p80; ☎055 293 78 11; www.facebook.com/ RedFeltrinelliFirenze/; Piazza della Repubblica 26; ⊙9am-11pm; 🛜) An abbreviation for 'Read, Eat, Drink', RED is a superb spot for lingering over a cappuccino between bookshelves on the ground floor of Florence's flagship Feltrinelli bookstore. The cafe has a great choice of cakes, gourmet *panini* (€4 to €9) and lunchtime dishes (€9.50 to €12.50), and also serves weekend brunch (€14 to €16).

Shake Café   CAFE
(Map p80; ☎055 21 59 52; www.shakecafe.bio; Via del Corso 28-32; ⊙7.30am-8pm) Smoothie bowls with protein powder, kale and goji berries, cold-pressed juices and vitamin-packed elixir shots – to eat in or take away – satisfy wellness cravings at this laid-back cafe on people-busy Via del Corso. International newspapers, mellow music and a relaxed vibe make it a hipster place to hang. All-day

> **WORTH A TRIP**
> ## WORTH THE WALK
> Known throughout Italy for the quality of its handmade gelato and sweet pastries, **Gelateria Pasticceria Badiani** (☎055 57 86 82; www.buontalenti.it; Viale dei Mille 20r; ⊙7am-1am summer, to midnight Sun-Thu, to 1am Fri & Sat winter) is located in the Campo de' Marte neighbourhood just outside the historic city centre but is – as any local will tell you – well worth the walk. The house speciality is Buontalenti gelato, a creamy concoction with flavourings that are a heavily guarded house secret.

wraps, salads and hearty, homemade soups (€6 to €7.50) too.

YAB
CLUB

(Map p80; ☎ 055 21 51 60; www.yab.it/en; Via de' Sassetti 5r; ⊗ 7pm-4am Mon & Wed-Sat Oct-May) Pick your night according to your age and tastes at this hugely popular nightclub with electric dance floor, around since the 1970s, behind Palazzo Strozzi.

 ## Santa Maria Novella

From historical cafes to literary cafe-bookshops, juice bars and modern wine bars, Santa Maria Novella offers some interesting drinking addresses and student-loved clubs.

★ Todo Modo
CAFE

(Map p80; ☎ 055 239 91 10; www.todomodo.org; Via dei Fossi 15r; ⊗ 10am-8pm Tue-Sun) This contemporary bookshop with hip cafe and pocket theatre at the back makes a refreshing change from the usual offerings. A salvaged mix of vintage tables and chairs sits between book- and bottle-lined shelves in the relaxed cafe, actually called 'UqBar' after the fictional place of the same name in a short story by Argentinian writer Jorges Luis Borges.

Sei Divino
WINE BAR

(Map p80; ☎ 055 21 57 94; Borgo d'Ognissanti 42r; ⊗ 6pm-1am Wed-Mon) This stylish wine bar tucked beneath a red-brick vaulted ceiling is a veteran on Florence's prolific wine-bar scene. Come here for music and occasional exhibitions as well as fine wine. *Aperitivi* 'hour' (with copious banquet) runs from 7pm to 10pm, with a buoyant crowd spilling outside onto the pavement in summer.

Space Club
CLUB

(Map p80; ☎ 055 29 30 82; www.facebook.com/spacefirenze2; Via Palazzuolo 37r; admission variable; ⊗ 10pm-4am) Sheer size alone at this vast nightclub in Santa Maria Novella impresses – dancing, drinking, video-karaoke in the bar, and a mixed student-international crowd.

San Lorenzo & San Marco

Nightlife is thin on the ground in this part of town, as are bars and cafes. That said, new venues are beginning to open up here, including one of Florence's best cocktail bars and coffee shops.

★ Ditta Al Cinema
CAFE, BAR

(Map p88; ☎ 055 045 71 63; Via Cavour 50r; ⊗ 8am-midnight Mon-Fri, 9am-midnight Sat & Sun;

☎) At home in Florence's historic La Compagnia cinema, the third and most recent space of iconic coffee roaster and gin bar Ditta Artigianale doesn't disappoint. Some 150 different labels of gin jostle for the limelight at the bar, while barman Lorenzo's cocktail list plays on the cinema's heritage with drinks named after movie classics. Breakfast, lunch, brunch and all-day tapas too.

Chillax Lounge Bar
BAR

(Map p94; ☎ 346 2656340; Via Fiesolana 8-10r; ⊗ 10pm-4am Tue-Sun) Kick back with a cocktail and chill in a predominantly wood interior at this lounge bar on the fringe of nightlife-hot Santa Croce. Music – both live and DJ sets – covers all sounds, including Latin, salsa, pop and rock. Wednesday is often karaoke night; check its Facebook page for events.

Rex Caffé
BAR

(Map p94; ☎ 055 248 03 31; www.rexfirenze.com; Via Fiesolana 25r; ⊗ 6pm-3am) A firm long-term favourite since 1990, down-to-earth Rex maintains its appeal. Behind the bar Virginia and Lorenzo shake a mean cocktail, using homemade syrups and artisanal spirits like ginger- or carrot-flavoured vodka, pepper rum and laurel vermouth. The artsy, Gaudi-inspired interior is as much art gallery and nightlife stage as simple bar. DJ sets at weekends and bags of fun events.

 ## Santa Croce

Be it lounging with locals, glass in hand, on Ponte alle Grazie as the sun softens and turns the river's romantic cascade of bridges a hazy mellow pink or quaffing cocktails in the city's hippest gin bar, Santa Croce more than delivers for after-dark explorers.

★ Ditta Artigianale
CAFE, BAR

(Map p94; ☎ 055 274 15 41; www.dittaartigianale.it; Via de' Neri 32r; ⊗ 8am-10pm Sun-Thu, 8am-midnight Fri, 9.30am-midnight Sat; ☎) With industrial decor and welcoming laid-back vibe, this ingenious coffee roastery and gin bar is a perfect place to hang at any time of day. The creation of three-times Italian barista champion Francesco Sanapo, it's famed for its first-class coffee and outstanding gin cocktails. If you're yearning a flat white, cold brew tonic or cappuccino made with almond, soy or coconut milk, come here.

Le Murate Caffè Letterario
BAR, CAFE

(Map p94; ☎ 055 234 68 72; www.lemurate.it; Piazza delle Murate Firenze; ⊗ 9am-1am; ☎) This artsy cafe-bar in Florence's former jail is where

DON'T MISS

ON-TREND CRAFT COCKTAILS

Mad Souls & Spirits (Map p96; ☑ 055 627 16 21; www.facebook.com/madsoulsandspirits; Borgo San Frediano 38r; ⊙ 6pm-2am Thu-Sun, to midnight Mon & Wed; 🛜) A this bar of the moment, cult alchemists Neri Fantechi and Julian Biondi woo a discerning fashionable crowd with their expertly crafted cocktails, served in a tiny aqua-green and red-brick space that couldn't be more spartan. A potted cactus decorates each scrubbed wood table and the humorous cocktail menu is the height of irreverence. Check the 'Daily Madness' blackboard for wild 'n' wacky specials.

Rasputin (Map p96; ☑ 055 28 03 99; www.facebook.com/rasputinfirenze; Borgo Tegolaio 21r; ⊙ 8pm-2am) The 'secret' speakeasy everyone knows about, it has no sign outside: disguised as a chapel of sorts, look for the tiny entrance with two-seat wooden pew, crucifix on the wall, vintage pics and tea lights flickering in the doorway. Inside, it's back to the 1930s with period furnishings, an exclusive vibe and barmen mixing Prohibition-era cocktails. Reservations (phone or Facebook page) recommended.

Lo Sverso (Map p88; ☑ 335 5473530; www.facebook.com/losverso.firenze; Via Panicale 7-9r; ⊙ 5pm-1am Mon-Sat, to midnight Sun) In a part of town where drinking holes are unusually scarce, stylish Lo Sverso is a real gem. Bartenders shake cocktails using homemade syrups (any cocktail using their feisty basil syrup is a winner), the craft beers – several on tap – are among the best in Florence and their home-brewed ginger ale is worth a visit in its own right.

Mayday (Map p80; ☑ 055 238 12 90; Via Dante Alighieri 16; cocktails €8; ⊙ 7pm-2am Tue-Sat) Strike up a conversation with passionate mixologist Marco at Mayday. Within seconds you'll be hooked on his homemade mixers and astonishing infusions, all handmade using wholly Tuscan ingredients. Think pancetta-infused whisky, saffron limoncello and porcini liqueur. Marco's cocktail list is equally impressive – or tell him your favourite flavours and let yourself be surprised.

literati meet to talk, create and perform over coffee, drinks and light meals. The literary cafe hosts everything from readings and interviews with authors – Florentine, Italian and international – to film screenings, debates, live music and art exhibitions. Tables are built from recycled window frames and in summer everything spills outside into the brick courtyard.

Beer House Club   CRAFT BEER
(Map p94; ☑ 055 247 67 63; www.beerhouseclub.eu; Corso dei Tintori 34r; ⊙ noon-3am) Sample the best of Italian craft beer at this young, fun beer bar in Santa Croce. Pick from 10 craft beers on tap and another 100 bottled beers, local, Italian and international. Big sports matches are screened here, the bar has a party-packed social agenda – check its Facebook page for events – and it serves food.

Eby's Bar   BAR
(Map p94; Via dell'Oriulolo 5r; ⊙ 11am-3am Mon-Sat) A lively student crowd packs out this young, fun, colourful address with wooden benches tucked outside in a covered alleyway. The kitchen is Mexican and the barmen are known far and wide for their shots, flaming included.

Off the Hook   BAR
(Map p94; ☑ 055 1999 1333; www.offthehook.it; Via Giuseppe Verdi 47; ⊙ noon-2.30am; 🛜) A buoyant all-rounder, this busy pub rocks with young Florentines tucking into craft beers, cocktails and a mind-boggling choice of creative burgers (€7 to €12) – vegan and vegetarian included. DJ sets and live bands every Tuesday and Friday from 10pm.

Lion's Fountain   IRISH PUB
(Map p94; ☑ 055 234 44 12; www.thelionsfountain.com; Borgo degli Albizi 34r; ⊙ 10am-3am) If you have the urge to hear more English than Italian – or to hear local bands play for that matter – this is the place. On a pretty pedestrian square, Florence's busiest Irish pub buzzes in summer when the beer-loving crowd spills across most of the square. Live music and a canary-yellow food 'truck' serving burgers, nachos, clubs, wings and brunch (€5 to €10).

Bamboo   CLUB
(Map p94; ☑ 339 4298764; www.bamboolounge club.com; Via Giuseppe Verdi 59r; ⊙ 7pm-4am Fri, Sat & Mon, to 3am Thu) A hipster crowd looks beautiful in this Santa Croce lounge and dance club with chintzy red seating, steely grey bar and a mix of hip-hop and R&B on the turntable.

HISTORIC CAFES

Caffè Giacosa (Map p80; ☑ 055 277 63 28; www.caffegiacosa.it; Via della Spada 10r; ⊗ 7.45am-8.30pm Mon-Fri, 8.30am-8.30pm Sat, 12.30-8.30pm Sun; 🖘) This chic cafe with 1815 pedigree was the inventor of the Negroni cocktail and hub of Anglo-Florentine sophistication during the interwar years. Today it is the hip cafe of local hotshot designer Roberto Cavalli, whose flagship boutique is next door. Giacosa is known for its refreshingly unelevated prices, excellent coffee and buzzing street terrace on fashionable Via de' Tournabuoni.

Caffè Rivoire (Map p80; ☑ 055 21 44 12; www.rivoire.it; Piazza della Signoria 4; ⊗ 7am-midnight Tue-Sun summer, to 9pm winter) This golden oldie with an unbeatable people-watching terrace has produced some of the city's most exquisite chocolate since 1872. Black-jacketed barmen with ties set the formal tone. Save several euros by joining the local Florentine crowd standing at the bar rather than sitting down at a table.

Gilli (Map p80; ☑ 055 21 38 96; www.gilli.it; Piazza della Repubblica 39r; ⊗ 7.30am-1.30am) The most famous of the historic cafes on the city's old Roman forum, Gilli has been serving utterly delectable cakes, chocolates, fruit tartlets and *millefoglie* (sheets of puff pastry filled with rich vanilla or chocolate Chantilly cream) to die for since 1733 (it moved to this square in 1910 and sports a beautifully preserved art nouveau interior).

Procacci (Map p80; ☑ 055 21 16 56; www.procacci1885.it; Via de' Tornabuoni 64r; ⊗ 10am-9pm Mon-Sat, 11am-8pm Sun, closed 3 weeks Aug) The last remaining bastion of genteel old Florence, this tiny cafe was born in 1885 opposite an English pharmacy as a delicatessen serving truffles in its repertoire of tasty morsels. Bite-sized *panini tartufati* (truffle pâté rolls) remain the thing to order, best accompanied by a glass of *prosecco* (sparkling wine).

Dress up and look good to get in. (The dress code, if it helps, is 'smart, casual, sexy, chic'.)

Blob Club CLUB
(Map p94; ☑ 324 8043276; Via Vinegia 21r; ⊗ 11pm-3am Mon-Wed, to 5am Thu-Sat) This small and edgy Santa Croce club lures an international crowd with its music theme nights – loads of 1960s, hip-hop, alternative rock; all sounds in fact.

🍷 Oltrarno

Be it speciality coffee, cocktails, craft beer or exceedingly fine wine from Tuscany and elsewhere in Italy, the Oltrarno delivers. Drinking and nightlife this side of the river is ab fabulous; watch out for edgy new openings here, as this is the 'hood where it happens.

★ Santarosa Bistrot BAR
(☑ 055 230 90 57; www.facebook.com/santarosa.bistrot; Lungarno di Santarosa; ⊗ 8am-midnight; 🖘) The living is easy at this hipster garden bistro-bar, snug against a chunk of ancient city wall in the flowery Santarosa gardens. Comfy cushioned sofas built from recycled wooden crates sit beneath trees al fresco; food is superb (meals €30); and mixologists behind the bar complement an excellent wine list curated by Enoteca Pitti Gola e Cantina with serious craft cocktails.

★ Enoteca Pitti Gola e Cantina WINE BAR
(Map p96; ☑ 055 21 27 04; www.pittigolaecantina.com; Piazza dei Pitti 16; ⊗ 1pm-midnight Wed-Mon) Wine lovers won't do better than this serious wine bar opposite Palazzo Pitti, run with passion and humour by charismatic trio Edoardo, Manuele and Zeno – don't be surprised if they share a glass with you over wine talk. Floor-to-ceiling shelves of expertly curated, small-production Tuscan and Italian wines fill the tiny bar, and casual dining (excellent cured meats and pasta *fatta in casa*) is around a handful of marble-topped tables.

★ Il Santino WINE BAR
(Map p96; ☑ 055 230 28 20; Via di Santo Spirito 60r; ⊗ 12.30-11pm) Kid sister to top-notch restaurant Il Santo Bevitore two doors down the street, this intimate wine bar with exposed stone walls and marble bar is a stylish spot for pairing cured meats, cheeses and Tuscan staples with a carefully curated selection of wine – many by local producers – and artisan beers.

Kawaii COCKTAIL BAR
(Map p96; ☑ 055 28 14 00; www.ristorantemomoyama.it; Borgo San Frediano 8r; ⊗ 6pm-1am) Head to this smart new Japanese cocktail bar for an inventive Blood Meray (tomato juice, Japanese Sochu, fresh ginger, soy sauce and Wasabi) or one of several creative sake-based fusion cocktails in the company of Japanese

tapas. Dress smartly and be prepared to try at least a couple of the 30-odd types of sake, 15 Japanese beers and 15 whiskeys.

Ditta Artigianale   CAFE, BAR

(Map p96; 📞 055 045 71 63; www.dittaartigianale. it; Via dello Sprone 5r; ⊙ 8am-midnight Mon-Fri, 9am-midnight Sat & Sun; 🛜) The second branch of Florence's premier coffee roaster and gin bar treats its faithful hipster clientele to full-blown dining in a 1950s-styled interior alongside its signature speciality coffees, gin cocktails and laid-back vibe. Think bright geometric-patterned wallpaper, comfy gold and pea-green armchairs, a mezzanine restaurant up top, buzzing ground-floor bar with great cocktails down below, and a tiny street terrace out the back.

Volume   BAR

(Map p96; 📞 055 238 14 60; www.volumefirenze. com; Piazza Santo Spirito 3r; ⊙ 8.30am-1.30am) Armchairs, recycled and upcycled vintage furniture, books to read, juke box, crepes and a tasty choice of nibbles with coffee or a light lunch give this hybrid cafe-bar-gallery real appeal – all in an old hat-making workshop with tools and wooden moulds strewn around. Watch for various music, art and DJ events.

La Cité   BAR

(Map p96; 📞 055 21 03 87; www.lacitelibreria.info; Borgo San Frediano 20r; ⊙ 2pm-2am Mon-Sat, 3pm-2am Sun; 🛜) A hip cafe-bookshop with an eclectic choice of vintage seating, La Cité makes a wonderful, intimate venue for book readings, after-work drinks and fantastic live music – jazz, swing, world music. Check its Facebook page for the week's events.

Dolce Vita   BAR

(Map p96; 📞 055 28 45 95; www.dolcevitaflorence. com; Piazza del Carmine 6r; ⊙ 7pm-1.30am Sun-Wed, to 2am Thu-Sat, closed 2 weeks Aug) Going strong since the 1980s, this veteran bar with a distinct club vibe is an Oltrarno hot spot for after-work drinks, cocktails and DJ sets. Its chic, design-driven interior gets a new look every month thanks to constantly changing photography and contemporary art exhibitions. In summer, its decked terrace is the place to be seen (shades obligatory). Live bands too.

🍷 Boboli & San Miniato al Monte

Being enviably riverside or on a hill with some of the finest city views in town, this neighbourhood predictably serves up some appealing drinking holes.

★ Le Volpi e l'Uva   WINE BAR

(Map p102; 📞 055 239 81 32; www.levolpieluva. com; Piazza dei Rossi 1; ⊙ 11am-9pm Mon-Sat) This unassuming wine bar hidden away by Chiesa di Santa Felicità remains as appealing as the day it opened over a decade ago. Its food and wine pairings are first class – taste and buy boutique wines by small producers from all over Italy, matched perfectly with cheeses, cold meats and the best *crostini* in town. Wine-tasting classes too.

Flò   LOUNGE, CLUB

(Map p102; 📞 055 65 07 91; www.flofirenze.com; Piazzale Michelangelo 84; ⊙ 7.30pm-4am summer) Without a doubt the hottest and hippest place to be seen in the city on hot sultry summer nights is Flò, a truly ab fab seasonal lounge bar that pops up each May on Piazzale Michelangelo. Different themed lounge areas include a dance floor and VIP area (where you have no chance of reserving a table unless you're in the Florentine in-crowd). Dress the part to get past the bouncers.

Il Lounge   LOUNGE

(Map p102; 📞 055 553 56 77; www.borgoin thecity.com; Lungarno Benvenuto Cellini 69r; ⊙ 2pm-midnight Tue-Sat, noon-3pm Sun; 🛜) When the madding crowd and raucous Tuscan *fiaschetteria* get too much, recharge your batteries in this stylish lounge – a chic haven of peace and tranquillity. The wine list is outstanding, a fireplace makes it winter cosy, and bar snacks are straight out of the gourmet kitchen of Michelin-starred chef Antonella Sardi (his restaurant is next door).

Zoé   BAR

(Map p102; 📞 055 24 31 11; www.facebook.com/ zoebarfirenze; Via dei Renai 13r; ⊙ 8.30am-3am; 🛜) This savvy Oltrarno bar knows exactly what its hip punters want – a relaxed, faintly industrial space to hang out in all hours (well, almost). Be it breakfast, lunch, cocktails or after-dinner party, Zoé is your gal. Come springtime's warmth, the scene spills out onto a wooden decked street terrace out the front. Watch for DJs spinning tunes and parties; check its Facebook page.

🍸 Out of Town

Tenax   CLUB

(📞 335 5235922; www.tenax.org; Via Pratese 46; admission varies; ⊙ 10pm-4am Thu-Sun Oct-Apr) The only club in Florence on the European club circuit, with great international guest DJs and wildly popular 'Nobody's Perfect' house parties on Saturday night; find the warehouse-style building out of town near Florence airport. Take bus 29 or 30 from Stazione di Santa Maria Novella.

☆ Entertainment

Opera di Firenze OPERA

(☑ 055 277 93 09; www.operadifirenze.it; Piazzale Vittorio Gui, Viale Fratelli Rosselli 15; ⊙ box office 10am-6pm Tue-Fri, to 1pm Sat) Florence's strikingly modern opera house with glittering contemporary geometric facade sits on the green edge of city park Parco delle Cascine. Its three thoughtfully designed and multifunctional concert halls seat an audience of 5000 and play host to the springtime Maggio Musicale Fiorentino (p103).

Teatro della Pergola THEATRE

(Map p94; ☑ 055 2 26 41; www.teatrodellapergola. com; Via della Pergola 18) Beautiful city theatre with stunning entrance; host to classical concerts October to April.

🔒 Shopping

Tacky mass-produced souvenirs (boxer shorts emblazoned with *David's* packet) are everywhere, not least at city market **Mercato Nuovo** (Map p80; Piazza del Mercato Nuovo; ⊙ 8.30am-7pm Mon-Sat), awash with cheap imported handbags and other leather goods. But for serious shoppers keen to delve into a city synonymous with craftsmanship since medieval times, there are plenty of workshops and boutiques to visit.

🔒 Duomo & Piazza della Signoria

★ Benheart FASHION & ACCESSORIES

(Map p80; ☑ 055 046 26 38; www.benheart.it; Via dei Cimatori 25r; ⊙ 10am-8pm) The flagship store of Benheart, this gorgeous shop showcases the handmade leather designs – shoes, jackets, belts and bags for men and women – of local superstar Ben, a young Florentine fashion designer who set up the business with Florentine schoolmate Matteo after undergoing a heart transplant. The pair swore that if Ben survived, they'd go it alone – which they did with huge success.

Fabriano Boutique ARTS & CRAFTS

(Map p80; ☑ 055 28 51 94; www.fabrianobout ique.com; Via del Corso 59r; ⊙ 9am-7.30pm) Luxurious writing paper, origami and pop-up greeting cards and other lovely paper products entice customers into this thoroughly

modern stationery boutique – a refreshing change from the traditional norm. Watch for occasional card-making, calligraphy and origami workshops.

Angela Caputi JEWELLERY

(Map p80; ☑ 055 29 29 93; www.angelacaputi. com; Borgo SS Apostoli 42-46; ⊙ 10am-1pm & 3.30-7.30pm Mon-Sat) The bold and colourful resin jewellery of Angela Caputi, at work in Florence since the 1970s, is much loved by Florentines. Eye-catching costume gems and jewels are her forté, shown off to perfection against one-of-a-kind women's fashion labels uncovered during her worldwide travels.

🔒 Santa Maria Novella

The web of streets immediately west of designer-studded Via de'Tornabuoni (p82) proffers super-stylish shopping for fashion, crafts, homewares and unique design: Via della Vigna Nuova and Via della Spada are lined with superb boutiques.

★ Officina Profumo-Farmaceutica di Santa Maria Novella BEAUTY, GIFTS

(Map p80; ☑ 055 21 62 76; www.smnovella.it; Via della Scala 16; ⊙ 9.30am-8pm) In business since 1612, this exquisite perfumery-pharmacy began life when Santa Maria Novella's Dominican friars began to concoct cures and sweet-smelling unguents using medicinal herbs cultivated in the monastery garden. The shop, with an interior from 1848, sells fragrances, skincare products, ancient herbal remedies and preparations for everything from relief of heavy legs to improving skin elasticity, memory and mental energy.

Grevi FASHION & ACCESSORIES

(Map p80; ☑ 055 26 41 39; www.grevi.it; Via della Spada 11-13r; ⊙ 10am-2pm & 3-8pm Mon-Sat) It was a hat made by Siena milliner Grevi that actress Cher wore in the film *Tea with Mussolini* (1999); ditto Maggie Smith in *My House in Umbria* (2003). So if you want to shop like a star for a hat by Grevi, this hopelessly romantic boutique is the address. Hats range in price from €30 to possibly unaffordable.

Aprosio & Co ACCESSORIES, JEWELLERY

(Map p80; ☑ 055 21 01 27; www.aprosio.it; Via del Moro 75-77r; ⊙ 10am-7pm Mon-Fri, 10.30am-7.30pm Sat) Ornella Aprosio fashions teeny tiny glass and crystal beads into dazzling pieces of jewellery, hair accessories, animal-shaped brooches, handbags, even glass-flecked cashmere. It is all quite magical.

Letizia Fiorini   ARTS & CRAFTS
(Map p80; ☎ 055 21 65 04; Via del Parione 60r; ⊗ 10am-7pm Tue-Sat) This charming shop is a one-woman affair – Letizia Fiorini sits at the counter and makes her distinctive puppets by hand in between assisting customers. You'll find Pulchinella (Punch), Arlecchino the clown, beautiful servant girl Colombina, Doctor Peste (complete with plague mask), swashbuckling Il Capitano and many other characters from traditional Italian puppetry.

Pineider   ARTS & CRAFTS
(Map p80; ☎ 055 28 46 56; www.pineider.com; Piazza de' Rucellai 4-7r; ⊗ 10am-7pm) Stendhal, Byron, Shelley and Dickens are among the literary luminaries who have chosen to purchase top-quality stationery from this company.

Richard Ginori   HOMEWARES
(Map p80; ☎ 055 21 00 41; www.richardginori1735.com; Via de' Rondinelli 17r; ⊗ 10am-7pm Mon-Wed, 10am-7.30pm Thu-Sat, noon-7pm Sun) The maze of rooms at this elegant porcelain shop is well worth exploring. Showcasing tableware produced by Richard Ginori, a Tuscan company established in 1735, the showroom is one of the city's most beautiful retail spaces: think original parquet flooring, moulded ceilings, papered walls and an 18th-century glass conservatory filled with plants.

Marioluca Giusti   HOMEWARES
(Map p108; ☎ 055 239 95 27; www.mariolucagiusti.com; Via della Vigna Nuova 88r; ⊗ 10am-7.30pm)

The jugs, beakers, glasses and other colourful tableware items in this eye-catching boutique look like glass – but are not. Everything created by designer Marioluca Giusti is crafted from synthetic material. Young, fresh and a mix of pop and vintage in style, these homewares make great gifts to take home. Find a second boutique (Map p108; ☎ 055 21 45 83; Via della Spada 20r; ⊗ 10am-7.30pm) nearby.

🎒 San Lorenzo & San Marco

The Mercato Centrale (p106) is obviously the place to shop for fresh fruit, veg, olive oil, salami to take home and so on. Otherwise, gourmet temple Eataly is here and the neighbourhood has a thin sprinkling of interesting independent fashion boutiques.

★**Street Doing**   FASHION, VINTAGE
(Map p88; ☎ 055 538 13 34; www.streetdoingvintage.it; Via dei Servi 88r; ⊗ 2.30-7.30pm Mon, 10.30am-7.30pm Tue-Sat) Vintage couture for men and women is what this extraordinary rabbit warren of a boutique is about. Carefully curated garments and acessories are in excellent condition and feature all the top Italian designers: beaded 1950s Gucci clutch bags, floral 1960s Pucci dresses, Valentino shades from every decade. Fashionistas, *this* is heaven.

Penko   JEWELLERY
(Map p80; ☎ 055 21 16 61; www.paolopenko.com; Via Ferdinando Zannetti 14-16r; ⊗ 9.30am-7pm Mon-Sat) Renaissance jewels and gems

---

TOP THREE: GOURMET SHOPS

Shopping for culinary products is a sheer joy in foodie Florence, a city where locals live to eat. Mercato Centrale (p106) and open-air Mercato di Sant'Ambrogio (Map p94; Piazza Ghiberti; ⊗ 7am-2pm Mon-Sat) aside, these are Florentines' favourites for food shopping.

La Bottega Della Frutta (Map p80; ☎ 055 239 85 90; Via dei Federighi 31r; ⊗ 8.30am-7.30pm Mon-Sat, closed Aug) Follow the trail of knowing Florentines, past the flower-and veg-laden bicycle parked outside, into this enticing food shop bursting with boutique cheeses, organic fruit and veg, biscuits, chocolates, conserved produce, excellent-value wine et al. Mozzarella oozing raw milk arrives fresh from Eboli in Sicily every Tuesday, and if you're looking to buy olive oil this is the place to taste. Simply ask Elisabeta or husband Francesco.

Eataly (Map p80; ☎ 055 015 36 01; www.eataly.net; Via de' Martelli 22r; ⊗ 10am-10.30pm; 🔊) A one-stop food shop for everything Tuscan. Peruse beautifully arranged aisles laden with olive oils, conserved vegetables, pasta, rice, biscuits and so on. There are fresh bakery and deli counters, fridges filled with seemingly every cheese under the Italian sun and a coffee bar.

Obsequium (Map p96; ☎ 055 21 68 49; www.obsequium.it; Borgo San Jacopo 17/39; ⊗ 10am-10pm Mon, to 9pm Tue & Wed, to midnight Thu-Sat, noon-midnight Sun) Tuscan wines, wine accessories and gourmet foods, including truffles, in one of the city's finest wine shops – on the ground floor of one of Florence's best-preserved medieval towers to boot. Not sure which wine to buy? Linger over a glass or indulge in a three-wine tasting with (€20 to €40) or without (€15 to €30) an accompanying *taglieri* (board) of mixed cheese and salami.

inspire the designs of third-generation jeweller Paolo Penko who works with his son in the atelier his grandfather opened in the 1950s. Everything is handmade, as the mass of vintage tools strewn on the workbench attests. Drop in at the right moment and Paolo can mint you your very own Florentine florin in bronze, silver or gold.

Scriptorium   ARTS & CRAFTS
(Map p80; ☑ 055 238 26 20; www.facebook.com/scriptoriumatelier/; Via de' Pucci 4; ☺ 10am-1pm & 3.30-7pm Mon-Fri, 10am-1pm Sat) A mooch around this upmarket boutique is worth it, if only to dip into the utterly cinematic courtyard of 16th- to 18th-century Palazzo Pucci in which it's hidden. Scriptorium crafts exquisite leather boxes and books, calligraphy nibs and pens, and old-world wax seals in every colour under the sun.

Mrs Macis   FASHION & ACCESSORIES
(Map p94; ☑ 055 247 67 00; Borgo Pinti 38r; ☺ 4-7.30pm Mon, 10.30am-1pm & 4-7.30pm Tue-Sat) Workshop and showroom of the talented Carla Macis, this eye-catching boutique – dollhouse-like in design – specialises in very feminine 1950s, '60s and '70s clothes and jewellery made from new and recycled fabrics.

Scarpelli Mosaici   ART
(Map p88; ☑ 055 21 25 87; www.scarpellimosaici.it; Via Ricasoli 59r; ☺ 9.30am-6.30pm Mon-Fri, to 1pm Sat) The entire Scarpelli family works hard to preserve the art of *pietre dure,* the puzzle-like marble mosaics, at this beautiful boutique and workshop tucked beneath a red-brick vaulted ceiling. If staff have time, they'll give you a quick introduction to this beautiful yet incredibly painstaking craft.

🔒 Santa Croce

Santa Croce is definitely a 'hood for atmospheric open-air market meanderings more than window shopping for chic designer goods.

★ Aquaflor   COSMETICS
(Map p94; ☑ 055 234 34 71; www.florenceparfum.com; Borgo Santa Croce 6; ☺ 10am-7pm) This elegant Santa Croce perfumery in a vaulted 15th-century *palazzo* exudes romance and exoticism. Artisan scents are crafted here with tremendous care and precision by master perfumer Sileno Cheloni, who works with precious essences from all over the world, including Florentine iris. Organic soaps, cosmetics and body-care products make equally lovely gifts to take back home.

Boutique Nadine   VINTAGE
(Map p94; ☑ 055 247 82 74; www.boutiquenadine.com; Via de' Benci 32r; ☺ 2.30-7.30pm Mon, 10.30am-7.30pm Tue-Sat, 2-7.30pm Sun) There is no more elegant and quaint address to shop for vintage clothing, jewellery, homewares and other pretty little trinkets. From the wooden floor and antique display cabinets to the period changing cabin, Nadine's attention to detail is impeccable. Find a second, riverside boutique near **Ponte Vecchio** (Map p80; ☑ 055 28 78 51; Lungarno degli Acciaiuoli 22r; ☺ 2.30-7.30pm Mon, 10am-7.30pm Tue-Sat).

🔒 Oltrarno

A delight to mooch around in, vintage lanes hide tiny workshops with Florentine artisans at work, art galleries and unique independent boutiques. Shopping strips Borgo San Jacopo and Via Santo Spirito are top for avant-garde fashion, and jewellery shops fill Ponte Vecchio (p96).

★ Lorenzo Perrone   ART
(Map p96; ☑ 340 274402; www.libribianchi.info; Borgo Tegolaio 59r; ☺ hours vary) Every book tells a different story in this absolutely fascinating artist's workshop, home to Milan-born Lorenzo Perrone who creates snow-white *Libri Bianchi* (White Books) – aka sublime book sculptures – out of plaster, glue, acrylic and various upcycled objects. His working hours are, somewhat predictably, erratic; call ahead.

★ &Co   ARTS & CRAFTS
(And Company; Map p96; ☑ 055 21 99 73; www.andcompanyshop.com; Via Maggio 51r; ☺ 10.30am-1pm & 3-7pm Mon-Sat) Souvenir shopping at its best! This Pandora's box of beautiful objects is the love child of Florence-born, British-raised callligrapher and graphic designer Betty Soldi and her vintage-loving husband, Matteo Perduca. Their extraordinary boutique showcases Betty's customised cards, decorative paper products, upcycled homewares and custom fragrances alongside work by other designers (including super-chic leather-printed accessories by Danish design company Edition Poshette).

Byørk   FASHION & ACCESSORIES
(Map p96; ☑ 333 9795839; www.bjorkflorence.com; Via della Sprone 25r; ☺ 2.30-7.30pm Mon, 10.30am-1.30pm & 2.30-7.30pm Tue-Sat) Cutting-edge fashion plus 'Zines, books, magazines' is what this trendy concept store, incongruously wedged between tatty old artisan workshops on an Oltrarno backstreet, sells.

It is the creation of well-travelled Florentine and fashionist Filippo Anzaione, whose taste in Italian and other contemporary European designers is impeccable.

Officine Nora   JEWELLERY
(Map p96; www.officinenora.it; Via dei Preti 2-4; ⊙11am-1pm, 3.30-7.30pm Mon-Fri) Once a mechanic's shop, this seriously cool workspace for contemporary jewellery-makers brings Florence's rich history of expert goldsmithing right up to date. The large, luminous loft is filled with well-loved desks used by the resident artisans who make a dazzling array of wearable art. Visitors are welcome watch them at work and purchase pieces, but it's best to email or call in advance.

Giulio Giannini e Figlio   ARTS & CRAFTS
(Map p96; ☑055 21 26 21; www.giuliogiannini.it; Piazza dei Pitti 37r; ⊙10am-7pm Mon-Sat, 11am-6.30pm Sun) This quaint old shopfront has watched Palazzo Pitti turn pink with the evening sun since 1856. One of Florence's oldest artisan families, the Gianninis – bookbinders by trade – make and sell marbled paper, beautifully bound books, stationery and so on. Don't miss the workshop upstairs.

🏛 Boboli & San Miniato al Monte

With neighbouring Oltraro dominating the shopping scene on this side of the river, Boboli and San Miniato are known for a handful of highly specialised, upmarket boutiques rather than generous shopping strips to browse.

★ Lorenzo Villoresi   PERFUME
(Map p102; ☑055 234 11 87; www.lorenzovilloresi.it; Via de' Bardi 14; ⊙10am-7pm Mon-Sat) Artisan perfumes, bodycare products, scented candles and stones, essential oils and room fragrances crafted by Florentine perfumer Lorenzo Villoresi meld distinctively Tuscan elements such as laurel, olive, cypress and iris with essential oils and essences from around the world. His bespoke fragrances are highly sought after and visiting his elegant boutique, at home in his family's 15th-century *palazzo,* is quite an experience.

Antica Bottega Degli Orafi   JEWELLERY
(Map p102; ☑055 246 90 32; www.marcobaroni firenze.com; Via dei Renai 3; ⊙9.30am-1pm & 3.30-7pm) Duck into this old-fashioned atelier to watch revered Florentine goldsmith Marco Baroni at work. Using all types of gold as well as iron, he crafts exquisite rings, bracelets,

pendants and earrings embedded with rare, precious and semi-precious gems and stones.

Legatoria Il Torchio   ARTS & CRAFTS
(Map p102; ☑05 5234 2862; www.legatoriailtor chio.com; Via de' Bardi 17; ⊙10am-1.30pm & 2.30-7pm Mon-Fri, 10am-1pm Sat) Peek into Erin Ciulla's cosy workshop for an insight into her contemporary approach to the traditional Florentine art of bookbinding. Inside you'll find a treasure trove of gifts, including hand-sewn leather books, marbled-paper photo frames and journals in the shape of musical instruments. Order in advance of your visit and she'll make a personalised item to your specifications.

Madova   FASHION & ACCESSORIES
(Map p102; ☑055 21 02 04; www.madova.com; Via Guicciardini 1r; ⊙9.30am-7.30pm Mon-Sat) Cashmere lined, merino lined, silk lined, lambs wool lined, unlined – gloves in whatever size, shape, colour and type of leather you fancy by glovemakers in the biz since 1919. Count on anything between €35 and €185 a pair.

Stefano Bemer   SHOES
(Map p102; ☑055 046 04 76; www.stefanobemer.com; Via di San Niccolò 2; ⊙10am-7pm Mon-Sat) Bespoke shoes for gents – complete with original sixpence coin embedded in the sole of the left shoe for good luck – is what this Florentine shoemaker does best. Pick from 40 basic styles, fashioned in a remarkable choice of leather, including deer, bull, shark, hippopotamus or Russian reindeer, preserved since 1786 using traditional tanning methods.

ℹ Information

EMERGENCY

Police station (Questura; ☑055 4 97 71, English-language service 055 497 72 68; http://questure. poliziadistato.it; Via Zara 2; ⊙24hr daily, English-language service 9am-2pm Mon-Fri)

MEDICAL SERVICES

Twenty-Four Hour Pharmacy (☑055 21 67 61; Stazione di Santa Maria Novella; ⊙24hr) This pharmacy inside Florence's central train station opens 24 hours. There is usually at least one member of staff who speaks English.

Dr Stephen Kerr: Medical Service (☑335-836 16 82, 055 28 80 55; www.dr-kerr.com; Piazza Mercato Nuovo 1; ⊙3-5pm Mon-Fri, or by appointment 9am-3pm Mon-Fri) Resident British doctor.

Hospital (Ospedale di Santa Maria Nuova; ☑055 6 93 81; www.asf.toscana.it; Piazza di Santa Maria Nuova 1; ⊙24hr)

WORTH A TRIP

FIESOLE DAY TRIPPER

One of the joys of Florence is leaving it behind and Fiesole provides the perfect excuse. Perched in the hills 9km northeast of the city, this bijou hilltop village has seduced for centuries with its cooler air, olive groves, scattering of Renaissance-styled villas and spectacular views of the plain. Boccaccio, Marcel Proust, Gertrude Stein and Frank Lloyd Wright, among others, raved about it.

10am

Founded in the 7th century BC by the Etruscans, Fiesole was the most important city in northern Etruria and its Area Archeologica (www.museidifiesole.it; Via Portigiani 1; adult/reduced Fri-Sun €10/6; ☉9am-7pm summer, shorter hours winter), off central square Piazza Mino di Fiesole, provides the perfect flashback. Buy a ticket from the tourist office (☎055 596 13 11, 055 596 13 23; www.fiesoleforyou.it; Via Portigiani 3; ☉10am-6.30pm summer, to 5.30pm winter) a couple of doors away, then meander around the ruins of an Etruscan temple, Roman baths and archaeological museum. Later, pause for thought on the stone steps of the 1st-century-BC Roman amphitheatre, the summer stage for Italy's oldest open-air festival, Estate Fiesolana (www.estatefiesolana.it).

Afterwards pop into neighbouring Museo Bandini (☎055 596 12 93; www.museidifiesole. it; Via Giovanni Dupré; adult/reduced €5/3, with Area Archeologica €12/8; ☉9am-7pm summer, shorter hours winter) to view early Tuscan Renaissance art, including fine medallions (c 1505–20) by Giovanni della Robbia and Taddeo Gaddi's luminous *Annunciation* (1340–45).

Noon

From the museum, a 300m walk along Via Giovanni Dupré brings you to the Museo Primo Conti (☎055 59 70 95; www.fondazioneprimoconti.org; Via Giovanni Dupré 18; adult €3; ☉9am-2pm Mon-Fri), where the eponymous avant-garde 20th-century artist lived and worked. Inside hang more than 60 of his paintings and the views from the garden are inspiring. Ring to enter.

1pm

Meander back to Piazza Mino di Fiesole, host to an antiques market on the first Sunday of each month, where cafe and restaurant terraces tempt. The pagoda-covered terrace of Villa Aurora (☎055 5 93 63; www.villaaurorafiesole.com; Piazza Mino da Fiesole 39; meals €30; ☉noon-2.30pm & 7-10.30pm), around since 1860, is the classic choice for its view. For rustic Tuscan partaken at a shared table, Vinandro (☎055 5 91 21; www. vinandrofiesole.com; Piazza Mino da Fiesole 33; meals €25; ☉noon-midnight) is popular, but not a patch on La Reggia degli Etruschi (☎055 5 93 85; www.lareggiadeglietruschi.com; Via San Francesco; meals €30; ☉7-9.30pm Mon-Wed, 12.30-1.30pm & 7-9.30pm Thu-Sun), an outstanding spot with swoon-worthy views where knowing Florentines lunch on Sunday.

3pm

Wander around Cattedrale di San Romolo (Piazza Mino di Fiesole; ☉7.30am-noon & 3-5pm) FREE, begun in the 11th century. A glazed terracotta statue of San Romolo by Giovanni della Robbia guards the entrance inside. Afterwards, make your way up steep walled Via San Francesco and be blown away by the staggeringly beautiful panorama of Florence that unfolds from the terrace adjoining 15th-century Chiesa e Convento di San Francesco (Via San Francesco; ☉9am-noon & 3-6pm). Grassy-green afternoon-nap spots abound and the tourist office has brochures outlining walking trails (1km to 3.5km) from here.

5pm

Enjoy an *aperitivo* with Florentines at local hangout JJ Hill (☎055 5 93 24; Piazza Mino da Fiesole 40; ☉6pm-midnight Mon-Wed, 5pm-1am Thu-Sat, 5-11pm Sun), an atmospheric Irish pub with a tip-top beer list, excellent burgers and other quality pub grub. Or fire up the romantic in you with in a 2½-hour, 21km guided bike ride (€50 including bike hire) at sunset back to Florence with FiesoleBike (☎345 3350926; www.fiesolebike.it), a creative bike rental/guiding outfit run with passion by local Fiesole lad Giovanni Crescioli (a qualified biking and hiking guide to boot). His 'sunset' tour departs daily from Piazza Mino di Fiesole at 5pm in season.

TOURIST INFORMATION

Airport Tourist Office (☑ 055 31 58 74; www.firenzeturismo.it; Florence Airport, Via del Termine 11; ⊙9am-7pm Mon-Sat, to 2pm Sun)

Infopoint Bigallo (Map p80; ☑ 055 28 84 96; www.firenzeturismo.it; Piazza San Giovanni 1; ⊙9am-7pm Mon-Sat, to 2pm Sun)

Tourist Office (Map p88; ☑ 055 21 22 45; www.firenzeturismo.it; Piazza della Stazione 4; ⊙9am-6.30pm Mon-Sat, to 1.30pm Sun)

Tourist Office (Map p88; ☑ 055 29 08 32; www.firenzeturismo.it; Via Cavour 1r; ⊙9am-1pm Mon-Fri)

Getting There & Away

AIR

Also known as Amerigo Vespucci or Peretola airport, **Florence airport** (Aeroporto Amerigo Vespucci; ☑ 055 3 06 15, 055 306 18 30; www.aeroporto.firenze.it; Via del Termine 11) is 5km northwest of the city centre and is served by both domestic and European flights.

BUS

Services from the **bus station** (Autostazione Busitalia-Sita Nord; Map p80; ☑ 800 373760; Via Santa Caterina da Siena 17r; ⊙5.30am-8.30pm Mon-Sat, 6am-8pm Sun), just west of Piazza della Stazione, are limited; the train is better. Destinations operated by Sitabus (www.sitabus.it) include the following:

Siena (€7.80, 1¼ hours, at least hourly)

Greve in Chianti (€4.20, one hour, hourly)

TRAIN

Florence's central train station is **Stazione di Santa Maria Novella** (Piazza della Stazione). The **left-luggage counter** (Deposito Bagagliamano; Stazione di Santa Maria Novella; 1st 5hr €6, then per hour €0.90; ⊙6am-11pm) is located on platform 16. Tickets for all trains are sold in the main ticketing hall, but skip the permanently long queue by buying tickets from the touch-screen automatic ticket-vending machines; they have an English option and accept cash and credit cards.

Florence is on the Rome–Milan line. Services include the following:

DESTI-NATION	COST (€)	DURATION	FREQUENCY
Bologna	26	1hr-1¾hr	every 15 to 30 minutes
Lucca	7.50	1½hr-1¾hr	twice hourly
Milan	54-64	2¼hr-3½hr	at least hourly
Pisa	8.40	45min-1hr	every 15 minutes
Pistoia	4.40	45min-1hr	every 10 minutes
Rome	45-55	1¾hr-4¼hr	at least twice hourly
Venice	49-54	2¾hr-4½hr	at least hourly

ⓘ Getting Around

TO/FROM THE AIRPORT
Bus

ATAF operates a **Volainbus** (☑ 800 373760; www.fsbusitalia.it) shuttle (single/return €6/10, 30 minutes) between Florence airport and Florence bus station every 30 minutes between 6am and 8.30pm, then hourly from 8.30pm until 11.30pm (from 5.30am to 11.45pm from the airport).

Taxi

A taxi between Florence's Vespucci airport and the city centre costs a flat rate of €20 (€24 on Sundays and holidays, €25.30 between 10pm and 6am), plus €1 per bag and €1 supplement for fourth passenger. Exit the terminal building, bear right and you'll come to the taxi rank.

CAR & MOTORCYCLE

Nonresident traffic is banned from central Florence for most of the week and our advice, if you can, is to avoid the whole irksome bother of having a car in the city.

BICYCLE

Milleunabici (www.bicifirenze.it; Piazza della Stazione; 1hr/5hr/1 day €2/5/10; ⊙10am-7pm Mar-Oct) Violet-coloured bikes to rent in front of Stazione di Santa Maria Novella; leave ID as a deposit.

Florence by Bike (☑ 055 48 89 92; www.florencebybike.com; Via San Zanobi 54r; 1hr/5hr/1 day €3/9/12; ⊙9am-1pm & 3.30-7.30pm Mon-Sat, 9am-5pm Sun summer, closed Sun winter) Top-notch bike shop with bike rental (city, mountain, touring and road bikes), itinerary suggestions and organised bike tours (two-hour photography tours of the city by bike, and day trips to Chianti).

PUBLIC TRANSPORT

Buses and electric minibuses run by public transport company ATAF serve the city. Most buses – including bus 13 to Piazzale Michelangelo – start/terminate at the ATAF bus stops opposite the southeastern exit of Stazione di Santa Maria Novella. Tickets are valid for 90 minutes (no return journeys) cost €1.20 (€2 onboard – drivers don't give change!) and are sold at kiosks, tobacconists and at the **ATAF ticket & information office** (Map p88; ☑ 800 424500, 199 104245; www.ataf.net; Stazione di Santa Maria Novella, Piazza della Stazione; ⊙6.45am-8pm Mon-Sat) inside the main ticketing hall at Stazione di Santa Maria Novella. A travel pass valid for one/three/seven days is €5/12/18. Upon boarding, time stamp your ticket (punch on board) or risk an on-the-spot €50 fine.

TAXI

For a taxi, call ☑ 055 42 42 or ☑ 055 43 90.

Siena & Central Tuscany

Best Places to Eat

➜ Il Leccio (p170)

➜ L'Osteria di Casa Chianti (p149)

➜ Osteria del Castello (p154)

➜ La Taverna di San Giuseppe (p141)

➜ La Terrazza del Chiostro (p172)

➜ Dopolavoro La Foce (p171)

Best Wine Tasting

➜ Antinori nel Chianti Classico (p149)

➜ Castello di Ama (p153)

➜ Poggio Antico (p167)

➜ Fattoria Le Capezzine (p175)

➜ Vignamaggio (p146)

Why Go?

When people imagine classic Tuscan countryside, they usually conjure up images of central Tuscany. But there's more to this popular tourist region than gently rolling hills, sun-kissed vineyards and artistically planted avenues of cypress tress. The real gems are the historic towns and cities, most of which are medieval and Renaissance time capsules magically transported to the modern day.

This privileged pocket of the country has maintained a high tourist profile ever since the Middle Ages, when Christian pilgrims followed the Via Francigena from Canterbury to Rome. Towns on the route catered to the needs of these pilgrims and prospered as a result. Today not a lot has changed: tourism is the major industry, closely followed by wine and olive-oil production, and travellers are thick on the ground.

Come here for art, for Unesco-recognised architecture and landscapes, and for gastronomy. But most of all, come here for enchantment.

Road Distances (km)

	Montepulciano	Siena	San Gimignano	Volterra
Siena	70			
San Gimignano	112	46		
Volterra	120	50	30	
Greve in Chianti	102	48	33	53

SIENA

POP 53,903

Siena is a city where the architecture soars, as do the souls of many of its visitors. Effectively a giant, open-air museum celebrating the Gothic, Siena has spiritual and secular monuments that have retained both their medieval forms and their extraordinary art collections, providing the visitor with plenty to marvel at. The city's historic *contrade* (districts) are marvellous too, being as close-knit and colourful today as they were in the 17th century, when their world-famous horse race, the Palio, was inaugurated. And within each *contrada* lie vibrant streets populated with artisanal boutiques, sweet-smelling *pasticcerie* (pastry shops) and tempting restaurants. It's a feast for the senses and an essential stop on every Tuscan itinerary.

History

Legend tells us Siena was founded by the son of Remus, and the symbol of the wolf feeding the twins Romulus and Remus is as ubiquitous in Siena as it is in Rome. In reality the city was probably of Etruscan origin, although it didn't begin growing into a proper town until the 1st century BC, when the Romans established a military colony here called Sena Julia.

In the 12th century, Siena's wealth, size and power grew along with its involvement in commerce and trade. Its rivalry with neighbouring Florence grew proportionately, leading to numerous wars during the 13th century between Guelph Florence and Ghibelline Siena. In 1230 Florence besieged Siena and catapulted dung and donkeys over its walls. Siena's revenge came at the Battle of Montaperti in 1260, when it defeated its rival decisively. But victory was short-lived. Only 10 years later, the Tuscan Ghibellines were defeated by Charles of Anjou and Siena was forced to ally with Florence, the chief town of the Tuscan Guelph League.

In the ensuing century, Siena was ruled by the Consiglio dei Nove (Council of Nine), a bourgeois group constantly bickering with the feudal nobles. It enjoyed its greatest prosperity during this time, and the Council commissioned many of the fine buildings in the Sienese-Gothic style that give the city its striking appearance, including lasting monuments such as the duomo (cathedral) (p130), Palazzo Pubblico (p134) and Piazza del Campo (p134).

The Sienese school of painting also had its origins at this time and reached its peak in the early 14th century, when artists such as Duccio di Buoninsegna and Ambrogio Lorenzetti were at work.

SIENA & CENTRAL TUSCANY SIENA

THREE PERFECT DAYS

Day One

Prime your palate by touring the ultra-modern Antinori nel Chianti Classico (p149) winery (perhaps lunching at Rinuccio 1180 (p149) before exploring a historic one; try La Bottega di Badia a Passignano (p147) or Vignamaggio (p146). Next, navigate vine-lined back roads to Greve in Chianti to browse the Antica Macelleria Falorni (p146). Motor south to Panzano in Chianti (p148), visiting the Pieve di San Leolino (p148), dining at a Dario Cecchini (p148) eatery then checking into a local *agriturismo* or villa hotel.

Day Two

Explore the cobbled streets of Volterra (p163), admiring artefacts in the Museo Etrusco Guarnacci (p163) and visiting the workshops of alabaster artisans. Lunch might be at Ristorante-Enoteca Del Duca (p165), for fine dining, or cafe-style L'Incontro (p165). Next, head to the perfectly preserved medieval town of San Gimignano (p155) for art that balances the gravitas of the old (Collegiata; p155) with the exhilaration of the new (Galleria Continua; p157).

Day Three

On your final day, visit the majestic medieval abbey of Sant'Antimo (p167) then drive alongside ranks of Sangiovese grapes for lunch alongside local winemakers at Il Leccio (p170). Next comes Montalcino (p166), home to blockbuster Brunello wines; climb the Fortezza (p166)'s battlements, taste vintages in the town's many *enoteche*, then enjoy a modern Tuscan dinner at Drogheria Franci (p167).

Siena & Central Tuscany Highlights

1 Siena (p127) Gorging on Gothic architecture, sublime art and sweet almond biscuits.

2 Chianti (p145) Eating, drinking and sleeping in style while exploring one of the world's most famous wine regions.

3 San Gimignano (p155) Wandering the streets of this magically preserved medieval city.

4 Montepulciano (p173) Savouring Vino Nobile and locally raised Chianina beef in this atmospheric hilltop wine town.

5 Volterra (p163) Discovering Etruscan artefacts and alabaster workshops.

6 Montalcino (p166) Taste-testing Brunello, Tuscany's most famous wine, in one of the town's many *enoteche* (wine bars).

7 Val d'Orcia (p166) Detouring onto scenic back roads in this World Heritage–listed landscape.

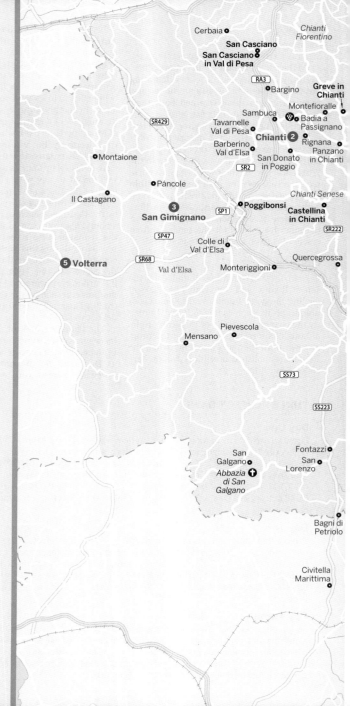

TOP SIGHT
OPERA DELLA METROPOLITANA DI SIENA

Siena's _duomo_ is one of Italy's greatest Gothic churches, and the focal point of important ecclesiastical buildings that include a museum, baptistry and crypt. All are embellished with wonderful art – Giovanni and Nicola Pisano, Pinturicchio, Jacopo della Quercia, Ghiberti, Donatello and (most famous of Sienese painters) Duccio di Buoninsegna are some of the artists whose works glorified their city and their god.

Duomo

Construction of the _duomo_ started in 1215 and work continued well into the 14th century. The magnificent facade of white, green and red marble was designed by Giovanni Pisano; the statues of philosophers and prophets are copies; you'll find the originals in the Museo dell'Opera. The interior is truly stunning, with walls and pillars continuing the black-and-white-stripe theme of the exterior.

Libreria Piccolomini

Through a door from the north aisle is this enchanting library (Piccolomini Library; Map p138; summer/winter free/€2), built to house the books of Enea Silvio Piccolomini, better known as Pope Pius II. Its walls are decorated with richly detailed frescoes painted between 1503 and 1508 by Bernardino (di Betto) Pinturicchio and depicting events in the life of Piccolomini, including his ordination as pope.

Pisano's Pulpit

The _duomo_'s exquisitely crafted marble-and-porphyry pulpit was created between 1265 and 1268 by Nicola Pisano, who had previously carved the famed pulpit in Pisa's

DON'T MISS
➔ Libreria Piccolomini
➔ Duomo
➔ Battistero di San Giovanni
➔ Cripta
➔ Museo dell'Opera
➔ Panorama del Facciatone

PRACTICALITIES
➔ Cattedrale di Santa Maria Assunta
➔ Map p138
➔ ☑ 0577 28 63 00
➔ www.operaduomo.siena.it
➔ Piazza Duomo
➔ summer/winter €4/free, when floor displayed €7
➔ ⊙ 10.30am-7pm Mon-Sat, 1.30-6pm Sun summer, to 5.30pm winter

duomo. Assisted by his son Giovanni and assistant Arnolfo di Cambio, Pisano depicted powerful scenes including the Last Judgement.

The Floor Panels

The inlaid-marble floor, decorated with 56 panels by about 40 artists and executed from the 14th to the 19th centuries, depicts historical and biblical subjects. Unfortunately, about half of the panels are obscured by protective covering, and are revealed only between late August and October each year (extra fee applies).

Battistero di San Giovanni

Behind the *duomo,* down a steep flight of steps, is the frescoed baptistry (Map p138; Piazza San Giovanni; €4). At its centre is a hexagonal marble font (c 1417) by Jacopo della Quercia, decorated with bronze panels depicting the life of St John the Baptist by artists including Lorenzo Ghiberti (*Baptism of Christ* and *St John in Prison;* 1427) and Donatello (*The Head of John the Baptist Being Presented to Herod;* 1427).

Cripta

This space (Map p138; Piazza San Giovanni; incl audioguide €6) below the cathedral's pulpit was rediscovered and restored in 1999 after having been filled to the roof with debris in the 1300s. The walls are completely covered with *pintura a secco* ('dry painting', better known as 'mural painting') dating back to the 1200s. There's some 180 sq metre–worth, depicting biblical stories including the Passion of Jesus and the Crucifixion.

Museo dell'Opera

The collection at Museo dell'Opera (Map p138; €8) showcases artworks that formerly adorned the *duomo,* including 12 statues of prophets and philosophers (1285–87) by Giovanni Pisano that decorated its facade. Also notable is the vibrant stained-glass window by Duccio di Buoninsegna (1287–90) and his striking *Maestà* (1308–11), painted on both sides as a screen for the *duomo's* high altar.

Panorama del Facciatone

In 1339 the city's leaders decided to transform the cathedral into one of Italy's biggest churches, but the plague of 1348 scotched their plan to build an immense new nave with the present church as the transept. Known as the Duomo Nuovo (New Cathedral), all that remains of the project is this panoramic terrace (Map p138), accessed through the museum.

PORTA DEL CIELO

To enjoy spectacular bird's-eye views of the interior and exterior of Siena's cathedral, buy a ticket for the 'Gate of Heaven' escorted tour (Map p138; http://opera duomo.siena.it; Duomo; €15 Mar-Oct, €10 Nov-Feb; ☺10.30am-7pm Mon-Sat & 1.30-6pm Sun summer, 10.30am-5.30pm Mon-Sat & 1.30-5.30pm Sun winter) up, into and around the building's roof and dome. Tour groups are capped at 18 participants and depart at fixed times throughout the day – purchase your ticket from the office in Museale Santa Maria della Scala (p134). Note that you'll need to arrive at the meeting point at least five minutes before your allocated tour time.

You'll save money (up to €9) by purchasing a combined OPA SI or Acropoli Pass, valid for three days, rather than individual tickets.

GUIDED TOURS

The excellent two-hour, guided 'Classic Siena' walking tour offered by Centro Guide Turistiche Siena e Provincia (p139) includes a tour of the *duomo* (Mon-Sat) or cripta (11am daily April to October).

SIENA & CENTRAL TUSCANY OPERA DELLA METROPOLITANA DI SIENA

TOP SIGHT
MUSEO CIVICO

Showcasing rooms richly frescoed by artists of the Sienese school in the early decades of the 14th century, this museum on the first floor of the Palazzo Pubblico (p134) is one of Siena's greatest attractions. The frescoes are unusual in that they were commissioned by the governing body of the city, rather than the Church, and depict secular rather than religious subjects.

Entrance Rooms

Enter via the Sala del Risorgimento, which is decorated with late-19th-century frescoes celebrating the life of the first king of Italy, Vittorio Emanuele II, and serialising key events in the Risorgimento (unification of Italy). Next to it is the Sala di Balia (Room of Authority), with 15th-century frescoes recounting the life of Pope Alexander III (the Sienese Rolando Bandinelli).

Anticappella & Cappella

Taddeo di Bartolo painted the frescoes in the Anticappella (Chapel entrance hall) in 1415, illustrating the virtues needed for the proper exercise of power (Justice, Magnanimity, Strength, Prudence Religion) as well as depictions of leading Republicans in ancient Rome.

DON'T MISS

➡ Sala del Mappamondo
➡ Sala dei Nove
➡ Anticappella
➡ Loggia dei Nove

PRACTICALITIES

➡ Civic Museum
➡ Map p138
➡ ☑ 0577 29 22 32
➡ Palazzo Pubblico, Piazza del Campo 1
➡ adult/reduced €9/8
➡ ⏱10am-6.15pm summer, to 5.15pm winter

The adjoining Capella (chapel) has a wooden choir carved and inlaid by Domenico di Niccolò (1415–28). Each of its 21 seats represents an article of the Credo.

Simone Martini's Maestà

Simone Martini's magnificent *Maestà* (Virgin Mary in Majesty; 1315) holds court in the Sala del Mappamondo (Hall of the World Map; pictured above); it is Martini's first known work.

The Surrender of Giuncarico Castle

Another fresco to be admired in the Sala del Mappamondo is this early 14th-century depiction of a representative of Giuncarico (shown to his right) handing over his sword to a member of the Sienese republic after its successful siege of the castle. Attributed to Duccio di Boninsegna, parts of the fresco were painted over at a later date.

Allegories of Good and Bad Government

Sienese artist Ambrogio Lorenzetti painted these huge frescoes in the Sala dei Nove (Hall of the Nine) around 1338–40. The central allegory features figures representing virtues including Justice, Wisdom and Peace. On the east and west walls are two scenes: one depicting an idyllic city filled with joyous citizens; the other presided over by a devilish-looking tyrant and filled with vice, crime and disease.

Loggia dei Nove

Views of Siena's southern valleys from this wide panoramic balcony are wonderful.

A plague outbreak in 1348 killed two-thirds of Siena's 100,000 inhabitants, leading to a period of decline that culminated in the city being handed over to Florence's Cosimo I de' Medici, who barred inhabitants from operating banks, thus severely curtailing its power.

But this centuries-long economic downturn was a blessing in disguise, as the lack of funds meant that Siena's city centre was subject to very little redevelopment or new construction. In WWII the French took Siena virtually unopposed, sparing it discernible damage. Hence the historic centre's listing on Unesco's World Heritage list as the living embodiment of a medieval city.

👁 Sights

★ Piazza del Campo   SQUARE
(Map p138) Popularly known as 'Il Campo', this sloping piazza has been Siena's civic and social centre since being staked out by the ruling Consiglio dei Nove (Council of Nine) in the mid-12th century. Built on the site of a Roman marketplace, its paving is divided into nine sectors representing the number of members of the *consiglio* and these days acts as a carpet on which young locals meet and relax. The cafes around its perimeter are the most popular coffee and *aperitivo* spots in town.

The Fonte Gaia (Happy Fountain; Map p138; Piazza del Campo) is located in the upper part of the square.

Palazzo Pubblico   HISTORIC BUILDING
(Palazzo Comunale; Map p138; Piazza del Campo) Built to demonstrate the enormous wealth, proud independence and secular nature of Siena, this 14th-century Gothic masterpiece is the visual focal point of the Campo, itself

---

---

the true heart of the city. Architecturally clever (notice how its concave facade mirrors the opposing convex curve) it has always housed the city's administration and been used as a cultural venue. Its distinctive bell tower, the Torre del Mangia (Map p138; ☑ 0577 29 23 43; www.enjoysiena.it; €10; ☺ 10am-6.15pm summer, to 3.15pm winter), provides magnificent views to those who brave the steep climb to the top.

The municipal offices are closed to visitors, but the major historical *sale* (halls) and rear loggia now form the unmissable Museo Civico (p132).

★ Museale Santa
Maria della Scala   MUSEUM
(Map p138; ☑ 0577 53 45 11, 0577 53 45 71; www.santamariadellascala.com; Piazza Duomo 1; adult/reduced €9/7; ☺ 10am-5pm Mon, Wed & Thu, to 8pm Fri, to 7pm Sat & Sun, extended hours in summer) Built as a hospice for pilgrims travelling the Via Francigena, this huge complex opposite the *duomo* dates from the 13th century. Its highlight is the upstairs Pellegrinaio (Pilgrim's Hall), featuring vivid 15th-century frescoes by Lorenzo di Pietro (aka Vecchietta), Priamo della Quercia and Domenico di Bartolo. All laud the good works of the hospital and its patrons; the most evocative is di Bartolo's *Il governo degli infermi* (*Caring for the Sick*; 1440–41), which depicts many activities that occurred here.

There's so much to see in the complex that devoting half a day is barely adequate. Don't miss the hugely atmospheric Archaeological Museum set in the basement tunnels; the medieval *fienile* (hayloft) on level three, which showcases Jacopo della Quercia's original 1419 sculptures from Siena's central Fonte Gaia (p134) fountain; and the *Sagrestia Vecchia* (Old Chapel) of the Chiesa SS Annunziata to the right near the main entrance, which houses di Bartolo's *Madonna della Misericordia* (1444–45) and a fresco cycle by di Pietro illustrating the Articles of the Creed.

There's an excellent gift shop on site, as well as a pleasant cafe that can be accessed from Piazza Duomo.

★ Pinacoteca Nazionale   GALLERY
(Map p138; ☑ 0577 28 11 61; http://pinacoteca nazionale.siena.it; Via San Pietro 29; adult/reduced €4/2; ☺ 8.15am-7.15pm Tue-Sat, 9am-1pm Sun & Mon) An extraordinary collection of Gothic masterpieces from the Sienese school sits inside the once grand but now sadly dishevelled 14th-century Palazzo Buonsignori.

Siena

N 0 ———— 500 m
0 ———— 0.25 miles

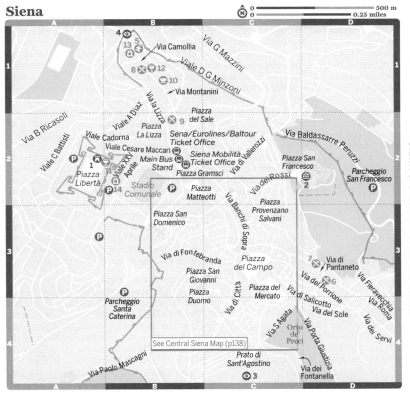

Siena

◎ Sights
1 Fortezza Medicea	A2
2 Oratorio di San Bernardino	D2
3 Orto Botanico	C4
4 Porta Camollia	B1

⊕ Activities, Courses & Tours
Siena Francigena Walking Tour	(see 4)
5 Siena Urban Running	B1

⊗ Eating
6 La Prosciutteria	D3

7 Lievito M@dre
7 Lievito M@dre	D3
8 Osteria Il Vinaio	B1
9 Ristorante Enzo	B2

☕ Drinking & Nightlife
10 Carta Zucchero	B1
11 Enoteca Italiana	B2
12 Mad in Italy	B1

⊙ Shopping
13 Il Maratoneta	B1
14 Wednesday Market	B2

The highlights are on the 2nd floor, where magnificent works by Guido da Siena, Duccio (di Buoninsegna), Simone Martini, Niccolò di Segna, Lippo Memmi, Ambrogio and Pietro Lorenzetti, Bartolo di Fredi, Taddeo di Bartolo and Sano di Pietro are housed.

The collection demonstrates the gulf cleaved between artistic life in Siena and Florence in the 15th century. While the Renaissance flourished 70km to the north, Siena's masters and their patrons remained firmly rooted in the Byzantine and Gothic precepts born of the early-13th century. Religious images and episodes predominate, typically pasted lavishly with gold and generally lacking any of the advances in painting (perspective, emotion, movement) that artists in Florence were exploring. That's not to say that the works here are second-rate – many are among the most beautiful and important creations of their time.

Artworks to hunt out include Duccio's *Madonna and Child* (Room 2) and *Madonna with Child and Four Saints* (Room 4); Simone Martini's *Madonna della Misericordia* and *Madonna with Child* (both in Room 4), *Madonna and Child* (Room 6) and *Blessed Agostino* altarpiece (Room 6); Bartolo di Fredi's huge and utterly magnificent *Adoration of the Magi* (Room 6); Lippo Memmi's *Madonna col Bambino* (Room 6); Ambrogio Lorenzetti's luminous *Annunciation* and *Madonna with Child* (both in Room 8); Pietro Lorenzetti's *Madonna Enthroned with Saint Nicholas and the Prophet Elia* (Room 8); Taddeo di Bartolo's *The Annunciation of the Virgin Mary* (Room 11); and Jacopo della Quercia's *Angelo Annunciante* (Room 18).

The gallery occasionally rearranges its exhibits; we've cited the room numbers at time of writing.

Palazzo Chigi Saracini   MUSEUM
(Map p138; ☑ 333 9180012, 0577 2 20 91; http://eng.chigiana.it; Via di Città 89; adult/student €7/5; ⊙ tours 11.30am Mon-Wed & Sat, 11.30am & 4pm Thur & Fri) Few buildings have pedigrees as splendid as this 13th-century palace. Home of the Piccolomini family (of which Pope Pius II was the most prominent member) during the Renaissance, it was acquired by the powerful Saracini family in the 18th century and inherited a century later by a scion of the wealthy Roman Chigi family. Today it houses the Fondazione Accademia Chigiana and its art-adorned interiors are a testament to the wealth, erudition and taste of the Saracini and Chigi families.

Highlights include the Rococco concert hall, the dining room with its unusual 'painted tapestry' walls and the *salotti* (salons), which house paintings produced between the 13th and 18th centuries. Valuable decorative arts and furniture include antique musical instruments, such as Liszt's piano and the oldest harpsichord in existence. A collection of photographs of famous artists who have been guests here is a testament to the musical taste of the last Chigi owner, Guido Chigi Saracini, who established the fondazione in 1932. These have included Arthur Rubinstein, Pietro Mascagni, Zubin Mehta and Daniel Barenboim.

The only way to visit the palace's interior is to join a one-hour guided tour. Note that these are sometimes postponed in winter, and when musical master classes are in progress. For tours in English, it is essential to book in advance by email or telephone.

Basilica di San Domenico   CHURCH
(Map p138; www.basilicacateriniana.com; Piazza San Domenico; ⊙ 7am-6.30pm Mar-Oct, 9am-6pm Nov-Feb) FREE St Catherine was welcomed into the Dominican fold within this huge and austere 13th-century basilica. Inside, the Cappella di Santa Caterina (halfway down the wall to the right of the altar) contains frescoes by Il Sodoma and Andrea Vanni depicting events in the saint's life. Also here are 15th-century reliquaries containing Catherine's head and one of her fingers, as well as a nasty-looking chain that she is said to have flagellated herself with.

The Cappella delle Volte (Chapel of the Vaults) to the right of the main entrance

---

GREEN ESCAPES

Orto Botanico (Botanical Garden; Map p135; ☑ 0577 23 28 77; www.simus.unisi.it; Via Pier Andrea Mattioli 4; adult/reduced €5/2.50; ⊙ 10am-7pm July-Sep, to 5pm Mar-Jun, to 4pm Oct-Feb) The tranquil terraces of this botanical garden, which is spread over 2.5 hectares of the verdant Sant'Agostino Valley, provide a welcome escape from the tourist crowds and gorgeous views across the valley. Owned by the University of Siena, which operates a scientific field here, it features hothouses filled with tropical and sub-tropical species, a genus terrace, fruit trees and gardens planted with aromatic, medicinal and food plants. In total, over 1000 species are represented. Native and endangered species are also represented.

Orto de' Pecci (Map p138; ☑ 0577 22 22 01; www.ortodepecci.it; Via Porta Giustizia; ⊙ 8.30am-10pm summer, reduced hours winter; ⬆) Operated by a social cooperative that gives support and employment to people with disabilities or dependency problems, this urban oasis is home to a small vineyard with clones of medieval vines, a cooperative organic farm that supplies the on-site restaurant with fruit and vegetables, plenty of animals (geese, goats, ducks and donkeys) and a scattering of site-specific contemporary artworks.

ℹ MUSEUM PASSES

If you're planning to visit Siena's major monuments (and we highly recommend that you do), several combined passes will save you money:

➡ OPA SI Pass: covers the duomo (p130), Libreria Piccolomini (p130), Museo dell'Opera (p131), Battistero di San Giovanni (p131) and Cripta (p131); €13 March to October, €8 November to February, valid for three days.

➡ OPA SI + Pass: covers the list above plus Porta del Cielo (p131) tour; €20 March to October, €15 November to February, valid for three days.

➡ Acropoli Pass: covers the duomo, Libreria Piccolomini, Museo dell'Opera, Battistero di San Giovanni, Cripta and Museale Santa Maria della Scala (p134); €18 March to October, €13 November to February, valid for three days.

➡ Acropoli + Pass: covers the list above, plus Porta del Cielo tour; €25 March to October, €20 November to February, valid for three days.

➡ Museo Civico (p132) and Museale Santa Maria della Scala: €13, tickets available at the museums.

➡ Museo Civico, Museale Santa Maria della Scala and Torre del Mangia (p134): €20, tickets available at the museums.

All of the passes can be purchased at the ticket office at Santa Maria della Scala. Note that children under 12 years of age receive free entry at the *duomo* sites and at Santa Maria della Scala, and that both the OPA SI and Acropoli passes include entry to the Oratorio di San Bernardino when it opens for the summer period.

---

was where the saint is said to have had many mystical experiences. It now houses a portrait of the saint by her contemporary Andrea Vanni. Other works of note in the basilica include a *Nativity* by Francesco di Giorgio Martini, a triptych of the *Madonna and Child with Saints Jerome and St John the Baptist* by Matteo di Giovanni and a *Maestà* by Guido da Siena.

Casa Santuario
di Santa Caterina   CHRISTIAN SITE
(Map p138; ☑ 0577 28 08 01; www.caterinati.org; Costa di Sant'Antonio 6; ☺ 9am-6pm Mar-Nov, 10am-6pm Dec-Feb) FREE St Catherine once lived here with her parents and 24 siblings (locals joke her mother must have been a saint too). Now a pilgrimage site overseen by nuns of the Benedictine order, the home's original kitchen and sleeping area were frescoed and converted into chapels in the 15th century. The larger Chiesa del Crocifisso (closed between 12.30pm and 3pm) was added in the 17th century. The downstairs Orotorio della Camera includes the saint's untouched, nearly bare cell.

Oratorio di San Bernardino   GALLERY
(Map p135; ☑ 0577 28 63 00; http://operaduomo. siena.it; Piazza San Francesco 10; €3; ☺ 10.30am-7pm Mon-Sat & 1.30-6pm Sun Mar–Oct) Nestled in the shadow of the huge Gothic church of San Francesco, this 15th-century oratory is dedicated to St Bernardino and decorated with Mannerist frescoes by Il Sodoma, Domenico (di Pace) Beccafumi and Girolamo del Pacchia. Upstairs, the small Museo Diocesano di Arte Sacra has some lovely paintings, including *Madonna del Latte* (*Nursing Madonna;* c 1340) by Ambrogio Lorenzetti.

Museo delle
Tavolette di Biccherna   MUSEUM
(Map p138; ☑ 0577 24 71 45; www.archiviostato. si.it; 4th fl, Banchi di Sotto 52; ☺ guided tours 9.30am, 10.30am & 11.30am Mon-Sat) FREE Housed in the Renaissance-era Palazzo Piccolomini, Siena's state archives aren't a usual stop on the standard tourist itinerary, but provide ample reward for those who choose to visit. The small on-site museum takes its name from the pride of the archive's collection: 103 small late-13th-century painted and gilded wooden panels known as the 'Tavolette di Biccherna'. Created as covers for the municipal accounts books, the *tavolette* were painted by Sienese artists including Ambogio Lorenzetti and Taddeo di Bartolo.

These and other evocative, historically significant documents (many medieval) can be seen on a compulsory guided tour (in Italian only). You'll want to linger in front of the cabinets containing the *tavolette,* enjoying

Central Siena

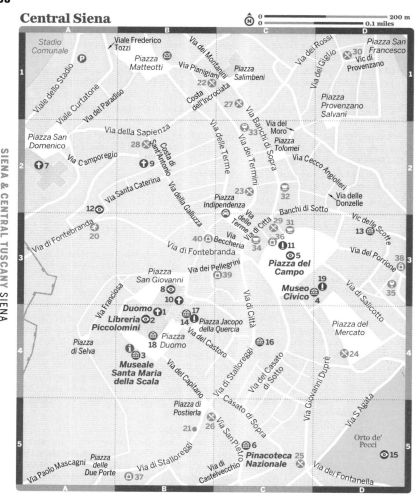

their scenes of Sienese life between the 13th and early-18th centuries and marvelling at the skill of their artists, but should ensure that you also view the illuminated *Constitution of Siena* (c 1310), which was written in Italian rather than Latin – very unusual for the time. There are also historical documents about the city's *contrade* (districts) and the Palio (p140), including drawings of costumes and processional floats.

To find the museum's entrance, head to the rear left-hand-side of the courtyard and take the elevator to the 4th floor.

🏃 Activities & Courses

Scuola di Cucina di Lella   COOKING
(Map p138; ☎0577 4 66 09; www.scuoladicucina dilella.net; Via di Fontebranda 69; classes from €80; ⊙10am-2pm & 4-8pm daily in summer by reservation) Lella Cesare Ciampoli is Sienese through and through, and clearly enjoys imparting the secrets of local dishes during her well-regarded cooking classes. At her professional kitchen near the historic Fontebranda fountain (p142) she demonstrates techniques and oversees participants as they prepare a four-course meal and then enjoy

Central Siena

it over lunch or dinner with wine. Assistant chef Francesco translates into English.

Siena Urban Running   RUNNING
(Map p135; ☎0577 4 42 77; maratoneta.sport@ libero.it; Via Camollia 201; run €25; ⊘7.45am Mon, Wed & Fri Jul-Oct) Guided 90-minute run through the historic centre organised by the Il Maratoneta (Maratoneta Sport; Map p135; ⊘9.30am-8pm Mon-Sat) walking and running shop. From November to mid-May there's a two-hour guided run in the early evening on Thursday. Running kits are available for €35.

Accademia Musicale Chigiana   MUSIC
(Map p138; ☎0577 2 20 91; www.chigiana.it; Via di Città 89; from €130) Competitive-entry, classical-music masterclasses and workshops are held in in the historic Palazzo Chigi Saracini (p136) during July and August.

Tuscan Wine School   WINE
(Map p138; ☎0577 22 17 04; www.tuscanwine school.com; Via di Stalloreggi 26) Two-hour wine-tasting classes introducing Italian and Tuscan wines (€45, 4-6pm Mon-Fri). Also offers a three-hour foodie walking tour (€45, noon-2pm Mon-Fri) and tours into neigh-

bouring wine regions (from €150, Mar-Oct). Advance bookings essential.

 Tours

**Centro Guide Turistiche
Siena e Provincia**   CULTURAL
(☎0577 4 32 73; www.guidesiena.it) This association of accredited guides offers guaranteed daily departures of a two-hour 'Classic Siena' Walking Tour (adult/child under 12 €20/ free) at 11am between April to October. This features key historical and cultural landmarks and includes entrance to the duomo (p130) or cripta (p131). Tours departs from outside the tourist information office in Santa Maria della Scala (p134) and are conducted in both Italian and English.

Siena Francigena Walking Tour   WALKING
(Map p135; ☎347 6137678; www.enjoysiena.it; adult/child under 11yr €20/10; ⊘9am early May–late Jun & Sep–mid-Oct) Introduced in 2017, this three-to-four-hour guided tour (Italian and English) departs from Porta Camollia (Map p135; Via Camollia) on the northern edge of the historic centre and follows the medieval pilgrim route for 4km to the *duomo* before continuing to Porta Romana. The tour

stops to visit the Museale Santa Maria della Scala (p134; ticket price included). Bookings essential.

Festivals & Events

Accademia Musicale Chigiana   MUSIC
(www.chigiana.it; ⊙Nov-Apr, Jul & Aug) The Accademia Musicale Chigiana presents two highly regarded concert series featuring classical musicians from around the world: Micat in Vertice from November to April and the Chigiana International Festival in July and August. Venues include the Teatro dei Rinnovati in the Campo, the *duomo*, Teatro dei Rozzi in Piazza Indipendenza, Chiesa di Sant'Agostino and Palazzo Chigi Saracini.

Eating

There are plenty of dining option in Siena, ranging from budget bakeries, *enoteche* (wine bars) and cafes popular with local university students to long-established, elegant and expensive restaurants that are the choice of cashed-up locals and visitors.

What all of these share is a strict adherence to regional cuisine. Among the many traditional Sienese dishes they serve are *panzanella* (summer salad of soaked bread, basil, onion and tomatoes), *ribollita* (a rich vegetable, bean and bread soup), *pappardelle alla lepre* (ribbon pasta with hare), *panforte* (a rich cake of almonds, honey and candied fruit) and *ricciarelli* (sugar-dusted chewy almond biscuits). Keep an eye out for

dishes featuring the region's signature *cinta senese* (indigenous Tuscan pig).

★ Osteria Il Vinaio   TUSCAN $
(Map p135; ☑0577 4 96 15; Via Camollia 167; antipasti €6-13, pasta €6-7; ⊙10am-10pm Mon-Sat) Wine bars are thin on the ground here in Siena, so it's not surprising that Bobbe and Davide's neighbourhood *osteria* (casual tavern serving simple food and drink) is so popular. Join the multi-generational local regulars for a bowl of pasta or your choice from the generous antipasto display, washed down with a glass or two of eminently quaffable house wine.

Osteria la Chiacchera   TUSCAN $
(Map p138; ☑0577 28 06 31; www.osterialachiacchera.it; Costa di San Antonio 4; €18; ⊙12.20-2.30 & 7-10pm Wed-Mon) Forgoing fuss, this unassuming *osteria* has a limited number of shared tables but a lot of charm. The menu (Italian only) offers hearty local dishes – *crostini* and *pici* with various sauces are always on offer, as are dishes with *fagioli* (white beans) – and these are enjoyed with the cheap house wine. Book ahead to be sure of snaffling a spot.

La Finestra   TUSCAN $$
(Map p138; ☑0577 22 35 02; www.ristorantelafinestra.it; Piazza del Mercato 14; meals €26; ⊙11.30am-3pm & 6.30-10.30pm Mon-Sat; ☑) A *finestra* (window) onto Siena's historic open-air marketplace, this family-run business is notable for its pleasant streetside

---

THE PALIO

Dating from the Middle Ages, spectacular Palio (Piazza del Campo; ⊙2 Jul & 16 Aug) includes a series of colourful pageants and a wild horse race in Piazza del Campo (p134). Ten of Siena's 17 contrade (town districts) compete for the coveted *palio* (silk banner). Each *contrada* has its own traditions, symbol and colours, plus its own church and *palio* museum.

From about 5pm on race days, representatives from each *contrada* parade in historical costume, all bearing their individual banners. For scarcely one exhilarating minute, the 10 horses and their bareback riders tear three times around a temporarily constructed dirt racetrack with a speed and violence that makes spectators' hair stand on end.

The race is held at 7.45pm in July and 7pm in August. Join the crowds in the centre of the Campo at least four hours before the start if you want a place on the rails, but be aware that once there you won't be able to leave for toilet or drink breaks until the race has finished. Alternatively, the cafes in the Campo sell places on their terraces; these cost between €350 and €400 per ticket, and can be booked through the tourist office (p143) up to one year in advance.

Note that during the Palio, hotels raise their rates between 10% and 50% and enforce a minimum-stay requirement. To join a Palio-focused guided tour and learn all about the event from a local, contact the Centro Guide Turistiche Siena e Provincia (p139).

TOP FIVE QUICK EATS

Lievito M@dre (Map p135; ☑0577 28 80 28; www.lievitomadresiena.it; Via di Pantaneto 59; pizza slice €2.2.50, panino €1.50-3.50; ☺7.30am-1am; 🖥) Close to the Campo, this popular bakery and cafe offers filled *panini* and slices of pizza to take away, as well as €5 lunch dishes to enjoy at one of the inside tables. Its €5 *aperitivo* offer includes a drink and your choice from a spread of snacks.

La Prosciutteria (Map p135; ☑0328 5414325; www.laprosciutteria.com; cnr Via Pantaneto & Vicolo Magalotti; panino €4-7, tasting board €5-15; ☺11.30am-9.30pm; 🖥) The name says it all. Prosciutto is the focus here, served in *panini* or on a *taglieri* (tasting board) – cheese is an optional extra. Order to take away (the **Orto de' Pecci** (p136) is close by), or claim one of the tables on the street and enjoy a glass of wine (€2.50) too.

Consorzio Agrario di Siena (Map p138; www.capsi.it; Via Pianigiani 9-13; ☺8am-8.30pm Mon-Sat, 9.30am-8pm Sun) Operating since 1901, this farmer's co-op is a rich emporium of food and wine, much of it locally produced. Self-caterers can source meat from the on-site butcher, as well as cheese, bread, vegetables, fruit and pasta. There's also a bar area where you can purchase and eat a *panino* (€2.50 to €5) or freshly cooked pizza (€12 to €14.30 per kg).

Morbidi (Map p138; ☑0577 28 02 68; www.morbidi.com; Via Banchi di Sopra 75; lunch/aperitivo buffet €12/from €7; ☺8am-8pm Mon-Thu, to 10pm Fri & Sat) A classy deli famed for its top-quality produce, Morbidi's excellent-value basement lunch buffet (€12; 12.15-2.30pm Mon-Sat) allows you to choose from freshly prepared antipasti, salads, risotto, pasta and dessert. Bottled water is supplied, wine and coffee cost extra. Buy your ticket upstairs before heading down. The cost of the *aperitivo* buffet (6-10pm Fri & Sat) depends on your choice of drink.

Te Ke Voi? (Map p138; ☑0577 4 01 39; Vicolo di San Pietro 4; burgers €9-14, pizza €7-10, pasta €8-10; ☺noon-1am; ✎) The name means 'Whaddya want?' and the answer is simple – cheap and tasty food prepared fast and served in pleasant surrounds. Beloved of local students, it serves focaccias, salads, risottos, pastas, pizzas and burgers (including veggie options). The *pasta cresciuta* (fried pasta) goes down a treat with a cold beer or glass of wine. Order at the counter.

terrace and for the larger-than-usual number of vegetarian options on its menu. Other than this there are few surprises – expect traditional decor and dishes, a predominantly local wine list and efficient service.

Ristorante Enzo   TUSCAN **$$**
(Map p135; ☑0577 28 12 77; www.daenzo.net; Via Camollia 49; meals €40; ☺noon-2.30pm & 7.30-10pm Tue-Sun) The epitome of old-fashioned Sienese dining, Da Enzo, as it is popularly called, welcomes guests with a complimentary glass of *prosecco* and follows up with traditional dishes made with skill and care. There's fish on the menu, but most locals head here for the handmade pasta and meat dishes. Consider opting for one of the traditional menus (€28 to €35).

Enoteca I Terzi   TUSCAN **$$**
(Map p138; ☑0577 4 43 29; www.enotecaiterzi.it; Via dei Termini 7; meals €35; ☺11am-3pm & 6.30pm-1am Mon-Sat, shorter hrs in winter) Close to the

Campo but off the well-beaten tourist trail, this *enoteca* (wine bar) is located in a vaulted medieval building but has a contemporary feel. It's popular with sophisticated locals, who linger over working lunches, *aperitivi* sessions and slow-paced dinners featuring Tuscan *salumi* (cured meats), delicate handmade pasta, grilled meats and wonderful wines (many available by the glass).

★**La Taverna di San Giuseppe**   TUSCAN **$$$**
(Map p138; ☑0577 4 22 86; www.tavernasangiuseppe.it; Via Dupré 132; meals €45; ☺noon-2.30pm & 7-10pm Mon-Sat) Any restaurant specialising in beef, truffles and porcini mushrooms attracts our immediate attention, but not all deliver on their promise. Fortunately, this one does. A favoured venue for locals celebrating important occasions, it offers excellent food, an impressive wine list with plenty of local, regional and international choices, a convivial traditional atmosphere and efficient service. Love it.

ⓘ SIENA FOR CHILDREN

This is a great choice of destination for those travelling with children. Toddlers will enjoy running around the Campo (p134), climbing the ramparts of a castle – the **Fortezza Medicea** (Map p135; Piazza Caduti delle Forze Armate; ⊙ 24hr) FREE – and exploring the Orto de' Pecci (p136) with its grassy lawns, outdoor artworks, trees and farm animals.

They will also adore playing the uniquely Sienese Game of the Palio, which involves an exciting race of wooden balls called *barberi* around a tiered circular stone course called a *pista*. The balls, which are painted in the colours of the city's 17 *contrade* (districts), can be purchased at shops including **Antica Siena** (Map p138; ☑ 0577 4 64 96; Piazza del Campo 28; ⊙ 9am-8.30pm) in the Campo and there are marble *pistas* at the Fortezza Medicea and opposite the **Fontebranda** (Map p138; Vicolo del Tiratoio).

Older children will enjoy the cultural tours and activities offered as part of the Siena for Kids and #SienaFrancigenaKids programmes, which are offered during the winter months. Check www.enjoysiena.it/en/attrattore/Siena-for-Kids-00002/ or contact the tourist office (p143) for details.

★ Tre Cristi
SEAFOOD $$$

(Map p138; ☑ 0577 28 06 08; www.trecristi.com; Vicolo di Provenzano 1-7; meals €45, tasting menus €40-65; ⊙ 12.30-2.30pm & 7.30-10pm Mon-Sat) Seafood restaurants are thin on the ground in this meat-obsessed region, so the long existence of Tre Cristi (it's been around since 1830) should be heartily celebrated. The menu here is as elegant as the decor, and touches such as a complimentary glass of *prosecco* at the start of the meal add to the experience. Exemplary service.

🍷 Drinking & Nightlife

Via Camollia and Via di Pantaneto are Siena's major bar and coffee strips. Though atmospheric, the bars lining the Campo (p134) are expensive if you sit at a table – consider yourself warned.

Caffè Fiorella
CAFE

(Torrefazione Fiorella; Map p138; www.torrefazionefiorella.it; Via di Città 13; ⊙ 7am-6pm Mon-Sat) Squeeze into this tiny, heart-of-the-action space to enjoy some of Siena's best coffee. In summer, the coffee granita with a dollop of cream is a wonderful indulgence.

Bar Il Palio
CAFE

(Map p138; ☑ 0577 28 20 55; Piazza del Campo 47; ⊙ 8am-10pm, later in summer) Arguably the best coffee on the Campo; drink it standing at the bar or suffer the financial consequences. Service on the terrace, which is a popular *aperitivo* spot, can be excruciatingly slow.

Bar Pasticceria Nannini
CAFE

(Map p138; ☑ 0577 23 60 09; www.pasticcerienannini.it/en; Via Banchi di Sopra 24; ⊙ 7.30am-9.30pm Mon-Fri, to 11pm Sat, to 10pm Sun) Established in 1886, Nannini's good coffee and location near the Campo ensure that it remains a local favourite. It's a great place to sample Sienese treats including *cantuccini* (crunchy, almond-studded biscuits), *cavallucci* (chewy biscuits flavoured with aniseed and other spices), *ricciarelli* (chewy, sugar-dusted almond biscuits), *panforte* (dense spiced cake with almonds and candied fruit) and *panpepato* (*panforte* with the addition of pepper and hazlenuts).

Carta Zucchero
CAFE

(Map p135; ☑ 0577 28 47 69; www.cartazucchero.it; Via Camollia 92-94; ⊙ 12.30-7.30pm Mon, from 10am Tue-Sat; 🛜) The reason why this bookshop-cafe is named after traditional paper sugar bags is a mystery, but its popularity is easily explained: it offers an extensive range of new and secondhand books (some in English), hosts literary and musical events and has a tranquil cafe serving a wide range of leaf tea (including organic and herbal choices), single-origin coffee, *panini* and salads.

Mad in Italy
WINE BAR

(Map p135; ☑ 0577 4 39 81; Via Camollia 136-138; ⊙ 11am-4pm Mon-Thu, to midnight Fri & Sat) About as hip as Siena gets, this laid-back 'bio-bar' is popular with the student set. Decor is thrift-shop quirky, the vibe is friendly and there's often live music on Fridays and Saturdays. Choose from a good range of wine and spirits and consider eating, too – many of the imaginatively presented dishes (€6-10) are vegetarian and organic.

Enoteca Italiana
WINE BAR

(Map p135; ☑ 0577 22 88 43; www.enoteca-italiana.it; Fortezza Medicea, Piazza Libertà 1; ⊙ noon-7.30pm Mon & Tue, to midnight Wed-Sat) The former munitions cellar and dungeon of this Medici fortress (p142) has been artfully transformed into a classy *enoteca* that carries more than 1500 Italian labels. You can take a bottle with you, ship a case home or just enjoy a glass in the attractive courtyard or vaulted interior.

Cacio e Pere   CLUB
(Map p138; ☑0577 151 07 27; Via dei Termini 70; ◷7pm-1am) If you're a university student studying in Siena, you're likely to be a regular at this hybrid bar and club, which is known for its live music, cheapish food and free-flowing drinks. Those who head here for *aperitivi musicali* tend to stay on to closing time – it's that type of place. Check its Facebook page for events info.

UnTUBO   CLUB
(Map p138; ☑0577 27 13 12; www.untubo.it; Via del Luparello 2; cover charge varies; ◷6.30pm-3am Tue-Sat) Live jazz acts regularly take the stage at this intimate club near the Campo, which is popular with students and the city's boho set. Check the website for a full events programme – blues, pop and rock acts pop in for occasional gigs too. Note that winter hours are often reduced.

🛍 Shopping

⭐ Il Magnifico   FOOD
(Map p138; ☑0577 28 11 06; www.ilmagnifico.siena. it; Via dei Pellegrini 27; ◷7.30am-7.30pm Mon-Sat) Lorenzo Rossi is Siena's best baker, and his *panforte, ricciarelli* (sugar-dusted chewy almond biscuits) and *cavallucci* (chewy biscuits flavoured with aniseed and other spices) are a weekly purchase for most local households. Try them at his bakery and shop behind the *duomo,* and you'll understand why.

Bottega d'Arte   ART
(Map p138; www.arteinsiena.it; Via di Stalloreggi 47; ◷hours vary) Inspired by the works of Sienese masters of the 14th and 15th centuries, artists Chiara Perinetti Casoni, Paolo Perinetti Casoni and Michelangelo Attardo Perinetti Casoni create exquisite icons in tempera and 24-carat gold leaf. Expensive? Yes. Worth it? You bet.

Brocchi   ANTIQUES
(Map p138; ☑347 4346393; brocchi1815@libero. it; Via del Porrione 41-43; ◷4-7.30pm Mon-Fri) A brass door knocker may seem a strange choice of souvenir, but the examples made by Laura Brocchi are attractive, well priced and authentically Sienese. Continuing a family tradition (Brocchi has been in business since 1815), Laura works from an historic nearby forge and is known throughout the city for the traditional pieces she makes for the city's *contrade* (districts).

Il Pellicano   CERAMICS
(Map p138; ☑0577 24 79 14; www.siena-ilpellicano. it; Via Diaccето 17a; ◷10.30am-7pm summer, hours vary in winter) Elisabetta Ricci has been making traditional hand-painted Sienese ceramics for over 30 years. She shapes, fires and paints her creations, often using Renaissance-era styles or typical *contrade* (district) designs. Elisabetta also conducts lessons in traditional ceramic techniques.

Wednesday Market   MARKET
(Map p135; ◷7.30am-2pm) **FREE** Spreading around Fortezza Medicea and towards the Stadio Comunale, this is one of Tuscany's largest markets and is great for cheap clothing; some food is also sold.

ℹ️ Information

Tourist Office (Map p138; ☑0577 28 05 51; www.enjoysiena.it; Piazza Duomo 1, Santa Maria della Scala; ◷9am-6pm summer, to 5pm winter) Siena's tourist information office is located in the Museale Santa Maria della Scala, and can provide free maps of the city. The entrance is on the right (western) side of the museum building.

Police Station (Questura; ☑0577 20 11 11; http://questure.poliziadistato.it/Siena; Via del Castoro 6; ◷8am-8pm Mon-Sat)

Azienda Ospedaliera Universitaria Senese (☑0577 58 51 11; www.ao-siena.toscana.it; Strada della Scotte) Hospital just north of Siena at Le Scotte.

ℹ️ Getting There & Away

BUS
Sena/Eurolines/Baltour

Tickets for Siena bus services operated by the Sena/Eurolines/Baltour group are also available

SIENA & CENTRAL TUSCANY SIENA

LOCAL KNOWLEDGE

LOCAL LIFE

Organised by a group of Central Tuscan municipalities, Be Tuscan for a Day (☑338 5829179; www.betuscanforaday.com) programmes offers visitors a chance to get a taste of 'authentic' local life on the farm, in the kitchen, in artisans' studios and outdoors. It includes cooking classes, vineyard and photography tours, horse riding, trekking and cycling.

from a **ticket office** (Map p135; ☑ 0861 1991900; Piazza Gramsci; ☺ 9am-6.20pm Mon-Fri, 9am-12.30pm & 1.45-4.30pm Sat, 4-7pm Sun) underneath the bus station in Piazza Gramsci.

Ticket prices vary according to availability and demand. Routes include the following:

DESTINA-TION	FARE (€)	TIME	FREQUENCY (DAILY)
Bologna	13-24	3hr	6
Milan	17-29	4¼hr	7
Naples	18-30	6¼hr	6
Perugia	13-20	1½hr	1
Rome	13-25	3½hr	13
Turin	17-34	7¼hr	3
Venice	17-30	5½hr	2

CAR & MOTORCYCLE

To drive between Siena and Florence, take the Siena–Florence autostrada or the more scenic SR222.

TRAIN

Siena's rail links aren't that extensive; buses can be a better option. There is a direct *regionale* service to Florence (from €9.10, 1½ hours, hourly). Rome requires a change of train at Chiusi-Chianciano Terme. For Pisa, change at Empoli.

A free *scala mobile* (escalator) connects the **train station** (Piazza Carlo Rosselli) with Viale Vittorio Emanuele II, near Porta Camollia in the historical centre.

ℹ Getting Around

BUS

Within Siena, **Tiemme** (☑ 0577 20 41 11; www.tiemmespa.it) operates *pollicino* (city centre), *urbano* (urban) and *suburbano* (suburban) buses (€1.20 per one hour). Buses 3 and 9 run between the train station and Piazza Gramsci.

CAR & MOTORCYCLE

There's a ZTL (Limited Traffic Zone) in Siena's historic centre, although visitors can often drop off luggage at their hotel; ask reception to report your licence number in advance, or risk a hefty fine.

There are large car parks operated by **Siena Parcheggi** (☑ 0577 22 87 11) at the Stadio Co-munale and around the Fortezza Medicea, both just north of Piazza San Domenico. Hotly contested free street parking (look for white lines) is available in Viale Vittorio Veneto on the Fortezza Medicea's southern edge. The paid car parks at San Francesco and Santa Caterina (aka Fontebranda) each have a free *scala mobile* (escalator) going up into the centre.

Most car parks charge €2 per hour between 7am and 8pm. There's more parking information at www.sienaparcheggi.com.

TAXI

Call **Radio Taxi Siena** (☑ 348 3892305, 0577 4 92 22; www.taxisiena.it) to order a taxi, or head

---

SIENA MOBILITÀ BUSES

Siena Mobilità (☑ 800 922984; www.sienamobilita.it), part of the Tiemme network, links Siena with the rest of Tuscany. It has a ticket office (Map p135; www.sienamobilita.it; Piazza Gramsci; ☺ 6.30am-7.30pm Mon-Fri, from 7am Sat) underneath the main bus station (Map p135; Piazza Antonio Gramsci); there's also a daytime-only left-luggage office here (bag between 7am and 7pm, €5.50).

Routes operated by Siena Mobilità from Monday to Saturday include the following:

DESTINATION	FARE (€)	TIME	FREQUENCY	NOTES
Arezzo	6.60	1½hr	8 daily	
Colle di Val d'Elsa	3.40	30min	hourly	Onward connections for Volterra (€2.75, four daily)
Fiumicino Airport (Rome)	22	3¾hr	2 daily	
Florence (*Corse Rapide/* Express service via the *autostrada*).	7.80	1¼hr	frequent	'Corse Ordinarie' services don't use the *autostrada* and take at least 20 extra minutes
Montalcino	4.90	70min	6 daily	Departs train station
Montepulciano	6.80	1½hr	2 daily	Departs train station
Monteriggioni	6.10	75min	frequent	
Pienza	5.50	70min	2 daily	Departs train station
San Gimignano	6	1-1½hr	10 daily	Often changes in Poggibonsi (€4.35, 1hr, hourly)

to the **taxi stand** (Map p138; Piazza Independenza) on Piazza Independenza.

CHIANTI

The vineyards in this postcard-perfect part of Tuscany produce the grapes used in namesake Chianti and Chianti Classico: world-famous reds sold under the Gallo Nero (Black Cockerel/Rooster) trademark. It's a landscape where you'll encounter historic olive groves, honey-coloured stone farmhouses, dense forests, graceful Romanesque *pievi* (rural churches), handsome Renaissance villas and imposing stone castles built in the Middle Ages by Florentine and Sienese warlords.

Though now part of the province of Siena, the southern section of Chianti (Chianti Senese) was once the stronghold of the Lega del Chianti, a military and administrative alliance within the city-state of Florence that comprised Castellina, Gaiole and Radda.

Chianti's northern part sits in the province of Florence (Chianti Fiorentino) and is a popular day trip from that city. The major wine and administrative centres are Greve in Chianti, Castellina in Chianti and Radda in Chianti.

For regional information, including festivals and special events, see www.wechianti. com and www.chianti.com.

Greve in Chianti

POP 13,862

The main town in the Chianti Fiorentino, Greve is a hub of the local wine industry and has an amiable market-town air. It's not picturesque (most of the architecture is modern and unattractive), but it does boast an attractive, historic central square and a few notable businesses. The annual Expo del Chianti Classico (Chianti Classico Expo; www.expochianti classico.com/en/; ⊙ 2nd weekend of Sep) (wine fair) is held in early September – if visiting

Chianti

at this time, book accommodation here and throughout the region well in advance.

👁 Sights & Activities

Vignamaggio
WINERY, GARDEN

(📞 0558 54 66 24; www.vignamaggio.com; Via Petriolo 5; ⊙ Apr-Oct) Mona Lisa Gherardini, subject of Leonardo da Vinci's world-famous painting, married into the family that built this villa in the 14th century. More recently, the villa and its magnificent formal gardens featured in Kenneth Branagh's film adaptation of *Much Ado About Nothing*. Restored in 2017, it offers accommodation, a restaurant, cooking classes, wine tastings (two hours, €27) and a three-hour tour of the gardens, organic vineyard and historic wine cellars (€59 including four-course lunch with wines). Bookings essential.

The estate is located 5km southeast of Greve in Chianti and 9km northeast of Panzano in Chianti.

Enoteca Falorni
WINE

(📞 055 854 64 04; www.enotecafalorni.it; Piazza delle Cantine 6; ⊙ 10.30am-7.30pm spring & autumn, to 8pm summer, closed Wed winter) This *enoteca* is a perfect place to let your palate limber up before visiting individual wineries. It stocks more than 1000 wines and offers 100 for tasting, including Chianti, Chianti Classico, IGTs, Grappa and Vin Santo made by a variety of producers. Buy a prepaid wine card (€5 to €25) and use it to test your tipple of choice.

Castello di Verrazzano
WINE

(📞 0558 5 42 43; www.verrazzano.com; Via Citille, Greti; tours €18-62; ⊙ 9.30am-6pm Mon-Sat, 10am-1pm & 3-6.30pm Sun) This hilltop castle 3km north of Greve was once home to Giovanni da Verrazzano (1485–1528), who explored the North American coast and is commemorated in New York by the Verrazano-Narrows Bridge (the good captain lost a 'z' from his name somewhere in the mid-Atlantic). Today it presides over a 225-hectare wine estate offering a wide range of tours.

Each tour incorporates a short visit to the historic wine cellar and gardens, plus tastings of the estate's wines (including its flagship Chianti Classico) and other products; perhaps honey, olive oil or balsamic vinegar. The 'Classic Wine Tour' (€18, 1½ hours, 10am & 3pm Monday to Friday) includes a tasting of several wines; the 'Chianti Tradition Tour' (€32, 2½ hours, 11am Monday to Friday) includes a tasting of wine and gastronomic specialities; while the 'Wine and Food Experience' (€58, three hours, noon Monday to Friday) includes a four-course lunch with estate wines. Tour bookings are recommended.

🍴 Eating

Bistro Falorni
DELI $

(📞 0558 53029; www.falorni.it; Piazza Giacomo Matteotti 71; taglieri €7-16, bruschetta €4, panino €5; ⊙ 10.30am-7pm) Italians do fast food differently, and what a wonderful difference it is. Greve's famous *macelleria* (butcher) and gourmet-provision shop opened this cafeteria attached to the *macelleria* in 2013, and it was an instant success with both locals and tourists. Choose from the range of *taglieri* (tasting boards), *panini* and bruschettes on offer, and order a glass of wine (€4), too.

🛍 Shopping

Antica Macelleria Falorni
FOOD

(📞 0558 5 30 29; www.falorni.it; Piazza Giacomo Matteotti 71; ⊙ 9am-1pm & 3.30-7pm Mon-Sat from 10am Sun) This atmospheric *macelleria* (butcher shop) in the main square was

ℹ CYCLING CHIANTI

Exploring Chianti by bicycle is a true highlight. The Greve in Chianti tourist office (p147) can supply information about local cycling and walking routes, and the town is home to the well-regarded Discovery Chianti, which runs guided cycling and walking tours. It's also possible to rent bicycles from Ramuzzi (p147) in Greve's town centre.

A number of companies offer guided cycling tours leaving from Florence:

Discovery Chianti (📞 328 6124658; www.discoverychianti.com; Via I Maggio 32; price on application; ⊙ Mar-Oct)

Florence By Bike (📞 0554 8 89 92; www.florencebybike.it; adult/reduced €83/75; ⊙ daily Mar-Oct)

I Bike Italy (📞 342 9352395; www.ibikeitaly.com; road/electric bike €450/550; ⊙ Mon, Wed & Fri mid-Mar–Oct)

I Bike Tuscany (📞 335 812 07 69; www.ibiketuscany.com; €120-160)

established by the local Falorni family way back in 1806. Known for its *finocchiona briciolona* (pork salami made with fennel seeds and Chianti), it also sells wine, cheese and other gourmet food provisions.

ℹ Information

The **tourist office** (☑ 390 55853606, 0558 54 52 71; www.helloflorence.net; Piazza Matteotti 10; ⊙ 10.30am-1.30pm late Mar–mid-Oct, to 6.30pm Easter-Aug) is located in Greve's main square.

ℹ Getting There & Around

BICYCLE
Rent two wheels in Greve from **Ramuzzi** (☑ 055 85 30 37; www.ramuzzi.com; Via Italo Stecchi 23; mountain/hybrid bike per day/week €20/130, scooter €55/290; ⊙ 9am-1pm & 3-7pm Mon-Fri, 9am-1pm Sat).

BUS
Buses travel between Greve in Chianti and Florence (€3.30, one hour, hourly) and between Greve and Panzano in Chianti (€1.30, 15 minutes, frequent). The bus stop is on Piazza Trento, 100m from Piazza Giacomo Matteotti.

CAR & MOTORCYCLE
Greve is on the Via Chiantigiana (SR222). Find parking in the two-level, open-air car park on Via Luca Chini, on the opposite side of the main road to Piazza Matteotti (this is free on the top level). On Fridays, don't park overnight in the paid spaces in Piazza Matteotti – your car will be towed away to make room for Saturday market stalls.

Badia a Passignano

Chianti doesn't get much more atmospheric than Badia a Passignano, a hamlet built around a Benedictine Vallombrosan abbey and vineyards run by the legendary Antinori dynasty. Head here to visit its historic church and abbey buildings, admire the views over the vineyards and taste Antinori wines in the classy *osteria* (casual tavern).

◉ Sights & Activities

Chiesa di San Michele Arcangelo CHURCH
(Abbey of Passignano; Via di Passignano; admission by donation; ⊙ guided tours in Italian 10am-noon & 3-5.30pm Fri, Sat & Mon-Wed summer, 3-5.30pm Sun, reduced hrs winter) An 11th-century church on this site was destroyed in the 13th century and replaced by this structure, which was subsequently heavily altered over

MONTEFIORALLE

Medieval Montefioralle crowns a rise just east of Greve, and can be accessed via a 2km walking path from Greve town centre (head up Via San Francesco, off Via Roma). Surrounded by olive groves and vineyards, the hilltop village was home to Amerigo Vespucci (1415–1512), an explorer who followed Columbus' route to America. Vespucci wrote so excitedly about the New World that he inspired cartographer Martin Waldseemüller (creator of the 1507 *Universalis Cosmographia*) to name the new continent in his honour.

End your village meander with lunch at La Castellana (☑ 0558 5 31 34; www.ristorantelacastellana.it; Via di Montefioralle 2, Montefioralle; meals €40; ⊙ noon-2pm & 7.30-9.30pm Tue-Sun summer, hours vary winter). Cooking is home-style Tuscan; the wine list reads like a map of Chianti's highlights; and seating is inside or on the hillside terrace with romantic panorama of cypresses, olive trees and vines.

the centuries. Dedicated to St Michael the Archangel (look for the 12th-century statue of him slaying a dragon next to the high altar), it is home to frescoes and paintings of varying quality – the best are by Domenico Cresti (known as 'Il Passignano') in the central chapel in the apse.

Monastery MONASTERY
(☑ 0558 07 23 41 (English), 0558 07 11 71 (Italian); Abbey of Passignano, Via di Passignano; admission by donation; ⊙ guided tours in Italian 10am-noon & 3-5.30pm Fri, Sat & Mon-Wed summer, 3-5.30pm Sun, reduced hrs winter) The four Vallombrosan monks who call this medieval abbey home open their quarters to visitors on regular guided tours. The highlight is the refectory, which was remodelled in the 15th century and is presided over by Domenico Ghirlandaio's utterly marvellous, recently restored 1476 fresco *The Last Supper*. The tours also visit the monastery's garden cloister and historic kitchen. It's best to book in advance.

La Bottega di Badia a Passignano WINE
(☑ 0558 07 12 78; www.osteriadipassignano.com; Via di Passignano 33; ⊙ 10am-7.30pm Mon-Sat) Taste or purchase Antinori wine in this *enoteca* beside the prestigious Osteria di Passignano restaurant (p148). A tasting of three

TUSCANY'S CELEBRITY BUTCHER

The small town of Panzano in Chianti, 10km south of Greve in Chianti, is known throughout Italy as the location of L'Antica Macelleria Cecchini (☑0558 5 20 20; www.dariocecchini.com; Via XX Luglio 11; ☉9am-4pm), a butcher's shop owned and run by the ever-extroverted Dario Cecchini. This Tuscan celebrity has carved out a niche for himself as a poetry-spouting guardian of the *bistecca* (steak) and other Tuscan meaty treats, and he operates three eateries clustered around the *macelleria*: Officina della Bistecca (☑0558 5 21 76; www.dariocecchini.com; Via XX Luglio 11; set menu adult/child under 10 €50/10; ☉sittings at 1pm & 8pm), with a set menu built around the famous *bistecca*; Solociccia (☑0558 5 27 27; www.dariocecchini.com; Via XX Luglio; set meat menus €30 & €50; ☉sittings at 1pm, 7pm & 9pm), where guests sample meat dishes other than steak; and Dario DOC (☑0558 5 21 76; www.dariocecchini.com; Via XX Luglio 11; burgers €10 or €15, meat sushi €20; ☉noon-3pm Mon-Sat), his casual lunchtime-only eatery. Book ahead for the Officina and Solociccia. When we last visited, Cecchini had plans to add a fourth eatery to his empire – check the website for an update.

Don't leave Panzano in Chianti without visiting one of Chianti's most beautiful churches, Romanesque Pieve di San Leolino (Strada San Leolino, Località San Leolino; ☉7.30am-noon) located on a hilltop just outside Panzano in Chianti. Artworks inside the church include a 1421 polyptych behind the high altar by Mariotto di Nardo (1421), two glazed terracotta tabernacles by Giovanni della Robbia, and a luminous 13th-century triptych by the master of Panzano depicting the Virgin and Child next to saints including St Catherine of Alexandria, the patron saint of philosophers.

wines by the glass will cost between €25 and €55 and there is a variety of guided tours of the cellars and vineyards on offer – check the website for details.

Eating & Drinking

★ L'Antica Scuderia   TUSCAN $$

(☑335 8252669; www.ristorolanticascuderia.com; Via di Passignano 17; meals €45, pizza €8-12; ☉12.30-2.30pm & 7.30-10.30pm Wed-Mon; 🖶) The large terrace at this ultra-friendly restaurant overlooks one of the Antinori vineyards and is perfect for summer dining. In winter, the elegant dining room comes into its own. Lunch features antipasti, pastas and traditional grilled meats, while dinner sees plenty of pizza-oven action. Kids love the playground set; adults love the fact that it keeps the kids occupied.

La Cantinetta di Rignana   TUSCAN $$

(☑0558 5 26 01; www.lacantinettadirignana.com; Rignana; meals €36; ☉noon-3pm & 7-10pm Wed-Mon summer, hours vary winter) You might wonder, as you settle onto the terrace here, whether you've found your perfect Chianti lazy lunch location. A historic mill forms the backdrop, vine-lined hills roll off to the horizon and rustic dishes are full of local ingredients and packed with flavour. It's 4km from Badia a Passignano at the end of an unsealed, rutted road.

Osteria di Passignano   MODERN ITALIAN $$$

(☑055 807 12 78; www.osteriadipassignano.com; Via di Passignano 33; meals €85, tasting menus €80-90, with wine €100-140; ☉12.15-2.15pm & 7.30-10pm Mon-Sat; 🅿) Badia a Passignano sits amid a landscape scored by row upon row of vines, and the elegant Michelin-starred eatery in the centre of the hamlet has long been one of Tuscany's best-loved dining destinations. Intricate, Tuscan-inspired dishes fly the local-produce flag and the wine list is mightily impressive, with Antinori offerings aplenty (by the glass €7 to €35).

❶ Getting There & Away

There is no public transport connection to Badia a Passignano. The easiest road access is via Strada di Badia off the SP94.

San Casciano in Val de Pesa

POP 17,062

Almost totally destroyed by Allied bombs in 1944, San Casciano in Val di Pesa, to the south of Florence, was fully rebuilt and is now a busy hub for the local wine and olive-oil industries. There are no sights of note within the town itself, but the surrounding countryside is home to a number of impressive *agriturismi* and villas.

🏃 Activities

⭐ **Antinori nel Chianti Classico**   WINE
(☑0552 35 97 00; www.antinorichianticlassico.it; Via
Cassia per Siena 133, Località Bargino; tour & tasting
€25-50, bookings essential; ☉10am-5pm Mon-Fri, to
5.30pm Sat & Sun winter, 6.30pm Sat & Sun summer)
Marco Casaminti's sculptural building set into
the hillside is a landmark sight on the *auto-strada* just south of Florence, and is one of
the world's most impressive examples of con-
temporary winery design. Daily guided tours
(in English and Italian) visit the wine-making
and fermentation areas before heading to one
of the glass tasting rooms cantilevered over
the barriques in the cathedral-like ageing
cellar for a tutored tasting of Antinori wines.
Tours (90 minutes/1½ hours) cost €30/50 for
three/five wines; bookings essential.

The Antinori family has been in the
wine-making business since 1180. At the stylish bar beside the shop you can taste 16 of
their recent vintages (€4 to €15 per tasting) or
have a sommelier-led 'guided tasting' of three
wines (€9 or €12). Afterwards, you can also
enjoy lunch or a glass of wine in the Rinuccio 1180 restaurant (p149). Alternatively, book
for the 2½-hour wine tour and lunch (€150),
which includes tastings of seven cru wines.

Bargino is 7km south of San Casciano in
Val di Pesa and 20km northwest of Greve.

🍴 Eating & Drinking

You're close to Florence in San Casciano,
so there's much to be said for popping into
that gourmet city for a meal. The local hotels
have restaurants; the one at **Villa I Barronci**
(☑0558 2 05 98; www.ibarronci.com; Via Sorripa
10) is particularly impressive but must be
booked in advance.

Rinuccio 1180   TUSCAN $$
(☑0552 35 97 20; www.antinorichianticlassico.it;
Via Cassia per Siena 133, Bargino; meals €40, tast-
ing platters €14-15; ☉noon-4pm) Built on the
rooftop of the sleek Antinori winery, this
restaurant seats diners on an expansive out-
door terrace with a 180-degree Dolby-esque
surround of hills, birdsong and pea-green
vines. In cooler weather, the dining action
moves into a glass dining space. Cuisine is
Tuscan, modern, seasonal and sassy (Chianti
burger, anyone?) and the wine list is (natu-
rally) fabulous. Book ahead.

⭐ **L'Osteria di Casa Chianti**   TUSCAN $$
(☑0571 66 96 88; www.osteriadicasachianti.it; Lo-
calità Case Nuove 77, Fiano; meals €38; ☉7-10pm
Tue-Sat, 12.30-2.30pm & 7-10pm Sun) The type

of restaurant that fuels fantasies of moving
permanently to Tuscany, this ultra-friendly
eatery bakes its own bread, makes pasta by
hand, grills *bistecca* on a wood fire, specialises in truffle and porcini mushroom dishes, and has an exceptional wine list. It also
imparts the secrets of its delectable cooking
in 4½-hour classes (€95 including lunch).
Book ahead.

You'll find it on the SP79 between Fiano
and Certaldo, 14km southwest of San Casciano in Val di Pesa.

ℹ️ Getting There & Away

San Casciano is on the SP92, just off the
Florece–Siena autostrada. **Busitalia/Autolinee
Chianti Valdarno (ACV)** (☑800.373760; www.
acvbus.it) operates services between San Casciano and Florence (€2.30, 20 minutes, 10 daily)
and between San Casciano and Greve in Chianti
(€2.30, 30 minutes, three daily).

Castellina in Chianti
POP 2859

Established by the Etruscans and fortified
by the Florentines in the 15th century as
a defensive outpost against the Sienese,
sturdy Castellina in Chianti is now a major
centre of the wine industry, as the huge silos brimming with Chianti Classico on the
town's approaches attest. The town's location on the SR222 makes it a convenient

---

ℹ️ GETTING AROUND CENTRAL TUSCANY

Car & Motorcycle Siena is Central
Tuscany's major transport hub, with
traffic zooming up and down the Siena–Florence Raccordo Autostradale
and other major highways linking the
city with other key Italian cities. Car is
by far the best way to get around the
legendary Chianti region, criss-crossed
by a picturesque network of *strade provinciale* (provincial roads) and *strade
secondarie* (secondary roads), some of
which are unsealed, narrow and tricky
to navigate. Most towns have strictly
enforced Limited Traffic Zones (ZTLs) in
their historic centres.

Bus Buses travel between Siena and
smaller towns throughout the area,
although services can be infrequent and
connections convoluted.

ROAD TRIP >
WINE TOUR OF CHIANTI

• •

Little matches the glorious indulgence of a leisurely drive along cypress alleys and vineyard-clad lanes in the ancient wine region of Chianti. Not only is the scenery intoxicating, but the region is also peppered with outstanding restaurants, fine ruby-red wine and a portfolio of historic wine-producing estates. This tour requires some planning: tastings and cellar tours must be booked in advance.

❶ Antinori nel Chianti Classico
From Florence, head 22km south along the *superstrada* (expressway), exit at Bargino and follow signs to **Antinori nel Chianti Clas-**

sico (p149), a state-of-the-art wine estate featuring an architecturally innovative ageing cellar. Take a tour, prime your palate with a wine tasting and enjoy an alfresco lunch

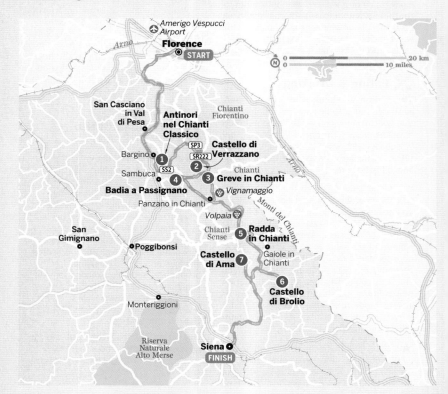

with sensational Chianti vineyard view in the estate's **Rinuccio 1180** (p149) restaurant.

❷ Castello di Verrazzano

Head southeast along the SS2, SP3 and SS222 towards Greve in Chianti. Stop at historic **Castello di Verrazzano** (p146), a half-hour drive (19km) from Bargino, for a themed tasting. Tours of the hilltop castle's 225-hectare wine estate include a fascinating visit of the historic wine cellar and gardens.

❸ Greve in Chianti

On the next day, test your new-found knowledge over a self-directed tasting at **Enoteca Falorni** (p146). For lunch, eat a Tuscan-style burger at **Dario DOC** (p148) in Panzano in Chianti, 7km south along the SR222, or a memorable four-course lunch with perfectly paired wines at **Vignamaggio** (p146), 4.5km south off the same road. Combine lunch at the beautiful 14th-century villa with a tour of its magnificent gardens, organic vineyard and historic wine cellar. Curious chefs can book a cooking class.

❹ Badia a Passignano

Devote the afternoon to exploring Badia a Passignano, an 11th-century, still-functioning Vallombrosian abbey surrounded by an An-

tinori wine estate. Enjoy a tasting in the *enoteca* (wine bar) and consider an early pizza dinner at **L'Antica Scuderia** (p148) opposite the abbey, where you'll be able to watch the sun set over the vineyards.

❺ Radda in Chianti

On day three, drive south to the hilltop hamlet of Volpaia near Radda in Chianti and take a tour of the **Castello di Volpaia** (p153) cellars. Afterwards, backtrack 9km north for a lazy lunch and glass of Volpaia's Chianti Classico or Riserva at **Bar Ucci** (p153) in the historic wine town of Radda in Chianti.

❻ Castello di Brolio

On your final day, motor south to **Castello di Brolio** (p154), ancestral home of the aristocratic Ricasoli family. Their wine estate dates from the 11th century and is the oldest in Italy. Visit the castle museum and formal garden, then sample some Baron Ricasoli Chianti Classico in the estate's *cantina* (cellar) or over a sensational modern Tuscan lunch in its **osteria** (p154).

❼ Castello di Ama

Devote the afternoon to investigating award-winning wines and contemporary art at nearby **Castello di Ama** (p153), a straightforward 12km drive along the SP484.

overnight or meal stop for those travelling between Florence and Siena.

◉ Sights & Activities

Museo Archeologico del Chianti Senese MUSEUM
(☑ 0577 74 20 90; www.museoarcheologicochianti. it; Piazza del Comune 17; adult/reduced €5/3; ☺ 10am-6pm daily Apr, May, Sep & Oct, 11am-7pm Jun-Aug, 10am-5pm Sat & Sun Nov-Mar) Etruscan archaeological finds from the local area are on display at this museum in the town's medieval *rocca* (fortress). Room 4 showcases artefacts found in the 7th-century-BC **Etruscan Tombs of Montecalvario** (Ipogeo Etrusco di Monte Calvario; ☺ 24hr) **FREE**, which are on the northern edge of town off the SR222.

Via delle Volte WALKING
From Castellina's southern car park, follow Via Ferruccio alongside the town's eastern defensive walls. These incorporate the atmospheric Via delle Volte, an 800m-long arched medieval passageway that was originally used for ancient sacred rites and later enclosed with a roof and incorporated into the Florentine defensive structure.

✖ Eating & Drinking

Ristorante Taverna Squarcialupi TUSCAN $$
(☑ 0577 74 14 05; www.tavernasquarcialupi.it; Via Ferruccio 26; meals €38; ☺ noon-3pm & 7-10pm Thu-Mon & noon-3pm Tue) Interesting and highly successful flavour combinations characterise the menu at this huge *taverna* (tavern) in the centre of Castellina. The handmade pasta

---

① OUTLET SHOPPING

Follow local bargain-hunters to the Valdarno area in northeast Chianti to unleash your inner fashionista (and your credit cards). Bargains from the previous season's collections can be sourced at the **Mall** (www.themall.it; Via Europa 8, Leccio Reggello; ☺ 10am-7pm, to 8pm Jun-Aug) in Leccio Regello; **Dolce & Gabbana** (☑ 055 833 13 00; www.dolce-gabbana.it; Via Pian dell'Isola 49, Località Santa Maria Maddalena, Incisa in Valdarno; ☺ 9am-7pm Mon-Sat, 10am-7pm Sun), off the SR69 near Incisa Val d'Arno; and **Prada** (☑ 0552 8 34 39; Space Factory Outlets, Via Levanella Becorpi, Località Levanella; ☺ 10.30am-7.30pm Mon-Fri & Sun, 9.30am-7.30pm Sat), off the SR69 on the southern edge of Montevarchi.

---

dishes are delicious – grab a seat on the panoramic rear terrace enjoy one with a glass or two of wine from the nearby La Castellina wine estate.

Ristorante Albergaccio TUSCAN $$$
(☑ 0577 74 10 42; www.ristorantealbergaccio.com; Via Fiorentina 63; meals €50; ☺ 12.30-2.30pm & 7.30-9.30pm, closed parts of Dec-Mar; ✍) Albergaccio bills its culinary approach as 'the territory on the table' and local seasonal produce certainly holds sway here. Once the proud possessor of a Michelin accolade, its star has waned (literally) in recent times but it's still a satisfying albeit pricey place to dine. Find it 1km northeast of Castellina on the San Donato in Poggio road.

Antica Fattoria la Castellina WINE
(☑ 0577 74 04 59; www.lacastellina.it; Via Ferruccio 28; ☺ 10am-7.30pm) The town's best-known wine shop sells wines from its La Castellina estate and also offers tastings from €5.

① Information

Castellina's **tourist office** (☑ 0577 74 13 92; www.amocastellinainchianti.it; Via Ferruccio 40; ☺ 10am-1pm Apr-Jun, 10am-1pm & 4-7 Tue-Fri July-Sep) can book visits to wineries and cellars. It also provides maps, accommodation suggestions and other information.

① Getting There & Away

BUS
Tiemme (p144) bus 125 links Castellina in Chianti with Radda in Chianti (€1.60, 10 minutes, 3-5 daily Mon-Sat) and with Siena (€3.40, 40 minutes, seven daily Mon-Sat). The most convenient bus stops are on the main road near Via delle Mura.

CAR & MOTORCYCLE
Castellina is on the Via Chiantigiana (SR222). The most convenient car park is at the southern edge of town off Via IV Novembre (€1/5 per hour/day).

Radda in Chianti

POP 1613

The age-old streets in pretty Radda in Chianti fan out from its central square, where the shields and escutcheons of the 16th-century Palazzo del Podestà add a touch of drama to the scene. A historic wine town, it's the home of the Consorzio di Chianti Classico and is an appealing if low-key base for visits to some classic Tuscan vineyards.

WORTH A TRIP

VOLPAIA

Wines, olive oils and vinegars have long been produced at wine estate **Castello di Volpaia** (☑ 0577 73 80 66; www.volpaia.it; Località Volpaia), 7km north of Radda in Chianti in the medieval hamlet of Volpaia (the name is misleading, as there's no actual castle here). Book ahead to enjoy a tasting and tour of the cellars (price on application), or purchase from the *enoteca* (noon to 7pm Thursday to Tuesday) inside the hamlet's main tower.

Post-visit, consider a light lunch of salami made by the owner's father and a glass of Volpaia's Chianti Classico or Riserva at **Bar Ucci** (☑ 0577 73 80 42; www.bar-ucci.it; Piazza Della Torre 9, Volpaia; snacks €4-8, meals €18; ⊙8am-9pm Tue-Sun); modern Tuscan cuisine using herbs and veg from the estate's organic garden at the highly regarded **Osteria Volpaia** (☑ 0577 73 80 66; www.osteriavolpaia.com; Vicolo della Torre 2, Volpaia; meals €36; ⊙12.30-3pm & 7.30-9.30pm Thu-Tue) ✦; or *cucina contadina* (food from the farmers' kitchen) on a tree-shaded terrace with sweeping views of the Chianti hills at family-run **Ristorante La Bottega** (☑ 0577 73 80 01; www.labottegadivolpaia.it; Piazza della Torre 1, Volpaia; meals €28; ⊙noon-2.30pm & 7.30-9.30pm Wed-Mon Easter-Jan).

⊙ Sights & Activities

Casa Chianti Classico   MUSEUM
(☑ 0577 73 81 87; www.chianticlassico.com; Monastery of Santa Maria al Prato, Circonvallazione Santa Maria 18; ⊙museum 11.30am-1pm & 3-6pm Mon-Sat Apr-Oct) **FREE** Occupying an 18th-century convent complex attached to a 10th-century church, this facility is operated by the Consorzio di Chianti Classico and pays homage to the region's favourite product. Book to visit the **Wine Museum** on the first floor to learn all about the history of the denomination, purchase a glass of wine (€5) and then compare your tasting notes to an expert's in a clever multimedia quiz. Or sign up for a 90-minute **wine class** (Italian or English; €35).

The complex also has a **restaurant** (meals €35; ⊙12.30-2.30 & 7.30-9.30pm Tue-Sat, 12.30-2.30pm Sun Mar-Dec) and a well-stocked **enoteca** (antipasti €8-16, pastas €10-13; ⊙11.30am-6pm Tue-Sat & 11.30-2.30pm Sun Mar-Dec). The latter has a lovely terrace overlooking vineyards – perfect for a leisurely lunch or late afternoon glass of wine. To find it, head downhill from Radda in Chianti's main piazza.

✕ Eating

La Botte di Bacco   TUSCAN $$$
(☑ 0577 73 90 08; www.ristorantelabottedibacco.it; Viale XX Settembre 23; meals €50; ⊙12.30-2.30pm & 7.30-10.30pm Fri-Wed, closed 2 weeks Nov; ✳) A long-standing favourite, this romantic choice on the main road through Radda has a traditional interior but the menu has an untraditional tinge, probably because chef Flavio D'Auria hails from Naples and isn't afraid to make unobtrusive tweaks to Tuscan classics. The impressive wine list is dominated by local drops.

⊙ Information

Tourist Office (☑ 0577 73 84 94; www.chiantiradda.it; Piazza del Castello 2; ⊙10am-1pm & 3-6.30pm summer, 10.30am-12.30pm winter) The Radda tourist office can book accommodation and tours for this pocket of Chianti, and also supplies information about walks in the area.

⊙ Getting There & Away

Radda is linked with Siena by the SP102 and with Castellina in Chianti by the SR429. **Tiemme** (p144) buses link the town with Castellina (€1.60, 10 minutes, three to five daily Mon-Sat) and with Siena (€4.20, one hour, four daily Mon-Sat). There are also services to/from Florence (€4, 95 minutes, two to four daily Monday to Saturday); you'll need to change at Lucarelli on some of these. Buses stop on Via XX Settembre (SR429) near the Monte dei Paschi di Siena bank.

Gaiole in Chianti
POP 2758

Surrounded by majestic medieval castles and atmospheric *pievi* (rural churches), this small town has few attractions but is sometimes visited en route to Castello di Brolio (p154) or Castello di Ama.

⊙ Sights & Activities

★**Castello di Ama**   SCULPTURE, WINE
(☑ 0577 74 60 69; www.castellodiama.com; Località Ama; guided tours adult/child under 16yr €15/free; ⊙by appointment) At Castello di Ama centuries-old wine-making traditions meet cutting-edge contemporary art in a 12th-century *borgo* (agricultural estate). As well as vineyards and a winery producing internationally acclaimed wines such as 'L'Apparita' merlot, the estate also features a

CHIANTI WINES

The ruby-red Chianti and Chianti Classico DOCGs have a minimum Sangiovese component: 75% for Chianti and 80% for Chianti Classico. They're undoubtedly the region's blockbuster wines, but they're not the only quality vintages produced here: the Colli dell'Etruria Centrale; Pomino; Vin Santo del Chianti and Vin Santo del Chianti Classico DOCs are top local drops too.

The biggest wine-producing estates have *cantine* (cellars) where you can taste and buy wine, but few vineyards – big or small – can be visited without reservations. For a comprehensive list and map of wine estates, buy a copy of *Le strade del Gallo Nero* (€2.50) at the tourist offices in Greve in Chianti, Radda in Chianti and Castellina in Chianti.

The Consorzio Vino Chianti Classico (www.chianticlassico.com) is a high-profile consortium of local producers; its website has more information on its members (96% of local producers), the wines themselves and related events.

boutique hotel, a restaurant and a sculpture park showcasing 14 impressive site-specific pieces by artists including Louise Bourgeois, Chen Zhen, Anish Kapoor, Kendell Geers and Daniel Buren. This can be visited on a guided tour; advance bookings essential.

Castello di Brolio   CASTLE

(☑0577 73 02 80; www.ricasoli.it; Località Madonna a Brolio; garden, chapel & crypt €5, guided tours €8; ⊙10am-5.30pm mid-Mar–Nov, guided tours 10.30am-12.30pm & 2.30-5pm Tue-Sun) The ancestral estate of the aristocratic Ricasoli family dates from the 11th century and is the oldest winery in Italy. Currently home to the 32nd baron, it opens its formal garden, panoramic terrace and museum to day trippers, who often adjourn to the excellent on-site *osteria* for lunch after a guided tour of the castle's small but fascinating museum.

Occupying three rooms in the castle's tower, the museum is dedicated to documenting the life of the extravagantly mustachioed Baron Bettino Ricasoli (1809–80), the second prime minster of the Republic of Italy and a true polymath (scientist, farmer, winemaker, statesman and businessman). A leading figure in the Risorgimento, one of his other great claims to fame is inventing

the formula for Chianti Classico that is enshrined in current DOC regulations.

The *castello*'s chapel dates from the early 14th century; below it is a crypt where generations of Ricasolis are interred. The estate produces wine and olive oil, and the huge terrace commands a spectacular view of the vineyards and olive groves.

The Classic Tour (€28, two hours) takes in the wine-making facilities and features a tasting; it runs daily from Friday to Wednesday (book online). The Vineyard Tour (€45, two hours, 3.30pm Thursday) sees you exploring three of the estate's different terroirs and sampling vintages beside the vines; advance bookings are essential.

A *bosco inglese* (English garden) surrounds the estate, in it (near the car park) you'll find the estate's Osteria del Castello (☑0577 73 02 90; osteria@ricasoli.it; meals €40; ⊙noon-2.30pm & 7-9.30pm Fri-Wed Apr-Oct; noon-2.30pm Sun-Wed plus 7-9.30pm Fri & Sat 2nd half of Mar, Nov & Dec). Just outside the estate's entrance gates, on the SP484, is a modern *cantina* (cellar; p154) where you can taste the Castello di Brolio's well-regarded Chianti Classico.

Barone Ricasoli Cantina   WINE

(Località Madonna a Brolio; ⊙10am-7pm Apr-Oct) Head to this *cantina* just outside the gates of Castello di Brolio (p154) to taste and purchase the estate's wines. One taste of an entry-level wine is included in entry tickets to the castle; you can taste three more for €5. Consider purchasing a bottle of the estate's flagship wine, the Chianti Classico DOCG Gran Selezione, to enjoy at a later date.

Parco Sculture del Chianti   SCULPTURE

(Chianti Sculpture Park; ☑0577 35 71 51; www.chiantisculpturepark.it; Località La Fornace; adult/child €10/5; ⊙10am-dusk; 🚶) Site-specific contemporary artworks created by artists from 24 countries are scattered throughout this 7-hectare wood, including a glass labyrinth by Jeff Saward that children in particular will adore. Between June and August weekly sunset jazz and opera concerts are staged in the park's marble-and-granite amphitheatre.

The park is 11km southwest of Gaiole in Chianti. When here, be sure to visit the neighbouring village of Pievasciata, which is full of site-specific outdoor artworks.

Eating

The in-house Il Pievano restaurant in the ritzy Hotel Castello di Spaltenna (www.spaltenna.it) on the edge of Gaiole is one of the very few restaurants in Chianti to possess a Michelin star. Outside town, the best options are the *osteria* at the Castello di Brolio (p154) and the restaurant at Castello di Ama (☑0577 74 61 91; www.castellodiama.com; Castello di Ama, Località Ama; meals €30; ⊙noon-3pm & 7-9pm Wed-Mon).

ⓘ Getting There & Away

Gaiole is on the SP408 between Siena and Montevarchi. **Tiemme** (p144) bus 127 travels between Gaiole and Via Lombardi behind Siena's railway station (€1.60, 40 minutes, nine daily Mon-Sat). The bus stop is on the main road, opposite the elementary school.

SAN GIMIGNANO

POP 7820

As you crest the nearby hills, the 14 towers of the walled town of San Gimignano rise up like a medieval Manhattan. Originally an Etruscan village, the settlement was named after the bishop of Modena, San Gimignano, who is said to have saved the city from Attila the Hun. It became a *comune* (local government) in 1199, prospering in part because of its location on the Via Francigena. Building a tower taller than their neighbours' (there were originally 72) became a popular way for prominent families to flaunt their power and wealth. In 1348 plague wiped out much of the population and weakened the local economy, leading to the town's submission to Florence in 1353. Today, not even the plague would deter the swarms of summer day trippers, who are lured by a palpable sense of history, intact medieval streetscapes and enchanting rural setting.

◉ Sights

San Gimignano's triangular Piazza della Cisterna is named after the 13th-century cistern at its centre. In Piazza del Duomo, the cathedral looks across to the late-13th-century Palazzo Vecchio del Podestà (Piazza del Duomo) and its tower, the Torre della Rognosa.

★ Collegiata   CHURCH
(Duomo; Basilica di Santa Maria Assunta; ☑0577 94 01 52; www.duomosangimignano.it; Piazza del Duomo; adult/reduced €4/2; ⊙10am-7pm Mon-Sat, 12.30-7pm Sun summer, 10am-4.30pm Mon-Sat, 12.30-4.30pm Sun winter) Parts of San Gimignano's Romanesque cathedral were built in the second half of the 11th century, but its remarkably vivid frescoes, depicting episodes from the Old and New Testaments, date from the 14th century. Look out, too, for

the Cappella di Santa Fina, near the main altar – a Renaissance chapel adorned with naive and touching frescoes by Domenico Ghirlandaio depicting the life of one of the town's patron saints. These featured in Franco Zeffirelli's 1999 film *Tea with Mussolini*.

Entry is via the side stairs and through a loggia that was originally covered and functioned as the baptistry. Once in the main space, face the altar and look to your left (south). On the wall are scenes from Genesis and the Old Testament by Bartolo di Fredi, dating from around 1367. The top row runs from the creation of the world through to the forbidden-fruit scene. This leads to the next level and fresco, the expulsion of Adam and Eve from the Garden of Eden, which sustained some damage in WWII. Further scenes include Cain killing Abel, and the stories of Noah's ark and Joseph's coat. The last level continues with the tale of Moses leading the Jews out of Egypt, and the story of Job.

On the right (north) wall are scenes from the New Testament by the workshop of Simone Martini (probably led by Lippo Memmi, Martini's brother-in-law), which were completed in 1336. Again, the frescoes are spread over three levels, starting in the six lunettes at the top. Starting with the Annunciation, the panels work through episodes such as the Epiphany, the presentation of Christ in the temple and the massacre of the innocents on Herod's orders. The subsequent panels on the lower levels summarise the life and death of Christ, the Resurrection and so on. Again, some have sustained damage, but most are in good condition.

On the inside wall of the front facade, extending onto adjoining walls, is Taddeo

SIENA & CENTRAL TUSCANY SAN GIMIGNANO

ⓘ **CENT SAVERS**
....

Three combined tickets can save you money in San Gimignano:

Civic Museums Ticket (adult/reduced €9/7) Gives admission to the Palazzo Comunale (p156) and its attractions, the Polo Museale Santa Chiara (p157) and San Lorenzo in Ponte (p157). Valid 48 hours; one visit per site.

San Gimignano Pass (adult/child €13/10) Includes all of the above plus the Collegiata and Museo d'Arte Sacra (p158). Valid 48 hours; one visit per site.

Collegiata & Museo d'Arte Sacra (adult/child €6/3)

San Gimignano

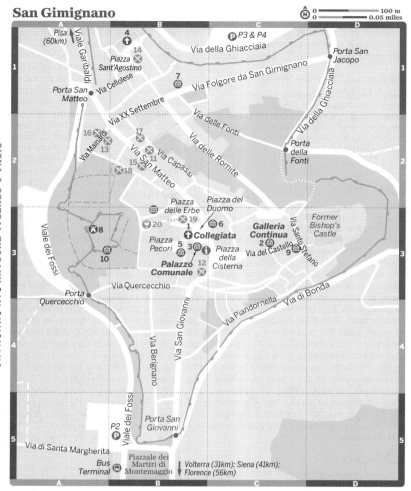

di Bartolo's striking depiction of the Last Judgment – on the upper-left side is a fresco depicting *Paradiso* (Heaven) and on the upper-right *Inferno* (Hell). The fresco of San Sebastian under them is by Benozzo Gozzoli.

The church is commonly known as the 'Collegiata', a reference to the college of priests that originally managed it.

★ **Palazzo Comunale**   MUSEUM
(⌨ 0577 99 03 12; www.sangimignanomusei.it; Piazza del Duomo 2; combined Civic Museums ticket adult/reduced €9/7; ⊘ 10am-7.30pm summer, 11am-5.30pm winter) The 13th-century Palazzo Comunale has always been the centre of San Gimigna-

no's local government; its magnificently frescoed Sala di Dante is where the great poet addressed the town's council in 1299 and its Camera del Podestà and Pinacoteca (Art Gallery) once housed government offices – now they are are home to wonderful artworks. Be sure to climb the 218 steps of the *palazzo*'s 54m Torre Grossa for a spectacular view over the town and surrounding countryside.

The Sala di Dante (also known as the Sala del Consiglio) is home to Lippo Memmi's early-14th-century *Maestà*, which portrays the enthroned Virgin and Child surrounded by angels, saints and local dignitaries – the kneeling noble in red-and-black stripes was

San Gimignano

the *podestà* (magistrate) of the time. Other frescoes portray jousts, hunting scenes and castles. Gadget fans are likely to enjoy the augmented reality glasses that superimpose digital medieval characters over the frescoes; hire them from the gift shop (€5).

Upstairs is the Camera del Podestà with its meticulously restored and slightly saucy cycle of frescoes by Memmo di Filippuccio – in this morality tale the rewards of marriage are shown in the scenes of the husband and wife naked in the bath and in bed. On the other side of the staircase are rooms housing the town's small but charming *pinacoteca*. Its highlights include two large *Annunciation* panels (1482) by Filippino Lippi; a huge altarpiece (1511) by Pinturicchio; *Madonna of Humility Worshipped by Two Saints* (1466) and *Madonna and Child with Saints* (1466) by Benozzo Gozzoli; and an altarpiece by Taddeo di Bartolo (1401) illustrating the life of St Gimignano.

⭐ Galleria Continua   GALLERY
(🖉0577 94 31 34; www.galleriacontinua.com; Via del Castello 11; ⊙10am-1pm & 2-7pm) FREE It may seem strange to highlight contemporary art in this medieval time capsule of a town, but there's good reason to do so. This is one of the best commercial art galleries in Europe, showing the work of big-name artists such as Ai Weiwei, Daniel Buren, Antony Gormley and Mona Hatoum. Spread over four venues (an old cinema, a medieval tower, a vaulted cellar and an apartment on Piazza della Cisterna), it's one of San Gimignano's most compelling attractions.

San Lorenzo in Ponte   MUSEUM
(🖉0577 28 63 00; www.sangimignanomusei.it; Via del Castello; combined Civic Museums ticket adult/

reduced €9/7; ⊙10am-7.30pm summer, 11am-5.30pm winter) The name of this 13th-century church refers to its original location next to a drawbridge (*ponte* means bridge) leading to the bishop's castle. The drawbridge has long since gone, but the castle still stands (now empty, it has functioned as a monastery and as a prison). Inside, a cycle of recently restored frescoes depicts scenes of St Benedict and a large 15th-century fresco by Cenni di Francesco di Ser Cenni shows Christ in Glory with the Virgin and 12 apostles.

Chiesa di Sant'Agostino   CHURCH
(Piazza Sant'Agostino; ⊙10am-noon & 3-7pm summer, to 6pm & closed Mon morning winter) FREE This late-13th-century church is best known for Benozzo Gozzoli's charming fresco cycle (1464–65) illustrating the life of St Augustine. You'll find it in the choir behind the altar. Gozzoli also painted the fresco featuring San Sebastian on the north wall, which shows the saint protecting the citizens of San Gimignano during the 1464 plague. What makes the image highly unusual is that he's helped by a bare-breasted Virgin Mary; this symbolises her maternal love for humanity.

Polo Museale Santa Chiara   MUSEUM
(Santa Chiara Museum Centre; 🖉0577 94 03 48; www.sangimignanomusei.it; Via Folgore da San Gimignano 11; combined Civic Museums ticket adult/reduced €9/7; ⊙10am-7.30pm summer, 11am-5.30pm winter) There are three museums in this complex. The ground floor is home to a part-reconstructed 15th- to 18th-century pharmacy known as the Speziera di Santa Fina, which features shelves stacked with brightly painted ceramic jars and half-empty potion bottles. Next to it is an Archaeological Museum showcasing Roman finds,

including tiny bronze figurines, etched mirrors and piles of brightly coloured mosaic tiles. Upstairs, the Gallery of Modern and Contemporary Art features works by Italian artists.

Vernaccia Wine Experience   MUSEUM

(📞 0577 94 12 67; www.sangimignanomuseo vernaccia.com; Via della Rocca 1; ⏰ 11.30am-6.30pm Apr-Oct) FREE San Gimignano's famous wine, Vernaccia, is celebrated in this small museum next to the rocca (fortress; Via della Rocca; ⏰ 24hr) FREE. Interactive exhibits on the 1st floor trace the history of the product and the surrounding land; there's also a ground-floor *enoteca* where you can taste Vernaccia and other varietals produced in the region (per taste €1-6) or buy a glass to enjoy on a terrace with a panoramic view.

Museo d'Arte Sacra   MUSEUM

(📞 0577 94 01 52; www.duomosangimignano.it; Piazza Pecori 1; adult/child €3.50/2; ⏰ 10am-7pm Mon-Sat, 12.30-7pm Sun summer, 10am-4.30pm Mon-Sat, 12.30-4.30pm Sun winter) Works of medieval religious art from San Gimignano's key churches are on display in this modest museum. Particularly beautiful items made from precious metals include crafted chalices and thuribles (censers); there are also some exquisitely embroidered textiles.

🏃 Activities

The tourist office takes bookings for a range of English-language guided nature walks amid the hills surrounding San Gimignano, along 6km to 9km stretches of the Via Francigena and through the Riserva Naturale di Castelvecchio to the southwest of town. These run according to demand and cost between €15 and €25.

★ Vernaccia Master Class   WINE

(Via della Rocca 1; €25; ⏰ noon, 4pm & 6pm) Organised by the Vernaccia Wine Experience, these daily master classes include a guided tour of the 1st-floor Vernaccia exhibition and a tasting of four wines accompanied by typical local foods. Book through the tourist office.

👉 Tours

★ Vernaccia di San Gimignano Vineyard Visit   WINE

(€20; ⏰ 5-7pm Tue & Thu Apr-Oct) These highly enjoyable tastings of local foods and wines are delivered by English-language guides. Book at the tourist office (p159) at least a day in advance.

🎊 Festivals & Events

Ferie delle Messi   CULTURAL

(www.cavalieridisantafina.it; ⏰ 3rd weekend Jun) San Gimignano's medieval past is evoked through re-enacted battles, archery contests and plays.

Festival Barocco di San Gimignano   MUSIC

(www.sangimignano.com; ⏰ Sep-Oct) A high-quality season of baroque music concerts staged in the historic Teatro Leggieri.

🍴 Eating & Drinking

Many of San Gimignano's restaurants are solely geared to the tourist trade and serve mediocre food at inflated prices. Those that have higher standards tend to focus on fresh local produce, including the town's famous *zafferano* (saffron). You can purchase meat, vegetables, fish and takeaway food at the Thursday morning market (Piazza delle Erbe; ⏰ 8am-1.30pm) held in and around Piazzas Cisterna, Duomo and Erbe.

★ Gelateria Dondoli   GELATO $

(📞 0577 94 22 44; www.gelateriadipiazza.com; Piazza della Cisterna 4; gelato €2.20-6; ⏰ 9am-11pm summer, to 7.30pm winter, closed mid-Dec–mid-Feb) Think of it less as ice cream, more as art. Former gelato world champion Sergio Dondoli is a member of Italy's Ice Cream World Championship team and among his most famous creations are Crema di Santa Fina (saffron cream) gelato and Vernaccia sorbet. His creations are so delicious that some devotees even sign up for a two-hour gelato-making workshop (€400).

Dal Bertelli   SANDWICHES $

(📞 348 3181907; Via Capassi 30; panini €4-6, glasses of wine €3; ⏰ 1-7pm Apr-Dec) The Bertelli family has lived in San Gimignano since 1779, and its current patriarch is fiercely proud of both his heritage and his sandwiches. Salami, cheese, bread and wine are sourced from local artisan-producers and is sold in generous portions in a determinedly un-gentrified space with marble work surfaces, wooden shelves and curious agricultural implements dangling from stone walls.

D!Vineria   WINE BAR

(📞 0577 94 30 41; www.divineria.it; Via della Rocca 2c; ⏰ 10am-10pm mid-Mar–Oct) Massimo Delli, the owner of this tiny wine bar on the street leading up to the rocca (p158), will enthusiastically suggest local wines to try (consider ordering Montenidoli's Fiore or Rubicini's

Etherea – both excellent Vernaccias). He also stocks a good range of local salami and cheese (*taglieri* €18).

⭐ **Ristorante La Mandragola**   TUSCAN **$$**
(☑ 348 3023766; www.locandalamandragola.it; Via Diaccetto 26; meals €35; ☺ noon-3pm & 7-10pm; 🔊) Nestled beneath the crumbling walls of the rocca (p158), La Mandragola (The Mandrake) is deservedly popular – book ahead, especially if you're keen to dine in the gorgeous courtyard. It's not exactly tourist-free, but the welcome is genuine and the food is delicious, especially the handmade pasta dishes, which feature unusual sauces and stuffings. The set menus (€15-25) offer excellent value.

Locanda Sant'Agostino   TUSCAN **$$**
(☑ 0577 94 31 41; Piazza Sant'Agostino 15; meals €35, pizza €8-10; ☺ noon-3pm & 7-10pm Thu-Tue) It's a bit like eating in an Italian grandmother's kitchen: there's a family vibe, knick-knacks stack the shelves and the food is tasty. Homemade *pici* (thick, hand-rolled pasta) and tomato-slathered pizza are popular choices. In summer, seating on the piazza is hotly contested.

Olivieri Bistrot   MODERN ITALIAN **$$**
(☑ 0577 94 07 90; Via San Matteo 55; meals €30; ☺ 11am-10pm Tue-Sun, closed Tue winter) There's nothing traditional about this newcomer to the San Gimignano dining scene. Located on the major pedestrian spine, it has an attractive modern interior, friendly staff and a menu incorporating plenty of twists on Tuscan favourites. We love the homemade bread served with good-quality olive oil, and we like the fact that it serves *merende* (afternoon snacks) between meal services.

Osteria delle Catene   TUSCAN **$$**
(☑ 0577 94 19 66; www.osteriadellecatene.it; Via Mainardi 18; set menus €21-29; ☺ noon-2pm & 7-10pm Mon, Tue & Thur-Sat, noon-3pm Sun) 'The Prison' is as popular with San Gimignano locals as it is with visitors, something that can't be said of many places in this tourist-driven town. The menu is full of delightful surprises – dishes are seasonally driven and many utilise local saffron and Vernaccia wine.

La Mangiatoia   TUSCAN **$$**
(☑ 0577 94 10 94; Via Mainardi 5; meals €36; ☺ 12.30-2.30pm & 7.30-9.30pm Wed-Mon) There's confidence in their craft among the chefs at La Mangiatoia – they offer only five options in each antipasto, *primo* and *secondo*. Luck-

THE VIA FRANCIGENA

Devise a holiday with a difference by walking or driving parts of the Via Francigena, a medieval pilgrimage route connecting Canterbury with Rome. In Central Tuscany, the route goes past or through towns including San Gimignano, Monteriggioni, San Quirico d'Orcia and Radicòfani. Touring Club Italiano publishes *Via Francigena Toscana* (€8), an English-language guide and hiking map (1:175,000) – you'll find it for sale in tourist offices and bookshops throughout the region. Also check www.viafrancigenatoscana.org (in Italian) or www.viefrancigene.org/en/. The latter is packed with information and has an interactive map.

ily they're all good, with assured treatments of traditional Tuscan ingredients such as beef, venison and wild boar.

Perucà   TUSCAN **$$**
(☑ 0577 94 31 36; www.peruca.eu; Via Capassi 16; meals €35; ☺ 12-2.30pm & 7-10.30pm Fri-Wed) The owner is as knowledgeable about regional food and wine as she is enthusiastic, and the menu offers plenty of dishes inspired by local ingredients – try the duck breast with San Gimignano beer and plum sauce, or the rabbit with saffron and Vernaccia.

ℹ Information

San Gimignano's **tourist office** (☑ 0577 94 00 08; www.sangimignano.com; Piazza del Duomo 1; ☺ 10am-1pm & 3-7pm summer, 10am-1pm & 2-6pm winter) organises tours, supplies maps and can book accommodation. It also has information on the Strada del Vino Vernaccia di San Gimignano (Wine Road of the Vernaccia di San Gimignano).

ℹ Getting There & Away

BUS

San Gimignano's **bus station** (Piazzale dei Martiri di Montemaggio) is next to the Carabinieri (Police Station) at Porta San Giovanni. The tourist office (p159) sells bus tickets.

Florence (€6.80, 1¼ to two hours, 14 daily) Change at Poggibonsi.

Siena (€6, one to 1½ hours, 10 daily Monday to Saturday)

Monteriggioni (€4.20, 55 minutes, eight daily Monday to Saturday)

1. Collegiata (p155), San Gimignano 2. Detail of the *Maestà*
3. Abbazia di Sant'Antimo interior 4. Torre del Mangia and
Palazzo Pubblico (p134), Siena

Medieval Masterpieces

We reckon the Middle Ages get a bad rap in the history books. This period may have been blighted by famines, plagues and wars, but it also saw an extraordinary flowering of art and architecture. Cities such as Siena, San Gimignano and Volterra are full of masterpieces dating from this time.

Palazzo Pubblico, Siena

Built on the cusp of the Middle Ages and the Renaissance, Siena's city hall (p134) is a triumph of Gothic secular architecture. Inside, the Museo Civico (p132) showcases a collection that is modest in size but monumental in quality.

Abbazia di Sant'Antimo

Benedictine monks have been performing Gregorian chants in this Romanesque abbey (p167) near Montalcino ever since the Middle Ages. Dating back to the time of Charlemagne, its austere beauty and idyllic setting make it an essential stop on every itinerary.

Collegiata, San Gimignano

Don't be fooled by its modest facade. Inside, the walls of this Romanesque cathedral (p155) are adorned with brightly coloured frescoes resembling a vast medieval comic strip.

Duccio di Buoninsegna's *Maestà*, Siena

Originally displayed in Siena's *duomo* (cathedral) and now the prize exhibit in the Museo dell'Opera (p131), Duccio's altarpiece portrays the Virgin surrounded by angels, saints and prominent Sienese citizens of the period.

Head to Colle di Val d'Elsa (€3.40, 35 minutes) to take a connecting bus to Volterra (€2.75, 50 minutes). These run four times daily from Monday to Saturday.

CAR & MOTORCYCLE

To arrive in San Gimignano from Florence and Siena, take the Siena–Florence autostrada, then the SR2 and finally the SP1 from Poggibonsi Nord. From Volterra, take the SR68 east and follow the turn-off signs north to San Gimignano on the SP47.

Parking is expensive here. The cheapest option (€1.50/6 per hour/24 hours) is at Parcheggio Giubileo (P1) on the southern edge of town; the most convenient is at Parcheggio Montemaggio (P2) next to Porta San Giovanni (€2/20 per hour/24 hours).

TRAIN

The closest train station to San Gimignano is Poggibonsi (by bus €2.50, 30 minutes, frequent).

Monteriggioni

POP 9810

The local tourism office markets Monteriggioni as a 'Gateway to the Middle Ages', and though hackneyed, the description fits. Enclosed by monumental walls with ramparts and 14 watchtowers, the physical structure of this fortified village has changed little since it was established in the 13th century and became a popular stop on the Via Francigena pilgrim trail. Sights include the walls, a small armour museum and the 13th-century Church of Santa Maria Assunta. There are also plenty of touristy boutiques to browse. In June and July, the streets are full of colourfully clad characters participating in one of Italy's oldest medieval festivals.

◎ Sights

Ramparts   CASTLE

(adult/child under 8yr €3/free; ⊘ 9.30am-1.30pm & 2-7.30pm summer, to 6pm mid–Sep-Oct, closed Tue winter) Built by the Republic of Siena in the 13th century as a defensive outpost against Florence, Monteriggioni's castle resisted a number of sieges and attacks but fell into disrepair after Siena fell to its rival in the 16th century. Reconstructed in the 19th century, the ramparts can now be accessed from two locations within the town and offer wonderful views over the countryside.

The ticket also includes entry to the four-room armour museum in the tourist office building.

Abbadia a Isola   ABBEY

(⊘ 335 6651581; www.badiaisola.it; SP74; ⊘ 9am-1pm Mon-Fri, 9am-1pm & 3-6pm Sat & Sun summer) FREE The name ('isola' means island) reflects the fact that until the 18th century, this 11th-century abbey was surrounded by swampland. It has hosted many pilgrims on the Via Francigena over the centuries and a modern hostel continues that tradition. Its Chiesa di San Salvatore features a 14th-century fresco by Taddeo di Bartolo and a polyptych by 15th-century painter Sano di Pietro. An Etruscan sarcophagus to the right of the altar contains the bones of St Chirino, the church's patron saint.

The abbey is 4km from the Monteriggioni fortress, and it is possible to walk between the two on an original stretch of the Via Francigena.

✦ Festivals & Events

Medieval Festival   CARNIVAL

(Festa Medievale; ⊘ 0577 30 48 34; www.monteriggionimedievale.com; daily pass adult/reduced €12/10; ⊘ Jun & Jul) This popular festival includes feasts, jousts, a market, musical performances, falconry and battle re-enactments.

✗ Eating

★ **Bar dell'Orso**   TUSCAN $

(⊘ 0577 30 50 74; www.bardellorso.it; Via Cassia Nord 23, La Colonna di Monteriggioni; meals €24, panino €4; ⊘ 5am-midnight) Known throughout the region for the affordability and excellence of its food, the Bear Bar bustles from morning to night and is a great place to grab a quick *panino* or a lunch of handmade pasta or hearty stew. Later in the day, order a *merende* (afternoon snack) of cured meats, cheese and pickled vegetables – best enjoyed with a glass of *vino*.

Antico Travaglio   TUSCAN $$

(⊘ 0577 30 47 18; www.anticotravaglio-monteriggioni.com; Piazza Roma 6a; meals €39; ⊘ closed Nov-Mar) Boasting seating on the main piazza, on a rear terrace and in a former blacksmith's forge and stable, this sprawling business place has multiple strings to its bow: it's a restaurant, *gelateria*, bar, cafe and social hub. The homemade pasta and gelato are renowned, and service is both friendly and efficient.

❶ Information

The **tourist office** (⊘ 0577 30 48 34; www.monteriggioniturismo.it; Piazza Roma 23; ⊘ 9.30-1.30 & 2-7.30pm daily summer, 10am-1.30pm &

ABBAZIA DI SAN GALGANO

About 45km southwest of Siena via the SS73 are the evocative ruins of the 13th-century Cistercian Abbazia di San Galgano (www.sangalgano.info; San Galgano; adult/reduced €2/1; ⊙9am-7pm summer, 9.30-5.30pm winter), in its day one of the country's finest Gothic buildings. Today, the abbey's roofless ruins are a compelling sight, with remarkably intact walls interspersed with soaring arches and empty, round spaces where the windows would have been.

On a hill overlooking the abbey is the tiny, round Romanesque Cappella di Monte Siepi, home to badly preserved frescoes by Ambrogio Lorenzetti depicting the life of local soldier and saint, San Galgano, who lived his last years here as a hermit.

Near the approach to the abbey is a *fattoria* (farmhouse) with a cafe (*panino* €4 to €5) and restaurant (meals €24).

If you are heading towards Siena, Montalcino, Pienza or Montepulciano after your visit here, be sure to take the SS73 south and then veer east onto the SP delle Pinete (direction San Lorenzo a Merse), a scenic drive through protected forest.

2-4pm Wed-Mon winter) inside Monteriggioni's walls can supply plenty of information about the town and surrounding area

ⓘ Getting There & Away

BUS

Tiemme (p144) buses link Monteriggioni with Florence (€6.10, 75 minutes, frequent services Monday to Saturday, two daily Sunday), San Gimignano (€4.20, 55 minutes, eight daily Monday to Saturday) and Siena (€2.50, 25 minutes, frequent services Monday to Saturday), stopping at the roundabout at Colonna Di Monteriggioni.

TRAIN

Trains between Monteriggioni and Siena (€2.60, 15 minutes, hourly) stop at Castellina Scala, on the SR2 and 2.6km from the castle. Change at Empoli for Florence.

VOLTERRA

POP 10,519

Volterra's well-preserved medieval ramparts give the windswept town a proud, forbidding air that author Stephenie Meyer deemed ideal for the discriminating tastes of the planet's principal vampire coven in her wildly popular *Twilight* series. Fortunately, the reality is considerably more welcoming, as a wander through the winding cobbled streets attests.

History

The Etruscan settlement of Velathri was an important trading centre and senior partner of the Dodecapolis group of Etruscan cities. It's believed that as many as 25,000 people

lived here in its Etruscan heyday. Partly because of the surrounding inhospitable terrain, the city was among the last to succumb to Rome – it was absorbed into the Roman confederation around 260 BC and renamed Volaterrae. The bulk of the old city was raised in the 12th and 13th centuries under a fiercely independent free *comune* (city-state). The city first entered Florence's orbit in 1361, but the people of Volterra fought hard against Medici rule – their rebellion was brought to a brutal end when Lorenzo il Magnifico's soldiers sacked the city in 1472. There was another rebellion in 1530 – again brutally crushed by the Florentines – but Volterra would never again achieve self-government, moving from Florentine rule to that of the Grand Duchy of Tuscany before Italian unification in 1860.

Since Etruscan times the people of Volterra have been famous for carving alabaster mined from nearby quarries, artistry still in evidence locally today.

◉ Sights & Activities

The Volterra Card (adult/reduced/family €14/12/22, valid 72hr) gives admission to Volterra's Museo Etrusco Guarnacci, the Pinacoteca Comunale (p164), Ecomuseo dell'Alabastro (p165), Palazzo dei Priori (Piazza dei Priori; adult/reduced €5/3; ⊙10.30am-5.30pm summer, 10am-4.30pm Sat & Sun winter), Acropoli and Teatro Romano. It's available at all of the museums.

★ Museo Etrusco Guarnacci   MUSEUM
(☎0588 8 63 47; Via Don Minzoni 15; adult/reduced €8/6; ⊙9am-7pm summer, 10am-4.30pm winter) The vast collection of artefacts exhibited here makes this one of Italy's most impressive

Volterra

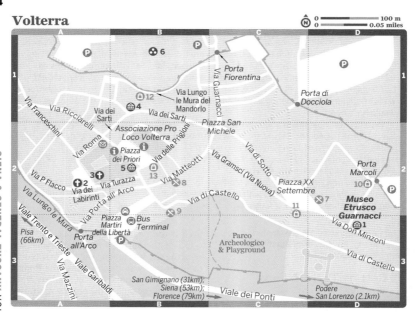

Volterra

Etruscan collections. Found locally, they include some 600 funerary urns carved mainly from alabaster and tufa – perhaps the pick is the Urn of the Sposi, a strikingly realistic terracotta rendering of an elderly couple. The finds are displayed according to subject and era; the best examples (those dating from later periods) are on the 2nd and 3rd floors.

Make sure you track down the crested helmet excavated from the Tomba del Guerruccia at nearby Poggio alle Croci; and the *L'Ombra della Sera (Shadow of the Evening)*, an elongated bronze nude figurine that bears a striking resemblance to the work of the Swiss sculptor Alberto Giacometti.

**Cattedrale di Santa
Maria Assunta**　　　　　　　　　CATHEDRAL
(Duomo di Volterra; Piazza San Giovanni; ☺ 8am-noon & 2-6pm summer, to 5pm winter) A handsome coffered ceiling is the most striking single feature of Volterra's *duomo,* which was built in the 12th and 13th centuries and remodelled in the 16th. The **Chapel of Our Lady of Sorrows**, on the first chapel to the left as you enter from Piazza San Giovanni, has two sculptures by Andrea della Robbia and a small fresco of the *Procession of the Magi* by Benozzo Gozzoli. In front of the *duomo,* is a 13th-century **baptistry** (☺ 8am-noon & 2-6pm summer, to 5pm winter) featuring a Sansovino font (1502).

Pinacoteca Comunale　　　　　　GALLERY
(📞 0588 8 75 80; Via dei Sarti 1; adult/reduced €8/6; ☺ 9am-7pm summer, 10am-4.30pm winter) Local, Sienese and Florentine art holds sway in this modest collection in the Palazzo Mi-

nucci Solaini. Taddeo di Bartolo's *Madonna Enthroned with Child* (1411) is exquisite, while Rosso Fiorentino's *Deposition from the Cross* (1521) appears strikingly modern. The gallery shares an entrance with the Ecomuseo dell'Alabastro.

Ecomuseo dell'Alabastro   MUSEUM
(✍ 0588 8 63 47; Via dei Sarti 1; adult/reduced €8/6; ⊙ 9am-7pm summer, 10am-4.30pm winter) As befits a town that's hewn the precious material from nearby quarries since Etruscan times, Volterra is the proud possessor of an alabaster museum. It's an intriguing exploration of everything related to the rock, from production and working to commercialisation. Contemporary creations feature strongly; there are also choice examples from Etruscan times onwards, as well as a re-created artisan's workshop.

Roman Theatre   ARCHAEOLOGICAL SITE
(✍ 0588 8 63 47; Via Francesco Ferrucci; adult/reduced €5/3; ⊙ 10.30am-5.30pm summer, 10am-4.30pm Sat & Sun winter) The grassy ranks of seating and towering columns of Italy's finest and best-preserved Roman theatre makes this a particularly evocative archaeological site. It was commissioned in the 1st century BC and could hold up to 2000 spectators. Today the *cavea* (sloping seating area), orchestra pit and stage are still clearly discernible. Note that there's also a great – and free – view of the theatre from Via Lungo Le Mura del Mandorlo.

👉 Tours

Volterra Walking Tour   WALKING
(✍ 347 1435004; www.volterrawalkingtour.com; €10; ⊙ 12.30pm Mon & Wed, 6pm Tue, Thu-Sun Apr-Jul & Sep-Oct) An enjoyable one-hour English-language exploration of the city's Etruscan, Roman and Medieval past leaves from Piazza Martiri della Libertà. Bookings aren't necessary but tours only commence with a three-person/€30 minimum; payment is cash only.

🎊 Festivals & Events

Volterra AD 1398   CULTURAL
(www.volterra1398.it; day pass adult/reduced €10/6; ⊙ 3rd & 4th Sun Aug) The citizens of Volterra roll back the calendar some 600 years, take to the streets in period costume and celebrate all the fun of a medieval fair.

🍴 Eating & Drinking

Decent dining options are somewhat limited in Volterra. Those that we have recommended tend to serve local specialities including white Marzuolo truffles, mushrooms (porcini and ovuli), *zuppa volterrana* (thick vegetable and bread soup), *pappardelle* with hare or wild boar sauce, *trippa alla volterrana* (tripe cooked with tomato, sausage and herbs) and *ossi di morto* (bones of the dead) almond biscuits.

⭐ **L'Incontro**   CAFE $
(✍ 0588 8 05 00; Via Matteotti 18; panini €1.80-3.50, biscuits €1.50-2.50; ⊙ 6am-midnight, closed Wed winter; 🛜) L'Incontro's rear *salone* is a top spot to grab a quick antipasto plate or *panino* for lunch, and its front bar area is always crowded with locals enjoying a coffee or *aperitivo*. The house-baked biscuits are noteworthy – try the chewy and nutty *brutti mai buoni* ('ugly but good') or their alabaster-coloured cousin, *ossi di morto* (bones of the dead).

La Carabaccia   TUSCAN $$
(✍ 0588 8 62 39; www.lacarabacciavolterra.it; Piazza XX Settembre 4-5; meals €25; ⊙ 12.30-2.30pm Tue-Sat & 12.30-2.30pm summer, 12.30-2.30pm Tue-Thu & Sun & 12.30-2.30pm & 7.30-9pm Fri & Sat winter; 🛜🌿) Mother and daughters Sara, Ilaria and Patrizia have put their heart and soul into this charming trattoria with a country-style interior and attractive front terrace. Named after a humble Tuscan vegetable soup (one of the specialities of the house), it's the city's best lunch option. The small seasonal menu changes daily and always features fish on Fridays.

Ristorante-Enoteca Del Duca   TUSCAN $$$
(✍ 0588 8 15 10; www.enoteca-delduca-ristorante.it; Via di Castello 2; meals €45; ⊙ 12.30-3pm & 7.30-10pm Wed-Mon, closed Jan-early Mar; 🌿) Volterra's acclaimed fine-dining establishment serves traditional Tuscan dishes on well-spaced tables in its vaulted 15th-century dining areas; there's also a lovely rear courtyard. The wine list is dominated by tipples from the owner's Marcampo vineyard, but also includes some pricey IGTs. The attached *enoteca* offers simple and well-priced dishes (€8-15) at lunch.

🛍 Shopping

Volterra's centuries-old heritage as an alabaster-mining and -working town ensures plenty of shops specialise in hand-carved alabaster items. The **Società Cooperativa Artieri Alabastro** (✍ 0588 8 61 35; www.artieri alabastro.it; Piazza dei Priori 4-5; ⊙ 10am-7pm) showcases the impressive work of 23 local alabaster artisans in a roomy town-centre shop. To watch alabaster being carved, head to **Alab'Arte** (✍ 340 7187189, 340 9816908;

www.alabarte.com; Via Orti di San Agostino 28; ⊙10am-12.30pm & 3-6pm Mon-Sat).

For more information about artisans in Volterra, see www.arteinbottegavolterra.it.

Boutique del Tartufo   FOOD
(☑348 7121883; www.boutiquedeltartufo.it; Vicolo Ormanni 1; ⊙10.30am-7.30pm Wed-Mon summer, 10.30-12.30 & 2.30-6.30pm winter) Stefania Socchi's husband is a professional truffle hunter, and sources the tasty fungi that are used to produce the products sold in her shop just off Piazza XX Settembre. Purchase whole truffles or opt for honey, polenta, pasta, oil or pastes made or infused with them. You can also order a *panino* made with truffle paste or truffle-infused cheese.

Email trufflehunting@boutiquedeltartufo. it to enquire about the possibility of going on a truffle hunt with Stefania's husband and his dog – this is sometimes possible.

Fabula Etrusca   JEWELLERY
(☑0588 8 74 01; www.fabulaetrusca.it; Via Lungo Le Mura del Mandorlo 10; ⊙10am-7pm Easter-Christmas) Distinctive pieces in 18-carat gold – many based on Etruscan designs – are handmade in this workshop on Volterra's northern walls.

ℹ Information

Volterra's extremely efficient **tourist office** (☑0588 8 60 99; www.volterratur.it; Piazza dei Priori 19; ⊙9.30am-1pm & 2-6pm) provides free maps, offers a free hotel-booking service and rents out an audioguide tour of the town (€5).

The equally helpful, volunteer-run **Associazione Pro Loco Volterra** (☑0588 8 61 50; www.provolterra.it; Piazza dei Priori 10; ⊙9am-12.30pm & 2.30pm Mon-Sat, 9am-12.30pm Sun) gives tourist advice, sells bus tickets and provides luggage storage (2hr/extra hr/day €3/1/6).

ℹ Getting There & Around

BUS
Volterra's **bus station** (Piazza Martiri della Libertà) is in Piazza Martiri della Libertà. Buy tickets at *tabacchi* or the volunteer-run Associazione Pro Loco Volterra (p166) office. Note bus services are greatly reduced on Sundays.

CTT (☑800 570530; www.pisa.cttnord.it) buses connect Volterra with Pisa (€5.50, two hours, up to 10 Monday to Saturday) via Pontedera (€3.85).

You'll need to go to Colle di Val d'Elsa (€2.75, 50 minutes, four Monday to Saturday) to catch one of four connecting Tiemme (p144) services (Monday to Saturday) to San Gimignano (€3.40,

35 minutes), Siena (€3.40, two hours) or Florence (€5.60, two hours).

CAR & MOTORCYCLE
Volterra is accessed via the SR68, which runs between Cecina on the coast and Colle di Val d'Elsa, just off the Siena–Florence autostrada.

A ZTL (Limited Traffic Zone) applies in the historic centre. The most convenient car park is beneath Piazza Martiri della Libertà (€1.80/15 per hour/day). Whether charges apply in other car parks encircling the town is seasonal and subject to change. The tourist office can give updates.

TAXI
Taxi rank (Piazza Martiri della Libertà)

VAL D'ORCIA

The picturesque agricultural valley of Val d'Orcia is a Unesco World Heritage site, as is the town of Pienza on its northeastern edge. Its distinctive landscape features flat chalk plains, out of which rise almost conical hills topped with fortified settlements and magnificent abbeys that were once important staging points on the Via Francigena.

Montalcino

POP 5093
Known globally as the home of one of the world's great wines, Brunello di Montalcino, the attractive hilltop town of Montalcino has a remarkable number of *enoteche* lining its medieval streets, and is surrounded by hugely picturesque vineyards. There's history to explore too: the town's efforts to hold out against Florence even after Siena had fallen earned it the title 'the Republic of Siena in Montalcino', and there are many well-preserved medieval buildings within the historic city walls.

⊙ Sights & Activities

To save a couple of euros for your wine fund, purchase a combined ticket (adult/reduced €6/4.50) for entry to the fortezza's ramparts and the Museo Civico e Diocesano d'Arte Sacra. These are available from the tourist office (p170).

Fortezza   HISTORIC BUILDING
(Piazzale Fortezza; courtyard free, ramparts adult/reduced €4/2; ⊙9am-8pm Apr-Oct, 10am-6pm Nov-Mar) This imposing 14th-century structure was expanded under the Medici dukes and now dominates Montalcino's skyline.

ABBAZIA DI SANT'ANTIMO

This serenely beautiful, Romanesque abbey (☑0577 28 63 00; www.antimo.it; Castelnuovo dell'Abate; ⊙10am-1pm & 3-7pm summer, till 5pm winter) FREE lies in an isolated valley just below the village of Castelnuovo dell'Abate, 11km from Montalcino.

Tradition tells us Charlemagne founded the original monastery here in 781. The exterior, built in pale travertine stone, is simple except for the stone carvings, which include various fantastical animals. Inside, study the capitals of the columns lining the nave, especially the one representing Daniel in the lion's den (second on the right as you enter). Below it is a particularly intense polychrome 13th-century Madonna and Child and there's a haunting 12th-century Crucifixion above the main altar.

Three to four buses per day (€1.50, 15 minutes, Monday to Saturday) connect Montalcino with the village of Castelnuovo dell'Abate.

It's a two- to three-hour walk from Montalcino to the abbey. The route starts next to the police station near the main roundabout in town; many visitors choose to walk there and return by bus – check the timetable with the tourist office (p170).

You can sample and purchase local wines in its enoteca (☑0577 84 92 11; www.enotecalafortezza.com; ⊙9am-8pm, reduced hours in winter) and also climb up to the fort's ramparts. Buy a ticket for the ramparts at the bar.

Museo Civico e Diocesano d'Arte Sacra MUSEUM
(☑0577 84 60 14; Via Ricasoli 31; adult/reduced €4.50/3; ⊙10am-1pm & 2-5.30pm Tue-Sun) Occupying the former convent of the neighbouring Chiesa di Sant'Agostino, this collection of religious art from the town and surrounding region includes a triptych by Duccio and a *Madonna and Child* by Simone Martini. Other artists represented include the Lorenzetti brothers, Giovanni di Paolo and Sano di Pietro.

★**Poggio Antico** WINE
(☑restaurant 0577 84 92 00, 0577 84 80 44; www.poggioantico.com; Località Poggio Antico, off SP14; ⊙cantina 10am-6pm, restaurant noon-2.30pm & 7-9.30pm Tue-Sun, closed Sun evening winter) Located 5km outside Montalcino on the road to Grosseto, Poggio Antico is a superb foodie one-stop-shop. It makes award-winning wines (try its Brunello Altero or Riserva), conducts free cellar tours in Italian, English and German, offers paid tastings (approx €25 depending on wines) and has an on-site restaurant (p167). Book tours in advance.

✗ Eating & Drinking

★**Trattoria L'Angelo** TUSCAN $
(☑0577 84 80 17; Via Ricasoli 9; meals €20; ⊙noon-3pm Wed-Mon Sep-Jun, noon-3pm & 7-11pm Wed-Mon Jul & Aug) We thought about keeping shtum about this place (everyone loves to keep a secret or two), but it seemed selfish not to share our love for its pasta dishes with our loyal readers. Be it vegetarian (ravioli stuffed with ricotta and truffles) or carnivorous (*pappardelle* with wild-boar sauce), the handmade *primi* here are uniformly excellent. *Secondi* aren't as impressive.

★**Enoteca Osteria Osticcio** WINE BAR
(☑0577 84 82 71; www.osticcio.it; Via Giacomo Matteotti 23; antipasto & cheese plates €7-17, meals €40; ⊙noon-4pm & 7-11pm Fri-Wed, plus noon-7pm Thu summer) In a town overflowing with *enoteche*, this is definitely one of the best. Choose a bottle from the huge selection of Brunello and its more modest sibling Rosso di Montalcino to accompany a meal, or opt for a tasting of three Brunelli (€16) or a Brunello and Rosso (€9). The panoramic view, meanwhile, almost upstages it all.

Drogheria Franci MODERN ITALIAN $$
(☑0577 84 81 91; www.locandafranci.com; Piazzale Fortezza 6; meals €42; ⊙12.30-3pm & 7.30-10pm, later in Jul & Aug; 🖘) A perfect example of the sleekly styled wine bar that is trending in Tuscany today, Franci offers a menu that takes more than a few liberties when presenting traditional dishes – think exciting flavour combinations, refined plating and pared-back serving sizes. Seating is in an old *drogheria* (grocery store) that has been given a modern makeover, or on two outdoor terraces.

Ristorante di Poggio Antico MODERN ITALIAN $$$
(☑0577 84 92 00; www.poggioantico.com; Località Poggio Antico, off SP14; meals €50, tasting menus €50-80; ⊙noon-2.30pm & 7-9.30pm Tue-Sun, closed Sun dinner winter; 🖉) The fine-dining

ROAD TRIP >
EXPLORING THE VAL D'ORCIA

Few valleys are as magnificent as this – but then, the valley is a Unesco World Heritage site. Stitched from vine-covered rolling hills, medieval abbeys and celebrity wine towns, the Val d'Orcia is among Tuscany's most beautiful road trips. Pilgrims following the Via Francigena to Rome trod the same route in medieval times and the rewards remain unchanged: peace, serenity, soul-soaring views, sensational food and wine...

❶ Abbazia di Sant'Antimo

From the medieval town of Montalcino, cruise along the SP55 south past vineyard after vineyard planted with the grapes used in Tuscany's most-famous wine, Brunello. Arriving in Castelnuovo dell'Abata 11km later, get set for the ultimate swoon: the village looks down on the hauntingly beautiful, Romanesque church of **Abbazia di Sant'Antimo**

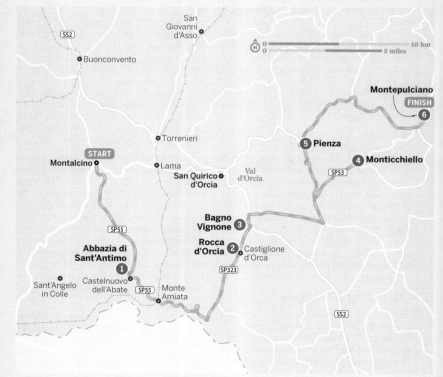

One day 70km

Great for... Outdoors, History & Culture, Food & Drink

Best Time to Go May to October

(p167), Built in pale travertine stone, the abbey church positively glistens in the sunlight. If you're lucky, catch monks singing Gregorian chants.

➋ Rocca d'Orcia

Continue south on the SP55 and north on the SP323 towards Castiglione d'Orcia. These roads ride a ridge providing sweeping Val d'Orcia views, before twisting down then up through a quintessentially Tuscan landscape: honey-yellow farmhouses set amid rows of cypress trees and vines. Near Castiglione d'Orcia the crisply geometric lines of the Rocca d'Orcia (also called the Rocca di Tentennano) loom into view. This part-13th-century fortress clings to a limestone spur: follow signs to park beneath it and clamber up for a closer look, both at the castle and the landscape laid out like a living map far below.

➌ Bagno Vignoni

Next, the SP323 swoops down amid more panoramic views. Detour to Bagno Vignoni to stroll the fine town square, which frames a vast thermal water-filled basin.

➍ Monticchiello

Back on the SP323, take the (signed) right turn towards Monticchiello on the SP53 to enter the valley you saw from the high hills. Here a series of minor roads, straight as arrows and lined with cypresses, sweep past farms. In the tiny village of Monticchiello, take in the narrow streets, picturesque squares and panoramic views of the Val d'Orcia; these are best appreciated over lunch on the terrace of **Osteria La Porta** (📋0578 75 51 63; www.osterialaporta.it/en/osteria-la-porta-restaurant; Via del Piano 3; meals €40; ⊙cafe 9am-12.30pm & 3-7pm, restaurant 12.30-3pm & 7.30-10pm Fri-Wed, closed Jan & Thu winter); book ahead.

➎ Pienza

Pick up signs for Pienza; a comfortable cruise that sees the town's *duomo*-dominated skyline become ever more impressive as you climb nearer. Stop to admire its World Heritage–listed Piazza Pio II, enjoy a coffee or aperitivo at **Bar Il Casello** (p172) or **La Terrazza del Chiostro** (p172).

➏ Montepulciano

Head to your final destination: the enchanting medieval town of Montepulciano, teetering on a narrow ridge of volcanic rock and seducing horses of visitors with its exceptional portfolio of accommodation, dining options and wine-tasting opportunities – most with spectacular views over the Val di Chiana and Val d'Orcia.

DON'T MISS

TRATTORIA PERFECTION
....
Sometimes simple dishes are the hardest to perfect. And perfection is the only term to use when discussing **Il Leccio** (☑0577 84 41 75; www.illeccio. net; Via Costa Castellare 1/3, Sant'Angelo in Colle; meals €30, 4-course set menu €36; ⊙noon-2.30pm & 7-9pm Thu-Tue; ☑) in Brunello heartland. Watching the chef make his way between his stove and kitchen garden to gather produce for each order puts a whole new spin on the word 'fresh', and both the results and the house Brunello are spectacular.

Be sure to order the *grande antipasti* (it's large enough for two to share) and always ask about daily specials.

Sant'Angelo in Colle is 10km south-west of Montalcino along Via del Sole (or 10km west of the Abbazia di Sant'Antimo along an unsealed but signed road through vineyards).

---

restaurant on this highly regarded wine estate (p167) is one of the best in the area, serving a menu of creative, contemporary Italian cuisine. Order à la carte, or opt for a tasting menu – there are four, one of which is vegetarian. You'll dine inside a converted barn building or on the scenic terrace.

Caffè Fiaschetteria Italiana 1888 CAFE
(☑0577 84 90 43; Piazza del Popolo 6; ⊙7.30am-11pm, closed Thu winter) You could take a seat in the slender square outside this atmosphere-laden *enoteca*-cafe, but then you'd miss its remarkable 19th-century decor – all brass, mirrors and ornate lights. It's been serving coffee and glasses of Brunello to locals since 1888 and is still chock-full of charm.

❶ Information

Montalcino's **tourist office** (☑0577 84 93 31; www.prolocomontalcino.com; Costa del Municipio 1; ⊙10am-1pm & 2-5.50pm, closed Mon winter) is just off the main square. It can supply free copies of the *Consorzio del Vino Brunello di Montalcino* map of wineries and also books cellar-door visits and winery accommodation.

❶ Getting There & Away

BUS

Tiemme (p144) buses run between Montalcino and Siena (€4.50, 75 minutes, six daily Monday to Saturday). The bus stop is near the **Hotel**

Vecchia Oliviera (☑0577 84 60 28; www.vecchiaoliviera.com; Via Landi 1; s €85, d €150-170; ⓟ❊🛜❊).

CAR & MOTORCYCLE

To reach Montalcino from Siena, take the SS2 (Via Cassia); after Buonconvento, turn off onto the SP45. There's plenty of parking around the *fortezza* and in Via Pietro Strozzi (€1.50 per hour, 8am to 8pm).

Pienza
POP 2107

Once a sleepy hamlet, pretty Pienza was transformed when, in 1459, Pope Pius II began turning his home village into an ideal Renaissance town. The result is magnificent – the church, papal palace, town hall and accompanying buildings in and around Piazza Pio II went up in just three years and haven't been remodelled since. In 1996 Unesco added the town to its World Heritage list, citing the revolutionary vision of urban space. On weekends, Pienza draws big crowds; come midweek if you possibly can.

⊙ Sights

Piazza Pio II PIAZZA
Stand in this magnificent square and spin 360 degrees. You've just taken in an overview of Pienza's major monuments. Gems of the Renaissance constructed in a mere three years between 1459 and 1462, they're arranged according to the urban design of Bernardo Rossellino, who applied the principles of Renaissance town planning devised by his mentor, Leon Battista Alberti.

The space available to Rossellino was limited, so to increase the sense of perspective and dignity of the great edifices he'd been commissioned to design, he set them off at angles to the cathedral around a magnificently paved piazza.

★**Duomo** CATHEDRAL
(Piazza Pio II; ⊙8.30am-1pm & 2.15-6.30pm) Pienza's *duomo* was built on the site of the Romanesque Chiesa di Santa Maria, of which little remains. The Renaissance church with its handsome travertine facade was commissioned by Pius II, who was so proud of the building that he issued a papal bull in 1462 forbidding any changes to it. The interior is a strange mix of Gothic and Renaissance styles and contains a superb marble tabernacle by Rossellino housing a relic of St Andrew the Apostle, Pienza's patron saint.

There's a small museum in the crypt (admission €2) The Casa dei Canonici (House of the Church Canons) sits next door to the *duomo*.

★ **Palazzo Piccolomini** PALACE
(☑ 0577 28 63 00; www.palazzopiccolominipienza.
it; Piazza Pio II; adult/reduced with guided tour €7/5;
⊙ 10am-6.30pm Tue-Sun summer, to 4.30pm winter, closed early Jan–mid-Feb & 2nd half Nov) This magnificent palace was the residence of Pope Pius II, and is considered Bernardo Rossellino's masterpiece. Built on the site of the pope's family houses, it features a fine courtyard, handsome staircase and the former papal apartments, which are filled with period furnishings and minor art. To the rear, a three-level loggia offers a spectacular panorama over the Val d'Orcia far below. Guided tours leave at 30-minute intervals but not between 12.30pm and 2pm; peeking into the courtyard is free.

Palazzo Borgia PALACE
(Palazzo Vescovile; Piazza Pio II) The future Pope Alexander VI, then just Cardinal Roderigo Borgia, was gifted this palace by Pius II and subsequently modified and enlarged it in 1492. It's home to the Museo Diocesano (☑ 0578 74 99 05; http://palazzoborgia.it; Corso il Rossellino 30; adult/reduced €4.50/3; ⊙ 10.30am-1.30pm & 2.30-6pm Wed-Mon summer, 10am-4pm

---

WORTH A TRIP

IRIS ORIGO & THE GARDENS AT LA FOCE

Of the many foreigners who chose to make Tuscany their home in the early decades of the 20th century, Iris Origo made one of the greatest impacts. Born in 1902, her wealthy American father died when she was only seven years old and she was raised by her neurotic Anglo-Irish mother, Sybil. Choosing to live in Fiesole, Sybil rented a villa built by the Medicis and threw herself into the intellectual and artistic circles of the Anglo-Florentines, which were dominated by the charismatic figure of art historian Bernard Berenson. Iris grew up in a privileged and artistic milieu populated with expats, extroverts and eccentrics. By the time she turned 21, she had decided to marry an urbane Florentine, Antonio Origo, and settle down permanently in the countryside with him to lead a more meaningful life.

In 1924, Iris and Antonio purchased a run-down farm estate called La Foce (☑ 0578 6 91 01; www.lafoce.com; Strada della Vittoria 61, off SP40; adult/child under 12yr €10/free; ⊙ tour & entry 3pm, 4pm, 5pm & 6pm Wed, 11.30am, 3pm & 4.30pm Sat & Sun last weekend Mar–1 Nov) in the Val d'Orcia and set about restoring its main 16th-century building and improving the long-neglected farm. Having grown up in one of Fiesole's most beautiful villas, Iris was keen to make improvements to her new house, which had originally been used as an inn for pilgrims walking the Via Francigena between Canterbury and Rome. She engaged one of her oldest friends, fashionable English architect Cecil Pinsent (1884–1963), to first renovate the house and then – over a period of 15 years – create a series of splendid landscaped gardens that have been lovingly maintained and can now be visited on guided tours. The tours visit the elegant *limonaia* (greenhouse where lemon trees are protected over winter); the fountain garden with its travertine water feature, manicured hedges and flower beds; a fragrant wisteria walk; and a stunning lower garden with geometric plantings of cypress trees, double box hedges and a distant backdrop of Monte Amiata.

In the tours, guides describe the lives of Iris and Antonio; their collaboration with Pinsent; their experiences at La Foce during WWII, when they sheltered and aided partisans, refugees and allied troops (recounted by Iris in her celebrated 1947 memoir *War in Val d'Orcia*); and their socially progressive initiatives in education and health care for the estate's workers. As extraordinary as it sounds, Iris was able to do all of this, raise two children (a third died in his infancy), travel across the globe, conduct two passionate extra-marital affairs and write 12 books across a wide variety of subjects, including an autobiography, *Images and Shadows* (1970). Her last work, a book of essays titled *A Need to Testify,* was published in 1984, only a few years before her death in 1988, aged 86.

Post-tour, indulge in a long and lazy al fresco lunch at Dopolavoro La Foce (☑ 0578 75 40 25; www.dopolavorolafoce.it; Strada della Vittoria (SP40) 90; meals €28, sandwiches €4-5; ⊙ 8am-11pm; P 🤖 📶), a textbook exercise in Tuscan chic with its idyllic back garden for summer dining and an on-trend menu featuring vegetarian pasta, burgers, flatbread sandwiches, craft beers and organic juices.

Sat & Sun winter) and the tourist office. Enter via the courtyard onto Corso il Rossellino.

Pieve di Corsignano   CHURCH
(off SP18; ⊙ 9am-6pm summer, from 10am winter) Look out for this Romanesque church at the western edge of Pienza. It dates from the 10th century, when Pienza was called Corsignano, and boasts a strange circular bell tower with eight arched windows. Close inspection reveals the carving of a two-headed siren over the main doorway and scenes of the Three Kings and Nativity over the side door on to the right. Inside the church is the baptismal font where Pope Pius II was christened.

✖ Eating & Drinking

Coffee breaks in Pienza are best spent at one of the cafes around Piazza Pio II. For sunset drinks, it's hard to beat casual Bar Il Casello (🖰 0578 74 91 05; Via del Casello 3; ⊙ noon-8pm Wed, Thu & Sun, 6pm-midnight Fri, noon-midnight Sat) or ritzy La Terrazza del Chiostro (🖰 349 5676148, 0578 74 81 83; www.laterrazzadelchiostro. it; Via del Balzello; ⊙ 3.30-6.30pm Thu-Tue, closed mid-Nov–mid-Mar, open Wed in high summer).

Osteria Sette di Vino   TUSCAN $
(🖰 0578 74 90 92; Piazza di Spagna 1; meals €16; ⊙ noon-2.30pm & 7.30-10pm Thu-Tue) Known for its *zuppa di pane e fagioli* (bread and white-bean soup), *bruschette* and range of local *pecorino* (sheep's-milk cheese), this simple place is run by the exuberant Luciano, who is immortalised as Bacchus in a copy of Caravaggio's famous painting hanging above the main counter. There's a clutch

BAGNI SAN FILIPPO

Medieval pilgrims walking the Via Francigena from Canterbury to Rome loved pausing in this part of central Tuscany to enjoy a long therapeutic soak in its thermal springs. If you're keen to do the same, consider avoiding the famous thermal institute in Bagno Vignoni and instead head to the open-air cascades (⊙ 24hr) FREE in this tiny village 16km southwest of Pienza. You'll find them just uphill from Hotel le Terme – follow signs to 'Fosso Bianco' down a lane for about 150m. Your destination is a series of mini pools, fed by hot, tumbling cascades of water. A free al fresco spa.

of tables inside and a scattering outside – book ahead.

Pummarò   PIZZA $
(🖰 0578 74 85 68; www.pummaropizzeria.it; Piazza Martiri della Libertà 2-3; slice €2-2.50, pizza €7-9; ⊙ 11.30am-3pm & 6-10pm, closed Jan-Mar; 🛜 🖊) Located next to the city walls on bustling Piazza Martiri della Libertà, this pizzeria has a streetside terrace that is inevitably packed – you may have to wait for a table. There's an innovative range of pizzas and *calzoni,* including all-vegetable offerings; the *pizza pummarò* (with cherry tomatoes, *mozzarella di bufala* and basil) is superb.

⭐ **Townhouse Caffè**   MODERN ITALIAN $$
(🖰 0578 74 90 05; www.la-bandita.com/townhouse/the-restaurant; Via San Andrea 8; meals €40; ⊙ noon-2.30pm Tue-Sun, 7-10pm daily early Apr–early Jan) The menu at this chic eatery is pared back in more ways than one: there are around four choices per course, presentation is minimalist and the emphasis is on the quality of the produce rather than clever culinary tricks – bravo! In summer, guests dine in an atmospheric medieval courtyard; in winter, the action moves into a two-room space with open kitchen.

Trattoria Latte di Luna   TUSCAN $$
(🖰 333 8467808; Via San Carlo 2-4; meals €30; ⊙ noon-2pm & 7-10pm Thu-Tue) Famed for its succulent *maialino da latte arrosto* (roasted suckling pig), this much-loved trattoria is an excellent dining option, especially if you are lucky enough to score a table on its streetside terrace.

⭐ **La Terrazza del Chiostro**   MODERN ITALIAN $$$
(🖰 0578 74 81 83, 349 5676148; www.laterrazzadelchiostro.it; Via del Balzello; meals €50; ⊙ 12.30-2.30pm & 7.30-10pm Thu-Tue, closed mid-Nov–mid-Mar, open Wed in high summer) Chef Alessandro Rossi was one of the youngest-ever recipients of an Italian Michelin star and clearly has ambitions to reprise his success here. Dining on the gorgeous terrace with its panoramic view is the stuff of which lasting travel memories are made, and the food has plenty of pizzazz – to fully appreciate it, opt for a set menu (4-/6-/9-courses €50/75/125).

ⓘ Information

Tourist Office (🖰 0578 74 99 05; info.turismo @comune.pienza.si.it; Corso il Rossellino 30; ⊙ 10.30am-1.30pm & 2.30-6pm Wed-Mon summer, 10am-4pm Sat & Sun winter) Located off the ground-floor courtyard in Palazzo Borgia. It supplies a town map but offers few other services.

Getting There & Away

BUS

Two **Tiemme** (p144) buses run Monday to Saturday between Siena and Pienza (€5.50, 70 minutes) and nine travel to/from Montepulciano (€2.50, 20 minutes). The bus stops are just off Piazza Dante Alighieri. Buy tickets at one of the nearby bars.

CAR & MOTORCYCLE

On summer weekends finding a parking space in Pienza can be a real challenge as the car park near the centre (€1.50/5 per one/four hours) fills quickly. There is a limited number of free parking spaces on Via Circonvallazione below the *duomo*, but these are hotly contested.

MONTEPULCIANO

POP 14,097

Exploring the medieval town of Montepulciano, perched on a reclaimed narrow ridge of volcanic rock, will push your quadriceps to failure point. When this happens, self-medicate with a generous pour of the highly reputed Vino Nobile while also drinking in the spectacular views over the Val di Chiana and Val d'Orcia.

◉ Sights

Il Corso   STREET

Montepulciano's main street – called in stages Via di Gracciano, Via di Voltaia, Via dell'Opio and Via Poliziano – climbs up the eastern ridge of the town from Porta al Prato and loops to meet Via di Collazzi on the western ridge. To reach the centre of town (Piazza Grande) take a dog-leg turn into Via del Teatro.

In Piazza Savonarola, up from the Porta al Prato, is the Colonna del Marzocca (Piazza Savonarola), erected in 1511 to confirm Montepulciano's allegiance to Florence. The late-Renaissance Palazzo Avignonesi (Via di Gracciano nel Corso 91) is at No 91; other notable buildings include the Palazzo di Bucelli (Via di Gracciano nel Corso 73) at No 73 (look for the recycled Etruscan and Latin inscriptions and reliefs on the lower facade), and Palazzo Cocconi (Via di Gracciano nel Corso 70) at No 70.

Continuing uphill, you'll find Michelozzo's Chiesa di Sant'Agostino (www.montepulciano chiusipienza.it; Piazza Michelozzo; ⊘9am-noon &

3-6pm), with its lunette above the entrance holding a terracotta Madonna and Child, John the Baptist and St Augustine. Opposite, the Torre di Pulcinella (Piazza Michelozzo), a medieval tower house, is topped by the town clock and the hunched figure of Pulcinella (Punch, of Punch and Judy fame), which strikes the hours. After passing historic Caffè Poliziano (🕿 0578 75 86 15; www. caffepoliziano.it; Via di Voltaia 27; ⊘7am-8pm Mon-Fri, to 11pm Sat, to 9pm Sun; 🛜), the Corso continues straight ahead and Via del Teatro veers off to the right.

Piazza Grande   PIAZZA

Elegant Piazza Grande is the town's highest point and main meeting place. If you think it looks familiar, it might be because it featured in *New Moon,* the second movie in the *Twilight* series based on Stephanie Meyer's vampire novels. They shot the main crowd scene here, despite the book being set in Volterra. More recently, it features in episodes of the television series *Medici: Masters of Florence.*

Palazzo Comunale   PALACE

(Piazza Grande; terrace & tower adult/reduced €5/2.50, terrace only €2.50; ⊘10am-6pm) Built in the 14th-century in Gothic style and remodelled in the 15th century by Michelozzo, the Palazzo Comunale still functions as Montepulciano's town hall. Head up the 67 narrow stairs to the tower to enjoy extraordinary views – you'll see as far as Pienza, Montalcino and even, on a clear day, Siena.

Duomo   CATHEDRAL

(www.montepulcianochiusipienza.it; Piazza Grande; ⊘8am-7pm) Montepulciano's 16th-century *duomo* is striking, largely because its unfinished facade gives the building an organic, heavily weathered look. Inside, don't miss Taddeo di Bartolo's ornate *Assumption* triptych (1401) behind the high altar.

★Museo Civico
& Pinacoteca Crociani   ART GALLERY, MUSEUM
(🕿 0578 71 73 00; www.museocivicomontepulciano. it; Via Ricci 10; adult/reduced €5/3; ⊘10.30am-6.30pm Wed-Mon summer, reduced hours winter) It was a curatorial dream come true: in 2011 a painting in the collection of this modest art gallery was attributed to Caravaggio. The work, *Portrait of a Man,* is thought to portray Cardinal Scipione Borghese, the artist's patron. It's now accompanied by a touch-screen interpretation that allows you to explore details of the painting, its restoration and diagnostic attribution. Other works

Montepulciano

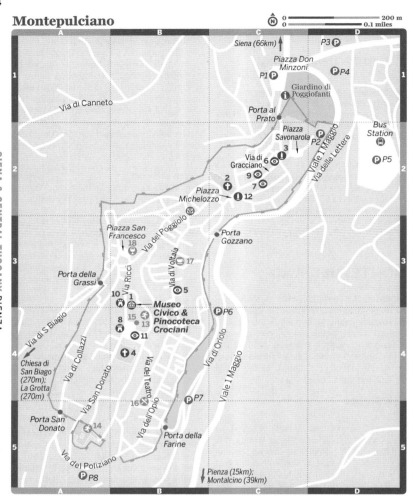

here include two terracottas by Andrea Della Robbia, and Domenico Beccafumi's painting of the town's patron saint, Agnese.

Activities

★ **Cantina de' Ricci**   WINE
(📞0578 75 71 66; www.cantinadericci.it; Via Ricci 11; per tasting €3; ⏱10.30am-7pm mid-Mar–early Jan, Sat & Sun only early Jan–mid-Mar) **FREE** The most evocative of Montepulciano's wine cellars, this *cantina* lies at the foot of a steep winding staircase in the Renaissance-era Palazzo Ricci (www.palazzoricci.com; Via Ricci 9-11). Immense vaulted stone encasements

surround two-storey-high barrels. Dimly lit and hushed, it's like a cathedral of wine. Entry is free, but tastings are charged.

★ **Enoliteca Consortile**   WINE
(www.consorziovinonobile.it; Fortezza di Montepulciano, Via San Donato 21; ⏱11am-5pm Mon-Thu, noon-7pm Fri & Sat) Operated by Montepulciano's consortium of local wine producers, this recently opened showcase of Vino Nobile on the ground floor of the Medicean fortress has a modern tasting room offering over 70 wines for tasting and purchase. Buy a €10 or €15 card, use it to pour the tipples of your choice and direct your own tasting.

Montepulciano

Cantina Storica Talosa WINE
(☑ 0578 75 79 29; www.talosa.it; Via Talosa 8; ⊙ 10am-7.30pm Apr-Dec, 10am-7pm Sat & Sun Jan-Mar) **FREE** The underground tunnels in this *cantina* were hewn out of tufa by the Etruscans and are now filled with huge oak barriques. Look out for the sea fossils in the tufa – they're five million years old. There's also an Etruscan tomb dating from the 6th century BC to visit. Tastings are free, but the expectation is that you'll buy at least one bottle.

★ **Palazzo Vecchio Winery** WINE
(☑ 0578 72 41 70; palazzovecchio@vinonobile.it; Via Terra Rossa 5, Valiano) Idyllic is the first word that comes to mind when describing this wine estate. Its large 14th-century stone farmhouse is surrounded by fruit trees, the winery is in converted outbuildings and 25 hectares of vineyards planted with Sangiovese, Canaiolo and Mammolo grapes cascade down the hillsides. Visits are by reservation only; tastings cost €20 and a five-course lunch with wine €80.

You'll find the estate atop a hill outside the town of Valiano, 15km northeast of Montepulciano. The excellent La Dogana *enoteca,* part of the same estate, is nearby.

Fattoria Le Capezzine WINE
(☑ 0578 72 43 04; www.avignonesi.it; Via Colonica 1, Valiano; ⊙ 10am-7pm Mon-Sat, noon-6pm Sun, to 6pm May & Oct, 10am-6pm Mon-Fri Mar-Apr, 10am-5pm Mon-Fri Nov & Dec, closed Jan & Feb) Part of the legendary Avignonesi company, this 19-hectare estate is known for its 'Round Vineyard', which was designed to establish to what extent the quality of wine is influenced by density of planting and type of rootstock. Tastings of its Nobile, Rosso, Vin Santo and grappa in the *cantina* are free if you eventually purchase a bottle of wine.

Book in advance to enjoy a two-hour tour of the vineyards, ageing cellars and *vinsantaia* (where Vin Santo is aged), followed by a tasting of Avignonesi wines. The estate is 15km northeast of Montepulciano.

Courses & Tours

Strada del Vino Nobile di Montepulciano e dei Sapori della Valdichianna Senese TOURS
(☑ 0578 75 78 12; www.stradavinonobile.it; Piazza Grande 7; ⊙ 9.30am-1.30pm & 2.30-6pm Mon-Fri, 10am-1pm & 2-5pm Sat, 10am-1pm Sun) This office organises a huge range of tours and courses, including cooking courses (€59 to €90), vineyard tours (€49 to €115) and walking tours in the vineyards culminating in a wine tasting (€29 to €49). Book in advance online or at its information office in Piazza Grande.

Festivals & Events

Bravio delle Botti CULTURAL
(www.braviodellebotti.com; ⊙ Aug) Members of Montepulciano's eight *contrade* (districts) push 80kg wine barrels uphill in this race held on the last Sunday in August. There are also Renaissance-themed celebrations during the week before.

Eating & Drinking

Dining in Montepulciano is a highlight – particularly if you opt for the local Chianina beef washed down with a glass or two of the famous Vino Nobile.

★ **La Dogana** MODERN ITALIAN $$
(☑ 339 5405196; Strada Lauretana Sud 75, Valiano; meals €32, cheese & salumi platter €9; ⊙ 10am-10.30pm Wed-Sun, closed Jan) Chef and cookbook writer Sunshine Manitto presides over the

OFF THE BEATEN TRACK

SACRED SOLITUDE

Concealed amidst dense forest on the edge of the Castelnuovo Berardenga region, 14th-century Abbazia di Monte Oliveto Maggiore (☑0577 70 76 11; www.monteoliveto maggiore.it; Monte Oliveto Maggiore; ⊕9.15am-noon & 3.15-5pm Mon-Sat, to 6pm summer) FREE was founded by Giovanni (John) Tolomei – later Saint Bernardo Tolomei – and is still a retreat for Benedictine monks. The cloister features a fresco series by Luca Signo-relli and Giovanni Antonio Bazzi (Il Sodoma) illustrating events in the life of St Benedict, founder of the order. There is also a church with magnificent choir stalls of inlaid wood and a refectory frescoed by Fra' Paolo Novelli.

A donation is requested to visit the abbey's library, museum and pharmacy; visits to the historic cantina (Historic Wine Cellar; www.agricolamonteoliveto.com; Monte Oliveto Mag-giore; ⊕10am-1pm & 2.30-6.30pm summer), where you can enjoy a wine tasting, are free. Parking costs €1.

kitchen of this super-chic *enoteca* overlooking the Palazzo Vecchio Winery. Windows frame vistas of vines and cypress trees, but the best seats in the house are on the grassed rear ter-race. The menu showcases seasonal produce (much of it grown in the kitchen garden) and offers both snacks and full meals.

Sunshine also conducts hands-on cooking classes on Tuesdays (€150 including dinner). When here, be sure to try a glass of Palazzo Vecchio wine (try the Terra Rossa).

Osteria Acquacheta   TUSCAN $$
(☑0578 71 70 86; www.acquacheta.eu; Via del Teatro 22; meals €25-30; ⊕12.30-3pm & 7.30-10.30pm Wed-Mon mid-Apr–Dec) Hugely pop-ular with locals and tourists alike, this bustling *osteria* specialises in *bistecca alla fiorentina* (chargrilled T-bone steak), which comes to the table in huge, lightly seared and exceptionally flavoursome slabs (don't even *think* of asking for it to be served oth-erwise). Book ahead.

★ La Grotta   RISTORANTE $$$
(☑0578 75 74 79; www.lagrottamontepulciano.it; Via di San Biagio 15; meals €40; ⊕12.30-2pm & 7.30-10pm Thu-Tue, closed mid-Jan–mid-Mar) The dishes here may be traditional, but their fla-vour and presentation is refined – artfully arranged Parmesan shavings and sprigs of herbs crown delicate towers of pasta, vegeta-bles and meat. The service is exemplary and the courtyard garden divine. It's just below town, overlooking the Renaissance splendor of the Chiesa di San Biago (☑0578 75 72 90; www.parrocchiemontepulciano.org; Via di San Bia-go; incl audioguide €3.50; ⊕7am-8pm).

★ E Lucevan Le Stelle   WINE BAR
(☑0578 75 87 25; www.lucevanlestelle.it; Piazza San Francesco 5; ⊕11.30-11.30pm mid-Mar–Dec;

☎) The decked terrace of this ultra-friendly *osteria* is the top spot in Montepulciano to watch the sun go down. Inside, squishy sofas, modern art and jazz on the sound system give the place a chilled-out vibe. Its food (antipasto plates €4.50 to €8, *piadine* (flat-bread sandwiches) €6, pasta €6.50 to €9) isn't a strength – stick to a glass or two of Nobile (€5 to €7).

ℹ Information

Strada del Vino Nobile di Montepulciano Information Office (p175) Books accommo-dation in Montepulciano and arranges a wide range of courses and tours.

Tourist Office (☑0578 75 73 41; www.proloco montepulciano.it; Piazza Don Minzoni 1; ⊕9am-1pm) Reserves-last-minute accommo-dation (in person only), supplies town maps and sells bus tickets.

ℹ Getting There & Away

BUS

The Montepulciano **bus station** (Piazzo Pietro Nenni) is next to Car Park No 5. **Tiemme** (p144) runs four buses daily to/from Siena's train station (€6.60, 1½ hours) stopping at Pienza (€2.50, 20 minutes) en route.

CAR & MOTORCYCLE

To reach Montepulciano from Florence, take the Valdichiana exit off the A1 (direction Bettolle–Sinalunga) and then follow the signs; from Siena, take the Siena–Bettolle–Perugia Super Strada.

A 24-hour ZTL applies in the historic centre between May and September; in October and April it applies from 8am to 8pm, and from November to March it applies from 8am to 5pm. Check whether your hotel can supply a permit. Otherwise, there are plenty of paid car parks circling the historic centre.

Southern Tuscany

Best Places to Eat

➡ Taverna del Vecchio Borgo (p182)

➡ Antica Trattoria Aurora (p194)

➡ Il Tufo Allegro (p188)

Best Etruscan Sights

➡ Parco Archeologico 'Città del Tufo' (p189)

➡ Museo Civico Archeologico 'Isidoro Falchi' (p184)

➡ Scavi di Città (p184)

➡ Museo Civico Archeologico di Pitigliano (p185)

➡ Museo Archeologico all'Aperto 'Alberto Manzi' (p185)

Why Go?

Despite being barely a blip on many visitors' radars, Southern Tuscany is really a region for the Italy connoisseur. Here you'll encounter the intensely atmospheric Città del Tufo, a trio of still-inhabited hill towns that have been sculpted from volcanic rock since Etruscan times. Further north, more Etruscan gems await at Roselle and Vetulonia, and one of Tuscany's most charming hilltop towns, Massa Marittima. Around all of these destinations, extraordinary archaeological sites, Renaissance settlements, churches and museums lie waiting to be explored.

An embarrassment of natural riches means you can travel from sandy beaches to snowy mountains in just a few hours, passing wildlife-packed marshes and vine-covered slopes en route. The activities on offer are irresistible: swim, hike, horse ride and mountain bike by day before recharging over flavoursome Maremmese food and wine in secluded *agriturismi* (farmstays) by night.

Road Distances (km)

Massa Marittima	38			
Grosseto	52	48		
Pitigliano	129	120	75	
Parco Regionale della Maremma	28	67	20	56
	Vetulonia	Massa Marittima	Grosseto	Pitigliano

Southern Tuscany Highlights

1 **Parco Regionale della Maremma** (p192) Hiking, bicycling, horse-riding and swimming in this wild and wonderful national park.

2 **Massa Marittima** (p180) Joining the *passeggiata* (evening stroll) in one of Tuscany's most magnificent piazzas.

3 **Parco Archeologico 'Città del Tufo'** (p189) Walking in the footsteps of Etruscans along the mysterious rock-carved sunken roads known as *vie cave* (sunken roads).

4 **Pitigliano** (p184) Admiring spectacular views over the countryside from this hilltop stronghold hewn out of volcanic rock.

5 **Monte Amiata** (p183) Discovering towns and a sculpture garden amid forests of beech and chestnut.

6 **Riserva Naturale Provinciale Diaccia Botrona** (p191) Following tens of thousands of migrating birds to this evocative marshland.

7 **Vetulonia** (p184) Exploring Etruscan excavations at the archaeological sites.

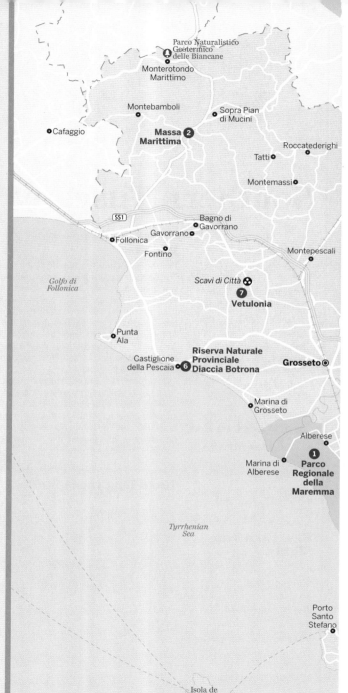

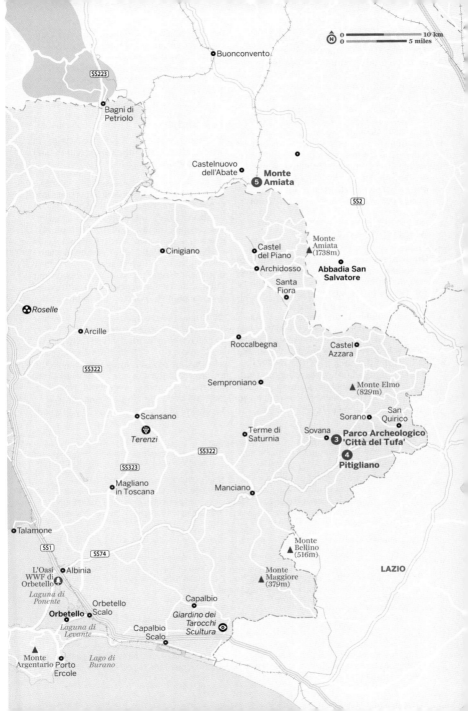

THE ALTA MAREMMA

The Alta (Upper) Maremma starts south of Livorno and continues down to Grosseto, incorporating Massa Marittima and the surrounding Colline Metallifere (metal-producing hills). The ancient mining history and unique landscape of these hills have been acknowledged by inclusion in Unesco's European Geopark Network, and the surrounding area is rich in Etruscan history, too. Inland territory includes the hill towns south of the Crete Senesi and the mountainous terrain surrounding Monte Amiata, all of which make excellent stops for those travelling between South and Central Tuscany.

Massa Marittima

POP 8380

Drawcards at this tranquil hill town include an eccentric yet endearing jumble of museums, an extremely handsome central piazza and largely intact medieval streets that are blessedly bereft of tour groups.

Briefly under Pisan domination, Massa Marittima became an independent *comune* (city-state) in 1225 but was swallowed up by Siena a century later. A plague in 1348 was followed by the decline of the region's lucrative mining industry, reducing the town to the brink of extinction, a situation made even worse by the prevalence of malaria in surrounding marshlands. Fortunately, the draining of marshes in the 18th century and the re-establishment of mining shortly afterwards brought it back to life.

The town is divided into three districts: the Città Vecchia (Old Town), Città Nuova (New Town) and Borgo (Borough). Entry to the Città Vecchia is via the massive Arco Senese.

⊙ Sights

A cumulative ticket (€10) gives access to all of Massa Marittima's museums and monuments.

★ Cattedrale di San Cerbone   CATHEDRAL
(Piazza Garibaldi; ⊙ 8am-noon & 3-7pm summer, to 6pm winter) Presiding over photogenic Piazza Garibaldi (aka Piazza Duomo), Massa Marittima's asymmetrically positioned 13th-century *duomo* is dedicated to St Cerbonius, the town's patron saint, who's always depicted surrounded by a flock of geese. Inside, don't miss the free-standing *Maestà* (Madonna and Child enthroned in majesty; 1316), attributed by some experts to Duccio di Buoninsegna.

★ Museo di Arte Sacra   MUSEUM
(Complesso Museale di San Pietro all'Orto; ☑ 0566 90 22 89; www.museiartesacra.net; Corso Diaz 36; adult/reduced €5/3; ⊙ 10am-1pm & 4-7pm Tue-Sun summer, 11am-1pm & 3-5pm Tue-Sun winter) In the former monastery of San Pietro all'Orto, this museum houses a splendid *Maestà* (c 1335–37) by Ambrogio Lorenzetti as well as sculptures by Giovanni Pisano that original-

THREE PERFECT DAYS

Day One

Explore Etruscan necropolises and walk along mysterious *vie cave* (sunken roads) at the Parco Archeologico 'Città del Tufo' (p189) before visiting the *duomo* (cathedral) and museum in Sovana (p188) and then heading to Pitigliano (p184) to wander centuries-old streets, visit an ancient Jewish enclave and dine in one of the town's excellent restaurants.

Day Two

Your destination today is the Parco Regionale della Maremma (p192), where you can walk, cycle or canoe through wild scenery and have a beach break at Marina di Alberese. At the end of the day, relax over a bottle of Morellino di Scansano at the welcoming *agriturismo* on the Terenzi (p190) wine estate.

Day Three

Cruise north to Massa Marittima (p180) to admire its handsome piazzas and the Cattedrale di San Cerbone (p180), eating lunch at one of its three Slow Food–acknowledged restaurants. Work off some calories exploring the geological sites around Parco Naturalistico Geotermico delle Biancane (p182) and then check into the Montebelli Agriturismo & Country Hotel (p184), one of the region's best *agriturismo* options.

Massa Marittima

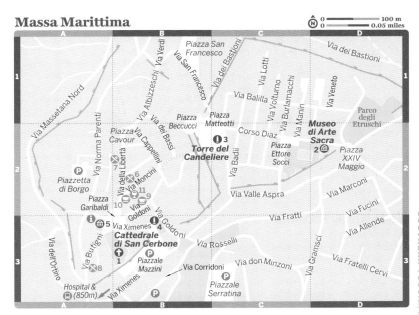

ly adorned the facade of the *duomo*. The collection of primitive grey alabaster bas-reliefs also came from the *duomo*, but originally date from an earlier era.

Museo Archeologico MUSEUM
(Piazza Garibaldi 1; adult/reduced €3/1.50; ⊙10am-1pm & 4-7pm Tue-Sun summer, 11am-1pm & 3-5pm Tue-Sun winter) The 13th-century **Palazzo del Podestà**, the historic residence of the town's chief magistrate, houses a dusty archaeological museum. The noteworthy exhibit is *La Stele del Vado all'Arancio*, a simple but compelling stone stela (funeral or commemorative marker) dating from the 3rd millennium BC.

Albero della Fecondità MONUMENT
(Via Ximenes, off Piazza Garibaldi) FREE A rather risqué surprise lurks underneath this 13th-century former wheat store. Its loggia shelters the Fonte dell'Abbondanza (Fountain of Abundance), a now decommissioned public drinking fountain that features an extraordinary fresco known as the *Albero della Fecondità* (Fertility Tree) that might well make you blush. Look closely to see what type of fruit the tree bears!

★ **Torre del Candeliere** TOWER
(Candlestick Tower; Piazza Matteotti; adult/reduced €3/2; ⊙10.30am-1.30pm & 3-6pm Tue-Sun summer,

Massa Marittima

11am-1pm & 2.30-4.30pm Tue-Sun winter) Climb to the top of this 13th-century, 74m-high tower for stupendous views over the old town.

Arco Senese ARCHITECTURE
(Piazza Matteotti) Massa Marittima's immense, medieval Arco Senese (Sienese Arch) peels away from the old city walls to soar overhead as you pass between the Città Vecchia and Città Nuova.

WORTH A TRIP

THE COLLINE METALLIFERE

Massa Marittima's handsome buildings and artistic treasures are the legacy of the town's location in the centre of Tuscany's Colline Metallifere (metal-producing hills). Mining occurred here for three millennia, and has shaped the region's physical and cultural landscapes – something acknowledged by the addition of the Parco delle Colline Metallifere (www.parks.it/parco.colline.metallifere) to Unesco's European Geopark Network.

The national park incorporates many sites, including **Parco Naturalistico Geotermico delle Biancane** ([📞] 0566 91 70 39; www.parks.it/parco.colline.metallifere; Strada Provinciale Bagnolo, Monterotondo Marittimo; ⊙ information office 9.30am-12.30pm & 2.30-4.30pm Tue-Fri late Mar-Oct) **FREE** in Monterotondo Marittimo, a geothermal park 21km north of Massa Marittima where steam has been transformed into power by vapour turbines since 1916, supplying electricity to one million Tuscan households (meeting 25% of Tuscany's energy needs). Visitors can take a two-hour walk through wooded terrain, where steam belches from the earth's crust and clumps of sulphur crystals form.

✸ Festivals & Events

Balestro del Girifalco　　　　　　CULTURAL
(Contest of the Falcon's Heart; www.societaterzieri massetani.it) This crossbow competition is held twice yearly on the first Sunday after 20 May and on a Sunday in either July or August (usually the second Sunday in August). Twenty-four competitors from the town's three *terzieri* (districts) dress in medieval costume and compete for a golden arrow.

Lirica in Piazza　　　　　　　　MUSIC
(www.liricainpiazza.it; ⊙ Aug) Three operas are staged under the stars in this annual festival held in Piazza Garibaldi.

✖ Eating

The three eateries in town are recognised as Slow Food destinations; all serve local specialities including *tortelli alla maremma* (pasta parcels filled with ricotta and spinach).

★Taverna del Vecchio Borgo　　TUSCAN **$$**
([📞] 0566 90 21 67; taverna.vecchioborgo@libero.it; Via Norma Parenti 12; meals €32; ⊙ 7.30-10pm Tue-Sun summer, 7.30-10pm Tue-Sat, 12.30-2.30pm Sun winter) Massa's best restaurant is as atmospheric as it is delicious. You'll sit in a dimly lit brick-vaulted wine cellar dating from the 16th century and dine on top-quality beef grilled on the wood-fired oven or unusual dishes such as *testaroli* pasta with a pistachio sauce. The set four-course menu (€30) is a steal.

La Tana dei Brilli　　　　　　TUSCAN **$$**
([📞] 0566 90 12 74; www.latanadeibrilli.it; Vicolo del Ciambellano 4; meals €26; ⊙ noon-2.30pm & 7-10pm Thu-Tue Dec-Oct) Billed as the 'smallest *osteria* in Italy' and seating a mere 10 people at four tables (another six can squeeze onto tiny alley tables outside), this friendly place ticks every box on the Slow Food checklist, featuring authentic Maremmese dishes made with local products. It also has a sensational and dirt-cheap *vino de casa* (€4 per litre).

L'Osteria da Tronca　　　　　　TUSCAN **$$**
([📞] 0566 90 19 91; Vicolo Porte 5; meals €28; ⊙ 6-9.45pm Thu-Tue Mar–mid-Dec) Squeezed into a side street, this stone-walled restaurant specialises in the rustic dishes of the Maremma. Specialities include *acquacotta* (a hearty vegetable soup with bread and egg), *tortelli alla maremma* (pasta parcels filled with ricotta and spinach) and *coniglio in porchetta* (roasted stuffed rabbit).

🍷 Drinking & Nightlife

There's a very strong coffee culture here, with a number of good cafes to choose from. For an *aperitivo*, grab one of the arcade tables at **Caffè Le Logge** ([📞] 0566 91 43 45; Piazza Garibaldi 11-13; ⊙ 7am-midnight Fri-Wed; 🛜).

★Il Bacchino　　　　　　　　WINE BAR
([📞] 0566 94 02 29; Via Moncini 8; ⊙ 10am-1pm & 4-7.30pm, closed Mon Nov-Feb) Owner Magdy Lamei may not be a local (he's from Cairo), but it would be hard to find anyone else as knowledgeable and passionate about local artisanal produce. Come to this classy *enoteca* (wine bar) he runs with his wife, Monica, to taste and buy local wines (€3.50 to €25 per glass), or to stock up on picnic provisions including jams, cheese and cured meats.

Bar Torrefazione　　　　　　　CAFE
(Via Goldoni 17; ⊙ 7.30am-12.30pm & 5-7.30pm Mon-Fri, 7.30am-12.30pm Sat) Gloria Dina makes the best coffee in town, which is why her diminutive cafe is always busy. The fact that it's the cheapest cup in town probably helps, too.

There's no official business name – look for the 'Bar Torrefazione' (Bar and Roastery) sign.

❶ Information

Tourist Office (☎ 0566 90 65 54; www.turismomassamarittima.it; Via Todini 3; ⊙10am-1pm & 3-5pm Wed-Fri, to 6pm Sat & Sun Apr-Jun & Oct, 10am-1pm & 4-7pm Wed-Mon Jul & Aug, 10am-1pm & 3-5pm Fri-Mon Nov-Mar) Down a side street beneath the Museo Archeologico. The website has plenty of information.

❶ Getting There & Away

BUS

The bus station is near the hospital on Piazza del Risorgimento, 1km down the hill from Piazza Garibaldi. Tiemme (www.tiemmespa.it) operates two buses to Grosseto (€5.20, 80 minutes, Monday to Saturday) and one to Siena (€6, two hours, Monday to Saturday) at 7.10am. To get to Volterra you'll need to change at Monterotondo Marittimo. **Massa Veternensis** (Piazza Garibaldi 18) sells bus and train tickets.

OFF THE BEATEN TRACK

MONTE AMIATA

Circling the extinct volcano of Mt Amiata (1738m), the heavily forested region of Monte Amiata links the Maremma with the Val d'Orcia and is an intriguing off-the-beaten-track destination for those travelling between Southern and Central Tuscany.

Sights & Activities

Garden of Daniel Spoerri (Il Giardino di Daniel Spoerri; ☎ 0564 95 08 05; www.danielspoerri.org; Strada Provinciale Pescina, Seggiano; adult/reduced €10/8; ⊙10.30am-7pm Easter-Nov, closed Mon Easter–mid-Jun & mid-Sep–Nov) Opened in 1997, this sculpture garden is the passionate project of Romanian–Swiss artist Daniel Spoerri (b 1930), who created many of the 112 artworks spread over its 16 hectares. The landscape here is glorious – wildflowers carpet the fields and olive groves surround the property – and the site-specific works address the theme of how art should complement nature rather than overwhelm it. The standout piece is Olivier Estoppey's 2001 work *Dies Irae* (Judgement Day) – don't miss it.

Mineral Park Museum (Parco Museo Minerario di Abbadia San Salvatore; ☎ 0577 77 83 24; www.museominerario.it; Piazzale Renato Rossaro 6, Abbadia San Salvatore; adult/reduced €12/10; ⊙9.30am-12.30pm & 3.30-6.30pm mid-Jun–Oct) Cinnabar, the red-coloured mineral from which mercury or quicksilver is extracted, was mined in the hills around Abbadia San Salvatore from Etruscan times until quite recently. This now-defunct mercury mine was once the largest employer in Monte Amiata and it has now been converted into a fascinating museum documenting the mine's role in shaping both the local economy and the life of the community. It offers displays, artworks, audiovisual presentations and even a train ride through the mine tunnels.

Abbadia San Salvatore (☎ 0577 77 73 52; www.abbaziasansalvatore.it; Via del Monastero; donation to enter crypt €2; ⊙7am-1pm & 3-6pm) Founded by the Lombards in the 8th century, this abbey was originally entrusted to the Benedictines but later passed to the Cistercians. An important stop on the Via Francigena, it is notable primarily for its hugely atmospheric crypt, which has a forest of 44 columns, each featuring unique decorations on their capitals.

Dzogchen Community & Cultural Association (☎ 0564 96 68 37; www.dzogchen.it; Merigar West; prices on application) A community of Tibetan Buddhists in rural Tuscany? Yes, you read that correctly. This Buddhist centre near Archidosso was established in 1981 and offers workshops in Yantra yoga, meditation and sacred and modern Tibetan dancing to those interested in investigating techniques for living in a more mindful way. These are held in the centre's richly decorated temple.

The community has also opened an extremely impressive multimedia **Museum of Asian Art and Culture** (www.dzogchen.it/museo-di-arte-contemporanea-orientale; Fortezza, Archidosso; combined ticket with Archidosso Castle adult/reduced €7/5; ⊙10am-1pm & 4-7pm Tue-Sun summer, closed weekdays winter), near the medieval castle in Archidosso, 5km away.

Getting There & Away

Local bus services are extremely limited. You'll need a car to explore the area.

CAR & MOTORCYCLE

There's a convenient car park (€1 per hour during the day, free at night) close to Piazza Garibaldi; head up the hill and you'll find it on your left.

TRAIN

The nearest train station is in Follonica, 22km southwest of Massa; it's served by a regular shuttle bus (€2.60, 25 minutes, 10 daily).

Vetulonia

Originally an important Etruscan settlement, this windswept hilltop village 23km northwest of Grosseto was colonised by the Romans in 224 BC. It retains important traces of both eras, which can be investigated at the Museo Civico Archeologico 'Isidoro Falchi' and by visiting the Scavi di Città archaeological site.

◉ Sights & Activities

To horse ride between vines and olive groves, head 7km north to Montebelli Agriturismo & Country Hotel (☑ 334 2206929; www.montebelli.com; Località Molinetto, Caldana), a biodynamic wine and olive-oil estate with sensational facilities.

★ Museo Civico
Archeologico 'Isidoro Falchi'   MUSEUM
(☑ 0564 94 80 58; museo-vetulonia@libero.it; Piazza Vatluna; adult/reduced €5/2.50; ◎ 10am-2pm & 4-8pm Tue-Sun Jun-Sep, 10am-4pm Tue-Sun Oct-Feb, 10am-6pm Tue-Sun Mar-May) Vetulonia's main piazza boasts spectacular views over the surrounding countryside and is home to this small but extremely impressive museum bringing Etruscan history to life through a rich display of artefacts excavated from local Etruscan tombs and settlements. Highlights include the furnishings of the tomb of the *Fibula d'Oro* (Golden Brooch).

Scavi di Città   ARCHAEOLOGICAL SITE
(◎ 10am-6pm Tue-Sun Mar-May) FREE In 2009 a small team of archaeologists began excavating

---

❶ GETTING AROUND SOUTHERN TUSCANY

Bus Tiemme buses (www.tiemmespa.it) travel to many towns and villages, but services are infrequent.

Car & Motorcycle Undoubtedly the best way to explore.

Train A major train line links Grosseto with Rome, Livorno and Pisa.

---

these foundations of a 2300-year-old Etruscan *domus* (house), on the main road just below Vetulonia. The team uncovered dry-stone walls, a brick floor, a small terracotta altar, plenty of amphorae and a small fragment of wall fresco. It's thought this is the most intact Etruscan–Roman-era villa in existence, and there may be other undiscovered sites nearby.

✖ Eating

Delicious organic meals are cooked up at Il Baciarino (☑ 347 9344943; www.baciarino.com; Via della Fonte), a designer *agriturismo* on the edge of Vetulonia. It's much-loved by Florentines and Livornese who adore the tranquil surrounds, sensational views and minimalist decor. There are cooking classes too.

La Vecchia Osteria   TUSCAN $$
(☑ 0566 84 49 80; Viale Marconi 249, Bagno di Gavorrano; meals €31; ◎ noon-2.30pm & 7-10pm Fri-Wed, daily Jul-Sep; 🗢) The unassuming exterior of this neighbourhood eatery on Bagno di Gavorrano's main street gives no clue as to the excellence of its kitchen. The handmade pasta is sensational (especially the *tortelli di ricotta*) and the rustic mains pack a flavoursome punch. Bagno di Gavoranno is 22km south of Massa Marittima and 18km northwest of Vetulonia.

❶ Getting There & Away

Driving to Vetulonia, exit the SS1 at Montepescali/Braccagni (heading towards Braccagni) and follow the SP152 and SP72 uphill to the village.

CITTÀ DEL TUFO

The picturesque towns of Pitigliano, Sovana and Sorano form a triangle enclosing a dramatic landscape where local buildings have been constructed from the volcanic porous rock called tufo since Etruscan times. This area is known as the Città del Tufo (City of the Tufo) or, less commonly, the Paese del Tufo (Land of the Tufo).

Pitigliano
POP 3820

Organically sprouting from a volcanic rocky outcrop towering over the surrounding country, this spectacularly sited hilltop town is surrounded by gorges on three sides, constituting a natural bastion completed to the east by a fort. Within the town, twisting

VIE CAVE

There are at least 15 *vie cave* (sunken roads) hewn out of tufo in the valleys below Pitigliano. These enormous passages – up to 20m deep and 3m wide – are popularly believed to be sacred routes linking Etruscan necropolises and other religious sites. A more mundane explanation is that these strange ancient corridors were used to move livestock or as some kind of defence, allowing people to flit from village to village unseen. The **Torciata di San Giuseppe** (☉19 Mar) is a procession through the Via Cava di San Giuseppe marking the end of winter.

Two particularly good examples of *vie cave*, the **Via Cava di Fratenuti** and the **Via Cava di San Giuseppe**, are found 500m west of Pitigliano on the road to Sovana. Fratenuti has high vertical walls and Etruscan markings, and San Giuseppe passes the **Fontana dell'Olmo**, a fountain carved out of solid rock. From it stares the sculpted head of Bacchus, the god of wine and fertility.

There's a fine **walk** from Pitigliano to Sovana (8km) that incorporates parts of the *vie cave*. For a description and map, go to www.trekking.it and download the pdf in the Maremma section. There's also an enjoyable 2km walk from the small stone bridge in the gorge below Sorano along the **Via Cava San Rocco** to the **Necropoli di San Rocco**, another Etruscan burial site.

The open-air **Museo Archeologico all'Aperto 'Alberto Manzi'** (Alberto Manzi Open-Air Archaeology Museum; ☏0564 61 40 67; Strada Provinciale 127 Pantano, off SS74; adult/reduced €4/2; ☉10am-7pm Tue-Sun Apr-Oct), south of Pitigliano on the road to Saturnia, contains sections of *vie cave* and several necropolises.

stairways disappear around corners, cobbled alleys bend tantalisingly out of sight beneath graceful arches and reminders of the town's once-considerable Jewish community remain in the form of a 16th-century synagogue and a unique Jewish-flavoured local cuisine.

◉ Sights

For Etruscan heritage savings, buy the combined ticket (adult/reduced €6/3) giving entry to the Museo Civico Archeologico di Pitigliano and the Museo Archeologico all'Aperto 'Alberto Manzi' outside town.

La Piccola Gerusalemme MUSEUM
(Little Jerusalem; ☏0564 61 42 30; www.lapiccolagerusalemme.it; Vicolo Manin 30; adult/reduced €5/4; ☉10am-1pm & 2.30-6pm Sun-Fri summer, 10am-noon & 3-5pm Sun-Fri winter) Head down Via Zuccarelli and turn left at a sign indicating 'La Piccola Gerusalemme' to visit this fascinating time capsule of Pitigliano's rich but sadly near-extinct Jewish culture. It incorporates a tiny, richly adorned synagogue (established in 1598 and one of only five in Tuscany), ritual bath, kosher butcher, bakery, wine cellar and dyeing workshops.

Museo di Palazzo Orsini MUSEUM
(☏0564 61 60 74; www.palazzo-orsini-pitigliano.it; Piazza della Fortezza 25; adult/child €4/3; ☉10am-1pm & 3-7pm Tue-Sun summer, to 5pm winter) Enlarged by the ruling Orsinis in the 16th century, this

13th-century castle later became the residence of the local bishop and is now a museum. Its rooms are filled with an eclectic collection of artworks and local ecclesiastical oddments. Don't miss the 15th-century painted wooden sculpture of the Madonna with baby Jesus by Jacopo Della Quercia.

Museo Civico Archeologico di Pitigliano MUSEUM
(☏0564 61 40 67; Piazza della Fortezza; adult/reduced €3/2; ☉10am-7pm Mon, Thu & Fri, to 6pm Sat & Sun Jun-Aug, 10am-5pm Sat & Sun Easter-May) Head up the stone stairs to this small but well-run museum, which has rich displays of finds from local Etruscan sites. Highlights include some huge intact *bucchero* (black earthenware pottery) urns dating from the 6th century BC and a collection of charming pinkish-cream clay oil containers in the form of small deer.

✕ Eating & Drinking

La Rocca TUSCAN, PIZZA $
(☏0564 61 42 67; Piazza della Repubblica 12; meals €28, pizzas €4-8.50; ☉9.30am-10pm Tue-Sat, later summer) Generous pourings of local wine are on offer at this cavernous restaurant and wine bar next to one of the panoramic viewpoints on Piazza della Repubblica. It's run by the local agricultural consortium, so the range of *prodotti tipici* (typical local products) showcased on the menu is impressive.

1. Pitigliano (p184)
This spectacular hilltop village sprouts from a volcanic rocky outcrop that towers over the surrounding country.

2. Cattedrale di San Cerbone (p180), Massa Marittima
Don't miss the *Maestà* inside Massa Marittima's *duomo;* attributed by some to be the work of Duccio di Buoninsegna.

3. Scavi di Città (p184), Vetulonia
Foundations of a 2300-year-old Etruscan house were uncovered in 2009.

DON'T MISS

TERME DI SATURNIA

Terme di Saturnia (☎ 0564 60 01 11; www.termedisaturnia.it; day €25, after 2pm €20; ⊗ 9.30am-7pm summer, to 5pm winter) is about 2.5km south of the village of Saturnia. You can spend a whole day dunking yourself in the hot pools and signing on for ancillary activities such as the alluring 'four-hand massage shower' or the somewhat sinister-sounding 'infiltration of gaseous oxygen to reduce excess fat'.

On weekends, the place sometimes morphs into a club after the dinner service.

★ **Il Tufo Allegro**   TUSCAN $$
(☎ 0564 61 61 92; www.iltufoallegro.com; Vicolo della Costituzione 5; meals €42; ⊗ noon-2.30pm & 7.30-9.30pm Wed-Sun) The aromas emanating from the kitchen door off Via Zuccarelli should be enough to draw you down the stairs and into the cosy dining rooms, which are carved out of tufo. Chef Domenico Pichini's menu ranges from traditional to modern and all of his creations rely heavily on local produce for inspiration. It's near La Piccola Gerusalemme.

Hostaria del Ceccottino   ITALIAN $$
(☎ 0564 61 42 73; www.ceccottino.com; Piazza San Gregorio VII 64; meals €45; ⊗ 12.30-3pm & 7-10pm Fri-Wed mid-Mar–mid-Jan) Specialising in *piatti tipici* (typical dishes), Ceccottino serves delicious versions of Tuscan classics such as *spezzatino di cinghiale* (wild boar stew), but also offers less-common dishes inspired by local produce. There might be a tagliatelle made with *bottarga* (salted dried cod roe) from Orbatello, or a *tortelli* stuffed with fresh ricotta and *ortica* (nettles).

★ **Angiolina Vineria**   WINE BAR
(☎ 0564 61 52 91; angiolina.pitigliano@libero.it; Piazza della Repubblica 209; bruschetta €12, cheese & salumi platter €15; ⊗ noon-8.30pm Mon-Fri, to midnight Fri & Sat Mar-Dec) It may be modest in size, but this wine bar is ambitious in its aspirations. There's a small but stellar list of wines by the glass (order the Roccapesta Morellino di Scansano if it's on offer), and a similarly styled food menu. Try the *merenda Toscana* platter of local delicacies (€18).

ℹ Information

The **tourist office** (☎ 0564 61 71 11; www.comune.pitigliano.gr.it; Piazza Garibaldi 12; ⊗ 10am-12.30pm & 3-5.30pm Tue-Sat,

10am-12.30pm Sun summer, 10am-12.30pm & 3-5.30pm Sat, 10am-12.30pm Sun winter) is in the piazza just inside the Old City's main gate.

ℹ Getting There & Away

Tiemme buses (www.tiemmespa.it) leave from Via Santa Chiara, just off Piazza Petruccioli. They tend to operate Monday to Saturday only; buy tickets at Bar Guastini in Piazza Petruccioli. Services include the following:

Grosseto (€7.90, two hours, three daily)

Siena (€10.10, three hours, one daily)

Sorano (€1.50, 10 to 20 minutes, one to three daily)

Sovana (€1.50, 10 to 20 minutes, two daily)

Sovana

The main attractions at this postcard-pretty town are a cobbled main street that dates from Roman times, two austerely beautiful Romanesque churches and a museum.

◉ Sights & Activities

Duomo   CATHEDRAL
(Antica Cattedrale di San Pietro; Via del Duomo; adult/child €2/1; ⊗ 10am-1pm & 3-7pm summer, 11am-1pm & 2.30-5.30pm winter, weekends only mid-Jan–mid-Feb) Built over a 200-year period starting in the 12th century, this Romanesque–Gothic cathedral was commissioned by local boy-made-big Pope Gregory VII (Hildebrand of Sovana; c 1015–85). Its strangely positioned doorway is decorated with carvings of people, animals and plants, and its huge interior has a beauty that owes nothing to artworks and everything to the genius of its architect.

Museo di San Mamiliano   MUSEUM
(Piazza del Pretorio; adult/child €2/free; ⊗ 10am-1pm & 3-7pm Thu-Tue Mar-Oct, 10am-1pm & 2-5pm Sat & Sun Nov & Dec) In 2004 archaeologists excavating beneath the ruined 9th-century Church of St Mamiliano made the discovery of a lifetime – a cache of 498 gold coins buried in a vase under the church floor in the 5th century AD. Most are now displayed in this small museum of Roman times, which occupies the restored church.

Santa Maria Maggiore   CHURCH
(Piazza del Pretorio; ⊗ 9am-5pm) Designed in a Romanesque–Gothic transitional style, the 16th-century frescoes in the apse of this church are perhaps the main reason to head inside; there's also an unusual stone *ciborium* (vaulted canopy over the altar) dating from the 9th century.

★ **Parco Archeologico**
'Città del Tufo'   ARCHAEOLOGICAL SITE
(Necropoli di Sovana; www.leviecave.it; €5; ⊙ 10am-7pm summer, to 6pm Oct, to 5pm Sat & Sun Nov-Mar) At Tuscany's most significant Etruscan tombs, 1.5km east of town, signs in Italian and English guide you around four elaborate burial sites. The headline exhibit is the Tomba Ildebranda, named after Gregory VII, which preserves traces of its carved columns and stairs. The Tomba dei Demoni Alati (Tomb of the Winged Demons) features a recumbent headless terracotta figure.

La Biagiola   WINE
(☑ 366 676 64 00; www.labiagiola.it; Località Pianetti; ⊙ by appointment) Those interested in wine and archaeology might want to combine the two by visiting this wine estate 7km north of Sovana. Recently, the remains of an imperial Roman villa were discovered in the vineyard and the archaeologists excavating it welcome visitors to join them for a one-hour hands-on experience on the dig, followed by a tasting of the estate's wines. Price on application.

✕ Eating & Drinking

★ Vino al Vino   TUSCAN $
(☑ 0564 61 71 08; vinoalvino@virgilio.it; Via del Duomo 10; cheese & salumi plates €14; ⊙ 10.30am-9pm Wed-Mon mid-Mar–Dec, 10.30am-9pm Sat & Sun Jan–mid-Mar) Mellow jazz plays on the soundtrack, art adorns every wall and the vibe is friendly at this hybrid cafe and *enoteca* (wine bar) on Sovana's main street. The speciality-roast coffee is good; cakes (sourced in Pitigliano) are even better. At lunch or dinner, glasses of wine and tasting plates of local produce reign supreme.

❶ Information

The extremely helpful **tourist office** (☑ 0564 61 40 74; ⊙ 10am-1pm & 3-7pm Wed-Mon mid-Mar–Oct, 10am-1pm & 2-5pm Sat & Sun Nov & Dec) is in the Palazzo Pretorio on the main piazza.

❶ Getting There & Away

Between Monday and Saturday, Tiemme buses (www.tiemmespa.it) travel to/from Pitigliano (€1.50, 10 to 20 minutes, two daily) and Sorano (€1.50, 15 minutes, once or twice daily).

Sorano
POP 3430

Sorano's setting is truly dramatic – sitting astride a rocky outcrop, its weatherworn stone houses are built along a ridge over-looking the Lente River and Gorge. Below the ridgeline are *cantine* (cellars) dug out of tufo, as well as a tantalising series of terraced gardens, many part-hidden from public view.

◉ Sights

Fortezza Orsini   FORT
(☑ 0564 63 34 24; adult/reduced €4/2; ⊙ 10am-1pm & 3-7pm Tue-Sun summer,10am-1pm & 2-5pm Sat & Sun Nov & Dec) Work on this massive fortress started in the 11th century. Today it still stands sentinel over the town, its sturdy walls linking two bastions surrounded by a dry moat. The highlight of any visit is undoubtedly a guided tour of the evocative subterranean passages (11am, 3.30pm, 4.30pm and 5.30pm in summer, 11am and 3pm in November and December), which are noticeably chilly even in the height of the Tuscan summer.

Area Archeologica
di Vitozza   ARCHAEOLOGICAL SITE
(⊙ 10am-dusk) [FREE] More than 200 caves pepper a high rock ridge here, making it one of the largest troglodyte dwellings in Italy. The complex was first inhabited in prehistoric times. To explore the site, you'll need two hours and sturdy walking shoes. It's 4km due east of Sorano; there's a signed walking path between Sorano and the site.

✕ Eating & Drinking

Ristorante Fidalma   TUSCAN $$
(☑ 0564 63 30 56; www.ristorantefidalma.com; Piazza Busatti 5; meals €26; ⊙ 12.30-3.30pm & 7.30-10.30pm Thu-Tue; ✸) There's a lot to like at this barn-like restaurant just off Sorano's main piazza. The menu is dominated by home-style Maremmese dishes (expect lots of meat), the pasta is hand-made by *nonna,* and the family members waiting on tables are incredibly friendly. There's even a well-priced set menu of two courses, *contorno* (side dish) and a coffee for €20.

Cantina L'Ottava Rima   WINE BAR
(☑ 349 8024196; www.cantinaottavarima.com; Via del Borgo 25; ⊙ noon-3pm & 6pm-midnight

❶ **CENT SAVER**
· ·
If you're planning to visit the Museo di San Mamiliano and the Parco Archeologico 'Città del Tufo' in Sovana, and the Fortezza Orsini in Sorano, a combined ticket (adult/reduced €8/5) will save you money.

TERENZI

Awarded the 'Emerging Winery of the Year' accolade in Gambero Rosso's 2013 *Vini d'Italia* (Wines of Italy) guide, Terenzi (☑ 0564 59 96 41; www.terenzi.eu; Località Montedonico, Scansano; ☉ 9.30am-7.30pm May-Oct, 9.30am-5.30pm Mon, Tue, Thu & Fri, 9.30am-1pm & 2-5.30pm Wed, 10am-6pm Sat & Sun Nov-Apr) wine estate is now well established among the top producers of Morellino di Scansano. Call ahead to book a free tour of the vineyards and winery, or visit the *cantina* for a tasting (non-vintage wines free, *gran selezione* €2–3 per 150ml).

You'll find Terenzi on a scenic road just outside the town of Scansano, a 50-minute drive from Pitigliano on a secondary route to Grosseto.

Thu-Sun summer, reduced hours winter) Here you'll sip your drink surrounded by carved rock walls – this casual *cantina* has been hacked out of the tufo. Add rickety tables and it's an atmospheric spot to sample local wines and simple dishes that highlight quality Maremmese produce. It's on a terraced walkway towards the foot of town.

ℹ Information

The best source of tourism information is the **tourist office** (☑ 0564 63 30 99; Fortezza; ☉ 10am-1pm & 3-7pm Thu-Sun mid-Mar–Oct, 10am-1pm & 2-5pm Sat & Sun Nov-Dec) in the *fortezza*.

ℹ Getting There & Away

From Monday to Saturday, Tiemme (www.tiem mespa.it) operates services to/from Pitigliano (€1.50, 10 to 20 minutes, one to three daily) and Sovana (€1.50, 15 minutes, two daily).

THE BASSA MAREMMA

The Bassa (Lower) Maremma starts at Grosseto and sweeps along the coast, incorporating the peninsula of Monte Argentario and the mountains and marshes of the Parco Regionale della Maremma. It's a wonderland for nature lovers, full of pristine landscapes with abundant local flora and fauna, and it's also a hugely popular spot for outdoor activities including walking, horse riding and birdwatching.

Grosseto

POP 82,100

Poor Grosseto. Its uninviting name, unattractive surrounds and lack of headline sights lead to it being ignored by most tourists, relegated to a mere navigational marker for those taking the coastal highway to Rome. Those who buck this trend will find a city with some lively places to eat and drink and a vaguely counterculture vibe.

One of the last Sienese-dominated towns to fall into Medici hands (in 1559), Grosseto's bastions, fortress and hexagonal-shaped, 2.5km-long walls were raised by the Florentines in order to protect what was then an important grain and salt depot for the grand duchy. Today, the city is the provincial capital of the Maremma, and its *centro storico* (historic centre) is a perfect place to stroll and experience the *passeggiata* along Corso Carducci.

The city is renowned for its heavy winter rainfalls, which have caused catastrophic floods in the past.

◉ Sights

Roselle   ARCHAEOLOGICAL SITE
(☑ 0564 40 24 03; SS223; adult/reduced €4/2; ☉ 8.30am-7pm May-Aug, to 6.30pm Mar, Apr, Sep & Oct, to 5.30pm Nov-Feb) In the 7th century BC Roselle (Rusellae) was already an Etruscan town; it fell under Roman control in the 3rd century BC. Although there are no great monuments, you do get a clear idea of the town's layout from the remaining Roman defensive walls, amphitheatre, traces of houses and baths, forum, workshops and streets. When here, be sure to take the 1km walk alongside the settlement's massive, still intact 8000-year-old walls. It's located 11km northeast of Grosseto off the E78.

★ Museo Archeologico e d'Arte della Maremma   MUSEUM
(☑ 0564 48 87 50; http://maam.comune.grosse to.it; Piazza Baccarini 3; adult/reduced €5/2.50; ☉ 10am-6pm Tue-Fri, 10am-1pm & 5-8pm Sat & Sun Jun-Sep, 9.30am-4pm Tue-Fri, 10am-1pm & 4-7pm Sat & Sun Apr-May, 9am-2pm Tue-Fri, 10am-1pm, 4-7pm Sat & Sun Oct-Mar) Grosseto's major tourist drawcard features an archaeological museum on the ground floor and a museum of ecclesiastical art upstairs. Items unearthed from Roselle are given pride of place downstairs – don't miss the statues of the family of the Emperor Augustus. There's also an impressive collection of Etruscan funerary urns. The 2nd floor is home to artworks spanning

the 13th to 19th centuries, including Stefano di Giovanni's *Madonna delle ciliege* (Madonna with Cherries; c 1445), which originally hung in the city's *duomo*.

Cattedrale di San Lorenzo   CATHEDRAL
(www.diocesidigrosseto.it; Piazza del Duomo; ☉10am-6pm Mon-Sat, 9.30-11am & 12.15-6pm Sun) Grosseto's late-13th-century *duomo* has a distinctive Sienese character and a particularly beautiful rose window. Much of the facade was renewed along neo-Romanesque lines during the 19th century. Inside, look for Matteo di Giovanni's *Madonna delle grazie* (Our Lady of Grace) in the left transept, the 1470 baptismal font and the 15th-century stained-glass windows depicting saints.

🎉 Festivals & Events

Festa di San Lorenzo   CULTURAL
(☉9 & 10 Aug) The festival celebrates Grosseto's patron saint, St Lawrence. Most events are staged in or around the *duomo*.

🍴 Eating & Drinking

The main bar and cafe strips are Via San Martino, Via Ricasoli and Via degli Aldobrandeschi in the *centro storico*.

★ Gelateria Key West   GELATO $
(Via San Martino 25; gelato €2-5.50; ☉8.30am-10.30pm Sun-Fri, to midnight Sat) Grosseto's local population seems like a happy lot, and the presence of this sensational *gelateria* in the centre of the city may well have something to do with this. Fresh ingredients are used to create some of the best icy treats in Tuscany – it's an essential stop on any city itinerary. Choose from gelato, frozen yoghurt or crepes (€2.50).

Al Numero Nove   TUSCAN $
(☑0564 42 76 98; Via degli Aldobrandeschi 9; meals €24; ☉noon-3pm & 6-10pm Tue-Sun; ☝) Grosseto's bohemian set congregates at this hybrid restaurant and wine bar near the *duomo*, drawn by the arty decor, laid-back atmosphere and well-priced food and drinks. Pastas are largely vegetarian, and there are *spuntini* (snacks) to graze on if you don't feel like a full meal.

L'Uva e il Malto   MODERN ITALIAN $$
(☑0564 41 12 11; www.luvaeilmalto.it; Via Mazzini 165; meals €42; ☉12.30-2.30pm & 7.30pm-midnight Mon-Sat) Chef Moreno Cardone takes great pride in his dishes, using quality local produce to create tasty, attractively presented meals. There are fish and meat options aplenty, but few vegetarian choices. Wife Samantha runs front of house and is always happy to guide you through the predominantly local wine list.

Vineria da Romolo   TUSCAN $$
(☑0564 27 55 1; Via Vinzaglio 5; meals €25; ☉10am-3pm & 6pm-midnight Thu-Mon, 6pm-midnight Wed) Wine barrels turned into tables and benches set the scene at this casual trattoria. Inside it's a mass of bottles, plastic grapes and the odd fake parrot. The food is flavourful and traditional – expect country-style pastas and platters piled-high with meat and cheese. The same owners operate the popular Pizzaria da Romolo (Via Vinzaglio 18; pizzas €5-9; ☉7pm-midnight Wed-Mon), opposite.

Caffè Ricasoli   BAR
(☑0564 2 62 20; Strada Ricasoli 20; ☉7am-midnight Tue-Sat; ☝) Old vinyl records may dangle from the ceiling, but the music at this beatnik cafe-bar is bang up to date. DJs spin Italian pop towards the end of the week and it hosts occasional live music. There's an

SOUTHERN TUSCANY GROSSETO

WORTH A TRIP

DIACCIA BOTRONA NATURE RESERVE

The marshes surrounding the coastal town of Castiglione della Pescaia are an important shelter for migrating birds, and 12.7-sq-km Riserva Naturale Provinciale Diaccia Botrona (☑348 774 32 01, 389 003 13 69; www.maremma-online.it) off the SS322 is a wonderful chance to explore this flat yet fascinating landscape. Boat tours (adult/child €12/6; 5pm and 6.30pm Tuesday to Sunday mid-June to mid-September) enable you to spot waterfowl, heron, flamingo and other species; book in advance.

Boat tours leave from the visitor centre (Riserva Naturale Provinciale Diaccia Botrona; €2.50; ☉3pm-sunset Thu-Sun mid-Sep–Mar, 3.30-7pm Thu-Sun Apr–mid-Jun, 4-8.30pm Tue-Sun mid-Jun–mid Sep) in the Casa Rossa Ximenes, a handsome sluice-house commissioned in the mid-18th century by Grand Duke Pietro Leopoldo I of Lorraine to help reclaim the marshes for agriculture and reduce the area's horrifyingly high levels of malaria. The visitor centre features a multimedia display (in Italian only) about the reserve's wildlife, the building and the reclamation.

internet cafe at the back and the free wi-fi, like the coffee, comes fast and strong.

❶ Information

There is a **tourism information point** (☑ 0564 42 79 18; www.turismoinmaremma.it; Corso Carducci 5; ☉ hours vary) on pedestrianised Corso Carducci.

❶ Getting There & Away

BUS

Buses usually leave from the train station. Buy tickets at the **Tiemme ticket office** (Grosseto Train Station; ☉ 7.30am-6.45pm Mon-Sat) next door. Monday to Saturday services include:

Florence (€11.70, two hours, six daily)
Massa Marittima (€5.20, one hour, four daily)
Pitigliano (€7.90, two hours, three daily)
Porto Santo Stefano (€5.80, one hour, one daily)
Rome Airport (€17, two hours, two daily)
Siena (€7.80, 80 minutes, 10 daily)

CAR & MOTORCYCLE

A Zona a Traffico Limitato (ZTL; Limited Traffic Zone) applies in the *centro storico*. There's plenty of paid car parking surrounding the city walls; the most convenient is at Porta Corsica, next to the city gate on Viale Zimenes (€0.70 per hour).

TRAIN

The main coastal train line runs between Pisa, Livorno and Rome via Grosseto. Services include the high-speed (*Alta Velocità*) *Frecciabianca*. Regular (roughly hourly) connections from Grosseto include:

Genoa (Intercity €36, four hours)
Livorno (*Regionale* €11.50, 1¾ hours)
Pisa (*Regionale* €12.70, two hours)
Rome (Intercity €24, 1¾ hours)

Parco Regionale della Maremma

Hundreds of acres of forests, pristine coasts, countless activities and your chance to be a cowboy are all on offer in this wild and wonderful national park. It's also a popular destination for beachgoers, who enjoy safe swimming at the 8km-long sandy beach at Marina di Albarese.

◉ Sights & Activities

⭐ Parco Regionale
della Maremma   NATURE RESERVE
(☑ 0564 39 32 38; www.parco-maremma.it; adult/reduced from €6/4; ☉ 8.30am-4pm Apr–mid-Mar, to 6pm mid-Jun–Oct, to 2pm Nov-Mar) This spec-

tacular regional park incorporates the Uccellina Mountain Range, a 600-hectare pine forest, marshy plains and 20km of unspoiled coast. Park access is limited to 13 signed walking trails ranging in length from 2.5km to 13km; the most popular is A2 ('Le Torri'), a 5.8km walk to the beach. From mid-June to mid-September you can only visit on a guided tour because of possible bushfires; call ahead to check times. An entry fee is paid at the main, Alberese visitor centre.

Terre Regionali Toscani   HORSE RIDING
(☑ 0564 40 71 80; www.alberese.com; Strada del Mare 25, Spergolaia, Alberese; ☉ 10am-1pm Thu Jul & Aug, other times by reservation) Parts of the park are farmed, mainly to graze the Maremma's famous cattle. This 400-hectare organic farm offers visitors a superb insight into the work of the local *butteri* (traditional cowboys), who herd the property's cows; experienced riders can take a four-hour '*butteri experience*' and join the cowboys in their herding work (€60).

The property is also the regional headquarters of the Slow Food organisation and offers tastings of its produce in summer. Book at least 24-hours ahead.

Il Gelsomino   HORSE RIDING
(☑ 0564 40 51 33; www.ilgelsomino.com; Via Strada del Barbicato 4, Alberese; treks from €40) Horse-riding treks through the park are suitable for all skill levels – beginners welcome.

🍴 Eating

La Bottega Maremmana   DELI $
(Alberese; ☉ 7am-8pm Mon-Sat, to 7pm Sun Apr-Oct, 8am-4pm Mon-Fri & 8.30am-12.30pm Sat & Sun Nov-Mar) This store opposite the park's Alberese visitor centre stocks a range of local produce and will also make up *panini* on request.

Osteria Il Mangiapane   TUSCAN $$
(☑ 0564 40 72 63; Strada Cerretale 9, Alberese; meals €28; ☉ noon-2.30pm & 7-10pm Easter-Sep) You can't get more Maremmese than this. Vowing to 'stay in touch with nature and deliver authentic, old-fashioned meals', the chef here successfully does just that. There are tables inside, but everyone prefers to sit in the garden, where there are trees and a children's play area. Try the beef, which is sourced from the Terre Regionali Toscani farm.

🛍 Shopping

⭐ Bottega Terre
Regionali Toscani   FOOD & DRINKS
(Via dell'Artigliere 4, Alberese; ☉ 7am-7pm Jun-Sep, closed Wed & Sun Oct-May) Showcasing produce

SOUTHERN TUSCANY PARCO REGIONALE DELLA MAREMMA

from the local farm (p192) of the same name, this shop is manna from heaven for self-caterers – look out for top-quality Maremmana beef, honey, dried pasta made with wheat grown on the farm, olive oils, *pecorini* (sheep's cheese), *salumi* (meats) and DOCG wines. One robust Morellino di Scansano costs a mere €1.80 per litre, so bring bottles to fill.

ℹ Information

Main Visitor Centre (☏ 0564 39 32 38; Via del Bersagliere 7-9, Alberese; ☺8am-6pm mid-Jun–mid-Sep, to 4pm mid-Sep–mid-Nov, to 2pm mid-Nov–mid-Jun) In Alberese.
Seasonal Visitor Centre (☏ 0564 88 71 73; Via Nizza 12, Talamone; ☺9am-noon & 3-5pm Jul & Aug) A summer-only visitor centre that adjoins the Talamone Aquarium at the park's southern edge (the aquarium showcases the local lagoon environment and works to protect local turtles).

ℹ Getting There & Away

Tiemme buses travel between Alberese and Grosseto (€1.80, eight daily). Buy tickets at Caffè Hawaii near the bus stop.

Orbetello

POP 14,900

Set on a balance-beam isthmus running through a lagoon south of the Parco Regionale della Maremma, Orbetello is a relatively laid-back destination with some appealing, if low-key, historic buildings and a bird-packed nature reserve.

◉ Sights

L'Oasi WWF di Orbetello NATURE RESERVE
(☏0564 89 88 29; www.wwf.it; SS Aurelia, Località Ceriolo; ☺guided visits 9.30am & 1.30pm Sat & Sun Sep-Apr) FREE An extraordinary 140 species of birds have been seen on Orbetello Lagoon. The best place to spot some of them is at the L'Oasi WWF di Orbetello north of town. As well as winter weekend visits, you can also explore the reserve in July and August (by appointment only) on Tuesday and Saturday at 5.30pm.

ℹ Information

Tourist Office (☏ 0564 86 04 47; www.proloco-orbetello.it; Piazza della Repubblica 1; ☺10am-1pm & 4-6pm) Opposite the cathedral.

ℹ Getting There & Away

BUS
Between Monday and Saturday infrequent Tiemme buses connect Orbetello and Orbetello-Monte

GIARDINO DEI TAROCCHI

Twenty-two oversized Gaudí-influenced sculptures tumble down a hillside at fantastical sculpture garden Giardino dei Tarocchi Scultura (http://ilgiardinodei tarocchi.it/en; Località Garavicchio-Capalbio; adult/reduced €12/7; ☺2.30-7.30pm summer) created by Franco-American artist Niki de Saint Phalle (1930–2002). The whimsical, mosaic-covered creations merge with the surrounding park, creating what the artist called a 'garden of joy'. It's a colossal effort that depicts characters from the tarot card pack (think the Moon, Fool and Justice) and even includes a sculpture lived in by De Saint Phalle while the garden was being built.

Sculptor Jean Tinguely contributed to many of the figures, and the visitor centre was designed by Swiss architect Mario Botta. The sculpture garden is 25km east of Orbetello; take the Pescia Fiorentina exit from the SS1.

Argenteria train station with Porto Santo Stafano and Porto Ercole on Monte Argentario (€2.50).

TRAIN
Frequent services travel between Grosseto and Orbetello-Monte Argenteria (€4.40, 25 minutes).

Monte Argentario

POP 12,700

Once an island, this rugged promontory became linked to the mainland by three slender, 6km-long accumulations of sand, one of which now forms the isthmus of Orbetello. Overdevelopment has spoiled the promontory's northern side, particularly around crowded Porto Santo Stefano. Porto Ercole on the promontory's less-frenetic southern side is a smaller and more attractive harbour, with three historic forts and a long sandy beach known as Feniglia. Traffic on the promontory is simply horrendous and accommodation prices head into the stratosphere during the high season – avoid visiting at this time.

◉ Sights & Activities

Old Town HISTORIC SITE
(Porto Ercole) Porto Ercole's *centro storico* stretches up the hillside, past the sandwiched-in Chiesa di Sant'Erasmo and

> **OFF THE BEATEN TRACK**
>
> ## MAGLIANO IN TOSCANA
>
> A 23km drive inland from Orbetello leads to this hilltop town, fortified by monumental walls built between the 14th and 16th centuries. Specific sights are limited to the Romanesque churches of San Martino and San Giovanni Battista (the latter has a remodelled Renaissance facade). But the trip is well rewarded by lunch in the pretty garden at Antica Trattoria Aurora (☑0564 59 27 74; Via Chiasso Lavagnini 12, Magliano in Toscana; meals €45; ☉noon-2.30pm & 7.30-10pm Thu-Tue Mar-Dec), a restaurant serving excellent modern Tuscan cuisine. To get here, take the Albinia exit off the SS1 and then turn left onto the SS323.

up towards the largest of the three Spanish forts that surround the town.

Forte Stella   FORT
(Porto Ercole; €2; ☉10am-1pm & 6-9pm daily Jul-Aug, Sat & Sun only Jun) Built by the Spanish, this 16th-centry fort, an unusual star shape (hence its name), is the only Porto Ercole fort open to the public.

Via Panoramica   SCENIC DRIVE
Signs point you towards this narrow route that encircles the entire Monte Argentario prom-ontory. It offers sweeping sea views across to the hazy whaleback of the Isola de Giglio. The road can get dangerously busy in summer.

Caravaggio's Tomb   TOMB
(Via Caravaggio, Porto Ercole) One of the greatest painters of the Renaissance, Michelangelo Merisi Caravaggio died in Porto Ercole on 18 July, 1610 after a tempestuous and short life. In 2014, authorities 'found' his bones in a local crypt and DNA tested them to prove their authenticity. They then constructed this extremely strange tomb in the centre of town. Not everyone approved – many locals were shocked at the reliquary-like structure, which they deemed more suited to a saint than the sinner Caravaggio undoubtedly was.

✖ Eating & Drinking

Don't expect too much from eateries here – quality is generally on the low side.

★**Baretto**   BAR, CAFE
(☑0564 83 26 54; Lungomare Andrea Doria 39, Porto Ercole; ☉8am-3am, reduced hours winter) One of the few bars in Porto Ercole open year-round, Baretto has a lovely terrace overlooking the marina. In summer, tables here are the most sought-after in town. The friendly bar staff are multi-talented, making good coffees and excellent cocktails.

Bar Giulia   CAFE
(Via del Molo 16, Porto Santo Stefano; ☉daily summer, 7am-2am Tue-Sun rest of yr) The terrace of Bar Giulia is a popular locals' haunt, sitting as it does right beside the sea overlooking a harbour framed by buildings stacked up on the slopes behind. All in all it's a picturesque spot for a morning coffee, *panino* or late-afternoon *aperitivo*. It's right at the far (west) end of the *lungomare* (port promenade).

❶ Information

There are tourist offices in both Porto Santo Stefano and Porto Ercole. Both can supply the handy *Hiking Through Argentario* map, which outlines 27 hiking trails on Monte Argentario.
Porto Santo Stefano Tourist Office (☑0564 81 19 79; www.prolocomonteargentario.com; Piazzale Sant'Andrea 1, Porto Santo Stefano; ☉3-6pm Fri, 9am-12.30pm & 3-6pm Sat, 9am-12.30pm Sun Easter–mid-Jun & Oct, 9.30am-1pm & 4.30-7pm daily mid-Jun–Sep) Set at the far eastern end of the port.
Porto Ercole Tourist Office (☑0564 81 19 79; www.prolocomonteargentario.com; Piazza Roma, Porto Ercole; ☉3-6pm Fri, 9am-12.30pm & 3-6pm Sat, 9am-12.30pm Sun Easter–mid-Jun & Oct, 9.30am-1pm & 4.30-7pm daily mid-Jun–Sep) On Piazza Roma near the port.

❶ Getting There & Away

BOAT
Maregiglio (www.maregiglio.it) and Toremar (www.toremar.it) operate year-round ferry services between Porto Santo Stefano and the island of Giglio, one hour away. Fares cost around €26 return per passenger and €90 re-turn per car.

BUS
Between Monday and Saturday infrequent Tiemme buses connect Porto Santo Stefano and Porto Ercole with central Orbetello and its train station (€2.50). They also run to Grosseto (€5.80).

Central Coast & Elba

Best Places to Eat

➜ Vetto alle Vaglie (p201)
➜ La Barrocciaia (p201)
➜ Enoteca Tognoni (p204)
➜ Osteria di Suvereto da l'Ciocio (p208)
➜ Ristoro Agricolo Montefabbrello (p214)
➜ Enoteca de Centro (p204)

Best Wine Tasting

➜ Petra Wine (p208)
➜ Tenuta Argentiera (p205)
➜ Tenuta La Chiusa (p214)
➜ La Regola (p204)

Why Go?

Despite possessing the types of landscapes that dreams are made of, much of this part of Tuscany feels far away from well-beaten tourist trails. Here you can investigate the multicultural past and extraordinary cuisine of port city Livorno and then follow the Strada del Vino e dell'Olio Costa degli Etruschi south, visiting vineyards, olive groves, medieval villages and scenic archaeological sites along the way.

And then there's Elba: ripe for alfresco frolics, this Mediterranean island has a landscape dotted with orange trees, palms, vineyards and sandy covers begging you to lay down a beach towel. It's the perfect place to wind down after a stretch of busy Tuscan travelling.

Road Distances (km)

	Suvereto	Livorno	Piombino	Bogheri
Livorno	79			
Piombino	24	86		
Bolgheri	39	50	38	
Portoferrario	24+1hr	86+1hr	1hr	38+1hr

Central Coast & Elba Highlights

1 Livorno
(p198) Sampling superb seafood and investigating Tuscany's multicultural past in this historic port city.

2 Strada del Vino e dell'Olio Costa degli Etruschi
(p206) Taste-testing local drops at wineries and *enoteche* (wine bars) while following this scenic wine route along the Etruscan coast.

3 Parco Archeologico di Baratti e Populonia
(p209) Picnicking between Etruscan tombs and enjoying majestic sea views.

4 Elba (p209)
Emulating Napoleon and spending a far-too-brief sojourn on

Ligurian Sea

Gorgona

TYRRHENIAN SEA

Crespina

Lari

Lorenzana

Casciana Terme

Chianni

Riparbella

Montescudaio

Monteverdi Marittimo

6 Terme de Sasseta

Castagneto Carducci

Sassetta

Donoratico

San Guido

2 Bolgheri

Strada del Vino e dell'Olio Costa degli Etruschi [SS243]

Bibbona

[SS68]

Forte di Bibbona

Marina di Bibbona

Rosignano Marittimo

Vada

Cecina

Marina di Cecina

Rosignano Solvay

[SS1]

Castiglioncello

Fortullino

Castelnuovo Misericordia

Quercianella

Montenero Gabbro

Antignano

[A12]

[A12]

[SS206]

[SS1]

Livorno 1

the most magical
island in the Tuscan
Archipelago.

5 Suvereto
(p205) Exploring the
streets and stairways
of this medieval time-
capsule of a village.

**6 Terme di
Sassetta** (p208)
Soaking in a mineral-
rich thermal spa set in
dense chestnut forest.

Capraia
Capraia ▲
Monte
Castello
(447m)
San
Stéfano
Monte
Arpagna
(415m)

Ferry to Corsica

Ferry to Olbia (Sardinia)

Ferry to Corsica

Punta
Brigantina

Pianosa

Chiessi
Monte
Capanne
(1018m) ▲
Fetovaia
Cavoli
La Pila
Marciana
Marina
La
Biodola
Marina
di Campo
Lacona
Elba 4
Portoferraio
Le Grotte
Porto
Azzurro
Porto
Azzurro
Capoliveri
Cavo
Rio Marina

Golfo di
Follonica

Ferry to Giglio

Ferry to Giglio

Follonica

Venturina
SS398
SS1
Campiglia
Marittima
San Vincenzo
Baratti
SP23
Populonia
Piombino
**Parco Archeologico di
Baratti e Populonia 3**

Parco Archeominerario
di San Silvestro
Cafaggio
5 Suvereto
Belvedere

N

10 miles
20 km

LIVORNO

POP 159,219

Tuscany's third-largest city is a quintessential port town with a colourful history and cosmopolitan heritage. Declared a free port in the 17th century, Livorno (Leghorn in English) attracted traders from across the globe, who brought with them new customs and habits, exotic goods, slaves and foreign forms of worship. The result was a city famed throughout Europe for its multiculturalism. Today its seafood is the best on the Tyrrhenian coast, its shabby historic quarter threaded with Venetian-style canals is full of character and its elegant belle époque buildings offer evocative reminders of a prosperous past. An easy train trip from Florence, Pisa and Rome, it makes an understated but undeniably worthwhile stop on any Tuscan itinerary.

History

The earliest references to Livorno date from 1017. The port was ruled by Pisa and Genoa for centuries, until Florence took control in 1421. It was still tiny; by the 1550s it had only 480 residents. But all that changed under Cosimo I de' Medici, who converted the scrawny settlement into a heavily fortified bastion – to the point that even today it's known throughout Italy as a 'Medici town'.

The 17th-century declaration of Livorno as a free port sparked swift development and the 19th century saw even more development. But as parts of the local community became more and more prosperous, issues of social inequity arose, leading to the 1921 founding of the Italian Community Party.

As one of Fascist Italy's main naval bases, Livorno was bombed heavily during WWII and many of its historic buildings were destroyed.

◉ Sights

Save money when you're in Livorno by purchasing a Livorno Card (1/2/3 days for €3/4/5), which gives free local bus transport, full entry to the Museo Civico Giovanni Fattori and discounted entry to the Museo di Storia Naturale del Mediterraneo, Acquario di Livorno and boat tours. Each adult pass also gives one accompanying child aged 11 and under the same benefits. The cards are available at *tabacchi,* some hotels, the train station and the tourist office (p203).

★ **Santuario della Madonna di Montenero**   CHRISTIAN SITE
(☑ 0586 57 96 27; www.santuariomontenero.org; Piazza di Montenero 9; ⊘ 8.30am-12.30pm & 2.30-6pm summer, 8.30am-5pm Mon-Fri & 7.30am-5.30pm Sat & Sun winter) The story goes like this: in 1345, the Virgin Mary appeared to a shepherd, who led her to black mountain *(monte nero)*, a haven of brigands. Needless to say, the brigands immediately saw the error of their ways and built a chapel on the mountain. Soon pilgrims arrived and the chapel was extended in stag-

---

THREE PERFECT DAYS

Day One

Livorno (p198) does seafood like nowhere else in Tuscany. Examine raw specimens bright and early at the Mercato Centrale (p202), stay around for lunch at Vetto alle Vaglie (p201) or La Barrocciaia (p201) and then head to the waterfront to join the *passeggiata* (evening stroll) along the black-and-white chequered Terrazza Mascagni (p199) before dinner and a glass or two of vino at friendly Cantina Nardi (p201).

Day Two

From Livorno head south, wending your way through a rolling hinterland strung with medieval villages and vines. Famous foodie stops include Bolgheri (p204), where Enoteca Tognoni (p204) and Enoteca de Centro (p204) are top picks. Next, pop into Tenuta Argentiera (p205) and Petra Wine (p208) to taste local Val di Cornia DOC wines before overnighting in postcard-perfect Suvereto (p205).

Day Three

On day three, head across the water to the paradisaical island of Elba. Catch the ferry from Piombino to Portoferraio, explore the waterfront, visit Napoleon-related sites and lunch in the Old Town. You might also squeeze in a trip up Monte Capanne (p215) before enjoying a farmhouse dinner at Ristoro Agricolo Montefabbrello (p214) and then checking into a nearby hotel.

THE CITY OF NATIONS

Livorno's declaration as a free port in the 17th century made it a magnet for British, Dutch and other merchants trading between Europe and the Middle East. The long and prosperous involvement of these merchants with the city is reflected in the churches still standing in the town's centre: the Greek community's **Chiesa dei Greci Uniti**; (Chiesa della Santissima Annunziata; Via della Madonna) Armenian community's **Chiesa di San Gregorio Armeno** (San Gregorio Illuminatore; Via della Madonna); Dutch-German community's **Chiesa Olandese-Alemanna** (Scali degli Olandesi 20); and multinational **Chiesa della Madonna** (Via della Madonna 22). Sadly, the original 17th-century synagogue where the city's then-300-strong Jewish community worshipped was destroyed during WWII; a modern concrete **synagogue** (Piazza Elijah Benamozegh) was built as a replacement after the war.

The traders weren't the only foreigners to live in Livorno: the Medicis were involved in the slave trade, and African slaves formed part of the labour force that built the canal system in Piccola Venezia and feature in the 17th-century **Monumento dei Quattro Mori** (Monument of the Four Moors; Map p200; Piazza Giuseppe Micheli) opposite the port. Though commissioned to commemorate the victories of Grand Duke Ferdinand I of Tuscany over the Ottomans, its depiction of the Grand Duke elevated above the chained, subjected African slaves is a disturbing reminder of this dark episode in the city's history.

es; it reached its present form in 1774. Rooms and corridors surrounding the church house a fascinating collection of 20,000 historic ex-votos thanking the Virgin for miracles.

The best time to visit is on 8 September, for the Festa del Madonna. To get here by public transport, take the LAM Rosso bus (direction: Montenero) and get off at the last stop, Piazza delle Carrozze in Montenero Basso. From there, take the historic funicular (€2, every 10 to 20 minutes) up to the sanctuary.

Terrazza Mascagni STREET
(Viale Italia; ☺24hr) FREE No trip to Livorno is complete without a stroll along this seafront terrace with its dramatic black-and-white chessboard-style pavement. When it was built in the 1920s, it was called Terrazza Ciano after the leader of the Livorno fascist movement; it now bears the name of Livorno-born opera composer Pietro Mascagni (1863–1945).

Acquario di Livorno AQUARIUM
(☑0586 26 91 11; www.acquariodilivorno.com; Piazzale Mascagni 1; adult/child €14/8; ☺10am-6pm Apr-Jun & Sep, to 7.30pm Jul & Aug, tour 4pm) The main attraction here is a 45-minute 'Behind the Tanks' tour that visits the aquarium's kitchen, laboratory and tanks. Offered daily, it is unexpectedly fascinating (who knew that a turtle eats kilos of salad every day?). Front of house, the stars of the show are reef sharks, seahorses and huge green sea turtles Ari and Cuba. The Napoleon fish with their prominent and familiar profiles provide a laugh. Upstairs there's a reptile area featuring a chameleon and gloriously green iguana.

Piccola Venezia AREA
(Little Venice) Piccola Venezia is a tangle of small canals built during the 17th century using Venetian methods of reclaiming land from the sea. At its heart sits the remains of the Medici-era **Fortezza Nuova** (New Fort; ☺24hr) FREE. Canals link this with the slightly older waterfront **Fortezza Vecchia** (Old Fort; infofortezzavecchia@portolivorno.it; ☺9am-7pm Tue-Sun) FREE. The waterways can be explored by canal-side footpaths but a boat tour is the best way to see its shabby-chic panoramas of faded, peeling apartments draped with brightly coloured washing, interspersed with waterside cafes and bars.

Chiesa di Santa Caterina CHURCH
(☑0586 89 40 90; www.chiesadisantacaterina.it; Piazza dei Domenicani; ☺9am-12.30pm & 3-6.30pm Mon-Sat, 9am-12.30pm Sun) This early-18th-century Domenican church with its thick stone walls and prominent dome stands sentry on the western side of Piazza dei Domenicani as it did for the Medicis, who commissioned its construction. Sadly, they ran out of money before the facade could be covered in marble. The main altar features a painting of *The Coronation of the Virgin* by Giorgio Vasari, and there's a gallery of ex-votos to its right.

Chiesa di San Ferdinando Re CHURCH
(☑0586 88 85 41; Piazza Anita Garibaldi 1) Constructed between 1704 and 1714 but extensively damaged during WWII and subsequently rebuilt, this church was named after the King of Castille. Its ornate interior features stucco and marble decoration, as well as statues by

Central Livorno

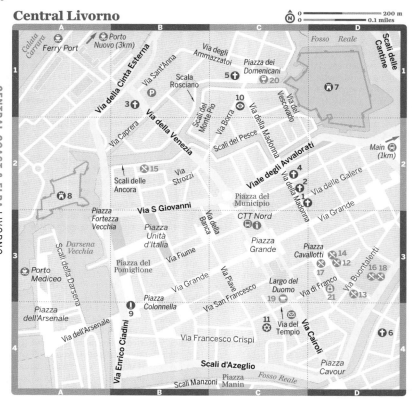

Central Livorno

Giovanni Baratta. The main marble altar includes Baratta's sculpture of an angel freeing two slaves and acknowledges the role of this congregation in paying the ransom of Christian slaves in North Africa during the 17th century.

Museo Civico Giovanni Fattori GALLERY
(☑ 0586 82 46 20; museofattori@comune.livorno.it; Via San Jacopo in Acquaviva 65; adult/reduced €6/4; ☉ 10am-1pm & 4-7pm Tue-Sun) The highlight of a visit here is the 19th-century building. Known as Villa Mimbelli, it has an ornately decorated

interior featuring an extraordinary staircase with balustrades in the form of naked cherubs. Works in the collection include a few medieval and Renaissance pieces, but the main focus is on works by the 19th-century Italian Impressionist Macchiaioli school led by Livorno-born Giovanni Fattori (1825–1908). Artists in this group worked directly from nature, emphasising naturalness through patches, or 'stains' *(macchia),* of colour.

🏃 Activities

The city's beach clubs open from May to September.

Bagni Pancaldi   SWIMMING

(☑0586 80 55 66; www.pancaldiacquaviva.it; Viale Italia 56, Terrazza Mascagni; adult/child €6/5; ⊙8am-8pm May-Sep, later high summer) The elegant soft-apricot facade of Bagni Pancaldi shelters old-fashioned baths where you can swim, rent canoes, relax under rented umbrellas and frolic in the sun. The baths were the height of sophistication, hosting tea dances and musical soirées, when they first opened in 1840 and they're still a popular place to see and be seen.

👉 Tours

Livorno in Battello   BOATING

(☑333 1573372; www.livornoinbattello.it; adult/child €12/5) Three local companies offer daily one-hour guided tours of Livorno's Medicean waterways by boat, but this is the only one that operates year-round (up to four departures daily in summer, limited departures December to February). Boats leave from Scali Finocchietti in summer and from Piazza Giuseppe Micheli in winter. Buy tickets and check schedules/departure points at the tourist office (p203).

🍴 Eating

Livornonese cuisine – particularly traditionally prepared seafood – is known throughout Italy for its excellence. Indeed, sampling the city's signature dish of *cacciucco* (pronounced kar-*choo*-ko), a mixed seafood stew, is reason enough to visit the city. Preferably made using the local Slow Food–accredited San Vincenzo tomatoes, it packs more than its fair share of flavour.

★**Antica Torteria Al**
Mercato Da Gagarin   SANDWICHES $

(☑0586 88 40 86; Via del Cardinale 24; ⊙8am-2pm & 4.30-8.30pm Mon-Sat) There's only one treat on offer here: a simply sensational sandwich known as a *cinque e cinque* (five and five)

that is filled with scrumptious *torta di ceci* (chickpea pancake). When ordering, choose between bread or focaccia and consider adding the traditional accompaniment of a *spuma bionda* (traditional carbonated drink).

★**Antica Friggitoria**   SWEETS $

(☑0586 88 45 71; www.anticafriggitoria.it; Piazza Cavalotti 9; ⊙8.30am-12.30pm & 4-7.30pm Mon-Sat) It's rare to encounter a Livornese who isn't a fan of the delectable *frati* (doughnuts) and *scagliozzi* (fried polenta) that have been made at this simple place on the city's major market square since 1920. In the lead-up to the Festival of San Giuseppe in March, customers flock here to buy *frittelle di riso* (sweet fried rice balls).

★**Gelateria Populare 2**   GELATO $

(☑0586 26 03 54; www.gelateriapopolare2.it; Via Carlo Meyer 11; gelato €2.20-3.70; ⊙8am-1am Tue-Sun summer, to 8pm winter; 🤙) Many locals stop at this local institution for a sugar hit after enjoying a late-afternoon *passeggiata* (stroll) on the Terrazza Mascagni, and we strongly recommend you do the same. Made fresh each day, its gelato is undoubtedly the best in town. Also serves crepes, frappès and hot chocolate (the latter in winter only).

★**Vetto alle Vaglie**   TUSCAN $

(☑347 7487020; www.allevettovaglie.com; Counter 111, Mercato Centrale; mains €5-15; ⊙8am-3pm Tue-Thu & Sat, 8am-3pm & from 7pm Fri) Owned by three sommeliers, this wine bar in the historic Mercato Centrale has a menu that changes according to what produce is fresh and plentiful on the day – it's just as likely to feature *triglie alla Livornese* (mullet in a tomato sauce) as it is pasta with an aromatic pesto sauce. It also – unsurprisingly – offers an impressive selection of wine.

★**La Barrocciaia**   OSTERIA $

(☑0586 88 26 37; www.labarrocciaia.it; Piazza Cavallotti 13; meals €24, panini €5-7; ⊙11am-3pm & 6-11pm Tue-Sat, 6-11pm Sun) Locals speak of La Barrocciaia with great fondness – partly because of a homely interior that's alive with banter, but also because of its simple but flavour-packed food. Stews fluctuate between wild boar and *cacciucco,* there's always a choice of *mare* (sea) or *terra* (land) antipasti and it's perfectly acceptable to drop in for a simple *panino* and glass of wine.

★**Cantina Nardi**   TUSCAN $

(☑0586 80 80 06; Via Cambini 6-8; bar snacks from €1, meals €22; ⊙10am-3.30pm & 4.45-9.30pm

DON'T MISS

AT THE MARKET

Mercato Centrale (Mercato Centrale detto Vettovaglie; Via Buontalenti; ⊙ 6am-2pm Mon-Sat) The largest covered market in Italy, this 95m-long neoclassical building miraculously survived Allied WWII bombing. Arresting both gastronomically and architecturally, it has a particularly impressive fish hall that has recently undergone a sensitive restoration. Famed Italian painter Amedeo Modigliani (1184–1920) once had an atelier on the upper floor (now offices).

Mercato di Piazza Cavallotti (Piazza Cavallotti; ⊙ 6am-1pm Mon-Sat) Head here in the morning to join the local shoppers making their purchases from open-air stalls full of violet artichokes, golden courgette flowers, hot red peppers and seasonal fruit and veg.

VAD Formaggi (☑ 0586 88 41 06; www.vadformaggi.com; Via di Franco 36; ⊙ 7.45am-12.45pm Mon & Wed, 7.45am-12.45pm & 4.45-7.45pm Thu-Sat) The walls of this extraordinary cheese shop, in business since 1955, are lined floor-to-ceiling with giant rounds of Parmesan; on market days, the queue of customers often spills out the door.

Mon-Thu, to 11pm Fri & Sat) They've been in business since 1965, so the friendly Nardis know how to keep their customers happy. As much an *enoteca* as Slow Food–hailed eatery, Cantina Nardi has a 400-bottle wine list (an amazing 100 wines are offered by the glass) and is one of the city's best *aperitivo* spots. Sit between bottle-filled shelves inside, or at a streetside table.

Surfer Joe's Diner   AMERICAN $
(☑ 0586 80 92 11; www.surferjoe.it; Terrazza Mascagni; meals €20; ⊙ 11am-midnight Sun-Thu, to 1am Fri & Sat, shorter hours winter) What a burst of dynamism this zesty surf bar attached to Livorno's aquarium adds to the city's drinking and dining scene. American burgers, onion rings, pancakes and smoothies form its culinary core; 1950s diner is its 'look'; and surf music reigns supreme on the sound system. A huge terrace licked by the sea breeze and shaded with bamboo huts is the icing on the cake.

L'Ancora   SEAFOOD $$
(☑ 0586 88 14 01; www.ristoranteancoralivorno.com; Scali delle Ancore 10; meals €35; ⊙ noon-2.30pm & 7-10.30pm, closed Tue winter) Its name means 'the Anchor', an acknowledgement of this building's history as a 17th-century marine workshop. The vaulted-brick interior is atmospheric, but the best seating is on the canalside terrace in summer. You can order *cacciucco* here, but there are plenty of other fishy choices on the menu.

Cantina Senese   OSTERIA $$
(☑ 0586 89 02 39; Borgo dei Cappuccini 95; meals €30; ⊙ noon-2.30pm & 7.30-10pm Mon-Sat) Harbour workers are the first to fill the long wooden tables at this wonderfully unpretentious eatery, with other locals following close behind. Ordering is frequently done via faith in your server, rather than by menu. The mussels are exceptional, as is the *cacciucco* (Fridays only), both served with piquant garlic bread.

Osteria del Mare   SEAFOOD $$
(☑ 0586 88 10 27; Borgo dei Cappuccini 5; meals €30; ⊙ 12.30-2.30pm & 7.30-10pm Fri-Wed) The list of *secondi* is almost purely fish at this smart old-world *osteria* near the water. The traditional, home-style cooking lures the punters: many opt for the signature *riso nero* (black rice) with the catch of the day, or a simple plate of *fritto misto* (a battered and deep-fried mix of thumb-sized fish).

🍷 Drinking & Nightlife

Piazza Grande is surrounded by cafes where locals meet for coffee or an *aperitivo*. There are also plenty of cafes and terrace bars near the Terrazza Mascagni (p199) and overlooking the canals in Piccola Venezia (p199).

Caffè Duomo   CAFE
(☑ 0586 89 11 13; Via Cairoli 6; ⊙ 6.30am-8.30pm Mon-Sat) Locals have been enjoying the well-made coffee at this friendly cafe behind the *duomo* (cathedral) since 1945. In summer, the tables in the arcade are blissfully cool.

La Bodeguita   BAR
(☑ 346 6100832; Piazza dei Domenicani 20; ⊙ 6.30pm-1.30am Wed-Sat & Mon, 12.30-3pm & 6.30pm-1.30am Sun) This red-brick cellar bar has a sun-drenched wooden-decking terrace afloat the canal in Piccolo Venezia. Enjoy a cocktail and generously topped bruschetta while members of the local rowing club ply the water with oars in front of you, or join the city's younger set as they party here on Friday and Saturday nights.

ℹ️ Information

Tourist Office (☑ 0586 89 42 36; www.co-mune.livorno.it/portaleturismo; Via Pieroni 18; ⏱ 9am-4pm summer, to 3pm Apr & Oct-Dec, to 1pm Jan-Mar) Hands out free maps and books boat tours.

ℹ️ Getting There & Away

BOAT

Livorno is a major port. Regular ferries for Sardinia and Corsica depart from the **ferry port** (Map p200; Calata Carrara); and ferries to Capraia use the smaller **Porto Mediceo** (Map p200; Via del Molo Mediceo) near Piazza dell'Arsenale. Boats to Spain use Porto Nuovo, 3km north of the city.

Corsica Ferries (☑ per min €0.15 825 095095; www.corsica-ferries.co.uk) Two to seven services per week to Bastia, Corsica (from €33, four hours) and Golfo Aranci, Sardinia (from €61, 9½ hours).

Grimaldi Lines (☑ 081 49 64 44; www.grimaldi-ferries.com) Daily sailings to/from Olbia, Sardinia (from €25, nine hours) and Palermo, Sicily (from €43, 18 hours).

Moby (www.moby.it) Year-round it runs at least two services a day to Olbia, Sardinia (from €48, seven to 10 hours). Plus in the summer, several crossings a week to Bastia, Corsica (from €30, four hours).

Toremar (www.toremar.it) Several crossings per week, year-round to Capraia (€17, 2¾ hours).

CAR & MOTORCYCLE

The A12 runs past the city; the SS1 connects Livorno with Rome. There are several car parks near the waterfront; these charge between €0.30 (Nuovo Mercatale Americano) and €1 per hour (Piazza Mazzini).

TRAIN

From the **main train station** (Piazza Dante) walk westwards (straight ahead) along Viale Carducci, Via de Larderel and Via Grande to access Piazza Grande, Livorno's central square.

Services include the following:

Florence (*regionale veloce* from €9.60, 1¼ hours, hourly).

Pisa (€2.60, 15 minutes, frequent).

Rome (*regionale veloce* from €22.75, three to four hours, at least seven daily).

A taxi between the train station and the centre of town costs €16.

ℹ️ Getting Around

BUS

LAM Blu buses operated by **CTT Nord** (Map p200; www.livorno.cttnord.it; Via Bellatalla 1) travel from the main train station into the city centre, stopping at Piazza Grande before continuing to Porto Mediceo and then along the seafront (€1.20, on board €1.70, valid for 75 minutes). If you're catching a ferry to Sardinia or Corsica, take bus 1 to Piazza Grande then bus 5 from Via Cogorano, just off Piazza Grande.

THE ETRUSCAN COAST

The coastline south from Livorno to just beyond Piombino lives up to its historically charged name, the Costa degli Etruschi (Etruscan Coast), thanks to the Etruscan tombs unearthed on its shores. Its basic bucket-and-spade beaches are often unstartling, but those who venture inland will discover a swathe of pretty hilltop villages and some lesser-known but very good wines.

Castiglioncello

POP 3900

Diminutive Castiglioncello, 30km south of Livorno, is an agreeably unpretentious seaside resort where Italian art critic Digo Martelli held court in the late 19th century. He played host to the Florentine Impressionist artists of the period, giving birth to the artistic movement known as La Scuola di Castiglioncello (Castiglioncello School). These days, the town is popular with summer visitors, who flock to its sandy beaches; the best of these are on the town's northern fringe.

⊙ Sights & Activities

Castello Pasquini   CASTLE
(Piazza della Vittoria; ⏱ 24hr) **FREE** Crenellated Castello Pasquini was built in the late 19th century. Today it is surrounded by lovely tree-shaded grounds and a great play park.

✗ Eating & Drinking

Seafood is the thing to eat here. There are plenty of restaurants on Via Aurelia and along the seafront at Punta Righini.

Caffè Ginori   CAFE
(☑ 0586 75 90 55; www.caffeginori.it; Via Aurelia 947; ⏱ 6.30am-1am, reduced hours winter) This 1940s bar and cafe was the favourite haunt of Italian heart-throb Marcello Mastroianni when he had a summer villa in Castiglioncello, and it remains the most popular cafe in town. Join the locals relaxing and chatting on the tree-shading terrace facing Piazza Vittoria, order one of the delectable cakes to accompany your coffee and embrace *la dolce vita*.

LUNCH BREAK

Motoring from Castiglioncello towards Bolgheri along the SS1, it's worth breaking for tasting and lunch at one of the region's most innovative, organic wineries; 16km south of Castiglioncello, turn left (east) onto the SR68 to Riparbella.

Brothers Flavio and Lucca Nuti bottled their first vintage in 1997, and now their 25-hectare organic vineyard **La Regola** (☑ 0586 69 81 45; www.laregola.com; Località Altagrada, near Riparbella; ⊙ 10am-1pm & 3-7pm Mon-Fri, 10am-1pm Sat May-Oct, extended hours Sat Jun-Aug), in the Cecina Valley, yields more than 1000 bottles of wine per year. A location close to the sea on mineral-rich soil gives their wines a distinctive taste that can be appreciated during a tour and tasting (€10) in the modern winery building.

A highlight of the tour is seeing (and hearing) Stefano Tonelli's evocative multimedia artwork Somnium (2016) in the ageing cellar. It's one of a number of site-specific artworks on the estate.

ⓘ Information

The **tourist office** (☑ 0586 75 32 41; www.castiglioncello.it; Via Aurelia 632; ⊙ 9am-10pm & 3-8pm Mon-Fri, 9am-8pm Sat, reduced hours winter) is at the train station and can provide free town maps.

ⓘ Getting There & Away

There are hourly train services between Castiglioncello and Livorno (€3.50, 20 minutes).

Bolgheri

Every serious wine buff knows the name of Bolgheri, largely due to the fact that it is where the first of the internationally famous 'Super Tuscans', Sassicaia, was produced. A bijou town approached via a spectacular avenue of cypress trees, it is dominated by a storybook-style castle which incorporates the main town gate and the part-Romanesque Chiesa di SS Giacomo e Cristoro. The main – really only – reason to head here is to taste local wines and dine on seasonal produce in one of its excellent *enoteche* (wine bars).

◉ Sights

Cypress Alley   LANDMARK
Made famous by Tuscan poet Giosuè Carducci in his 1874 poem *Davanti a San Guido,* this avenue of 2540 cypress trees is 5km long and dead straight, providing a truly stunning entry to town.

✖ Eating & Drinking

★ Enoteca Tognoni   TUSCAN $
(☑ 0565 76 20 01; www.enotecatognoni.it; Via Lauretta 5; pasta €11-14, wine by taste €4.50-14, by small glass €9-28; ⊙ noon-2.30pm & 7-10pm Thu-Tue) This wine-lined *enoteca* is a temple to

taste, both gastronomic and oenological. Sassicaia (€28 per 100mL) is among dozens of local wines available to sample – others are more affordable. The menu is limited but delectable, changing daily according to what is fresh at the market. There's always a few pasta dishes on offer, as well as a range of quality *salumi* and cheese.

★ Enoteca de Centro   TUSCAN $$
(☑ 0565 76 21 78; Via Giulia 3; meals €30) When a wine bar is as friendly as this, the fact that it also serves great food comes as a delightful surprise. Michele Innocenti is a genial host and expert on local wine, and he will gladly guide you in a tasting (from €4). Alternatively, choose a bottle, order the succulent *bistecca alla Fiorentina* and dine on the pretty streetside terrace.

La Taverna del Pittore   TUSCAN $$
(☑ 0565 76 21 84; www.latavernadelpittore.it; Largo Nonna Lucia 4; meals €40; ⊙ noon-2.30pm & 7.30-10.30pm, closed Mon) The Painter's Tavern has a rustic dining room that's full of charm, but the best tables are under the orange trees outside. The menu specialises in local game – expect plenty of duck, pigeon, pheasant and boar, expertly cooked and packed with flavour. Owner Goffredo is a jazz fan, so there's always great music on the sound system.

ⓘ Information

La Strada del Vino e dell'Olio Visitor Centre
(☑ 0565 74 97 68; www.lastradadelvino.com; Castegneto Carducci 45, San Guido; ⊙ 10am-1pm & 2-5pm Mon-Sat summer, 10am-5pm Mon-Fri winter) Supplies free maps showing wine estates where you can taste and buy, and can also arrange visits or guided tours to wineries, olive farms and honey producers. Book at least a few days in advance. It's just off the SS1.

ℹ Getting There & Away

Between Monday and Saturday, one daily Tiemme bus (www.tiemmespa.it) travels between Castagneto Carducci and Bolgheri (€2.10, 30 minutes), continuing and terminating in San Guido. There is a car park on Via degli Orti, downhill from the main gate.

San Vincenzo

POP 6911

Italian visitors flock to this moderately attractive seaside town in summer to flop on sandy beaches backed by herb-scented *macchia* (wild scrubland) and pine forest. Yachties moor their vessels in the town's smart modern Marina di San Vincenzo, while the plains inland are rich in industrial heritage and soothing thermal springs.

◉ Sights & Activities

**Parco Archeominerario
di San Silvestro**   ARCHAEOLOGICAL SITE
(www.parchivaldicornia.it; Via di San Silvestro 34b, Campiglia Marittima; adult/reduced €16/12; ⊙10am-7pm Tue-Sun Jun & Sep, 9.30am-7.30pm daily Jul & Aug, reduced hours Oct-May) The area's 3000-year mining history is explored at this intriguing industrial site in Campiglia Marittima, approximately 10km inland from San Vincenzo. Here you can explore the ruins of the 14th-century mining town Rocca di San Silvestro, reached via an underground train that passes through the Temperino copper and lead mines. Guided tours depart roughly hourly.

Calidario Terme Etrusche   HOT SPRINGS
(☑0565 85 15 04; www.calidario.it; Via del Bottaccio 40, Venturina; pool entry per day adult/child €20/10, spa package per person €29-55; ⊙1-4pm & 4.30-7.30pm Mon-Fri, 9.30am-12.30pm, 1-4pm & 4.30-7.30pm Sat & Sun, closed early Jan-early Mar & weekends Jul & Aug) What a treat: a thermal spa where you can enjoy a swim or pamper yourself with a spa package including include use of the sauna, hamam and multi-sensory shower. Magnesium- and calcium-rich waters, at a toasty 36°C, flow into a mini-lake where bathers take relaxing and therapeutic dips. There are also comfortable bedrooms in a converted outbuilding (doubles from €89).

The *terme* are 15km south of San Vincenzo.

Tenuta Argentiera   WINE
(☑0565 77 31 76; www.argentaria.eu; Via Aurelia 412, Località Pianali; ⊙9am-7pm Mon-Sat, to 5pm Nov-Mar) Known for its Bordeaux-style cabernet sauvignon, franc and merlot, this sprawling estate on the coastal road 6.5km north of San Vincenzo is one of the largest wine producers in the region, with 75 hectares of vineyards extending from forested hills down to the sea. Book via email to take a tour, or pop into its *enoteca* just off the highway, where you can enjoy a tasting of three red wines (€10). This includes the estate's flagship drop, Bolgheri Superiore.

✖ Eating & Drinking

During the high season restaurants are expensive and heavily booked. Many are closed over winter.

Zanzi Bar   BAR
(☑0565 179 43 53; zanzibar.sanvincenzo@gmail.com; Piazza del Porto 2; ⊙5.30pm-2am) Those in the know remain staunchly loyal to shabby-chic Zanzibar, drawn by vintage decor, designer nourishment and DJ sets after dark. It's in a former fisherman's hut at the northern end of the marina.

ℹ Getting There & Away

Frequent trains link San Vincenzo and Livorno (€6.10, 40 minutes to one hour).

Suvereto

POP 3072

On weekends and over summer, day-trippers flock to this almost magically preserved medieval village to meander along its narrow cobbled streets and climb its steep, cream-stone stairways brightened by balconies brimming with flowers. Surrounded by countryside planted with olive trees, vineyards and the *suvere* (cork oak) trees that give the village its name, it's one of the most delightful destinations on the Etruscan coast.

◉ Sights & Activities

There are 80km of signed walking, biking and horse-riding trails in the countryside around Suvereto. Access 18 dedicated itineraries at www.suveretotrekking.it.

Rocca Aldobrandesca   CASTLE
(Via Corta; ⊙9am-dusk) Suvereto's crowning glory is this part-15th-century *rocca* (castle), abandoned in the 1600s and slowly being restored. The climb to it up winding village streets is steep but rewards with a magnificent panorama of surrounding fields and olive groves. On dusky pink summer evenings it's particularly enchanting.

ROAD TRIP >
THE WINE AND OIL ROAD

• •

Tasting wine on coastal estates and motoring along avenues lined with olive groves and cypress trees strikes is the essence of the Strada del Vino e dell'Olio Costa degli Etruschi (www. lastradadelvino.com). The 150km-long tourist route stretches south from Livorno to Piombino, and across to Elba, and passes cellars, wineries and farms offering wine and olive-oil tastings. Enticing places to eat pepper the trail; book tastings in advance.

❶ Bolgheri

Wine map and other information from the San Guido **visitor centre** (p204) in hand, hit the road in San Guido along the famous 5km-long **Cypress Alley** (p204) to bijou

Bolgheri. Park in the car park on Via degli Orti, then stroll through the fortified arch to explore this historic town where the first of the internationally famous 'Super Tuscans', Sassicaia, was produced. Consider staying

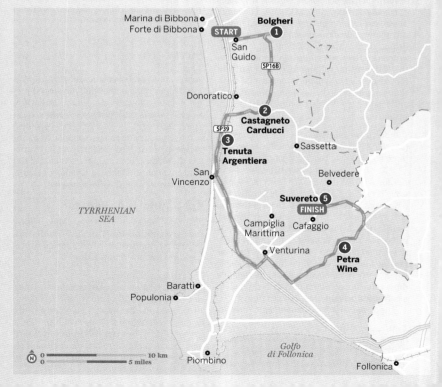

Great for... Food & Drink, Outdoors

Time to Go Spring, summer or autumn

for lunch and a wine tasting at **Enoteca de Centro** (p204) or **Enoteca Tognoni** (p204), and be sure to taste a couple of the local IGT tipples. There are literally hundreds of vintages to choose from.

❷ Castagneto Carducci

Next, head 1km back down the Cypress Alley before taking the SP16B leading south past neatly planted vineyards and scattered olive groves. A series of switchbacks later, the pale yellow buildings of Castagneto Carducci appear ranged on the ridge above. Park on the village edge and follow one of the lanes heading upwards. Most lead to the 13th-century **Propositura di San Lorenzo**, a dimly lit affair with faded frescoes and ornate beams inside and a view of the sun-dappled Etruscan Coast from the terrace.

❸ Tenuta Argentiera

Continue west towards the coast, turning left (south) and heading down the SP39 for 5km to reach **Tenuta Argentiera** (p205), one of this region's largest, best-known and most spectacularly sited wineries – 75 hectares of majestic vineyards extend from forested hills down to the sea. Enjoy a tasting in the *cantina* or in the fortress-like hilltop winery with its views to the coast; book ahead for the latter.

❹ Petra Wine

Continue south towards Venturina and on to the architecturally distinctive **Petra Wine** (p208) in San Lorenzo Alto, a temple-like modern structure designed by celebrity Swiss architect Mario Botta and built into the side of a hill. The impressively environmentally sustainable winery produces 100% organic wines. Learn all about the hi-tech winery and its extraordinary vintages on guided a tour, ending with a tasting; again, you'll need to book in advance.

❺ Suvereto

Finish your tour in the miraculously intact medieval hamlet of Suvereto, where you can explore the cobbled streets and hike up to the 15th-century **Rocca Aldobrandesca** (p205) to admire a sweeping panorama of the medieval village and surrounding vineyard-clad lands. Given the accolades of 'Slow Food town', 'wine town' and 'oil town' that it bears, Suvereto is a predictably wonderful place to discover local Val di Cornia DOC wines and to dine well. Come dusk, relax over a delectable dinner of modern Tuscan cuisine Slow Food–style at **Osteria di Suvereto da l'Ciocio** (p208) or **Ristorante dal Cacini** (p208).

OFF THE BEATEN TRACK

TERME DI SASSETTA

Head to **Terme di Sassetta** (☑0565 79 43 52; https://lacerreta.it/le-terme; Via Campagna Sud 143, Pian delle Vigne; 4hr Mon-Fri or 3hr Sat & Sun adult/child €30/20; ⊙10am-7.30pm Mon-Fri, 9.30am-8pm Sat & Sun; ⛱) to spend a therapeutic hour or two relaxing in the popular *terme* (baths) in a chestnut wood outside the tiny settlement of Sassetta. It features a cascade of indoor and outdoor rock pools filled with hyperthermal water that springs from the ground at a constant temperature of 51°C. Children aged under five years of age aren't admitted.

★ **Petra Wine** WINE
(☑0565 84 53 08; www.petrawine.it; Località San Lorenzo Alto 131; ⊙daily by appointment) On first sight, Petra resembles a huge pink Mayan temple that has been mysteriously transported to this rural pocket of Tuscany. Designed by acclaimed Swiss architect Mario Botta, the building is inserted into the hillside and houses an environmentally sustainable winery producing 100% organic wines under the Petra and Belvento labels.

Email to book a tour of the building, which features an extraordinary purple-lit underground ageing tunnel among other state-of-the-art features, followed by a tasting of the company's wines. Tours are conducted in English, Italian and Russian. You can tour the vineyard and cellar and then taste three wines in the *cantina* (€35, 90 minutes); add some local produce to the tasting (€45, two hours); or enjoy a tour, tasting and lunch (€80 to €100, two hours).

★ Festivals & Events

Le Serate Medievali CULTURAL
(Medieval Evenings; http://suvereto.net/serate-medievali; ⊙mid-Jul) For two nights each year in mid-July the Serate Medievali transforms the Romanesque cloister of the Convento di San Francesco into a medieval marketplace complete with locals dressed in traditional costume, fire eaters, minstrels, a medieval banquet, and plenty of art, craft and food stalls.

✗ Eating & Drinking

Given the accolades of 'Slow Food town', 'wine town' and 'oil town' that it bears, Suvereto is a predictably wonderful place to discover local Val di Cornia DOC wines and dine

well. Most restaurants are closed in January and February.

Il Gallo Golosone GELATERIA $
(Via Roma 4; gelato €1.50-3) On busy weekends, staff here do an excellent job filling cups and cones with the house-made gelato. They also make coffee and serve it to customers on the small streetside terrace.

Enoteca dei Difficili TUSCAN $
(☑0565 82 70 87; Via San Leonardo 2; panini €4, bruschette €4-5; ⊙6pm-2am Mon-Wed, to 3am Fri-Sun; ☎) Suvereto's younger generation loves this spirited *osteria*. No wonder: the brick ceiling and vintage chairs ensure it's stylish, there's live music on weekends and tasty treats include soup (€7.50) and €12 *taglieri* (wild boar, salami and cheese platters). There are plenty of local drops on the wine list.

Ristorante dal Cacini TUSCAN $$
(☑0565 82 83 13; www.ilcacini.it; Via del Crocifisso 3; set menus €30-55; ⊙12.30-2.30pm & 7-9.30pm, closed Tue) The chef here buys fish fresh every day and cooks it however his fancy dictates – hence the compulsory set menu rather than an à la carte array. Tables sport driftwood and filmy drapes, while the vine-shaded terrace and garden have sea glimpses – the perfect spots to linger over lunch.

★ **Osteria di Suvereto da l'Ciocio** TUSCAN $$$
(☑0565 82 99 47; www.osteriadisuvereto.it; Piazza dei Giudici 1; meals €45; ⊙12.30-2.30pm & 7.30-10.30pm Tue-Sun) Worthy recipient of a Slow Food accolade (the only Suvereto eatery so honoured), this *osteria* opposite the handsome 13th-century *palazzo comunale* (town hall) has a beautiful terrace lined by honey-coloured stone walls and a stylish dining room adorned with modern art. The menu, meanwhile, is aimed firmly at foodies – modern dishes that also manage to respect centuries-old local food traditions.

ℹ Information

There's a **tourist information point** (☑0565 82 93 04; www.commune.suvereto.li.it; Via Magenta 14; ⊙hours vary Easter–1 Jan) sharing a building with the Museo Artistico della Bambola (Doll Museum).

ℹ Getting There & Away

Regular Tiemme buses link Suvereto with the Campiglia Marittima train station at Venturina (€2.10, 20 minutes), where trains to/from Livorno stop.

Golfo di Baratti

The crescent-shaped Baratti Gulf sits at the southern tip of the Etruscan Coast, at the end of a 12km dead-straight road lined by sandy beaches and sky-high parasol pines. The main draws here are the beaches, which are packed in summer, and the sprawling Parco Archeologico di Baratti e Populonia, which is set on a promontory overlooking the sea.

◉ Sights & Activities

★ **Parco Archeologico
di Baratti e Populonia** ARCHAEOLOGICAL SITE
(Archaeological Park of Baratti & Populonia; ✆0565 22 64 45; www.parchivaldicornia.it; Baratti; Acropolis adult/reduced €9/6/4, Necropoli €9/7, Acropolis & Necropoli €14/10, entire park €16/12; ☺9.30am-7.30pm Jul & Aug, 10am-7pm Jun & early Sep, limited hours late Sep-May) The Etruscan sites on display here are some of Tuscany's finest. Four marked walking trails lead through a vast green park, revealing a ruined town and well-preserved prehistoric tombs. The gigantic circular tumulus tombs in the Necropoli di San Cerbone are among the most impressive and are visited on a one-hour Italian-language guided tour that enters the Tomba dei Carri, which is a whopping 28m in diameter. The Acropolis can be visited on a self-guided 90-minute tour.

A 90-minute Va del Ferro trail explores tumulus tombs and the ruins of ancient buildings.

The two-hour Via delle Cave trail leads through shady woodland to ranks of chamber tombs that have been hacked out of the soft ochre sandstone; ancient quarries are also dotted around. The scenic Via del Monastero trail (2½ hours) breaks off from the Via della Cave trail and continues to the Benedictine Monastery of San Quirico and on towards the Acropoli of Populonia.

The Via della Romanella (Metal Working Trail; 2½ hours) leads to the Etruscan Acropoli di Populonia (settlement of Populonia). Digs here have revealed the foundations of a 2nd-century-BC Etruscan temple; you'll see the remains of Roman temples, the city's central square, some towering terracing and an evocative, roughly paved road.

✕ Eating & Drinking

There are beach bars and eateries along the road linking the main highway and Porto di Baratti, as well as at the port and in Baratti itself. There's also an eatery in the archaeological park's reception building.

Canessa SEAFOOD $$
(✆0565 2 95 30, 320 9328353; www.ristorantecanessa.com; Località Baratti 43; meals €40; ☺12.30-2.30pm & 7.30-10pm, closed mid-Oct–early Apr) What makes this seafood restaurant at Porta di Baratti so unique is the 15th-century watchtower that the modern building is wrapped around. The freshly made pasta is delicious, as are the many fishy choices. Best of all is the view, with huge windows overlooking the lapping waves. There are also four upstairs guest rooms (http://canessacamere.it; doubles €80 to €100). No breakfast.

ℹ Getting There & Away

Four buses travel between Piombino and Baratti every day except Sunday (€2.10, 30 minutes).

THE TUSCAN ARCHIPELAGO

POP 34,389

A local legend says that when Venus rose from the waves seven precious stones fell from her tiara, creating seven islands off the Tuscan coast. These little-known gems range from tiny Gorgona, just 2.23 sq km in size, to the biggest and busiest island, 224-sq-km Elba (Isola d'Elba), best known as the place where Napoleon was exiled.

Elba

Napoleon would think twice about fleeing Elba today. Dramatically more congested than when the emperor was exiled here in 1814 (he managed to engineer an escape within a year), the island is an ever-glorious paradise of beach-laced coves, vineyards, azure waters, hairpin-bend motoring, a 1018m mountain (Monte Capanne) and mind-bending views. It's all supplemented by a fine seafaring cuisine, lovely island wines, and land and seascapes just made for hiking, biking and sea kayaking.

With the exception of high season (actually only August), when the island's beaches and roads are jam-packed, Elba is something of a Robinson Crusoe paradise. In springtime, early summer and autumn, when grapes and olives are harvested, there are plenty of tranquil nooks on this stunningly picturesque, 28km-long, 19km-wide island.

There is a wealth of information about the island at www.infoelba.com.

History

Elba has been inhabited since the Iron Age and the extraction of iron ore and metallurgy were the island's principal sources of economic wellbeing until well into the second half of the 20th century. In 1917 some 840,000 tonnes of iron were produced, but in WWII the Allies bombed the industry to bits.

Ligurian tribespeople were the island's first inhabitants, followed by Etruscans and Greeks. Centuries of peace under the Pax Romana gave way to more uncertain times during the barbarian invasions, when Elba became a refuge for those fleeing mainland marauders. By the 11th century, Pisa (and later Piombino) was in control and built fortresses to help ward off attacks by Muslim raiders and pirates operating out of North Africa.

In the 16th century, Cosimo I de' Medici grabbed territory in the north of the island, where he founded the port town of Cosmopolis, today's Portoferraio.

🏃 Activities

The Parco Nazionale dell'Archipelgo Toscana office (p213) in Portoferraio can advise on Elba's many walking trails, biking paths and other outdoor activities. There are also offices in Marciana and Rio d'Elba.

Given its crystal-clear waters, diving and snorkelling are big on Elba between June and September; diving schools Diving in Elba (✆347 3715788; www.divinginelba.com; Hotel Club Airone, Località San Giovanni), with offices in Portoferraio, La Biodola and Procchio, and Enfola Diving Center (✆338 6893949, 347 2713187; www.enfoladivingcenter.it; Enfola;

⊙ 9am-7pm Jun-Sep), 6km west of Portoferraio on Enfola beach, can set you up with gear, tuition and guides. Otherwise, explore the island's sea-locked beaches and coves by motor boat, kayak or yacht.

ⓘ Getting There & Away

AIR

Elba's airstrip, **Aeroporto Isola d'Elba** (www. elbaisland-airport.it), is 2km north of Marina di Campo in La Pila. Czech airline Silver Air (www. silverairitalia.it) has a local office and services destinations including Pisa, Milan, Lugana and Florence.

BOAT

Getting to Elba involves a ferry crossing from Piombino or San Vincenzo on the mainland. Ferry companies include **Moby** (✆199 303040; www. mobylines.com), **Toremar** (✆199 117733; www. toremar.it), **Blu Navy** (✆0565 22 58 33, 0565 26 97 10; www.blunavytraghetti.com) and **Aquavision** (✆0565 97 60 22; www.aquavision.it). Most passengers arrive in Portoferraio on services from Piombino (at least hourly, foot passenger/car and driver €17/50 one way). There are also services to/from Cavo and Rio Marina.

ⓘ Getting Around

BUS

CTT Nord (www.livorno.cttnord.it) runs reasonably regular services linking all of Elba's main towns (€1.20 to €2.50). In Portoferraio, buses leave from the bus station, opposite the main Piombino ferry jetty.

CAR

Car is the easiest way to get around Elba, except in August when roads are jammed. The island's southwest coast offers the most dramatic and scenic motoring. With no traffic, expect to take

---

THE TUSCAN ARCHIPELAGO NATIONAL PARK

The Parco Nazionale dell'Arcipelago Toscano (Tuscan Archipelago National Park; www. islepark.it) safeguards the delicate ecosystems of Elba's seven islands as well as the 600 sq km of sea that washes around them. It's Europe's largest protected marine area and is home to rare species such as the Neptune's shaving brush seaweed, unique to the archipelago.

Monk seals, driven from other islands by humans, still gambol in the deep underwater ravines off Montecristo. The islands serve as an essential rest stop for birds migrating between Europe and Africa. The shy red partridge survives on Elba and Pianosa and the archipelago supports more than a third of the world's population of the Corsican seagulls, adopted as the national park's symbol.

On Elba, the park runs a visitor centre (p213) in Portoferraio.

Divided into two seasons (April and late September to early October), the Walking Festival (✆0565 90 82 31; www.tuscanywalkingfestival.it) is staged by the Parco Nazionale dell'Arcipelago Toscano and includes plenty of guided hikes across the island. Hikes last from two to five hours and are graded easy, medium and challenging.

Elba

0   2.5 miles
0   5 km

Tyrrhenian Sea

Capraia

Piombino

Piombino

Piombino

Cavo

Rio Marina

Museo dei Minerali e dell'Arte Mineraria

Rio dell'Elba

Rio

Nisporto

Ortano

Bagnaia

Cima del Monte (516m)

Ottone

Magazzini

Schiopparello

Nisportino

Portoferraio

Le Grotte

San Giovanni

Spiaggia la Padulella

Spiaggia di Capo Bianco

Spiaggia di Sansone

Spiaggia di Sorgente

Capo d'Enfola

Enfola

Viticcio

La Biodola

Golfo della Biodola

Spiaggia di Scaglieri

Spiaggia di Spartaia

Procchio

San Martino

Villa Napoleonica di San Martino

Museo

Via Colle Reciso

Lacona

Golfo della Lacona

Porto Azzurro

Capoliveri

Spiaggia di Naregno

Calamita: Miniere di Capoliveri

Monte Calamita (413m)

Punta della Calamita

Spiaggia dello Stagnone

Spiaggia di Zuccale

Spiaggia di Barabarca

Spiaggia di Morcone

Spiaggia di Pareti

Spiaggia dell'Innamorata

Spiaggia della Paolina

Marciana Marina

Poggio

Monte Perone (630m)

SP37

Monte Maolo (749m)

Marmi

Aeroporto Isola d'Elba

La Pila

Marina di Campo

Acquario dell'Elba

Golfo di Campo

Montecristo (35km)

Tyrrhenian Sea

Marciana

Santuario della Madonna del Monte

Colle d'Orano

Capo Sant'Andrea

Monte Capanne (1018m)

Sant'Ilario in Campo

San Piero in Campo

Cavoli

Le Piscine

Seccheto

Punta di Fetovia

Fetovaia

Pomonte

Chiessi

Spiaggia delle Tombe

ⓘ BIKING & HIKING ON ELBA

A dizzying network of walking and mountain-biking trails blankets Elba. Many start in Portoferraio, but some of the best, far-flung trailheads kick off elsewhere.

Monte Capanne Circular A three-hour, 20km adventure on the slopes of Elba's highest mountain, which sees you cycling on paved and unpaved routes past scented *maquis* and pines. Total climb: 540m.

Marciana to Chiessi A 12km (six-hour) hike starts high up in Marciana and dribbles downhill past ancient churches, sea vistas and granite boulders to the seaside in Chiessi.

The Great Elba Crossing This three- to four-day, 60km east–west island crossing includes Monte Capanne, Elba's highest point (1018m), before overnighting on the coast (camping isn't allowed beside paths). The highlight is the final 19km leg from Poggio to Pomonte, passing the Santuario della Madonna del Monte (p215) and the **Masso dell'Aquila** rock formation.

one hour to motor the 35km from Procchio to Cavoli. Parking in blue bays on the island costs between €1 and €1.50 per hour and fees usually only apply between June and September.

Portoferraio

POP 11,992

Known to the Romans as Fabricia and later Ferraia (an acknowledgement of its important role as a port for iron exports), this small harbour was acquired by Cosimo I de' Medici in the mid-16th century, when its distinctive fortifications took shape.

Portoferraio can be a hectic place, especially in August when holidaymakers pour off the ferries from Piombino on the mainland every 20 minutes or so. But wandering the streets and steps of the historic centre, indulging in the exceptional eating options and haggling for sardines with fishermen more than makes up for the squeeze.

◉ Sights

The Old Town's spiderweb of narrow streets and alleys staggers uphill from the old harbour to Portoferraio's defining twinset of forts, **Forte Falcone** and **Forte Stella** (☑0565 91 69 89; Via della Stella; adult/reduced €2/1.50; ⊙9am-7pm Easter-Sep), revealing deserted 16th-century ramparts to wander and seagulls freewheeling overhead.

From waterside square **Piazza Cavour** head uphill along Via Garibaldi to the foot of the monumental **Scalinata Medici**, a fabulous mirage of 140 wonky stone steps cascading up through every sunlit shade of amber to the dimly lit, 17th-century **Chiesa della Misericordia** (Via della Misericordia; ⊙8am-5pm). Inside is Napoleon's death mask. Continue to the top of the staircase to reach the forts and **Villa dei Mulini**, where Napoleon lived when in Portoferraio.

Museo Nazionale della Residenze Napoleoniche MUSEUM
(Villa dei Mulini; ☑0565 91 58 46; Piazzale Napoleone; adult/reduced €5/2.50; ⊙8.30am-7pm Mon & Wed-Sat, to 1pm Sun) Villa dei Mulini was home to Napoleon during his stint in exile on this small isle. With its Empire-style furnishings, splendid library, fig-tree-studded Italianate gardens and unbeatable sea view, the emperor didn't want for creature comforts – contrast this with the simplicity of the camp bed and travelling trunk he used when on campaigns. While that history lesson is nice, the dearth of actual Napoleonic artefacts here is a tad disappointing.

Area Museale della Linguelle ARCHAEOLOGICAL SITE
(Torre della Linguella; Calata Buccari; adult/reduced €4/3; ⊙10am-4.40pm Fri-Wed Apr-Oct, to midnight Jun–mid-Sep) The 16th-century Torre del Martello was where Napoleon was 'imprisoned' at the start of his fleeting exile on Elba in 1814 and the russet-red, hexagonal tower remained a prison until 1877. It and the archaeological ruins next door (part of a luxurious Roman villa known as 'La Linguella' built between the 1st and 5th centuries AD) are now part of this museum. Also of interest are terracotta friezes from the Villa de Romana delle Grotte in the main museum building.

★ Museo Villa Napoleonica di San Martino MUSEUM
(☑0565 91 58 46; San Martino; adult/reduced €5/2.50; ⊙8.30am-7pm Tue-Sat, to 1pm Sun summer, 9am-3pm Tue-Sat, to 1pm Sun winter) Napoleon personally supervised the transformation of what had been a large farmhouse

in the hills 5km southwest of Portoferraio into an elegant villa where he could escape the summer heat. Romanticism and hubris both came into play as he sought to give his new residence a Parisian sheen – the pretty Room of the Love Knot and grand Egyptian Room were particular triumphs. In the 1850s, a Russian nobleman purchased the villa and built a grandiose gallery at its base.

Eating

Eateries in town aren't among the island's best. That said, they are always packed to the gills in August – reserve your table well in advance of dining.

Il Castagnacciaio PIZZA $
(☑ 0565 91 58 45; www.ilcastagnacciaio.com; Via del Mercato Vecchio 5; pizza €5-8; ☺ 10.30am-2.30pm & 4.30-10.30pm) They work the pizza chef so hard here the dining room sometimes has a smoky tinge. To go local, start with a lip-smacking plate of *torta di ceci* (chickpea 'pizza'), then watch your rectangular, thin-crust supper go in and out of the wood-fired oven. But save space for dessert – *castagnaccio* (chestnut 'cake') baked over the same flames.

Osteria Libertaria TUSCAN $$
(☑ 0565 91 49 78; Calata Giacomo Matteotti 12; meals €35; ☺ noon-2.30pm & 7-10.30pm summer) Fish drives the menu of this traditional *osteria* – no wonder, as the boats that land it are moored right outside. Traditional dishes such as fried calamari or *tonno in crosta di pistacchi* (pistachio-encrusted tuna fillet) are super-fresh and very tasty. Dine at one of two tile-topped tables on the traffic-noisy street or on the back-alley terrace.

Trattoria e Pizzeria Da Zucchetta TRATTORIA $$
(☑ 0565 91 53 31; Piazza della Repubblica 40; meals €35; ☺ 11.30am-3pm & 6-11.30pm Wed-Mon) The setting is homely rather than smart (a couple of TVs show the nightly news), but the seafood here is top-notch. The gnocchi or *pappardelle* are packed with crustaceans and fishy flavour, while the garlicky catch of the day is a winner: char-grilled, dotted with rocket and laced with lemon and olive oil.

Bitta 20 SEAFOOD $$$
(☑ 0565 93 02 70; ristorantebitta20@gmail.com; Calata Mazzini 20; meals €50; ☺ noon-2.30pm & 7-11pm Tue-Sun Easter–mid-Oct) A Portoferraio favourite, this harbourside eatery has a long terrace overlooking a string of bobbing yachts. White napery and efficient service combine with fresh fish and seafood to make it a good choice for lunch or dinner. Book for the latter.

ⓘ Information

Parco Nazionale dell'Archipelgo Toscana Office (Info Park; ☑ 0565 90 82 31; www.parcoarcipelago.info; Calata Italia 4; ☺ 9am-7pm Apr-Oct, to 10pm Tue & Thu Aug, 9am-4pm Mon-Sat, to 3pm Sun Nov-Mar) Helpful staff have abundant information on walking and biking on the island. Find the office on the seafront, near the ferry docks

ⓘ Getting There & Around

BOAT
Year-round, regular car and foot passenger ferries sail at least hourly between Stazione Marittima (ferry port) in Piombino and Elba's main town, Portoferraio. Unless it's August or a summer weekend, there's no need to book a ticket in advance; simply buy one from a booth

---

HAGGLING FOR FISH

Hanging out with locals, waiting for the fishing boats to come in, is a quintessential Portoferraio pastime. The crowd starts forming on the quay around 9.30am and by the time the first boats dock at 10am there's a line-up of punters waiting to exchange hand-crumpled bank notes for the catch of the day.

The larger industrial fishing boats dock midway between the ferry terminal and the old-town harbour on Banchina d'Alto Fondale. Occasionally they'll catch a huge tuna – which draws a real crowd – but in the main it's wooden crates of sardines, mackerel and anchovies the crews sell from the sides of their boats (€5 for a plastic-bag full).

Smaller vessels with just one or two fishermen moor alongside Calata Giacomo Matteotti at the old harbour each morning any time from 8am onwards. And these are the guys who get the real catch – octopus, lobster, eel and swordfish on good days.

If haggling for fish is simply not your cup of tea, there's always harbourside fishmonger Pescheria del Porto (☑ 0565 91 87 29; www.pescheriadelporto.it; Via Delle Galeazze 20; ☺ 8am-12.30pm Mon-Sat).

ℹ CENT SAVERS

The Portoferraio Card (€10) gives entry to the Villa de Romana delle Grotte, Area Museale della Linguelle, Teatro dei Vigilanti and Fortezze e Forte Falcone. It's available at all four sites.

There's also a joint ticket for the Museo Nazionale della Residenze Napoleoniche in Villa Mulini and the Museo Villa Napoleonica di San Martino (adult/reduced €8/4, valid 72 hours), which gives a saving of €2. It's available at both museums.

---

at the port. Fares (one way around €17/50 per person/car and driver) vary according to the season. Sailing time is one hour.

Aquavision (www.aquavision.it) Seasonal services only.

Blunavy (www.blunavytraghetti.com) Seasonal services only.

Moby (www.mobylines.com)

Toremar (www.toremar.it)

BUS

Buses travel within Portoferraio and from the port to various destinations around the island. Tickets for trips up to 10km cost €1.40; for longer distances they cost €2.50.

CAR & MOTORCYCLE

TWN Rent (☑ 0565 91 46 66; www.twn-rent.it; Viale Elba 32) Offers cars, scooters, electric bicycles, mountain bikes and city bikes from the office next to the port in Portoferraio, Also has offices in Marina di Campo, Lacona and Porto Azzurro.

Schiopparello, Magazzini & Otone

So close to Portoferraio that they are generally considered to be its suburbs, this cluster of settlements around pebbled coves and on rich agricultural land east of the ferry docks dates back to the Roman period, when the powerful owners of the island's iron mines built ornate seaside villas here. These days, the coves shelter hotels and the hinterland is planted with olive trees, grapes, citrus and wheat. It's a much more peaceful and attractive sleeping option than Portoferraio itself.

🏃 Activities

Tenuta La Chiusa   WINE
(☑ 0565 93 30 46; www.tenutalachiusa.it; Località Magazzini 93, Magazzini; ⊙ 8.30am-2.30pm & 4-8pm Mon-Sat summer, to 5pm winter) La Chiusa is idyllically located on the edge of the water

---

at Magazzini, some 8km east of Portoferraio. In the history books because it was where Napoleon stayed on the night he landed on Elba in 1814, it's the oldest and possibly largest wine and olive-oil estate on the island, with 11.5 hectares of vineyards and 700 olive trees.

Montefabbrello   FOOD & DRINKS
(☑ 339 8296298; www.montefabbrello.it; Località Schiopparello 30; ⊙ daily) The farm-gate shop of this family-owned estate sells its own wine (Trebbiano Toscano, Ansonica, Passito and Vermentino) and extra-virgin olive oil, as well as dried 'Pasta dell' Elba' made using wheat grown in nearby fields.

🍴 Eating & Drinking

★ **Ristoro Agricolo**
Montefabbrello   TUSCAN $$
(☑ 339 8296298; www.montefabbrello.it; Località Schiopparello 30; meals €38; ⊙ 7.30-10pm Jun-Sep, 7.30-10pm Fri & Sat, noon-3pm Sun Oct–May) A model of slow and sustainable cuisine, this rustic restaurant on the Montefabbrello farm grows its own wheat to make pasta, grapes to make wine and olives to produce oil. Fruit and veggies are homegrown too. Tasty pasta dishes, home-made bread and plenty of meat and game choices (unusual on Elba) make it an essential stop on every foodie itinerary.

ℹ Getting There & Away

Bus 118 travels between Portoferraio and Bagnaia (€2.50; 25 minutes) stopping at Schiopparello and Magazzini (€1.40) en route, but services are few and far between.

Marciana Marina, Marciana & Poggio
POP 1977

Unlike many modern cookie-cutter marinas, the attractive resort of Marciana Marina has character and history to complement its pleasant pebble beaches. The port is 18km west along the coast from Portoferraio. From it, a twisting 9km mountain road winds inland up to Marciana, the island's oldest and highest village (375m).

Marciana's stone streets, arches and stone houses with flower boxes and petite balconies are as pretty as a picture, and it's worth exploring them before heading uphill from the village to Elba's most important pilgrimage site: the Santuario della Madonna del Monte.

Between the two Marcianas, along a twisting and precipitous road, is the mountain village of Poggio. Set on the SP25, it's famous for its spring water and has steep cobblestone alleys and stunning coastal views.

◎ Sights & Activities

⭐**Cabinovia Monte Capanne**   FUNICULAR
(Cableway; ☑ 0565 90 10 20; www.cabinovia-isoladelba.it; Località Pozzatello; adult/reduced/child return €18/13/9; ⊙ 10am-1pm & 2.20-5pm mid-Apr–mid-Oct) Elba's famous cable-car transports passengers up to the island's highest point, Monte Capanne (1018m), in open, barred baskets – imagine riding in a canary-yellow parrot cage and you'll get the picture. After a 20-minute ride, passengers alight and can scramble around the rocky peak to enjoy an astonishing 360-degree panorama of Elba, the Tuscan Archipelago, Etruscan Coast and Corsica 50km away. Keen hikers can buy a cheaper one-way ticket and take the 90-minute walk back down a rocky path.

Santuario della Madonna del Monte CHAPEL
(⊙ 24hr) FREE To enjoy a invigorating 40-minute hike, head up through Marciana along Via della Madonna to reach this much-altered hilltop chapel with its 13th-century fresco of the Madonna painted on a slab of granite. A remarkable coastal panorama unfolds as you make your way here past scented parasol pines, chestnut trees, wild sage and thyme. Once you reach the chapel (627m), emulate Napoleon and drink from the old stone fountain across from the church – a plaque commemorates his visit in 1814.

Monte Perone   MOUNTAIN
Just south of Poggio, the SP37 winds to a well-signed picnic site at the foot of Monte

Perone (630m). To the left (east) you can wander up the mountain to take in spectacular views across much of the island. To the right (west) you can scramble fairly quickly to a height affording broad vistas down to Poggio, Marciana and Marciana Marina.

✖ Eating

There are plenty of choices in Marciana Marina, but few in Poggio and Marciana. In summer (especially August) make reservations at all restaurants.

⭐**Ristorante Salegrosso**   SEAFOOD **$$**
(☑ 0565 99 68 62; salegrossoristo@hotmail.com; Piazza della Vittoria 14, Marciana Marina; meals €40; ⊙ 12.30-2.30pm & 7.30-10pm Tue-Sun Mar-Dec) Those on the hunt for Elba's best fish dish need look no further – the fish stew here is a flavoursome pile of shellfish, tomato and saffron topped by a garlicky slice of bruschetta. Delicious! Dine on it or other fishy treats, including excellent homemade pasta, while watching locals take their evening *passeggiata* along the waterfront.

⭐**Osteria del Noce**   SEAFOOD **$$**
(☑ 0565 90 12 84; www.osteriadelnoce.it; Via della Madonna 19, Marciana; meals €30; ⊙ noon-2pm & 7.30-9.30pm late-Mar–Sep) This family-run bistro in hilltop Marciana is the type of place where the bread is homemade and flavoured with fennel, chestnut flour and other seasonal treats. The pasta and seafood dishes and the sweeping views from the terrace are truly memorable. To find it, follow the Madonna del Monte walking signs to the top of the village.

DON'T MISS

MARCIANA MARINA: A TRADITIONAL PASSEGGIATA

The loveliest moment of the day in laid-back Marciana Marina is early evening, when the entire town seems to wander beside the waterfront for that oh-so-Tuscan *passeggiata*.

Start at the seafront's eastern end where the gigantic palm trees and bars of Piazza della Vittoria provide prime places to watch the walking get underway. Follow the local custom and treat yourself to a gelato while you walk; those sold at La Svolta (☑ 0565 9 94 79; www.gelaterialasvolta.it; Via Cairoli 6, Marciana Marina; ⊙ 10.30am-late Tue-Sun Apr-Oct) are the best on the island.

Walk west a few minutes along waterside Viale Margherita, then make a quick detour a block inland to take in the pretty peach-painted church and pristine carpet cobblestones in Piazza Vittorio Emanuele. There are plenty of bars, cafes and restaurants here to return to later in the evening.

Backtrack to the water and continue meandering west past boutiques and a mini marina before, as the sun sinks, you find yourself at the far end of the waterfront on Spiaggia di Capo Nord, a handsome beach of large smooth pebbles overlooked by a 12th-century Saracen tower. It's the perfect spot to watch the sun sink over the Tyrrhenian Sea.

LAZY DAYS

There is no more perfect spot in the Tuscan woods to wind down after a busy stretch of sightseeing and touring than the island of Elba, a Mediterranean paradise.

GOURMET ESCAPE

Utterly tranquil despite being just a few minutes from the Portoferraio–Magazzini road, **Agriturismo Due Palme** (☎0565 93 30 17, 338 7433736; www.agriturismoelba.it; Via Schiopparello 28, Schiopparello) is part of the only olive plantation on Elba to produce quality-stamped IGP olive oil. Simple, well-maintained self-catering cottages are dotted amid flowerbeds, citrus trees and 100-year-old olive groves. Don't leave without tasting and buying the silky fresh-green oil.

BEACH LIFE

Life is a beach on the island of Elba where snorkellers mingle with wave-frolicking kids in crystal-clear waters, while further out at sea, kayaking couples paddle peacefully from secret cove to secret cove, in search of their own private spot to romance under the hot Tuscan sun. Sun fish, barracudas and eagle rays reward the most of patient of divers. Beach hot spots: Spaggia di Spartaia, Innamorata and Sorgente.

SENSATIONAL SUNSETS

End the day on a sea-facing terrace with glass of velvety red Aleatico DOCG wine, island-distilled grappa or tangy, Elba-lemon limoncino in hand. Watch the sun sink into the Med in one of the restaurants at the island's swishest James Bond-style address, **Hotel Hermitage** (☎0565 97 40; www.hotelhermitage.it; La Biodola; ⊙late Apr–early Oct), both by the sand in La Procchio.

1. Cavoli beach (p218), Marina di Campo
2. Seafood dish, Elba
3. Al fresco diners, Capoliveri (p218)

Publius   TUSCAN **$$$**
(🖉 0565 9 92 08; www.ristorantepublius.it; Piazza del Castagneto 11, Poggio; meals €46; ⊘ 7.30-10.30pm Mon, noon-2pm & 7.30-10.30pm Tue-Sun late-Apr–Oct) The floor-to-ceiling windows at this formal, hillside restaurant at the lower end of Poggio village create the sense of eating in a classy treehouse, while the vistas from the stylish roof terrace make you feel you're suspended above the sea. The refined Tuscan menu profiles fish and mountain produce.

ℹ Information

There is a tiny summer-only tourist information point on Piazza della Vittoria in Marciana Marina.

ℹ Getting There & Away

Bus 116 links Marciana Marina and Marciana with Portoferraio at least eight times per day (€2.50).

Marina di Campo
POP 4805

A small fishing harbour on the south side of the island, Marina di Campo is Elba's second-largest town. Here a curling, picturesque bay dotted with bobbing boats adds personality to what is otherwise very much a holiday-oriented town. Its beach of bright, white sand pulls in holiday-makers by the thousands; coves further west, though less spectacular, are more tranquil.

◉ Sights & Activities

Cavoli   BEACH
The shingle-sand beach at Cavoli, just 6km west of Marina di Campo, is particularly family-friendly, thanks to its beach cafe, sun loungers, pedalos and kids' playground.

Acquario dell'Elba   AQUARIUM
(🖉 0565 97 78 85; www.acquarioelba.com; Traversa di Via Segagnan 245; adult/reduced €8/7; ⊘ 9am-7pm Apr–mid-Oct, to 11.30pm Jun–mid-Sep) More than 150 Mediterranean species inhabit this modest aquarium, making it a good grey-day option. It's 2km northeast of town, signposted off the SP30 to Lacona.

Il Viottolo   TREKKING, CYCLING
(🖉 329 7367100; www.ilviottolo.com; Via Albarelli 60) Well-regarded adventure specialists offering a wide range of treks, mountain biking, whale watching, sailing and sea kayaking. Contact them for a tailored itinerary or to check dates and prices of organised tours.

✖ Eating & Drinking

Il Cantuccio   TRATTORIA **$**
(🖉 0565 97 67 75; Largo Garibaldi 6; pizza €6-9, meals €25; ⊘ noon-3pm & 7-11pm) Ignore the waterfront's menu-touting waiters and instead duck into Largo Garibaldi to find this unassuming trattoria. In business since 1930, the place is excellent value (a rarity on Elba), serving seafood, homemade pasta, wood-fired pizza and 18 different varieties of olive oil.

Da Mario   BAR
(Lungomare Generale Fabio Miribelli 29; ⊘ 8am-11pm) The full name is Yacht Club Da Mario, but everyone shortens this to Da Mario – that's the kind of place it is. Pouring drinks and making coffee since 1952, it's friendly and has decking overlooking a cluster of fishing boats and a long curl of sand.

ℹ Getting There & Away

Bus 116 links Marina di Campo with Procchio and Portoferraio at least eight times per day (€2.50).

Capoliveri
POP 4033

Picturesque Capoliveri sits in the high hills of Elba's southeast corner. Its steep alleys are lined with narrow houses, while the panorama of rooftops and sea that fans out from the old stone terrace on its central square, Piazza Matteotti, is absolutely lovely.

◉ Sights

Calamita: Miniere di Capoliveri   MINE
(🖉 0565 93 54 92; www.minieredicalamita.it; museum adult/reduced €2.50/1.50, tours adult €18-24, reduced €12-18; ⊘ hourly tours from 10am-4.30pm late May–Aug, reduced tours & hours late Apr & Sep-Nov) Guided tours take visitors from a small site museum in Vallone, 11km south of Capoliveri, to the Genevro mine where magnetite was extracted until the operation closed in 1981. You'll walk through dark underground tunnels to see huge cathedral-like caverns where the metal was extracted.

✖ Eating & Drinking

★ **Fandango**   WINE BAR
(🖉 389 8407711; Via Cardenti 1; ⊘ Tue-Sun Easter-Oct) Steps lead down from the panoramic terrace at the far end of the central Piazza Matteotti to this lively *enoteca,* which offers atmospheric seating under a vine-clad pergola. We love the well-made cocktails, excellent local wine list, live music and *piccolo cucina* (little snacks) made with local produce.

LOCAL KNOWLEDGE

ELBA'S FINEST BEACHES

Given the wide range of bays on Elba's 147km-long coast, it pays to know your *spiagge* (beaches). You'll find sandy strands on the south coast and in the Golfo della Biodola, on the western side of Capo d'Enfola. The beach town of Procchio, and adjoining resort area of La Biodola, is the nearest sandy beach to Portoferraio, 10km west, and draws big summertime crowds thanks to its long stretch of golden sand. West from Procchio, the road hugs cliffs above Spiaggia di Spartaia and Spiaggia della Paolina, beautiful little beaches requiring a steep clamber down – as is the case with many of Elba's finest beaches. Parking is invariably roadside and scant.

Colle d'Orano & Fetovaia

The standout highlight of these two gorgeous swathes of golden sand on Elba's western coast is the dramatic drive between the two. Legend has it Napoleon frequented Colle d'Orano to sit and swoon over his native Corsica, which is visible across the water. A heavenly scented, promontory covered in *maquis* (herbal scrubland) protects sandy Fetovaia, where nudists flop on nearby granite rocks known as Le Piscine.

Enfola

Just 6km west of Portoferraio, it's not so much the grey pebbles as the outdoor action that lures crowds to this tiny fishing port. There are pedalos to rent, a beachside diving school, and a family-friendly 2.5km-long circular hiking trail around the green cape.

Morcone, Pareti & Innamorata

Find this trio of charming sandy-pebble coves framed by sweet-smelling pine trees some 3km south of Capoliveri in southeast Elba. Rent a kayak and paddle out to sea on Innamorata, the wildest of the three; or fine dine and overnight on Pareti beach at Hotel Stella Maris (☑ 0565 96 84 25; www.albergostellamaris.it; Località Pareti; d €145-190; P ❀ ☎), one of the few three-star hotels to be found on the sand.

Sansone & Sorgente

This twinset of cliff-ensnared, white-shingle and pebble beaches stands out for crystal-clear, turquoise waters just made for snorkelling. By car from Portoferraio, follow the SP27 towards Enfola. Parking is challenging.

Lo Sgarbo SEAFOOD $
(☑ 348 2987970; Via Silvio Pellico 3; meals €22; ☉ 7.30-10.30pm) No resort-style glamour or pretension at this popular *spaghetteria* – just exceptionally tasty seafood pasta served in the dining room or at one of the outdoor tables.

La Taverna dei Poeti TUSCAN $$$
(☑ 0565 96 83 06; www.latavernadeipoeti.com; Via Roma 14; meals €46; ☉ 7.30-11.30pm daily summer) Much-loved by locals, this traditional address sees chef Massimo cook up the very best of Tuscan produce with a generous peppering of simplicity. The menu splits dishes into *mare* (sea) and *terre* (literally 'earth', meaning meat), and a €70 tasting menu pairs each of the four courses with a different wine.

ℹ Information

Visit Elba Tourist Information Office (☑ 0565 96 76 50; www.infoelba.com; Viale Australia 1; ☉ 9am-1.30pm Jun-Oct) The island's main tourist office.

ℹ Getting There & Away

Bus 117 connects Capoliveri with Portoferraio, Porto Azzurro, Rio Elba, Rio Marina and Cavo at least eight times daily (€2.50).

Porto Azzurro

POP 3751

Fittingly (considering its name), Porto Azzurro's glittering blue harbour fronts a palm-dotted pedestrianised square; a compact maze of flower-framed lanes, lined with restaurant and cafe terraces, spreads out behind. It makes for an atmospheric place to sample local seafood and wine, and a sweep of good beaches is found nearby.

✖ Eating

L'Osteria dei Quattro Gatti SEAFOOD $$
(☑ 0565 9 52 40; Piazza del Mercato 4; meals €40; ☉ 7.30-10pm Tue-Sun, closed Mon mid-Sep–May) In the maze of lanes leading off from the main

WORTH A TRIP

RIO DELL'ELBA & RIO MARINA

Mountainous and relatively remote, north-east Elba was the heart of the island's mining operation, and heritage attractions here bring that industrial history to life vividly. The two main towns, hill-top Rio dell'Elba (population 1212) and coastal Rio Marina (population 2233), sit amid a network of plunging, twisting roads that will test your nerve and driving skills.

Rio's mining history dates from Etruscan times, with open-cast working continuing right up until 1982 when the mines closed. Museo dei Minerali e dell'Arte Mineraria (☑0565 96 20 88; www.parcominelba.it; Via Magenta 26, Rio Marina; adult/reduced €2.50/1.50; ⊙9.30am-12.30pm & 3.30-6.30pm Apr-Jun, Sep & Oct, 9.30am-12.30pm & 4.30-7.30pm Jul & Aug) charts that story and runs guided tours (adult/reduced €12/7.50) of the mining area by electric train – these include a chance to dig for minerals yourself. Book a few days in advance.

square (Piazza Matteotti), hunt out the flow-er-framed deck of this *osteria,* which sets the scene for excellently executed fish-themed dishes, often featuring treats such as *bot-targa* (salted fish roe). There aren't many tables, so it's a good idea to make a reservation.

Tamata   MODERN ITALIAN $$$
(☑0565 94 00 48; www.tamataristorante.it; cnr Vias Cesare Battisti & Cavalloti; meals €55; ⊙12.30-2pm & 7.30-10pm Mar–mid-May & mid-Oct–Nov, 7.30-10pm mid-May–mid Oct) This is as close as Elba gets to a temple of gastronomy. The exciting contemporary dishes that emerge from the kitchen have plenty of visual va-va-voom and taste great too – to truly appreciate the chef's inventiveness, opt for the tasting menu (€90). Wonderful wine list.

❶ Getting There & Away

Bus 117 connects Porto Azzurro with Capoliveri, Portoferraio, Rio Elba, Rio Marina and Cavo at least eight times daily (€2.50).

Giglio, Gorgona & Pianosa

Giglio (population 1442) is the second-largest of the seven islands in the Tuscan Archipelago. Located south of Elba, it comprises 21 sq km of predominantly hilly terrain and is a popular hiking destination. There are also a number of sheltered bays popular with swimmers. These days, most people know the island as the place where the cruise ship *Costa Concordia* met its tragic end in 2012, but it's a lovely place to spend a day and can easily be accessed by ferry from Porto Santo Stefano on Monte Argentario – Maregiglio (www.maregiglio.it) and Toremar (www.toremar.it) operate year-round services (passenger/car €26/90 return). There are also weekly services from Elba's Porta Azzurro on Aquavision (www.aquavision.it: adult/child return €35/20, two hours).

Pinprick Pianosa (population 10), south-west of Elba, served as a penal colony until 1997. It's not geared to tourism so there's no compelling reason to visit.

North of Elba, the island of Gorgona (population 220) hosts a high-security prison and is pretty well off-limits to day-trippers.

Capraia

POP 415

This tiny island in the Tyrrhenian Sea is a mere 31km from the French island of Corsica. Only 8km long and 4km wide, its highest point is Monte Castello (447m). It is a popular day-tripping destination in summer, when its few hotels and restaurants open, but is eerily quiet at other times of the year.

The island's great walks include the trail to Lake Stagnone – Capraia's tourist office (☑338 1509312, 0586 90 52 35; www.prolococapraiaisola.it; Via Assunzione 42; ⊙9.30am-12.30pm & 6.30-7.30pm Jul & Aug, reduced hours Jun & Sep) has maps of hiking and biking routes around the island. A chequered history has seen Genoa, Sardinia, the Saracens from North Africa and Napoleon all have a bash at running Capraia.

❶ Getting There & Away

Once a week, **Aquavision** (p210) runs a day trip (adult/child return €30/15, 2½ hours each way) from Portoferraio and Marciana Marina on Elba to Capraia, which leaves you five hours to explore the island. It also offers services from San Vincenzo on the mainland to the island (adult/child return €35/20, two hours), with a seven-hour stop. **Toremar** (☑0586 90 50 69; www.toremar.it) operates ferries between Livorno and Capraia (€40 return, 2¾ hours each way, one or two daily in summer, less frequently in winter); in high season schedules can allow a return trip in a day, but triple-check before setting out.

Northwestern Tuscany

Best Places to Eat

➡ Filippo Mud Bar (p261)

➡ Pepenero (p251)

➡ Osteria Il Papero (p250)

➡ Magno Gaudio (p249)

➡ Sergio Falaschi (p251)

➡ Locanda di Mezzo (p255)

Best Crowd-Free Treasures

➡ Barbialla Nuova (p251)

➡ Osteria Il Papero (p250)

➡ Museo di Palazzo Pretorio (p247)

➡ Al Benefizio (p257)

➡ Villa Bongi (p239)

➡ Palazzo Pfanner (p237)

Why Go?

There's far more to this green corner of Tuscany than Italy's iconic Leaning Tower. Usually hurtled through en route to Florence and Siena's grand-slam queue-for-hours sights, this is the place to take your foot off the accelerator and go slowly – on foot or by bicycle or car. Allow for long lunches of regional specialities to set the pace for the day, before meandering around a medieval hilltop village or along an ancient pilgrimage route.

University hub Pisa and 'love at first sight' Lucca – with its 16th-century walls ensnaring a labyrinth of butter-coloured buildings, Romanesque palaces and gracious piazzas – have an air of tranquillity and tradition that begs the traveller to linger. Lesser-known Pistoia, Prato and Pietrasanta, all off the beaten tourist track, provide a welcome reprieve in high season from the crowds (dead-easy half- or full-day trips by train from Florence, incidentally). This is snail-paced Italy, and impossible not to love.

Road Distances (km)

	Pistoia	Pisa	Lucca	San Miniato
Pisa	55			
Lucca	40	23		
San Miniato	64	47	70	
Pietrasanta	68	31	30	77

North-western Tuscany Highlights

1 Lucca (p234) Pedalling and picnicking on delicious local treats atop this handsome city's Renaissance city walls.

2 Leaning Tower (p226) Meandering through medieval Pisa and scaling its iconic tower at sunset.

3 Truffle hunts (p251) Hunting white truffles with a dog in autumnal woods near outrageously foodie San Miniato.

4 Pistoia (p243) Fleeing the crowds by delving into the treasure trove of museums in this vibrant European City of Culture.

5 Pietrasanta (p260) Revelling in exciting contemporary art, cuisine and boutique shopping in this gem of a small art town.

6 Garfagnana (p252) Losing yourself in green rural Tuscany in chestnut-rich forests.

7 Carrara (p256) Seeing where Michelangelo sourced his marble and visiting the extraordinary quarries.

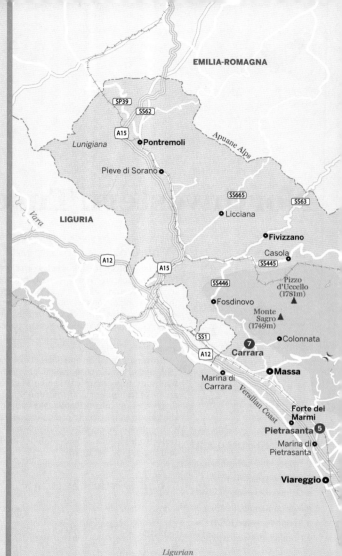

EMILIA-ROMAGNA

Enza

Pietra di
Bismantova
(1047m) ▲

Monte
Vecchio
(1982m) ▲

Monte Alto   Foce di Radici
(1538m) ▲   (1529m)
San Romano   SS324
in Garfagnana   San Pellegrino
        6   in Alpe (1525m)
● Garfagnana
Serchio   Castiglione
Monte   di Garfagnana
Umbriano ▲   Lago di
(1229m)   Pontecosi   ● Abetone
Lago   SS12
di Vagli   ● Castelnuovo
           di Garfagnana   Vico
Pania Della   ● Barga   Pancellorum   San Marcello
Croce   San   Pistoiese   SS632
(1858m) ▲   Cassiano   Ponte   Popiglio
Monte   Parco Regionale   Bagni di   Coccia   SS64   Badia a
Croce   delle Alpi ♨   Lucca   SS12   Taona
(1314m) ▲ Apuane   ●
Monte   Margine di
Piglione ▲   ● Borgo a   Momigno ●
(1232m)   Mozzano   Fattoria
                                                            di Celle
Monsagrati   SS12   Villa Oliva &   ◉
              Villa Grabau   4 ● Pistoia
A11   ◎ ● Marlia   ● Pescia   Montecatini
A12   ◎   Villa Reale   Terme   A11   Prato ●
                         SS435   4
        ● Lucca   Lamporecchio
Montuolo   1   ●
              ● Altopascio
Torre ●   Lago di
del Lago   Massaciuccoli   SS12
A11   SS439   SS436
Parco Regionale
Migliarino ♨   Arno   SS67
San Rossore   Sta Maria
Massaciuccoli   a Monte ●
                                                                  CHIANTI
           2 ● Pisa   Cascina   ● Montópoli
Pisa   3
International SS206   ● Pontedera   SS67   ● San Miniato
Airport   SS67b   La Serra ●   SS429
              ● Ponsacco   Collebrunacchi ●

La Sterza (6km);   Montaione
Lajatico (6.2km) ↓   3

PISA

POP 89,200

Once a maritime power to rival Genoa and Venice, Pisa now draws its fame from an architectural project gone terribly wrong. But the world-famous Leaning Tower is just one of many noteworthy sights in this compelling city. Education has fuelled the local economy since the 1400s, and students from across Italy compete for places in its elite university. This endows the centre of town with a vibrant cafe and bar scene, balancing an enviable portfolio of well-maintained Romanesque buildings, Gothic churches and Renaissance piazzas with a lively street life dominated by locals rather than tourists – a charm you will definitely not discover if you restrict your visit to Piazza dei Miracoli.

History

Pisa became an important naval base and commercial port under Rome and remained a significant port for centuries. The city's golden days began late in the 10th century, when it became an independent maritime republic and a formidable rival of Genoa and Venice. A century on, the Pisan fleet was sailing far beyond the Mediterranean, successfully trading with the Orient and bringing home new ideas in art, architecture and science. At the peak of its power (the 12th and 13th centuries), Pisa controlled Corsica, Sardinia and the Tuscan coast. Most of the city's finest buildings date from this period, when the distinctive Pisan-Romanesque architectural style with its use of coloured marbles and subtle references to Andalucian architectural styles flourished. Many of these buildings sported decoration by the great father-and-son sculptural team of Nicola and Giovanni Pisano.

Pisa's support for the imperial Ghibellines during the tussles between the Holy Roman Emperor and the pope brought the city into conflict with its mostly Guelph Tuscan neighbours, including Siena, Lucca and Florence. The real blow came when Genoa's fleet inflicted a devastating defeat on Pisa at the Battle of Meloria in 1284. After the city fell to Florence in 1406, the Medici court encouraged great artistic, literary and scientific endeavours and re-established Pisa's university, where the city's most famous son, Galileo Galilei, taught in the late 16th century. During WWII about 40% of old Pisa was destroyed.

◉ Sights & Activities

Many visitors to Pisa arrive by train at Pisa San Rossore and don't get any further than neighbouring Piazza dei Miracoli; those in the know arrive or depart using Stazione Pisa Centrale, allowing casual discovery of the *centro storico* (historic centre).

Away from the crowded heavyweights of Piazza dei Miracoli, along the Arno river

---

THREE PERFECT DAYS

Day One

In lovely **Lucca** (p234) hire a bike, stock up on the city's finest picnic fare and free-wheel along the city's medieval streets. Picnic atop the monumental **city wall** (p234) or pedal east to lunch alfresco in **Renaissance villa grounds** (p243). Come evening, enjoy a Puccini recital in a **medieval church** (p237).

Day Two

Fall in love with backstreet Pisa, saving **Piazza dei Miracoli** (p226) for last – the best tower shots are from the cloister garden of **Museo dell'Opera del Duomo**, once it eventually reopens after renovation work. In the late afternoon, leave Pisa for Slow Food town **San Miniato** (p250). Sip an *aperitivo* with valley view in a quaint old-world cafe and dine at **Pepenero** (p251) or out-of-town **Osteria Il Papero** (p250). Overnight at truffle farm **Barbialla Nuova** (p251).

Day Three

Shop for a picnic of local forest produce in **Castelnuovo di Garfagnana** (p252), then motor up and over the **Apuane Alps** (p252) – allow time for pulling over to soak up vistas of monumental marble blocks being cut out of the mountainside. Picnic on the **Passo del Vestito** (p253) and visit its botanical garden, then drop down to the sea. In Massa, head north to **Carrara** (p256) to see a marble quarry or south to **Pietrasanta** (p260) for fine art and creative drinking and dining at **Filippo Mud Bar** (p261).

banks, Pisa comes into its own. Splendid *palazzi,* painted a multitude of hues, line the southern *lungarno* (riverside embankment), from where shopping boulevard Corso Italia legs it to the central train station, Stazione Pisa Centrale. Don't miss the waterside, triple-spired Chiesa di Santa Maria della Spina (p232); closed for restoration work, it's an exquisite Pisan-Gothic church encrusted with tabernacles and statues. It was built between 1230 and 1223 to house a reliquary of a *spina* (thorn) from Christ's crown.

Pisa's medieval heart lies north of the water: from Piazza Cairoli, with its evening bevy of bars and gelato shops, meander along Via Cavour and get lost in the surrounding lanes and alleys. A daily fresh-produce market fills Piazza delle Vettovaglie, ringed with 15th-century porticoes and cafe terraces.

Museo Nazionale di San Matteo MUSEUM
(⌨050 54 18 65; Piazza San Matteo in Soarta 1; adult/reduced €5/2.50; ⊙8.30am-7.30pm Tue-Sat, to 1.30pm Sun) This inspiring repository of medieval masterpieces sits in a 13th-century Benedictine convent on the Arno's northern waterfront boulevard. The museum's collection of paintings from the Tuscan school (c 12th to 14th centuries) is notable, with works by Lippo Memmi, Taddeo Gaddi, Gentile da Fabriano and Ghirlandaio. Don't miss Masaccio's *St Paul,* Fra' Angelico's *Madonna of Humility* and Simone Martini's *Polyptych of Saint Catherine.*

Palazzo Blu GALLERY
(www.palazzoblu.it; Lungarno Gambacorti 9; ⊙10am-7pm Tue-Fri, to 8pm Sat & Sun) FREE Facing the river is this magnificently restored 14th-century building with a striking dusty-blue facade. Inside, its over-the-top 19th-century interior decoration is the perfect backdrop for the Foundation Pisa's art collection – predominantly Pisan works from the 14th to the 20th centuries on the 2nd floor, plus various temporary exhibitions (adult/reduced €6/4) on the ground floor. Admission also includes an archaeological area in the basement and the noble residence of this aristocratic palace, furnished as it would have been in the 19th century, on the 1st floor.

☆ Festivals & Events

Palio delle Quattro Antiche Repubbliche Marinare CULTURAL
(Regatta of the Four Ancient Maritime Republics; ⊙early Jun) The four historical maritime rivals – Pisa, Venice, Amalfi and Genoa – take turns

FLEE THE CROWDS

For a Zen respite from the Piazza dei Miracoli crowd, explore Orto e Museo Botanico (Botanical Garden & Museum; ⌨050 221 13 10; Via Roma 56; adult/reduced/family €4/2/6; ⊙8.30am-8pm Apr-Sep, 9am-5pm Mon-Sat, to 1am Sun Oct-Mar), a peaceful walled garden laced with centurion palm trees, flora typical to the Apuane Alps, a fragrant herb garden, vintage greenhouses and 35 orchid species. Showcasing the botanical collection of Pisa University, the garden dates from 1543 and was Europe's first university botanical garden, tended by the illustrious botanist Luca Ghini (1490–1556). The museum, inside Palazzo della Conchiglie, explores the garden's history, with exquisite botanical drawings, catalogues, maquettes etc.

to host this historic regatta. The regatta sailed into Pisa in 2017 and will do so again in 2021.

Luminaria di San Ranieri LIGHT SHOW
(⊙16 Jun) The night before the day of Pisa's patron saint is magical: thousands upon thousands of candles and blazing torches light up the river and riverbanks while fireworks bedazzle the night sky.

Gioco del Ponte CULTURAL
(⊙last Sun Jun) During Gioco del Ponte (Game of the Bridge), two teams in medieval costume battle it out over the Ponte di Mezzo.

✗ Eating

Pisa has a good range of eating places, especially around Borgo Stretto – the university on cafe-ringed Piazza Dante Alighieri – and south of the river in the trendy San Martino quarter. Avoid the touristy restaurant strip on Via Santa Maria.

Local specialities include fresh *pecorino* (sheep's milk cheese) from San Rossore, *zuppe di cavolo* (cabbage soup), *pan ficato* (fig cake) and *castagnaccio* (chestnut-flour cake enriched by nuts).

★ Gelateria De' Coltelli GELATO $
(⌨345 481 19 03; www.decoltelli.it; Lungarno Pacinotti 23; cones/tubs €2.30-4.50; ⊙11.30am-10.30pm Sun-Thu, to 11.30pm Fri & Sat) Follow the crowd to this world-class *gelateria* across from the river, famed for its sensational artisanal, organic and 100% natural

TOP SIGHT
PIAZZA DEI MIRACOLI

No Tuscan sight is more immortalised in kitsch souvenirs than the iconic tower teetering on the edge of this vast green square, also known as Piazza del Duomo (Cathedral Sq). Its lawns provide an urban carpet on which Europe's most extraordinary concentration of Romanesque buildings lounge: the *duomo* (cathedral), *battistero* (baptistry) and *campanile* (bell tower, aka the Leaning Tower).

DON'T MISS

➡ Leaning Tower

➡ Camposanto

➡ Battistero

➡ Duomo

PRACTICALITIES

➡ Campo dei Miracoli

➡ 📞 050 83 50 11

➡ www.opapisa.it

Leaning Tower

One of Italy's signature sights, the Torre Pendente (€18; ⊘ 8am-8pm Apr-Sep, 9am-7pm Oct, to 6pm Mar, 10am-5pm Nov-Feb) truly lives up to its name, leaning a startling 3.9 degrees off the vertical. The 56m-high tower, officially the *duomo*'s *campanile* (bell tower), took almost 200 years to build, but was already listing when it was unveiled in 1372.

Access is limited to 45 people at a time – children under eight are not allowed in/up and those aged eight to 10 years must hold an adult's hand. To avoid disappointment, book in advance online. Visits last 35 minutes and involve a steep climb up 251 steps. All bags, handbags included, must be deposited at the free left-luggage desk next to the central ticket office – you can take cameras up.

Duomo

Pisa's huge 11th-century duomo (Duomo di Santa Maria Assunta; ⊘ 10am-8pm Apr-Sep, to 7pm Oct, to 6pm Nov-Mar) FREE with its striking cladding of green and cream marble (a 13th-century addition) was the blueprint for Romanesque churches throughout Tuscany. The elliptical dome, the first of its kind in Europe at the time, dates from 1380 and the wooden ceiling decorated with 24-carat gold is a legacy of Medici rule.

San Ranieri

Admire the Portale di San Ranieri, copies of the 12th-century bronze doors illustrating the life of Christ, facing the Leaning Tower. The doors are named after Pisa's patron saint, Ranieri. His preserved skeleton is inside the cathedral in a glass-sided marble 'urn' in the Cappella di San Cappella Ranieri. Arab-sculpted decorative elements in the chapel demonstrate how influential the Islamic world was on Pisa at this time; the 11th-century bronze griffin that stood atop the cathedral until 1828 was booty, probably Egyptian in origin.

Giovanni Pisano's Pulpit

The extraordinary octagonal pulpit in the north aisle was sculpted from Carrara marble by Pisano between 1302 and 1310; it was inspired by his father's pulpit in the Battistero and also features nude and heroic figures.

Battistero

Construction of the cupcake-style Battistero (Battistero di San Giovanni; €5, combination ticket with Camposanto or Museo delle Sinopie €7, Camposanto & Museo €8; ☺8am-8pm Apr-Sep, 9am-7pm Oct, to 6pm Mar, 10am-5pm Nov-Feb) began in 1152, but the building was remodelled and continued by Nicola and Giovanni Pisano more than a century later and finally completed in the 14th century. Don't leave without climbing to the Upper Gallery to listen to the custodian demonstrate the double dome's remarkable acoustics and echo effects.

Camposanto

Soil shipped from Calvary during the Crusades is said to lie within the white walls of this hauntingly beautiful cloistered quadrangle (€5, combination ticket with Battistero or Museo delle Sinopie €7, Battistero & Museo €8; ☺8am-8pm Apr-Sep, 9am-7pm Oct, to 6pm Mar, 10am-5pm Nov-Feb) where prominent Pisans were once buried. Some of the sarcophagi here are of Graeco-Roman origin, recycled during the Middle Ages. During WWII, Allied artillery unfortunately destroyed many of the 14th- and 15th-century frescoes that once covered the cloister walls.

Museo delle Sinopie

This museum (€5, combination ticket with Battistero or Camposanto €7, Battistero & Camposanto €8; ☺8am-8pm Apr-Sep, 9am-7pm Oct, to 6pm Mar, 10am-5pm Nov-Feb) safeguards several *sinopie* (preliminary sketches) drawn by artists in red earth pigment on the walls of the Camposanto in the 14th and 15th centuries before frescoes were painted over them. It offers a compelling study in fresco painting technique, with short films and scale models filling in the gaps.

NORTHWESTERN TUSCANY PIAZZA DEI MIRACOLI

TOP TIPS

There are limited admissions to the Leaning Tower: book in advance online or grab the first available slot as soon as you arrive; ticket desks are behind the tower and in the Museo delle Sinopie.

Admission to the *duomo* is free, but you need to show a ticket – either for one of the other sights or a *duomo* coupon distributed at ticket offices.

Inside the Battistero, a hexagonal marble pulpit (1260) by Nicola Pisano is the undoubted highlight. Inspired by the Roman sarcophagi in the Camposanto, Pisano used powerful classical models to enact scenes from biblical legend. His figure of Daniel, who supports one of the corners of the pulpit on his shoulders, is particularly extraordinary.

THE TRIUMPH OF DEATH

Among the few of the Camposanto's frescoes to survive was this remarkable illustration of Hell (1333–41) attributed to Buonamico Buffalmacco. Fortunately the mirrors once stuck next to the graphic images of the damned being roasted alive on spits have been removed – originally, viewers would have seen their own faces in the horrific scene.

Why Pisa Leans

In 1160 Pisa boasted 10,000-odd towers, but no *campanile* (bell tower) for its cathedral. Loyal Pisan, Berta di Bernardo, righted this in 1172 when she died and left a legacy of 60 pieces of silver in her will to the city to get cracking on a *campanile*.

Ironically, when Bonnano Pisano set to work on the world's most famous *campanile* in 1173, he did not realise what shaky ground he was on: beneath Piazza dei Miracoli's lawns lay a treacherous mix of sand and clay, 40m deep. And when work stopped five years on, with just three storeys completed, Italy's stump of an icon had already tilted. Building resumed in 1272, workers compensating for the lean by building straight up from the lower storeys to create a subtle banana curve. By the 19th century, many were convinced the tower was a mere whimsical folly of its inventors, built deliberately to lean.

In 1838 a clean-up job to remove muck oozing from the base of the tower exposed, once and for all, the true nature of its precarious foundations. In the 1950s the seven bells inside the tower, each sounding a different musical note and rung from the ground by 14 men since 1370, were silenced for fear of a catastrophic collapse. In 1990 the tower was closed to the public. Engineers placed 1000 tonnes of lead ingots on the north side to counteract the subsidence on the south side. Steel bands were wrapped around the 2nd storey to keep it together.

Then in 1995 the tower slipped a whole 2.5mm. Steel braces were slung

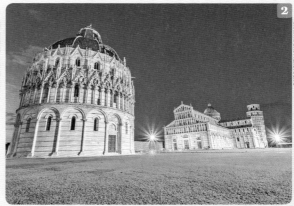

1. Leaning Tower (Torre Pendente) **2.** Battistero di San Giovanni and the *duomo* **3.** Chiesa di San Nicola's *campanile*

around the 3rd storey of the tower and attached to heavy hydraulic A-frame anchors some way from the northern side. The frames were replaced by steel cables, attached to neighbouring buildings. The tower held in place, engineers gingerly removed 70 tonnes of earth from below the northern foundations, forcing the tower to sink to its 18th-century level – and correct the lean by 2011 to 43.8cm. Success...

Every year scientists carry out tests on Pisa's pearly white leaning tower to measure its lean and check it's stable. Ironically, results in 2013 showed that the world's most famous leaning tower had, in fact, lost 2.5cm of its iconic lean, with some scientists even predicting a complete self-straightening by the year 2300. Let's hope not.

LEANING CITY

Duomo & Battistero (p226 & p227) The tower's neighbours lean 25cm and 51cm respectively.

Chiesa di San Nicola (Via Santa Maria) Nicola Pisano's octagonal *campanile* (bell tower) is another sacred edifice that is not dead straight.

Chiesa di San Michele degli Scalzi (Via San Michele degli Scalzi) Note the wonky red-brick square tower.

Pisa

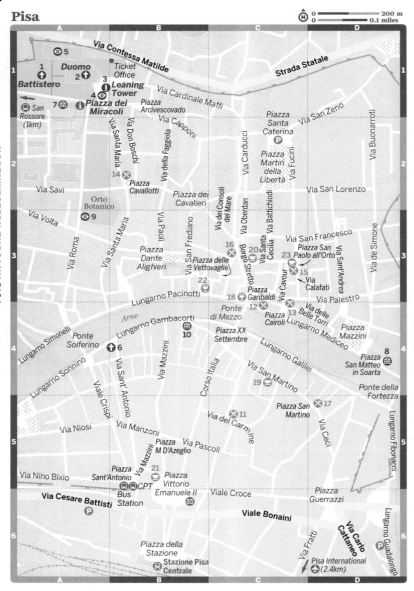

N 0 ▬▬▬▬▬ 200 m
  0 ▬▬▬▬▬ 0.1 miles

Via Contessa Matilde
Strada Statale

1 Battistero
Duomo 2
Ticket Office 3
Leaning Tower 4
5
7 Piazza dei Miracoli
San Rossore (1km)

Via Cardinale Maffi
Piazza Arcivescovado
Via Capponi

Piazza Santa Caterina
Via San Zeno
Via Buonarroti

Via Don Boschi
Via della Faggiola
Via Carducci
Piazza Martiri della Libertà
Via Fucini
Via San Lorenzo

Via Savi
Via Santa Maria
14 Piazza Cavallotti
Piazza dei Cavalieri
Orto Botanico
9

Via Volta
Via Roma
Via Santa Maria
Via Paoli
Piazza Dante Alighieri
Via San Frediano
Piazza delle Vettovaglie
Via dei Consoli del Mare
Via Oberdan
Via Santa Cecilia
Via Battichiodi
16
20 Borgo Stretto
23 Piazza San Paolo all'Orto
Via San Francesco
15 Via Calafati
Via Cavour
Via Sant'Andrea
Via de Simone
Via San Francesco

22
18 Piazza Garibaldi
12 Piazza Cairoli
13 Via delle Belle Torri
Lungarno Mediceo
Via Palestro
Piazza Mazzini

Arno
Lungarno Pacinotti
Lungarno Gambacorti
10
Ponte di Mezzo
Piazza XX Settembre
8 Piazza San Matteo in Soarta

Ponte Solferino
6
Via Mazzini
Corso Italia
Lungarno Galilei
Ponte della Fortezza

Lungarno Simonelli
Lungarno Sonnino
Viale Crispi
Via Sant'Antonio
Via San Martino
19
17 Piazza San Martino
Via Ceci
Lungarno Fibonacci

Via Niosi
Via Manzoni
Via del Carmine
11

Via Nino Bixio
Via Mazzini
Piazza M D'Azeglio
Via Pascoli
21 CPT
Piazza Sant'Antonio
Bus Station
Piazza Vittorio Emanuele II
Viale Croce
Piazza Guerrazzi
Via Carlo Cattaneo

Via Cesare Battisti
Viale Bonaini
Via Fratti
Pisa International (2.4km)
Lungarno Guadalongo

Piazza della Stazione
Stazione Pisa Centrale

---

gelato. Flavours are as zesty and appealing as its bright-orange interior. The hard part is choosing: ginger, ricotta cheese with pine nuts and honey, candied chestnuts, almond with candied lemon peel, cashew with Maldon salt, kiwi, or ricotta with candied orange peel and chocolate chips.

L'Ostellino SANDWICHES **$**

(Piazza Cavallotti 1; panini €3.50-7; ⊘noon-4.30pm Mon-Fri, to 6pm Sat & Sun) For a gourmet *panino* (sandwich) wrapped in crunchy waxed paper, this minuscule deli and *panineria* delivers. Take your pick from dozens of different combos written by hand on the black-

Pisa

◉ Top Sights

◉ Sights

◉ Eating

◉ Drinking & Nightlife

board (*lardo di colonnata* with figs or cave-aged *pecorino* with honey and walnuts are sweet favourites), await construction, then hit the green lawns of Piazza dei Miracoli to picnic with the crowds.

Pizzeria Il Montino   PIZZA $
(☑ 050 59 86 95; www.pizzeriailmontino.com; Vicolo del Monte 1; pizza €6-8.50, foccacine €2.50-5; ☺ 10.30am-3pm & 5-10pm Mon-Sat) There's nothing fancy about this down-to-earth pizzeria, an icon among Pisans, students and sophisticates alike. Take away or order at the bar then grab a table, inside or out, and munch on house specialities such as *cecina* (chickpea pizza), *castagnaccio* (chestnut cake) and *spuma* (sweet, nonalcoholic drink). Or go for a *focaccine* (small flat roll) filled with salami, pancetta or *porchetta* (suckling pig).

Capodimonte   PIZZA $
(☑ 334 949 72 24, 050 87 06 90; www.facebook.com/capodimontepisa; Via del Carmine 14; pizza €4-12, meals €30; ☺ noon-3pm & 7pm-1.30am Tue-Sun) For generous-sized pizza *forna a legna* (cooked in a proper, wood-burning oven) in

Pisa, washed down with a local craft beer, you won't do better than this stylish diner with red-brick ceiling, zebra-print cushions and funky music. The relaxed vibe is bar-like, and the food – a huge choice of pizza as well as steaks and pasta – doesn't disappoint.

Green & Go   HEALTH FOOD $
(☑ 050 893 21 50; www.facebook.com/Greenand GoPisa; Lungarno Mediceo 46; meals €4-10; ☺ 10.30am-3.30pm Mon-Sat) Concoct your own bespoke, lunchtime salads and sandwiches at this green fast-eat joint, a hymn to fresh fruit and veg with its lengthy list of potential ingredients waiting to be popped between bread or atop a bowl of lettuce leaves, couscous or other zesty grains. Homemade soups, fruit juices and smoothies too.

Ir Tegame   ITALIAN $
(☑ 050 57 28 01; www.facebook.com/irtegamepisa; Piazza Cairoli 9; meals €10-20; ☺ noon-2.30pm & 7.45-11.15pm) When the urge for a swift bowl of pasta strikes, hit this stylish *spaghetteria* on one of Pisa's buzziest squares. A riot of faux flowers, strung on red and white ladders, decorate the low ceiling and the menu only features *primi* (first courses) – pasta *primi* to be precise, all fresh and handmade. The *taglioni* with black truffle shavings is spot on.

The 'Giro Pasta' menu (€20), comprising four different pasta dishes brought to the tables in pans, dessert, water and house wine, is unbeatable value.

Ristorante Galileo   TUSCAN $$
(☑ 050 2 82 87; www.ristorantegalileo.com; Via San Martino 6-8; meals €25; ☺ 12.30-2.30pm & 7.30-10.30pm Wed-Mon) For good, honest, unpretentious Tuscan cooking, nothing beats this classical old-timer. From the cork-covered wine list to the complimentary plate of warm homemade focaccia and huge platters of tempting *cantuccini* (almond-studded biscuits), Galileo makes you feel welcome. Fresh pasta is strictly hand- and home-made, and most veggies are plucked fresh that morning from the restaurant's veggie garden.

Osteria Bernardo   TUSCAN $$
(☑ 050 57 52 16; Piazza San Paolo all'Orto 1; meals €40; ☺ 8-11pm Tue-Sat, 12.30-2.30pm & 8-11pm Sun) This small bistro on a pretty square, well away from the Leaning Tower crowd, is the perfect fusion of easy dining and gourmet excellence. Its menu is small – just four or five dishes per course – and cuisine is creative. Think pistachio-crusted lamb, beef in beer sauce or a tasty risotto with stilton

NORTHWESTERN TUSCANY PISA

cheese, lettuce and crisp leek. Reservations recommended.

Drinking & Nightlife

Most drinking action takes place on and around Piazza delle Vettovaglie, while the university on cafe-ringed Piazza Dante Alighieri is always student-packed.

Look out for local wines produced in the surrounding Pisan hills under the DOCG Chianti delle Colline Pisane label or Bianco Pisano di San Torpè, a Trebbiano-dominated wine with a delicate, dry flavour.

Keith CAFE
(☑050 50 31 35; www.facebook.com/keithcafe; Via Zandonai 4; ⊘7am-11pm summer, to 9pm winter; ⊛) This trendy cafe stares face to face with Tuttomondo (1989), a mural on the facade of a Pisan church – and the last mural American pop artist Keith Haring painted just months before his death. Sip a coffee or cocktail on the terrace and lament the fading, weather-beaten colours of Haring's 30 signature prancing dancing men.

La Stafetta CRAFT BEER
(www.lastafetta.com; Lungarno Pacinotti 24; ⊘5pm-1am, to 2am Fri & Sat) Squat on a bench outside or grab a pew inside this funky riverside tap room, the creation of three ale-loving Pisan students: Matteo, Davide and Francesco. Inside, order one of the small microbreweries own brews: taste English hops in Wilson (a dark-red bitter with hints of coffee, chocolate and liquorice) or go for a light and golden May Ale.

Bazeel BAR
(☑349 088 06 88; www.bazeel.it; Lungarno Pacinotti 1; ⊘7am-1am Sun-Thu, to 2am Fri & Sat) A dedicated all-rounder, Bazeel is a hot spot from dawn to dark. Laze over breakfast, linger over a light buffet lunch or hang out with the A-list crowd over a generous *aperitivo* spread, live music and DJs. Its chapel-like interior is nothing short of fabulous, as is its pavement terrace out the front. Check its Twitter feed for what's on.

Sottobosco CAFE
(☑050 314 20 84; www.facebook.com/sottobosco. libricafe; Piazza San Paolo all'Orto 3; ⊘noon-3pm & 6pm-midnight Tue-Fri, 6pm-1am Sat, to midnight Sun summer, reduced hours winter) This creative book-cafe is a breath of fresh air. Tuck into an end-of-day sugar doughnut and cappuccino or an early-evening *aperitivo* at a glass-topped table filled with artists' crayons perhaps, or a button collection. Salads, *panini,* salami or cheese *taglieri* (tasting boards) and oven-baked cheese are simple and home-made. Come dark, jazz bands play or DJs spin tunes.

Its summertime wooden terrace is one of the city's loveliest.

Caffè Letteraria Volta Pagina CAFE
(☑050 520 27 16; http://caffeletterariovoltapagina. it; Via San Martino 71; ⊘noon-6pm Tue-Sun) Kick back over a smoothie, juice or something stronger at this edgy literary cafe with red-brick vaulted ceiling, achingly cool vintage furnishings and laid-back lounge vibe. Breakfast and brunch (including gluten-free pasta and other dishes) are menu regulars, and weekly readings, concerts and other cultural happenings set the place buzzing. Check its Facebook page for what's on.

Caffè Pasticceria Salza CAFE
(☑050 58 01 44; Borgo Stretto 44; ⊘8am-8.30pm Tue-Sun) This old-fashioned cake shop has

---

❶ HOW TO FALL IN LOVE WITH PISA

Sure, the iconic Leaning Tower is the reason everyone wants to go to Pisa. But once you've put yourself through the Piazza dei Miracoli madness (littered lawns, football-playing school groups, photo-posing pandemonium...) most people simply want to get out of town.

To avoid leaving Pisa feeling oddly deflated by one of Europe's great landmarks, save the Leaning Tower and its oversized square for the latter part of the day – or, better still, an enchanting visit after dark (mid-June to late August/early September) when the night casts a certain magic on the glistening white monuments and the tour buses have long gone.

Upon arrival, indulge instead in peaceful meanderings along the Arno river, over its bridges and through Pisa's medieval heart. Discover the last monumental wall painting Keith Haring did before he died, enjoy low-key architectural and art genius at the Chiesa di Santa Maria della Spina (Lungarno Gambacorti) and Palazzo Blu (p225), and lunch with locals at Sottobosco or Osteria Bernardo (p231).

And only once you've fallen in love with the other Pisa, should you head for the tower.

DESTINATION SPAGHETTI: LARI

For foodies keen to meander off the beaten track between Pisa and Livorno, there is no finer destination than medieval Lari, a fortified village with 11th-century castle and a pasta factory no gastronome should miss.

Here's an interesting fact for you: the Barilla company makes as much pasta in 20 minutes as family-run **Martelli Pasta Factory** (☑ 0587 68 42 38; www.famigliamartelli.it; Via dei Pastifici 3; ☺ 9am-1pm & 3-5pm Mon, Tue & Thu-Sat, closed 2 weeks Aug) **FREE** makes in a year – it's an authentically artisanal operation. Established in 1926 and self-described as the smallest pasta factory in the world, it exports internationally (Germany and Australia are the biggest importers) and is happy to give its devoted customers a free 10-minute tour showcasing its hands-on production methods.

On the tour, you'll see slowly kneaded dough being fed through traditional bronze moulds to create spaghetti and spaghettini, penne, macaroni and fusilli – the best days to visit are Tuesday and Friday, when spaghetti is made. The pasta is then air-dried for 50 hours (compared to three hours industrially) before being cut and packaged by hand in Martelli's trademark canary-yellow paper packets. These are designed to evoke the pre-1960s paper that loose, market-bought pasta was wrapped in before industrialisation changed it all.

Chewier and coarser in texture than many, Martelli's pasta marries particularly well with meat sauces and game. In Lari itself, buy it for €4.50 per kilogram at village cafe and tobacconist **La Bottega delle Specialità** (☑ 0587 68 71 12; Via Diaz 12-14; ☺ 7.30am-8pm Mon-Sat; ☎) or eat the pasta for lunch at **Antica Osteria al Castello** (☑ 329 2088155; Piazza Giacomo Matteotti 13; pasta €10-20, meals €36; ☺ 12.30-2pm & 7.30-10pm Wed-Sun, also Mon Jun-Aug) in the main piazza.

Getting There & Away

There are no direct public transport links between Lari and Livorno or Pisa, so you'll need your own wheels.

been tempting Pisans into sugar-induced wickedness since 1898. It's an equally lovely spot for a cocktail – any time. Check its Facebook page for enticing foodie events and happenings.

ℹ Information

Tourist Office (☑ 050 55 01 00; www.turismo.pisa.it/en; Piazza dei Miracoli 7; ☺ 9.30am-5.30pm) Provides city information, free maps and various services including guided tours, left luggage (€3/4 per small/large bag per day), bicycle rental (€3/15 per hour/day), and a computer terminal to check train times and sign up for city bike-sharing scheme Ciclopi etc. Also sells public transport tickets.

ℹ Getting There & Away

AIR

Pisa International Airport (Galileo Galilei Airport; ☑ 050 84 93 00; www.pisa-airport.com) Tuscany's main international airport is a 10-minute drive south of Pisa; there are flights to major European cities.

BUS

From its **bus station** (Piazza Sant'Antonio 1) hub, Pisan bus company **CPT** (☑ 050 50 55 02;

www.cpt.pisa.it; Piazza Sant'Antonio 1; ☺ ticket office 7am-8.15pm Mon-Fri, to 8pm Sat & Sun) runs buses to/from Volterra (€6.10, two hours, up to 10 daily with change of bus in Pontedera).

TRAIN

There is a handy **left-luggage counter** (Deposito Bagagli; ☑ 050 261 52; www.depositobagaglipisa.it; Pisa Centrale; bag per day €5; ☺ 6am-9pm) at **Pisa Centrale** (Piazza della Stazione) train station – not to be confused with north-of-town **Pisa San Rossore** (Via Giunta) station. Regional train services to/from Pisa Centrale:

Florence (€8.40, 1¼ hours, frequent)
Livorno (€2.60, 15 minutes, frequent)
Lucca (€3.50, 30 minutes, every 30 minutes)
Viareggio (€3.50, 15 minutes, every 20 minutes)

ℹ Getting Around

TO/FROM THE AIRPORT

Fully automated, super-speedy **PisaMover** (http://pisa-mover.com) trains link **Pisa International Airport** (p233) with Pisa Centrale train station (€2.70, five minutes, every five minutes from 6am to midnight).

The LAM Rossa (red) bus line (€1.20, 10 minutes, every 10 to 20 minutes) run by CPT passes through the city centre and the train station en route to/from the airport. Buy tickets from the blue ticket machine, next to the bus stops to the right of the train station exit.

A taxi between the airport and city centre should cost no more than €10. To book, call **Radio Taxi Pisa** (☑ 050 54 16 00; www.cotapi.it).

BICYCLE
Some hotels lend bikes to their guests. Otherwise pedal around town on a silver bicycle courtesy of Pisan bike-sharing scheme **Cicopli**, with an **info point** (☑ 800 005 640; www.ciclopi.eu; Piazza Vittorio Emanuele II; 1st hr free, 2nd/3rd/4th half-hour €0.90/1.50/2.50; ☯ 9.30am-1pm) on Piazza Vittorio Emanuele II. Pick-up/drop-off at 14 stations dotted around the city, including at Pisa Centrale and Pisa San Rossore train stations, Pisa airport and Piazza Manin (adjoining Piazza dei Mracoli).

Toscana In Tour (☑ 333 260 21 52; www.toscanaintour.it; Via della Faggiola 41) rents decent bicycles (€16 to €20 per day), scooters and stylish vespas. Touristy stands at the northern end of Via Santa Maria and other streets off Piazza dei Miracoli rent touristy four-wheel rickshaws for up to three/six people (€10/15 per hour) and regular bicycles (€3.50 to €5 per hour).

CAR & MOTORCYCLE
Parking costs around €2 per hour; don't park in the historic centre's Limited Traffic Zone (ZTL). There's a free car park outside the zone on Lungarno Guadalongo, near Fortezza di San Gallo on the south side of the Arno.

LUCCA
POP 89,000

Lovely Lucca endears itself to everyone who visits. Hidden behind imposing Renaissance walls, its cobbled streets, handsome piazzas and shady promenades make it a perfect destination to explore by foot – as a day trip from Florence or in its own right. At the day's end, historic cafes and restaurants tempt visitors to relax over a glass or two of Lucchesi wine and a slow progression of rustic dishes prepared with fresh produce from nearby Garfagnana.

If you have a car, the hills to the east of Lucca demand exploration. Home to histor-

ⓘ CENT SAVER
If you plan to visit the Museo della Cattedrale, Chiesa de SS Giovanni e Reparata and the sacristy inside Cattedrale di San Martino, buy a cheaper combined ticket (adult/reduced €9/5) at any of the sights.

ic villas and belle époque Montecatini Terme where Puccini lazed in warm spa waters, they are easy and attractive day-trip destinations from Lucca.

History
Founded by the Etruscans, Lucca became a Roman colony in 180 BC and a free *comune* (self-governing city) during the 12th century, when it enjoyed a period of prosperity based on the silk trade. In 1314 it briefly fell to Pisa, but regained its independence under the leadership of local adventurer Castruccio Castracani degli Anterminelli, and began to amass territories in western Tuscany, including marble-rich Carrara. Castruccio died in 1328 but Lucca remained an independent republic for almost 500 years.

Napoleon ended all this in 1805 when he created the principality of Lucca and placed one of the seemingly countless members of his family in need of an Italian fiefdom (this time his sister Elisa) in control of all of Tuscany. Ten years later the city became a Bourbon duchy before being incorporated into the Kingdom of Italy. It miraculously escaped being bombed during WWII, so the fabric of the *centro storico* has remained unchanged for centuries.

◉ Sights & Activities
Stone-paved Via Fillungo, with its fashion boutiques and car-free mantra, threads its way through the medieval heart of the old city. East is one of Tuscany's loveliest piazzas, oval cafe-ringed Piazza Anfiteatro, named for the amphitheatre that was here in Roman times. Spot remnants of the amphitheatre's brick arches and masonry on the exterior walls of the medieval houses ringing the piazza.

★ City Wall   HISTORIC SITE
Lucca's monumental *mura* (wall) was built around the old city in the 16th and 17th centuries and remains in almost perfect condition. It superseded two previous walls, the first built from travertine stone blocks as early as the 2nd century BC. Twelve metres high and 4.2km long, today's ramparts are crowned with a tree-lined footpath looking down on the historic centre and – by the Baluardo San Regolo (San Regolo Bastion) – the city's vintage botanical gardens (☑ 0583 44 21 61; Casermetta San Regolo; adult/reduced €4/3; ☯ 10am-7pm Jul-Sep, to 6pm May & Jun, to 5pm Mar, Apr & Oct) with its magnificent centurion cedar trees.

The wall-top path is a favourite location for the locals' sacrosanct *passeggiata* (evening stroll). Childen's climbing frames, swings and picnic tables beneath shady plane trees add a buzz of weekend activity to Baluardo San Regolo, Baluardo San Salvatore and Baluardo Santa Croce – a trio of 11 bastions studding the way. Older kids kick footballs around on the green lawns of Baluardo San Donato.

★ **Cattedrale di San Martino**   CATHEDRAL
(🖉0583 49 05 30; www.museocattedralelucca.it; Piazza San Martino; adult/reduced €3/2, incl Museo della Cattedrale & Chiesa e Battistero dei SS Giovanni & Reparata €9/5; ⊙9.30am-6pm Mon-Fri, to 6.45pm Sat, noon-6pm Sun summer, 9.30am-5pm Mon-Fri, to 6.45pm Sat, noon-6pm Sun winter) Lucca's predominantly Romanesque cathedral dates from the 11th century. Its stunning facade was constructed in the prevailing Lucca-Pisan style and designed to accommodate the pre-existing *campanile* (bell tower). The reliefs over the left doorway of the portico are believed to be by Nicola Pisano, while inside, treasures include the Volto Santo (literally, Holy Countenance) crucifix sculpture and a wonderful 15th-century tomb in the sacristy. The cathedral interior was rebuilt in the 14th and 15th centuries with a Gothic flourish.

Legend has it that the *Volto Santo,* a simply fashioned image of a dark-skinned, life-sized Christ on a wooden crucifix, was carved by Nicodemus, who witnessed the crucifixion. In

NORTHWESTERN TUSCANY LUCCA

THE PUCCINI TRAIL

Lucca has a particular lure for opera buffs: it was here, in 1858, that the great Giacomo Puccini was born, and baptised the following day in the Chiesa e Battistero dei SS Giovanni e Reparata. The maestro, who came from a long line of Lucchesi musicians, grew up in an apartment at Corte San Lorenzo 9, now the house-museum Casa Puccini (🖉0583 58 40 28; www.puccinimuseum.org; Corte San Lorenzo 9; adult/reduced/family €7/5/13; ⊙10am-7pm May-Sep, to 6pm Mar, Apr & Oct, to 1pm & 3-5pm Wed-Mon Nov-Feb) – look for the imposing statue of the maestro at the front. During his teenage years, Puccini played the organ in Cattedrale di San Martino (p235) and performed as a piano accompanist at Teatro del Giglio (www.teatrodelgiglio.it; Piazza del Giglio 13-15), the 17th-century theatre where the curtain would later rise on some of his best-known operas: *La Bohème* (1896), *Tosca* (1900) and *Madame Butterfly* (1907).

In 1880 Puccini left Lucca to study at Milan's music conservatory. After his studies, he returned to Tuscany to rent a lakeside house in Torre del Lago, 15km west of Lucca on the shore of Lago di Massaciuccoli. Nine years later, after the successes of *Manon Lescaut* (1893) and *La Bohème,* he had a villa built on the same lakeshore, undertaking the Liberty-style interior decoration himself. It was here that Puccini with his wife, Elvira, spent his time working, hunting on the lake and carousing with a diverse group of hunters, fishermen and bohemian artists. *Madame Butterfly, La fanciulla del West* (1910), *La Rondine* (1917) and *Il Trittico* (1918) were composed on the Forster piano in his front study, and he wrote his scores on the walnut table in the same room.

Villa di Torre del Lago, now the Museo Villa Puccini (🖉0584 34 14 45; www.giacomopuccini.it; Viale Puccini 266, Torre del Lago; adult/reduced €7/3; ⊙2.30-5.50pm Mon, 10am-12.40pm & 3-6.20pm Tue-Sun), has been preserved as it was during Puccini's residence and is hence fascinating to visit (by guided tour every 40 minutes). In summer the villa grounds and lakeshore buzz with the world-famous Puccini Festival (www.puccinifestival.it), which sees three or four of the great man's operas performed in a purpose-built outdoor theatre. Tickets are like gold dust and sell out months in advance.

Puccini was a frequent visitor to Montecatini Terme, a charming spa resort 56km east, known for its mineral-rich waters. From May to October, spa lovers still flock here to wallow in warm waters and indulge in beauty treatments at its *terme* (thermal baths) in grand old buildings overlooking a beautiful park. The tourist office (🖉0573 77 22 44; www.montecatiniturismo.it; Viale Verdi 66-68, Montecatini Terme; ⊙9am-12.30pm & 3-6pm Mon-Sat, plus 9am-noon Sun summer) has details.

In 1921 Puccini and Elvira moved to a villa in nearby Viareggio where the composer became a regular fixture at Gran Caffè Margherita (p262). He worked on his last opera, the unfinished *Turandot,* here. After Puccini's death in 1924, Elvira and son Antonio added a chapel to the Torre del Lago villa; Puccini's remains were interred there in 1926.

Lucca

200 m
0.1 miles

Via del Bacchettoni

Baluardo San Salvatore

Strada del Vino e dell'Olio

Porta Elisa

Baluardo della Libertà

Via della Quarquonia

Via Paoli

Via Elisa

Via del Bacchettoni

Baluardo San Regolo

Piazza San Francesco

Via Santa Chiara

●13

Via San Micheletto

◉11

Via del Fosso

Via Rosi

Via Santa Gemma Galgani

Via della Fratta

Via del Fosso

Via San Nicolao

🏛9

Porta San Gervasio

Via del Giardino Botanico

Via del Fosso

Piazza San Pietro Somaldi

Via Canuleia

Via dell'Angelo Custode

Via della Rosa

Via della Quarquonia

Via Santa Croce

Via Guinigi

(500m)

Passeggiata della Mura

Via Fillungo

Piazza San Frediano

Piazza degli Scalpellini

Piazza Anfiteatro

Via Mordini

Torre Guinigi
◉5

Piazza dei Servi

Via Vallisneri

Via del Fosso

Via della Quarquonia

Via della Cavallerizza

Piazza del Collegio

Piazza Anfiteatro

Piazza San Frediano

Via della Anfiteatro

Piazza del Carmine

Via Sant'Andrea

Piazza Bernardini

Museo della Cattedrale

Via Antelminelli

Cattedrale di San Martino

Via degli Asili

Via Battisti

Via degli Angeli

Via del Moro

Via Fillungo

Via Cenami

Via del Battistero

Piazza San Martino

Piazza San Giovanni

City Wall
◉2

Palazzo Pfanner
🏛4

Piazza Sant'Agostino

Via Bura

✕18

●12

🏛26

Via del Molinetto

🏛3

Cattedrale

Piazza del Giglio

Via San Giorgio

Via del Loreto

Via Tegrimi

✕20

Via della Caldera

Via Santa Lucia

✕24
15
28
23
27

Piazza San Michele

Via Roma

Piazza XX Settembre

✕19

Piazza del Giglio

◉22

Piazza Napoleone

Via dei Giglio

🎫8

Via del Duomo

Via Galli Tassi

🏛10

✕25

Via Santa Giustina

Via del Toro

6
17

Via di Poggio

Piazza della Cittadella

Via della Cervia

Corte Campana

Via Veneto

Piazza San Romano

Passeggiata della Mura

Via delle Conce

Piazzale San Donato

Porta San Donato

Via San Paolino

Piazzale Verdi

Piazzale Boccherini

Porta Sant'Anna

Via Vittorio Emanuele II

Moat

Lucca

NORTHWESTERN TUSCANY LUCCA

fact, it has been dated to the 13th century. A major object of pilgrimage, the sculpture is carried through the streets every 13 September at dusk during the Luminaria di Santa Croce, a solemn torch-lit procession marking its miraculous arrival in Lucca.

The cathedral's many other works of art include a magnificent *Last Supper* by Tintoretto above the third altar of the south aisle and Domenico Ghirlandaio's 1479 *Madonna Enthroned with Saints*. This impressive work by Michelangelo's master is currently located in the sacristy. Opposite lies the exquisite, gleaming marble tomb of Ilaria del Carretto carved by Jacopo della Quercia in 1407. The young second wife of the 15th-century lord of Lucca, Paolo Guinigi, Ilaria died in childbirth aged only 24. At her feet lies her faithful dog.

★ Museo della Cattedrale   MUSEUM
(Cathedral Museum; ☑ 0583 49 05 30; www.museo cattedralelucca.it; Piazza San Martino; adult/reduced €4/3, with cathedral sacristy & Chiesa e Battistero dei SS Giovanni e Reparata €9/5; ⊙10am-6pm summer, to 5pm Mon-Fri, to 6pm Sat & Sun winter) The cathedral museum safeguards elaborate gold and silver decorations made for the cathedral's Volto Santo, including a 17th-century crown and a 19th-century sceptre.

Chiesa e Battistero dei
SS Giovanni e Reparata   CHURCH
(☑0583 49 05 30; www.museocattedralelucca. it; Piazza San Giovanni; adult/reduced €4/3, with cathedral sacristy & Museo della Cattedrale €9/5; ⊙10am-6pm summer, to 5pm Mon-Fri, to 6pm Sat & Sun winter) The 12th-century interior of this deconsecrated church is a hauntingly atmospheric setting for summertime opera and concert recitals (www.puccinielasua lucca.com), staged daily at 7pm; buy tickets (adult/reduced €20/16) in advance inside the church. In the north transept, the Gothic baptistry crowns an archaeological area comprising five building levels going back to the Roman period. Don't miss the hike up the red-brick bell tower.

★ Palazzo Pfanner   PALACE
(☑0583 95 21 55; www.palazzopfanner.it; Via degli Asili 33; palace or garden adult/reduced €4.50/4, both €6/5; ⊙10am-6pm Apr-Nov) Fire the romantic in you with a stroll around this beautiful 17th-century palace where parts of *Portrait of a Lady* (1996), starring Nicole Kidman and John Malkovich, were shot. Its baroque-styled garden – the only one of substance within the city walls – enchants with ornamental pond, lemon house and 18th-century statues of Greek gods posing between potted lemon trees. Summertime chamber-music concerts hosted here are absolutely wonderful.

Climb the grand outdoor staircase to the frescoed and furnished piano *nobile* (main reception room), home to Felix Pfanner, an Austrian émigré who first brought beer to Italy – and brewed it in the mansion's cellars from 1846 until 1929. From the copper

LOCAL KNOWLEDGE

A WALL-TOP PICNIC

When in Lucca, picnicking atop its city walls – on grass or at a wooden picnic table – is as lovely (and typical) a Lucchese lunch as any.

Buy fresh-from-the-oven pizza and focaccia with a choice of fillings and toppings from fabulous bakery Forno Amedeo Giusti (☑0583 49 62 85; www.facebook.com/PanificioGiusti; Via Santa Lucia 20; pizzas & filled focaccias per kg €10-15; ☉7am-7.30pm Mon-Sat, 4-7.30pm Sun), then nip across the street for a bottle of Lucchesi wine and Garfagnese *biscotti al farro* (spelt biscuits) at La Bodega di Prospero (Via Santa Lucia 13; ☉9am-7pm); look for the old-fashioned shop window stuffed with sacks of beans, lentils and other local pulses.

Complete the perfect picnic with a slice of *buccellato,* a traditional sweetbread loaf with sultanas and aniseed seeds, baked in Lucca since 1881. Devour the rest at home, with butter, dipped in egg and pan-fried, or dunked in sweet Vin Santo. Buy it at pastry shop Taddeucci (☑0583 49 49 33; www.buccellatotaddeucci.com; Piazza San Michele 34; buccellato loaf per 300/600g €4.50/9; ☉8.30am-7.45pm, closed Thu winter) for €4.50/9 per 300/600g loaf. Or seduce taste buds with truffles, white-chocolate spread and other artisanal chocolate creations almost too beautiful to eat from Caniparoli (www.caniparolicioccolateria.it; Via San Paolino 96; ☉9.30am-1pm & 3.30-7.30pm), the finest chocolate shop in town.

Swill down the picnic with your pick of Italian craft beers at microbrewery De Cervesia (☑0583 49 30 81; www.decervesia.it; Via Fillungo 90; ☉10.30am-1pm & 3.30-7.30pm Tue-Sat), which has a small shop on Lucca's main shopping street and a tap room for serious tasting (open 5pm to 10pm Tuesday to Sunday) a few blocks away at Via Michele Rosi 20. Should a shot of something stronger be required to aid digestion, nip into historic pharmacy Antica Farmacia Massagli (☑0583 49 60 67; Piazza San Michele 36; ☉9am-7.30pm Mon-Sat) for a bottle of China elixir, a heady liqueur of aromatic spices and herbs first concocted in 1855 as a preventive measure against the plague. Lucchese typically drink the natural alcoholic drink (no colouring or preservatives) at the end of a meal.

pots strung above the hearth in the kitchen to the dining-room table laid for lunch, the rooms vividly evoke daily life in an early-18th-century Lucchese *palazzo* (mansion).

Chiesa di San Michele in Foro   CHURCH

(Piazza San Michele; ☉7.40am-noon & 3-6pm summer, 9am-noon & 3-5pm winter) One of Lucca's many architecturally significant churches, this glittering Romanesque edifice marks the spot where the city's Roman forum was. The present building with exquisite wedding-cake facade was constructed over 300 years on the site of its 8th-century precursor, beginning in the 11th century. Crowning the structure is a figure of the archangel Michael slaying a dragon. Inside the dimly lit interior, don't miss Filippino Lippi's 1479 painting of Sts Helen, Jerome, Sebastian and Roch (complete with plague sore) in the south transept.

★ Torre Guinigi   TOWER

(Via Sant'Andrea 45; adult/reduced €4/3; ☉9.30am-7.30pm Jun-Sep, to 6.30pm Apr & May, to 5.30pm Oct & Mar) The bird's-eye view from the top of this medieval, 45m-tall red-brick tower adjoining 14th-century Palazzo Guinigi is predictably magnificent. But what impresses even more are the seven oak trees planted in a U-shaped

flower bed at the top of the tower. Legend has it that upon the death of powerful Lucchese ruler Paolo Guinigi (1372–1432) all the leaves fell off the trees. Count 230 steps to the top.

A combination ticket covering the Torre del'Ore and the Orto Botanico (p234) costs €9/6.

Torre del'Ore   TOWER

(Via Fillungo; adult/reduced €4/3; ☉9.30am-7.30pm Jun-Sep, to 6.30pm Apr & May, to 5.30pm Oct & Mar) Legend has it that Lucca's 13th-century clock tower – at 50m tall, the highest of the city's 130 medieval towers – is inhabited by the ghost of Lucida Mansi, a Lucchese lass who sold her soul to the devil in exchange for remaining young and beautiful for three decades. On 14 August 1623 the devil came after her to pay her debt, only for Lucida to climb up the clock tower to try and stop time. The devil caught her and took her soul.

Lucca Center of Contemporary Art   MUSEUM

(☑0583 49 21 80; www.luccamuseum.com; Via della Fratta 36; adult/reduced €9/7; ☉10am-7pm Tue-Sun) FREE Lucca's contemporary-art museum hosts some riveting exhibitions; check its website for details.

Museo Nazionale di Palazzo Mansi MUSEUM

(☑0583 5 55 70; www.luccamuseinazionali.it/en; Via Galli Tassi 43; adult/reduced €4/2; ☺8.30am-7.30pm Tue-Sat) This 16th-century mansion built for a wealthy Luccan merchant is a wonderful piece of rococo excess. The private apartments are draped head to toe in tapestries, paintings and chintz. The elaborate, gilded bridal suite must have inspired many high jinks in its time.

👉 Tours

Tuscany Ride A Bike CYCLING

(☑0583 47 17 79; www.tuscanbike.it; Via Elisa 28; ☺9.30am-7.30pm) Explore the region by bike with a full-day guided bike tour: from Lucca, along the river Serchio, to Pisa (34km; from €55 per person); a bike tour around Lucca city followed by a riverside pedal to an organic farm for lunch with farmer Paolo (20km; from €65); or an exhilarating bike ride along back roads to the Versilian Coast (45km; from €98).

Bike and wine tours too and regular bike rental (€5/15 per hour/day).

⭐ Festivals & Events

Lucca Summer Festival MUSIC

(www.summer-festival.com; ☺Jul) This month-long festival brings rock and pop stars to Lucca.

🍴 Eating

Lucca is known for its traditional cuisine and prized olive oil. Garfagnana is not far away and local chestnuts, porcini mushrooms, honey, *farro* (spelt), sheep's-milk cheese and *formenton* (ground corn) are abundant – and a perfect match with a delicate white Colline Lucchesi or a red Montecarlo di Lucca wine.

⭐ Gustevole GELATO $

(☑366 896 03 46; www.facebook.com/gelateria gustevolelucca; Via di Poggio Seconda 26; cones & tubs €2.30-3; ☺1.30-7pm Tue-Thu, noon-7pm Fri, to 8pm Sat) With enticing flavours like liquorice and mint, ricotta with fig and walnut, or pine kernel made with local Pisan kernels (nuts in sweet, crunchy caramelised clumps), the most recent addition to Lucca's artisan gelato scene is pure gold. Gelato is organic, natural and gluten-free. The key to entering gelato heaven: ask for a dollop of thick whipped cream on top.

Da Felice PIZZA $

(☑0583 49 49 86; www.pizzeriadafelice.it; Via Buia 12; focaccia €1-3, pizza slices €1.30; ☺11am-8.30pm Mon, 10am-8.30pm Tue-Sat) This buzzing spot behind Piazza San Michele is where the locals come for wood-fired pizza, *cecina* (salted chickpea pizza) and *castagnacci* (chestnut cakes). Eat in or take away, *castagnaccio* comes wrapped in crisp white paper, and my, it's good married with a chilled bottle of Moretti beer.

L'Hamburgheria di Eataly BURGERS $

(☑0583 42 92 16; www.facebook.com/hambur gheriadieatalylucca; Via Fillungo 91a; burgers €9.80-13.80; ☺11am-midnight Mon, 8.30am-midnight Tue-Sat, 9.30am-midnight Sun; 🐾) A clever mix of fast and slow food, this modern Eataly eatery cooks up gourmet burgers crafted from Tuscany's signature Chianina beef alongside a tantalising mix of hot dogs, grilled meats and *taglieri* (wooden chopping boards) loaded with salami, cold meats and cheeses. Begin with a focaccia (€9.50 to €19.50) to share beneath red-brick vaults inside or among potted lemon trees in the courtyard.

LOCAL KNOWLEDGE

SUNDAY LUNCH WITH LOCALS

Ask locals where to lunch on Sunday or to escape the city's stifling summer heat and the reply is invariably Villa Bongi (☑0583 51 04 79; www.villabongi.it; Via di Cocombola 640, Montuolo; meals €40; ☺6.30-10.30pm Mon-Sat, noon-3pm & 6.30-10.30pm Jun-Sep, closed Tue Oct-May; 🚗), a dreamy salmon-pink mansion with a stone-balustrade verandah, 7km west of town. The grand old villa overlooks olive groves and has a wonderful tree-shaded terrace on which diners feast alfresco on Tuscan cuisine with green views of soft rolling Lucchesi hills.

Pasta is strictly homemade and traditional dishes enjoy a creative seasonal twist – red-cabbage risotto with gorgonzola fondue, saffron-scented tagliatelle (ribbon pasta) with prosciutto and prawns. Come winter, dining is all about snuggling up, glass of wine in hand, in front of a roaring fire. Its tasting menus (€35 and €45) are good value. Reservations are essential, especially on Sunday when Lucchese families flock here for Villa Bongi's outstanding-value lunch.

NICO BERNIERI/SHUTTERSTOCK ©

1. Apuane Alps (p252)
Isolated farmhouses, medieval hermitages and hilltop villages make up a hiking trail through the Apuane Alps.

2. Castelnuovo di Garfagnana (p252)
Fresh porcini, chestnuts and sacks of farro (spelt) fill autumnal markets in this medieval eyrie.

3. Piazza Anfiteatro (p234), Lucca
Cafe-ringed Piazza Anfiteatro is named for the amiphteatre here in Roman times.

4. Basilica della Madonna dell'Umiltà (p246), Pistoia
Giorgio Vasari designed the dome as an imitation of Florence's famous dome.

Trattoria da Leo
TRATTORIA $

(☎ 0583 49 22 36; http://trattoriadaleo.it/; Via Tegrimi 1; meals €25; ☺ 12.30-2pm & 7.30-10.30pm Mon-Sat) A much-loved veteran, Leo is famed for its friendly ambience and cheap food – ranging from plain-Jane acceptable to grandma delicious. Arrive in summer to snag one of 10 tables covered with chequered tablecloths and crammed beneath parasols on the narrow street outside. Otherwise, it's noisy dining inside among typically nondescript 1970s decor. No credit cards.

★ Ristorante Giglio
TUSCAN $$

(☎ 0583 49 40 58; www.ristorantegiglio.com; Piazza del Giglio 2; meals €40; ☺ noon-2.30pm & 7.30-10pm Thu-Mon, 7.30-10pm Wed) Splendidly at home in the frescoed 18th-century Palazzo Arnolfini, Giglio is stunning. Dine at white-tableclothed tables, sip a complimentary *prosecco*, watch the fire crackle in the marble fireplace and savour traditional Tuscan with a modern twist: think fresh artichoke salad served in an edible parmesan-cheese wafer 'bowl', or risotto simmered in Chianti. End with Lucchese *buccellato* (sweetbread) filled with ice cream and berries.

Tasting menus (€40 and €60) are the best value.

Buca di Sant'Antonio
TUSCAN $$$

(☎ 0583 5 58 81; www.bucadisantantonio.com; Via della Cervia 3; meals €45; ☺ 12.30-3pm & 7.30-10pm Tue-Sat, 12.30-3pm Sun) Gosh, what a fabulous collection of copper pots is strung from the wood-beamed ceiling! This atmosphere-laden restaurant has wooed romantic diners since 1782 and is still going strong. The Tuscan cuisine does not quite live up to the exceptional wine list, but it remains a favourite nonetheless. Service is formal – think gents of a certain age in black suits

---

❶ LOST IN VINES
....

At the **Strada del Vino e dell'Olio** (☎ 0583 49 51 69; www.stradavinoeoliolucca.it; Porta Elisa; ☺ 9.30am-7pm) pick up maps and details of wine-tasting, dining and sleeping opportunities at wineries and olive farms along the **Strada del Vino e Olio** (Wine and Oil Road), a network of idyllic driving itineraries between Lucca, the rich vineyard-stiched hills of Colline Lucchesi (north), the chic hilltop village of Montecarlo (east) overlooking a sea of vineyards and olive groves, and Viareggio (west) on the coast.

---

and dicky bows – and opens with a glass of *prosecco* on the house as *aperitif*.

★ Bistrot Undici Undici
CAFE

(☎ 0583 189 27 01; www.facebook.com/und1c1und1c1; Piazza Antelminelli 2; ☺ 10am-8pm Tue-Thu, to 1am Fri-Sun) With one huge cream-coloured parasol providing shade and a tinkling fountain providing an atmospheric soundtrack, cafe terraces don't get much better than this. And then there is the view at this bucolic cafe (the only cafe) on Piazza San Miniato of the almighty facade of Lucca's lovely cathedral. Live music sets the place rocking after dark.

🛍 Shopping

★ Benheart
SHOES

(☎ 0583 152 43 85; www.benheart.it; Via Santa Lucia 5; ☺ 10.30am-6.30pm Mon-Fri, to 8pm Sat & Sun) For an exquisite pair of handmade leather shoes, look no further than this fashionable boutique of rapidly rising Florentine designer Ben. The young designer set up shop with his friend and business partner, Matteo, after surviving a heart transplant.

❶ Information

Tourist Office (☎ 0583 58 31 50; www.turismo.lucca.it; Piazzale Verdi; ☺ 9am-7pm Apr-Sep, to 5pm Mar-Oct) Free hotel reservations, left-luggage service (two bags €1.50/4.50/7 per hour/half-day/day) and guided city tours in English departing at 2pm daily in summer and on Saturdays and Sundays in winter. The two-hour tour is €10/free per adult/child under 15 years.

❶ Getting There & Away

BUS

From the **bus stops** around Piazzale Verdi, **Vaibus Lucca** (www.lucca.cttnord.it) runs services throughout the region, including to the following destinations:

Bagni di Lucca (€3.40, 50 minutes, eight daily)

Castelnuovo di Garfagnana (€4.20, 1½ hours, eight daily)

Pisa airport (€3.40, 45 minutes to one hour, 30 daily)

CAR & MOTORCYCLE

The A11 runs westwards to Pisa and Viareggio and eastwards to Florence. To access the Garfagnana, take the SS12 and continue on the SS445.

In Lucca it's easiest to park at Parcheggio Carducci, just outside Porta Sant'Anna. Within the walls, most car parks are for residents only, indicated by yellow lines. Blue lines indicate where anyone, including tourists, can park (€2

WORTH A TRIP

A VILLA TOUR

Between the 15th and 19th centuries, successful Lucchesi merchants flaunted their success to the world by building opulent summer residences in the hills around the city, and though a few have crumbled away or been abandoned, many are still inhabited.

Villa Reale (☑0583 3 01 08; www.parcovillareale.it; Via Fraga Alta 2, Marlia, Capannori; adult/ reduced €9/7; ◷10am-6pm Mar-Oct, by appointment only Nov-Feb) Elisa Bonaparte, Napoleon's sister and short-lived ruler of Tuscany, once lived in handsome Villa Reale, 7km north of Lucca in Marlia. The house isn't open to the public, but the statuary-filled gardens can be visited. Bring your own picnic.

Villa Grabau (☑0583 40 60 98; www.villagrabau.it; Via di Matraia 269, San Pancrazio; guided tour adult/child €7/free; ◷10am-1pm & 3-7pm Tue-Sun Apr, Jun-Aug & Sep-Nov, 11am-1pm & 2.30-5.30pm Nov-Mar) Neoclassical Villa Grabau, 11km north of Lucca in San Pancrazio, sits among a vast parkland with sweeping traditional English- and Italian-styled gardens, splashing fountains, more than 100 terracotta pots with lemon trees and a postcard-pretty lemon house – host to fashion shows, concerts and the like – dating from the 17th century. It even has a clutch of self-catering properties to rent in its grounds should you happen to fall in love with the estate. Guided villa and garden visits last 45 minutes.

Villa Oliva (☑330 44 62 52, 0583 40 64 62; www.villaoliva.it; Via delle Ville, San Pancrazio; ◷9.30am-12.30pm & 2-6pm mid-Mar–mid-Nov) In San Pancrazio, 11km north of Lucca, the gardens of Villa Oliva, surrounding a 15th-century country residence designed by Lucchesi architect Matteo Civitali, demand a springtime stroll. Retaining its original design, the fountain-rich park staggers across three levels and includes a romantic cypress alley and stables reckoned to be even more beautiful than those at Versailles. Watch for summertime concerts here.

Getting There & Away

To reach these villas, take the SS12 northeast from Lucca (direction Abetone) and exit onto the SP29 to Marlia. From Marlia, San Pancrazio is a mere 1.2km north.

per hour). If you are staying within the city walls, contact your hotel ahead of your arrival and enquire about the possibility of getting a temporary resident permit during your stay.

TRAIN

The train station is south of the city walls: take the path across the moat and through the (dank and grungy) tunnel under Baluardo San Colombano. Regional train services:

Florence (€7.50 to €9.60, 1¼ to 1¾ hours, hourly)

Pietrasanta (€4.40 to €6.10, 50 minutes, hourly)

Pisa (€3.50, 30 minutes, half-hourly)

Pistoia (€5.50, 45 minutes to one hour, half-hourly)

Viareggio (€3.50, 25 minutes, hourly)

ⓘ Getting Around

Rent wheels (ID required) to pedal the 4.2km circumference of Lucca's romantic city walls:

Biciclette Poli (☑0583 49 37 87; www. biciclettepoli.com; Piazza Santa Maria 42; per hr/day €3/15; ◷9am-7pm summer) Just across from the city walls, this seasonal bike-

rental outfit has regular city bikes as well as mountain bikes (€4/20 per hour/day), racing bikes (€7/35 per hour/day) and tandems (€6.50/32.50 per hour/day). Kids' bikes too.

Cicli Bizzarri (☑0583 49 66 82; www.cicli bizzarri.net; Piazza Santa Maria 32; per hr/day €3/15; ◷8.30am-7.30pm summer, to 12.30pm & 2-7.30pm winter) Every type of bike imaginable for rent – tandems and e-bikes included.

Tourist Center Lucca (☑338 821 39 52 0583 49 44 01; www.touristcenterlucca.com; Piazzale Ricasoli 203; bike per 3hr/day €8/12; ◷9am-7pm) Exit the train station and bear left to find this handy bike-rental outlet, with kids' bikes, tandems, trailers and various other gadgets. It also has left-luggage facilities (€3/5 per bag up to three hours/day).

PISTOIA

POP 90,300

Pretty Pistoia sits snugly at the foot of the Apennines. An easy day trip from Pisa, Lucca or Florence, it thoroughly deserved its 2017 status as European City of Culture. A town that has grown well beyond its medieval ramparts,

Pistoia

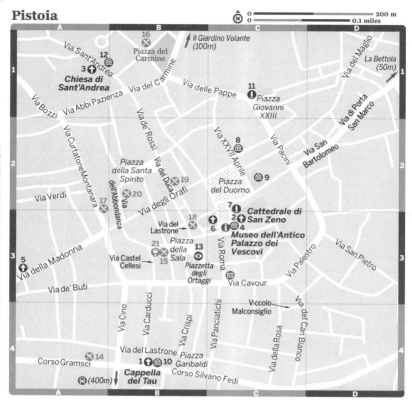

Pistoia

its *centro storico* is well preserved and stands guardian to striking contemporary art.

On Wednesdays and Saturdays a morning market transforms Pistoia's main square, Pi-

azza del Duomo, as well as its surrounding streets, into a lively sea of blue awnings and jostling shoppers. Otherwise, on Monday to Saturday peruse open-air stalls heaped with seasonal fruit and vegetables on tiny Piazza della Sala.

◉ Sights

Pistoia's key sights are clustered around its beautiful cathedral square, Piazza del Duomo, which is hemmed by a maze of narrow pedestrian streets made for meandering. Avoid Monday when many of the key sights are shut.

⭐ **Cattedrale di San Zeno** CATHEDRAL
(☑ 0573 2 50 95; Piazza del Duomo; cathedral free, chapel adult/reduced €4/2; ⊙ 8.30am-12.30pm & 3-7pm, chapel 10.30am-noon & 3-5.30pm) This cathedral with beautiful Pisan-Romanesque facade safeguards a lunette of the Madonna and Child between two angels by Andrea della Robbia. Its other highlight, in the gated **Cappella di San Jacopo** off the north aisle (right of the main entrance), is the dazzling silver **Dossale di San Giacomo** (Altarpiece of St James), begun by artisan silversmiths by hand in 1287 and finally finished two centuries later by Brunelleschi. Buy tickets for the chapel in the Battistero di San Giovanni.

When the baptistry is closed, buy a ticket for the chapel from the cathedral custodian – poke your head around the door next to the **Capella di Sant' Atto**, at the far end of the north aisle. The Capella di San Jacopo also safeguards a much-treasured, silver reliquary containing part of the jawbone of Saint James.

Campanile della Cattedrale TOWER
(Cathedral Bell Tower; ☑ 0573 2 50 95; Piazza del Duomo; adult/reduced €7/5; ⊙ guided tours noon-3.30pm Tue-Fri, hourly 11am-5pm Sat & Sun) Scale the sky-high, red-brick *campanile* (bell tower) of the Cattedrale di San Zeno for a wonderful bird's eye view of Pistoia's iconic cathedral square. Buy tickets at the battistero across the square.

⭐ **Museo dell'Antico Palazzo dei Vescovi** MUSEUM
(☑ 0573 36 92 75; Piazza del Duomo; adult/reduced €5/3; ⊙ 10.15am-4pm Tue, Thu & Fri, to 6pm Sat & Sun) The bishops' palace, wedged next to the cathedral, provides a fascinating tour of Pistoia's urban history, ranging from touchable scale models of architectural gems such as the cathedral and the baptistry on the 1st floor to archaeological treasures in the basement. The indisputable highlight is *L'Arazzo Mille Fiori* (*Thousand Flowers Tapestry;* 1530), a rare, late-Gothic tapestry originally laid in front of the main altar in the cathedral

on Good Friday, upon which a crucifix with crucified Christ on it would be venerated.

Subsequently known as the 'tapestry of the Adoration', the enchanting cloth is a dazzling mirage of mythical unicorns, dogs and birds prancing through flower-filled meadows.

Visits to the bishops' palace are strictly by guided tour, which depart at 10.15am, 11.45am, 1.15pm & 2.45pm weekdays and 10.15am, 11.45am, 1.15pm, 3pm and 4.30pm on weekends.

Battistero di San Giovanni CHRISTIAN SITE
(Baptistry; ☑ 0573 2 50 95; Piazza del Duomo; ⊙ 10am-1pm & 3-6pm Tue-Sun 7pm) FREE Across the square from the Cattedrale di San Zeno is this 14th-century octagonal baptistry, elegantly banded in green-and-white marble to a design by Andrea Pisano. An ornate square marble font and soaring dome enliven the otherwise bare, red-brick interior. Buy tickets here for the Capella di San Jacopo and bell tower, both in the Cattedrale di San Zeno.

Museo Civico GALLERY
(☑ 0573 37 12 96; www.comune.pistoia.it/museo civico; Piazza del Duomo 1; adult/reduced €3.50/2; ⊙ 10am-4pm Tue-Fri, to 6pm Sat & Sun) Pistoia's Gothic **Palazzo Communale** is strung with works by Tuscan artists from the 13th to 20th centuries. Don't miss Bernardino di Antonio Detti's *Madonna della Pergola* (1498) with its modern treatment of St James, the Madonna and Baby Jesus; spot the mosquito on Jesus' arm.

NORTHWESTERN TUSCANY PISTOIA

WORTH A TRIP

A SERIOUS ART LOVER'S DETOUR

A teahouse, an aviary and other romantic 19th-century follies mingle with cutting-edge art installations created by the world's top contemporary artists at **Fattoria di Celle** (☑ 0573 47 99 07; www.goricoll.it; Via Montalese 7, Santomato di Pistoia; ⊙ by appointment only May-Sep) FREE, 5km west of Pistoia. The extraordinary private collection and passion of local businessman Giuliano Gori, this unique sculpture park showcases 70 site-specific installations sprinkled around his vast family estate. Visits – reserved for serious art lovers – require reservation via email at least 30 days in advance and entail a guided four- to five-hour hike around the estate (no rest stops!).

Chiesa di San Salvatore　HISTORIC BUILDING

(Via San Tomba di Catilina) Just steps from Piaz-za del Duomo is this beautiful gem of a Ro-manesque church, thought to originally date from the 8th to 10th centuries within the an-cient city walls (spot the small section of cob-blestone wall) and reconstructed to gain its current appearance in 1270. The church was abandoned in 1784 and subsequently used as a warehouse and artist's studio. Following a complete restoration in 2017–18, it will reo-pen as an innovative arts and cultural centre.

★**Chiesa di Sant'Andrea**　CHURCH

(Via Sant'Andrea 21; ⊗ 8.30am-5.30pm) FREE This 12th-century church was built outside the original city walls, hence its windowless (fortified) state. The partly white-and-green marble-striped facade is enlivened by a relief of the *Journey and Adoration of the Magi* (1166) by Gruamonte and Adeodato. But the highlight – Pistoia's most prized art work – is within the gloomy interior: an imposing marble pulpit carved by Giovanni Pisano (1298–1301). Two lions and a bent human figure bear the heavy load of the seven-columned masterpiece, and sibyls and the Prophets decorate the capitals.

Palazzo Fabroni　MUSEUM

(⤷ 0573 37 18 17; Via Sant'Andrea 18; adult/reduced €3.50/2; ⊗ 10am-2pm Tue-Fri, to 6pm Sun & Sun) Take a breather from the ancient with this airy contemporary-art museum, host to riveting temporary exhibitions and a per-manent collection amassed through exhib-iting artists donating works to the gallery. Highlights include the shadow wall painting *Scultura d'Ombra* (2007) by iconoclastic Italian artist Claudio Parmiggiani (b 1943) and rooms dedicated to Pistoia-born art-ists Mario Nigro (1917–1992) and Fernando

Melani (1907–85). Don't miss the photo of sculptor Marino Marini on the beach with his horse at Forte dei Marmi in 1973.

Should you get completely hooked, upon advance request it is possible to visit the nearby casa-studio (⤷ 800 01 21 46, 0573 37 18 17; Corso Gramsci 159; ⊗ by appointment only 10.30-11.15am & 11.30am-12.15pm last Sat of month) FREE of Fernando Melani where the abstract artist lived and worked.

Piazzetta degli Ortaggi　PIAZZA

Don't miss this beautiful small square, with its laid-back cafe life and striking, life-size sculpture of three blindfolded men, Giro di Sole (Around the Sun; Piazzetta degli Orgaggi) (*Around the Sun;* 1996), by contemporary Pistoia artist Roberto Barni (b 1939). In the 18th century the market square, adjoining Piazza della Sala and once home to a brothel, was the entrance to Pistoia's Jewish ghetto.

Basilica della Madonna dell'Umiltà　CHURCH

(⤷ 0573 2 20 45; Via della Madonna; ⊗ 8am-1pm & 4-6pm) FREE For anyone familiar with Florence, it is impossible not to notice the bright red-tiled dome of this 15th-century backstreet church, built by Ventura Vitoni to house the Madonna of Humility (1350), a fresco said to have shed real tears in 1498, following which it became an object of de-vout worship. In 1563 Giorgio Vasari was commissioned to build a domed roof for the church – which he did, designing it as an exact (albeit smaller) imitation of the mag-nificent cupola crowning Florence's *duomo*.

Ospedale del Ceppo　MONUMENT

(⤷ 0573 36 80 23; www.irsapt.it; Piazza Giovan-ni XXIII; underground tour adult/reduced €9/7; ⊗ 10am-6pm Apr-Sep, to 5pm Oct-Mar) The beau-tifully restored facade of this former hospi-

---

VESPA TOUR

There's a certain romance to touring Tuscany on the back of a Vespa, Italy's iconic scoot-er, which revolutionised travel when Piaggio launched it from its factory in Pontedera, 25km southeast of Pisa, in 1946. The 'wasp', as the two-wheeled utility vehicle was affec-tionately known, has been restyled 120 times since, culminating most recently in Piag-gio's vintage-inspired GTV and LXV models. Yet the essential design remains timeless.

The complete Vespa story, from the Genovese company's arrival in Tuscany in 1921 to its manufacturing of four-engine aircraft and hydroplanes, to its WWII destruction and re-birth as Europe's exclusive Vespa producer, is grippingly told in Pontedera's Museo Piag-gio (⤷ 0587 2 71 71; www.museopiaggio.it; Viale Rinaldo Piaggio 7; ⊗ 10am-6pm Tue-Fri, to 1pm & 2-6pm Sat, to 8pm Aug & 2nd & 4th Sun of other months) FREE, in a former factory building.

Should Vespa's free-wheeling, carefree spirit take hold, hook up with Tuscany by Vespa (www.tuscanybyvespa.com) – operated by Florence Town (p102) in Florence – for your very own Hepburn-style Vespa tour.

PRATO

It is off the beaten tourist track, yes. But the historical town of Prato (pop 191,150) is conveniently 'on the track' when it comes to savouring this unexplored town on a crowd-free foray by train from Pistoia (€2.60, 15 minutes) or Florence (€2.60, 30 minutes).

Tuscany's second-largest town after Florence, this traditional textile-producing centre has a compact old town girded by near-intact city walls. From Prato's Stazione Porta al Serraglio it is a five-minute walk to Piazza del Duomo and 12th-century Cattedrale di Santo Stefano (☑ 0574 2 62 34; Piazza del Duomo; ☺ 9am-3am Mon-Sat) FREE, with its magnificent frescoes by Filippo Lippi behind the altar and Agnolo's fresco cycle of the *Legend of the Holy Girdle* (1392–95) in the chapel to the left of the entrance. The unusual protruding pulpit (1428) on the cathedral's Pisan-Romanesque facade was designed by Donatello and Michelozzo to publicly display the *sacra cintola*, a deeply venerated girdle believed to have been given to St Thomas by the Virgin and brought to Prato from Jerusalem after the Second Crusade. Brought out five times a year today, the gossamer-fine wool rope brocaded with gold thread is locked away in the chapel in a gold reliquary with three keys.

Learn more about the Virgin's girdle in the cathedral's Museo dell'Opera del Duomo (☑ 0574 2 93 39; www.diocesiprato.it/museo-dellopera-del-duomo; Piazza del Duomo 49; adult/reduced €5/4; ☺ 10am-1pm & 2-5pm Mon & Wed-Sat, 2-5pm Sun), accessed via the foot of the cathedral bell tower, and at the nearby Museo di Palazzo Pretorio (☑ 0574 193 49 96; www.palazzopretorio.prato.it; Piazza del Commune; adult/reduced €8/6; ☺ 10.30am-6.30pm Wed-Mon), an impressive hulk of a history museum. The tourist office (☑ 0574 2 41 12; www.pratoturismo.it; Piazza Buonamici 7; ☺ 9am-1pm & 3-6pm Mon-Fri, 10am-1pm Sat & Sun) is just around the corner from here. Dedicated museum buffs can continue to local textile museum Museo del Tessuto (☑ 0574 61 15 03; www.museodeltessuto.it; Via Puccetti 3; adult/reduced €7/5; ☺ 10am-3pm Tue-Thu, to 7pm Fri & Sat, 3-7pm Sun), at home in the former Campolmi textile mill. If contemporary art is more your cup of tea, head 3km out of town to the dazzling Centro Per l'Arte Contemporanea Pecci (☑ 0574 53 17; www.centropucci.it; Viale della Repubblica 277; adult/reduced/family €10/7/28; ☺ noon-8pm Tue & Wed, to midnight Thu-Sun), a curvaceous gold piece of contemporary architecture by Holland-based, Indonesian architect Maurice Nio with exciting art exhibitions.

Post-sightseeing, excite taste buds with a sweet shopping spree at Antonio Mattei (☑ 0574 2 57 56; www.biscottimatteideseo.it; Via Ricasoli 20; ☺ 8am-7.30pm Tue-Fri, to 1pm & 3.30-7.30pm Sat, to 1pm Sun, closed 2nd Sun of month & Jul), Prato's famed *biscottificio* where the city's signature *biscotti di Prato* (twice-baked almond biscuits made for dunking in sweet wine) have been made since 1858. To see the bakers in action, visit in the morning. The biscuits (€16.50 per kg), not sealed but simply wrapped in waxy royal-blue paper and tied with string, are best eaten within five days.

Round off your Prato visit with a local craft beer at artisan brewery Mostodolce (☑ 0574 06 36 52; www.facebook.com/mostodolcepo; Via dell'Arco 6; ☺ 7.30pm-2am Mon-Wed, to 2.30am Thu-Sat) or a memorable glass of wine and lunch, *apericena* (meal-sized *aperitivo* buffet) or dinner at Le Barrique (☑ 0574 3 01 51; www.lebarriquewinebar.it; Corso Mazzoni 19; ☺ noon-12.30am; ☎). This fashionable wine bar, with stylish red-brick interior and excellent Tuscan kitchen, is one of the few places in town to taste *mortadella di Prato*, a heavily seasoned, rose-coloured sausage spiced up with Alchermes liqueur and only produced by two butchers in Prato today.

tal stuns with its 16th-century polychrome terracotta frieze by Giovanni della Robbia. It depicts the *Sette Opere di Misericordia* (Seven Works of Mercy), and the five medallions represent the *Virtù Teologali* (Theological Virtues). The 13th-century hospital building cannot be visited, but you can delve into its underground belly of passageways and subterranean rivers decorated with old surgical tools, scalpels and all sorts with a one-hour Pistoia Sotterranea guided tour.

Museo Marino Marini   MUSEUM
(☑ 0573 3 02 85; www.fondazionemarinomarini.it; Corso Silvano Fedi 30; adult/reduced €3.50/2; ☺ 10am-6pm Mon-Sat, 2.30-7.30pm Sun Apr-Sep, 10am-5pm Oct-Mar) This gallery inside Palazzo del Tau is devoted to Pistoia's most famous modern son, eponymous sculptor and

AN OPERA BUFF'S DETOUR

Some 35km west of both Barbialla Nuova and San Gimignano, ringed by a natural amphitheatre of soul-stirring hills, is **Lajatico** (population 1336). This tiny village is the birthplace and family home of opera singer Andrea Bocelli (b 1958) who, each year in July or August, returns to his village to sing – for just one evening.

His stage is the astonishing **Teatro del Silenzio** (www.teatrodelsilenzio.it), a specially constructed, open-air 'Theatre of Silence' built in a green meadow on the fringe of the village where the natural silence is broken once a year – by the Tuscan tenor and his friends (Placido Domingo, José Carreras, Sarah Brightman and Chinese pianist Lang Lang have all performed here). Each year different sculptures by contemporary artists are added to the ensemble, to striking effect. Listening to the tenor sing to an audience of 10,000 against a backdrop of gently rolling green hills is an overwhelming experience. Tickets, usually released each year in March, cost €80 to €400 and are sold by **Vivaticket** (www.vivaticket.it).

Opera buffs with a penchant for a fine vintage can continue 5km to **La Sterza** to buy wine and olive oil produced on Bocelli's family estate at **Cantina Bocelli** (☑ 0587 64 30 27; www.bocellifamilywines.com; Via Volterrana 57, La Sterza; ⊙ 10am-12.30pm & 4-7pm Mon-Fri), a red-brick vaulted cellar at the southern end of the village on the SR439.

painter Marino Marini (1901–80). Dozens of his drawings and paintings – mainly of female nudes (pear-shaped, evoking goddess of fertility Pomona) and horses – hang here.

★ **Cappella del Tau** CHAPEL
(Tau Chapel; ☑ 0573 3 22 04; Corso Silvano Fedi 70; ⊙ 8.15am-1.30pm Mon-Sat) FREE Adjoining the Museo Marino Marini (p247) is this tiny 14th-century chapel, frescoed Gothic-style from top to bottom by the School of Giotto and a dramatic guardian to Marino Marini's monumental equestrian sculpture *The Miracle* (1952). The frescoes illustrate tales from the New and Old Testaments and the story of Saint Anthony Abbot, depicted as an old man with white beard, staff and pig by his side. On his feast day, January 17, local farmers used to bring their animals to the chapel to get them blessed by their patron saint.

Il Giardino Volante GARDENS
(The Flying Garden; ☑ 0573 37 18 19; www.ilgiardino volante.it; Via degli Armeni 5a; ⊙ 9am-12.30pm & 3.30-7pm Jul & Aug, 9am-12.30pm & 3-7pm Wed-Sun May & Jun, shorter hours winter) FREE Break between sights with a frolic in this whimsical city park designed by local artists where contemporary works of art mingle with playful slides, climbing frames, miniature wooden huts, a sand pit and so forth. A black steel cub marks the entrance.

★ Festivals & Events

Pistoia Blues MUSIC
(www.pistoiablues.com; ⊙ Jul) Going strong for at least three decades, Pistoia's annual blues festival lures big names. BB King, Miles Davis,

Sting and Santana have all taken to the stage here – an electrical fresco affair that packs out Piazza del Duomo. Tickets costs €25 to €75.

Giostra dell'Orso CULTURAL
(⊙ 25 Jul) Translated as Joust of the Bear, this medieval event sees jousting and other equestrian pranks fill Piazza del Duomo during Pistoia's celebration of its patron saint San Giacomo.

✗ Eating

Pistoia's foodie street is pedestrian-only **Via del Lastrone**, lined with cafes, wine bars and traditional restaurants serving *carcerato* (a type of offal), *frittata con rigatino* (omelette with salt-cured bacon), *farinata con cavalo* (chickpea pancake with cabbage), *migliacci* (fritters made with pig's blood) and other specialities. End with *berlingozzo*, a sweet traditionally served with a glass of local Vin Santo.

Carmine ITALIAN $
(☑ 0573 2 26 00; www.bio-barpasticceriacarmine. it; Corso Gramsci 4; meals €15; ⊙ 6am-8pm Mon-Fri, 4am-8pm Sat, to 1.30pm & 3-8pm Sun) Blink and you could well miss the fact that this enticing cake shop and bakery with exquisite sweet bites displayed in rows beneath glass is, in fact, 100% gluten-free. A daily menu chalked on the board features a decent choice of savoury *primi* and *secondi*, pizza included, making it a hot spot in town for gluten-free breakfast, brunch and lunch.

Osteria Pizzeria Apicio PIZZA $
(☑ 334 758 19 91; Via del Duca 8; meals €20; ⊙ 7pm-12.30am Tue-Sun) Squirrelled away in

a yet another wonderful old building down a side street, this hybrid pizzeria-*osteria* is a staunchly local affair. Its cavernous, chapel-like interior is a mesmerising collage of original features – sky-high vaulted ceiling, exposed stone, red brick, water well – and its oven-fired pizzas are the best in town. A tip-top choice of craft beers is the icing on the cake.

La Bettola   TRATTORIA $

(🖉0573 296 62; www.facebook.com/la.bettola.79; Via Porta San Marco 69; meals €20; ☺12.30-2.30pm & 7-11pm Tue-Sun) A backstreet treasure that you really won't find unless you know about it, this stalwart no-frills trattoria cooks up some of the most traditional and tastiest Tuscan cuisine in town beneath age-old, red-brick vaults. Just as remarkable are its low prices. Try the once-eaten-never-forgotton *zuppa del carcerato* (a local offal soup) followed by *collo di pollo ripieno* (stuffed chicken neck) perhaps or the *lampredotto con salse* (tripe with salsa).

★I Salaioli   DELI $$

(🖉0573 2 02 25; www.isalaioli.it; Piazza della Sala 20-22; meals €30; ☺6.30am-midnight Mon-Sat, 8am-midnight Sun) One glance at the delectable salami wedges and cheese rounds on the counter begging to be eaten and you'll be smitten. This is one of those fabulous deli-restaurants that suits naturally gourmet Tuscany so, so well: products are fresh, local and seasonal, and can be bought to take away or eat in, either on the stylish deli mezzanine or on the people-watching pavement terrace.

★Magno Gaudio   ITALIAN $$

(🖉0573 2 69 05; Via Curtatone Montanoro 12; meals €30; ☺7am-11pm Mon-Sat; 🕾) If it is local Pistoians you're looking for, snag a table at this brilliant all-rounder. Be it breakfast, brunch, dinner or an *aperitivo* on the street terrace, this hybrid delivers, with free wi-fi, creative cuisine – lots of fish, imaginative pasta dishes and sesame-seed-encrusted tuna carpaccio to die for – and friendly unpretentious service.

Wall and ceiling lamps threaded with tin pots and pans add a touch of funk.

Osteria La BotteGaia   OSTERIA $$

(🖉0573 36 56 02; www.labottegaia.it; Via del Lastrone 17; meals €30; ☺noon-3pm & 7-11pm Tue-Sat, 7-11pm Sun) Dishes range from staunchly traditional to experimental at this Slow Food–hailed *osteria,* famed for its finely butchered cured meats and interesting wine list. Aubergine and ricotta strudel in tomato sauce is one of a few interesting vegetarian options.

Reserve in advance, or if you don't get a table, opt for wine and snacks at La BotteGaia's *vineria* (wine bar) on the same street.

Trattoria dell'Abbondanza   TRATTORIA $$

(🖉0573 36 80 37; Via dell'Abbondanza 10; meals €25; ☺noon-2.30pm & 7-10.30pm Thu-Tue) Dine beneath coloured parasols in an atmospheric alley outside or plump for a table inside where homey collections of doorbells, pasta jars and so on catch the eye. The cuisine, once you've deciphered the handwriting on the menu, is simple tasty Tuscan.

Il Carbonile   SEAFOOD $$

(🖉331 843 49 15, 347 043 41 53; www.ilcarbonileristorante.com; Piazza del Carmine 6b; meals €30; ☺7.30-10.30pm Tue-Sat, 12.30-2.30pm & 7.30-10.30 Sun) When the urge for a creative and contemporary culinary experience strikes, head for this delightful fish restaurant, tucked away in a walled courtyard off Piazza del Carmine. Interior design – both inside and al fresco – is intimate and smart. Much of the seasonal produce is sourced at zero kilometres, and there are a handful of meat and veg creations as well as the enticing *Mare* (Sea) menu.

🍷 Drinking & Nightlife

Car-free market square Piazza della Sala (and its surrounding web of narrow streets) is the hot spot in town for atmospheric drinks in trendy bars – wonderfully al fresco in summer.

ⓘ GETTING AROUND NORTHWESTERN TUSCANY

Bus With the exception of a couple of daily buses linking Lucca with Bagni di Lucca and Castelnuovo di Garfagnana, bus routes are practically non-existent.

Car & Motorcycle Your own wheels, two or four, are indispensable for rubbing souls with this rural region. Road links are excellent and varied: the toll-free FI-PI-LI (SS67) provides a fast link between Pisa, Livorno and Florence; and the north-south A12, A11 and SS1 all skirt the region. Driving in the Apuane Alps, Garfagnana and Lunigiana is a dramatically scenic affair, across glorious mountain passes (snow-blocked some winters) and along sinuous, hairpin-laced country lanes.

Train Excellent rail links connect key towns Pisa, Lucca, Pietrasanta and Viareggio.

★ **Caffètteria Museo Marino Marini** CAFE (www.fondazionemarinomarini.it; Corso Silvano Fedi 32; ⊙7am-9pm Mon-Thu, to 11pm Fri & Sat) This warm, vibrant cafe with its own bakery (superb breads) and flowery, courtyard garden buzzes with local life. Sip an espresso at the bar, chat with friends over cappuccino at one of four tables in the cosy interior, or flop on a country-style sofa in the covered porch and admire the blooming hydrangeas in the fabulous cloister garden – utterly gorgeous in summer.

Fiaschetteria La Pace WINE BAR (☑ 0573 2 31 39; www.fiaschetteriapistoia.com; Via dei Fabbri 7-9; meals €25; ⊙5.30-11pm) 'Everything is going to be all right' is the strapline of this hip bar and bistro. And indeed, be it shelling free peanuts around a wooden table in the vintage interior or perched on a stone slab of a window sill outside, everything *is* good at this trendy eating-drinking address. Creative Tuscan cuisine and traditional tasting boards of salami and cheese keep everyone happy any time of day.

❶ Information

Tourist Office (☑ 0573 2 16 22; www.pistoia.turismo.toscana.it; Piazza del Duomo 4; ⊙9am-1pm & 3-6pm) Pop in for a city map and information on biking and hiking itineraries around Pistoia. Two-hour guided walking tours around town (€10) depart from here at 10.30am and 3.30pm daily in July and August, and at 3.30pm Friday, 10.30am and 3.30pm weekends the rest of the year.

❶ Getting There & Around

From the train station, head straight along Viale XX Settembre, across the roundabout, and beyond

---

OFF THE BEATEN TRACK

WORTH THE DRIVE

Lost in the hills above San Miniato, family-run **Osteria Il Papero** (☑ 338 4302267; www.osteriailpapero.com; Piazza 1 Maggio 1, Balconevisi; meals €30; ⊙8-11pm Wed-Sat, noon-3pm Sun) stuns with its unexpectedly creative, top-quality Tuscan cuisine. Local farm products rule in the kitchen where young photographer-musican-turned-self-trained-chef Leandro Gaccione applies his artistic talent to astonishing effect. Don't miss the fabulous themed tastings accompanied by live music on the first Thursday evening of each month. Book ahead.

---

along Via Atto Vannucci (which becomes Via Cino) to get to the Old Town. Regional train services:

Florence (€4.40, 45 minutes, every 20 minutes)

Lucca (€5.50, 45 minutes to one hour, half-hourly)

Pisa (€6.80 to €9.60, two hours, one daily or change at Lucca)

Prato (€2.60, 15 minutes, every 20 minutes)

Viareggio (€6.80, one hour, hourly)

SAN MINIATO

POP 27,900

There is one delicious reason to visit this enchantingly sleepy, medieval hilltop town almost equidistant (50km) between Pisa and Florence: to eat, hunt and dream about the *Tuber magnatum pico* (white truffle).

San Miniato town's ancient cobbled streets, burnt soft copper and ginger in the hot summer sun, are a delight to meander along. Savour a harmonious melody of magnificent palace facades, 14th- to 18th-century churches and an impressive Romanesque cathedral with 12th-century bell tower (Piazza del Duomo; adult/child €3/free; ⊙11am-2pm Mon-Fri, to 2pm & 3-6pm Sat & Sun Apr-Sep, 10am-1pm & 2-5pm Sat, 2-5pm Sun Oct-Mar) to scale, ending with the stiff hike up San Miniato's reconstructed medieval fortress tower, Torre di Frederico II (Tower of Frederick II; Via di Rocca; €3.50; ⊙11am-5pm Tue-Sun), to enjoy a great panorama. Before setting off, buy a combined ticket to all the key sites (adult/reduced €5/4) at the tourist office (p252).

✖ Eating & Drinking

With an abundance of exceptional local produce, dining out in San Miniato is second to none, whatever your budget. Devour *carciofo San Miniatese* (locally grown artichokes) in April and May; chestnuts and wild mushrooms in autumn; and *formaggio di capra delle colline di San Miniato* (the local goat's cheese) and locally raised Chianina beef whatever the month.

Mercato della Terra di San Miniato MARKET (www.mercatidellaterra.it; Piazzale Dante Alighieri; ⊙9am-2pm 3rd Sun of month) Don't leave town without experiencing the foodie buzz of this vibrant farmers market, humming with fresh fruit, veg, meat, raw milk and other local produce from small-scale farmers and artisan producers. It spills across Piazzale Dante Alighieri on the third Sunday of each month.

HUNTING WHITE TRUFFLES

An integral part of local culture since the Middle Ages, some 400 *tartufaio* (truffle hunters) in the trio of small valleys around San Miniato snout out the precious fungus, pale ochre in colour, from October to mid-December. The paths and trails they follow are a family secret, passed along generations. The truffles their dogs sniff out are worth a small fortune after all, selling for anything between €1500 and €3000 per kilogram in Tuscany and four times as much in London and other European capitals.

There is no better time to savour the mystique of this cloak-and-dagger truffle trade than during San Miniato's Mostra Mercato Nazionale del Tartufo Bianco (National White Truffle Market), on the last three weekends in November, when restaurateurs and truffle tragics come from every corner of the globe to purchase supplies, sample truffle-based delicacies in the town's shops and restaurants, and breathe in one of the world's most distinctive aromas. San Miniato tourist office has a list of truffle dealers and can help you join a truffle hunt.

The best are the early-morning truffle hunts at Barbialla Nuova (☑0571 67 70 04; www.barbialla.it; Via Casastada 49, Montaione; 2-/4-/6-/8-person apt €110/175/240/350, minimum 2/7 nights winter/summer; ☉Mar-Dec; P☎☒) ⌕, a 500-hectare farm, 20km south of San Miniato near Montaione, run by new-generation farmer Guido Manfredi. Truffle hunts (€60 to €80 per person, 2½ hours, October to mid-December) on the estate with truffle-hunter Giovanni end with a glass of Chianti and a tasting of local organic cheese and salami – or go to a local restaurant and savour your truffle shaved over pasta followed by a *bistecca alla fiorentina* (chargrilled T-bone steak). Famed far and wide for its enviable success rate when it comes to uncovering these nuggets of 'white' gold, Barbialla's *tartufaio* and its dogs unearth some 20kg or so of edible booty in a season.

NORTHWESTERN TUSCANY EATING & DRINKING

Birra e Acciughe — CRAFT BEER
(☑329 0026905; www.facebook.com/birraeacciughe; Via Augusto Conti 29; ☉5pm-12.30am Mon-Sat, to midnight Sun) 'Beer & Anchovies' is the enticing name of this uber-cool craft-beer shop, its pocket-sized interior packed to the rafters with craft beers from Tuscany and Italy. Grab a bottle and appease hunger pangs with a gourmet panini (€3 to €5), filled perhaps with anchovies and butter, anchovies marinated in beer or chilli-spiced anchovies. Brie, honey and truffle butter is another favourite.

⭐**Sergio Falaschi** — TUSCAN $
(☑0571 4 31 90; www.sergiofalaschi.it; Via Augusto Conti 18-20; meals €25; ☉7.30am-3pm & 4-8pm Mon-Tue & Thu-Sat, 9am-3pm Sun; ☎) The most famous *macelleria* (butcher's shop) in town, run by the same family for three generations, is where most local restaurants buy their outstandingly excellent meat. Forge your way past the counter, into the back of the ceramic-tiled shop, to feast on feisty dishes of the day made from local Chianina beef and *cinta senese* (indigenous Tuscan pork from Siena).

San Miniato Prosciutteria — TUSCAN $
(☑0571 41 91 95; www.prosciutteriasanminiato.it; Via Ser Ridolfo 8; meals €15; ☉noon-3pm & 7-10pm Tue-Sun) A fashionably spartan, appealingly retro interior ensures nothing distracts from the business at hand at this *bottega con cucina* (shop with kitchen): savouring local cheeses, salami, faithfully traditional offal dishes like *lampredotto* and *trippa* (tripe), and various seasonal dishes cooked up from zero-kilometre produce. Not sure what to try? Marco will advise.

Pepenero — TUSCAN $$$
(☑0571 41 95 23; www.pepenerocucina.it; Via IV Novembre 13; meals €50, menus €30-50; ☉7.30-10pm Sat, 12.30-2pm & 7.30-10pm Sun & Wed-Fri) Chef and TV star Gilberto Rossi is one of the new breed of innovative Tuscan chefs using traditional products to create modern, seasonally driven dishes at this much-lauded restaurant. To share some of his secrets, sign up for one of his half-day cooking classes followed by an informal lunch on the restaurant's terrace. Reservations essential.

Peperino — TUSCAN $$$
(☑0571 41 95 23; Via IV Novembre 1; menu incl bottle champagne & wine €246; ☉by appointment only) Book the only table – a table for two – at Peperino, the world's smallest restaurant plum in the heart of Tuscany's most gourmet village, next to big brother, Pepenero. Decor is in-your-face romantic (think pink silk), furnishings are period and the waiter only comes when diners ring the bell. Reserve months in advance.

ℹ️ Information

Tourist Office (📞 0571 4 27 45; www.sanmini atopromozione.it; Piazza del Popolo 1; ⏱9am-1pm Mon, to 1pm & 2-5pm Tue-Sun)

ℹ️ Getting There & Away

Take a train to San Miniato-Fuecchio, then hop on a shuttle bus (€1, every 20 minutes) to the Old Town.

Regional train services:

Florence (€5.50, 45 minutes, hourly)
Pisa (€4.40, 30 minutes, hourly)

THE APUANE ALPS & GARFAGNANA

Rearing up inland from the Versilian Riviera are the Apuane Alps, a rugged mountain range protected by the Parco Regionale delle Alpi Apuane (Apuane Alps Regional Park; www.parcapuane.it) that beckons hikers with a trail of isolated farmhouses, medieval hermitages and hilltop villages.

Continue inland, across the Alps' eastern ridge, and three stunning valleys formed by the Serchio and its tributaries – the low-lying Lima and Serchio Valleys and the higher Garfagnana Valley, collectively known as the Garfagnana – take centre stage. Thickly forested with chestnut and acacia woods, this is a land where fruits of the forest (chestnuts, porcini mushrooms and honey) create a very rustic and fabulous cuisine.

The main gateway to this staunchly rural area is Castelnuovo di Garfagnana, home to the regional park's visitor centre.

Castelnuovo di Garfagnana

POP 5950

The medieval eyrie of Castelnuovo crowns the confluence of the Serchio and its smaller tributary, the Turrite. Its heart is pierced by the burnt-red Rocca Ariostesca (Ariosto's Castle), built in the 12th century and named after Italian poet Ariosto who lived here between 1522 and 1525 as governor of the Garfagnana for the House of Este. The town's quiet narrow lanes, arranged around the city's small duomo (Piazza del Duomo; ⏱hours vary), are a delight to meander along and local Slow Food dining is a real treat. Thursday morning is market day.

🍴 Eating & Drinking

Dining options are limited, but the outstanding quality of local produce shines through at a couple of outstanding eateries. One of Tuscany's finest gelato makers is also here.

Fuori dal Centro GELATO $
(📞 347 5971100; www.fuoridalcentro.com; Piazza Olinto Dini 1f; cones €2.30-4.30; ⏱1-8pm Tue-Sat, 11am-8pm Sun) Dare we say it: having tried and tested dozens of Tuscan *gelaterie,* this bright modern ice-cream shop comes out tops. Fuori dal Centro's regional-inspired flavours are magnificent. Try chestnut, fig and honey, pine kernel, cinnamon and local Lunigiana honey, meringue (truly sublime!) or – most unusually – *crema di farro,* which really does have grains of *farro* (spelt) in it.

⭐**Osteria Vecchia Mulino** OSTERIA $
(📞 0583 6 21 92; www.vecchiomulino.info; Via Vittorio Emanuele 12; tasting menu €18; ⏱11am-9pm Tue-Sun) Run with passion and humour by the gregarious Andrea Bertucci, this 160-year-old *osteria* has no menu but rather a symphony of cold dishes crafted from local products and brought to shared tables one at a time. Bottles of wine line the walls, floor to ceiling, and there are plenty of local, packaged culinary goodies to buy and take home with you.

Antica Pasticceria Fronte delle Rocca CAFE
(📞 0583 6 21 90; Piazzetta Ariosto 1; ⏱9am-1pm & 3.30-7.30pm Tue-Sun) This historic cake shop and chocolate-maker has been the hub of local life since 1885. Its atmospheric pavement terrace was clearly designed with 'go slow' lounging over a cappuccino stirred with a chocolate spoon or other sweet house delicacy in mind.

🛍️ Shopping

Alimentari Poli Roberto FOOD
(Via Olinto Dini 6; ⏱8.30am-1pm & 3.30-8.30pm) Across from the old city gate, sacks of beans, chickpeas, walnuts and *porcini* sit outside this grocer's shop – the chestnut beer, beer made from locally grown *farro, farro*-encrusted *pecorino* and honey are prerequisites for any respectable Garfagnana picnic, as is *castagnaccio* (chestnut cake) and *biroldo* (a type of pork salami spiced with wild fennel).

ℹ️ Information

Turismo Garfagnana (📞 0583 6 51 69, 0583 64 84 35; www.turismo.garfagnana.eu; Piazza delle Erbe 1; ⏱9am-1pm & 3-7pm summer, to 5.30pm winter; 📶) The region's prime park

OFF THE BEATEN TRACK

THREE PERFECT ROAD TRIPS

Nerves and stomach depending, dozens of narrow roads spaghetti from Castelnuovo into the Garfagnana's rural depths.

Across a Mountain Pass

Spiralling north from Castelnuovo, a concertina of hairpin bends along the SS324 lifts you up to Castiglione di Garfagnana and over the scenic Passo di Radici mountain pass, across the Apennines and into Emilia-Romagna. A minor parallel road to the south of the pass takes you to San Pellegrino in Alpe (www.sanpellegrino.org), a hilltop village at 1525m with a monastery and, in the old hospital, a Museo Etnografico (Ethnographic Museum; ☑ 0583 64 90 72; www.sanpellegrinoinalpe.it; Via del Voltone 14, San Pellegrino in Alpe; adult/reduced €2.50/1.50; ☉ 10am-1pm & 2-6.30pm summer, closed Mon & shorter hr winter) that brings traditional mountain life, scarcely changed for centuries, to life.

Alpine Flora & Marble Mountain

Head west towards the Med. The first 17km along the SP13 is straightforward, but once you fork right 2km south of Arni (follow signs for Massa along the SP4), motoring becomes a relentless succession of hairpins, unlit tunnels and breathtaking vistas of Carrara's marble quarries as you cross the Apuane Alps over the Passo del Vestito (1151m). Stop in Pian della Fioba to discover alpine flora in the Orto Botanico delle Alpi Apuane 'Pietro Pellegrini' (Apuane Alps Botanical Garden; ☑ 0585 49 03 49, 340 466 02 71; www.parcapuane.toscana.it/orto; Pian della Fioba; ☉ 9am-noon & 3-7pm late May–mid-Sep) FREE. From here the road drops down, through Antona and Altagnana, clinging to the hillside, to Massa on the Versilian Coast. The entire drive is 42km.

Subterranean Rivers & Lakes

The SS445 is a twisting route that leads you through lush green hills pocked with caves – completely worth the drive in itself, broken perhaps with a roadside picnic and plenty of photo stops. Allow time to visit the spectacular Grotta del Vento (☑ 0583 72 20 24; www.grottadelvento.com; Grotta del Vento 1, Vergemoli; adult/reduced 1hr guided visit €9/7, 2hr €14/11, 3hr €20/16; ☉ 10am-noon & 2-6pm), 9km west of the SS445 along a horribly narrow road. Inside is a world of underground abysses, lakes and caverns. April to October, choose between a one-, two- or three-hour guided tour – if you're up to the 800/1200 steps involved in the two-/three-hour tour, it's worth it. From November to March, the one-hour tour (300 steps) is the only choice.

information and tourist office has bags of info on farm accommodation, trekking, mountain biking, climbing, horse riding, white-water rafting and other activities in the Apuane Alps. It sells regional-park maps and has lists of local guides and mountain huts. It has a couple of sofas for lounging while using its free wi-fi, and it rents electric bikes (€4/10/15 per hour/half-day/day).

ⓘ Getting There & Away

Regional train services:

Lucca (€5.50, one hour, nine daily)
Pisa (€6.80, 1½ hours, four daily)

Barga

POP 10,030

This chic village, 12km south of Castelnuovo di Garfagnana, is one of those irresistibly slow Tuscan hilltop towns with a disproportionately large and dynamic English-speaking community – where else in Tuscany can you find a British, poppy-red telephone box upcycled as a free English book exchange? Churches, artisan workshops, attractive stone houses and palaces built by rich merchants between the 15th and 17th centuries lace the steep, photogenic streets leading up to Barga's elegant, Romanesque cathedral (☑ 0583 72 30 31; Piazza Beato Michele 1; ☉ 8.30am-6.30pm) FREE. Allow plenty of time for tranquil ambling between cafe terraces.

🍴 Eating & Drinking

Barga is another prime spot for sampling Garfagnana produce, including *necci* (chestnut crepes) and various local pasta made with sweet chestnut flour, stone-ground from the region's smoke-dried Carpinese chestnuts.

Apuane Alps & Garfagnana

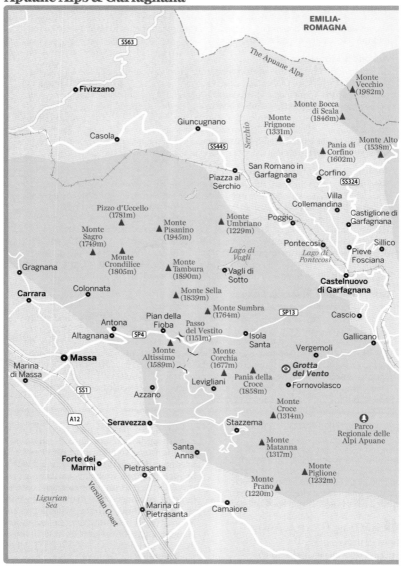

The old town of Barga squirrels away a couple of enchanting cafe pavement terraces. After dark, Barga's jazz club (☎0583 72 38 60; www.bargajazzclub.com; Via del Pretorio 23; annual membership card €8; ⊗9.30pm-1am Fri) is the liveliest spot for a Friday-night drink.

Sosta dei Diavoli　　　　TUSCAN $
(☎348 3643550; Via G Pascoli 140, Ponte di Catagnana; meals €20) It might seem to be just another humble, family-run cafe-bar in rural Tuscany, but the Devil's Stop is wickedly good. Come 7.30pm, owner Lorenzo Giuliani dons his chef's apron to cook up a

⭐ Locanda di Mezzo   TUSCAN **$$**

(📞0583 171 75 25; www.facebook.com/locandadi mezzobarga; Piazza Santissima Annunziata 7; meals €25; ⏱12.30-2.30pm daily, 7.45-10.30pm Tue-Sun; 📶) Local lads Giulio and Francesco provide the creative fun and energy behind Barga's top address, its tables enviably strewn in summer across photogenic Piazza Santissima Annunziata. Traditional Tuscan dishes get a distinctly creative kick, while paying homage to the ravishing local farm products they're invariably made from: think *farro* (spelt) ravioli in sage butter or *maltagliati* (pasta diamonds) with chickpea cream-laced baby squid.

ℹ️ Information

Tourist Office (📞0583 72 47 45; Via di Mezzo 47; ⏱9.30am-12.30pm Mon-Sat)

ℹ️ Getting There & Away

Take the SS12 from Lucca (direction: Abetone), veer left onto the SS445 and then turn right onto the SP7 at Fornaci di Barga. Barga is 5km further on.

Bagni di Lucca

POP 6160

Small-town Bagni di Lucca is 28km south of Castelnuovo di Garfagnana on the banks of the Lima river. Famed in the early 19th century for its thermal waters, which were enjoyed by the Lucca gentry and an international set (Byron, Shelley, Heinrich Heine and Giacomo Puccini were among the celebrity guests to take the waters), the spa town today is a pale shadow of its former splendid neoclassical self. In past years it had its own beautiful neoclassical casino (1837) with a music room where Strauss, Puccini and Liszt all performed, as well as a theatre and an atypically ornate Anglican church, now the municipal library (look for the stucco lion and unicorn motif above each window on the vivid burnt-red facade). In the small British cemetery, baroque tombs speak volumes.

👁 Sights & Activities

There are two distinct areas: the smaller casino-clad Ponte a Serraglio, clustered around a bridge that crosses the Lima river; and the main town, 2km east, where most shops, restaurants and hotels are. In the former, you'll find the Sorgente La Cova (Viale Casino Municipale 84) , a natural spring spouting out of a roadside wall.

small but sensational choice of antipasti and pasta *primi:* his local *pecorino* cheese with fresh pea-green broad beans and a pot of Lunigiana honey is simple but, oh, so good.

Find it at the bottom of the hill from Barga, 4km north in riverside Ponte di Catagnana.

In the tiny riverside hamlet of Borgo a Mozzano, 2km southwest of town, is the medieval stone Ponte del Diarolo – the so-called 'Devils' Bridge' with ancient stone paving dating from the 14th century.

✖ Eating

Circolo dei Forestieri   TUSCAN $
(☑0583 80 55 58; www.ristorantecircolodeiforestieri.it; Piazza Jean Varraud 10; meals €20; ⊙noon-3pm & 7.30-10pm Tue-Sun) Quell hunger pangs at the former home of the Foreigners' Club, an elegant belle époque building on the river side of Viale Umberto I, southeast of the casino. Its chandelier-lit dining room provides a splendid setting in which to enjoy quality Tuscan cuisine. The fixed, €11 lunchtime menu – including water, a glass of wine and coffee – is an absolute steal.

Buca di Baldabò   TUSCAN $
(☑0583 8 90 62; www.labucadibaldabo.it; Via Prati 11, Vico Pancellorum; meals €20; ⊙noon-3pm & 7-10pm Jun-Aug, lunch by reservation & 7-10pm Wed-Sun Sep-May) Perched on a hillock above chestnut and walnut forests, this is an iconic address every local foodie knows about. Hidden at the back of the village bar, it has no printed menu. Listen to what's cooking that day and take your pick from homemade pasta and sauces cooked up daily by chef Giovanni. Game is particularly big and side dishes are creative.

To get to Vico Pancellorum from Bagni di Lucca, head 9km northeast along the scenic SS12 towards Abetone and at the northern end of Ponte Coccia take the sharp turning on the left signposted 'Vico Pancellorum'; the restaurant is another 3km from here, at the foot of the hamlet, along a steep, narrow, curving road. Advance reservations are essential.

ℹ Information

Tourist Office (☑05 8380 5745; www.bagnidiluccaterme.info/en; Viale Umberto I 93; ⊙10am-1pm Mon & Wed-Sat)

ℹ Getting There & Away

Bagni di Lucca train station is in Fornoli, 4km southwest of the Bagni di Lucca Terme. Hope a local bus passes relatively soon after your arrival or arrange a taxi in advance through your hotel. Regional train services:

Lucca (€3.50, 30 minutes, seven daily)

Pisa (€5.50, 1¼ hours, five daily)

Carrara

POP 63,100

Many first-time visitors assume the white mountain peaks forming Carrara's backdrop are capped with snow. In fact, the vista provides a breathtaking illusion – the lunar white is 2000 hectares of marble gouged out of the foothills of the Apuane Alps in vast quarries, 5km out of town, that have been worked since Roman times.

The texture and purity of Carrara's white marble (derived from the Greek *marmaros,* meaning shining stone) is unrivalled, and it remains the world's most sought-after. Michelangelo selected marble here for masterpieces such as *Pièta* (the veined marble he used for his iconic *David* came from a quarry in neighbouring Pietrasanta), while Carrara marble was used for London's Marble Arch and by Rodin to sculpt *The Kiss.*

Bar the thrill of admiring its marble pavements, marble street benches, marble-clad post office and marble everything else, Carrara doesn't offer much for the visitor.

ℹ PLANNING: HIKING, BIKING, RAFTING ET AL

Tuscany Walking (www.tuscanywalking.com) Family-run, English-speaking set-up in Barga offering guided and self-guided hikes.

Ecoguide (☑340 6778356; www.eco-guide.it) This creative Lucca-based operation offers guided nature tours in the Garfagnana on foot and by bicycle, including magical night walks in the Garfagnana, kids' walks and photography treks.

Garfagnana Rafting (☑336 666795, 333 5282913; www.garfagnanarafting.com) Canyoning, kayaking, aqua-trekking and white-water rafting on the Lima and Serchio rivers; small-group hikes in the Apuane Alps too.

Sapori e Saperi (☑339 7636321, in the UK 07768 474 610; www.sapori-e-saperi.com) Embark on a bespoke culinary tour of the Garfagnana with knowledgeable foodie Erica or passionate chef, beekeeper and olive farmer Francesca. Learn how bread is traditionally baked, sausages are made, and *pecorino* cheese is produced as it's been done for generations. Visit olive farms, harvest chestnuts, hunt truffles, meet local cheesemakers and savour age-old recipes in local-endorsed restaurants.

MEET A BEEKEEPER

Squeeze your car along the narrow road to Al Benefizio (☑ 347 2703624; www.albene fizio.it; Via Ronchi 4, Ponte di Catagnana), a farm framed by fig trees, olive groves, vines, acacia and chestnut woods on a steeply terraced hillside near Barga, uphill from Ponte di Catagnana. Self-catering apartments with wood stoves, no TV and spectacular views sleep up to four, and the local baker, Maurizio, drives by each morning with fresh bread, pastries and scrumptious focaccia.

But the real reason to stay here is get acquainted with charismatic owner Francesca, a talented chef and beekeeper. With her you can visit the apiary with 100 hives beneath cherry trees, see how honey is extracted (Easter to September), sign up for a cooking course or olive-oil workshop, or help out with the olive harvest (by hand) in late November. In summer guests can swim, mountain bike, barbecue, play table tennis, help themselves to veg and herbs in the vegetable patch, pet the farm donkey Geubi, and collect fresh eggs. Or mingle, memorably so, with other guests at Francesca's wonderfully informal 'pizza parties' around the farm's old stone bread oven. No credit cards.

◉ Sights & Activities

The tourist office has information on walking trails with magnificent quarry views and also on a three-hour 'Michelangelo in White' biking itinerary – a 24km route that sees cyclists climb 550m up from Carrara-Avenza train station to the quarries and beyond to Colonnata.

Museo del Marmo   MUSEUM
(Marble Museum; ☑ 0585 84 57 46; www.muse odelmarmo.com; Viale XX Settembre 85; adult/ reduced €4.50/2.50; ⊙ 9am-12.30pm & 2.30-5pm Mon-Sat) Carrara's Marble Museum tells the full story of the marble quarries outside town, from the old chisel-and-hammer days to the 21st-century's high-powered industrial quarrying. A fascinating audiovisual history presentation documents the lives of quarry workers in the 20th century.

Cava di Fantiscritti   HISTORIC SITE
(Fantiscritti Quarry; Via Miseglia Fantiscritti) Head up the mountain to this dusty, truck-busy *cava de marmo* (marble quarry), through a dramatic series of tunnels used by trains to transport marble from 1890 until the 1960s when trucks took over. At the Fantiscritti Quarry entrance, pick a 40-minute guided tour by minibus and on foot of the Ravaccione 84 gallery inside the quarry, run by Marmotour (☑ 339 7657470; www.marmotour.com; adult/child €10/5; ⊙ 10am-6pm Jul & Aug, 11am-5pm Sep & Oct, 11am-5pm Mon-Fri, 10am-5pm Sat & Sun Apr-Jun, 10am-5pm Sat & Sun Mar & Nov), or pick a Bond-style 4WD tour of the open-cast quarries run by various unofficial operators lurking around on site. Or head ahead with Cave di Marmo Tours (☑ 328 0993322, 0585 181 00 37; www.cavedimarmotours. com; Viale G Galilei 122e; adult/child €40/20; ⊙ guided tours 9.20am & 2pm).

✖ Eating

The *only* place to lunch is in the hamlet of Colonnata, 2km from the Fantiscritti quarries, where one of Tuscany's greatest gastronomic treats, *lardo di colonnata* (thinner-than-wafer-thin slices of aromatic pig fat) sits ageing in marble vats of herby olive oil. Once you're hooked, purchase a vacuum-packed slab (€15 per kg) to take home from one of the many *larderie* (shops selling *lardo*) in the village.

Osteria nella Pia'   OSTERIA **$**
(☑ 338 8408173, 0585 75 80 97; www.osterianella pia.it; Via Fossa Cava 3, Colonnata; meals €20; ⊙ noon-3pm Tue-Thu & Sun, noon-3pm & 7.30-10pm Fri & Sat) It's worth getting lost in Colonnata's tangle of narrow lanes to find this family-run *osteria,* a local favourite for tasty *lardo* platters and imaginative pasta dishes. The *penne con lardo e pesto d'ortica* (penne with lardo and nettle pesto) is nothing short of superb. Kudos for the shaded summertime terrace wedged between old stone village houses and the hulk of marble mountain beyond.

ℹ Information

Tourist Office (☑ 0585 84 41 36; www. aptmassacarrara.it; Viale XX Settembre; ⊙ 8.30am-4.30pm summer, 9am-4pm Thu-Sun winter) Located opposite the stadium. Stop here to pick up a map of Carrara, its marble workshops and out-of-town quarries.

ℹ Getting There & Around

CAR & MOTORCYCLE
Travelling by car is the most convenient option, as you'll need one to reach the quarries and other nearby attractions.

ROAD TRIP >
THE VIA FRANCIGENA

•••

The medieval pilgrimage route of Via Francigena connected Canterbury with Rome by way of the rural Lunigiana region in northwestern Tuscany. It was so popular with pilgrims that in the 8th century the Lombard kings built churches, hospices and monasteries offering shelter and protection for pilgrims along its Lunigiana length. This tour, perfectly viable by car or bicycle, explores some of them.

1   Pieve di Soprano

From Pontremoli pick up the SS62 and follow it 8km towards Filattiera. In a grassy field on the left, admire the Romanesque Pieve di Sorano (1148), with traditional its *piagnaro* (stone slab) roof and a watchtower to signal its presence as a fortified stop on the pilgrimage route. Beyond the church, up high, is the old hilltop village.

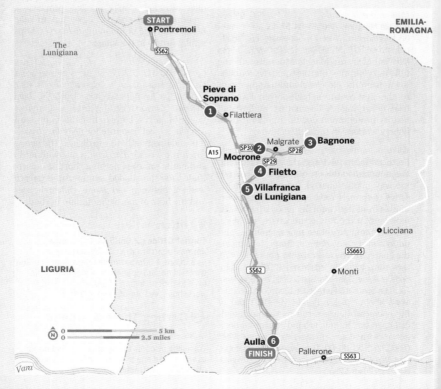

Two to three Hours 32km

Great for... Outdoors, History & Culture

Time to Go Spring, summer or early autumn

● ●

❷ Mocrone

Continue for 2.5km along the SS62 then turn left onto the SP30 (direction Bagnone) and drive 2.3km. In Mocrone enjoy great views of fortified Malgrate teetering on the hillside on your left; break for lunch at **Locanda Gavarini** (📞 0187 49 55 04; www.locandagavarini.it; Via Benedicenti 50, Mocrone; s/d/tr/q €70/90/95/120; ⊘ Mar-Dec; 🅿 ✉), an old-world village inn at the end of the narrowest street you're ever likely to drive along. A rural idyll where the only noise is twittering birds and the sunrise cry of the village cockerel, this countryside hotel-restaurant (meals €25) is a homage to local Lunigianese culinary tradition.

❸ Bagnone

About 4km after Mocrone, the road brings you into Bagnone, an important trading stop on the Via Francigena and distinctive for its castle, church and eateries. Stretch your legs with a scenic walk above the fiercely gushing river and its dramatic gorges; pick up the easy 15- or 30-minute trail from Piazza Roma and end on main street Via della Repubblica. The final leg across the medieval, stone-paved Ponte Vecchio (Old Bridge) is the stuff of poetry.

❹ Filetto

From Bagnone backtrack towards Mocrone and onwards towards Villafranca, veering slightly left onto the SP29 to reach Filetto. The walled medieval hamlet derives its name from the Greek word 'filakterion' and goes back in time each August with a fabulous Mercato Medioevale (Medieval Market); locals don medieval garb and set up street stalls selling local wares, demonstrating ancient crafts etc. Park outside its monumental gate and wander through its tiny piazzas and narrow lanes.

❺ Villafranca di Lunigiana

Arriving in Villafranca di Lunigiana 1.5km south, you're on another key stop on the pilgrim route. Set on the Magra river, it is an unassuming place with a small ethnographical museum in an old 15th-century flour mill.

❻ Aulla

End the tour 12km south in Aulla, known for its imposing Fortezza della Brunella (fortress) and abbey founded in AD 884. Originally part of a Benedictine monastery, the abbey served as a shelter to Via Francigena pilgrims on route to Rome for centuries and, to this day, safeguards the remains of St Caprasio, the hermit monk who inspired the spread of monastic life in Provence from the 5th century and subsequently was honoured with the title of patron saint of pilgrims.

DON'T MISS

MARBLE MOUNTAIN

Zipping down a dank, wet, unlit tunnel in a dusty white minibus, grubby headlights blazing, driver incongruously dolled up in a shiny shocking-pink bomber jacket...it is all somewhat surreal. Five minutes into the pitch-black marble mountain, everyone is told to get out.

It is 16°C (61°F), foggy, dirty and slippery under foot. And far from being a polished pearly white, it's grey – cold, wet, miserable grey. Rough-cut blocks, several metres long and almost as wide, are strewn about the place like toy bricks and marble columns prop up the 15m-high ceiling, above which a second gallery, another 17m tall, stands. The place is bigger than several football pitches, yet amazingly there is still plenty of marble left for the five workers employed at Cava di Fantiscritti (p257), 5km north of Carrara, to extract. With the aid of water and mechanical diamond-cutting chains that slice through the rock like butter, they take 10,000 tonnes of white marble a month.

To learn how the Romans did it (with chisels and axes – oh my!), visit the surprisingly informative, open-air Cava Museo (📞 393 3575925, 334 7870741; www.cavamuseo.com; Cava di Fantiscritti; ⏲ 11am-6pm) FREE, adjoining the souvenir shop across from the quarry entrance. Don't miss the B&W shots of marble blocks being precariously slid down the *lizza* (mountain pathway) to the bottom of the mountain where 18 pairs of oxen would haul the marble on carts to Carrara port. In the 1850s a rail network of 24 tunnels and seven bridges was built for trains to do the job – which they did until the 1960s. Cars can drive through many of these defunct train tunnels today (hence the tunnel that quarry tour groups use to drive into the mountain).

Carrara alone exploits 188 marble quarries today: the Apuane Alps safeguard the world's largest marble field, with the best Carrara marble selling for €4000 a tonne (exports alone are worth a handsome €360 million a year). Carrara's quarries employ 1200 men and another 700 truck drivers who zigzag each day up and down terrifyingly steep, mountain 'roads' transporting giant marble blocks. It's hard, dangerous work and on Carrara's central Piazza XXVII Aprile a monument remembers past workers who lost their lives up on the hills.

TRAIN

The nearest station is Carrara-Avenza, between Carrara and Marina di Carrara. Regional train services:

Pietrasanta (€2.60, 15 minutes, at least twice hourly)

Viareggio (€3.50, 25 minutes, twice hourly)

THE VERSILIAN COAST

The beaches from Viareggio northwards to Liguria are popular with local holidaymakers and some tourists, but have been blighted by beachfront development and get unpleasantly packed with Italy's beach-lovers during summer. We suggest steering clear of this coastal strip and instead heading inland to explore the hinterland town of Pietrasanta, known for its vibrant arts culture and *centro storico*.

Versilia is a major gateway to the Apuane Alps, Garfagnana and Lunigiana with roads from the coastal towns snaking their way deep into the heart of the mountains and connecting with small villages and walking tracks.

Pietrasanta

POP 24,000

Often overlooked by Tuscan travellers, this refined art town sports a bijou historic heart (originally walled) peppered with tiny art galleries, workshops and fashion boutiques – perfect for a day's amble broken only by lunch.

Founded in 1255 by Guiscardo da Pietrasanta, the *podestà* (governing magistrate) of Lucca, Pietrasanta was seen as a prize by Genoa, Lucca, Pisa and Florence, all of which jostled for possession of its marble quarries and bronze foundries. Florence won out and Leo X (Giovanni de' Medici) took control in 1513, putting the town's quarries at the disposal of Michelangelo, who came here in 1518 to source marble for the facade of Florence's San Lorenzo. Artists continue to work here, including internationally lauded Colombian-born sculptor Fernando Botero (b 1932), whose work can be seen here.

Pietrasanta is a great base for exploring the Apuane Alps and a lovely day trip from Pisa or Viareggio.

◉ Sights & Activities

From Pietrasanta train station on Piazza della Stazione head straight across Piazza Carducci, through the Old City gate and onto Piazza del Duomo, the main square, which doubles as an outdoor gallery for sculptures and other large works of art.

Duomo di San Martino   CATHEDRAL
(Piazza del Duomo; ⊙ hours vary) It is impossible to miss Pietrasanta's attractive cathedral, dating from 1256, on the central square. Its distinctive 36m-tall, red-brick bell tower is actually unfinished; the red brick was meant to have a marble cladding.

Chiesa di Sant'Agostino   CHURCH
(Piazza del Duomo; ⊙ hours vary) The far end of Piazza del Duomo is dominated by the 13th-century stone hulk of this deconsecrated church. Once dedicated to St Augustine, today the Romanesque space hosts seasonal art exhibitions.

Museo dei Bozzetti   MUSEUM
(✆ 0584 79 55 00; www.museodeibozzetti.it; Via Sant'Agostino 1; ⊙ 9am-1pm & 2-7pm Tue-Fri, 2-7pm Sat, 4-7pm Sun) FREE Inside the convent adjoining Chiesa di Sant'Agostino dozens of moulds of famous sculptures cast or carved in Pietrasanta are showcased by this small museum.

Via della Rocca   VIEWPOINT
(Piazza del Duomo) Next to Chiesa di Sant'Agostino, a steep path known as Via della Rocca leads up to what remains of Pietrasanta's ancient fortifications. The crenellated city walls date from the early 1300s and what remains of Palazzo Guinigi was built as a residence for the *signore* of Lucca, Paolo Guinigi, in 1408. Views of the city and the deep-blue Mediterranean beyond are worth the short climb.

Battistero di Pietrasanta   CHRISTIAN SITE
(Baptistery; Via Garibaldi 12; ⊙ variable) Around the corner from the cathedral on pedestrian Via Garibaldi is this atmospheric old-world baptistry. The pair of baptismal fonts – one originally in the cathedral in the 16th century and the other a hexagonal tub (1389) used two centuries before for full immersion baptisms – form a dramatic ensemble in the tiny candle-lit space.

Via Garibaldi   STREET
This quaint pedestrian strip is peppered with chic fashion boutiques and stylish art galleries. Highlights guaranteed to tempt include fashion designer Paolo Milani (✆ 0584 79 07 29; Via Garibaldi 11; ⊙ hours vary), whose studio is a riot of bold vibrant prints and a wild mix of textures covering the whole sombre-to-sequin spectrum; multibrand fashion queen and trendsetter Zoe (✆ 0424 52 21 25; www.zoecompany.eu; Via Garibaldi 29-33 & 44-46; ⊙ 10am-1pm & 4-8pm); vintage furniture design boutique Lei; and concept store Dada (✆ 0584 7 04 37; www.dadaconcept.it; Via Garibaldi 39; ⊙ 10am-1pm & 3.30-7.30pm Tue-Sun).

Chiesa della Misericordia   CHURCH
(✆ 0584 7 00 55; Via Mazzini 103; ⊙ hours vary) Squirrelled away on Via Mazzini is this precious chapel. Tucked between shops, the superb Chiesa della Misericordia is frescoed with the Gate of Paradise and Gate of Hell by Fernando Botero (b 1932). Spot the self-portrait of the Columbian artist – who lives in Pietrasanta – in Hell.

✕ Eating & Drinking

★ Filippo Mud Bar   TUSCAN $$
(✆ 0584 7 00 10; www.facebook.com/filippomud; Via Barsanti 45; 3-/5-course menu €35/55; ⊙ 12.30-2.15pm & 7pm-1am Wed-Sun, 7pm-1am Tue) Completely on trend, this chic open-plan space is part lounge, part cocktail bar (stunning paprika roasted almonds) and part formal restaurant with a sensational industrial-meets-lime-green-velour interior. Its menu, an ode to fusion cuisine, is equally fabulous: order a three- or five-course menu, or try the 'sensual experience for provocative souls' (€25) – aka a cocktail perfectly paired with a surprise dish. Reservations essential.

★ L'Enoteca Marcucci   WINE BAR
(✆ 0584 79 19 62; www.enotecamarcucci.it; Via Garibaldi 40; ⊙ 10am-1pm & 5pm-1am Tue-Sun) Taste fine Tuscan wine on bar stools at high wooden tables or beneath big parasols on the street outside. Whichever you pick, the distinctly funky, artsy spirit of Pietrasanta's best-loved *enoteca* enthrals.

Osteria Barsanti 54   TUSCAN $$
(✆ 0584 71 51 4; www.osteriabarsanti54.com; Via Barsanti 54; meals €35; ⊙ noon-2.30pm & 7-10.30pm) Tucked away on a quiet lane, a five-minute stroll from Piazza del Duomo, this *osteria* is a refined temple to good slow food and wine. 'Cook with love' is the strapline of culinary creatives Alessandro and Marco, and quality seasonal dishes packed with anchovies, sardines, purple potatoes, kale and the like seduce every time. Lunch on Thursday is posh *lampredotto* (tripe sandwich), served with a glass of red and bean salad.

NORTHWESTERN TUSCANY PIETRASANTA

La Brigata di Filippo   TUSCAN $$

(📞 0584 7 00 10; http://ristorantefilippo.com; Via Stagio Stagi 22; meals €40; ⊙12.30-2.30pm & 7.30pm-2am, closed Mon winter) 🍴 This exceptional foodie address never disappoints. From the homemade bread and focaccia brought warm to your table throughout the course of your meal to the contemporary fabric on the walls, to giant wicker lampshades and modern open kitchen, this bistro is chic. Cuisine is seasonal modern Tuscan and is perfect for a lazy lunch (two-/three-/four-course menus €25/35/45) inside or out.

ℹ Getting There & Away

Regional train services:

Pisa (€4.40, 30 minutes, every 30 minutes)

Viareggio (€2.60, 10 minutes, every 10 minutes)

Lucca (with change of train in Pisa or Viareggio; €6.10, one hour, every 30 minutes)

Viareggio

POP 62,500

This hugely popular sun-and-sand resort is known as much for its flamboyant Mardi Gras Carnevale, second only to Venice for party spirit, as for its dishevelled line-up of once-grand art-nouveau facades along its seafront, which recall the town's 1920s and '30s heyday.

Viareggio's vast golden-sand beachfront is laden with cafes, climbing frames and other kids' amusements and, bar the short public stretch opposite fountain-pierced Piazza Mazzini, is divided into *stabilimenti* (individual lots where you can hire cabins, umbrellas, loungers etc). Only a handful of waterfront buildings retain the ornate stylishness of the 1920s and '30s, notably Puccini's favourite cafe, 1929 **Gran Caffè Margherita** (📞 0584 58 11 43; www.ristorantemargherita.info; Viale Regina Margherita 30; ⊙7am-midnight) and neighbouring wooden Chalet Martini (1899).

◉ Sights & Activities

Literature lovers might like to pass by **Piazza Shelley**, the only tangible reference to the romantic poet who drowned in Viareggio; his body was washed up on the beach and his comrade-in-arts, Lord Byron, had him cremated on the spot.

La Citadella di Carnevale   MONUMENT

(📞 0584 5 30 48; Via Santa Maria Goretti; ⊙4-7pm Sat & Sun) FREE A couple of kilometres from the seafront is 'Carnival City' aka 16 gargantuan hangars that serve as workshops and garage space for the fantastic floats, crafted with

passion by each highly skilled and prized *carrista* (float-builder) for Viareggio's annual carnival. Carnevale history and the art of making *teste in capo* (the giant heads worn in processions) and *mascheroni a piedi* (big walking masks) is explained in the on-site **Museo del Carnevale** (Carnival Museum). Ask about its hands-on papier-mâché workshops.

✨ Festivals & Events

Carnevale di Viareggio   CULTURAL

(http://viareggio.ilcarnevale.com; ⊙Feb & Mar) Viareggio's annual moment of glory lasts four weeks in February to early March when the city goes wild during Carnevale – a festival of floats, many featuring giant satirical effigies of political and other topical figures. It also includes fireworks and rampant dusk-to-dawn spirit.

🍴 Eating & Drinking

La Barchina   FISH & CHIPS $

(📞 347 7212848; Lungomolo Corraldo del Greco; meals €8-10; ⊙noon-3pm Tue-Fri, to 11pm Sat & Sun) Join locals standing in line at this small white boat, moored at the harbour, which cooks up the morning's catch for lunch. The hot item to order is *fritto misto* (€8), a mix of squid, prawns and octopus battered, deep-fried and served with a huge friendly smile in plastic punnets. Friday cooks up *baccalà* (battered, salted cod) and veggie lovers are catered for with punnets of fried mushrooms.

Lettera 22   CAFE

(📞 0584 58 27 55; Via Mazzini 84; ⊙9am-8pm Tue-Sat, 3-8pm Sun & Mon; 📶) Mid-afternoon, lounge with hip locals at Lettera 22, a refreshingly stylish and up-to-the-minute literary cafe between the beach and the train station with free wi-fi, armchairs, books to browse, a kids' corner, cakes and wonderful pots of herbal and flavoured teas.

ℹ Information

Tourist Office (📞 0584 96 22 33; www.aptversilia.it; Viale Carducci 10; ⊙9am-1pm & 3-6pm Mon-Sat) Across from the clock on the waterfront.

ℹ Getting There & Away

To hit the seafront from the **train station** (Piazza Dante Alighieri), exit and walk straight ahead along Via Guiseppe Mazzini for 10 minutes to Piazza Giuseppe Mazzini and the sandy beach-fringed promenade beyond. Regional train services:

Florence (€9.60, 1½ hours, at least hourly)

Livorno (€5.50, 45 minutes, 16 daily)

Lucca (€3.50, 17 minutes, every 20 minutes)
Pietrasanta (€2.60, 10 minutes, every 10 minutes)
Pisa (€3.50, 18 minutes, every 20 minutes)
Pontremoli (€7.50, 1¼ hours, hourly)

THE LUNIGIANA

This landlocked enclave of territory is bordered to the north and east by the Apennines, to the west by Liguria and to the south by the Apuane Alps and the Garfagnana. The few tourists who make their way here tend to be lunching in Pontremoli, a real off-the-beaten-track gastronomic gem, or following in the footsteps of medieval pilgrims along the Via Francigena.

Autumnal visits reward with fresh, intensely scented porcini mushrooms that sprout under chestnut trees in fecund woods and hills. Wild herbs cover fields, and 5000 scattered hives produce the region's famous chestnut and acacia honey. These fruits of the forest and other regional delicacies – including Zeri lamb, freshly baked *focaccette,* crisp and sweet *rotella* apples, boiled pork shoulder, *caciotta* (a delicate cow's-milk cheese), *bigliolo* beans, local olive oil and Colli di Luni wines – are reason enough to visit.

Pontremoli

POP 7360

It may be small, but this out-of-the-way town presided over by the impressive bulk of Castello del Piagnaro has a decidedly grand air – a legacy of its strategic location on the pilgrimage and trading route of Via Francigena. Its merchants made fortunes in medieval times, and adorned the *centro storico* with palaces, piazzas and graceful stone bridges.

The *centro storico* is a long sliver stretching north–south between the Magra and Verde rivers, which have historically served as defensive barriers. Meandering its streets takes you beneath colonnaded arches, through former strongholds of opposing Guelph and Ghibelline factions, and past a 17th-century cathedral and an 18th-century theatre.

Sights

Castello del Piagnaro CASTLE
(Museo delle Statue Stele Lunigianesi; ☑0187 83 14 39; www.statuestele.org; adult/reduced €5/3; ☺10am-7.30pm Aug, to 6.30pm Jun & Sep, shorter hours Tue-Sun Oct-May) From central Piazza della Repubblica and adjacent Piazza del Duomo, walk along Via Garibaldi then bear left along Vietata l'Affissione or Sdrucciolo del Castello, two pretty alleys and staircases that stagger uphill to this ramshackle castle. A former military barracks, it takes its name from the *piagnaro* (stone slabs) that were once widely used to roof Lunigianese buildings. Views across town from the castle are impressive and the small Museo delle Statue Stele Lunigianesi showcases primitive stelae statues found nearby.

Eating & Drinking

In summer, come 5pm, what feels like the entire population of Pontremoli congregates on central Piazza della Repubblica to mingle on the terrace of Caffè degli Svizzeri (☑0187 83 01 60; Piazza della Repubblica 22; ☺7am-8pm Tue-Sun summer, shorter hours winter). The people gather to eat gelato and lap up the old-world charm that this tiny, overtly rural town exudes. Follow suit.

Trattoria Da Bussè TRATTORIA $
(☑0187 83 13 71; Piazza del Duomo 31; meals €25; ☺7.45-9.45pm Mon-Thu, 12.30-2.30pm & 7.45-9.45pm Sat & Sun) This Slow Food favourite has been run by the same family since the 1930s, and its original decor is charmingly old world. The regional menu includes *torta d'erbe della Lunigiana* (herb pie cooked over coals in a cast-iron pan lined with chestnut leaves to keep the mixture from sticking) and *testaroli* (thick crepe, cut in diamond shapes, boiled and often served with pesto). No credit cards.

Trattoria Pelliccia TRATTORIA $$
(☑0187 83 05 77; Via Garibaldi 137; meals €30; ☺noon-2pm & 7.30-10pm) This staunchly traditional trattoria, tucked at the end of the *centro storico,* is an ode to regional cuisine. Start with *testaroli della lunigiana al pesto* (a type of savoury crepe cut into diamonds, cooked like pasta and served with pesto), followed by oven-baked *agnello di Zeri* (lamb). End with an unjustly good sorbet (lemon and sage, pistachio and pepper, strawberry and port…).

Information

Tourist Office (☑0187 83 33 09; www.prolocopontremoli.it; Piazzetta della Pace; ☺10am-noon & 3.30-6pm Sat & Sun, daily Jul & Aug)

Getting There & Away

Regional train services:
La Spezia (€5.50, 50 minutes, frequent)
Pisa (€9.10, 90 minutes, hourly)

Eastern Tuscany

Best Places to Eat

➡ Le Chiavi d'Oro (p270)

➡ Il Cedro (p276)

➡ Ristorante Da Muzzicone (p281)

➡ Mest Osteria (p270)

➡ Beerbone Artburger (p282)

➡ Cremì (p270)

Best Hidden Gems

➡ Santuario della Verna (p277)

➡ Museo Michelangeliolesco (p280)

➡ Sacro Eremo e Monastero di Camaldoli (p280)

➡ Museo Madonna del Parto (p275)

➡ Il Cedro (p276)

➡ Osteria dell'Acquolina (p271)

Why Go?

The eastern edge of Tuscany is beloved by film directors who have immortalised its landscape and medieval hilltop towns in several critically acclaimed and visually splendid films. Yet the region remains bereft of tourist crowds and offers quiet trails for those savvy enough to explore here – or those simply in search of peace, tranquillity and mountains of natural beauty. Attractions are many and varied: spectacular mountain scenery and walks in the Casentino; magnificent art and architecture in the medieval cities of Arezzo, Sansepolcro and Cortona; one of Italy's most significant Catholic pilgrimage sites, Assisi; and Tuscany's best *bistecca alla fiorentina* (chargrilled T-bone steak) in the Val di Chiana. Your travels may be solitary and, for the most part, you'll need your own wheels to get around – but they'll always be rewarding.

Road Distances (km)

	Assisi	Arezzo	Cortona	Sansepolcro
Arezzo	94			
Cortona	65	29		
Sansepolcro	76	38	52	
Poppi	132	36	62	71

AREZZO

POP 99,540

Arezzo may not be a Tuscan centrefold, but those parts of its historic centre that survived merciless WWII bombings are as compelling as any destination in the region – the city's central square is as beautiful as it appears in Roberto Benigni's classic film *La vita è bella* (Life is Beautiful).

Once an important Etruscan trading post, Arezzo was later absorbed into the Roman Empire. A free republic as early as the 10th century, it supported the Ghibelline cause in the violent battles between pope and emperor and was eventually subjugated by Florence in 1384.

Today, the city is known for its churches, museums and fabulously sloping Piazza Grande (p269), across which a huge antiques fair (p270) spills each month. Come dusk, Arentini (locals of Arezzo) spill along the length of shop-clad Corso Italia for the ritual late-afternoon *passeggiata* (stroll).

◉ Sights

★ **Cappella Bacci**   CHURCH

(☑ 0575 35 27 27; www.pierodellafrancesca.it; Piazza San Francesco; adult/reduced €8/5; ⊙ 9am-6pm Mon-Fri, to 5.30pm Sat, 1-5.30pm Sun) This chapel, in the apse of 14th-century Basilica di San Francesco, safeguards one of Italian art's greatest works: Piero della Francesca's fresco cycle of the *Legend of the True Cross*. Painted between 1452 and 1466, it relates the story of the cross on which Christ was crucified. Only 25 people are allowed in every half hour, making advance booking (by telephone or email) essential in high season. The ticket office is down the stairs by the basilica's entrance.

This medieval legend is as entertaining as it is inconceivable. The illustrations follow the story of the tree that Seth plants on the grave of his father, Adam, and from which the True Cross is made. One scene shows the long-lost cross being rediscovered by Helena, mother of the emperor Constantine; behind her, the city of Jerusalem is pictured as a medieval view of Arezzo. Other scenes show the victory of Heraclius over the Persian king Khosrau, who had been accused of stealing the cross; Constantine sleeping in a tent on the eve of his battle with Maxentius (note Piero's masterful depiction of the nocturnal light); and Constantine carrying the cross into battle.

Two of the best-loved scenes depict the meeting of the Queen of Sheba and King Solomon. In the first half she is kneeling on a bridge over the Siloam River and meeting with the king; she and her attendants are depicted wearing rich Renaissance-style gowns. In the second half, King Solomon's palace seems to be modelled on the designs of notable architect Leon Battista Alberti.

THREE PERFECT DAYS

Day One

Two major films are set in Arezzo. Day one, explore the historic streets and piazzas where Roberto Benigni filmed *La vita è bella* (Life is Beautiful). Pop into the Duomo (p269) and Chiesa di Santa Maria della Pieve (p268); see where Arezzo-born painter, architect and art historian Vasari lived and worked; and pay homage to Piero della Francesca's genius in Basilica di San Francesco's Cappella Bacci, where Anthony Minghella shot the most memorable scene of *The English Patient*.

Day Two

Tuscany's most famous family of sculptors, the Della Robbias, took ceramics way beyond teacups in the 15th century, creating magnificent devotional sculptures for churches throughout Tuscany. Devote your second day to visiting the medieval monasteries at Camaldoli (p280) and Santuario della Verna (p277) in the Parco Nazionale delle Foreste Casentinesi, Monte Falterona e Campigna (p277), to admire masterpieces in glazed terracotta by the family's most famous member, Andrea (1435–1525).

Day Three

On day three, dip into Val di Chiana (p281), well placed between Arezzo and Cortona (p281) and also en route to central Tuscany. Home to apple orchards, olive groves and lush pastures where creamy white Chianina cattle graze, the valley invites off-the-beaten-track meanderings. Explore hilltop town Castiglion Fiorentino (p281), allowing time for a meaty lunch stop at Ristorante Da Muzzicone (p281).

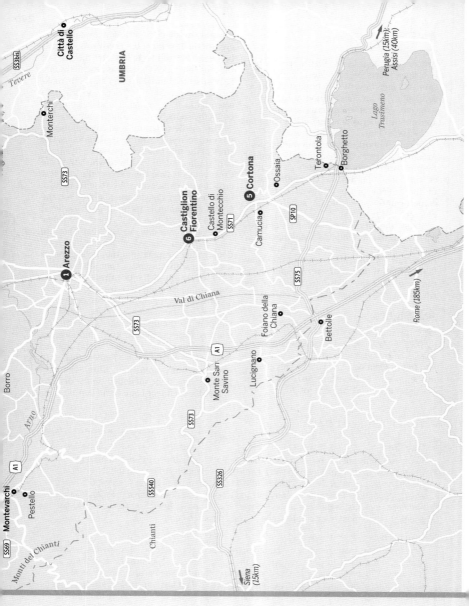

Eastern Tuscany Highlights

1 **Arezzo** (p265) Marvelling at Cappella Bacci's frescoes and one of Tuscany's most beautiful squares, Piazza Grande.

2 **Sansepolcro** (p274) Admiring the work of Renaissance painter Piero della Francesca at the Museo Civico.

3 **Poppi** (p276) Exploring a well-preserved medieval castle in this fortified hamlet.

4 **Parco Nazionale delle Foreste Casentinesi, Monte Falterona e Campigna** (p277) Communing with nature on a pilgrimage to secluded medieval monasteries in this remote national park.

5 **Cortona**

6 **Castiglion Fiorentino**

UMBRIA

Tevere

SS3bis

Città di Castello

Monterchi

SS73

Arezzo

Castello di Montecchio

SS71

Camucia

Ossaia

Terontola

Borghetto

Lago Trasimeno

Perugia (15km); Assisi (40km)

SP10

SS75

Val di Chiana

Foiano della Chiana

Bettolle

Rome (185km)

Monte San Savino

A1

Lucignano

SS73

SS326

Siena (15km)

SS540

Chianti

SS73

Arno

Borro

Monti del Chianti

Pestello

Montevarchi

A1

SS69

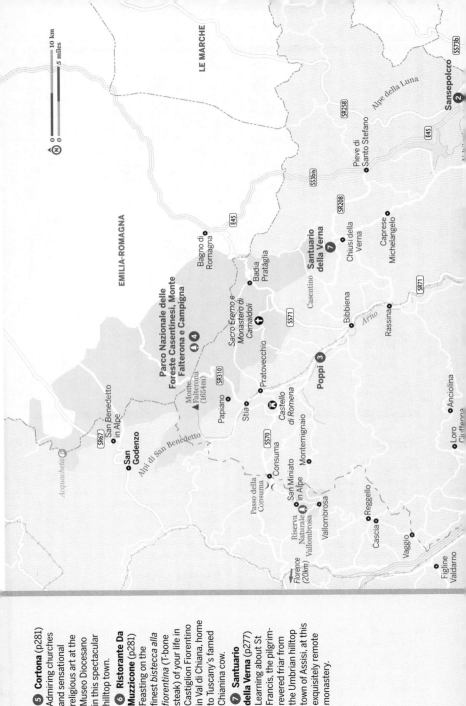

LE MARCHE

EMILIA-ROMAGNA

Parco Nazionale delle
Foreste Casentinesi, Monte
Falterona e Campigna

Casentino

5 Cortona (p281)
Admiring churches
and sensational
religious art at the
Museo Diocesano
in this spectacular
hilltop town.

6 Ristorante Da
Muzzicone (p281)
Feasting on the
finest *bistecca alla
fiorentina* (T-bone
steak) of your life in
Castiglion Fiorentino
in Val di Chiana, home
to Tuscany's famed
Chianina cow.

7 Santuario
della Verna (p277)
Learning about St
Francis, the pilgrim-
revered friar from
the Umbrian hilltop
town of Assisi, at this
exquisitely remote
monastery.

Sansepolcro

Pieve di
Santo Stefano

Alpe della Luna

Bagno di
Romagna

Badia
Prataglia

Chiusi della
Verna

Caprese
Michelangelo

Santuario
della Verna

Sacro Eremo e
Monastero di
Camaldoli

Monte
Falterona
(1654m)

Papiano

Stia

Pratovecchio

Castello
di Romena

Bibbiena

Arno

Rassina

Poppi

San Benedetto
in Alpe

San
Godenzo

Alpi di San Benedetto

Acquacheta

Montemignaio

Consuma

Passo della
Consuma

San Miniato
in Alpe

Vallombrosa

Riserva
Naturale
Vallombrosa

Florence
(20km)

Reggello

Cascia

Vaggio

Figline
Valdarno

Loro
Ciuffenna

Anciolina

10 km

5 miles

SR67

SR310

SS70

SR571

SS3bis

E45

SR258

SR208

SS73b

E45

SR71

Arezzo

Arezzo

★ **Chiesa di Santa
Maria della Pieve**   CHURCH
(Corso Italia 7; ⏰ 8am-12.30pm & 3-6.30pm) FREE
This 12th-century church – Arezzo's oldest –
has an exotic Romanesque arcaded facade
adorned with carved columns, each unique-

ly decorated. Above the central doorway are
13th-century carved reliefs called *Cyclo dei
Mesi* representing each month of the year. The
plain interior's highlight – removed for restoration work at the time of writing – is Pietro
Lorenzetti's polyptych *Madonna and Saints*

(1320–24), beneath the semidome of the apse. Below the altar is a 14th-century silver bust reliquary of the city's patron saint, San Donato.

Other treasures include a 13th-century crucifix by Margarito di Arezzo (left of the altar by the door to the sacristy) and a fresco on a column (across from the sacristy door) of Sts Francesco and Domenico by Andrea di Nerio (1331–69).

Piazza Grande PIAZZA
This lopsided and steeply sloping piazza is overlooked at its upper end by the porticoes of the Palazzo delle Logge Vasariane (Piazza Grande), completed in 1573. The churchlike Palazzo della Fraternità dei Laici (☑ 0575 2 46 94; www.fraternitadeilaici.it; Piazza Grande; adult/child €3/free; ⏱ 10am-6pm Thu-Mon, 11.30am-5.30pm Tue & Wed) in the northwest corner was started in 1375 in the Gothic style and finished after the onset of the Renaissance, and now houses a small museum.

Duomo di Arezzo CATHEDRAL
(Cattedrale di SS Donato e Pietro; Piazza del Duomo; ⏱ 7am-12.30pm & 3.30-6.30pm) FREE
Construction started in the 13th century but Arezzo's cathedral wasn't completed until the 15th century. In the northeast corner, next to the vestry door left of the intricately carved main altar, is Piero della Francesca's exquisite fresco, *Mary Magdalene* (c 1459), unfortunately dwarfed somewhat by the 13m-tall cenotaph of Arezzo bishop Guido Tarlati (moved to its current spot in 1783). Also notable are five glazed terracottas by Andrea della Robbia and his studio in the Cappella della Madonna del Conforto.

Museo Diocesano di Arte Sacra MUSEUM
(MuDAS; ☑ 0575 402 72 68; Piazza del Duomo 1; adult/reduced €5/3; ⏱ 10am-6.30pm summer, to 5pm winter) Across from Duomo di Arezzo (p269), inside a stunning 13th-century *palazzo* where the bishop of Arezzo, Guglielmino Ubertini, lived from 1256, is the Diocesan Museum of Sacred Art (also known as MuDAS). The ground floor exhibits 12th- to 16th-century works of sacred art, originally displayed in churches now destroyed or shut. At the top of the grandiose staircase, on the 1st floor, a series of beautifully frescoed rooms showcase the art collections of various resident bishops over the centuries.

Fortezza Medicea FORTRESS
(Viale Bruno Buozzi; ⏱ 10am-6pm Tue-Fri, 10am-12.30pm & 2-7.30pm Sat & Sun) Up high to the southeast of Duomo di Arezzo, across the peaceful gardens of the Passeggio del Prato (⏱ 24hrs), rears the Fortezza Medicea, built between 1538 and 1560 and offering grand views of the town and countryside from its surrounding park.

★ **Museo Archeologico Nazionale 'Gaio Cilnio Mecenate'** MUSEUM
(Gaius Cilnius Maecenas Archeological Museum; ☑ 0575 2 08 82; www.facebook.com/archeologio arezzo; Via Margaritone 10; adult/reduced €6/3, 1st Sunday each month free; ⏱ 8.30am-7.30pm, to 1.30pm Nov) Overlooking the remains of a Roman amphitheatre that once seated up to 10,000 spectators, this museum – named after Gaius Maecenas (68–8 BC), a patron of the arts and trusted advisor to Roman Emperor Augustus – exhibits Etruscan and Roman artefacts in a 14th-century convent building. The highlight is the *Cratere di Euphronios*, a 6th-century-BC Etruscan vase decorated with vivid scenes showing Hercules in battle.

Also of note is an exquisite tiny portrait of a bearded man from the second half of the 3rd century AD, executed in chrysography, a method in which a fine sheet of gold is engraved then encased between two glass panes.

Casa Museo di Ivan Bruschi MUSEUM
(☑ 0575 35 41 26; www.fondazionebruschi.it; Corso Italia 14; adult/reduced €8/6; ⏱ 10am-7pm Tue-Sun summer, 10am-1pm & 2-6pm Tue-Sun winter) Ivan Bruschi, a wealthy antiques dealer, restored 13th-century Palazzo del Capitano del Popolo in the 1960s. After his death, the *palazzo* (mansion) became a house-museum showcasing Bruschi's eclectic personal collection of furniture, art, coins, jewellery, costumes and ceramics dating from the prehistoric, Etruscan, Greek, Roman, medieval and Renaissance periods.

Museo di Casa Vasari MUSEUM
(Vasari House Museum; ☑ 0575 29 90 71; www.musei statialiarezzo.it/museo-casa-vasari; Via XX Settembre 55; adult/reduced €4/2; ⏱ 8.30am-7.30pm Mon & Wed-Sat, to 1.30pm Sun) Built and sumptuously decorated by Arezzo-born painter, architect and art historian Giorgio Vasari (1511–74), this museum is where Vasari lived and worked, and where the original manuscript of his *Lives*

EASTERN TUSCANY AREZZO

ⓘ **CENT SAVER**

A combined ticket (adult/reduced €15/12) covers admission to Cappella Bacci, Museo Archeologico Nazionale and Museo di Casa Vasari.

of the Most Excellent Painters, Sculptors and Architects (1550) – still in print under the title *The Lives of the Artists* – is kept. End on the bijou, Renaissance-style roof garden with flower beds, box hedges and a fountain in its centre. To access the museum, ring the bell.

⚜ Festivals & Events

Fiera Antiquaria di Arezzo — FAIR
(Arezzo Antique Fair; www.fieraantiquaria.org) Tuscany's most famous antiques fair is held in Piazza Grande (p269) on the first Sunday and preceding Saturday of every month.

Giostra del Saracino — CULTURAL
(Joust of the Saracino; www.giostradelsaracinoarezzo.it; ☉ Jun & Sep) This medieval jousting competition, held on Piazza Grande (p269) on the third Saturday of June and first Sunday of September, sees each of the city's four *quartieri* (quarters) put forward a team of 'knights'.

🍴 Eating & Drinking

Dining in Arezzo is a real treat, with a fantastic choice of eateries offering top-notch traditional and modern Tuscan cuisine. In warm weather, the action spills outside.

★ Cremì — GELATO $
(☑ 333 976 63 36; www.facebook.com/gelateriaartigianalecremì; Corso Italia 100; cones & tubs €1.80-5; ☉ 10am-7.30pm Tue-Sun) Follow the locals to this bright, modern *gelateria artigianale* (artisan ice-cream shop) on Arezzo's main *passeggiata* (late afternoon-strolling) strip.

ℹ WINE TALK

The Arezzo region boasts one DOCG (Denominazione di Origine Controllata e Garantita) and five DOC (Denominazione di Origine Controllata) wines: Chianti Colli Arentini DOCG, Vinsanto del Chianti Colli Arentini DOC, Vinsanto del Chianti Colli Arentini Occhio di Pernice DOC, Valdichiana DOC, Cortona DOC and Pietraviva DOC. To investigate these fully, follow the Strada del Vino Terre di Arezzo (www.stradadelvino.arezzo.it) driving itinerary past surrounding vineyards and wineries, or take advantage of local wines on restaurant menus across the region. For information and a map, pop into the Strada del Vino Terre di Arezzo Information Point (☑ 0575 29 40 66; www.stradadelvino.arezzo.it; Via Ricasoli 38-40; ☉ 9.30am-3pm Mon-Fri) in Arezzo.

Enticing seasonal flavours include pear and vanilla, strawberry cheesecake, peanut, and walnut and fig. Or opt for the luscious and wildly popular house speciality – *mousse di nutella* (a creamy, light-as-air chocolate- and hazelnut-flavoured mousse-cum-ice cream).

La Bottega di Gnicche — SANDWICHES $
(☑ 0575 182 29 26; www.bottegadignicche.com; Piazza Grande 4; panini €3.50-7; ☉ 11am-8pm Thu-Tue) Choose from a delectable array of artisan meats and cheeses to stuff in a *panino* at this old-fashioned *alimentari* (grocery store) on Arezzo's main piazza. Check the day's hand-written menu for hot dishes too, such as *ribollita* (traditional Tuscan veg-and-bread soup). Eat inside, between shelves of canary-yellow bags of Martelli pasta, or on the wooden terrace with a sweeping piazza view.

Antica Osteria Agania — TUSCAN $
(☑ 0575 29 53 81; www.agania.com; Via G Mazzini 10; meals €20; ☉ noon-3pm & 6-10.30pm Tue-Sun) Agania has been around for years and her fare is die-hard traditional; the tripe and *grifi con polenta* (lambs' cheeks with polenta) are sensational. Indeed it's timeless, welcoming restaurants like this, potted herbs on the doorstep, that remain the cornerstone of Tuscan dining. Begin with *antipasto misto* (mixed appetisers), then choose your *primo* (first course) from the six pasta types and eight sauces on offer.

Agania's *pici* (fat spaghetti) with wild boar sauce is legendary. Arrive by 1pm to beat the crowd of regulars, or join the crowd waiting outside.

★ Mest Osteria — TUSCAN $$
(☑ 0575 08 08 61; www.osteriamest.it; Via Giorgio Vasari 11; meals €35; ☉ 7-11.45pm Wed, noon-3pm & 7-11.45pm Thu-Sun) For a thoroughly contemporary Tuscan dining experience, snag a table at this edgy *osteria* (tavern) with fantastic gnarled old wooden shutters and dazzling stainless-steel kitchen. The lunch menu features light, smart bites such as 0km club sandwiches, lavishly topped *bruschette*, salmon burgers and creative pasta dishes. Dinner is all about ork with caramelised leeks and mustard-spiced potatoes and other creative mains.

★ Le Chiavi d'Oro — ITALIAN $$
(☑ 0575 40 33 13; www.ristorantelechiavidoro.it; Piazza San Francesco 7; meals €45; ☉ 12.30-2.30pm & 7.30-10.30pm Tue-Sun) Contemporary Italian cooking is on offer at this game-changing restaurant in central Arezzo. Design lovers

LUNCH EN ROUTE TO FLORENCE

Heading east from Florence to Arezzo, vivid pink Osteria dell'Acquolina (☑ 055 97 74 97; www.acquolina.it; Via Setteponti Levante 26, Terranuova Bracciolini; meals €30; ⊙ noon-4pm & 7-11pm Tue-Sun) is the perfect lunch stop, especially in summer when the dining action spills out onto the terracotta-brick terrace with its 360° view of olive trees, vines and hills beyond. Cuisine is Tuscan and there's no written menu – the chef cooks different dishes every day.

The mixed platter of *antipasti* (which includes delicious bread-and-tomato 'soup') is a mainstay, as are imaginative *primi* (green pepper and mint risotto) and the classic T-bone steak, *bistecca alla fiorentina* (€45 per kg). Advance reservations are recommended at weekends when Florentines flock here for a taste of the Tuscan countryside.

To find Acquolina, 34km west of Arezzo, take the Valdarno exit off the A1 and follow signs for 'Terranuova Bracciolini' and 'Arezzo' until you pick up 'Osteria dell'Acquolina' signs.

are wooed by the minimalist interior with part-resin, part-parquet floor and stylish 1960s Danish chairs, while foodies are quickly won over by the simplistic menu that reads something like a shopping list of ingredients. Bream with artichokes, saffron, breadcrumbs and lime anyone?

Il Cantuccio
TUSCAN $$
(☑ 0575 2 68 30; www.il-cantuccio.it; Via Madonna del Prato 76; meals €25; ⊙ noon-3pm & 7-11.30pm Thu-Tue) Tucked away from Arezzo's churches and museums, this much-loved trattoria is cosy in winter when its vaulted, red-brick cellar setting comes into its own. Cuisine is Tuscan, seasonal, and cooked with much love and pride. Begin with fresh artichoke salad in spring, followed by your pick of a dozen-odd mix-and-match pasta types and sauces, from tomato simple to truffle extravagant.

Caffè Vasari
CAFE
(☑ 0575 04 36 97; Piazza Grande 15; ⊙ 7.30am-9pm summer, 8.30am-6pm winter) Bathed in Tuscan sunrays from dawn to dusk, this traditional cafe really is the perfect spot for lapping up the ancient elegance and beauty of Piazza Grande (p269) over a coffee or *aperitivo*. Find it enviably squirrelled beneath the cinematic porticoes of Palazzo delle Logge Vasariane (p269).

ⓘ Information

Tourist Office (☑ 0575 40 19 45; Piazza della Libertà; ⊙ 2-4pm) Find another branch of the **tourist office** (☑ 0575 2 68 50; Piazza della Repubblica 22-23; ⊙ 10.30am-12.30pm) to the right as you exit the train station.

Una Vetrina per Arezzo e Le Sue Vallate (☑ 0575 182 27 70; www.arezzoturismo. it; Emiciclo Giovanni Paolo II, Scale Mobili di Arezzo; ⊙ 9am-6pm Mon-Fri, to 7pm Sat & Sun) Private tourist office on the *scala mobile*

(escalator) leading up to Piazza del Duomo; it has toilet facilities (€0.50).

ⓘ Getting There & Away

BUS

Buses operated by **Siena Mobilità** (www.siena mobilita.it) serve Siena (€7, 1½ hours, seven daily). **Etruria Mobilità** (www.etruriamobilita. it) buses serve Sansepolcro (€4.40, one hour, hourly) and Cortona (€3.50, one hour, frequent). Buy tickets from the **ticket point** (Via Piero della Francesca 1; ⊙ 6.10am-8pm Mon-Sat year-round, 6.30am-noon Sun summer, 8am-12.30pm Sun winter) to the left as you exit the train station; buses leave from the **bus bay** (Via Piero della Francesca) opposite.

CAR & MOTORCYCLE

To drive here from Florence, take the A1; the SS73 heads west to Siena. Parking at the train station costs €2 per hour.

TRAIN

Arezzo is on the Florence–Rome train line, and there are frequent services to Florence (*Regionale* €8.50, one to 1½ hours) and Rome (Intercity €27.50, 2¼ hours; *Regionale* €14.50, 2¾ hours). There are twice-hourly regional trains to Camucia–Cortona (€3.50, 20 minutes).

SANSEPOLCRO

POP 15,900

This hidden gem is a town that truly deserves that description. Dating from the year 1000, Sansepolcro (called 'Borgo' by locals) reached its current size in the 15th century and was walled in the 16th century. Its historic centre is littered with *palazzi* and churches squirrelling away Renaissance works of art or bejewelled with exquisite terracotta Andrea della Robbia medallions. Spend a day wandering from dimly lit church to church, following in

1

ROMBOSTUDIO/SHUTTERSTOCK ©

COME BENEDETTO
RISALDA LO CAPISTERO
CH'ERA ROTTO

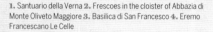

1. Santuario della Verna 2. Frescoes in the cloister of Abbazia di Monte Oliveto Maggiore 3. Basilica di San Francesco 4. Eremo Francescano Le Celle

3

COMPLEXLU/SHUTTERSTOCK ©

Magnificent Monasteries

Consider yourself warned: after visiting these medieval monasteries in Tuscany and nearby Umbria, you may well find yourself entertaining serious thoughts about leaving your fast-paced urban existence to embrace the contemplative life.

Basilica di San Francesco, Assisi

Every year, more than five million pilgrims make their way to the medieval hilltop town of Assisi, St Francis' birthplace in the Umbria region to visit the huge basilica (p284) and monastery that is dedicated to his legacy. Don't miss his ornamental tomb in the basilica crypt.

Santuario della Verna

St Francis of Assisi is said to have received the stigmata at this spectacularly located monastery (p277) on the southeastern edge of the Casentino. Pilgrims flock here to worship in the Cappella delle Stimmate and to admire the Andrea della Robbia artworks in the church.

Sacro Eremo e Monastero di Camaldoli

Deep in the forest of the Casentino, amid a landscape that has changed little for centuries, lie this Benedictine monastery and hermitage (p280). Treasures include paintings by Vasari and Bronzino, as well as one of Andrea della Robbia's greatest terracotta sculptures.

Abbazia di Monte Oliveto Maggiore

The Benedictine monks living in this medieval abbey (p176) southeast of Siena tend the vineyard and olive grove, study in one of Italy's most important medieval libraries and walk through a cloister frescoed by Luca Signorelli and Il Sodoma.

Eremo Francescano Le Celle

A babbling stream, old stone bridge and terraces of olive trees contribute to the fairy-tale feel of this picturesque Franciscan hermitage (p282) just outside Cortona.

❶ GETTING AROUND EASTERN TUSCANY

Bus Buses in this part of the region are few and far between – you can travel from Arezzo to Sansepolcro via Anghiari, or from Arezzo to Cortona via Castiglion Fiorentino, but that's it.

Car & Motorcycle To explore the Casentino and Val di Chiana, you need your own wheels.

Train Arezzo is on the Florence–Rome train line, as is Camucia, a 15-minute shuttle-bus ride from Cortona's historic centre. Regional rail lines link Arezzo with the Casentino, and Sansepolcro with Perugia.

the footsteps of Sansepolcro's greatest son, Renaissance artist Piero della Francesca.

◉ Sights

★ Museo Civico Piero della Francesca   MUSEUM

(✎ 0575 73 22 18; www.museocivicosansepolcro.it; Via Niccolò Aggiunti 65; adult/reduced €10/8.50, with Casa di Piero della Francesca €11/9; ⏱ 10am-1.30pm & 2.30-7pm mid-Jun–mid-Sep, to 6pm mid-Sep–mid-Jun) The town's flagship museum is home to a small but top-notch collection of artworks, including three Piero della Francesca masterpieces: *Resurrection* (1458–74), the *Madonna della Misericordia* (Madonna of Mercy) polyptych (1445–56) and *Saint Julian* (1455–58). Admire also works from the studio of Andrea della Robbia: a polychrome terracotta called *The Nativity and Adoration of the Shepherds* (1485) and a beautiful tondo (circular sculpture) known as the *Virgin and Child with Manetti Coat of Arms* (1503).

Casa di Piero della Francesca   MUSEUM

(✎ 0575 74 04 11; Via Niccolò Aggiunti 71; adult/child €5/3, with Museo Civico €11/9; ⏱ 10am-12.30pm & 2.30-5.30pm) Sansepolcro's most famous son, Renaissance painter Piero della Francesca, lived and worked at this modest 15th-century house in downtown Sansepolcro. Between lengthy visits to Italian courts, he slowly restored the house in a Renaissance style, painting some wonderful frescoes – such as his full-length portrait of a youthful Hercules – on the walls of the 1st floor, which was unfortunately detached in the 1860s. It was exported to the US in 1908, and is exhibited today at the Isabella Stewart Gardner Museum in Boston.

Cattedrale di San Giovanni Evangelista   CATHEDRAL

(Duomo di Sansepolcro; Via Giacomo Matteotti 4; ⏱ 10am-noon & 4-7pm) Sansepolcro's 14th-century *duomo* (cathedral) contains an *Ascension* by Perugino, a *Resurrection* by Raffaellino del Colle and a polyptych by Niccolò di Segna that is thought to have influenced Piero's *Resurrection*. Left of the main altar is the striking *Il Volto Santo* (Sacred Face), a wooden crucifix with a wide-eyed Christ in a blue gown that dates to the 9th century, and – nearby – a beautiful ceramic tabernacle (unfortunately badly chipped) by Andrea della Robbia.

Aboca Museum   MUSEUM

(✎ 0575 73 35 89; www.abocamuseum.it; Via Niccolò Aggiunti 75; adult/reduced €8/4; ⏱ 10am-1pm & 3-7pm Apr-Sep, 10am-1pm & 2.30-6pm Tue-Sun Oct-Mar) When magnificent art and churches tire, take a break in this medicinal plant museum inside 18th-century Palazzo Bourbon del Monte. Exhibits provide a fascinating insight into our relationship with herbs from prehistoric times to the present, with rooms dedicated to mortars, weighing scales, glassware and antique books chronicling ancient remedies. In the Poison Cellar deadly ingredients were skillfully crafted into medicinal remedies.

★✴ Festivals & Events

Palio della Balestra   CULTURAL

(www.balestrierisansepolcro.it; ⏱ 2nd Sun Sep) Crossbow tournament between local archers and rivals from nearby Gubbio, with contestants and onlookers in medieval costumes. It usually takes place on Piazza Torre di Berta.

✖ Eating

Sansepolcro has some delightful places to dine. Cuisine is staunchly Tuscan and faithful to its roots – no deviating from Nonna's cookbook in this traditional small town. Foodie street Via Lucca Pacioli, peppered with eating options, is a good starting point.

★ Il Giardino di Piero   TUSCAN $$

(✎ 0575 73 31 19; www.osteriailgiardinodipiero.it; Via Niccolò Aggiunti 98b; meals €30; ⏱ 12.30-2pm & 7.30-10pm Tue-Sun; 🕿 🍴) Be it the locally bred *cinta senese* pork, Chianina beef, *pecorino* cheese or fresh pasta, everything is 100% organic at this enticing restaurant. Summertime tables sit on a shaded terrace strung with fairy lights and cuisine is modern Tuscan. Think cinnamon-spiced Chianina tripe, beef *tagliata* (thin slices) with chili pepper and mint, and a mountain of vegetarian dishes.

★ **Ristorante Da Ventura**   TUSCAN **$$**
(🖉 0575 74 25 60; www.albergodaventura.it; Via
Niccolò Aggiunti 30; meals €30; ⊗12.30-2.15pm &
7.30-9.45pm Tue-Sat, 12.30-2.15pm Sun) This old-
world eatery is a culinary joy. Trolleys lad-
en with feisty joints of pork, beef stewed in
chianti classico and roasted veal shank are
pushed from table to table, bow-tied waiters
intent on piling plates high. The veal fillet
topped with wafer-thin slices of *lardo di col-
onnata* (cured pork fat) and the veal carpac-
cio with black truffle shavings are glorious.

Ristorante Fiorentino   ITALIAN **$$**
(🖉 0575 74 20 33; www.ristorantefiorentino.it; Via
Luca Pacioli 60; meals €35; ⊗noon-3pm & 7.30-
10.30pm Thu-Tue) An iconic address, this grandiose dining room dates to 1807. Sweep up the
marble staircase and into a historical world
of glass chandeliers, Renaissance wooden
coffered ceiling and original fireplace. Food is
traditional with an occasional modern twist.

Drinking & Nightlife

Cafe life is *bella* in this handsome, old-world
town where summertime pavement terrace
cafes bask in the shade of centuries-old
palazzi and public buildings adorned with
15th-century decorative medallions. Several
cafes and pubs line key *passeggiata* (late-
afternoon stroll) drag, Via XX Settembre.

Enoteca Guidi   WINE BAR
(🖉 0575 74 19 07; www.locandaguidi.it; Via Luca Pacioli 44-46; meals €20; ⊗11am-midnight Thu-Tue)

Owner Saverio presides over the teensy *enoteca* (wine bar) and rear dining space where
simple meals are served. Enjoy a local artisan
beer or *vino* (everything from local drops to
fashionable Super Tuscans). Should you be
unable to drag yourself away at the end of
the night, the bar has a handful of simple
rooms upstairs (single €45, double €90).

Caffè degli Appennini   BAR
(🖉 0575 74 17 55; Via XX Settembre 48; ⊗5pm-
1am Sun-Thu, to 2am Fri & Sat; 🖥) This young,
hybrid gastropub-pizzeria buzzes with
fun-loving locals at weekends who pile into
the cavernous space to guzzle decent beer
and every imaginable type of pizza (€6.50
to €9), cooked *forno à legna* (in a traditional wood-fired oven). In warm weather, the
drinking action spills outside onto the attractive, wood-decking pavement terrace on
the main pedestrian drag.

ⓘ Information

Tourist office (🖉 0575 74 05 36; www.valti
berinaintoscana.it; Via Giacomo Matteotti
8; ⊗9.30am-1pm & 2.30-6.30pm summer,
shorter hours winter; 🖥)

ⓘ Getting There & Away

Etruria Mobilità (www.etruriamobilita.it) operates regular buses to/from Arezzo (€4.40, one
hour), stopping in Anghiari (€1.60, 10 minutes)
en route. **Sulga** (www.sulga.it) operates a daily
service to Rome and Leonardo da Vinci Airport
(€25, 3½ to 4¼ hours); check schedules and

EASTERN TUSCANY SANSEPOLCRO

PIERO DELLA FRANCESCA

Though many details about his life are hazy, it is believed that the great Renaissance
painter Piero della Francesca was born around 1420 in Sansepolcro and died in 1492.
Trained as a painter from the age of 15, his distinctive use of perspective, mastery of light
and skilful synthesis of form and colour set him apart from his artistic contemporaries,
and the serene grace of his figures remains unsurpassed to this day. In his book *The
Lives of the Artists,* Piero's fellow Tuscan Giorgio Vasari called him the 'best geometri-
cian of his time' and lamented the fact that so few of his works were preserved for posterity, leading to him being 'robbed of the honour that [was] due to his labours'.

Piero's most famous works are the *Legend of the True Cross* in Arezzo's Cappella
Bacci (p265), his *Resurrection* in Sansepolcro's Museo Civico and his panel featuring
Federico da Montefeltro and Battista Sforza, the Duke and Duchess of Urbino in Florence's Uffizi (p68). But he is perhaps most fondly remembered for his luminous *Madonna del Parto* showcased in Museo Madonna del Parto (Pregnant Madonna Museum;
🖉 0575 7 07 13; www.madonnadelparto.it; Via della Reglia 1, Monterchi; adult/reduced €6.50/5;
⊗9am-1pm & 2-7pm summer, to 5pm Wed-Mon winter) in Monterchi, a village in the remote
Tiber Valley between Sansepolcro (15km north) and Arezzo (28km west). During the
time Piero lived in Sansepolcro, the painter had a home studio at Via Niccolò Aggiunti 71,
today the small Casa di Piero della Francesca museum.

For a complete itinerary, pick up the brochure Terre di Piero at tourist offices or
consult it online at http://terredipiero.it.

buy tickets online. Buses use the bus station off Via G Marconi, near Porta Fiorentina.

VALLE DEL CASENTINO

The northeastern corner of Tuscany is home to spectacular mountains, historic monasteries and hamlets where traditional customs and cuisine are proudly maintained. The Casentino (www.casentino.net) is a handy resource, with plenty of information on mountain biking and hiking.

Poppi

POP 6160

Seeming to float in the clouds above the Arno plain, Poppi Alta (the historic upper section of the town) is crowned by the commanding presence of the Castello dei Conti Guidi. The kiosk in the piazza outside the castle is the social hub during the summer months; at other times locals tend to socialise in Ponte a Poppi (the lower town).

⊙ Sights

Castello dei Conti Guidi   CASTLE
(📋0575 52 05 16; www.buonconte.com; Piazza della Repubblica 1; adult/reduced €6/4; ⊙10am-6pm summer, to 5pm Thu-Sun winter) Castello dei Conti Guidi was built in the 13th century by Count Simone da Battifolle, head of the Guidi family. Inside, there's a fairy-tale courtyard, a handsome staircase, a library

full of medieval manuscripts and a chapel with frescoes by Taddeo Gaddi. The scene of *Herod's Feast* shows Salome apparently clicking her fingers as she dances, accompanied by a lute player, while John the Baptist's headless corpse lies slumped in the corner.

✖ Eating

Dining in this rural part of Tuscany is traditional and local. There are a couple of dining options in Poppi Alta – or head out of town for a meal to remember in a timeless, family-run village inn.

Osteria Il Porto   TUSCAN $
(📋0575 52 92 33; www.osteriailporto.it; Via Roma 226; meals €20; ⊙7-11.30pm Mon-Fri, 12.30-3pm & 7-11.30pm Sat & Sun; 🛜🚻) Follow the locals to this wildly popular eatery, reminiscent of a German beer garden with its large summer garden strewn with bench-clad tables and a relaxed vibe. Cuisine is staunchly Tuscan, with lots of regional dishes: the *tortelli di patate* (potato-filled pasta cushions) made with local red Cetica potatoes, the wild boar stew and herb-stuffed rabbit are all hearty and delicious.

Craft beer is the thing to drink here. In a former life, the grandiose red-brick building with racing-green shutters was Poppi's fluvial harbour building; timber from the Casentino forests was transported from here, along the Arno River, to Florence and Pisa.

La Vite   TUSCAN $$
(📋0575 56 09 62; www.ristorantelavite.net; Piazza della Repubblica, Soci; meals €25; ⊙noon-2.30pm

---

CUCINA TIPICA CASENTINESE

Cuisine in this naturally rich part of Tuscany has its roots firmly ensnared in tradition and seasonal fruits of the rural land. Eating options are wholly traditional, with just a tiny pinch of modern Tuscan thrown in the cooking pot for good measure.

On the SP67, 9km north of Poppi towards Camaldoli, countryside hotel **I Tre Baroni** (📋0575 55 62 04; www.itrebaroni.it; Via di Camaldoli 52, Moggiona; s/d/tr/q €65/85/100/140; ⊙Easter-Oct; 🅿@🛜🚻) cooks up excellent gastronomic dining options (menus from €40) on a romantic summer terrace with a sweeping valley view.

Or track down the utterly fantastic, 100% homemade *cucina tipica Casentinese* (typical Casentino cuisine) at gem of a family-run village bistro **Il Cedro** (📋0575 55 60 80; www.ristoranteilcedro.com; Via di Camaldoli 20, Moggiona; meals €25; ⊙12.30-2pm Tue-Sun), squirrelled away in the tiny hamlet of Moggiona, 1km further north along the same sinuous road to Camaldoli. There is no menu – rather, seasonal, traditional dishes of the day are chalked on the board. Think the Casentino's signature *tortelli di patate* (potato-filled pasta cushions) or a hearty plate of *pappardelle* pasta laced with a hare or goat *ragù* (meat and tomato sauce), followed by local Chianina beef or autumnal game with porcini mushrooms from the nearby forest perhaps. Its *capriolo* (roe deer venison) cooked in white wine, and *cianghiale in umido* (wild boar, slowly braised in red wine with juniper berries and red peppers), are local legends.

TASTY PRATOVECCHIO

The town itself is unremarkable, but Pratovecchio does have a couple of tasty addresses well worth the 8km drive from Poppi.

La Tana degli Orsi (☑ 0575 58 33 77; Via Roma 1, Pratovecchio; meals €40; ⊘ 7.30pm-1am Thu-Tue, to 2am Fri & Sat) In the evening the dozen tables at La Tana degli Orsi (The Lair of the Bear), an unusual chalet-style building, are hotly contested, making advance reservations essential. Decor hovers between classy and kitsch, but cuisine is top quality Tuscan with many traditional Casentino dishes created here with local produce. An outstanding wine list lures oenophiles.

Toscana Twist (☑ 0575 58 21 20; Via della Libertà 3, Pratovecchio; meals €30; ⊘ 6am-7.30pm Tue-Thu, to 10pm Fri, to 9pm Sat) Toscana Twist is a rare and wonderful breed in rural Tuscany. This exceptionally contemporary address near the train station is a pedigree hybrid. Its day begins with breakfast – delicious cakes, cookies and pastries – and closes with dinner on Friday, and an *aperitivo* banquet (from 6.30pm) on Saturday. Both evenings set the place buzzing with savvy hobnobbing locals from surrounding villages.

& 6.30-10.30pm Wed-Mon, to 11pm Sat) This easy dine in Soci, 5km east of Poppi, is run by young dynamic sommelier Barbara and chef Cesare. It's a real favourite with locals – and travellers – hungry for a good-value feast of top-quality Tuscan food in the company of great wine. Under no circumstances skimp on *dolci* (dessert) – all homemade and fabulous. Kudos for the pretty summertime patio garden.

ⓘ Information

Tourist office (☑ 0575 52 05 11; www.casentino.ar.it; Via Roma 203, Ponte a Poppi; ⊘ 8am-6pm Mon-Fri)

ⓘ Getting There & Away

Frequent trains run by **Trasporto Ferroviario Toscano** (TFT; www.trasportoferroviariotoscano.it) link Poppi with Arezzo (€4, one hour), Bibbiena (€1.50, 10 minutes) and Stia (€1.50, 15 minutes).

Parco Nazionale delle Foreste Casentinesi, Monte Falterona e Campigna

One of three national parks in Tuscany, the Parco Nazionale delle Foreste Casentinesi, Monte Falterona and Campigna (Casentino Forests, Mount Falterona and Campigna National Park; www.parcoforestecasentinesi.it/en) straddles the Tuscany–Emilia-Romagna border and protects scenic stretches of the Apennines and Italy's largest forest and woodlands.

One of the highest peaks, Monte Falterona (1654m), marks the source of the Arno. The park is home to a rich assortment of wildlife, including nearly 100 bird species. Nine self-guided nature trails criss-cross the park:

the most popular is the 4.5km uphill hike (4½ hours return) from San Benedetto in Alpe to the spectacular Acquacheta Waterfall, made famous by Dante's *Divine Comedy*.

The major settlement in the park is Badia Pratáglia, a small village in the Alpe di Serra mountain range, near the border with Emilia-Romagna.

⊙ Sights

★ **Santuario della Verna** MONASTERY
(☑ 0575 53 41; www.laverna.it; Via del Santuario 45, Chiusi della Verna; ⊘ Sanctuary 6.30am-10pm summer, to 7.30pm winter, Cappella delle Stimmate 8am-7pm summer, to 5pm winter, Museo della Verna daily Jul & Aug, 10am-noon & 1-4pm Sat & Sun) FREE This remote Franciscan monastic complex is where St Francis of Assisi is said to have received the stigmata and is a major pilgrimage destination. The Corridoio delle Stimmate, decorated with modern frescoes recounting St Francis' life, leads to the Cappella delle Stimmate, built in 1263 on the spot where the saint supposedly received the stigmata two years before his death, aged 44. The monumental *Crucifixion* by Andrea della Robbia here is magnificent.

Across from the door to the chapel, steps lead outside to the Precipicio, the precipice – literally – from which the devil supposedly tried to hurl Francis down onto the rocks below. The narrow path is not for the vertiginously challenged.

The monastery basilica houses remarkably fine polychrome glazed ceramics by Andrea della Robbia and his studio: a *Madonna and Child Enthroned between Saints* to your right as you enter the church; a *Nativity* on the right before the altar; an

ROAD TRIP > GO SLOW IN THE VALLE DEL CASENTINO

Time stands still in the remote Valle del Casentino (Casentino Valley). Ancient Etruscan strongholds, Romanesque churches and isolated farmsteads have scarcely changed over the centuries, while the pace of local life – slow – follows the hypnotic beat of the seasons and the land. When the romantic call of the Tuscan wild beckons, this road trip – easily done in a day from Florence – is the one to take.

① Castello di Romena

From Florence head southeast (direction Firenze Sud) and drive alongside the Arno river through Pontassieve and over the **Passo della Consuma** (SS70), a scenic mountain pass over this Tuscan section of the Apennine Mountains (follow the signs for Consuma and Bibbiena). The road eventually brings you to the turn-off to the Castello di Romena, on the left-hand side of the road. Wander around

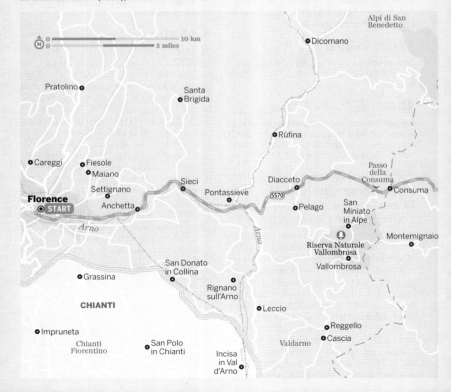

Great for... Outdoors, History & Culture

Best Time to Go Spring, summer or early autumn

this ruined 11th-century castle and let your imagination run riot Dantesque-style. Yes, Dante was a regular visitor from Florence.

2 Pieve di Romena

Walk or drive the 1.5km downhill to the Pieve di Romena, an exquisite Romanesque church, built in the mid-12th century. Inside capitals are sculpted with primitive carvings of human and animal figures. To gain entry, try knocking on the door of the adjoining building.

3 Stia

Follow road signs to Stia, the town where the Arno River meets its first tributary, the Staggia. The town was for many years the centre of the local wool industry and is now home to the **Museo dell'Arte della Lana – Lanificio di Stia** (☑ 0575 58 22 16; www.museodellalana.it; Via Sartori 2; adult/reduced €5/3; ☉10am-1pm & 4-7pm Tue-Sun Aug, shorter hours rest of yr), an impressive wool museum that occupies a handsome, centuries-old mill. The mill was the Casentino Valley's major employer from the 19th Century until 2000 when it closed down. Near the museum's entrance is Tessilnova, a shop selling examples of the brightly coloured and 'nubby' woollen blankets and clothing that the Casentino is famous for, as well as other top-quality, Italian-made woollen clothing.

4 Santuario di Santa Maria delle Grazie

Drive 4km northwest along the P556 (towards Fornace and Londa) to the Santuario di Santa Maria delle Grazie, a beautiful Renaissance church dating from 1432 and built, so local lore says, to commemorate the apparition of the Virgin Mary to a local peasant called Giovanna. If the church is not open, try to find a local who might be able to let you inside to admire its treasure chest of sacred art: a fresco by Ghirlandaio and two colourful ceramic lunettes by Benedetto Buglioni. The cloister adjoining the church is all that remains of a neighbouring monastery.

5 Poppi

Backtracking to Stia, proceed south through Pratovecchio and continue on to the regional centre of **Poppi** (p276), where you can visit the magnificent 13th-century **Castello dei Conti Guidi** (p276) and wander the picturesque streets of the upper town before heading to your accommodation for the night.

OFF THE BEATEN TRACK

AT HOME WITH MICHELANGELO

Art lovers can have a field day in the remote Tuscan outback of Casentino. *David*'s creator was born in the lost village of Caprese (today called Caprese Michelangelo, population 1500), 17km south of Chiusi della Verna, and the small stone house where the artist grew up can be visited. Right at the top of the hilltop village, next to Caprese's medieval castle, the Museo Michelangeliolesco (☑ 0575 79 37 76; Via Capoluogo 1, Caprese Michelangelo; adult/reduced €4/3; ⊘ 9.30am-7.30pm Aug, 10am-7pm Mon-Fri, 9.30am-7.30pm Sat & Sun Jun, Jul & Sep, shorter hours winter) employs a series of plaster casts to tell the tale of Michelangelo's childhood roamings in the countryside here and his subsequent artistic career.

So deeply was the artist inspired by the landscape here that he used the silhouette of Mt Penna, as seen from Chiusi della Verna, as the backdrop for the *Tondo Doni* in Florence's Uffizi (p68) and the *Creation of Adam* fresco in Rome's Sistine Chapel. Driving downhill from the Santuario della Verna towards Chiusi della Verna village, look for a brown sign on the left indicating 'La Roccia di Adamia'. Adam's Rock is just that – the rock that Michelangelo painted, and on which he set a reclining Adam holding out his left arm, fingers almost touching, towards a bearded God.

Adoration in the small chapel to the right of the altar; saints on either side of the altar; a huge *Ascension* (c 1480) in the chapel to the left of the altar; and a beautiful *Annunciation* in the second chapel to the left.

Don't miss the Cappella delle Reliquie, a small chapel on the right side of the basilica, safeguarding the habit that Francis wore when he recieved the stigmata in 1224. Other relics include the saint's girdle, a blood-stained cloth used to clean his stigmatic wounds, a whip used by Francis as an instrument of penance, and the stick he walked with when roaming the mountains. In the interesting Museo della Verna, monastic life is evoked by artefacts such as ancient Bibles and song books, manuscripts, sacred art, the re-creation of an old pharmacy and a huge cauldron above the old kitchen chimney and so on.

By car, follow signs just outside the hamlet of Chiusi della Verna for the monastery complex or take the way of the pilgrims along the taxing 30-minute uphill footpath from Chiusi della Verna – it is 23km east of Bibbiena, accessed via the SP208. There is a pilgrim guesthouse (€60 per person) with a refectory (set breakfast/lunch/dinner €5/16.50/16.50), and a cafe-bar selling monk-made products (chocolate, honey, liqueur, jams, conserved fruit) on site. Parking is €1/7 per hour/day.

Sacro Eremo e
Monastero di Camaldoli   MONASTERY
(Camaldoli Hermitage & Monastery; ☑ 0575 55 60 44, 0575 55 60 21; www.camaldoli.it; Località Camaldoli 14, Camaldoli; ⊘ hermitage 6-11am & 3-6pm, monastery 8am-1pm & 3.30-6pm, pharmacy 9am-12.30pm & 2-6pm) FREE Hidden in the dense forest of the national park are the Benedictine hermitage and monastery of Camaldoli, founded between 1024 and 1025 by St Romualdo and now home to a community of over 20 monks. From Poppi, follow Via Camaldoli (SR67) up through the forest; the *eremo* (hermitage), 6km uphill to the left where the road splits, and *monastero* (monastery), 2km straight downhill, are both clearly signposted.

At the remote hermitage, home to nine monks today, you can visit the baroque Chiesa del Sacro Eremo (1658), with a Bronzino altarpiece of the *Crucifixion and Four Saints*, and the Cappella di San Antonio Abate, left of the main entrance, with an exquisite ceramic altarpiece depicting the *Virgin, Child and Saints* by Andrea della Robbia. In the courtyard, opposite the church, is the 11th-century Cella di San Romualdo Abate (cell) where St Romualdo lived, worked and prayed. Before leaving the hermitage complex, admire the Porta Speciosa, a black bronze set of doors to the right of the main entrance chillingly adorned with a skull, headstone, cranium of a billy goat and a tree, all representing death; an owl represents a solitary monk praying at night, and the bell strung from the tree is a symbol of life. The unusual artwork is a contemporary piece by Claudio Parmiggiani (b 1943).

Continuing to the monastery, a 3km drive away through thick forest, admire a trio of paintings by Vasari in the Chiesa dei Monastero di Camaldoli (1501–24), restored in 1772. Don't miss the 15th-century Antica Farmacia (1450), an old-world pharmacy with beautiful wood-pannelled cabinets stocked with soap, perfumes, cosmetics and ancient natural remedies made by the 20 resident monks. A small museum displays wooden hand presses, stone milling machines, earthenware oil jars, copper alembics and other tools used by the monks since the 15th century. Don't miss the spooky 17th-century mirror, to the right of the doorway as you exit, in which you can see a reflection of your true self (aka a skeleton).

ℹ Information

Badia Pratáglia Visitor Centre (✆ 0575 55 94 77; www.parcoforestecasentinesi.it; Via Nazionale 14a, Badia Pratáglia; ⊙ 9am-12.30pm & 3.30-6pm summer, 9am-12.30pm Sat & Sun winter)

National Park Tourist Office (✆ 0575 5 03 01; Via G Brocchi 7, Pratovecchio; ⊙ 8am-1pm & 3-5pm Mon-Thu, 8am-1pm Fri)

ℹ Getting There & Away

Your own vehicle is essential for exploring the thickly forested and mountainous national park. Main access roads are the narrow and sinuous SR71 linking Bibbiena with Badia Pratáglia, and the hairpin-laced SP208 diving east from Bibbiena to Chiusi della Verna.

VAL DI CHIANA

This wide green valley stretches south from Arezzo into the province of Siena in central Tuscany, and is punctuated by gently rolling hills crowned with medieval villages. Its prized agricultural land is rich in orchards and olive groves, but it is primarily known as the home of Tuscany's famed Chianina cows, one of the oldest breeds of cattle in the world and the essential ingredient in Tuscany's signature dish, *bistecca alla fiorentina*.

If you're in the valley on the third Sunday in June, don't miss the Palio dei Rioni (www.facebook.com/PaliodeiRioniCodroipo) that sees jockeys on horseback race around Piazza Garibaldi in Castiglion Fiorentino – like Siena's *palio* on a smaller scale.

Castiglion Fiorentino

POP 13,250

Driving from Arezzo to Cortona, take a break in this picturesque walled town crowned with the impressively restored Cassero, a bulky medieval fortress with panoramic views of the Val di Chiana from both its grassy green grounds and atop its half-ruined tower, the Torre del Cassero (✆ 0575 65 94 57; www.musei castiglionfiorentino.it; Via del Tribunale 8; ⊙ 10am-

12.30pm & 3.30-6pm Fri-Sun) FREE. Next door, the Museo Civico Archeologico (✆ 0575 65 94 57; www.museicastiglionfiorentino.it; Via del Tribunale 8; ⊙ 10am-12.30pm & 3.30-6pm Fri-Sun) FREE is a well-put-together archaeological museum incorporating medieval prison cells and the subterranean remains of a 6th-century-BC Etruscan temple and an Etruscan house from the late 4th century BC.

The lower part of Castiglion Fiorentino's fortress plays sentry to a small collection of art including Taddeo Gaddi's *Virgin and Child* in the Pinacoteca Comunale (✆ 0575 65 94 57; www.museicastiglionfiorentino.it; Via del Cassero 6; ⊙ 10am-12.30pm & 3.30-6pm Fri & Sat) FREE.

ℹ Information

Find the small **tourist office** (✆ 0575 65 82 78; www.prolococastiglionfiorentino.it; Piazza Risorgimento 19; ⊙ 10am-noon Tue-Sun, 4-6pm Wed & Fri) at the bottom of the hill, by Porta Fiorentina.

ℹ Getting There & Away

Arriving by car, a Zona a Traffico Limitato (ZTL; Limited Traffic Zone) applies in the streets immediately surrounding the Torre del Cassero, but there is ample free parking on Piazza Garibaldi.

Cortona

POP 22,450

Rooms with a view are the rule rather than the exception in this spectacularly sited hilltop town. In the late 14th century Fra' Angelico lived and worked here, and fellow artists

---

LOCAL KNOWLEDGE

THE PERFECT STEAK

Ask any local where to sink your teeth into the perfect *bistecca alla fiorentina*, aka Tuscany's iconic T-bone steak, and the answer is always Ristorante Da Muzzicone (✆ 348 935 66 16, 0575 65 84 03; Piazza San Francesco 7; meals €30; ⊙ 12.15-2.15pm & 7.30-9.30pm). The restaurant is famed for its succulent, cooked-to-perfection beef (€45 per kg) grilled above a wood fire.

If T-bone traditionally cut from the Val di Chiana's famed Chianina cow does not appeal, there are grilled beef fillets in green pepper sauce or balsamic vinegar to tempt. In summer, tables spill onto the pretty square outside. Advance reservations essential.

EASTERN TUSCANY CASTIGLION FIORENTINO

Luca Signorelli and Pietro da Cortona were both born within the walls – all three are represented in the Museo Diocesano's small but sensational collection. Large chunks of *Under the Tuscan Sun,* the soap-in-the-sun film of the book by Frances Mayes, were shot here.

◉ Sights

★ Museo Diocesano
MUSEUM

(Piazza del Duomo 1; adult/reduced €5/3; ⊙10am-7pm Apr-Oct, to 5pm Tue-Sun Nov-Mar) Little is left of the original Romanesque character of Cortona's cathedral (⊙variable), rebuilt several times in a less-than-felicitous fashion. Fortunately, its wonderful artworks have been saved and displayed in this museum. Highlights include a moving *Crucifixion (*1320) by Pietro Lorenzetti and two beautiful works by Fra' Angelico: *Annunciation* (1436) and *Madonna with Child and Saints* (1436–37).

★ Museo dell'Accademia Etrusca e della Città di Cortona
MUSEUM

(MAEC; www.cortonamaec.org; Piazza Signorelli 9; adult/reduced €10/7; ⊙10am-7pm Apr-Oct, to 5pm Tue-Sun Nov-Mar) In the 13th-century Palazzo Casali, this fascinating museum displays substantial local Etruscan and Roman finds, Renaissance globes, 18th-century decorative arts and contemporary paintings. The Etruscan collection is the highlight, particularly those objects excavated from the tombs at Sodo, just outside town. The *palazzo*'s plain facade was added in the 17th century.

Basilica di Santa Margherita
CHURCH

(Piazza Santa Margherita; ⊙8am-noon & 3-7pm summer, 9am-noon & 3-6pm winter) For an effective cardiovascular workout, hike up to this largely 19th-century church through Cortona's warren of steep cobbled lanes. Inside, the remains of St Margaret, patron saint of Cortona, lie in a 14th-century glass-sided tomb above the altar.

Fortezza del Girifalco
LANDMARK

(⊠0575 164 53 07; www.fortezzadelgirifalco.it; Via di Fortezza; adult/reduced €5/3; ⊙10am-8pm mid-Jun–Aug, to 7pm mid-Apr–mid-Jun & Sep, to 6pm Oct, Nov & Mar–mid-Apr, 10am-6pm Sat & Sun Dec-Feb) Lap up the stupendous view over the Val di Chiana to Lago Trasimeno in Umbria from the remains of this Medici fortress, atop the highest point in town – count on a good 15 minutes for the steep hike up. Check the website for its fabulous season of events including yoga workshops, falconry shows, theatre performances, collective picnics, dinner concerts, DJ sets and dancing after dark.

Eremo Francescano Le Celle
MONASTERY

(⊠0575 60 33 62; Strada dei Cappuccini 1; ⊙7am-7pm) This Franciscan hermitage hides in dense woodland 3km north of Cortona. Its buildings sit next to a picturesque stream with an 18th-century stone bridge, and the only sounds to disturb the tranquil atmosphere are the bells that call the resident friars to vespers and mass in the cave-like Chiesa Cella di San Francesco.

★ Festivals & Events

Giostra dell'Archidado
CULTURAL

(www.giostraarchidado.com; ⊙May or Jun) A full week of medieval merriment (the date varies to coincide with Ascension Day) culminates in a crossbow competition.

Cortona on the Move
ART

(www.cortonaonthemove.com) International festival of contemporary photography, held each year from mid-July to late September.

Cortonantiquaria
FAIR

(⊠0575 63 06 10; www.cortonantiquaria.it; Piazza G Franciolini; ⊙late Aug or early Sep) Cortona's well-known antique furniture fair, an annual event since 1963, fills the period rooms of 18th-century Palazzo Vagnotti.

✕ Eating

Pasticceria Banchelli
PASTRIES $

(⊠0575 60 10 52; Via Nazionale 11; cakes & pastries from €1.50; ⊙7.30am-8pm Tue-Sun) For sinful cakes with coffee, this cake shop and cafe has been the place to go since 1930. Pay at the counter and grab a street table outside in the morning sun.

★ Beerbone Artburger
BURGERS $

(⊠0575 60 17 90; www.facebook.com/cortonaburger; Via Nazionale 55; burgers €9-14; ⊙11am-midnight Mon & Thu-Sun, 9am-5pm & 6pm-midnight Wed; ⊕) The feisty burgers cooked up at this contemporary restaurant on Cortona's main pedestrian drag are no ordinary burgers. Select your Tuscan meat – Chianina beef or *cinta senese* pork, smoked over apple wood – and choose between lavish toppings: truffles with truffle cream, fried egg and lettuce perhaps, or *pecorino* cheese with homemade syrah mayonnaise. Craft beer completes the tasty ensemble.

La Fett'unta
TUSCAN $

(⊠0575 63 05 82; www.winebarcortona.com; Via Giuseppe Maffei 3; meals €15; ⊙12.30-2.30pm & 5.30-10pm Thu-Tue; ⊕) Hanging baskets of flowers mark the entrance to this tiny, deli-style *fi-*

Cortona

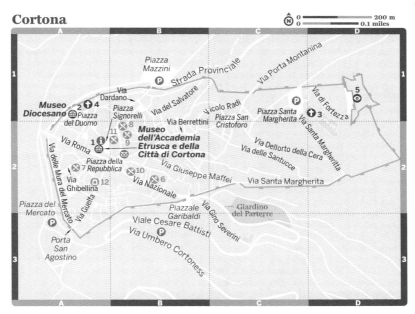

Cortona

aschetteria (simple wine bar) known for its first-class budget dining. Inside, tempting cold cuts and pre-prepared dishes sit beneath glass, begging to be gobbled up. Service is overwhelmingly friendly, there's a kids' corner, and traditional Tuscan cuisine – fresh from big sister Osteria del Teatro (☑0575 63 05 56; www.osteria-del-teatro.it; Via Giuseppe Maffei 2; meals €35; ⊙12.30-2.30pm & 7.30-9.30pm Thu-Tue) across the street – is spot on.

★La Bucaccia   TUSCAN $$
(☑0575 60 60 39; www.labucaccia.it; Via Ghibellina 17; meals €35; ⊙12.45-3pm & 7-10.30pm Tue-Sun) Cortona's finest address, this gourmet gem resides in the medieval stable of a Renaissance *palazzo*. Cuisine is Tuscan and Cortonese – much meat and handmade pasta

(chestnut ravioli!) – and the cheese course is superb, thanks to owner Romano Magi who ripens his own. Dedicated gourmets won't be able to resist the six *pecorino* types with fruit sauces, homemade salsas and honeys. Reservations essential.

Cooking classes and cheese-making workshops are offered too.

Taverna Pane e Vino   TUSCAN $$
(☑0575 63 10 10; www.pane-vino.it; Piazza Signorelli 27; meals €25; ⊙noon-11pm Tue-Sat) Simple seasonal dishes are the trademark of this vaulted cellar, a hot spot with local bon vivants who come to indulge in their pick of Tuscan and Italian wines in the company of *bruschette*, terracotta dishes of oven-baked cheese and bacon, and Tuscan soups and meats.

WORTH A TRIP

ASSISI

Thanks to St Francis, who was born here in 1182, the medieval hilltop town of Assisi (population 28,130) in the neighbouring region of Umbria is a major destination for millions of pilgrims. Its major drawcard is the Basilica di San Francesco (www.sanfrancescoassisi.org; Piazza di San Francesco; ⊙ upper church 8.30am-6.50pm, lower church & tomb 6am-6.50pm) FREE, which comprises two churches filled with magnificent Renaissance art. The Basilica Superiore (Upper Church) was built between 1230 and 1253 in the Italian Gothic style and features a superb fresco cycle by Giotto. Downstairs, in the dimly lit Basilica Inferiore (Lower Church), there's a series of colourful frescoes by Simone Martini, Cimabue and Pietro Lorenzetti. Stairs lead down to the crypt where the tomb of St Francis lies.

The basilica has its own information office (🖉 075 819 00 84; www.sanfrancescoassisi.org; Piazza di San Francesco 2; ⊙ 9am-5.30pm Mon-Sat), opposite the entrance to the lower church, where you pick up an audio guide in 10 languages (€4) or groups of 10 or more can schedule an hour-long tour in English or Italian, led by a resident Franciscan friar. To avoid disappointment at busy times, either call or email ahead.

Assisi is a popular overnight destination, so book ahead during peak times: Easter, August, September and the Feast of St Francis (4 October). Contact the tourist office (🖉 075 813 86 80; www.visit-assisi.it; Piazza del Comune 22; ⊙ 9am-6pm Mon-Fri, to 7pm Sat, to 6pm Sun, shorter hrs winter) for accommodation lists. For lunch, consider seasonal Umbrian cuisine peppered with Med-Asian touches at Osteria La Piazzetta dell'Erba (🖉 075 81 53 52; www.osterialapiazzetta.it; Via San Gabriele dell'Addolorata 15a; meals €30-35; ⊙ 12.30-2.30pm & 7.30-10.30pm Tue-Sun; 🛜) or feast on local cheese and *salumi* (cured meat) platters accompanied by painstakingly curated local wines at the rustic but excellent Bibenda Assisi (🖉 339 861 51 52; www.bibendaassisi.it; Vicolo Nepis 9; wines by the glass €3.50-10; ⊙ 11.30am-11pm Wed-Mon; 🛜).

Regular trains connect Assisi with Arezzo (€8.60, 1½ hours) and Florence (€15.70, 2½ hours). A Zona a Traffico Limitato (ZTL; Limited Traffic Zone) applies in the historic centre, but there are plenty of paid car parks just outside the walls.

🛍 Shopping

★ Falegnameria Rossi   ARTS & CRAFTS
(🖉 0575 6 27 45; www.facebook.com/giancarlo rossiwoodworker; Via Guelfa 28; ⊙ variable) An exquisitely carved shop sign depicting a horse hangs above the entrance to the workshop of Giancarlo Rossi, a third-generation carpenter and cabinetmaker who crafts beautiful objects for the home – both functional and decorative – from wood in the family workshop, established by grandfather Armando in the 1920s. Find a small showroom, open upon request, around the corner at Via Roma 2.

ℹ Information

Tourist office (🖉 0575 63 72 21; www.comune dicortona.it; Piazza Signorelli 9; ⊙ 9am-1pm & 2-6pm Mon-Fri, 9.30am-1pm Sat)

ℹ Getting There & Away

BUS
From Piazza del Mercato, **Etruria Mobilità** (www.etruriamobilita.it) buses connect the

town with Arezzo (€3.50, one hour, frequent) via Castiglion Fiorentino (€2.40).

CAR & MOTORCYCLE
Car is by far the easiest way to access hilltop Cortona. The city is on the north–south SS71 that runs to Arezzo. It's also close to the Siena–Bettolle–Perugia autostrada, which connects to the A1. There are paid car parks around the circumference of the city walls and a free car park at Parcheggio dello Spirito Santo that is connected to the historical centre by a *scala mobile* (escalator). A Zona a Traffico Limitato (ZTL; Limited Traffic Zone) applies inside the walls.

TRAIN
The nearest train station is 6km southwest in Camucia, accessible via bus (€1.40, 15 minutes, hourly). Camucia train station has no ticket office, only machines. If you need assistance purchasing tickets, go to the station at Terontola, 6.7km south of Camucia, instead. Destinations include:

Arezzo (€3.50, 25 minutes, hourly)
Florence (€10.70, 1¾ hours, hourly)
Rome (€11.55, 2¾ hours, eight daily)

Understand Florence & Tuscany

Florence & Tuscany Today

It's not all fabled romance in this land of super wines and enchanting stone farmsteads lost in cinematic rushes of pretty hills, pea-green vineyards and cypress alleys. The Tuscan cart still turns around the same 'go slow' spindle it did three millennia ago – but with diminishing state coffers, increasing globalisation and various economic woes to dodge en route.

Best on Film

Life is Beautiful (Robert Benigni; 1998) Oscar-winning Holocaust comedy set in Arezzo.

A Room with a View (James Ivory; 1985) Exquisitely rendered screen version of EM Forster's 1908 novel.

Tea with Mussolini (Franco Zeffirelli; 1999) Semi-autobiographical film, opening in Florence in 1935.

The English Patient (Anthony Minghella; 1996) Romantic drama starring Arezzo's Cappella Bacci.

Best in Print

The Stones of Florence (Mary McCarthy; 1956) Timeless portrait of Florence.

Tuscan Cities (William Dean Howells) Wonderful travel narrative penned by the American consul to Venice in 1883.

The Birth of Venus (Sarah Dunant; 2003) The daughter of a wealthy merchant falls in love with a fresco painter in 15th-century Florence.

The Decameron (Giovanni Boccaccio; 1353) A bawdy masterpiece.

A Tabernacle for the Sun (Linda Proud; 1997) Book One of the Botticelli Trilogy.

Modern Museology

As state funds diminish, museums are less able to afford a full quota of staff, and hence they sometimes open certain floors or rooms to visitors for limited hours only. Yet Tuscany remains committed to safeguarding its treasure chest of art.

In Florence, the €65-million 'New Uffizi' refurbishment project continues apace, climaxing in 2016 with the opening of the celebrated Botticelli rooms. All rooms on the 2nd floor are now finished. Dozens more rooms have opened on the 1st floor, bringing the permanent collection from 45 rooms to a staggering 101. State-of-the-art displays using multimedia, sound and film at Florence's outstanding new Museo degli Innocenti are an overdue nod to modern museology; the future Zeffirelli film school and museum, destined to open in the city's former San Firenze courthouse in Santa Croce, promises to be equally innovative. Historic Tuscan coffee-machine maker La Marzocco, headquartered in the Mugello in northeastern Tuscany, has pledged to invest €5 million in a coffee museum and an on-trend 'coffee academy' at its original industrial plant in Fiesole.

In Prato, delayed €9-million renovation works at the Centro per l'Arte Contemporanea Luigi Pecci have come to an end, and the results are stunning. Unveiled at the end of 2016, the sparkling-gold, spaceship-like piece of contemporary architecture marks a new milestone for contemporary art in a region known predominantly for its Renaissance masterpieces.

Economic Woes

Tuscany is feeling the strain of Europe's ongoing financial crisis. Italy's debt burden (133% of GDP in 2016) is the highest in the euro zone after Greece; and in 2016, for the first time since 1959, consumer prices in Italy fell as inflation – or, rather, deflation – notched a negative -0.1%. Yet Tuscany remains one of Italy's most prosperous regions, with Tuscan GDP declining by just 3.4% since 2008 (compared to 6.4% nationally) and expected to grow by 1% in 2017. Unemployment in Tuscany was 9.2% in early 2017, compared to 11.9% countrywide.

But Tuscany has a thorn in its side: its historic sugar daddy, Banca Monte dei Paschi di Siena, at home in a wonderful old *palazzo* in Siena since 1472 and the world's oldest bank. Floundering in bad loans and witness to several rounds of restructuring and injections of capital since 2013, when its economic woes first became apparent, the bank announced in December 2016 that it had just four months of liquidity left and needed a further €5 billion in capital to survive. Amid increasing fears of the bank's collapse, the EU accepted in June 2017 the massive rescue plan put forward by Italy's government that will effectively see the state bail out the bank. In return, the latter must accept an EU-approved, cutthroat restructure involving mass redundancies and pay cuts.

Preserving Tuscan Heritage
As Tuscany was born out of agriculture, sustainability and Slow Food are right at home here. And as the global pace accelerates, the region tenaciously preserves a grassroots heritage that begs travellers to sample aromatic slices of *lardo* (pig fat) or fennel salami over wine in a century-old wine bar, dine beneath dangling hams in the local butcher's shop and overnight on a neighbourhood farm.

Globalisation is being met with head-on defiance by Tuscan urban planners. In 2016 Florence's mayor refused a bid by McDonald's to open a branch within sight of the city's Unesco World Heritage–protected cathedral, following which the fast-food giant allegedly sued the city for losses of €17.8 million. More ingenious steps taken to preserve the essence (not to mention the dignity and decorum) of the region's overwhelmingly historic capital include hosing down church steps to scare off picnicking tourists; staging after-dark cinema screenings on piazzas otherwise plagued by illegal street hawkers; and creating alternative 'digital graffiti' stations at key monuments such as Brunelleschi's cupola in Florence where centuries-old stone walls otherwise tempt graffiti-happy visitors.

Farm to Table
Farm-to-table dining has always existed in this rich, green part of the world, but Tuscans are taking it one step further: witness Michelin-starred restaurants with organic farms, food trucks and burger restaurants serving local farm-sourced meat, gourmet bistros in countryside wineries... A dazzling contemporary Tuscan cuisine is fast emerging as talented young chefs reinvent the oldest recipes in the Tuscan world to sensational effect. But, then, this is a region so confident in its agricultural bounty that its capital city insists that restaurants and food shops in its historic centre use 70% local produce in their kitchens.

POPULATION: **3.74 MILLION**

AREA: **22,994 SQ KM**

GDP: **€105,151.5 MILLION**

ANNUAL INFLATION: **0%**

UNEMPLOYMENT RATE: **9.2%**

if Tuscany were 100 people

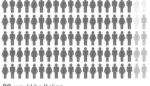

89 would be Italian
2 would be Albanian
would be Chinese
6 would be other

belief systems
(% of population)

Roman Catholic 85 — Other 15

population per sq km

FLORENCE — TUSCANY — ITALY

♦ ≈ 80 people

History

Tuscan history is an opera that quietly opens with the wine-loving Etruscans around the 9th century BC, staccatos with feisty clashes between medieval city states, and crescendos with Florence's powerful Medici dynasty and the birth of the Renaissance. To this day, it is the Renaissance, with its extraordinary art and architecture, that defines the region's largest city and remains the region's greatest moment; Tuscany has not been at the cusp of such momentous change since.

The Etruscans

No one knows exactly why the ancient Etruscans headed to Tuscany in the 9th century BC, but Etruscan artefacts give clues as to why they stayed: dinner. The wild boar roaming the Tuscan hills was a favourite on the menu, and boar hunts are a recurring theme on Etruscan ceramics and tomb paintings. In case the odd boar bristle tickled the throat while eating, Etruscans washed down their meals with wine, thereby introducing viticulture to Italy.

Tomb paintings show Etruscan women keeping pace with men in banquets so decadent they scandalised even the orgy-happy Romans. Many middle-class and aristocratic women had the means to do what they wished, including indulging in music and romance, participating in politics and overseeing a vast underclass of servants. Roman military histories boast of conquests of Etruscan women along with Etruscan territory starting in the 3rd century BC. According to recent genetic tests, Etruscans did not mingle much with their captors – their genetic material is distinct from that of modern Italians, who are the descendants of ancient Romans.

Etruscans didn't take kindly to Roman authority, nor were they keen on being enslaved to establish Roman plantations. They secretly allied with Hannibal to bring about the ignominious defeat of the Romans – one of the deadliest battles in all of Roman history – at Lago Trasimeno in neighbouring Umbria: 16,000 Roman soldiers were lost in approximately three hours.

After that Rome took a more hands-off approach with the Etruscans, granting them citizenship in 88 BC to manage their own affairs in the new province of Tuscia (Tuscany) and in return securing safe passage along the major inland Roman trade route via the Via Flaminia. Little did the Romans realise when they paved the road that they were also

Learn to speak Etruscan at Etruscology: www.etruskisch. de/pgs/vc.htm. Favourite words: *netshvis* (a fortune teller who reads animal entrails) and *thuta* (which can mean either 'chaste' or 'only married once').

TIMELINE	9th century BC	265 BC	88 BC
	Etruscans bring highly civilised wine, women and song to the hills of Tuscany – never has life been so good. Unfortunately, they fail to invite the Romans and war ensues.	Etruria falls to Rome, but it remains unruly and conspires with Hannibal against Rome during the Punic Wars.	The Romans establish the province of Tuscia (Tuscany), grant Etruscans citizenship and give them a free hand to run the province as they see fit.

paving the way for their own replacements in the 5th to 8th centuries AD: first came German emperor Theodoric, then Byzantine emperor Justinian, then the Lombards and finally Charlemagne in 800.

Medieval Scandal

Political power constantly changed hands in medieval Tuscany. Nevertheless, two notorious women wielded power effectively against a shifting backdrop of kings and popes. The daughter of a Roman senator and a notorious prostitute-turned-senatrix, Marozia already had one illegitimate son by her lover Pope Sergius III and was pregnant when she married the Lombard duke of Spoleto, Alberic I, in AD 909. He was hardly scrupulous himself: he'd achieved his position by murdering the previous duke, and he soon had Sergius III deposed. When Alberic was in turn killed, Marozia married Guy of Tuscany and conspired with him to smother Pope John X and install (in lethally rapid succession) Pope Leo VI and Stephen VIII.

After Guy's death, she wooed his half-brother Hugh of Arles, the new king of Italy. No matter that he already had a wife: his previous marriage was soon annulled. But at the wedding ceremony, Marozia's son, Alberic II, who had been named Pope John XI, had the happy couple arrested. Marozia spent the rest of her life in prison, but her legacy lived on: five popes were her direct descendants.

Countess Matilda of Tuscany (1046–1115) was another power woman. Rumour has it that she was more than just an ally to Pope Gregory VII, and there's no doubt she was a formidable strategist. To consolidate her family's Tuscan holdings, she married her own stepbrother, Godfrey the Hunchback. She soon arranged for him to be sent off to Germany, annulling the marriage and marrying a powerful prince 26 years her junior.

When Matilda's ally Pope Gregory VII excommunicated Holy Roman Emperor Henry IV in 1077 for threatening to replace him with an antipope, the emperor showed up outside her castle barefoot and kneeling in the snow to beg the pope's forgiveness. Gregory, who was Matilda's guest, kept him waiting for three days before rescinding the excommunication. Henry retaliated for what he saw as Matilda's complicity in his humiliation by conspiring with Matilda's neighbours to seize her property, and even turned her trophy husband against her – but Matilda soon dislodged Henry's power base in the north with the support of his son Conrad. Disgraced by his own family and humbled on the battlefield by a woman, Henry died in 1106.

A New Law & Order

By the 13th century Tuscans wanted change. Farmers who had painstakingly reclaimed their fields wanted to get their produce to market alive; merchants needed peaceful piazzas in which to conduct their business; and the populace at large began to entertain hopes of actually living past the age of 40.

Best Roman Relics

....

Area Archeologica (Fiesole)

....

Roman theatre (Volterra)

....

Vetulonia

HISTORY MEDIEVAL SCANDAL

Medieval Tuscany was violent: leaders of powerful families were stabbed by rivals while attending Mass; peasants were ambushed by brigands; and bystanders were maimed in neighbourhood disputes that all too easily escalated into murderous brawls. Petty crimes were punished with steep fines, corporal punishment and public flogging or mutilation.

59 BC	AD 570–774	773–74	1080
After emerging victorious from a corrupt election campaign for the position of Roman consul, Julius Caesar establishes a soldier-retiree resort called Florentia.	The Lombards rule Italy as far south as Florence and manage to turn the tiny duchy of Spoleto into a booming trade empire.	Charlemagne crosses the Alps into Italy, fighting the Lombards and having his ownership of Tuscany, Emilia, Venice and Corsica confirmed by Pope Hadrian I.	Henry IV deposes Pope Gregory VII for the second time, installing Clement III in his place and marching against Gregory's supporter Matilda of Tuscany, confiscating her territory.

FLAGELLATING MONKS & NUNS

The first known case of religious self-flagellation dates from the mid-13th century in Perugia in Tuscany's neighbour Umbria, when a strange, spontaneous parade of believers began whipping themselves while singing.

By 1260 roving bands of Flagellants appeared in major Tuscan cities, stripped to the waist, hooded and ecstatically whipping themselves while singing *laudi* (songs about the passion of Christ). They made quite an impression in Florence and Siena, where adherents formed *scuole di battuti* (schools of beatings) to build *case di Dio* (houses of God) that served as charity centres, hospices and hosts to mass flagellation sessions.

The Church remained neutral on the issue until the fledgling Flagellants claimed that their activities could grant temporary relief from sin. This posed direct competition to the Church's practice of confession, not to mention its steady business in indulgences, pardons and tithes. The Flagellant movement was banned in 1262, only to regain momentum a century later during the plague and recur periodically until the 15th century, when the Inquisition subjected Flagellants to the ultimate mortification of the flesh: burning at the stake.

Self-flagellation processions continued to be held in Tuscany under the Church's guidance into the late 19th century.

In a bid to reorganise their communities in a more civilised fashion, *comuni* (town councils) were established in Florence, Siena and other towns. In this new power-sharing arrangement, representatives were drawn from influential families, guilds and the merchant classes. Building projects were undertaken to give citizens a new sense of shared purpose and civic identity. Hospitals and public charities helped serve the needy, and new public squares, marketplaces and town halls became crucial meeting places.

Law and order was kept by a *podestà*, an independent judiciary often brought in from outside the city for limited terms of office to prevent corruption. Each *comune* (city state) developed its own style of government: Siena's was the most imaginative. To curb bloody turf battles among its *contrade* (neighbourhoods), Siena channelled its fighting spirit into organised boxing matches, bullfights and Il Palio, an annual horse race. Anyone who breached the peace was fined and the city's coffers soon swelled.

After Florence won yet another battle against Siena by cutting off the town's water supply, Siena's *comune* was faced with a funding choice: build an underground aqueduct to fend off Florence or a cathedral to establish Siena as the creative capital of the medieval world. The council voted unanimously for the latter.

Dante's Circle of Hell

In Dante Alighieri's *Inferno*, 1300 is an ominous year: our hero Dante (1265–1321) escapes from one circle of hell only to tumble into the next

1082	1136	1167	1296
Florence picks a fight with Siena over ownership of the Chianti region, starting a bitter rivalry that will last the next 400 years.	Scrappy, seafaring Pisa adds Amalfi to its list of conquests, which includes Jerusalem, Valencia, Tripoli and Mallorca, and colonies in Constantinople and Cairo.	Siena's *comune* (town council) establishes a written constitution, declaring that elected terms should be short and money should be pretty; it's soon amended to guarantee Sienese public boxing matches.	Building work begins on Florence's *duomo*. The cathedral takes 150 years to complete and, once capped with the largest dome in Italy since antiquity, becomes the ultimate symbol of Renaissance Florence.

– as was the case for the writer and his fellow Tuscans, who endured a hellish succession of famine, economic collapse, plague, war and tyranny throughout the 14th century.

Approximately two-thirds of the population was lost in cities across Tuscany in the bubonic-plague outbreak of 1348, and since the carriers of the plague (fleas and rats) weren't identified or eradicated, the Black Death ravaged the area for decades. Entire hospital and monastery populations were wiped out, leaving treatment to opportunists promising miracle cures. Flagellation, liquor, sugar and spices were prescribed, as was abstinence from bathing, fruit and olive oil.

Painful though those days must have been to record, writers such as Boccaccio, Dante and Marchionne di Coppo Stefani (c 1336–85) wrote frank assessments of their time, believing that their critiques might one day serve the greater good. More than any painterly tricks of perspective or shading, it's this rounded view of humanity that brought truth to Renaissance art.

Renaissance Belligerence & Beauty

The Renaissance was a time of great art and great tyrants, and there was an uneasy relationship between the two. The careful balance of power of the *comuni* became a casualty of the plague in the 14th century; political control was mostly left to those who survived and were either strong enough or unscrupulous enough to claim it. In *comuni* such as Florence and Siena, powerful families assumed control of the *signoria,* the city council ostensibly run by guild representatives and merchants.

Cities, commercial entities and individual families took sides with either the Rome-backed Guelphs or the imperial Ghibellines, loyalists of the Holy Roman Empire. Since each of these factions was eager to put itself on the map, this competition might have meant a bonanza for artists and architects – but shifting fortunes in the battlefield meant funds for pet art projects could disappear just as quickly as they appeared.

Tuscany began to resemble a chess game, with feudal castles appearing only to be overtaken, powerful bishops aligning with nobles before being toppled, and minor players backed by key commercial interests occasionally rising to power. Nowhere was the chess game harder to follow than in the Ghibelline *comune* of Pistoia: first it was conquered by the Florentine Guelphs, then it split into White and Black Guelph splinter groups, then it was captured by Lucca (which was at that time Ghibelline backed) before being reclaimed by the Florentines.

The Medicis

The Medici family were not exempt from the usual failings of Renaissance tyrants, but early on in his rise to power Cosimo the Elder (1389–1464) revealed a surprisingly enlightened self-interest and an exceptional eye for art. Although he held no elected office, he served as ambassador

Relive 14th-century Florence by visiting Dante's Florentine home, with a tripe shop and the chapel where he met his muse, Beatrice Portinari. For pop-culture Dante, read Sandow Birk and Marcus Sanders' *The Divine Comedy*, which sets the *Inferno* in Los Angeles' traffic, *Purgatorio* in foggy San Francisco and *Paradiso* in New York.

1314–21	1348–50	1469–92	1478–80
Dante Alighieri writes his *Divina Commedia*, told in the first person, using Tuscan dialect instead of the usual formal Latin. It's peppered with political satire, pathos, adventure and light humour.	Black Death ravages Tuscany, wiping out approximately two-thirds of the population in dense urban areas, and it doesn't stop there: further outbreaks are recorded until 1500.	Lorenzo de' Medici unofficially rules Florence, despite the 1478 Pazzi conspiracy, an attempted overthrow that left his brother Giuliano torn to shreds in the *duomo*.	A confusing set of overlapping wars breaks out among the papacy, Siena, Florence, Venice, Milan and Naples, as individual families broker secret pacts and the dwindling Tuscan population pays the price.

The Medici have nothing to hide – at least, not any more. Dig your own dirt on Florence's dynamic dynasty in the archives at www.medici.org.

for the Church, and through his behind-the-scenes diplomatic skills managed to finagle a rare 25-year stretch of relative peace for Florence. When a conspiracy led by competing banking interests exiled him from the city in 1433, some of Cosimo's favourite artists split town with him, including Donatello and Fra' Angelico.

But they weren't gone long: Cosimo's banking interests were too important to Florence, and he returned triumphant after just a year to crush his rivals, exert even greater behind-the-scenes control and sponsor masterpieces such as Brunelleschi's legendary dome for Florence's *duomo* (cathedral).

But sponsorship from even the most enlightened and powerful patrons had its downside: their whims could make or break artists and they attracted powerful enemies. Lorenzo de' Medici (Lorenzo il Magnifico; 1449–92) was a legendary supporter of the arts and humanities, providing crucial early recognition and support for Leonardo da Vinci, Sandro Botticelli and Michelangelo, among others.

HOW MACHIAVELLIAN!

Few names have such resonance as that of Niccolò Machiavelli (1469–1527), the Florentine scholar and political thinker who said 'the times are more powerful than our brains'. He was born into a poor offshoot of one of Florence's leading families and his essential premise – 'the end justifies the means' – is one that continues to live with disturbing vitality five centuries on.

Impoverished as Machiavelli's family was, his father had a well-stocked library, which the young Machiavelli devoured. When he was 29 Machiavelli landed a post in the city's second chancery. By 1500 he was in France on his first diplomatic mission in the service of the Florentine Republic. Indeed, so impressed was he by the martial success of Cesare Borgia and the centralised state of France that Machiavelli concluded Florence, too, needed a standing army – which he convinced the Republic to do in 1506. Three years later it was bloodied in battle against the rebellious city of Pisa.

The return to power of the Medici family in 1512 was a blow for Machiavelli. Suspected of plotting against the Medici, he was thrown into Florence's Le Stinche (the earliest known jail in Tuscany, dating from 1297 and among the first in Europe) in 1513 and tortured with six rounds of interrogation on the prison's notorious rack. Yet he maintained his innocence. Once freed, he retired a poor man to a small property outside Florence.

But it was during these years that Machiavelli did his greatest writing. *Il Principe* (The Prince) is his classic treatise on the nature of power and its administration, a work reflecting the confusing and corrupt times in which he lived and his desire for strong and just rule in Florence and beyond. He later wrote an official history of Florence, the *Istorie Fiorentine*.

In 1526 Machiavelli joined the papal army in its futile fight against imperial forces. By the time the latter had sacked Rome in 1527, Florence had again rid itself of Medici rule. Machiavelli hoped he would be restored to a position of dignity, but to no avail. He died frustrated and, as in his youth, impoverished.

1494	1497	1498	1527–30
The Medici are expelled by Charles VIII of France, and friar Savonarola declares a theocratic republic with his Consiglia di Cinquecento.	Savonarola sets fire to art in Florence. Books, paintings and musical instruments go up in flames on the pious preacher's 'Bonfire of the Vanities' on Florence's Piazza della Signoria.	To test Savonarola's beliefs, rival Franciscans invite him to a trial by fire. He sends a representative to be burned instead but is eventually tortured, hanged and burned as a heretic.	Florentines run the Medici out of town. The Republic of Florence holds out for three years, until the emperor's and pope's combined cannon power reinstalls the Medici.

SAVONAROLA'S LEGACY

Savonarola's theocratic rule over Florence (1494–98) only lasted four years, until his denunciation of decadence got him excommunicated and executed by Pope Alexander VI, who didn't appreciate Savonarola criticising his extravagant spending, illegitimate children and pursuit of personal vendettas. But Savonarola's short reign had an impact on Tuscany for centuries to come. It made the Church see a need to exert more direct control over the independent-minded region, and to guard against humanist philosophies that might contradict the Church's divine authority, hence the Inquisition: heretical ideas were made punishable by death, leading to an understandably chilling effect on intellectual inquiry. Celebrated universities in Pisa and Siena were subject to scrutiny, and the University of Pisa was effectively closed for about 50 years until Cosimo I de' Medici (1519–74) reinaugurated it in 1543.

But after Lorenzo escaped an assassination attempt arising from a conspiracy among the rival Florentine Pazzi family, the king of Naples and the pope, the artists he supported had to look elsewhere for sponsorship until Lorenzo could regain his position. Religious reformer Savonarola took an even darker view of Lorenzo and the classically influenced art he promoted, viewing it as a sinful indulgence in a time of great suffering. When Savonarola ousted the Medici in 1494, he decided that their decadent art had to go, too, and works by Botticelli, Michelangelo and others went up in flames in the massive 'Bonfire of the Vanities' on Florence's Piazza della Signoria.

Galileo

One of the most notable faculty members at the revitalised University of Pisa was a professor of mathematics named Galileo Galilei (1564–1642). To put it in mathematical terms, Galileo was a logical paradox: a Catholic who fathered three illegitimate children; a man of science with a poetic streak who lectured on the dimensions of hell according to Dante's *Inferno;* and an inventor of telescopes whose head was quite literally in the clouds but who kept in close contact with many friends who were the leading intellectuals of their day.

Galileo's meticulous observations of the physical universe attracted the attention of the Church, which by the 16th century had a difficult relationship with the stars. Pope Paul III kept several astrologers on hand, and no major papal initiative or construction project could be undertaken without first searching the sky with an astrolabe for auspicious signs. Yet theologian (and sometime astrologer) Tommaso Campanella was found guilty of heresy for dissenting views that emphasised observation. Research into the universe's guiding physical principles was entrusted

America was named after Amerigo Vespucci, a Florentine navigator who, from 1497 to 1504, made several voyages of discovery in what would one day be known as South America.

1633	1656	1737	1760s
Galileo Galilei is condemned for heresy in Rome. True to his observations of a pendulum in motion, the Inquisition's extreme measures yield an opposite reaction: Enlightenment.	The plague kills at least 300,000 people across central and southern Italy.	Habsburg Maria Theresa ends the Medici's dynastic rule by installing her husband as grand duke of Tuscany. She remains the brains of the operation, reforming Tuscany from behind the scenes.	Florence, along with Venice, Milan and Turin, becomes an essential stop for British aristocrats on the Grand Tour, a trend that continues until the 1840s.

by Paul III to his consulting theologians, who determined from close examination of the scriptures that the sun must revolve around the earth.

Equipped with telescopes that he'd adjusted and improved, Galileo came to a different conclusion. His observations supported Nicolaus Copernicus' theory that the planets revolved around the sun, and a cautious body of Vatican Inquisitors initially allowed him to publish his findings as long as he also presented a case for the alternative view. But when Galileo's research turned out to be dangerously convincing, the Vatican reversed its position and tried him for heresy. By then Galileo was quite ill, and his weakened state and widespread support for him may have spared him the usual heresy sentence of execution. Under official threat of torture, Galileo stated in writing that he may have overstated the case for the Copernican view of the universe, and he was allowed to carry out his prison sentence under house arrest. Pope Urban VIII alternately indulged his further studies and denied him access to doctors, but Galileo kept on pursuing scientific research even after he began losing his sight. Meanwhile, Tommaso Campanella was taken out of prison and brought to Rome, where he became Urban VIII's personal astrologer in 1629.

See Galileo's preserved middle finger (and other body parts) in Florence's superb and wholly interactive Museo Galileo, next to the Uffizi. Online, explore Galileo's life, times, religious context and scientific advances in The Galileo Project (http://galileo.rice.edu).

Gold Gilt: Going for Baroque

With his astrologers on hand, the pope might have seen Italy's foreign domination coming. Far from cementing the Church's authority, the Inquisition created a power vacuum on the ground while papal authorities were otherwise occupied with lofty theological matters. While local Italian nobles and successful capitalists vied among themselves for influence as usual, the Austrian Holy Roman Empress Maria Theresa took charge of the situation in 1737, and set up her husband, Francis, as the grand duke of Tuscany.

Napoleon Bonaparte took over swaths of Tuscany in 1799, and so appreciative was he of the area's cultural heritage that he decided to take as much as possible home with him. What he couldn't take he gave as gifts to various relatives – never mind that all those Tuscan villas and church altarpieces were not technically his to give. Following Napoleon's fall from grace in 1814, the emperor was exiled to the island of Elba in the Tuscan Archipelago and Habsburg Ferdinando III took over the title of grand duke of Tuscany. However, Napoleon's sister Elisa Bonaparte and various other relations refused to budge from the luxe Lucchesi villas they had usurped, so concessions were made to accommodate them all.

Still more upmarket expats arrived in Tuscany with the inauguration of Italy's cross-country train lines in 1840. Soon no finishing-school education would be complete without a Grand Tour of Italy, and the landmarks and museums of Tuscany were required reading. Trainloads of debutantes, dour chaperones and career bachelors arrived, setting the stage for EM Forster novels and Tuscan time-share investors.

1765–90	1796–1801	1805–14	1861
Enlightenment leader Leopold I continues his mother Maria Theresa's reforms. Moved by Cesare Beccaria's case for criminal-justice reform, he makes Tuscany the first sovereign state to outlaw the death penalty.	Italy becomes a battleground between Napoleon and their Russian allies: Tuscans witness much of their cultural patrimony divvied up as the spoils of war.	Napoleon establishes himself as king of Italy, with the military assistance of Italian soldiers he'd conscripted; when his conscripts desert, Napoleon loses Tuscany to Grand Duke Ferdinando III in 1814 and is exiled to Elba.	Two decades of insurrections culminate in a new Italian government, with a parliament and a king. Florence becomes Italy's capital in 1865, despite extensive poverty and periodic bread riots.

Red & Black: A Chequered Past

While an upper-crust expat community was exporting Romantic notions about Italy, the country was facing harsh realities. Commercial agriculture provided tidy sums to absentee royal Austrian landlords while reducing peasants to poverty and creating stiff competition for small family farms. In rural areas, three-quarters of the family income was spent on a meagre diet of mostly grains. The promise of work in the burgeoning industrial sector lured many to cities, where long working hours and dangerous working conditions simply led to another dead end, and 70% of family income was still spent on food. Upward mobility was rare, since university admissions were strictly limited, and the Habsburgs were cautious about allowing locals into their imperial army or bureaucratic positions. Increasingly, the most reliable means for Tuscans to support their families was emigration to the Americas.

Austrian rule provided a common enemy that united Italians across provinces and classes. The Risorgimento (reunification period) was not so much a reorganisation of some previously unified Italian states (which hadn't existed since Roman times) as a revival of city-state ideals of an independent citizenry. The secret societies that had flourished right under the noses of the French as a local check on colonial control formed a network of support for nationalist sentiment. During 1848 and 1849 revolution broke out, and a radical government was temporarily installed in Florence.

Nervous that the Austrians would invade, conservative Florentine leaders invited Habsburg Leopold II to return as archduke of Tuscany. But when rural unrest in Tuscany made Austria's return to power difficult, Austrian retaliation and brutal repression galvanised nationalist sentiment in the region. Although the country was united under one flag in 1861, this early split between radicals and conservatives would define the region's future political landscape.

HABSBURG & MEDICI LEGACIES

Austrian Holy Roman Empress Maria Theresa (mother of 16 children – including Marie Antoinette) was a self-taught military strategist who kept local potentates in check and pushed through reforms that curbed witch burning, outlawed torture, established mandatory education and allowed Italian peasants to keep a modest share of their crops. She also brought the Habsburgs' signature flashy style to Tuscany, and kicked off a frenzy of redecoration that included flamboyant frescoes packed with cherubs, ornate architectural details that were surely a nightmare to dust, and gilding whenever and wherever possible.

Perhaps fearing that her family's priceless art collection might factor into Maria Theresa's redecorating plans, Medici heiress Anna Maria Luisa de' Medici willed everything to the city of Florence upon her death in 1743, on the condition that it all must remain in the city.

1871	1915	1921	1940–43
After French troops are withdrawn from Rome, the forces of the Kingdom of Italy defeat the Papal States to take power in Rome; the capital moves there from Florence.	Italy enters WWI fighting a familiar foe: the Austro-Hungarian Empire. War casualties, stranded POWs, heating-oil shortages and food rationing make for a hard-won victory by 1918.	Mussolini forms the Fascist Party, and Tuscan supporters fall in line by 1922. The 1924 elections are 'overseen' by Fascist paramilitary groups, and the Fascists win a parliamentary majority.	The Fascist Italian Empire joins Germany in declaring war on Great Britain and France. Italy surrenders in 1943; Mussolini refuses to comply and war continues.

Unification didn't end unemployment or unrest; only 2% of Italy's population gained the right to vote in 1861. Strikes were held to protest working conditions, and their suppression gave rise to a new Socialist Party in 1881. The new Italian government's money-making scheme to establish itself as a colonial power in Abyssinia (modern-day Ethiopia and Eritrea) proved a costly failure: 17,000 Italian soldiers were lost near Adowa in 1896. When grain prices were raised in 1898, many impoverished Italians could no longer afford to buy food, and riots broke out. Rural workers unionised, and when a strike was called in 1902, 200,000 rural labourers came out en masse.

Finally Italian politicians began to take the hint and initiated some reforms. Child labour was banned, working hours set and the right to vote extended to all men over the age of 30 by 1912 (women would have to wait until 1945). But as soon as the government promised the Socialists to fund an old-age pension scheme, it reneged, and opted to invade Tunisia instead.

Italy got more war than it had budgeted for in 1914, when WWI broke out. A young, prominent Socialist firebrand named Benito Mussolini (1883–1945) led the call for Italy to intervene in support of the Allies, though most Socialists were opposed to such an action. As a result, Mussolini was expelled from the Socialist Party and went on to join the Italian army. After being injured and discharged, he formed the Italian Combat Squad in 1919, the forerunner of the National Fascist Party.

Inter-War Blues

Though Italy had been on the winning side in WWI, Tuscans were not in the mood to celebrate. In addition to war casualties, 600,000 of their countrymen served time as prisoners of war, and 100,000 died, primarily due to the Italian government's failure to send food, clothing and medical supplies to its own soldiers. Wartime decrees that extended working hours and outlawed strikes had made factory conditions in industrial centres so deplorable that women led mass strikes. Bread shortages and bread riots spread, and in 1919 violent uprisings broke out in the industrial towns of Viareggio and Piombino: the dismissal of 500 workers at the Piombino steel mills sparked a general strike that rapidly degenerated into full-scale bloodshed between workers and armed forces.

Mussolini had clearly found support for his call to order in disgruntled Tuscany, and by 1922 his black-shirted squads could be seen parading through Florence, echoing his call for the ousting of the national government and the purging of socialists and communists from all local positions of power. In 1922 the Fascists marched on Rome and staged a coup d'etat, installing Mussolini as prime minister.

No amount of purging prevented the country from plunging into recession in the 1930s after Mussolini demanded a revaluation of the Italian lira. While the free fall of wages won Mussolini allies among industrialists, it created further desperation among his power base. New military con-

Tuscany's regional government is headed by the president, elected every five years. He is aided by 10 ministers and a legislative regional council comprising 65 members, also elected by proportional representation for the same five-year term. Keep tabs on the regional government and council at www.regione.toscana.it and www.consiglio.regione.toscana.it.

1943–45	1946	1966	1969
The Italian Resistance joins the Allies against Mussolini and the Nazis; Tuscany is liberated. When civil warfare ends in 1945, a coalition government is formed.	Umberto II is exiled after a referendum to make Italy a republic is successful; 71.6% of Tuscans vote for a republic.	The Arno bursts its banks, submerging Florence in metres of mud and water. Some 5000 people are left homeless and thousands of artworks and manuscripts are destroyed.	Strikes and student uprisings demand social change and promote sweeping reforms, not just in working conditions but also in housing, social services, pensions and civil rights.

quests in Libya and Ethiopia initially provided a feeble boost to the failing economy, but when the enormous bill came due in the late 1930s, Mussolini hastily agreed to an economic and military alliance with Germany. Contrary to the bold claims of Mussolini's propaganda machine, Tuscany and the rest of Italy was ill-prepared for the war it entered in 1940.

WWII & Tuscan Resistance

Contrary to the deep-rooted Florentine belief that a city brimming with so many artistic treasures could not possibly be targeted (Florence had remained perfectly intact during WWI, being neither occupied nor attacked), Florence was badly damaged during WWII. Ironically, it was not until the end of the war, however, following the occupation of the city by German troops on 11 September 1943, that the first bombs were dropped. Allied forces broke through the German line south of Rome in May 1944 and promptly rushed north to liberate Rome and all the territory in between. Forced to retreat, the Germans built a new defensive line using forced labour further north: the Gothic Line ran east from the Pisan coast – via Pisa, Lucca, Florence and eastern Tuscany – to the Adriatic Coast. Allied bombers immediately retaliated by taking out Florence's train station and with it a precious supply line for the Germans; several hundred Florentine civilians were also killed. In neighbouring Pisa, the cathedral and Leaning Tower remained intact, but the Camposanto was ruined, along with much of the old town.

A powerful resistance movement emerged in Tuscany during WWII, but not soon enough to prevent hundreds of thousands of Italian casualties, plus a still-unknown number of Italians shipped to death camps in Germany and 23 Italian concentration camps, including one near Arezzo; in Florence a stone in front of the city synagogue memorialises the 248 Jews from Florence who died in the camps. Similar fates were shared by Jews in Siena, Pisa and other Tuscan towns.

German forces' final gift to the city of Florence before leaving in August 1944 was to destroy all the bridges across the River Arno in order to slow advancing Allied troops. Every bridge was blown up except for the Ponte Vecchio, which Hitler ordered to be spared: the timelessly seductive view down the Arno from the new window Mussolini had specially punched in the bridge section of the Vasari Corridor in anticipation of Hitler's visit to Florence in 1941 had obviously made a lasting impression on the Nazi leader.

Rise of the Tuscan Left

A new Italian government surrendered to the Allies in 1943, but Mussolini refused to concede defeat, and dragged Italy through two more years of civil war, Allied campaigns and German occupation. Tuscany emerged from these black years redder than ever and became a Socialist power base.

Immediately after the war, three coalition governments succeeded one another. Italy became a republic in 1946 and the newly formed

Tuscany's Renaissance legacy was almost lost in the 1966 Great Flood of Florence that left thousands homeless and three million manuscripts and thousands of artworks under mud, stone and sewage. Those heroes who helped dig the treasures from the mud are honoured as *gli angeli del fango* (angels of mud).

1970s–'80s	1993	1995	2005
The Anni di Piombo (Years of Lead) terrorise the country with extremist violence and reprisals; police kill anarchist Franco Serantini in Pisa, and the Red Brigades kill Florence's mayor in 1986.	A car bomb at the Uffizi kills six and causes US$10 million damage to artworks. The mafia is suspected but never indicted. The same year 200,000 people protest mafia violence.	Maurizio Gucci, heir to the Florence-born Gucci fashion empire, is gunned down outside his Milan offices. Three years later, his estranged wife, Patrizia Reggiani, is jailed for ordering his murder.	Regional elections in Tuscany see incumbent centre-left president Claudio Martini win a second term in office, reconfirming Tuscany as Italy's bastion of the left.

right-wing Democrazia Cristiana (Christian Democrats) won the first elections under the new constitution in 1948.

Until the 1980s the Partito Comunista Italiano (Italian Communist Party), despite being systematically kept out of government, played a crucial role in Tuscany's social and political development. The party was founded in the Tuscan port town of Livorno in 1921, and its huge popularity prompted the so-called Anni di Piombo (Years of Lead) in the 1970s, dominated by terrorism and social unrest. In 1978 the Brigate Rosse (Red Brigades, a group of young left-wing militants responsible for several bomb blasts and assassinations) claimed their most important victim – former Christian Democrat prime minister Aldo Moro. He was kidnapped in Rome, kept hostage for 54 days, then shot. A memorial next to Chiesa di San Francesco al Prato in Pistoia in northwestern Tuscany remembers Moro, his two bodyguards and three policemen killed during the initial kidnapping.

Despite the disquiet, the 1970s enjoyed positive change: divorce and abortion became legal, and legislation was passed allowing women to keep their own names after marriage. The Regione Toscana was one of 15 regional governments with limited powers to be formed across the country. And, in predictable Tuscan centre-left fashion, from its creation on it was the red left in Tuscany that dominated local political debate.

Trouble at the Bank

Europe's ailing economy limped from bad to dire from 2012 in a financial crisis considered to be the worst since the 1930s Great Depression. The Tuscan crunch came with a bank scandal. In 2013 the Banca Monte dei Paschi di Siena – Italy's third-largest lender and the world's longest-operating bank, in business in a gorgeous *palazzo* in Siena since 1472 – revealed losses of €730 million on a trio of derivative deals, made between 2007 and 2009 and hidden from regulators. While former high-ranking officials at the pedigree bank grappled with corruption, fraud and bribery allegations, the government came to the rescue with a €4.1-billion bailout and a €5-billion share sale 12 months later to raise capital. Yet the bank still managed to fail European regulator stress a year on, prompting another round of fundraising (€3 billion, with a promised 8% return on equity by 2018) from its shareholders in 2015.

Restructuring at the bank, essential for survival, saw hundreds of its 1900 countrywide branches close. But the fallout of the scandal reached far beyond job cuts. For decades 'il Monte' (as Tuscans know the bank) sustained Siena's vibrant cultural life. Through its foundation, the Fondazione Monte dei Paschi di Siena, it funded part of the city's university, hospital, football team and so on – effectively providing around 10% of Siena's local-government budget. For Siena (and Tuscany) the social and economic impact of their sugar daddy's dramatic fall from grace was cause for concern.

Best Historical Reads

Renaissance Florence on Five Florins a Day (2010), Charles FitzRoy

Tuscany: A History (2011), Alistair Moffat

Queen Bee of Tuscany: The Redoubtable Janet Ross (2013), Ben Downing

The Light in the Ruins (2013) by bestselling New York author Chris Bohjalian paints a vivid portrait of the 'innermost ring of Dante's inferno' that was Tuscany during WWII through the tale of the doomed love between an Italian noblewoman and a German soldier.

2008	2012	2015	2017
Silvio Berlusconi and his right-wing allies, in power since 2001, win the national election and a second seven-year term in office. Tuscany's traditional support of leftist candidates and parties is diluted.	Italian cruise ship *Costa Concordia* sinks off the Tuscan coast, claiming 32 lives. The eventual removal of the wreckage in 2015 from the island of Giglio is the most costly in maritime salvage history.	The left emerges stronger than ever in Tuscany in regional elections. Incumbent centre-left president Enrico Rossi's Democratic Party (PD) lands 48.03% of votes, ensuring a second term in office for Rossi.	Florentine fashion house Salvatore Ferragamo pays €1.5 million to restore *Neptune* on Piazza della Signoria and Gucci pledges €2 million to reinvent the city's Giardino di Boboli (Boboli Gardens).

The Tuscan Way of Life

Romanticised the world over, Tuscany has impassioned more writers, designers and film-makers than any other region. Yet what is it that makes the birthplace of Gucci, Cavalli and the Vespa scooter so inspiring, so *dolce* (sweet)? Florence takes the lead with its artistic heritage and tradition of master craftsmanship, but Tuscan style, grace and appreciation of beauty find expression in an extraordinary attention to detail, a quest for perfection and a dauntless pride in local dialect and history.

Rural Roots

Deeply attached to their patch of land, people in this predominantly rural neck of the woods, with only a dusting of small towns, are not simply Italian or Tuscan. Harking back to centuries of coexistence as rival political entities with their own style of architecture, school of painting, bell tower and so on, it is the *paese* (home town) or, in the case of Siena and other towns, the *contrada* (neighbourhood) in which one is born that reigns supreme. For most, such *campanilismo* (literally, 'loyalty to one's bell tower') is all-consuming. 'Better a death in the family than a Pisan at the door' says an old Florentine proverb with reference to the historic rivalry between the Tuscan towns.

Passionate, proud, reserved, hard-working, family-oriented, fond of food and wine, thrifty, extremely self-conscious and proud of their appearance are characteristics attributed to Tuscans across the board.

Brash, no, but in Florence Florentines like to make it known where they stand in society. From oversized doorknobs to sculpted stonework, overt statements of wealth and power are everywhere in this class-driven city, whose dialect – penned for the world to read by literary greats Dante, Boccaccio and Petrarch in the 14th century – is deemed the purest form of Italian.

Titled Florentines are still alive and well, accounting for a tiny fraction of contemporary Florentine society. From the 12th century until the Renaissance, when wealth and ability overtook aristocratic ranking, titles – prince, duke, marques, count, viscount, baron, patrician and noble – ruled the roost. Florentine nobility derived mainly from bankers and merchants, and many of the city's most wonderful properties and countryside estates remain in the hands of counts and barons – Europe's largest private walled garden, the Giardini di Torrigiani, is a prime example.

In the city, elderly nobles still gather each week at Florence's exclusive, elusive Circolo dell' Unione (aka 'club of nobles'), enthroned since 1852 in a *palazzo* on Florence's most aristocratic street, Via de' Tournabuoni. Membership is not hereditary and costs a (large) fee. Some 60% of the club's 400-odd members (of which just a handful are female) bear a title – though titles have not been recognised by the Italian state since 1948, following the fall of the Italian monarchy.

No title better delves into the essence of Tuscan life than *The Wisdom of Tuscany: Simplicity, Security and the Good Life – Making the Tuscan Lifestyle Your Own* by Ferenc Màté.

Unesco World Heritage Sites

Historic centre of Florence

Pisa's Piazza dei Miracoli

Historic centre of Siena

Val d'Orcia

Historic centre of San Gimignano

Historic centre of Pienza

Medici villas and gardens

A PEASANT'S LIFE

Mezzadria (sharecropping), a medieval form of land management in place until 1979, was the key to success in the Tuscan countryside. *Contadini* (peasants) lived and worked on the land, receiving in return a home for their traditionally large families (typically consisting of 10 people – the more hands the better) and 50% of the crops or profit reaped from the land they worked. The other half went to the *padrone* (land owner), who often did not live on his *fattoria* (agricultural estate) but in the city.

Post-WWII industrialisation saw the birth of the tractor and the first shift in the equal balance between landowner and peasant: farmers had no money to buy tractors, obliging owners to invest instead and so upsetting the apple cart in terms of who gave how much. Gradually farm workers gravitated towards towns in search of better-paid jobs, the 1960s witnessing a particularly large exodus and prompting the eventual collapse of sharecropping and many a Tuscan farm with it.

La Dolce Vita

Life is *dolce* (sweet) for this privileged pocket of Italy, one of the country's wealthiest enclaves, where the family reigns supreme, and tradition and quality trump quantity. From the great names in viticulture to the flower-producing industry of Pescia and the small-scale farms of rural Tuscany, it is family-run businesses handed down generations that form the backbone of this proud, strong region.

In Florence – the only city with a faint hint of the cosmopolitan – daily life is the fastest paced. Florentines rise early, drop their kids at school by 8am, then flit from espresso to the office by 9am. Lunch is a lengthy affair for these food- and wine-loving people, as is the early-evening *aperitivo,* enjoyed in a bar with friends to whet the appetite for dinner. For younger Florentines, who bear the brunt of Florence's ever-rising rent and salaries that scarcely increase, it is quite common to treat the lavish *aperitivo* spread like dinner – enter *apericena*. Smokers, fast dwindling, puff on pavements outside.

There is no better time of day or week than late Sunday afternoon to witness the *passeggiata* (early-evening stroll), a wonderful tradition that sees Tuscans in towns don a suitable outfit and walk – to get a gelato, chat, meet friends, mooch, contemplate the sunset and, quite simply, relish the close of the day at an exceedingly relaxed pace.

Theatre, concerts, art exhibitions (the free opening on Thursday evenings at Florence's Palazzo Strozzi is always packed) and *il calcio* (football) entertain after hours. Tuscany's top professional football club, ACF Fiorentina, has a fanatical fan base (check the memorabilia in Florence's Trattoria Mario).

Weekends see many flee their city apartments for less urban climes, where the din of *motorini* (scooters) whizzing through the night lessens and there's more space and light. Green countryside is a mere 15-minute getaway from lucky old Florence, unlike many urban centres where industrial sprawl really sprawls.

Best Passeggiata Strips

Via de' Tornabuoni & Ponte Vecchio (Florence)

Via Fillungo (Lucca)

Via Banchi di Sopra (Siena)

'The Corso' aka Corso Italia (Arezzo)

Corso Carducci (Grosseto)

Casa Dolce Casa

By their very nature, family-oriented Tuscans travel little (many live all their lives in the town of their birth) and place great importance on *casa dolce casa* (home, sweet home) – the rate of home ownership in Tuscany is among Europe's highest.

The rural lifestyle is driven by close-knit, ancient communities in small towns and villages, where local matters and gossip are more important than national or world affairs. Everyone knows everyone to the point of being clannish, making assimilation for outsiders hard – if not impossible. Farming is the self-sufficient way of life, albeit one that is becoming increasingly difficult – hence the mushrooming of *agriturismi* (farm-stay accommodation), as farmers stoically utilise every resource they have to make ends meet.

At one time the domain of Tuscany's substantial population of well-off Brits (there's good reason why playwright John Mortimer dubbed Chianti 'Chiantishire' in his 1988 novel and 1989 TV adaptation *Summer's Lease*), the region's bounty of stylish stone villas and farmhouses with terracotta floors, wood-burning fireplaces and terraces with views are now increasingly passing back into the hands of Tuscans eagerly rediscovering their countryside.

In both urban and rural areas, children typically remain at home until they reach their 30s, often only leaving the nest to wed. In line with national trends, Tuscan families are small, with one or two kids; around 20% of households are childless and 25% are single. Despite increasing numbers of working women, chauvinistic attitudes remain well entrenched in more rural areas.

Lose yourself in the culinary and cultural beauty of the Tuscan home with Emiko Davies' *Florentine* (2016), an inspirational cookbook with exquisite photography, a 'romantic nostalgia' vibe and plenty of astute musings on modern life in the Renaissance city.

La Festa

Delve into the mindset of a Tuscan and a holy trinity of popular folklore, agricultural tradition and religious rite of passage dances before your eyes – which pretty much translates as *la festa* (party!). No cultural agenda is more jam-packed with ancient festivities than theirs: patron saints alone provide weeks of celebration, given that every village, town, profession, trade and social group has a saint to call its own and venerate religiously.

La festa climaxes – not once but twice – with Siena's soul-stirring Il Palio, a hot-blooded horse race conceived in the 12th century to honour the Virgin Mary and revamped six centuries on to celebrate the miracles of the Madonna of Provenzano (2 July) and the Assumption (16 August). Deeply embroiled in its religious roots are a fierce *contrada* rivalry, not to mention a penchant for dressing up and a respect for tradition that sees horses blessed before the race, jockeys riding bareback and the silk banner for the winner of August's race ritually designed by Sienese artists and the July banner by non-Sienese. (Legend says that a Sienese bride marrying in far-off lands took with her earth from her *contrada* to put beneath the legs of her marital bed to ensure that her offspring would be conceived on home soil.)

Although it's by no means the social force it once was, Catholicism (the religion of 85% of the region) and its rituals nevertheless play a key role

COFFEE CULTURE

Coffee is not just a drink but a way of life for Tuscans, whose typical day is punctuated with caffeine, the type of coffee depending wholly on time of day and occasion.

The number-one cardinal rule: cappuccino (espresso topped with hot, frothy milk), *caffè latte* (milkier version with less froth) and *latte macchiato* (warmed milk 'stained' with a spot of coffee) are only ever drunk at breakfast or in the early morning. If you're truly Tuscan, though, the chances are you'll probably grab a speed espresso (short, sharp shot of strong, black coffee) or *caffè doppio* (double espresso) standing up at the bar with everyone else at your favourite cafe on the way to work.

Lunch and dinner only end one way: with *un caffè* (literally 'a coffee', meaning an espresso and nothing else), although come dusk it is quite acceptable to finish with *un caffè corretto* (espresso with a dash of grappa or another spirit).

Sitting down at a table in a cafe to have a coffee is four times more expensive than drinking it standing at the bar.

THE TUSCAN WAY OF LIFE LA FESTA

Tuscan Icons

The Vespa scooter

Gucci

Chianti wine

Michelangelo's David

Renaissance art

Italians Dance and I'm a Wallflower by Florence-based author Linda Malcone provides a cracking insight into local behaviour and cultural expression. It's published by The Florentine Press (www.theflor entinepress. com), a fabulous resource for pub- lications (print and ebook) in English covering everything from arts and culture to politics, travel and humour.

in daily lives: first Communions, church weddings and religious feast days are an integral part of Tuscan society.

Bella Figura

A sense of style is vital to Tuscans, who take great pride in their dress and appearance to ensure their *bella figura* (good public face). Dressing impeccably comes naturally to most, and for most Florentines chic is a byword. Indeed it was in their beautiful city that the Italian fashion industry was born and bred.

Guccio Gucci and Salvatore Ferragamo got the haute-couture ball roll- ing in the 1920s with boutiques in Florence. And in 1951 a well-heeled Florentine nobleman called Giovanni Battista Giorgini held a fashion soirée in his Florence home that spawned Italy's first prêt-à-porter fashion shows. The catwalk quickly shifted to Florence's Palazzo Pitti, where Europe's most prestigious fashion shows dazzled until 1971 (when the women's shows moved to Milan). The menswear shows stayed put, though, and top designers still leg it to Florence twice a year to unveil their menswear collections at the Pitti Immagine Uomo fashion shows and their creations for *bambini* (kids) at Pitti Bimbo.

Tuscan Design

Never has Italian design been so expressive as in 1963, when Piaggio in Pontedera, 25km east of Pisa, launched the Vespa 50, a motorised scoot- er requiring no driving licence. Overnight it became a 'must-have' item as Italy's young things snapped up the machine and the freedom and independence it gave. All of Europe's Vespas are still made in the Tuscan plant where the original 'wasp' was born in 1946.

While Audrey Hepburn was cruising around Rome side-saddle on a Vespa for Hollywood, a group of anti-establishment artists and archi- tects were busy building a reputation for Florence as the centre of 1960s avant-garde design. The groups Radical Design, Archizoom and Super- studio were all founded in Florence in 1966, and included hot-shot Flor- entines Massimo Morozzi (b 1941; buy his pasta set from Alessi) and Andrea Branzi (b 1938), whose furniture designs are timeless.

As with fashion, the design scene moved to Milan in the 1970s, starv- ing Tuscany of its cutting edge.

The Tuscan Table

Whether sinking your teeth into a beefy blue *bistecca alla fiorentina* (chargrilled T-bone steak), wine tasting in Chianti, savouring Livorno fish stew or devouring white truffles unearthed around San Miniato near Pisa, travelling in Tuscany is a memorable banquet of gastronomic and viticultural experiences.

A Country Kitchen

It was above an open wood fire in *la cucina contadina* (the farmer's kitchen) that Tuscan cuisine was cooked up. Its basic premise: don't waste a crumb.

During the 13th and 14th centuries, when Florence prospered and the wealthy started using silver cutlery instead of fingers, simplicity remained the hallmark of dishes served at lavish banquets thrown by feuding families as a show of wealth. And while the Medici passion for flaunting the finer things in life during the Renaissance gave Tuscan cuisine a fanciful kick, with spectacular sugar sculptures starring alongside spit-roasted suckling pig, ordinary Tuscans continued to rely on the age-old *cucina povera* (poor dishes) to keep hunger at bay.

Contemporary Tuscan cuisine remains faithful to these humble roots, using fresh local produce and eschewing fussy execution.

A Bloody Affair: Meat & Game

The icon of Tuscan cuisine is Florence's *bistecca alla fiorentina,* a chargrilled T-bone steak rubbed with olive oil, seared on the chargrill, seasoned, and served *al sangue* (blue and bloody). A born-and-bred rebel, this feisty cut of meat is weighed before it's cooked and priced on menus per *l'etto* or 100g. Traditionally it is butchered from creamy Chianina cows, one of the oldest breeds of cattle, originating from the wide green Val de Chiana in eastern Tuscany.

Tuscan markets conjure up animal parts many wouldn't dream of eating. In the past, prime beef cuts were the domain of the wealthy and offal was the staple peasant fare: tripe was simmered for hours with onions, carrots and herbs to make *lampredotto* or with tomatoes and herbs to make *trippa alla fiorentina* – two classics still going strong.

Pasto, an ancient mix of *picchiante* (cow's lungs) and chopped potatoes, is not even a gastronomic curiosity these days – due to lack of demand it has died a quiet death and is no longer possible to find on restaurant menus. Equally ancient *cibrèo* (chicken's kidney, liver, heart and cockscomb stew) and *colle ripieno* (stuffed chicken's neck) are both still cooked up, though. Another golden oldie featured on many a medieval fresco is *pollo al mattone* – boned chicken splattered beneath a brick, rubbed with herbs and baked beneath the brick. The end result is handsomely crispy.

Cinghiale (wild boar), hunted in autumn, is turned into *salsicce di cinghiale* (wild-boar sausages) or simmered with tomatoes, pepper and herbs to create a rich stew.

Best Traditional Tuscan

Il Teatro del Sale (Florence)

....

Trattoria Mario (Florence)

....

La Taverna di San Giuseppe (Siena)

....

Ristorante La Mandragola (San Gimignano)

....

La Bucaccia (Cortona)

....

Osteria La Porta (Val d'Orcia)

**Best
Bistecca
alla
Fiorentina**

Trattoria Mario
(Florence)

Officina della
Bistecca (Panzano
In Chianti)

Sergio Falaschi
(San Miniato)

Ristorante Da Muz-
zicone (Castiglion
Fiorentino)

Osteria Acquacheta
(Montepulciano)

Dopolavoro
(La Foce)

In Tuscany the family pig invariably ends up on the plate as a salty slice of *soprassata* (head, skin and tongue boiled, chopped and flavoured with garlic, rosemary and other herbs and spices), *finocchiona* (fennel-spiced sausage), prosciutto, nearly black *mallegato* (spiked with nutmeg, cinnamon, raisins and pine kernels from San Miniato) or *mortadella* (a smooth-textured pork sausage speckled with cubes of white fat). *Lardo di colonnata* (thin slices of local pork fat aged in a mix of herbs and oils for at least six months) is a treat hard to find outside Tuscany.

Best on Friday: Fish

The old Medici port of Livorno leads the region in seafood: *cacciucco* (one 'c' for each type of fish thrown into it) is the signature dish. Deriving its name from the Turkish *kukut*, meaning 'small fry', *cacciucco* is a stew of five fish simmered with tomatoes and red peppers, served atop stale bread. *Triglie alla livornese* is red or white mullet cooked in tomatoes, and *baccalà alla livornese,* also with tomatoes, features cod traditionally salted aboard the ships en route to the port. *Baccalà* (salted cod), not to be confused with *stoccofisso* (unsalted air-dried stockfish), is a trattoria mainstay, served on Fridays as tradition and old-style Catholicism demands.

Poor Man's Meat: Pulses, Grains & Veg

Pulses were poor man's meat to Tuscans centuries ago. Jam-packed with protein, cheap and available year-round (eaten fresh in summer, dried in winter), pulses go into traditional dishes like *minestra di fagioli* (bean soup), *minestra di pane* (bread and bean soup) and *ribollita* (a 'reboiled' bean, vegetable and bread soup with black cabbage that is left to sit for a day before being served).

Of the dozens of bean varieties, *cannellini* and dappled *borlotti* are the most common; both are delicious drizzled with olive oil to accompany

GO SLOW TUSCANY

Born out of a desire to protect the world from McDonaldisation, Slow Food (www.fondazi oneslowfood.com) preserves local food traditions and encourages interest in the food we eat, its origins and how it tastes. Created by Italian wine writer Carlo Petrini, it works in over 130 countries and has also given rise to Slow City (www.cittaslow.blogspot.com). Slow City towns in Tuscany – Anghiari, Barga, Castelnuovo Berardenga, Civitella in Val di Chiana, Greve in Chianti, Massa Marittima, Pratovecchio, San Miniato, San Vincenzo and Suvereto – have a visible and distinct culture; rely on local resources rather than mass-produced food and culture; work to reduce pollution; and increasingly rely on sustainable development, such as organic farming and public transport.

Industrialisation, globalisation and environmental dangers threaten traditional, indigenous edibles. Enter Slow Food's **Ark of Taste**, a project born and headquartered in Florence that aims to protect and promote endangered food products, including, in Tuscany: Chianina beef, *lardo di colonnata,* Certaldo onions, Casola chestnut bread, Cetica red potatoes, Garfagnana potato bread and *farro* (spelt), Carmignano dried figs, *cinta senese* (the indigenous Tuscan pig), Londa Regina peaches, Pistoian Mountain *pecorino* cheese, Orbetello *bottarga* (salted mullet roe) and Zeri lamb. Among the many cured meats that make the list: San Miniato *mallegato*, Prato *mortadella* (smooth-textured pork sausage made dull pink with drops of alkermes liqueur and speckled white with cubes of fat), Sienese *buristo* (a type of pork salami made in the province of Siena), Valdarno *tarese* (a 50cm- to 80cm-long pancetta spiced with red garlic and orange peel and covered in pepper), Florentine *bardiccio* (fresh fennel-flavoured sausage encased in a natural skin of pig intestine and eaten immediately) and *biroldo* (spiced blood sausage made in Garfagnana from pig's head and blood).

Sampling any of these Tuscan items guarantees an authentic tasting experience.

meat. The round, yellow *zolfino* from Pratomagno and the silky-smooth *sorano* bean from Pescia are prized. Of huge local pride to farmers in the Garfagnana is *farro della garfagnana* (spelt), an ancient grain grown in Europe as early as 2500 BC.

Tuscany's lush vegetable patch sees medieval vegetables grow alongside tomatoes. Wild fennel, black celery (braised as a side dish), sweet red onions (delicious when oven baked), artichokes and zucchini flowers (stuffed and oven baked), black cabbage, broad beans, chicory, chard, thistle-like cardoons and green tomatoes are among the ones to look out for.

Prized as one of the most expensive spices, saffron is all the rage around San Gimignano, where it was enthusiastically traded in medieval times. Fiery red and as fine as dust by the time it reaches the kitchen, saffron in its rawest state is the dried stigma of the saffron crocus.

Pass the Salt: Bread

One bite and the difference is striking: Tuscan *pane* (bread) is unsalted, creating a disconcertingly bland taste many a bread lover might never learn to enjoy.

Yet it is this centuries-old staple – deliberately unsalted to ensure it lasted for a good week and to complement the region's salty cured meats – that forms the backbone of Tuscany's most famous dishes: *pappa al pomodoro* (bread and tomato soup), *panzanella* (tomato and basil salad mixed with a mush of bread soaked in cold water) and *ribollita*. None sound or look particularly appetising, but the depth of flavour is extraordinary.

Thick-crusted *pane toscana* is the basis of two antipasti delights: *crostini* (lightly toasted slices of bread topped with liver pâté) and *fettunta* (a kind of Tuscan bruschetta that's also called *crogiantina;* toast fingers doused in garlic, salt and olive oil).

A Dowry Skill: Cheese

So important was cheesemaking in the past that it was a dowry skill. Still respected, the sheep's-milk *pecorino* crafted in Pienza ranks among Italy's greatest *pecorini*: taste it young and mild with fava beans, fresh pear or chestnuts and honey, or try it mature and tangy, spiked with *toscanello* (black peppercorns) or as *pecorino di tartufo* (infused with black-truffle shavings). *Pecorino* massaged with olive oil during the ageing process turns red and is called *rossellino*.

Festive Frolics: Sweets, Chocolate & Ice

Be it the honey, almond and sugar-cane sweets served at the start of 14th-century banquets in Florence or the sugar sculptures made to impress at the flamboyant 16th- and 17th-century feasts of the Medici, *dolci* (sweets) have always been reserved for festive occasions. In more humble circles street vendors sold *bomboloni* (doughnuts) and *pandiramerino* (rosemary-bread buns), while Carnevale in Florence was marked by *stiacchiata* (Florentine flat bread made from eggs, flour, sugar and lard, then dusted with icing sugar).

As early as the 13th century, servants at the Abbazia di Montecelso near Siena paid tax to the nuns in the form of *panpepato* (a pepper and honey flat bread), although legend tells a different tale: following a siege in Siena, Sister Berta baked a revitalising flat cake of honey, dried fruit, almonds and pepper to perk up the city's weakened inhabitants. Subsequently sweetened with spices, sprinkled with sugar and feasted on once a year at Christmas, Siena's *panforte* (literally 'strong bread') – a rich cake with nuts and candied fruit – is now eaten year-round. An adage says it stops couples quarrelling.

THE TUSCAN TABLE A COUNTRY KITCHEN

Pasta is as much Tuscan as it is Italian, and no Tuscan banquet would be quite right without a *primo* (first course) of home-made *maccheroni* (wide, flat ribbon pasta), *pappardelle* (wider flat ribbon pasta) or Sienese *pici* (a thick, hand-rolled version of spaghetti) served with a duck, hare, rabbit or boar sauce.

DINING ETIQUETTE

Dining out in Tuscany has its own set of unspoken rules – heed them to make your dining experience a whole lot smoother.

Dress Smart-casual is best, particularly in Florence and other cities and large towns, where working urbanites go home to freshen up between *aperitivo* and dinner.

Courses Don't feel obliged to order the Tuscan full monty; it's quite acceptable to order just one or two courses such as an *antipasto* (starter) and a *primo* (pasta course), or even just a *secondo* (main course).

Bread This is plentiful, unsalted and served without butter – or a side plate (put it on the table).

Spaghetti Twirl it around your fork as if you were born twirling – no spoons, please.

Young children It is perfectly acceptable to ask for a plate of plain pasta with butter and Parmesan.

Coffee Never order a cappuccino after 11am, and certainly not after a meal, when an espresso is the only respectable choice (with, perhaps, a digestif of grappa or another fiery spirit).

Il conto (the bill) Whoever invites pays.

Splitting the bill Common enough.

Tipping If there is no *servizio* (service charge), leave a 10% to 15% tip.

Tuscan *biscotti* (biscuits) – once served with candied fruit and sugared almonds at the start of and between courses at Renaissance banquets – are dry, crisp and often double baked. *Cantucci* are hard, sweet biscuits studded with almonds. *Brighidini di lamporecchio* are small, round aniseed-flavoured wafers; *ricciarelli* are almond biscuits, sometimes with candied orange; and *lardpinocchiati* are studded with pine kernels. In Lucca, locals are proud of their *buccellato* (a sweet bread loaf with sultanas and aniseed seeds), a treat given by godparents to their godchild on their first Holy Communion and eaten with alacrity at all other times.

Unsurprisingly, it was at the Florentine court of Catherine de' Medici that Italy's most famous product, gelato, first appeared, thanks to court maestro Bernardo Buontalenti (1536–1608), who engineered a way of freezing sweetened milk and egg yolks. For centuries, ice cream and sherbets – a mix of shaved ice and fruit juice served between courses at Renaissance banquets to aid digestion – only appeared on wealthy tables.

Celebrations

Be it harvest, wedding, birth or religious holiday, traditional celebrations are intrinsically woven into Tuscan culinary culture. They are not as raucous as festivals of the past, when an animal was sacrificed, but most remain meaty affairs.

Tuscans have baked breads and cakes, such as ring-shaped *berlingozzo* (Tuscan sweet bread) and *schiacciata alla fiorentina* (a flattish, spongy bread-cake best made with old-fashioned lard) for centuries during Carnevale, the period of merrymaking leading up to Ash Wednesday. Fritters are another sweet Carnevale treat: *cenci* are plain twists (literally 'rags') of fried, sweet dough sprinkled with icing sugar, *castagnole* look like puffed-up cushions, and *fritelle di mele* are slices of apple battered, deep fried and eaten warm with sugar.

On Easter Sunday families take baskets of hard-boiled white eggs covered in a white-cloth napkin to church to be blessed, and return home to a luncheon feast of roast lamb gently spiced with garlic and rosemary, preceded by the blessed eggs.

September's grape harvest sees grapes stuck on top of *schiacciata* to make *schiacciata con l'uva* (grape cake), and autumn's chestnut harvest brings a flurry of chestnut festivals and the appearance of *castagnaccio* (chestnut cake baked with chestnut flower, studded with raisins, topped with a rosemary sprig and served with a slice of ricotta) on the Tuscan table.

Come Christmas, *bollito misto* (boiled meat) with all the trimmings is traditional for many families: various animal parts, eg trotters, are thrown into the cooking pot and simmered for hours with a vegetable and herb stock. The meat is later served with mustard, green salsa and other sauces. A whole pig, notably the recently revived ancient white-and-black *cinta senese* indigenous breed, roasted on a spit, is the other option.

On the Wine Trail

There's far more to this vine-rich region than cheap, raffia-wrapped bottled Chianti – *that* was the 1970s, darling! Something of a viticulture powerhouse, Tuscany excites oenophiles with its myriad full-bodied, highly respected reds. Wine tasting is an endless pleasure and the region is peppered with *enoteche* (wine bars) and *cantine* (wine cellars) designed especially for tasting and buying.

Many are planted on Tuscany's *strade del vino* (wine roads): signposted itineraries that lead motorists and cyclists along wonderfully scenic back roads into the heart of Tuscan wine country.

Tuscan white amounts to one label loved by Renaissance popes and artists alike: the aromatic Vernaccia di San Gimignano, best drunk as an aperitif on a terrace in or around San Gimignano.

Brunello di Montalcino

Brunello di Montalcino is one of Italy's most prized wines: count on up to €15 for a glass, €30 to €100 for an average bottle and €5000 for a 1940s collectible. The product of Sangiovese grapes grown south of Siena, it must spend at least two years ageing in oak. It is intense and complex, with an ethereal fragrance, and it's best paired with game, wild boar and roasts. Brunello grape rejects go into Rossi di Montalcino, Brunello's substantially cheaper but wholly drinkable kid sister.

Vino Nobile di Montepulciano

Prugnolo Gentile grapes (a clone of Sangiovese) form the backbone of the distinguished Vino Nobile di Montepulciano (2006 was an exceptional year). Its intense but delicate nose and dry, vaguely tannic taste make it the perfect companion to red meat and mature cheese.

Best Creative Tuscan
....
Essenziale (Florence)
....
Filippo Mud Bar (Pietrasanta)
....
La Terrazza del Chiostro (Pienza)
....
Osteria di Passignano (Badia A Passignano)
....
Le Chiavi d'Oro (Arezzo)
....
La Dogana (Montepulciano)

THE TUSCAN TABLE ON THE WINE TRAIL

OLIVE OIL

Olive oil heads Tuscany's culinary trinity (bread and wine are the other two members) and epitomises the earthy simplicity of Tuscan cuisine: dipping chunks of bread into pools of this liquid gold or biting into a slice of oil-doused *fettunta* (bruschetta) are sweet pleasures here.

The Etruscans were the first to cultivate olive trees and press the fruit to make oil, a process refined by the Romans. As with wine, strict rules govern when and how olives are harvested (October to December), the varieties used, and so on.

The best Tuscan oils wear a Chianti Classico DOP or Terre di Siena DOP label and an IGP certificate of quality issued by the region's Consortium of Tuscan Olive Oil. In Florence look out for prize-winning oils from local producer Marchesi de' Frescobaldi.

Chianti

The cheery, full and dry Chianti is known the world over as being easy to drink, suited to any dish and wholly affordable. It was more famous than good in the 1970s, but contemporary Chianti gets the thumbs up from wine critics today. Produced in seven subzones from Sangiovese and a mix of other grape varieties, Chianti Classico – the traditional heart of this long-standing winegrowing area – is the best known, with a DOCG (Denominazione d'Origine Controllata e Garantita; Protected Designation of Origin and Quality) guarantee of quality and a Gallo Nero (Black Cockerel) emblem that once symbolised the medieval Chianti League. Young, fun Chianti Colli Senesi from the Siena hills is the largest subzone; Chianti delle Colline Pisane is light and soft in style; and Chianti Rùfina comes from the hills east of Florence.

Best Wine Bars

Le Volpi e l'Uva (Florence)

Il Santino (Florence)

L'Enoteca Marcucci (Pietrasanta)

Enoteca Tognoni (Bolgheri)

Enoteca Osteria Osticcio (Montalcino)

Cantina Nardi (Livorno)

Super Tuscans

One result of Chianti's 'cheap wine for the masses' reputation in the 1970s was the realisation by some Tuscans – including the Antinoris, Tuscany's most famous wine-producing family – that wines with a rich, complex, internationally acceptable taste following the New World tradition of blending mixes could be sold for a lot more than local wines. Thus, innovative, exciting wines were developed and cleverly marketed to appeal to buyers both in New York and in Florence. And when an English-speaking scribe dubbed the end product 'Super Tuscans', the name stuck. (Italian winemakers prefer the term IGT – *indicazione geografica tipica*.) Sassacaia, Solaia, Bolgheri, Tignanello and Luce are all super-hot Super Tuscans.

More and more international wine producers are turning to Tuscan soil to blend Super Tuscans and other modern wines. American-owned **Castello Banfi** (http://castellobanfi.com), in the Tuscan biz for over three decades, is one of the most state-of-the-art wineries in Italy and continues to impress the international wine world with its pioneering work, quietly underscoring the demise of winemaking as the exclusive domain of old, blue-blooded Tuscan families. These days, in this ancient land first cultivated by the Etruscans, Tuscany's oldest craft is open to anyone with wine-wizardry nous.

Celebrity Wine

Celebrity-backed wine followed hot on the heels of the Super Tuscans. English pop star Sting owns an organically farmed estate, **Tenuta Il Palagio** (www.palagioproducts.com), near Figline Valdarno in Chianti

---

TOP WINE & OIL ROADS

Meander past olive groves, vines and farms plump with local produce with these delightful *strade del vino e dell'olio* (wine and oil roads).

Strada del Vino e dei Sapori Colli di Maremma (www.stradavinimaremma.it) This route southeast of Grossetto highlights several DOC and DOCG wines, extra-virgin olive oil Toscano IGP, and the Maremma breed of cattle.

Strada del Vino e dell'Olio Lucca Montecarlo e Versilia (www.stradavinoeoliolucca.it) Seravezza in the Apuane Alps to Lucca, then east to Montecarlo and Pescia. This route features Lucca's famous DOP olive oil and the Colline Lucchesi and Montecarlo di Lucca DOCs.

Strada del Vino e dell'Olio Costa degli Etruschi (www.lastradadelvino.com) A scenic 150km itinerary along the Etruscan Coast from Livorno to Piombino and then over to the Tuscan island of Elba; Super Tuscan Sassicaia is the big tasting highlight.

WINE CLASSIFICATIONS

The quality and origin of Tuscan wine is flagged with these official classifications:

DOC (Denominazione d'Origine Controllata; Protected Designation of Origin) Must be produced within a specified region using defined methods to meet a certain quality; the rules spell out production area, grape varietals and viticultural/bottling techniques.

DOCG (Denominazione d'Origine Controllata e Garantita; Protected Designation of Origin and Quality) The most prestigious stamp of quality, DOCG wines are particularly good ones, produced in subterritories of DOC areas. Of Italy's 44 DOCGs, eight are Tuscan – Brunello di Montalcino, Carmignano, Chianti, Chianti Classico, Morellino di Scansano, Vernaccia di San Gimignano, Vino Nobile di Montepulciano and Elba Aleatico Passito.

IGT (Indicazione Geografica Tipica; Protected Geographical Indication) High-quality wines, such as Super Tuscans, that don't meet DOC or DOCG definitions.

where he produces various wines, each named after one of his songs: Message in a Bottle, When We Dance, and so forth. In 2016 Sting's full-bodied red wine Sister Moon – a winning blend of Sangiovese, cabernet sauvignon and merlot grapes – was listed as one of Italy's best 100 wines by American magazine *Wine Spectator*.

Super Tuscan reds are produced by the son of Florentine designer Roberto Cavalli at **Tenuta degli Dei** (www.deglidei.com), outside Panzano in Chianti, where top-of-the-range bottles are packaged in a typical Cavalli, flashy leopard-skin box. Wines produced southeast of Pisa on the family estate of opera singer Andrea Bocelli are sold at Cantina Bocelli (p248) in La Sterza.

If celebrity design is more your cup of tea, taste wine at the subterranean, design-driven **Rocca di Frassinello** (www.castellare.it/it/rocca-di-frassinello) winery near Grossetto by Renzo Piano; or the equally breathtaking **Petra** (www.petrawine.it) winery by Swiss architect Mario Botta in the Etruscan hills near Suvereto.

Then, of course, there is the spectacular Antinori cellar (p149), ground breaking in design – quite literally: an entire hillside in the heart of Chianti Classico was dug up, a designer cellar was popped inside and earthed over, and new vines were planted, leaving just two giant slashes (the panoramic terraces of the 26,000-sq-metre building) visible from the opposite Chianti hill.

Wine Tasting in Situ

Antinori nel Chianti Classico (Bargino)

Petra Wine (Suvereto)

Castello di Ama (Gaiole in Chianti)

Poggio Antico (Montalcino)

Tuscany on Page & Screen

Few destinations have such a rich history and landscape to draw on for inspiration as Tuscany – or offer writers, actors and crews such a sybaritic location in which to re-search, write and shoot their works. The birthplace of Italian literature (courtesy of the great Dante Alighieri) and the setting for the greatest Italian film of recent decades (*Life is Beautiful*), Tuscany offers the visitor plenty of options when it comes to pre-departure reading and viewing.

Tuscany in Print

The region's literary heritage is rich and varied, and it nurtures both local and foreign writers to this day.

Britons Abroad

....

Pictures from Italy (Charles Dickens; 1846)

....

Along the Road (Aldous Huxley; 1925)

....

Etruscan Places (DH Lawrence; 1932)

Local Voices

Prior to the 13th century, Italian literature was written in Latin. But all that changed with Florentine-born Dante Alighieri (c 1265–1321). One of the founders of the Dolce Stil Novo (Sweet New Style) literary movement, whose members wrote lyric poetry in the Tuscan vernacular, Dante went on to use the local language when writing the epic poem that was to become the first, and greatest, literary work published in the Italian language: *La grande commedia (The Great Comedy)*, published around 1317 and later renamed *La divina commedia (The Divine Comedy)* by his fellow poet Boccaccio. Divided into three parts – *Inferno, Purgatorio* and *Paradiso* – *The Divine Comedy* delivered an allegorical vision of the afterlife that made an immediate and profound impression on readers and, through its wide-reaching popularity, established the Tuscan dialect as the new standardised form of written Italian.

Another early adaptor to the new language of literature was Giovanni Boccaccio (1303–75), who hailed from Certaldo. His masterpiece, *Decam-eron*, was written in the years following the plague of 1348. A collection of 100 allegorical tales recounted by 10 characters, it delivered a vast pan-orama of personalities, events and symbolism to contemporary readers and was nearly as popular and influential as *The Divine Comedy*.

The remaining member of the influential triumvirate that laid down the course for the development of a rich literature in Italian was Petrarch (Francesco Petrarca; 1304–74), born in Arezzo to Florentine parents. Al-though most of his writings were in Latin, he wrote his most popular works, the poems, in Italian. *Il canzoniere (Songbook;* c 1327–68) is the distilled result of his finest poetry. Although the core subject is his un-requited love for a woman named Laura, the breadth of human grief and joy is treated with a lyrical quality unseen until then. His influence spread far and across time: the Petrarchan sonnet form, rhyme scheme and even subject matter was adopted by English metaphysical poets of 17th-century England such as John Donne.

Another outstanding writer of this period was Niccolò Machiavel-li (1469–1527), known above all for his work on power and politics, *Il Principe (The Prince;* 1532).

19th Century Onwards

After its stellar start during the Renaissance, Tuscany took a literary break in the 17th and 18th centuries. The scene regained momentum in the 19th century with Giosuè Carducci (1835–1907), a Maremma-born writer who spent the second half of his life in Bologna. The best of his poetry, written in the 1870s, ranged in tone from a pensive evocation of death (such as in 'Pianto antico') or memories of youthful passion ('Idillio Maremmano') to a nostalgia harking back to the glories of ancient Rome.

During the pre-WWI years Florence's Aldo Palazzeschi (1885–1974) was in the vanguard of the Futurist movement. In 1911 he published arguably his best work, *Il codice di Perelà (Perelà's Code),* a sometimes bitter allegory that in part becomes a farcical imitation of the life of Christ.

Another Florentine, Vasco Pratolini (1913–91), set four highly regarded neo-realist novels in his birthplace: *Le ragazze di San Frediano (The Girls of San Frediano;* 1949), *Cronaca familiare (Family Diary;* 1947), *Cronache di poveri amanti (Chronicle of Poor Lovers;* 1947) and *Metello* (1955).

Fiesole-born Dacia Maraini (b 1936), for many years the partner of author Alberto Moravia, is one of Italy's most lauded contemporary writers, with novels, plays and poetry to her credit. Her best-known works include *Buio* (1999), which won the Premio Strega, Italy's most prestigious literary award, and *La lunga vita di Marianna Ucrìa* (published in English as *The Silent Duchess;* 1990). Her most recent novel is *La bambina e il sognatore* (2015).

Through Foreign Eyes

The trend of setting English-language novels in Tuscany kicked off during the era of the Grand Tour, when wealthy young men from Britain and northern Europe travelled around Europe to view the cultural legacies of antiquity and the Renaissance, completing their liberal educations and being introduced to polite society in the process. The Grand Tour's heyday was from the mid-17th century to the mid-19th century.

With the advent of rail travel in the 1840s, the prospect of a cultural odyssey opened to the middle classes. Wealthy travellers from Britain,

Americans Abroad
Italian Hours (Henry James; 1909)
....
The Stones of Florence (Mary McCarthy; 1956)
....
The City of Florence (RWB Lewis; 1995)

TUSCAN MEMOIRS

Many people visit Tuscany and dream of purchasing their own piece of paradise. The following writers did just that, some establishing wildly successful literary franchises in the process.

Kinta Beevor (*A Tuscan Childhood;* 1993) Beautiful evocation of life in the Tuscan countryside between the two world wars, by the daughter of an English painter who bought a castle in Tuscany and hobnobbed with the likes of DH Lawrence, Aldous Huxley et al.

Eric Newby (*A Small Place in Italy;* 1994) The original Tuscan memoir; Newby bought a farmhouse in northeastern Tuscany in the 1960s and so came to pen this sensitive portrait of rural Tuscany, its people, seasons and ancient rituals.

Frances Mayes (*Under the Tuscan Sun: At Home in Italy; Bella Tuscany; In Tuscany; Every Day in Tuscany;* 1996–2010) Following the end of her marriage, American writer and poet (and subsequent Tuscan bard) bought a dilapidated house in Cortona, did it up and wrote about it in *Under the Tuscan Sun* – a classic today.

Ferenc Máté (*The Hills of Tuscany; A Vineyard in Tuscany: A Wine-Lover's Dream; The Wisdom of Tuscany;* 1999–2009) The author and his wife, a painter, left New York for Tuscany's Montalcino vineyards in 1990 – the abandoned farm they bought anchors a wine-producing estate today.

Mark Gordon Smith (*Tuscan Echoes; Tuscan Light: Memories of Italy;* 2003–2007) It's the tiny details of nature, season and cuisine that stand out in the short-story prose of this English writer who spent his early childhood in Tuscany.

America and Australasia flocked to Italy, and some wrote about their experiences. Notable among these were Henry James, who set parts of *The Portrait of a Lady* (1881) and *Roderick Hudson* (1875) here; George Eliot, whose *Romola* (1862) was set in 15th-century Florence; and EM Forster, who set *A Room with a View* (1908) in Florence and *Where Angels Fear to Tread* (1905) in San Gimignano (fictionalised as Monteriano).

Things slowed down in the early 20th century, with only a few major novelists choosing to set their work here. These included Somerset Maugham (*Up at the Villa*; 1941) and Aldous Huxley (*Time Must Have a Stop*; 1944).

In recent decades, a number of highly regarded novels have been set in Tuscany. Perhaps the best known of these is the Renaissance fiction by English writer Linda Proud, whose Botticelli trilogy – *A Tabernacle for the Sun, Pallas and the Centaur* and *The Rebirth of Venus* – is set in Renaissance Florence during the Pazzi conspiracy, the Medici exile and the rise of Savonarola. The historical detail in all three is exemplary, and each is a cracking good read. Her novel about Botticelli's master Fra' Filippo Lippi, *A Gift for the Magus,* was published in 2012.

Other writers who have used Renaissance Florence as a setting include Sarah Dunant (*The Birth of Venus*; 2003), Salman Rushdie (*The Enchantress of Florence*; 2008), Michaela-Marie Roessner-Hermann (*The Stars Dispose*; 1997, and *The Stars Dispel;* 1999) and Jack Dann (*The Memory Cathedral*; 1995). Of these, Dann wins the prize for constructing the most bizarre plot, setting his novel in a version of the Renaissance in which Leonardo da Vinci actually constructs a number of his inventions (eg the flying machine) and uses them during a battle in the Middle East while in the service of a Syrian general.

Also set in Florence are *Innocence* (1986), written by Booker Prize-winning novelist Penelope Fitzgerald and set during the 1950s; *The Sixteen Pleasures* (1994) by Robert Hellenga, set after the devastating flood of 1966; *The English Patient* (1992) by Michael Ondaatje; and *Inferno* (2013) by Dan Brown (author of *The Da Vinci Code*).

Tuscany on Film

Cinema heavyweight Franco Zeffirelli was born in Florence in 1923 and has set many of his films in the region. His career has taken him from radio and theatre to opera (both stage productions and film versions) and his films include *Romeo and Juliet* (1968), *Brother Sun, Sister Moon* (1972), *Hamlet* (1990) and the semiautobiographical *Tea with Mussolini* (1999). Watch snippets of the latter as part of an engaging cinematic montage of films set in Florence at the city's Museo Novecento.

Actor, comedian and director Roberto Benigni was born near Castiglion Fiorentino in 1952. He picked up four Oscars and created a genre all of his own – Holocaust comedy – with the extraordinarily powerful *La vita é bella* (*Life Is Beautiful;* 1998), a film shot in the east Tuscan town of Arezzo that he directed, co-wrote and starred in. Often compared with Charlie Chaplin and Buster Keaton, he has directed nine films (two set in Tuscany) and acted in many more, including three directed by American independent film-maker Jim Jarmusch.

Four films based on neo-realist novels by Vasco Pratolini were shot in Florence: *Le ragazze di San Frediano* (*The Girls of San Frediano;* Valerio Zurlini; 1954), *Cronache di poveri amanti* (*Chronicle of Poor Lovers;* Carlo Lizzani; 1954), *Cronaca familiare* (*Family Diary;* Valerio Zurlini; 1962) and *Metello* (Mauro Bolognini; 1970).

Award-winning film-makers Paolo and Vittorio Taviani were born in San Miniato and have set parts of three of their films in Tuscany: *La notte di San Lorenzo* (*The Night of the Shooting Stars;* 1982), *Le affinità elettive* (*Elective Affinities;* 1996) and *Good Morning Babylon* (1987).

In *Across the Big Blue Sea* (2017), Swiss writer Katja Meier shares the lessons she learnt during her time working in a home for refugees in the Tuscan hills; Maremma is the setting.

Best 'Shot in Tuscany'

The English Patient (Anthony Minghella; 1996)

Gladiator (Ridley Scott; 2000)

Much Ado about Nothing (Kenneth Branagh; 1993)

A Room with a View (James Ivory; 1985)

Inferno (Ron Howard; 2016)

Art & Architecture

In many respects, the history of Tuscan art is also the history of Western art. Browse through any text on the subject and you'll quickly develop an understanding of how influential the Italian Renaissance, which kicked off and reached its greatest flowering in Florence, has been over the past 500 years. Indeed, it's no exaggeration to say that architecture, painting and sculpture rely on its technical innovations and take inspiration from its major works to this very day.

The Etruscans

Roughly 2800 years before we all started dreaming of a hilltop getaway in Tuscany, the Etruscans had a similar idea: the hill towns that they founded are dotted throughout the countryside.

From the 8th to the 3rd centuries BC, Etruscans held their own against friends, Romans and countrymen, worshipped their own gods and goddesses, and farmed lowlands using sophisticated drainage systems of their own invention. How well they lived between sieges and war is unclear, but they sure knew how to throw a funeral. Etruscan *necropoli* (tombs) are found throughout southern, central and eastern Tuscany. Excavation of these tombs often yields a wealth of jewellery, cinerary urns (used for body ashes) made from terracotta and alabaster, earthenware pottery (particularly the glossy black ceramic known as *bucchero*) and bronze votive offerings.

Of course, the Romans knew a good thing when they plundered it. After conquering swaths of Etruscan territory in Tuscany in the 3rd century BC, they incorporated the Etruscans' highly refined, geometric style into their own art and architecture.

Enter Christianity

Roman centurions weren't in the area for long before Christianity began to take hold. After abandoning his studies and a promising career in Rome to adopt the contemplative life around AD 500, a young local man named Benedict went on to achieve a number of miracles, personally establish 12 monasteries and inspire the founding of many more. His story is visually narrated in great detail in the stunning fresco series (1497–1505) by Il Sodoma and Luca Signorelli in the Great Cloister at Abbazia di Monte Oliveto Maggiore, near Siena.

One early Benedictine monastery, San Pietro in Valle, was built in neighbouring Umbria by order of the Lombard duke of Spoleto, Faroaldo II. It kick-started a craze for the blend of Lombard and Roman styles known as Romanesque, and local ecclesiastical structures were built in this style. The basic template was simple: a stark nave stripped of extra columns ending in a domed apse, surrounded by chapels usually donated by wealthy patrons.

In the 11th century the Romanesque style acquired a distinctly Tuscan twist in Pisa, when the coloured marble banding and veneering of the city's *duomo* (cathedral) set a new gold standard for architectural decoration. This new style (sometimes described as Pisan) was then applied to a swath of churches throughout the region, including the Chiesa di San Miniato al Monte in Florence, and the Chiesa di San Michele in Foro and the Cattedrale di San Martino, both in Lucca.

Top Etruscan Museums

Museo Etrusco Guarnacci (Volterra)

Museo dell'Accademia Etrusca (Cortona)

Museo Civico Archeologico 'Isidoro Falchi' (Vetulonia)

Museo Archeologico Nazionale 'Gaio Cilnio Mecenate' (Arezzo)

Best Art Galleries

Galleria degli Uffizi (Florence)

Galleria dell'Accademia (Florence)

Pinacoteca Nazionale (Siena)

Museo Nazionale di San Matteo (Pisa)

Galleria Palatina, Palazzo Pitti (Florence)

Siena was not about to be outdone in the architectural stakes by its rivals Florence and Pisa, and so in 1196 its city council approved a no-expenses-spared program to build a new *duomo*. They certainly got their money's worth, ending up with a spectacular Gothic facade by Giovanni Pisano, a pulpit by Nicola Pisano and a rose window by Duccio di Buoninsegna.

While Tuscany's churches were becoming increasingly more spectacular, nothing prepared pilgrims for what they would find inside the upper and lower churches of the Basilica di San Francesco in Assisi, Umbria. Not long after St Francis' death in 1226, an all-star team of Tuscan artists was hired to decorate these churches in his honour, kicking off a craze for frescoes that wouldn't abate for centuries. Cimabue, Giotto, Pietro Lorenzetti and Simone Martini captured the life and gentle spirit of St Francis while his memory was still fresh in the minds of the faithful. For medieval pilgrims unaccustomed to multiplexes and special effects, entering a space that had been covered from floor to ceiling with stories told in living colour must have been a dazzling, overwhelming experience.

> **Best Gothic Churches**
> ....
> Duomo (Siena)
> ....
> Abbazia di San Galgano (south of Siena)
> ....
> Chiesa di Santa Maria della Spina (Pisa)

The Middle Ages: the Rise of the Comune

While communities sprang up around hermits and holy men in the hinterlands, cities began to take on a life of their own from the 13th and 14th centuries. Roman road networks had been serving as handy trade routes starting in the 11th century, and farming estates and villas began to spring up outside major trading centres as a new middle class of merchants, farmers and skilled craftspeople emerged. Taxes and donations sponsored the building of hospitals such as Ospedale Santa Maria della Scala in Siena. Streets were paved, town walls erected and sewerage systems built to accommodate an increasingly sophisticated urban population not keen on sprawl or squalor.

Once townsfolk came into a bit of money, they weren't necessarily eager to part with it, and didn't always agree on how their tax dollars should be spent. *Comuni* (local governments) were formed to represent the various interests of merchants, guilds and competing noble families, and the first order of business in major medieval cities, such as Siena, Florence and Volterra, was the construction of an impressive town hall to reflect the importance and authority of the *comune*.

In addition to being savvy political lobbyists and fans of grand architectural projects that kept their constituents gainfully employed, medieval *comuni* were masters of propaganda, and perfectly understood the influence that art and architecture could wield. A case in point is Ambrogio Lorenzetti's *Allegories of Good and Bad Government* fresco series in Siena's Palazzo Comunale, which is better and bigger than any political billboard could ever be. In the *Allegory of Good Government*, Lorenzetti's grey-bearded figure of Legitimate Authority is surrounded by an entourage that would certainly put White House interns to shame: Peace, Fortitude, Prudence, Magnanimity, Temperance and Justice. Above them flit Faith, Hope and Charity, and to the left Concord sits confidently on her throne while the reins of justice are held taut overhead.

Next to this fresco is another depicting the effects of good government: townsfolk make their way through town in an orderly fashion, pausing to do business, greet one another and dance a merry jig. But things couldn't be more different in the *Allegory of Bad Government*, where horned and fanged Tyrannia rules over a scene of chaos surrounded by winged vices, and Justice lies unconscious, her scales shattered. Like the best campaign speeches, this cautionary tale was brilliantly rendered but not always heeded.

> As madness and profligacy often run in families, so too does artistic genius. Italian artistic dynasties include the della Robbias (Luca, Marco, Andrea, Giovanni and Girolamo), the Lorenzettis (Ambrogio and Pietro) and the Pisanos (Nicola and Giovanni, Andrea and Nino).

On the World Stage

When they weren't busy politicking, late-medieval farmers, craftspeople and merchants did quite well for themselves. Elegant, locally made ceramics, tiles and marbles were showcased in churches across Tuscany and became all the rage throughout Europe and the Mediterranean when pilgrims returned home to England and France with examples after following the Via Francigena pilgrimage route from Canterbury to Rome. Artisans were kept busy applying their skills to civic-works projects and churches, which had to be expanded and updated to keep up with the growing numbers and rising expectations of pilgrims in the area.

With outside interest came outside influence, and local styles adapted to international markets. Florence became famous for lustrous, tinglazed *maiolica* (majolica ware) tiles and plates painted with vibrant metallic pigments that were inspired by the Islamic ceramics of Mallorca (Spain). The prolific della Robbia family started to create richly glazed ceramic reliefs that are now enshrined at the Museo del Bargello in Florence and in churches and museums across the region.

Modest Romanesque cathedrals were given an International Gothic makeover befitting their appeal to pilgrims of all nations, but the Italian take on the French style was more colourful than the grey-stone spires and flying buttresses of Paris. The local version often featured a simple layout and striped stone naves fronted by multilayer birthday-cake facades, which might be frosted with pink paint, glittering mosaics and rows of arches capped with sculptures. The most famous example of this confectionery approach is the *duomo* in Siena.

The evolution from solid Romanesque to airy Gothic to a yin-and-yang balance of the two can be witnessed in buildings throughout the region, many of which blend a relatively austere Romanesque exterior with high Gothic drama indoors. This set a new ecclesiastical architecture standard that was quickly exported into Italy at large and on to the rest of Europe.

Best Romanesque Churches

Collegiata (San Gimignano)

Abbazia di Sant'Antimo (near Montalcino)

Pieve di Corsignano (Pienza)

Duomo (Sovana)

Pieve di Santa Maria (Arezzo)

Dark Times

By the 14th century the smiling Sienese townsfolk of Ambrogio Lorenzetti's *Allegory of Good Government* must have seemed like the figment of a fertile imagination. After a major famine in 1329 and then a bank collapse, Siena's *comune* went into debt to maintain roads, continue work on the *duomo,* help the needy and jump-start the local economy. But just when the city seemed set for a comeback, the plague brought devastation in 1348. Three-quarters of Siena's population – including Pietro and Ambrogio Lorenzetti – died, and virtually all economic and artistic activity ground to a halt. Another plague hit in 1374, killing 80,000 Sienese, and was swiftly followed by a famine. It was too much – the city never entirely recovered.

Florence was also hit by the plague in 1348, and despite fervent public prayer rituals, 96,000 Florentines died in just seven months. Those who

GIOTTO DI BONDONE

The 14th-century Tuscan poet Giovanni Boccaccio wrote in the *Decameron* that his fellow Tuscan Giotto di Bondone (c 1266–1337) was 'a genius so sublime that there was nothing produced by nature...that he could not depict to the life'.

Boccaccio wasn't the only prominent critic of the time to consider Giotto extraordinary – Giorgio Vasari was also a huge fan, arguing that Giotto initiated the 'rebirth' (*rinascità* or *renaissance*) in art. In his paintings, Giotto abandoned popular conventions such as the three-quarter view of head and body, and presented his figures from behind, from the side or turning around, just as the story demanded. Giotto had no need for lashings of gold paint and elaborate ornamentation to impress the viewer with the significance of the subject. Instead, he enabled the viewer to feel the dramatic tension of a scene through a naturalistic rendition of figures and a radical composition that created the illusion of depth.

Giotto's important works in Tuscany include an altarpiece portraying the Madonna and Child among angels and saints in Florence's Galleria degli Uffizi, a painted wooden crucifix in the Basilica di Santa Maria Novella and frescoes in the Basilica di Santa Croce. His magnificent *Life of St Francis* fresco cycle graces the walls of the upper church of the Basilica di San Francesco in Assisi, Umbria.

survived experienced a crisis of faith, making Florence fertile territory for humanist ideals – not to mention macabre superstition, attempts to raise the dead, and a fascination with corpses that the likes of Leonardo da Vinci would call science and others morbid curiosity.

At the plague's end, a Florentine building boom ensued when upstart merchants such as Cosimo I de' Medici (Cosimo the Elder) and Palla Strozzi competed to put their stamp on a city that needed to be reimagined after the horrors it had undergone.

The Renaissance

It wasn't only merchants who were jockeying for power at this time. To put an end to the competing claims of the Tuscan Ghibelline faction that was allied with the Holy Roman Empire, the Rome-backed Guelph faction had marked its territory with impressive new landmarks, predominantly in Florence. Giotto – often described as the founding artist of the Renaissance – had been commissioned to design the city's iconic 85m-tall square *campanile* (bell tower) and one-up the 57m-tall tower under construction in Ghibelline Pisa that was already looking a bit off kilter. And this was only one of many such projects.

'Mess with Florence, and you take on Rome' was the not-so-subtle hint delivered by Florentine architects, who made frequent reference to the glories of the ancient power and its classical architecture when designing the new churches, *palazzi* and public buildings that started sprouting across the city during the *Trecento* (14th century) and proliferated in the *Quattrocentro* (15th century). This new Florentine style became known as Renaissance or 'rebirth', and it really started to hit its stride after architect Filippo Brunelleschi won a competition to design the dome of Florence's *duomo*. Brunelleschi was heavily influenced by the achievements of the classical masters, but he was able to do something that they hadn't

Masaccio's *Trinity*, a wall painting in the Basilica di Santa Maria Novella, is often described as one of the founding works of Renaissance painting and the inspiration for Leonardo da Vinci's *Last Supper* fresco.

FILIPPO BRUNELLESCHI

Many Renaissance men left their mark on Florence, but few did so with as much grace and glory as Filippo Brunelleschi (1377–1446). An architect, mathematician, engineer and sculptor, Brunelleschi trained as a master goldsmith and showed early promise as a sculptor – he was an entrant in the 1401 competition to design the doors of the baptistry in Florence (won by fellow goldsmith Lorenzo Ghiberti) and shortly after travelled to Rome with Donatello, another goldsmith by training, to study that city's ancient architecture and art. When he returned to Florence in 1419 he took up an architectural commission from the silk merchant's guild to design a hospital for foundlings on Piazza della Santissima Annunziata in San Marco. Known as the Ospedale degli Innocenti (Hospital of the Innocents – today a stunning museum), his classically proportioned and detailed building featured a distinctive nine-arched loggia and was a radical departure from the High Gothic style that many of his artistic contemporaries were still embracing. Its design was sober, secular and sophisticated, epitomising the new humanist age.

In 1419, after completing his work on the foundling hospital, Brunelleschi moved on to a commission that was to occupy him for the next 42 years – the dome of Florence's *duomo*. His mathematical brain and talent for devising innovative engineering solutions enabled him to do what many Florentines had thought impossible: deliver the largest dome to be built in Italy since antiquity.

Brunelleschi's other works in Florence include the Basilica di San Lorenzo, the Basilica di Santo Spirito and the Cappella de' Pazzi in the Basilica di Santa Croce. Vasari said of him: 'The world having for so long been without artists of lofty soul or inspired talent, heaven ordained that it should receive from the hand of Filippo the greatest, the tallest, and the finest edifice of ancient and modern times, demonstrating that Tuscan genius, although moribund, was not yet dead'. He is buried in the *duomo*, under the dome that was his finest achievement.

been able to do themselves – discover and record the mathematical rules by which objects appear to diminish as they recede from us. In so doing, he gave local artists and architects a whole new visual perspective and a means to glorious artistic ends.

To decorate the new buildings, artists enjoyed a bonanza of commissions to paint heroic battle scenes, fresco private chapels and carve busts of the latest power players – works that sometimes outlived their patrons' clout. A good example is the Peruzzi family, whose members had risen to prominence in 14th-century Florence as bankers, with interests reaching from London to the Middle East. They set the trend for art patronage by commissioning Giotto to fresco the family's memorial chapel in Santa Croce, completed in 1320. When Peruzzi client King Edward III of England defaulted on loans the family went bankrupt – but, as patrons of Giotto's precocious experiments in perspective and Renaissance illusionism, their legacy set the tone for the artistic flowering of Florence.

One Florentine family to follow the Peruzzis' lead was the prominent Brancacci, who commissioned Masolino da Panicale and his precocious assistant Masaccio to decorate a chapel in the Basilica di Santa Maria del Carmine in Florence. After Masaccio's premature death aged only 27, the frescoes were completed by Filippino Lippi. In these dramatic frescoes, framed in astonishingly convincing architectural sets, scenes from the life of St Peter allude to pressing Florentine concerns of the day: the new income tax, unfair imprisonment and hoarded wealth. Masaccio's image of the expulsion of Adam and Eve from the Garden of Eden proved especially prophetic: the Brancacci were allied with the Strozzi family, and were exiled from Florence by the Medici before they could see the work completed.

But the patrons with the greatest impact on the course of art history were, of course, the Medicis. Patriarch Cosimo the Elder was exiled in 1433 by a consortium of Florentine families who considered him a triple threat: powerful banker, ambassador of the Church, and consummate politician with the savvy to sway emperors and popes. But the flight of capital from Florence after his departure created such a fiscal panic that the banishment was hastily rescinded and within a year the Medicis were well and truly back in town. To announce his return in grand style, Cosimo funded the 1437 rebuilding of the Convento di San Marco (now Museo di San Marco) by Michelozzo, and commissioned Fra' Angelico to fresco the monks' quarters with scenes from the life of Christ. Another artist pleased to see Cosimo return was Donatello, who had completed his lithe bronze statue of *David* (now in the city's Museo del Bargello) with his patronage.

Through such commissions, early Renaissance innovations in perspective, closely observed realism and *chiaroscuro* (the play of light and dark) began to catch on throughout the region. In Sansepolcro, a painter named Piero della Francesca earned a reputation for figures who were glowing with otherworldly light, and who were caught in personal predicaments that people could relate to: Roman soldiers snoozing on the job, crowds left goggle-eyed by miracles and bystanders distressed to witness cruel persecution. His fresco series *Legend of the True Cross*, commissioned by the Bacci family for a chapel in Arezzo's Chiesa di San Francesco, was one of the supreme artistic achievements of the time.

The High Renaissance

The decades leading up to and beginning the *Cinquecento* (16th century) are often seen as a kind of university faculty meeting, with genteel, silver-haired sages engaged in a collegial exchange of ideas. A bar brawl might be closer to the metaphorical truth, with artists, scientists, politicians and clergy mixing it up and everyone emerging bruised. The debate was never as simple as Church versus state, science versus art or seeing versus believing; in those days, politicians could be clergy, scientists could be artists, and artists could be clergy.

Filippo Lippi (1406–69) entered the Carmelite order as a monk aged 14, but he renounced his vows after eloping with a novice who was sitting for the figure of the Madonna in a fresco he was painting for Prato's *duomo*. Their son Filippino (1457–1504) became a notable painter too.

ART & ARCHITECTURE THE HIGH RENAISSANCE

As well as endowing churches, building palaces and funding frescoes, the wealthy merchant families of the Renaissance commissioned plenty of portraits. Cosimo I de' Medici's favourite portrait painter was Agnolo di Cosimo (1503–72), called Bronzino because of his dark complexion. Look for his Medici portraits in the Uffizi, Florence.

318

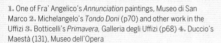
1. One of Fra' Angelico's *Annunciation* paintings, Museo di San Marco 2. Michelangelo's *Tondo Doni* (p70) and other work in the Uffizi 3. Botticelli's *Primavera*, Galleria degli Uffizi (p68) 4. Duccio's *Maestà* (131), Museo dell'Opera

VALERY VOENNYY/ALAMY ©

Tuscan Artists

Plenty of the big names jostle for precedence in the pantheon of Tuscan artists, so narrowing any list down to a 'Top Five' is a near impossible task. Here's our best attempt.

Michelangelo Buonarroti (1475–1564)

The quintessential Renaissance man: a painter, sculptor and architect with more masterpieces to his credit than any other artist either before or since. In Florence, view his *David* in the Galleria dell'Accademia (p90) and his *Tondo Doni* (Holy Family) in the Uffizi (p68).

Sandro Botticelli (c 1444–1510)

His Renaissance beauties charmed commissions out of the Medicis and continue to exert their siren call on the millions who visit the Uffizi Gallery (p68) each year. Don't miss his *Primavera* and *Birth of Venus*.

Giotto di Bondone (c 1266–1337)

Giotto kick-started the Renaissance with action-packed frescoes in which each character pinpoints emotions with facial expressions and poses that need no translation. Make the pilgrimage to Assisi (p284) to see his *Life of St Francis* fresco cycle.

Fra' Angelico (c 1395–1455)

Few artists are saints – they're far more likely to be sinners. One of the exceptions was Il Beato Angelico, who was canonised in 1982. His best-loved work is the *Annunciation*, versions of which are on display in Florence's Museo di San Marco (p88) and Cortona's Museo Diocesano (p282).

Duccio di Buoninsegna (c 1255–1318)

Head honcho of the Sienese school, he's known for his riveting Madonnas with level gazes and pale-green skin against glowing gold backgrounds. His masterwork is the *Maestà* in the Museo dell'Opera (p131) in Siena.

There were many artistic superstars during this period, and most were locals who ended up honing their skills in Florence and then moving elsewhere in Italy. Their careers were well documented by Giorgio Vasari in his gossipy *Lives of the Artists*.

To understand just how much of his life, passion and soul Michelangelo gave to sculpture – and the city of Florence – read Irving Stone's gripping biographical novel *The Agony and the Ecstasy* (1961).

Inspired by Masaccio, tutored by Fra' Filippo Lippi and backed by Lorenzo de' Medici, Sandro Botticelli was a rising Florentine art star who was sent to Rome to paint a fresco celebrating papal authority in the Sistine Chapel. The golden boy who'd painted the *Birth of Venus* for Lorenzo de' Medici's private villa in 1485 (now in Florence's Galleria degli Uffizi) could do no wrong until he was accused of sodomy in 1501. The charges didn't stick, but the rumours did, and Botticelli's work was critiqued as too decadently sensual for religious subjects. When religious reformer Savonarola ousted the Medici and began to purge Florence of decadent excess in the face of surely imminent Armageddon, Botticelli paintings went up in flames in the massive 'Bonfire of the Vanities'. Botticelli repudiated mythology and turned his attention to Madonnas, some of whom bear a marked family resemblance to his Venus.

Michelangelo, a Tuscan village lad from Caprese (today Caprese Michelangelo) in the remote Tuscan outback of Casentino in eastern Tuscany, was another of Lorenzo de' Medici's protégés. His classically inspired work was

RENAISSANCE FRESCOES

They may look like ordinary bible stories now, but in their heyday Renaissance frescoes provided running social commentary as well as religious inspiration. In them, human adversity looked divine, and vice versa.

Fantastic examples are found throughout Tuscany, but to see the very best head to the following churches and museums:

Collegiata, San Gimignano (p155) There are hardly any undecorated surfaces in this cathedral, with every wall sporting huge, comic-strip-like frescoes by Bartolo di Fredi, Lippo Memmi, Domenico Ghirlandaio and Benozzo Gozzoli. The highlight is Taddeo di Bartolo's gleefully grotesque *Final Judgment* (1396).

Libreria Piccolomini, Duomo, Siena (p130) Umbrian artist Bernardino Pinturicchio extols the glory of Siena in 10 vibrant fresco panels (c 1502–1507) celebrating Enea Silvio Piccolomini, aka the humanist Pope Pius II. St Catherine of Siena makes a cameo appearance.

Museo di San Marco, Florence (p88) Fra' Angelico's frescoes portray religious figures in all-too-human moments of uncertainty, reflecting the humanist spirit of the Renaissance. The highlight is his *Annunciation* (c 1440).

Museo Civico, Siena (p132) Magnificent is the only word to use when describing Ambrogio Lorenzetti's *Allegories of Good and Bad Government* (1338–40) and Simone Martini's *Maestà* (*Virgin Mary in Majesty;* 1315).

Cappella Brancacci, Florence (p97) Masaccio's *The Expulsion of Adam and Eve from Paradise* and *The Tribute Money* (c 1427) showcase architectural perspective and sly political satire.

Cappella Bacci, Chiesa di San Francesco, Arezzo (p265) Piero della Francesca's *Legend of the True Cross* (c 1452–66) displays a veritable encyclopaedia of Renaissance painting tricks (directional lighting, steep perspective etc).

Chiesa di Sant'Agostino, San Gimignano (p157) Benozzo Gozzoli's bizarre fresco of San Sebastian (c 1464) shows the fully clothed saint protecting the citizens of San Gimignano, helped by a bare-breasted Virgin Mary and a semi-robed Jesus. Wins the prize for the weirdest religious iconography.

Cappella dei Magi, Palazzo Medici-Riccardi, Florence (p87) More Gozzoli, but this time there's nothing strange about his subject matter, which has members of the Medici family making a guest appearance in the *Procession of the Magi to Bethlehem* (c 1459–63).

GIORGIO VASARI'S 'LIVES OF THE ARTISTS'

Painter, architect and writer Giorgio Vasari (1511–74) is rightly described as a 'Renaissance man'. Born in Arezzo, he gew up in what is now the small but fascinating house museum Museo di Casa Vasari. He later trained as a painter in Florence, working with artists such as Andrea del Sarto and Michelangelo (he idolised the latter). As a painter, he is best remembered for his floor-to-ceiling frescoes in the Salone dei Cinquecento in Florence's Palazzo Vecchio. As an architect, his most accomplished work was the elegant loggia of the Galleria degli Uffizi (he also designed the enclosed, elevated corridor that connected the Palazzo Vecchio with the Uffizi and Palazzo Pitti and was dubbed the 'Corridoio Vasari-ano' in his honour). But posterity remembers him predominantly for his work as an art historian. His *Lives of the Most Excellent Painters, Sculptors and Architects, from Cimabue to Our Time*, an encyclopaedia of artistic biographies published in 1550 and dedicated to Cosimo I de' Medici, is still in print (as *The Lives of the Artists*) and is full of wonderful anecdotes and gossip about his artistic contemporaries in 16th-century Florence.

Memorable passages include his recollection of visiting Donatello's studio one day to find the great sculptor staring at his extremely lifelike statue of the *Prophet Habakkuk* and imploring it to talk (we can only assume that Donatello had been working too hard). Vasari also writes about a young Giotto painting a fly on the surface of a work by Cimabue that the older master then tried to brush away.

uniformly admired until the Medicis were ousted by Savonarola in 1494. By some accounts, Savonarola tossed rare early paintings by Michelangelo onto his bonfires. Without his Medici protectors, Michelangelo seemed unsure of his next move: he briefly hid in the basement of San Lorenzo and then roamed around Italy. In Rome he carved a *Bacchus* for Cardinal Raffaele Riaro that the patron deemed unsuitable – but this only seemed to spur Michelangelo on to make a bigger and still more sensuous statue of *David* in 1501. It's now exhibited in Florence's Galleria dell'Accademia.

Leonardo, who hailed from Vinci, southwest of Florence, had so many talents that it is hard to isolate only a few for comment. In his painting, he took what some critics have described as the decisive step in the history of Western art – namely, abandoning the balance that had previously been maintained between colour and line and choosing to modulate his contours using shading. This technique is called *sfumato* and it is perfectly displayed in his *Mona Lisa* (now in the Louvre in Paris). Few of his works remain in his birthplace; the exceptions are his *Adoration of the Magi* and *Annunciation*, both in the Uffizi.

In 1542 the Inquisition arrived in Italy, marking a definitive end to the Renaissance exploration of humanity in all its glorious imperfections. Tuscan art and architecture would never again lead the world by example.

A Stop on the Grand Tour

A 'Grand Tour' of Italy became an obligatory display of culture and class status by the 18th century, and Tuscany was a key stop on the itinerary. German and English artists enraptured with Michelangelo, Perugino and other early High Renaissance painters took the inspiration home, kick-starting a neoclassicist craze. Conversely, trends from northern Europe (Impressionism, plein-air painting and Romanticism) became trendy among Italian artists, as witnessed in the collection at Florence's Galleria d'Arte Moderna in the Palazzo Pitti, which is dominated by late-19th-century works by artists of the Tuscan Macchiaioli school (the local equivalent of Impressionism). These include Telemaco Signorini (1835–1901) and Giovanni Fattori (1825–1908).

In architecture, the most fascinating case of artistic import–export is Italian art nouveau, often referred to as Liberty after the London store that put William Morris' Italian-inspired visual ideals into commercial action.

The term 'Macchiaioli' (the name given to a 19th-century group of Tuscan plein-air artists) was coined by a journalist in 1862. It mockingly implied that the artists' finished works were no more than sketches, and was drawn from the phrase *'darsi alla macchia'* (to hide in bushes or scrubland).

Tuscan Architecture

Italy has more than its share of great buildings, and a large percentage of these are in Tuscany. Brunelleschi and Michelangelo both designed masterpieces here, and every town and city seems to have at least one notable Romanesque, Gothic or Renaissance structure.

Churches

Tuscany's *chiese* (churches) are headline attractions where worship can take many forms. Every village, town and city has at least one church, and many are repositories of great art. Florence has masterpieces galore (don't miss Santa Maria Novella, Santa Croce and San Lorenzo), but Siena, Pisa and San Gimignano are richly endowed, too, with their respective *duomos* (cathedrals) being the best-loved and most distinctive buildings in town.

On the border of Tuscany and Umbria, Orvieto's *duomo* is one of the most beautiful in the country.

Baptistries

Important cathedrals often have a detached *battistero* (baptistry) with a dedicated altar and font. Pisa's cupcake-shaped example in the Piazza dei Miracoli, with its exquisite hexagonal marble pulpit carved by Nicola Pisano, is wonderful, as is Florence's Romanesque version with its famous door panels sculpted by Lorenzo Ghiberti.

Hospitals

Funded by the church, the *comune* (municipality) or wealthy philanthropists, *ospedali* (hospitals) have historically been among the largest and grandest of civic buildings. Siena's Santa Maria della Scala

1. Florence and its Duomo (p74)
2. Battistero di San Giovanni (p227), Pisa
3. Palazzo Pubblico, Torre del Mangia and Piazza del Campo (p134), Siena

is perhaps the best known, but architecture buffs adore Brunelleschi's Ospedale degli Innocenti in Florence.

Palaces

The Medicis weren't the only dynasty with a penchant for building *palazzi* (palaces). In the medieval and Renaissance periods, wealthy families in every city built houses aimed to impress, as did ambassadors, popes, cardinals and *podestàs* (chief magistrates). Architecturally notable examples include Palazzo Strozzi, Palazzo Pitti and Palazzo Medici-Riccardi in Florence; Palazzo Piccolomini, Palazzo Salimbeni and Palazzo Chigi-Saracini in Siena; and Palazzo Piccolomini in Pienza.

Piazzas

These triumphs of town planning are the lifeblood of every Tuscan community, the places where locals come to connect with their neighbours and where important institutions such as churches and town halls are almost inevitably situated. The two most famous examples, Piazzo Pio II in Pienza and Piazza dei Miracoli in Pisa, feature in Unesco's World Heritage List. Worthy of an honourable mention are Livorno's Piazza dei Domenicani, Arezzo's Piazza Grande and Massa Marittima's Piazza Garibaldi.

Town Halls

Built to showcase wealth and civic pride, the *palazzo comunale* (municipal palace) is often the most impressive secular building in a Tuscan town. Noteworthy examples include those on Siena's Piazza del Campo, Volterra's Piazza dei Priori and Florence's Piazza della Signoria.

The 20th Century

Best Sculpture Parks
....
Il Giardino di Daniel Spoerri (Seggiano)
....
Fattoria di Celle (Pistoia)
....
Giardino dei Tarocchi (southern Tuscany)
....
Forte Belvedere (Florence)
....
Chianti Sculpture Park (Chianti)
....
Castello di Ama (Chianti)

After centuries under the thumbs of popes and sundry imperial powers, Tuscany had acquired a certain forced cosmopolitanism, and local artists could identify with Rome, Paris and other big cities in addition to their own *contrada* (neighbourhood). The two biggest stars in the early decades of this century were Livorno-born painter and sculptor Amedeo Modigliani (1884–1920), who lived most of his adult life in Paris, and Greek-born painter Giorgio de Chirico (1888–1978), who studied in Florence and painted the first of his 'Metaphysical Town Square' series there.

Other than Modigliani and di Chirico, no Tuscan painters of note were represented within the major artistic movements of the century: Futurismo (Futurism), Pittura Metafisica (Metaphysical Painting), Spazialismo (Spatialism) and Arte Povera (conceptual art using materials of little worth). Architecture didn't have many local stars either, with the only exception being Giovanni Michelucci (1891–1990), whose buildings include Santa Maria Novella Railway Station in Florence (1932–34).

In the field of abstract art, installation art and sculpture, it was the small town of Pistoia that made itself heard in the 1950s and 1960s through a trio of artists. Pistoia-born Fernando Melani (1907–85) lived all his life in Pistoia, rarely exhibiting elsewhere. His playful works utilised an abundance of recycled materials, with thin metal wire being shaped and twisted in all directions to create the most extraordinary forms and models. His contemporary Mario Nigro (1917–1992) moved to Livorno when he was 12 and later, once the abstract-art bug bit, to the brighter lights of Milan. In the field of sculpture, Pistoia's Marino Marini (1901–80) drew on Tuscany's Etruscan heritage in his work, developing a strong equestrian theme – nudes and men on horseback are what Marini did best.

In the 1980s there was a return to painting and sculpture in a traditional (primarily figurative) sense. Dubbed 'Transavanguardia', this movement broke with the prevailing international focus on conceptual art and was thought by some critics to signal the death of avant-garde. Tuscan artists who were part of this movement include Sandro Chia (b 1946).

Contemporary Art

Best Modern Art Museums
....
Museo Novecento (Florence)
....
Galleria Continua (San Gimignano)
....
Palazzo Fabroni (Pistoia)
....
Museo Marino Mirini (Pistoia)
....
Lucca Centre of Contemporary Art (Lucca)
....
Palazzo Strozzi (Florence)

A heritage of rich artistic traditions spanning three millennia means job security for legions of Tuscan art-conservation specialists and art historians, but can also have a stultifying effect on artists attempting to create something wholly new. Fortunately, there's more going on than the daubs by pavement artists outside major museums and tourist attractions would indicate.

One of the most notable visual artists working here is Massimo Bartolini (b 1962), who radically alters the local landscape with just a few deceptively simple (and quintessentially Tuscan) adjustments of light and perspective that fundamentally change our experience: a bedroom where all the furniture appears to be sinking into the floor, Venice style; or a gallery where the viewer wears special shoes that subtly change the gallery's lighting with each step. Bartolini has also changed the local flora of the tiny Tuscan town of Cecina, near Livorno, where he lives and works, attracting colourful flocks of contemporary-art collectors and curators.

The bijou town of Pietrasanta in the hinterland of the Versilian coast in northwestern Tuscany has a vibrant arts community and is home to the much-lauded Colombian-born sculptor Fernando Botero (b 1932). In the Val d'Orcia, Volterra's homegrown sculptor Mauro Staccioli (b 1937) encourages visitors to admire the landscape from an alternative perspective with his series of monumental geometric installations scattered around town.

Also notable is San Gimignano's Galleria Continua, a world-class commercial gallery whose portfolio of artists includes Tuscans Giovanni Ozzola (b 1982) and Luca Pancrazzi (b 1961). In Prato, the contemporary-art flag is flown by the recently unveiled Centro per l'Arte Contemporanea Luigi Pecci.

Survival Guide

Directory A–Z

Climate

Florence

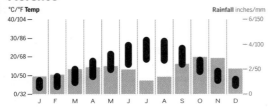

Elba

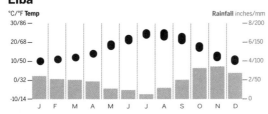

Customs Regulations

Visitors coming into Italy from non-EU countries can import the following items duty free:

➡ 1L spirits (or 2L wine)

➡ 200 cigarettes

➡ up to a total of €430 (€150 for travellers aged under 15) in value for other goods, including perfume and eau de toilette

Anything over these limits must be declared on arrival and the appropriate duty paid. On leaving the EU, non-EU citizens can reclaim any Value Added Tax (VAT) on any purchases over €154.94.

For more information, visit www.italia.it.

Discount Cards

Free admission to many galleries and cultural sites is available to youths under 18 and seniors over 65 years. EU citizens aged between 18 and 25 also often qualify for a 50% discount.

In many towns – Siena and San Gimignano includ-ed – you can save money by purchasing a **biglietto cumulativo**, a ticket that allows admission to a number of associated sights for less than the combined cost of separate admission fees.

Youth, Student & Teacher Cards

➡ The **European Youth Card** (Carta Giovani Europea; www.eyca.org/card/kiosk; €14, depending on place of purchase) is available to anyone, worldwide, under 30. It offers thousands of discounts at Italian hotels, museums, restaurants, shops and clubs, and can be bought online.

➡ Student, teacher or youth travel cards (www.isic.org) can save you money on accommodation, travel, food and drink. They're available online and worldwide from student unions, hostelling organisations and youth travel agencies such as STA Travel (www.statravel.com). Options include the International Student Identity Card (ISIC; for full-time students), International Teacher Identity Card (for full-time teachers) and the International Youth Travel Card (for travellers under 31).

➡ Many places in Italy give discounts according to age rather than student status. An ISIC may not always be accepted without proof of age (eg passport).

Firenze Card

When in Florence, consider purchasing a Firenze Card (€72; www.firenzecard.it), which is valid for 72 hours and covers admission to 72 museums, villas and gardens in Florence, as well as unlimited use of public transport and free wi-fi.

Electricity

Type F
230V/50Hz

Type L
220V/50Hz

Embassies & Consulates

Foreign embassies and consulates in Italy are listed under 'Ambasciate' or 'Consolati' in the telephone directory. In addition to their embassies or consulates, some countries run honorary consulates in other cities.

Food & Drink

For detailed information about eating in Tuscany. see Eat & Drink Like a Local (p41).

Gay & Lesbian Travellers

Homosexuality is legal in Italy and well accepted in the major cities. On the Tuscan coast, Viareggio and Torre del Lago have lively gay scenes.

Resources include the following:

Arcigay (www.arcigay.it) Bologna-based national organisation for the LGBTIQ community.

Azione Gay e Lesbica Firenze (☑055 22 02 50; www.azione gayelesbica.it; Via Pisana 32r) Active Florence-based organisation for gays and lesbians.

GayFriendlyItaly.com (www.gayfriendlyitaly.com) English-language site produced by Gay.it, featuring events and information on homophobia issues and the law.

Gay.it (www.gay.it) Website featuring LGBTIQ news, feature articles and gossip.

Pride (www.prideonline.it) National monthly magazine of art, music, politics and gay culture.

Health

Before You Go
HEALTH INSURANCE

➡ The free European Health Insurance Card (EHIC) covers EU citizens and those from Switzerland, Norway and Iceland for most medical care in public hospitals free of charge.

➡ The EHIC does not cover emergency repatriation home or non-emergencies.

➡ The EHIC is available from health centres and, in the UK, online (www.ehic.org.uk) and from post offices.

➡ Citizens from other countries should check whether there's a reciprocal arrangement for free medical care between their country and Italy – Australia, for instance, has such an agreement; carry your Medicare card.

➡ Additional health insurance should cover the worst possible scenario, such as an accident requiring an emergency flight home.

➡ Check in advance whether your insurance plan will make payments directly to providers or reimburse you later for overseas health expenditures.

VACCINATIONS

No jabs are required to travel to Italy. However, the World Health Organization (WHO) recommends that all travellers should be covered for diphtheria, tetanus, measles, mumps, rubella and polio, as well as hepatitis B.

EATING PRICE RANGES

The following price ranges refer to a meal consisting of two courses and a *bicchiere di vino della casa* (glass of house wine), and include a *coperto* (cover charge):

€ less than €25

€€ €25–45

€€€ more than €45

In Florence & Tuscany

AVAILABILITY & COST OF HEALTH CARE

Pharmacists can give you valuable advice and sell over-the-counter medication for minor illnesses. They can also advise you when more specialised help is required and point you in the right direction.

Pharmacies generally keep the same hours as other shops, closing at night and on Sundays. However, in big cities a handful remain open on a rotation basis *(farmacie di turno)* for emergency purposes. These are listed online at www.miniportale.it/mini portale/farmacie/Toscana. htm. You can also check the door of any pharmacy that is closed for business – it will display a list of the nearest emergency pharmacies.

If you need an ambulance, call 118. For emergency treatment, head straight to the *pronto soccorso* (casualty) section of a public hospital, where you can also get emergency dental treatment.

TAP WATER

Despite the Tuscan enthusiasm for consuming bottled mineral water with meals, tap water in the region is perfectly drinkable.

Insurance

A travel insurance policy to cover theft, loss and medical problems is a good idea. Some policies specifically exclude dangerous activities, which can include scuba div-

ing, motorcycling and even hiking – read the fine print.

Worldwide travel insurance is available at www.lonelyplanet.com/travel-insurance. You can buy, extend and claim online any time – even if you're already on the road.

Internet Access

Most locals have home connections and practically every hotel, B&B, hostel and *agriturismi* (accommodation on working farms or wine estates) offers free wi-fi (albeit patchy at times given many properties' centuries-old thick walls or deeply rural location). Specialised internet cafes are practically non-existent.

Legal Matters

The average tourist will only have a brush with the law if they're robbed by a bag-snatcher or pickpocket, or if their car is towed away.

In an emergency (to report theft, robbery, assault or accidents) call 113 or 112 – the latter has a reply service in a number of languages.

Maps

Once you meander off the main road and dip into rural Tuscany, a map definitely comes in handy. Several sheet maps cover the region, including Michelin's *Toscana* (1:200,000), Marco Polo's *Toscana/Tuscany* (1:200,000) and Touring Editore's *Toscana* (1:200,000).

Buy them from bookshops and some petrol stations.

If you're relying on digital maps, download off-line versions before departure: in rural Tuscany you will frequently find yourself with zero connectivity.

Money

ATMs widely available. Credit cards accepted at most hotels and many restaurants.

ATMs

Bancomats (ATMs) are widely available throughout Tuscany and are the best way to obtain local currency.

Credit & Debit Cards

International credit and debit cards can be used at any *bancomat* displaying the appropriate sign. Cards are also good for payment in most hotels, restaurants, shops, supermarkets and tollbooths.

If your card is lost, stolen or swallowed by an ATM, you can telephone toll free to have an immediate stop put on its use:

American Express ☑06 7290 0347

Diners Club ☑800 393939

MasterCard ☑800 870866

Visa ☑800 819014

Currency

The euro is Italy's currency. Notes come in denominations of €500, €200, €100, €50, €20, €10 and €5. Coins are in denominations of €2 and €1, and 50, 20, 10, five, two and one cents.

Money Changers

You can change money in banks, at the post office or in a *cambio* (exchange office). Post offices and banks tend to offer the best rates; exchange offices keep longer hours, but watch for high commissions and inferior rates.

Taxes & Refunds

A Value Added Tax (VAT) of around 22%, known as

Imposta di Valore Aggiunto (IVA), is slapped on most goods and services in Italy; a discounted rate of 10% applies in restaurants, bars and hotels. It's sometimes possible for non-EU residents to claim a refund of VAT paid on goods.

CLAIMING TAX REFUNDS

If you're a non-EU resident and spend more than €154.94 on a purchase, you can claim a refund when you leave. The refund only applies to purchases from affiliated retail outlets that display a 'tax free for tourists' (or similar) sign.

You have to complete a form at the point of sale, then have it stamped by EU customs as you leave the zone (if you are visiting one or more EU countries after visiting Italy, you'll need to submit the form at your final port of exit). For information and a list of refund offices in Florence, visit Tax Refund for Tourists (www.taxrefund.it).

Tipping

Taxis Round the fare up to the nearest euro.

Restaurants Many locals don't tip waiters, but most visitors leave 10% to 15% if there's no service charge.

Cafes Leave a coin (as little as €0.10 is acceptable) if you drank your coffee at the counter or 10% if you sat at a table.

Hotels Bellhops usually expect €1 to €2 per bag; it's not necessary to tip the concierge, cleaners or front-desk staff.

Opening Hours

Opening hours vary throughout the year. We've provided summer (high-season) and winter (low-season) opening hours, but be aware that hours might differ in the shoulder seasons.

Banks 8.30am to 1.30pm and 3.30pm to 4.30pm Monday to Friday

Restaurants 12.30pm to 2.30pm and 7.30pm to 10pm

Cafes 7.30am to 8pm

Bars and pubs 10am to 1am

Shops 9am to 1pm and 3.30pm to 7.30pm (or 4pm to 8pm) Monday to Saturday

Post

Le Poste (www.poste.it), Italy's postal system, is reasonably reliable, but if you are sending a package you might want to use DHL or FedEx, which can be safer.

Francobolli (stamps) are available at post offices and authorised *tabacchi* (tobacconists; look for the official sign: a big 'T', often white on black). Since letters often need to be weighed, what you get at the tobacconist for international airmail will occasionally be an approximation of the proper rate. If you've any concerns about ensuring an accurate stamp price, use a post office. *Tabacchi* keep regular shop hours.

Public Holidays

Most Italians take their annual holiday in August, with the busiest period occurring around 15 August, known locally as Ferragosto. This means that many businesses and shops close for at least a part of that month. Settimana Santa (Easter Week) is another busy holiday period for Italians.

Individual towns have public holidays to celebrate the feasts of their patron saints. National public holidays:

New Year's Day (Capodanno or Anno Nuovo) 1 January

Epiphany (Epifania or Befana) 6 January

Easter Sunday (Domenica di Pasqua) March/April

Easter Monday (Pasquetta or Lunedì dell'Angelo) March/April

Liberation Day (Giorno della Liberazione) 25 April – marks the Allied victory in Italy, and the end of the German presence in 1945

Labour Day (Festa del Lavoro) 1 May

Republic Day (Festa della Repubblica) 2 June

Feast of the Assumption (Assunzione or Ferragosto) 15 August

All Saints' Day (Ognissanti) 1 November

ITALY'S POLICE FORCES

There are six national police forces in Italy, as well as a number of local police forces. The main ones are shown in the table.

ORGANISATION	JURISDICTION	UNIFORM
polizia di stato (civil national police)	thefts, visa extensions and permits; based at the local *questura* (police station)	powder-blue trousers with a fuchsia stripe and a navy-blue jacket
arma dei carabinieri (military police)	general crime, public order and drug enforcement (often overlapping with the *polizia di stato*)	black uniform with a red stripe
polizia municipale (aka *vigili urbani;* municipal police)	parking tickets, towed cars, public order, petty crime	varies according to province

Feast of the Immaculate Conception (Immaculata Concezione) 8 December

Christmas Day (Natale) 25 December

Boxing Day (Festa di Santo Stefano) 26 December

Telephone

Mobile Phones

Local SIM cards can be used in European and Australian phones. Other phones must be set to roaming.

➡ Italy uses GSM 900/1800, which is compatible with the rest of Europe and Australia but not with North American GSM 1900 or the totally different Japanese system.

➡ Many modern smartphones are multiband, meaning they are compatible with a number of international networks – check with your service provider about using your phone in Italy.

➡ Beware of mobile calls being routed internationally; it can be very expensive for a 'local' call.

➡ You can get a temporary or prepaid account from several companies if you already own a GSM, dual- or multiband mobile phone.

➡ Always check with your provider in your home country to see whether your handset allows use of another SIM card. If yours does, it can cost as little as €20 to activate a local prepaid SIM card (sometimes with €10 worth of calls on the card). You'll need to register with a mobile-phone shop, bring your passport and wait for about 24 hours for your account to be activated.

➡ You can easily top up an Italian account with *ricarica* (prepaid minutes) from your selected mobile company at *tabacchi*, supermarkets and banks.

➡ TIM (www.tim.it), Vodafone (www.vodafone.it) and Wind (www.wind.it) have the densest networks of outlets across the country.

➡ If you have an internet-enabled phone, turn off data roaming when you're not using it, otherwise it devours credit.

Local Calls

➡ Italian telephone area codes all begin with 🕿0 and consist of up to four digits. The area code is followed by a number of anything from four to nine digits. The area code is an integral part of the telephone number and must *always* be dialled, even when calling from next door.

➡ Mobile-phone numbers begin with a three-digit prefix such as 🕿330.

➡ Toll-free (free-phone) numbers are known as *numeri verdi* and usually start with 🕿800.

➡ Nongeographical numbers start with 🕿840, 841, 848, 892, 899, 163, 166 or 199.

➡ Some six-digit national rate numbers are also in use (such as those for Alitalia and rail and postal information). As elsewhere in Europe, Italians choose from a host of providers of phone plans and rates, making it difficult to make generalisations about costs.

International Calls

➡ The cheapest options for calling internationally are free or low-cost computer programs such as Skype or Viber.

➡ Cut-price call centres can be found in all of the main cities; rates can be considerably lower than from Telecom Italia pay phones for international calls. Place your call from a private booth inside the centre and pay when you've finished.

➡ International calling cards, sold at newsstands and *tabacchi* (tobacconists), also

offer cheaper rates. They can be used at public telephones.

➡ To call another country from Italy, first dial 🕿00, then the relevant country and area codes, followed by the telephone number.

➡ To call Italy from abroad, call the international access number (🕿011 in the USA, 🕿00 from most other countries), Italy's country code (🕿39) and then the area code of the location you want, including the leading 0.

Pay Phones & Phonecards

➡ Telecom Italia public phones can be found on the streets, in train stations and in Telecom offices.

➡ Most pay phones accept only *carte/schede telefoniche* (phonecards), although some also accept credit cards. Prepaid phonecards (costing €1, €2.50, €3, €5 and €7.50) are sold at post offices, *tabacchi* and newsstands.

➡ Telecom offers a wide range of prepaid cards for both domestic and international use.

Time

Italy operates on a 24-hour clock. It is one hour ahead of GMT/UTC. Daylight-saving time starts on the last Sunday in March, when clocks are put forward one hour. Clocks are put back an hour on the last Sunday in October. This is especially valuable to know in Italy, as 'summer' and 'winter' hours at museums and other sights are usually based on daylight-saving time.

Toilets

Public toilets are non-existent. Your best bet, when the urge strikes, is to nip into the closest cafe, order an espresso at the bar and consider the cost of €1 the price for using their facilities. Can't turn on the tap to wash your hands? Press the floor pedal beneath the sink with your foot to get the water flowing.

Tourist Information

Visit Tuscany (www.visittuscany. com) is the website of Tuscany's regional tourist authority.

Travellers with Disabilities

Most Tuscan towns and cities are not easy for travellers with disabilities to navigate, and getting around can be a problem for wheelchair users – many streets are cobbled, and narrow pavements in historic centres are not wide enough for a wheelchair.

An increasing number of museums, including the Uffizi in Florence, include tactile models of major artworks for visitors with impaired vision.

Sage Traveling (www. sagetraveling.com) is a European accessible-travel specialist. Its website gives tips and advice on accessible travel in Florence, and it offers a range of wheelchair-accessible guided city tours; book online.

Download Lonely Planet's free *Accessible Travel* guide from http://lptravel.to/AccessibleTravel.

Visas

➡ European citizens of the 26 countries in the Schengen Area can enter Italy with nothing more than a valid identity card or passport.

British nationals only need a passport.

➡ Residents of 28 non-EU countries, including Australia, Brazil, Canada, Israel, Japan, New Zealand and the USA, do not require visas for tourist visits of up to 90 days.

➡ All non-EU and non-Schengen nationals entering Italy for more than 90 days, or for any reason other than tourism (such as study or work), may need a specific visa. For details, visit www.esteri.it or contact an Italian consulate.

➡ EU citizens do not require any permits to live or work in Italy but, after three months' residence, are supposed to register themselves at the municipal registry office where they live and offer proof of work or sufficient funds to support themselves.

➡ Non-EU foreign citizens with five years' continuous legal residence may apply for permanent residence.

➡ You should have your passport stamped on entry as, without a stamp, you could encounter problems if trying to obtain a residence permit *(permesso di soggiorno).* If you enter the EU via another member state, get your passport stamped there.

Permesso di Soggiorno

Non-EU citizens planning to stay at the same address for more than one week are supposed to report to the police station to receive a *permesso di soggiorno.*

Tourists staying in hotels are not required to do this.

A *permesso di soggiorno* only really becomes a necessity if you plan to study, work (legally) or live in Italy. Obtaining one is never a pleasant experience; it often involves long queues and the frustration of arriving at the counter only to find you don't have the necessary documents.

The exact requirements, such as specific documents and *marche da bollo* (official stamps), can change. In general, you will need a valid passport (if possible containing a stamp with your date of entry into Italy), a special visa issued in your own country if you are planning to study (for non-EU citizens), four passport photos and proof of your ability to support yourself financially. You can apply at the *ufficio stranieri* (foreigners' bureau) of the police station closest to where you're staying.

EU citizens do not require a *permesso di soggiorno.*

Study Visas

Non-EU citizens who want to study at a university or language school in Italy must have a study visa. These can be obtained from your nearest Italian embassy or consulate. You will normally require confirmation of your enrolment, proof of payment of fees and adequate funds to support yourself. The visa covers only the period of the enrolment. This type of visa is renewable within Italy but, again, only with confirmation of ongoing enrolment and proof that you are able to support yourself (bank statements are preferred).

Transport

GETTING THERE & AWAY

Flights, cars and tours can be booked online at lonelyplanet.com/bookings.

Air

→ High season for air travel to Italy is mid-April to mid-September.

→ Shoulder season runs from mid-September to the end of October and from Easter to mid-April.

→ Low season is November to March.

→ Tickets around Christmas and Easter often increase in price or sell out in advance.

Land

Border Crossings

If you are entering Italy from a neighbouring EU country, you do not require a passport check.

Bus

Buses are the cheapest overland option to Italy, but services are less frequent, less comfortable and significantly slower than the train.

Car & Motorcycle

Every vehicle travelling across the border should display a valid national licence plate and an accompanying registration card.

Train

→ Milan is the major rail hub in northern Italy. Most European services arrive there; onward connections include Florence and Pisa.

→ **Thello** (www.thello.com) overnight sleeper trains travel from Paris-Gare de Lyon to Venice via Milan.

→ From France, you can change at Turin for connecting services to Pisa.

AIRPORTS & AIRLINES

AIRPORT	ALTERNATIVE NAME/S	LOCATION	WEBSITE
Pisa International Airport (PSA)	Aeroporto Galileo Galilei	Pisa	www.pisa-airport.com
Florence Airport (FLR)	Amerigo Vespucci; Peretola	Florence	www.aeroporto.firenze.it
Umbria International Airport (PEG)	Perugia San Francesco d'Assisi	Perugia, Umbria	www.airport.umbria.it
Bologna Airport (BLQ)	Aeroporto G Marconi	Bologna, Emilia-Romagna	www.bologna-airport.it

Domestic flights into and out of the region:

Alitalia (✆from abroad 06 6 56 49 within Italy 89 20 10; www.alitalia.it) The national carrier. Flies from Pisa International Airport, Florence Airport and Bologna Airport to Rome and Catania.

Meridiana Fly (✆from abroad +39 0789 5 26 82 within Italy 89 29 28; www.meridiana.it) From Bologna Airport to Olbia and Cagliari.

Ryanair (www.ryanair.com) From Pisa International Airport to Trapani, Palermo, Bari, Brindisi and Cagliari; from Umbria International Airport to Brindisi, Cagliari and Trapani; from Bologna Airport to Bari, Brindisi, Trapani and Palermo.

EXPRESS TRAINS FROM CONTINENTAL EUROPE

FROM	TO	FREQUENCY	DURATION (HR)	COST (€)
Geneva	Milan	4 daily	4	79
Munich	Verona	5 daily	5½	62-89
Paris	Milan	4 daily	7-10	59-104
Ventimiglia	Milan	6 daily	4	32
Vienna	Florence	nightly	11	59-119
Zurich	Milan	7 daily	3¾	39-76

➡ For train times and fares, go to **Rail Europe** (www.raileurope-world.com). For rail passes, see **Eurail** (www.eurail.com).

Sea

Ferries connect Italy with its islands and with countries all across the Mediterranean. However, the only options for reaching Tuscany directly by sea are the ferry crossings to Livorno from Spain, Sardinia and Corsica.

For a comprehensive guide to ferry services into and out of Italy, consult **Traghettionline** (www.traghettionline.com). The website lists every route and includes links to ferry-company sites where you can buy tickets or search for deals.

GETTING AROUND

To/From the Airport

Pisa International Airport LAM Rossa (red) buses run into central Pisa (€1.20). PisaMover automated trains run to Pisa's Stazione Pisa Centrale (€2.70); regular trains run to Florence's Stazione di Santa Maria Novella (€8.40). Taxis cost €10 to central Pisa.

Florence Airport Buses run to central Florence (€6). Taxis cost a fixed €20 to central Florence (€23 on Sunday and holidays, €22 between 10pm and 6am), plus €1 per bag and €1 supplement for a fourth passenger.

Bicycle

Cycling is a national pastime in Italy. Bikes are prohibited on the *autostrada* (expressway), but there are few other special road rules.

Bikes can be taken on any train that carries the bicycle logo. The cheapest option is to buy a separate bicycle ticket: €3.50 for *regionale* (slow local train) services and €12 for international services. Tickets are valid for 24 hours and must be validated before boarding. Ferries allow free bicycle passage.

City-funded bike-sharing schemes are starting to take off in Tuscany: pick up a silver set of wheels in Pisa from one of 14 **Ciclopi** (☑800 005 640; www.ciclopi.eu; Piazza Vittorio Emanuele II; 1st hour free, 2nd/3rd/4th half-hour €0.90/1.50/2.50; ⊗9.30am-1pm) stations dotted around town. **SiPedala** (www.sien-aparcheggi.com/it/1125/Bike-sharing.htm) in Siena is the region's first electric-bike-sharing scheme, with 13 stations around town.

Boat

Year-round, regular ferries connect Piombino on the mainland with Portoferraio on Elba, and the smaller ports of Cavo and Rio Marina. From Livorno, ferries run to the island of Capraia, also year-round.

Bus

Although trains are the most convenient and economical way to travel between major towns, a bus is often the best public-transport link between small towns and villages. For a few intercity routes, such as the one between Florence and Siena, the bus is your best bet.

➡ Dozens of regional companies are loosely affiliated under the **Tiemme** (www.lfi.it) network.

➡ Most reduce or even drop services on holidays and at weekends, especially on Sunday.

➡ Local tourist offices often carry bus timetables.

➡ Buy tickets at ticket booths and dispensing machines at bus stations, or from *tabacchi* (tobacconists) and newsstands. Tickets can usually also be bought on board at a slightly higher cost.

➡ Validate tickets in the machine on board.

➡ In larger cities, ticket companies often have offices at the bus terminal; some offer good-value daily tourist tickets.

➡ Turn up on time: in defiance of deep-seated Italian tradition, buses are almost always punctual.

Car & Motorcycle
Car Hire

To rent a car you must be at least 25 years old and have a credit card. Car-rental agencies expect you to bring the car back with a full tank of petrol and will charge astronomically if you don't. You should also make sure that the office where you are returning your car will be open when you arrive – if not you will face fines.

Make sure you understand what is included in the price (unlimited kilometres, tax, insurance, collision damage waiver and so on). Also consider vehicle size carefully: high fuel prices, extremely narrow streets and tight parking conditions mean that smaller is always better.

Driving Licences

All EU member states' driving licences are fully recognised throughout Europe. Drivers with a non-EU licence are supposed to obtain an International Driving Permit (IDP) to accompany their national licence, though anecdotal testimonies indicate that this rule is rarely enforced.

Fuel & Spare Parts

Italy's petrol (gas) prices are among the highest in Europe and vary from one service station (*benzinaio, stazione di servizio*) to another. Lead-free gasoline (*senza piombo*; 95 octane) typically costs between €2.50 and €1.60 per litre, with diesel (*gasolio*) averaging €1.40 per litre. Many petrol stations are unattended at lunchtime, at night and at weekends; at these times credit cards can often be used for payment (note, though, that not all foreign cards are accepted).

Spare parts are available at many garages or via the 24-hour ACI motorist-

assistance number (⏻803 116).

Insurance

Always carry proof of vehicle ownership and evidence of third-party insurance. If driving an EU-registered vehicle, your home-country insurance is sufficient. Ask your insurer for a European Accident Statement (EAS) form, which can simplify matters in the event of an accident.

Motorcycle & Scooter Hire

Agencies throughout Tuscany rent everything from small Vespas to larger touring bikes.

Helmets are compulsory. Most firms won't hire motorcycles to under 18s. Many require a sizeable deposit, and you could be responsible for reimbursing the company for part of the cost of the bike if it is stolen.

You don't need a licence to ride a scooter under 50cc. The speed limit is 45km/h, you must be 14 or over and you can't carry passengers. To ride a motorcycle or scooter between 50cc and 125cc, you must be aged 16 or over and have a licence (a car licence will do). For motorcycles over 125cc you will need a motorcycle licence.

Mopeds below 150cc can't be ridden on motorways. Motorcycles can access some Zona a Traffico Limitato (ZTLs; Limited Traffic Zones).

SPEED LIMITS

For cars and motorbikes the following speed limits apply:

➡ Urban areas: 50km/h

➡ Secondary roads: 70km/h to 90km/h (look for signs)

➡ Main roads: 110km/h (90km/h in rain)

➡ Autostradas: 130km/h (110km/h in rain)

Speed limits are lower for towing vehicles (including caravans) and camper vans.

Parking

Parking spaces outlined in blue are designated for paid parking (look for a nearby ticket machine and display the ticket on your dashboard). White outlines indicate free parking; yellow outlines indicate that residential permits are needed. Traffic police generally turn a blind eye to motorcycles or scooters parked on footpaths.

Road Network

Tuscany has an excellent road network, including autostradas, superstradas (dual carriageways) and major highways. Most of these are untolled, with the main exceptions being the A11 and A12 (FI-PI-LI) autostrada connecting Florence, Pisa and Livorno and the A1 autostrada linking Milan and Rome via Florence and Arezzo. For information about driving times and toll charges on these, check www.auto strade.it/en.

There are several minor road categories, listed here in descending order of importance:

Strade statali (state highways) Represented on maps by 'S' or 'SS', they vary from toll-free, four-lane highways to two-lane

BUS COMPANIES IN TUSCANY

REGIONAL BUS COMPANY	WEBSITE (MOST IN ITALIAN ONLY)	SERVICES
ATL	www.atl.livorno.it	Livorno
CPT	www.cpt.pisa.it	Pisa & Volterra
Etruria Mobilità	www.etruriamobilita.it	Eastern Tuscany
Siena Mobilità	www.sienamobilita.it	Siena & around
SITA	www.sitabus.it	Florence & Chianti
Vaibus	www.vaibus.it	Lucca, Garfagnana & Versilia

main roads. The latter can be extremely slow, especially in mountainous regions.

Strade regionali (regional highways connecting small villages) Coded SR or R.

Strade provinciali (provincial highways) Coded SP or P.

Strade locali Often not even paved or mapped.

Road Rules

➡ Cars drive on the right and overtake on the left.

➡ Unless otherwise indicated, always give way to cars entering an intersection from a road on your right.

➡ Seatbelts (front and rear) are required by law; violators are subject to an on-the-spot fine.

➡ Children under 12 years must travel in the back seat, those under four must use child seats, and those under 1.5m must be in an approved restraint system or a suitable seat.

➡ Cars must carry a warning triangle and a reflective vest; they must be used in rural areas in the event of a breakdown or accident.

➡ Italy's blood-alcohol limit is 0.05% and random breath tests take place. Penalties can be severe.

➡ Speeding fines follow EU standards and are proportionate to the number of kilometres per hour over the speed limit you are travelling. The maximum penalty is a fine of €2000 and the suspension of your driving licence.

➡ Headlights are compulsory day and night for all vehicles on autostradas, and they are advisable for motorcycles even on smaller roads. Many Tuscan towns and cities have a Limited Traffic Zone (ZTL) in their historic centre. This means only local vehicles with parking permits can enter – all other vehicles must stay outside the ZTL or face fines. Hire cars are not exempt – travellers who unknowingly breach ZTLs can end up with hefty charges (fine plus administrative fee) on their credit cards.

Local Transport

Taxi

You can usually find taxi ranks at train and bus stations, or you can telephone for taxis. It's best to go to a designated taxi stand, as it's illegal for taxis to stop in the street if hailed. If you phone a taxi, bear in mind that the meter starts running from the moment of your call rather than when the taxi picks you up.

Tram

Florence is the only city where you might possibly use a tram, although the routes serve residential parts rather than touristy parts of town.

Train

➡ **Trenitalia** (📞from abroad 06 6847 5475 within Italy 89 20 21; www.trenitalia.com; ⏱call centre 7am-11.59pm) runs most of the services in Italy.

➡ The train network throughout Tuscany is limited.

Train Routes

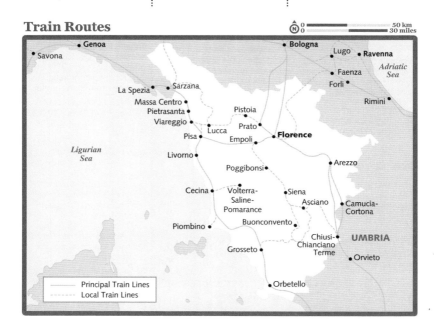

CLIMATE CHANGE & TRAVEL

Every form of transport that relies on carbon-based fuel generates CO_2, the main cause of human-induced climate change. Modern travel is dependent on aeroplanes, which might use less fuel per kilometre per person than most cars but travel much greater distances. The altitude at which aircraft emit gases (including CO_2) and particles also contributes to their climate change impact. Many websites offer 'carbon calculators' that allow people to estimate the carbon emissions generated by their journey and, for those who wish to do so, to offset the impact of the greenhouse gases emitted with contributions to portfolios of climate-friendly initiatives throughout the world. Lonely Planet offsets the carbon footprint of all staff and author travel.

➡ Tickets can be purchased from the ticket office, automated ticket machines at stations or via the Trenitalia app on your smartphone.

➡ Validate printed tickets before boarding by using the yellow *convalida* machines installed at the entrance to train platforms.

➡ Travelling without a validated ticket risks a fine of at least €50. It's paid on the spot to an inspector who will escort you to an ATM if you don't have the cash on you.

➡ Train timetables at stations generally display *arrivi* (arrivals) on a white background and *partenze* (departures) on a yellow one. Italy has several types of train:

Regionale (R) Slow and cheap, they stop at nearly all stations; *regionale veloce* (fast regional) trains stop at fewer stations.

InterCity (IC) Faster, more expensive services operating between major cities.

Alta Velocità (AV) State-of-the-art high-speed services travelling up to 350km/h. More expensive than InterCities, but journey times can be cut by half. The AV *Frecciarossa* stops at Florence, en route between Turin, Milan, Bologna, Rome and Salerno. Reservations are required.

Classes & Costs

There are 1st and 2nd classes on most Italian trains; a 1st-class ticket costs just under double the price of a 2nd-class one. There's not a huge amount of difference between the two – just a bit more space in 1st class, along with complimentary tea and coffee.

If you are taking a short trip, check the difference between the *regionale* and IC/AV ticket prices, as *regionale* tickets are always consid-

erably cheaper – you might arrive 10 minutes earlier on an IC or AV service, but you'll also pay at least €5 more. Check up-to-date prices on www.trenitalia.com.

Left Luggage

Most sizeable train stations have either a guarded left-luggage office or self-service lockers. The guarded offices are usually open 24 hours or 6am to midnight and charge around €5 per 12 hours for each piece of luggage.

Train Passes

Trenitalia offers various discount passes, including the Carta Verde (€40) for those aged 12 to 26 years and the Carta d'Argento (€30) for seniors (60-plus years). The passes give 10% to 15% off basic fares and 25% off international connections. See www.trenitalia.com for details.

Language

Modern standard Italian began to develop in the 13th and 14th centuries, predominantly through the works of Dante, Petrarch and Boccaccio – all Tuscans – who wrote chiefly in the Florentine dialect. The language drew on its Latin heritage and many dialects to develop into the standard Italian of today. Although many dialects are spoken in everyday conversation in Italy, standard Italian is understood throughout the country. Despite the Florentine roots of standard Italian – and the fact that standard Italian is widely used in Florence and Tuscany – anyone who has learned some Italian will notice the peculiarity of the local accent. In Florence, as in other parts of Tuscany, you are bound to hear the hard 'c' pronounced as a heavy 'h'. For example, *Voglio una cannuccia per la Coca Cola* (I want a straw for my Coca Cola) sounds more like *Voglio una hannuccia per la Hoha Hola*.

Italian pronunciation is relatively easy as the sounds used in spoken Italian can all be found in English. If you read our coloured pronunciation guides as if they were English, you'll be understood. The stressed syllables are indicated with italics. Note that ai is pronounced as in 'aisle', ay as in 'say', ow as in 'how', dz as the 'ds' in 'lids', and that r is a strong and rolled sound. Keep in mind that Italian consonants can have a stronger, emphatic pronunciation – if the consonant is written as a double letter, it should be pronounced a little stronger, eg *sonno son*·no (sleep) versus *sono so*·no (I am).

WANT MORE?

For in-depth language information and handy phrases, check out Lonely Planet's *Italian Phrasebook*. You'll find it at **shop.lonelyplanet.com**, or you can buy Lonely Planet's iPhone phrasebooks at the Apple App Store.

BASICS

Italian has two words for 'you' – use the polite form *Lei* lay if you're talking to strangers, officials or people older than you. With people familiar to you or younger than you, you can use the informal form *tu* too.

Hello.	*Buongiorno.*	bwon·*jor*·no
Goodbye.	*Arrivederci.*	a·ree·ve·*der*·chee
Yes./No.	*Sì./No.*	see/no
Excuse me.	*Mi scusi.* (pol)	mee *skoo*·zee
	Scusami. (inf)	*skoo*·za·mee
Sorry.	*Mi dispiace.*	mee dees·*pya*·che
Please.	*Per favore.*	per fa·*vo*·re
Thank you.	*Grazie.*	*gra*·tsye
You're welcome.	*Prego.*	*pre*·go

How are you?
Come sta/stai? (pol/inf)   *ko*·me sta/stai

Fine. And you?
Bene. E Lei/tu? (pol/inf)   *be*·ne e lay/too

What's your name?
Come si chiama?   *ko*·me see *kya*·ma

My name is ...
Mi chiamo ...   mee *kya*·mo ...

Do you speak English?
Parla/Parli   par·la/*par*·lee
inglese? (pol/inf)   een·*gle*·ze

I don't understand.
Non capisco.   non ka·*pee*·sko

ACCOMMODATION

Do you have a ... room?	*Avete una camera ...?*	a·*ve*·te oo·na *ka*·me·ra ...
double	*doppia con letto matrimoniale*	*do*·pya kon *le*·to ma·tree·mo·*nya*·le
single	*singola*	*seen*·go·la

KEY PATTERNS

To get by in Italian, mix and match these simple patterns with words of your choice:

When's (the next flight)?
A che ora è   a ke o·ra e
(il prossimo volo)? (eel pro·see·mo vo·lo)

Where's (the station)?
Dov'è (la stazione)? do·ve (la sta·tsyo·ne)

I'm looking for (a hotel).
Sto cercando   sto cher·kan·do
(un albergo).   (oon al·ber·go)

Do you have (a map)?
Ha (una pianta)?   a (oo·na pyan·ta)

Is there (a toilet)?
C'è (un gabinetto)? che (oon ga·bee·ne·to)

I'd like (a coffee).
Vorrei (un caffè). vo·ray (oon ka·fe)

I'd like to (hire a car).
Vorrei (noleggiare vo·ray (no·le·ja·re
una macchina).   oo·na ma·kee·na)

Can I (enter)?
Posso (entrare)?   po·so (en·tra·re)

Could you please (help me)?
Può (aiutarmi),   pwo (a·yoo·tar·mee)
per favore?   per fa·vo·re

How much is it per ...?	Quanto costa per ...?	kwan·to kos·ta per ...
night	una notte	oo·na no·te
person	persona	per·so·na

Is breakfast included?
La colazione è   la ko·la·tsyo·ne e
compresa?   kom·pre·sa

air-con	aria condizionata	a·rya kon·dee·tsyo·na·ta
bathroom	bagno	ba·nyo
campsite	campeggio	kam·pe·jo
guesthouse	pensione	pen·syo·ne
hotel	albergo	al·ber·go
youth hostel	ostello della gioventù	os·te·lo de·la jo·ven·too
window	finestra	fee·nes·tra

DIRECTIONS

Where's ...?
Dov'è ...?   do·ve ...

What's the address?
Qual'è l'indirizzo? kwa·le leen·dee·ree·tso

Could you please write it down?
Può scriverlo,   pwo skree·ver·lo
per favore?   per fa·vo·re

Can you show me (on the map)?
Può mostrarmi   pwo mos·trar·mee
(sulla pianta)?   (soo·la pyan·ta)

at the corner	all'angolo	a·lan·go·lo
at the traffic lights	al semaforo	al se·ma·fo·ro
behind	dietro	dye·tro
far	lontano	lon·ta·no
in front of	davanti a	da·van·tee a
left	a sinistra	a see·nee·stra
near	vicino	vee·chee·no
next to	accanto a	a·kan·to a
opposite	di fronte a	dee fron·te a
right	a destra	a de·stra
straight ahead	sempre diritto	sem·pre dee·ree·to

EATING & DRINKING

What would you recommend?
Cosa mi consiglia? ko·za mee kon·see·lya

What's in that dish?
Quali ingredienti   kwa·li een·gre·dyen·tee
ci sono in   chee so·no een
questo piatto?   kwe·sto pya·to

That was delicious!
Era squisito!   e·ra skwee·zee·to

Cheers!
Salute!   sa·loo·te

Please bring the bill.
Mi porta il conto, mee por·ta eel kon·to
per favore?   per fa·vo·re

I'd like to reserve a table for ...	Vorrei prenotare un tavolo per ...	vo·ray pre·no·ta·re oon ta·vo·lo per ...
(two) people	(due) persone	(doo·e) per·so·ne
(eight) o'clock	le (otto)	le (o·to)

I don't eat ...	Non mangio ...	non man·jo ...
eggs	uova	wo·va
fish	pesce	pe·she
nuts	noci	no·chee
(red) meat	carne (rossa)	kar·ne (ro·sa)

Key Words

bar	locale	lo·ka·le
bottle	bottiglia	bo·tee·lya
breakfast	prima colazione	pree·ma ko·la·tsyo·ne
cafe	bar	bar

cold	freddo	fre·do
dinner	cena	che·na
drink list	lista delle bevande	lee·sta de·le be·van·de
fork	forchetta	for·ke·ta
glass	bicchiere	bee·kye·re
grocery store	alimentari	a·lee·men·ta·ree
hot	caldo	kal·do
knife	coltello	kol·te·lo
lunch	pranzo	pran·dzo
market	mercato	mer·ka·to
menu	menù	me·noo
plate	piatto	pya·to
restaurant	ristorante	ree·sto·ran·te
spicy	piccante	pee·kan·te
spoon	cucchiaio	koo·kya·yo
vegetarian (food)	vegetariano	ve·je·ta·rya·no
with	con	kon
without	senza	sen·tsa

Meat & Fish

beef	manzo	man·dzo
chicken	pollo	po·lo
(dried) cod	baccalà	ba·ka·la
crab	granchio	gran·kyo
duck	anatra	a·na·tra
fish	pesce	pe·she
(cured) ham	prosciutto	pro·shoo·to
herring	aringa	a·reen·ga
lamb	agnello	a·nye·lo
lobster	aragosta	a·ra·gos·ta
meat	carne	kar·ne
mussels	cozze	ko·tse
octopus	polpi	pol·pee
oysters	ostriche	o·stree·ke
pork	maiale	ma·ya·le
prawn	gambero	gam·be·ro
rabbit	coniglio	ko·nee·lyo
salmon	salmone	sal·mo·ne
sausage	salsiccia	sal·see·cha
scallops	capasante	ka·pa·san·te
seafood	frutti di mare	froo·tee dee ma·re
shrimp	gambero	gam·be·ro
squid	calamari	ka·la·ma·ree
thinly sliced raw meat	carpaccio	kar·pa·cho
tripe	trippa	tree·pa
trout	trota	tro·ta

tuna	tonno	to·no
turkey	tacchino	ta·kee·no
veal	vitello	vee·te·lo

Vegetables

artichokes	carciofi	kar·cho·fee
asparagus	asparagi	as·pa·ra·jee
aubergine/ eggplant	melanzane	me·lan·dza·ne
beans	fagioli	fa·jo·lee
black cabbage	cavolo nero	ka·vo·lo ne·ro
cabbage	cavolo	ka·vo·lo
capsicum	peperone	pe·pe·ro·ne
carrot	carota	ka·ro·ta
cauliflower	cavolfiore	ka·vol·fyo·re
cucumber	cetriolo	che·tree·o·lo
fennel	finocchio	fee·no·kyo
lentils	lenticchie	len·tee·kye
lettuce	lattuga	la·too·ga
mushroom	funghi	foon·gee
nuts	noci	no·chee
olive	oliva	o·lee·va
onions	cipolle	chee·po·le
peas	piselli	pee·ze·lee
potatoes	patate	pa·ta·te
rocket	rucola	roo·ko·la
salad	insalata	een·sa·la·ta
spinach	spinaci	spee·na·chee
tomatoes	pomodori	po·mo·do·ree
vegetables	verdura	ver·doo·ra

Fruit & Gelato Flavours

apple	mela	me·la
cherry	ciliegia	chee·lee·e·ja
chocolate	cioccolata	cho·ko·la·ta
chocolate and hazelnuts	bacio	ba·cho
forest fruits (wild berries)	frutta di bosco	froo·ta dee bos·ko

Question Words

How?	Come?	ko·me
What?	Che cosa?	ke ko·za
When?	Quando?	kwan·do
Where?	Dove?	do·ve
Who?	Chi?	kee
Why?	Perché?	per·ke

fruit	frutta	froo·ta
grapes	uva	oo·va
hazelnut	nocciola	no·cho·la
lemon	limone	lee·mo·ne
melon	melone	me·lo·ne
orange	arancia	a·ran·cha
peach	pesca	pe·ska
pear	pere	pe·re
pineapple	ananas	a·na·nas
plum	prugna	proo·nya
strawberry	fragola	fra·go·la
trifle	zuppa inglese	tsoo·pa een·gle·ze
vanilla	vaniglia	va·nee·ya
wild/sour cherry	amarena	a·ma·re·na

tea	tè	te
(mineral) water	acqua (minerale)	a·kwa (mee·ne·ra·le)
white wine	vino bianco	vee·no byan·ko

Other

bread	pane	pa·ne
butter	burro	boo·ro
cheese	formaggio	for·ma·jo
cream	panna	pa·na
cone	cono	ko·no
cup	coppa	ko·pa
eggs	uova	wo·va
honey	miele	mye·le
ice	ghiaccio	gya·cho
jam	marmellata	mar·me·la·ta
noodles	pasta	pas·ta
oil	olio	o·lyo
pepper	pepe	pe·pe
rice	riso	ree·zo
salt	sale	sa·le
soup	minestra	mee·nes·tra
soy sauce	salsa di soia	sal·sa dee so·ya
sugar	zucchero	tsoo·ke·ro
truffle	tartufo	tar·too·fo
vinegar	aceto	a·che·to

Drinks

beer	birra	bee·ra
coffee	caffè	ka·fe
(orange) juice	succo (d'arancia)	soo·ko (da·ran·cha)
milk	latte	la·te
red wine	vino rosso	vee·no ro·so
soft drink	bibita	bee·bee·ta

EMERGENCIES

Help!
Aiuto!
a·yoo·to

Leave me alone!
Lasciami in pace!
la·sha·mee een pa·che

I'm lost.
Mi sono perso/a. (m/f)
mee so·no per·so/a

There's been an accident.
C'è stato un incidente.
che sta·to oon een·chee·den·te

Call the police!
Chiami la polizia!
kya·mee la po·lee·tsee·a

Call a doctor!
Chiami un medico!
kya·mee oon me·dee·ko

Where are the toilets?
Dove sono i gabinetti?
do·ve so·no ee ga·bee·ne·tee

I'm sick.
Mi sento male.
mee sen·to ma·le

It hurts here.
Mi fa male qui.
mee fa ma·le kwee

I'm allergic to ...
Sono allergico/a a ... (m/f)
so·no a·ler·jee·ko/a a ...

SHOPPING & SERVICES

I'd like to buy ...
Vorrei comprare ...
vo·ray kom·pra·re ...

I'm just looking.
Sto solo guardando.
sto so·lo gwar·dan·do

Can I look at it?
Posso dare un'occhiata?
po·so da·re oo·no·kya·ta

How much is this?
Quanto costa questo?
kwan·to kos·ta kwe·sto

It's too expensive.
È troppo caro/a. (m/f)
e tro·po ka·ro/a

Signs	
Entrata/Ingresso	Entrance
Uscita	Exit
Aperto	Open
Chiuso	Closed
Informazioni	Information
Proibito/Vietato	Prohibited
Gabinetti/Servizi	Toilets
Uomini	Men
Donne	Women

Can you lower the price?
Può farmi lo sconto?   pwo *far*·mee lo *skon*·to

There's a mistake in the bill.
C'è un errore nel conto.   che oo·ne·*ro*·re nel *kon*·to

ATM	Bancomat	ban·ko·mat
post office	ufficio postale	oo·*fee*·cho pos·*ta*·le
tourist office	ufficio del turismo	oo·*fee*·cho del too·*reez*·mo

TIME & DATES

What time is it?	Che ora è?	ke o·ra e
It's one o'clock.	È l'una.	e *loo*·na
It's (two) o'clock.	Sono le (due).	so·no le (*doo*·e)
Half past (one).	(L'una) e mezza.	(*loo*·na) e *me*·dza

in the morning	di mattina	dee ma·*tee*·na
in the afternoon	di pomeriggio	dee po·me·*ree*·jo
in the evening	di sera	dee *se*·ra

yesterday	ieri	ye·ree
today	oggi	o·jee
tomorrow	domani	do·*ma*·nee

Monday	lunedì	loo·ne·*dee*
Tuesday	martedì	mar·te·*dee*
Wednesday	mercoledì	mer·ko·le·*dee*
Thursday	giovedì	jo·ve·*dee*
Friday	venerdì	ve·ner·*dee*
Saturday	sabato	*sa*·ba·to
Sunday	domenica	do·*me*·nee·ka

January	gennaio	je·*na*·yo
February	febbraio	fe·*bra*·yo
March	marzo	*mar*·tso
April	aprile	a·*pree*·le
May	maggio	*ma*·jo
June	giugno	*joo*·nyo
July	luglio	*loo*·lyo
August	agosto	a·*gos*·to
September	settembre	se·*tem*·bre
October	ottobre	o·*to*·bre
November	novembre	no·*vem*·bre
December	dicembre	dee·*chem*·bre

Numbers

1	uno	*oo*·no
2	due	*doo*·e
3	tre	tre
4	quattro	*kwa*·tro
5	cinque	*cheen*·kwe
6	sei	say
7	sette	*se*·te
8	otto	*o*·to
9	nove	*no*·ve
10	dieci	*dye*·chee
20	venti	*ven*·tee
30	trenta	*tren*·ta
40	quaranta	kwa·*ran*·ta
50	cinquanta	cheen·*kwan*·ta
60	sessanta	se·*san*·ta
70	settanta	se·*tan*·ta
80	ottanta	o·*tan*·ta
90	novanta	no·*van*·ta
100	cento	*chen*·to
1000	mille	*mee*·lel

TRANSPORT

Public Transport

At what time does the ... leave/arrive?	A che ora parte/ arriva ...?	a ke o·ra *par*·te/ a·*ree*·va ...
boat	la nave	la *na*·ve
bus	l'autobus	*low*·to·boos
ferry	il traghetto	eel tra·*ge*·to
metro	la metro- politana	la me·tro- po·lee·*ta*·na
plane	l'aereo	la·e·re·o
train	il treno	eel *tre*·no

... ticket	un biglietto ...	oon bee·*lye*·to
one-way	di sola andata	dee *so*·la an·*da*·ta
return	di andata e ritorno	dee an·*da*·ta e ree·*tor*·no

bus stop	fermata dell'autobus	fer·*ma*·ta del *ow*·to·boos
platform	binario	bee·*na*·ryo
ticket office	biglietteria	bee·lye·te·*ree*·a
timetable	orario	o·*ra*·ryo
train station	stazione ferroviaria	sta·*tsyo*·ne fe·ro·*vyar*·ya

Does it stop at ...?
Si ferma a ...?   see *fer*·ma a ...

Please tell me when we get to ...
Mi dica per favore   mee *dee*·ka per fa·*vo*·re
quando arriviamo a ...   *kwan*·do a·ree·*vya*·mo a ...

I want to get off here.
Voglio scendere qui.   *vo*·lyo *shen*·de·re kwee

Driving & Cycling

I'd like	*Vorrei*	vo·*ray*
to hire	*noleggiare*	no·le·*ja*·re
a/an ...	*un/una ...* (m/f)	oon/*oo*·na ...
bicycle	*bicicletta* (f)	bee·chee·*kle*·ta
car	*macchina* (f)	*ma*·kee·na
motorbike	*moto* (f)	*mo*·to
bicycle	*pompa della*	*pom*·pa de·la
pump	*bicicletta*	bee·chee·*kle*·ta
child seat	*seggiolino*	se·jo·*lee*·no
helmet	*casco*	*kas*·ko

mechanic	*meccanico*	me·*ka*·nee·ko
petrol/gas	*benzina*	ben·*dzee*·na
puncture	*gomma bucata*	*go*·ma boo·*ka*·ta
service	*stazione di*	sta·*tsyo*·ne dee
station	*servizio*	ser·*vee*·tsyo

Is this the road to ...?
Questa strada porta a ...?   *kwe*·sta *stra*·da *por*·ta a ...

(How long) Can I park here?
(Per quanto tempo)   (per *kwan*·to tem·po)
Posso parcheggiare qui?   *po*·so par·ke·*ja*·re kwee

The car/motorbike has broken down (at ...).
La macchina/moto si è   la *ma*·kee·na/*mo*·to see e
guastata (a ...).   gwas·*ta*·ta (a ...)

I have a flat tyre.
Ho una gomma bucata.   o *oo*·na *go*·ma boo·*ka*·ta

I've run out of petrol.
Ho esaurito la   o e·zow·*ree*·to la
benzina.   ben·*dzee*·na

I've lost my car keys.
Ho perso le chiavi della   o *per*·so le *kya*·vee de·la
macchina.   *ma*·kee·na

Behind the Scenes

SEND US YOUR FEEDBACK

We love to hear from travellers – your comments keep us on our toes and help make our books better. Our well-travelled team reads every word on what you loved or loathed about this book. Although we cannot reply individually to your submissions, we always guarantee that your feedback goes straight to the appropriate authors, in time for the next edition. Each person who sends us information is thanked in the next edition – the most useful submissions are rewarded with a selection of digital PDF chapters.

Visit **lonelyplanet.com/contact** to submit your updates and suggestions or to ask for help. Our award-winning website also features inspirational travel stories, news and discussions.

Note: We may edit, reproduce and incorporate your comments in Lonely Planet products such as guidebooks, websites and digital products, so let us know if you don't want your comments reproduced or your name acknowledged. For a copy of our privacy policy visit lonelyplanet.com/privacy.

OUR READERS

Many thanks to the travellers who used the last edition and wrote to us with helpful hints, useful advice and interesting anecdotes: Deidre Terzian, Efrat Blum, Lisa Sarasohn, Trevor Matthews.

WRITER THANKS
Nicola Williams

Grazie mille to those in situ who shared their love and insider knowledge with me: wine-tasting double-act Manuele Giovanelli & Zeno Fioravanti (Pitti Gola e Cantina), Angela Banti (Lorenzo Villoresi), Doreen & Carmello (Hotel Scoti), Georgette Jupe (@girlinflorence), serial foodie Coral Sisk (@curiousappetite), Nardia Plumridge (@lostinflorence), family tour guide & art historian Molly McIlwrath, Cailin Swanson and Betti Soldi, Caroline (Raw), Duccio di Giovanni and Marco Mantonavi. Finally, kudos to my very own expert, trilingual, family-travel research team: Niko, Mischa & Kaya.

Virginia Maxwell

So many locals assisted me in my research for this trip. Many thanks to Tiziana Babbucci, Fernando Bardini, Maricla Bicci, Niccolò Bisconti, Enrico Bracciali, Rita Ceccarelli, Cecilia in Massa Marittima, Stefania Colombini, Ilaria Crescioli, Martina Dei, Paolo Demi, Federica Fantozzi, Irene Gavazzi, Francesco Gentile, Francesca Geppetti, Maria Guarriello, Benedetta Landi, Freya Middleton, Alessandra Molletti, Sonai Pallai, Luigi Pagnotta, Valentina De Pamphilis, Franco Rossi, Fabiana Sciano, Maria Luisa Scorza, Raffaella Senesi, Coral Sisk, Carolina Taddei and Luca Ventresa. Many thanks, too, to my travelling companions: Peter Handsaker, Eveline Zoutendijk, Max Handsaker, Elizabeth Maxwell, Matthew Clarke and Ella Clarke.

ACKNOWLEDGEMENTS

Climate map data adapted from Peel MC, Finlayson BL & McMahon TA (2007) 'Updated World Map of the Köppen-Geiger Climate Classification', Hydrology and Earth System Sciences, 11, 1633–44.

Illustrations p72-3 by Javier Zarracina.

Cover photograph: Farmhouse in Val d'Orcia, Francesco Riccardo Iacomino/AWL ©

THIS BOOK

This 10th edition of Lonely Planet's *Florence & Tuscany* guidebook was curated by Nicola Williams and re-searched and written by Nicola and Virginia Maxwell. The previous edition was written by Nicola and Belinda Dixon.

This guidebook was produced by the following:

Destination Editor Anna Tyler
Product Editors Kathryn Rowan, Anne Mason
Senior Cartographer Anthony Phelan
Book Designer Clara Monitto
Assisting Editors Sarah Bailey, James Bainbridge, Michelle Coxall, Pete Cruttenden, Jodie Martire, Kristin Odijk, Monique Perrin, Simon Williamson
Cartographer Valentina Kremenchutskaya
Cover Researcher Naomi Parker
Thanks to Will Allen, Nigel Chin, Lauren Keith, Catherine Naghten, Lauren O'Connell, Tony Wheeler

Index

Map Legend

Sights
- Beach
- Bird Sanctuary
- Buddhist
- Castle/Palace
- Christian
- Confucian
- Hindu
- Islamic
- Jain
- Jewish
- Monument
- Museum/Gallery/Historic Building
- Ruin
- Shinto
- Sikh
- Taoist
- Winery/Vineyard
- Zoo/Wildlife Sanctuary
- Other Sight

Activities, Courses & Tours
- Bodysurfing
- Diving
- Canoeing/Kayaking
- Course/Tour
- Sento Hot Baths/Onsen
- Skiing
- Snorkelling
- Surfing
- Swimming/Pool
- Walking
- Windsurfing
- Other Activity

Sleeping
- Sleeping
- Camping
- Hut/Shelter

Eating
- Eating

Drinking & Nightlife
- Drinking & Nightlife
- Cafe

Entertainment
- Entertainment

Shopping
- Shopping

Information
- Bank
- Embassy/Consulate
- Hospital/Medical
- Internet
- Police
- Post Office
- Telephone
- Toilet
- Tourist Information
- Other Information

Geographic
- Beach
- Gate
- Hut/Shelter
- Lighthouse
- Lookout
- Mountain/Volcano
- Oasis
- Park
- Pass
- Picnic Area
- Waterfall

Population
- Capital (National)
- Capital (State/Province)
- City/Large Town
- Town/Village

Transport
- Airport
- Border crossing
- Bus
- Cable car/Funicular
- Cycling
- Ferry
- Metro station
- Monorail
- Parking
- Petrol station
- S-Bahn/Subway station
- Taxi
- T-bane/Tunnelbana station
- Train station/Railway
- Tram
- Tube station
- U-Bahn/Underground station
- Other Transport

Routes
- Tollway
- Freeway
- Primary
- Secondary
- Tertiary
- Lane
- Unsealed road
- Road under construction
- Plaza/Mall
- Steps
- Tunnel
- Pedestrian overpass
- Walking Tour
- Walking Tour detour
- Path/Walking Trail

Boundaries
- International
- State/Province
- Disputed
- Regional/Suburb
- Marine Park
- Cliff
- Wall

Hydrography
- River, Creek
- Intermittent River
- Canal
- Water
- Dry/Salt/Intermittent Lake
- Reef

Areas
- Airport/Runway
- Beach/Desert
- Cemetery (Christian)
- Cemetery (Other)
- Glacier
- Mudflat
- Park/Forest
- Sight (Building)
- Sportsground
- Swamp/Mangrove

Note: Not all symbols displayed above appear on the maps in this book

OUR STORY

A beat-up old car, a few dollars in the pocket and a sense of adventure. In 1972 that's all Tony and Maureen Wheeler needed for the trip of a lifetime – across Europe and Asia overland to Australia. It took several months, and at the end – broke but inspired – they sat at their kitchen table writing and stapling together their first travel guide, *Across Asia on the Cheap*. Within a week they'd sold 1500 copies. Lonely Planet was born.

Today, Lonely Planet has offices in Franklin, London, Melbourne, Oakland, Dublin, Beijing and Delhi, with more than 600 staff and writers. We share Tony's belief that 'a great guidebook should do three things: inform, educate and amuse'.

OUR WRITERS

Nicola Williams

Border-hopping is a way of life for British writer, runner, foodie, art aficionado and mum-of-three Nicola Williams who has lived in a French village on the southern side of Lake Geneva for more than a decade. Nicola has authored more than 50 guidebooks on Paris, Provence, Rome, Tuscany, France, Italy and Switzerland for Lonely Planet and covers France as a destination expert for the *Telegraph*. She also writes for the *Independent, Guardian,* lonelyplanet.com, *Lonely Planet* magazine, *Cool Camping France* and others. Catch her on the road on Twitter and Instagram at @tripalong.

Virginia Maxwell

Though based in Melbourne, Australia, Virginia spends at least three months of every year in Europe and the Middle East researching guidebooks and other travel-related content for a variety of publishers. She caught the travel bug during her first overseas trip to London, where she lived for a couple of years after finishing an Arts degree at university, and she's been travelling regularly ever since. For the past 13 years Virginia has been working full-time as a travel writer and occasional book reviewer; before that she worked as a journalist, book and magazine editor, museum curator and film festival programmer. Recent assignments for Lonely Planet have included the north and west coasts of Tasmania, Istanbul (her favourite destination) and Turkey's Aegean coast, the Atlantic coast in Morocco and Tuscany.

Published by Lonely Planet Global Limited
CRN 554153
10th edition – January 2018
ISBN 978 1 78657 261 5
© Lonely Planet 2018   Photographs © as indicated 2018
10 9 8 7 6 5 4 3 2 1
Printed in China